THE

TIMBER TREES, TIMBER AND FANCY WOODS

THE
TIMBER TREES,
TIMBER AND FANCY WOODS,
AS ALSO,
THE FORESTS,
OF
India and of Eastern and Southern Asia.

BY

EDWARD BALFOUR, L. R. C. S. E.

GYAN

Published by

Gyan Publishing House
5, Ansari Road
Daryaganj, New Delhi-110002
Phone: 011-47034999, 9811692060
E-mail: books@gyanbooks.com

Distribution Network
gyanbooks.com
India, USA, Canada, UK, Australia, France

ISBN: 978-81-212-8298-7 (PB)
First Published, 1862

2nd Impression 2023

Printed at: Gyan Press, Delhi.

THE TIMBER TREES, TIMBER AND FANCY WOODS
Author: EDWARD BALFOUR

THE
TIMBER TREES, TIMBER AND FANCY WOODS,

AS ALSO,

THE FORESTS,

OF

India and of Eastern and Southern Asia.

BY

EDWARD BALFOUR, L. R. C. S. E.,

SURGEON MAJOR, MADRAS ARMY,

CORRESPONDING MEMBER OF THE IMPERIAL GEOLOGICAL INSTITUTE, VIENNA.

Madras:

PRINTED AT THE UNION PRESS, BY COOKSON AND CO.

1862.

PREFACE TO THE FIRST EDITION.

It had been suggested to me that persons whose avocations require them to attend to matters connected with the forests and with the timber trees, timber and fancy woods of India and of Eastern and Southern Asia, would find assistance in a manual indicating the botanical and vernacular names of the plants that furnish these useful products and which would also give some information regarding the characters of their different woods and their other economic products, noticing also the forests in which they grow and remarking on those plants towards the greater extension of which attention should be chiefly directed.

I too do not doubt but that there are people who would like to have such a hand-book; but what a private individual who would publish it must look to, is, how to secure himself from loss, and from the scanty European population residing in these countries, it may be questioned whether such a work would find buyers sufficient to cover the expense of properly producing it, an expense which would certainly not be inconsiderable. With a view therefore of ascertaining the public wants for such a work, when writing the article Timber in my "Cyclopædia of India and of Eastern and Southern Asia," I extended the notice to a length somewhat greater perhaps than the subject merited in a work of that character, and have now reconstructed the same into the present form. Those who have the former work need not therefore possess themselves with this, which is but a little more than a reprint of the article "Timber" in my "Cyclopædia of India," but if it be found that a work of this kind is indeed needed, the materials in my possession are amply sufficient greatly to extend this volume so as to supply the want.

EDWARD BALFOUR, *Surgeon, Madras Army.*

133, Mount Road, Madras, *23rd Feb.* 1858.

PREFACE TO THE SECOND EDITION.

THE increasing difficulty of procuring timber of suitable dimensions and quality has been so much felt, that the Military Finance Department recently deemed it advisable to propose the establishment, in British Burmah, of a timber purchasing agency on behalf of the Government of India. The Right Honorable the Governor-General in Council entirely approved of that scheme, and resolved that it should be carried out with as little delay as possible: and, at the same time, I was requested to arrange all the information respecting forest trees, which might be in my possession or which I could obtain from public or private sources, to be printed in a compendious form, for general use; hence, the appearance of this second edition of a work which was published in 1858. The form has been approved of by the Honorable the Governor of Madras in Council, in G. O. No. 2145 of 21st June 1861. In the former edition, the timbers and woods were arranged according to districts, which necessitated repetitions, but the work has been re-written with a view of condensing and, by additions, bringing our information on the subject up to the present time. The trees and shrubs producing timbers and fancy woods have now all been arranged alphabetically, according to their recognized botanical or, where such has been unascertained, their vernacular names. From the many tongues spoken in India, it seems impossible to follow any other plan, if repetitions under different local names and under the names of the trees of different localities, are to be avoided. The Index should, therefore, invariably be referred to, as every name and synonym is there given. The Honorable the Governor of Madras, in Order No. 2145 of 21st June 1861, commanded for me, free access to the records of Government in all departments: and I record, along with the authors whose writings have been consulted, the names of the officers of Government who have further helped me. The distances from other Presidencies have prevented me applying there, but in the course of inquiries during the past 20 years, the officers of Government have given a ready response to my applications for information and when this small work on one class of the useful products of the country shall be circulated amongst them, I feel sure, that they will also accept my present invitation for help towards a third edition, with any information in their power. For, in my letter to the Government of Madras, undertaking this revision, I have mentioned that though the edition of 1858, was declared useful, it was but a first attempt to bring together all existing information, and that careful emendations through two or three successive editions, in the next ten years, will be required to make it a complete or exhaustive work

It will be observed that I have placed under the scientific name which is recognized at the present day, the synonyms which are quoted by authors as names under which former authors have described the tree. With the increasing facilities for communication and the greater number of scientific botanists, a few years may now suffice to establish the correctness of these synonyms, the numbers of which have been owing to the difficulties which, as Dr. Wight explains* a residence in this country presented to the freedom of intercourse amongst the learned inquirers.

* Scientific botany in India commenced with the arrival of Kœnig, a Danish physician: previous to this, plants had been collected and transmitted to Europe, of which descriptions had been inserted by Linnæus, and others in their various publications; but, until Kœnig made his appearance, no one in India had studied the vegetation according to the Linnæan rules. His example was soon followed by many eminent individuals: among whom may be mentioned Jones, Fleming, Hunter, Anderson, Berry, John, Roxburgh, Heyne, Klein, Buchanan Hamilton, and the venerable Rottler, the only survivor of the illustrious group. Most of these formed themselves into a society for the purpose of promoting Botany: plants were industriously collected throughout all the Peninsula, as well as in Ceylon, and were not unfrequently examined and named by the society in common; to such was usually added the word "*nobis.*" By degrees, however, their opportunities of meeting grew less frequent, and their confidence in themselves greater, so that Roxburgh, Klein and Rottler commenced attaching names without consulting with their friends: an interchange of specimens, however, still continued, so that it was rarely difficult for the one to know what was intended by the other. The value of such specimens was

It will also be seen that I have largely given the vernacular synonyms by which the trees are said to be known to the various people of these countries and in the several localities in which they grow: and I have done this because some inquirers put a high value on such synonyms. But, a reference to the notices under black wood, ebony, rose wood, sandal wood, iron wood, poon wood, red wood, &c., &c., will satisfy the mind that commercial names have relation merely to the physical appearances or characters of the woods, and with regard to local names, it is not probable that uneducated and often little civilized nations can be more suggestful in their designations: and I may here refer to the synonyms under "Tree" and to the article "Sumatra," to the names applied by many of the Malaya-nesian nations and races in the Archipelago from Sumatra eastwards to Borneo, to show that the name for one of our most famed woods of India, the "Poon," merely signifies, in those wide regions, any tree. It is said that the island of Luzon got its name from a voyager asking the name of that island of a woman who was grinding corn with a hand-mill. Imagining that the, to her, indispensable hand-mill was the object of his inquiries, she answered "Luzon" and gave the name by which the island is now known. Many similar errors must ever occur in the inter-communications of educated and uneducated people, and though useful to the extent of directing inquirers, I deprecate any unbounded reliance on vernacular names.*

---

quickly felt, nor were they slow in transmitting them to Europe. Many of these plants were published in different works, sometimes under the name given by the donors: in other instances the name was changed, sometimes on the supposition that what was considered by the Indian botanists as a mere variety, was in reality a distinct species; sometimes on the still cruder idea, that a plant named by one of the Missionaries must be different from another of the same name sent by some other of the society. Frequently the change has been made without even quoting the original name as a synonym, a practice which has created much confusion, and given rise to great difficulty in unravelling the synonyms.—*Wight and Arnott's Prodromus, Vol. I, p. XI.*

* It may perhaps be objected that we have not given native names; these we have intentionally omitted partly for the reasons stated, and in accordance with the observations made by Dr. Wallich at page 99 of the 2nd volume of his edition of the Flora Indica. "I avail myself of this opportunity for remarking that the names which are given to plants by the natives of Nepaul are in general very uncertain, and fluctuating; and that I shall only make use of them on occasions when I have reason to be tolerably satisfied as to their correctness." The soundness of which is further proved by a remark of Dr. Carey, at p. 415 of the same volume, in a note on the word *Mun-ko-khoshee.* "The name here given as a Newar name, is, in the extract of Dr. Buchanan's letter, written *Mun-ko-khoshee,* and is one out of hundreds which might easily be produced, of the mistakes which constantly occur when persons unacquainted, in some measure at least, with the languages, set down words from the mouths of natives. Dr. Buchanan spoke only Hindoosthanee, and a Newar man gave him, as a reply to a question *Mun-ko-khoshee,* a Hindoosthanee word, which means *pleasure or delight to the mind.* This might be the Hindoosthanee word by which the tree is designated by the Nepalese, but it is much more probable the man only intended to say, *it was a delightful tree.* The abovementioned circumstance, and likewise the great number of native names of plants, seemingly obtained with the utmost ease by other gentlemen who have merely run through a country as collectors (which however was not the case with Dr. Buchanan), added to the difficulty, I have myself found in obtaining names, and the uncertainty of those commonly obtained, fully dispose me to coincide with the suggestion of my friend Wallich in his note at the foot of page 99." The supposed native names given to De Candolle and Jussieu by Leschenault, along with the specimens collected by him in the southern parts of the peninsula, corroborate strongly the opinion of Dr. Carey: they are in general a mere burlesque on names, meaning often that the natives *had no name for the plant* or *did not know it:* in other instances, it appears to have been not the name of the plant but the name of the village near which it was found, which had been marked down. Dr. Wight has frequently received six or eight names, totally distinct from each other, and formed from very different roots, for the same plant, within a few miles of each other: in short, the natives seem to have no rule either for nomenclature or orthography, they have no means of producing an uniformity of names, and very frequently confound one name with another, so that our inserting these would only tend to mislead, in place of proving an aid in the investigation of an unknown plant, by one acquainted with Botany. Owing to very different plants having the same native name, we have occasionally known dangerous mistakes originate, by erroneously substituting active medicines when those of an opposite kind were intended, and *vice versa.* On these last grounds particularly, we not only think it useless but injurious, nay even dangerous, to insert these names, unless the natives themselves shall have discovered some method by which a plant shall be known throughout by but one name, and that name shall be restricted to the individual plant.—*Wight and Arnott's Prodromus, Vol. I, p. XXIII.*

Fine flowering and useful plants being general favourites among people of every tongue, each nation seems desirous that every known plant (50,000 in number) should have a name in its own language: and no people insist on this privilege more strongly than the English, nor any with less reason, since they have not English names for many of their own indigenous plants, though the whole English flora

Under the circumstances in which many of the trees were scientifically named and from the varied modes in use of spelling vernacular names with the Roman character, it will readily be supposed that, in the one case, doubts exist as to some trees and, in the other, as to whether others are not repeated under different spellings of the same word. In some places my notes will be observed inquiring as to the correct scientific name or the correct spelling of the vernacular name. But, a general list of *Desiderata* is given—for which I have been indebted to Dr. Francis Appavoo in charge, in Madras, of the office of the Conservator of Forests, and of those who have the opportunity I ask assistance in supplying the required information. Also in my references to Dr. Roxburgh's Flora Indica, *Ed.* 1832, I have observed many large trees mentioned and many described as yielding valuable timber of which I have failed to discover any notices in other authors: I have not inserted such in the body of the work, as it is not apparent whether Dr. Roxburgh was, in so doing, describing solitary trees or trees common in a district: but, a general alphabetical list of such will be found arranged by me under the heading "*Roxburgh,*" included in Dr. Appavoo's list the list of *Desiderata*.

In addition to quoting in an abbreviated form, the authorities for the notice of each timber tree, there will be found, at the end of the volume the full titles of the authors or other sources of information, as most inquirers will naturally desire to consult the originals, whenever available.

EDWARD BALFOUR,

MADRAS, 20*th December* 1862. *Surgeon Major, Madras Army.*

---

scarcely furnishes 1,500 flowering species, nor for above a few hundreds (apart from mere translations of botanical names) for upwards of 20,000 exotics now in cultivation in their stoves and conservatories. We must bear in mind that in India, as in England, the same plants have different names in different provinces, and not unfrequently the same name is given to a variety of plants, or *vice versa*, a great variety of names to the same plant, rendering the knowledge of very difficult acquisition, and when acquired of comparatively little value. Added to these impediments to the acquisition of a correct knowledge of vernacular names of plants, we know that these names, being preserved not by description and figures which limit them invariably to the same species, but by tradition, are therefore in course of time, through mistakes of persons repeating them, liable to change by being applied to plants different from those, to which they were originally given, the only way indeed to account for the wide discrepancies often found in the names given to the same plants by different persons speaking the same language. For these, in my opinion, weighty reasons, I trust I shall not be blamed from seldom introducing native names into the body of this work and indulging the hope, that those desirous of obtaining a correct knowledge of Indian plants, will for the future, as much as possible, adopt their botanical nomenclature. Being at the same time aware, that one, and not the least important, object of Botany is to fix these vacillating vernacular names, and render them useful towards the advancement of science by connecting them with their comparatively stable botanical ones, I am most desirous of receiving lists in different native languages, of the plants figured in this work, as well as the collections mentioned above, with a view to the formation of a comprehensive catalogue and index of both.—*Wight, Ill. Ind. Bot. Vol.* i. *Int. Notice, p.* ii.

I may mention that care is required against placing undue reliance on native terms. It is a very prevalent, though erroneous, impression that uneducated, and even wild, races possess accurate knowledge of natural objects, when in truth the whole of their thoughts through life are directed to procuring their own subsistence. In the preface to the Flora Andhrica, Mr. Walter Elliot gives as authorities Drs. Royle and Griffiths in favor of, and Drs. Wight, Wallich and Carey against, the use of vernacular names, yet he remarks that it is the "commonest and most useful plants that are known by definite and generally received appellations." Dr. Waring observes, in a recent number of the Madras Quarterly Journal, that an entire dependance on native names, without reference to botanical characters or sensible properties, will often lead into error, and Dr. Hooker, in his Himalayan Journals, mentions that throughout his travels he had been struck with the undue reliance placed on the native names for plants. A reference to the article Bulbul will show how variously a vernacular name is applied in Southern Asia, and it is the same everywhere. With the English in India, the rose-woods are products of different species, different genera and even different families of plants. The Iron-wood of Ceylon is from the Mesua ferrea, that of the Canara forests is from two species of Memecylon; in Pegu, the Inga xylocarpa and the Inga bijemina, both afford woods known by this name; that brought from Australia, is from a species of Eucalyptus, and the Chinese Iron-wood is from the Metrosideros vera. And innumerable examples of a similar character could be given. The same specific term is often applied by non-scientific people, to a whole genus, often to plants or animals having or supposed by them to have some similar characters or qualities. And in illustration of these remarks, if we turn to Mr. Elliot's Flora Andhrica, we find several names current amongst the Tiling people, for almost every plant. Thus, for the Abelmoschus ficulneus, the Andropogon muricatus, the A. schœnanthus, the Abrus precatorius, the Abutilon Indicum, the Acacia Arabica, all plants in every day use, these are various. The A. muricatus has eight, and the Abrus precatorius, six. The country through which Telugu is spoken is extensive and to this, perhaps, is owing such diversity of terms.—*Balfour's Cyclopædia of India, 2nd Supplement, Preface, p.* iv.

AUTHORITIES CONSULTED.

ADAMS, BAIKIE, BARRON, a Manual of Natural History for the use of Travellers, London 1854.

AINSLIE, WHITELAW, M. D., Materia Medica of Hindostan, Madras 1813.

Do. do., M. R. A. S., Materia Indica, London 1826.

ANDERSON, BERESFORD Esq., Civil Engineer, Madras Railway, MSS.

BALFOUR, on the Iron Ores, the manufacture of Iron and Steel, and on the Coals of the Madras Presidency, in Report on the Government Central Museum, Madras 1855.

Do. Cyclopædia of India and of Eastern and Southern Asia, Commercial, Industrial and Scientific, Madras 1857.

Do. do., 1st Supplement, Madras 1858.

Do. do., 2nd do. do. 1862.

Do. Commercial Products of the Madras Presidency, as shewn by its exports and imports, their quantities and values, for the four years 1852-53 to 1855-56 inclusive, Madras 1857.

Do. The timber trees, timber and fancy woods, also the forests of India, and of Eastern and Southern Asia, Madras 1858.

BALFOUR, Colonel, C. B., Report to the Government of India.

BARLOW, PETER, an Essay on the strength and stress of timber, London 1817.

BEDDOME, Lieutenant, Timber trees of the Godavery, in Madras Exhibition Juries Reports.

BENNET'S Wanderings in N. S. Wales.

BENSON, Major, Madras Army, Report on the woods of Tenasserim.

BLUNDELL, Mr. Commissioner, Catalogue of woods of Tavoy in Catalogue Exhibition 1851.

BOOK of trees, descriptive of the principal timber trees, and the larger species of palms, London 1839.

BRANDIS, Dr., Conservator of Forests in No. XXVIII, Records of Govt. of India.

BRANDIS, Dr., Conservator of Pegu Forests, woods sent to the London Exhibition of 1862.

BROWN, Mr. ROBERT, Catalogue of plants of Madras.

BURTON, Journey to the city of the Salt Lakes.

CALCUTTA, Engineers' Journal.

CHETTY, SIMON CASEE, Esq., Member of the Legislative Council of Ceylon, Botanical Dictionary, containing the names of all the plants of the Tamil Flora, printed in the Literary Magazine Press, Madras 1844.

CLEGHORN, Dr. HUGH, Jury's Reporter on the woods in the Madras Exhibition of 1855.

Do. Conservator's Reports, to Madras Government for 1857, 1858, 1859 and 1860.

Do. The Forests and Gardens of Southern India, London 1861.

CRAWFURD'S Dictionary of Indian Archipelago 1861.

DANCE, Captain, in letter to Military Board, Madras; and Juries Reports of Madras Exhibition.

DRURY, Major HEBER, the Useful Plants of India, Madras 1858.

EARL, Esq., G. WINDSOR, in Journal Indian Archipelago.

EDYE, JOHN Esq., description of the Sea ports, on the coast of Malabar * * * * of the produce of the adjacent forests, Article XVII, pages 324 to 377, vol. ii, Journal of the Royal Asiatic Society, London 1835.

ELLIOT, WALTER, F. L. S., Flora Andhrica, a Vernacular and Botanical list of plants met with in the Telugu districts of the Northern Circars.

ELWIN, Esq., R. P., Agent Madras Railway.

ENGLISH Cyclopædia, by Charles Knight.

ENGLISH Forests and Forest trees London 1853.

EXHIBITION, London of 1851, Catalogue and Juries Reports.

Do. Madras, of 1855, 1857 and 1859, do. do.

Do. of 1851, Singapore Catalogue.

Do. of 1862, Calcutta and Madras Catalogues.

Do. London, of 1862, Dr. BRANDIS, Catalogue of woods of British Burmah sent to the London Exhibition of 1862.

Do. do. Mr. DOWLEANS, Catalogue of Bengal contributions to the Exhibition.

Do. do. Madras, do. do.

FALCONER, H., Report on the Teak plantations of Burmah, Report No. XXV, of 1857.

FAULKNER, Esq, ALEXANDER, Dictionary of Commercial Terms.

FORTUNE'S, Report on the Tea cultivation of the Himalayas.

Do. Wanderings in China.

Do. Tea districts.

Do. Residence in China.

FRITH, Lieut.-Colonel, Madras Artillery, woods in the Madras Arsenal, and in Catalogue of Exhibition of 1851.

GERARD'S Account of Kunawar.

GIBSON, DR. ALEXANDER, List of the woods of the Malabar forests, in Catalogue of the London Exhibition of 1851.

Do. do. on the woods of the Bombay forests in Bombay Geographical Society's Journal.

Do- do. Conservator's Reports to Bombay Government 1849 to 1856 and 1857 to 1859.

Do do. on the timber trees, of Canara and Sunda.

HAWKES, Captain, in Madras Catalogue Exhibition of 1855.

HERSCHELL, Sir JOHN, F. W. Bart, a Manual of Scientific Enquiry, London 1849.

HODGSON'S Nagasaki.

HOGG, ROBERT, the Vegetable Kingdom, London 1858.

HOLTZAPFEL on Turnery.

HONIGBERGER, JOHN MARTIN, Thirty-five years in the East, London 1852.

HOOKER'S, Dr. Himmalayan Journal.

HOOKER, J. D. M. D. R. N. F. R. S. and THOMSON, THOMAS, M. D. F. L. S., Surgeon H E. I. C. Flora Indica, London 1855.

HUNTER, DR. A., in Catalogue of Madras Exhibition of 1855.

IRVINE, DR., General Medical Topography of Ajmire.
JACKSON, Colonel J. R., F. R. S., What to observe, London 1845.
JAFFREY, ANDREW THOMAS, Hints to Amateur Gardeners, Madras 1855.
JAMESON'S W., Report on the Government Garden Saharunpore, 1855.
JOHNS, the Rev. C. A., The forest trees of Britain, London 1846.
JOURNAL Indian Archipelago.
KEPPEL, Captain, the Hon'ble G., Visit to the Indian Archipelago.
LOW'S Sarawak.
MACDONALD, Captain, On the woods of Ganjam and Gumsur, in M. E. Juries reports.
MADRAS Literary Society's Journal.
Do. Agri-Horticultural Society's Catalogue.
MAITLAND, Colonel JOHN, Superintendent Gun Carriage Manufactory, Madras, in the Proceedings of the Madras Exhibition of 1859, and Records of Gun Carriage Manufactory.
MALCOLM'S, Rev. H., Travels in South Eastern Asia 1839.
MARQUART, Captain, Chittagong woods in Catalogue of London Exhibition of 1861.
MARSHALL, Colonel HUBERT, Secretary to Government of Madras.
MASON, Rev. F. A. M., Tenasserim or Notes on the Fauna, Flora, minerals and nations of British Burmah and Pegu, Maulmain, 1852.
MASON, Rev. F. D. D. M. R. A. S., Burmah, its people and natural productions, Rangoon 1860.
MAYNE, D. Esq, list of Cuddapah woods in Catalogue of London Exhibition.
McCLELLAND, DR. J Superintendent of the Forests of Pegu, in No. IX, of Selections from the Records of the Government of India, Calcutta 1855.
McGILLIVRAY, MR., Narrative of the voyage in the Rattlesnake.
McIVOR, Mr., in Proceedings Madras Exhibition of 1855.
McCULLOCH'S Dictionary of Commerce.
MENDIS, Mr. ADRIAN, list of Ceylon woods sent to the Government Central Museum, Madras, through Sir George Anderson.
MORGAN, Major, Acting Conservator of Forests, Report 1860-61.
Do. Major, Acting Conservator of Forests, Report 1861-62. (*Note*—I observe that I have inadvertently in one or two places quoted Dr. Cleghorn as the Forest Reporter for 1860-61 and 1861-62. The reports of these two years, were by Major Morgan and corrections should be made accordingly.)
MORRISON the Hon'ble, Compendious description.
MUSEUM, Records of the Government Central Museum, Madras.
ORDNANCE, Records of Ordnance Department, Madras.
O'RILEY, Esq., E., in Journal, Indian Archipelago
O'SHAUGHNESSY, W. B., M. D. F. R. S. The Bengal Pharmacopœia, Calcutta 1844.
Do. W. B. M. D., Bengal Dispensatory Calcutta 1842.
PHILIPS, Captain CHARLES, on the Kimedy forests.
PINSON Esq., JOHN A. Acting Chief Engineer, Madras Railway.
POOLE, BRAITHWAITE Esq., Statistics of British Commerce, London 1852.
PRENDERGAST, Captain HUGH, Royal Engineers.
PUCKLE, Captain, Madras Catalogue Exhibition, 1862.
RAFFLES' History of Java.
RIDDLE, R., A Manual of Gardening for Western and Southern India, 3rd Edition, Madras 1856.
ROHDE, J. Esq., on the woods of the Madras Presidency, in Proceedings of the Madras Central Committee for the Exhibition of 1841.
Do. do. MSS. Trade and Arts Dictionary.
ROXBURGH'S Coromandel plants London 1795, 1798 and 1819.
Do. Flora Indica, Calcutta 1832.
ROYLE, M. D. V. P. R. S., J. FORBES, Illustrations of the Botany and other branches of the Natural History of the Himalaya mountains and of the Flora of Cashmere 2 Vols. London 1839.
Do. Fibrous plants.
Do. Materia Medica.
SANKEY, Captain, in Records of Madras Ordnance Department.
SCINDIAN, Newspaper.
SEEMAN, on Palms.
Do. Fiji islands.
SHUBRICK, CHARLES Esq., Collector of Sea Customs, Madras, Imports and Exports of timber into Calcutta, Madras and Bombay.
SIMMONDS, Commercial products.
SIMPSON, Colonel, Inspector General of Ordnance and Magazines in Artillery Records, and Records of Inspector General.
SINGAPORE, Catalogue Exhibition.
SMART Esq., W. G. Engineer Madras Railway.
SPRY, HENRY HARPUR, M. D. F. R. S. F. G. S., Suggestions for cultivation and introduction of useful and ornamental plants, Calcutta, 1841.
ST. JOHN, SPENCER, Life in the forest of the far East, London 1862.
THUNBERG Esq, History of Japan.
THWAITES, G. H. K. Esq., F. L. S., Enumeratio Pl. Zeylanicæ, parts I to IV, London 1859 to 1861.
TOMLINSON'S Cyclopædia of arts and manufactures.
TREDGOLD, on carpentry, Edition of 1843, published by Weale.
VOIGT, J. O., Hortus Suburbanus Calcuttensis, Calcutta 1845.
WALL, Mr., Report in Madras G. O., 17th July 1849.
WALLICH, Dr., List of Indian woods in Catalogue of Exhibition of 1851.
WARING'S Dr. Therapeutics.
WIGHT, Dr. ROBERT, on the woods of the Madras Presidency, in Proceedings of the Madras Central Committee for the Exhibition of 1851, being observations on the Forest trees of Southern India by Dr. Wight, with notes by Mr. Rohde, Madras 1850.
WIGHT, ROBERT, M. D. F. L. S. and ARNOTT, G. A. WALKER, A. M. F. L. S. and R. S., Prodromus Floræ Peninsulæ Orientalis: containing abridged descriptions of the plants found in the Peninsula of British India, London 1834.
WIGHT, Dr. ROBERT, M. D. F. L. S., Illustrations of Indian Botany, Madras 1840.
WIGHT'S Icones, Dr. Cleghorn's Index.
WILLIAM'S Rev., Middle Kingdom.
WILSON'S Hindu Theatre.

THE

TIMBER TREES, TIMBER AND FANCY WOODS,

AS ALSO,

THE FORESTS

OF

India and of Eastern and Southern Asia.

GENERAL OBSERVATIONS.

THE preservation of the forests of India and the search for the timbers and fancy woods, suitable for the purposes of the State and the wants of its people, have long been objects of attentive interest to the Governments of the several Presidencies, and many reports have been written on the forest trees of Southern Asia and their products. Amongst the best known of the scientific investigators we find recorded the names of Drs. Roxburgh, Ainslie, Wallich, Royle, Gibson, Falconar, McClelland, Mr. Graham, Dr. Wight, Dr. Cleghorn, the Revd. Dr. Mason, Dr. Stocks, Dr. Brandis, and Captain Beddome, while Captain Macdonald, Mr. Edye, Colonel Frith, Mr. Rohde, Colonel Simpson, Captain Sankey and Captain Dance may each be mentioned as having applied a large practical knowledge of the qualities of timber, to ascertain the woods suitable for the manufacturing industries of the country. The course generally adopted by the scientific inquirers has been to endeavour to identify the trees botanically, and then supply the names by which they are familiarly known to the people of the country. And, there is no doubt that if not the only proper mode, such a method is more correct than to endeavour to trace out the botanical name of a plant from its native name. In following the latter course, from the twenty or thirty languages spoken throughout British India, it must happen that the same plant will come to be described repeatedly under different names, and true progress will not be made until, having properly identified the botanical relations of the plant, the subject be completed by endeavouring to supply all the synonyms under which it is known. The latter is the course that will be followed here, in arranging the names of the trees producing the Timber and Fancy Woods of India and of Eastern and Southern Asia.

Even in this course, however, practical men should keep under view the vast extent of these regions and recognise that from the various physical conditions it is impossible that the same tree, botanically, can produce the same quality of timber in every locality where it grows. This indicates the necessity of not pinning the faith on the capabilities of any one wood, merely because a wood from a tree, of the same botanical name, but the growth of another district, may have been found highly suitable for the work to which it was put. The ordnance department should carefully keep this point in view and not use a timber, however lauded, unless it have been brought from the same place it was obtained from by those whose praises they act upon, or until severe trials have proved that the timber of the new locality, is equal to all that is required of it. As one instance of the variations to which the timber of the same botanical plant is liable, we may cite the majestic teak tree which grows to an immense height alike in Malabar, on the Godavery, in Pegu and in Tenasserim; which is met with far in the interior of India, and may be seen in the mountains of Bundelcund, though there only in the form of a moderate sized shrub. But even where it presents the same form of a gigantic tree, as in Malabar and Pegu, the qualities and colour of the timbers it yields in the two countries are certainly dissimilar, and it has been said that the timber of the Malabar teak tree, differs from that of the neighbouring Ana Mallai. It would appear from the remarks of Captain Dance that the Saul "Shorea robusta" of northern India has different properties from that of Amherst. But, in all countries, trees growing in the shelter of a deep valley or in a dense forest present a different appearance, and have different qualities from plants exposed to the winds and storms. In Gumsur, Dr. Cleghorn tells us that the Saul tree grows remarkably tall and straight in the forests, while, in open places, it yields a thick trunk, throws out branches and becomes umbrageous. But, if such differences exist even where the wood spoken of is the product of the same botanical plant, growing under different physical conditions, still greater caution is necessary when using the commercial terms by which woods are known. For, in all countries, most of the woods in general use have a variety of names; and, the *local* name varies often in the same district. Many have likewise, a *commercial* name, by which they are known in the market, as "Trincomallee" wood, "Coromandel" wood, &c., which are sometimes given from the place of export, but often it is impossible to trace their derivation. The Iron-woods, the Poons, the Ebonies, the Black-woods, the Rose-woods even of this small part of the world, are products of different species, different genera, and of different families of plants. The Iron-wood of Ceylon, is from the Mesua ferrea: that of the Canara forests, is from two species of Memecylon; in Pegu, the Inga xylocarpa and the Inga bijemina both afford woods known by this name; in Australia, it is got from a species of Eucalyptus, in the Archipelago, from the Casuarina equisitifolia and in China from Metrosideros vera. The Poon spars from the Canara and other forests of Southern India, are said to be obtained from three or four trees, the Calysaccion angustifolium according to Dr. Gibson in Canara; the Sterculia fœtida according to Dr. Cleghorn, in the Juries Reports, and Dr. Wight names, doubtingly, a species of Calophyllum and Dillenia pentagyna: though the best Poon spars would indeed seem to be from the Calophyllum; for, Dr. Cleghorn, in his recently re-published edition of his former reports &c., says it is the C. angustifolium of Roxburgh. The Blackwoods are obtained from species of Dalbergia, the Bombay Blackwood is from the Cassia Sumatrana; the Ebonies from species of Diospyros, Dombeya? and Bauhinia, and the Rosewoods, from species of Dalbergia and Pterocarpus. Mahogany, the name usually given to the wood of the West Indian Swietenia mahogani, is applied by the colonists of Western Australia, to the timber of the Eucalyptus rostrata, also known to them as Jarrah or Yarra. Where the educated people of Europe thus delight in applying the same commercial term to woods which are products of dissimilar plants, it is impossible to believe that the illiterate native races of half civilized countries can be more happy in their nomenclature. And, in a recent work, of immense labour and research, we find six Telugu names given for the Abrus precatorius, three for the Acacia Arabica, four for the Nauclea cadamba, three for Nauclea cordifolia, and so on.

The knowledge of such facts renders it obvious that in any observations on the Timber trees, Timber and Fancy Woods of India and of Eastern and Southern Asia, we should not only describe the trees generally, but indicate also the names of such as are found useful in different localities. These remarks will therefore embrace observations on the uses of timber; a list of all the trees known to produce timber in some part or other of the regions under notice; and, separate lists of the trees of particular districts. In this arrangement, the botanical names, with the various native synonyms, will be found arranged alphabetically. And, only when the botanical name has not been ascertained or is doubtful, will any notice be found under a vernacular designation.

At the time of the Great Exhibition of 1851, the total annual importation of timber into Great Britain was nearly two million loads, or one hundred million of cubic feet, entered under the several designations of "timber or unsawn wood," "deals and planks or sawn wood;" "teak," "staves," and "lath wood," and the following Table shows the countries from which the wood was chiefly imported, into England, in the year 1849.

	Timber.	Deals.	Teak.	Staves.	Lathe wood
Russia	41,419	173,586	—	325	15,539
Sweden	28,679	79,843	—	150	1,119
Norway	28,930	50,805	—	95	103
Prussia	117,470	35,006	—	19,213	6,169
Hanse Towns	2,441	68	—	1,012	—
Tuscany	2,299	9	—	—	—
Papal Territories	2,106	4	—	—	—
Western Africa	1	—	9,596	—	—
British India	1	2	17,459	56	—
Australia	977	540	1	4	—
British North America	578,748	468,572	9	45,614	14,813
British Guiana	4	19	4	103	—
United States	13,832	839	—	13,309	—
Miscellaneous	1,002	491	633	36	57
Total Loads	817,909	809,783	27,702	79,917	37,800

Of the chief woods employed in English ship-building seven had long been acknowledged as first-rate by the authorities at Lloyd's. But, there are now eight descriptions of timber admitted by the English as first-rate for ship-building purposes, and one of these has only been so ranked since the opening of the Great Exhibition of 1851. They are:—1, English oak; 2, American live-oak; 3, African oak; 4, Morung saul; 5, East Indian teak; 6, Green heart; 7, Morra; and 8, Iron-bark (the newly admitted wood). Of the above, the Morung saul is a tree of India, as well as the better known valuable Teak. The Iron-bark is from New South Wales, and has a density of 1426, and a strength of 1557—English oak being called 1000.

During the last thirteen years, a greater attention has been given to the character of the East Indian woods. The first stimulus occurred at the time of the Great Exhibition of 1851, where the collection exhibited by the Honorable East India Company was by far the most extensive series of woods in the whole Exhibition, and constituted a very valuable part of the great collection of Indian raw produce. It was declared remarkable for the large number of specimens, the excellence of many of them, and the valuable practical information to be gained by their examination. The collection consisted of many hundred specimens, and included several minor or local collections of great interest. Amongst them were the valuable collections of Drs. Roxburgh and Wallich (884, 885); an extensive series of the woods of the Malay Peninsula, Amherst, Tavoy, Tenasserim, Prince of Wales' Island, Assam, Cuddapah, Madras, Orissa, &c. And the Jury awarded a Prize Medal to Mr. Commissioner Blundell (p. 885) for a very valuable collection of Amherst woods, and one to Messrs. Almeida of Singapore (p. 890) for fine specimens of Lingoa-wood and Kaya-buka.

The smaller series of woods contributed by Messrs. A. P. Onslow, of Ganjam; D. Mayne, of Cuddapah (p. 188); General Tulloch, Madras; Captain Ogilvie of Masulipatam; Major Maitland, and Colonel Balfour, of Madras; Dr. Hunter, of Madras; Dr. Wight, of Coimbatore; Captain Marquart, of Chittagong; and J. R. Colvin, of Moulmein (pp. 888, 891), received Honorable Mention. The nature and properties of many of these Indian woods were then very little known in Britain, and though it was not deemed probable that it would be found worth while to import many of them into Europe, yet their importance to India was recognized to be every year increasing with the demand for timber for Indian railways and other engineering works.

Since then, there has been increased attention to the subject in consequence of the large quantities of sleepers required for the railways in progress throughout the country. In 1855, only, twenty-two trees were authorized to be used for the sleepers of the Madras Railways, but afterwards the trees deemed eligible were increased considerably, and again greatly diminished in number, as further experience has been gained. The trees recommended at times have been

1. Tectona grandis..........Teak.
2. Vatica robusta............Sal.
3. Dalbergia sissoo.........Sissoo.
4. Pterocarpus Indicus.....Pedowk.
5. Terminalia glabra........Karra marda.
6. ,, alata.........Maruthi maram.
7. Hardwickia binata.......Acha maram.
8. Pterocarpus marsupium.Vengé maram.
9. Terminalia chebula......Kadukai maram.
10. Conocarpus species......Nikani maram.
11. Soymida febrifuga.......Som maram, also Chor-kalli, also Somida wood.
12. Acacia odoratissima......Karru Venge, also Chella Wunge maram.
13. Prosopis spicigera.......Perambe maram.
14. Inga xylocarpa............Erruvalu maram, also Erool.
15. Acacia Arabica...........Karuvelu maram.
16. Bassia longifolia.........Dud Ilupe maram.
17. Acacia speciosa..........Kat vai maram, also Velvengé maram.
18. Kumbadri maram?
19. Aré wood.
20. Artocarpus hirsutus.......Angili.
21. Acacia sundra.............Karangalli.
22. Terminalia catappa......Nat vadam kotte.
23. Bignonia xylocarpa......Vaden Kume.
24. Conocarpus latifolia......Vella Nage.
25. Grewia tiliæfolia.........Sadachu.
26. Brièdelia spinosa.........Mullu venge.
27. Garuga pinnata...........Ani Karra.
28. Bignonia chelonoides....Padri maram.
29. Schleichera trijuga......Puvu maram.
30. Feronia elephantum.....Vilagam.
31. Hym.

Amongst those approved of, in 1855, which have since been removed from the list at present authorized, are the

Zizyphus glabrata............Karkatta.
Bauhinia diphylla............Acha maram.
Artocarpus integrifolia.
Kombadri.

But, in the Madras Railway, the experience of the Engineers has satisfied them that the timbers valuable for sleepers are so few, that iron-pot sleepers have been substituted for wooden ones on the Northern parts of their line.

In 1859-60, the number of sleepers delivered to the Madras Railway Company, in the Salem district, was 2,45,743. The largest number was from the genera Terminalia and Conocarpus of the Natural Family, Combretaceæ, and remarkable for the height and size of their trunks and the toughness of their timber. Their durability under ground has not been satisfactorily established, and the Terminalia chebula (Kadukai) appears to be liable both to the attacks of fungi and the carpenter bee, and, therefore, to be excluded from the specification list. Dr. Cleghorn, in his report for 1859-60, mentions that "Railway Sleepers which ought to have stood five or six years at least, have been found useless after being laid down not more than one-third of that time: in fact there are some parts of the Madras line where it was necessary that they should be taken up and replaced before the District itself was completed." It may be doubted whether any Indian forests or any Railway Company can long bear so great a tax as this, and iron sleepers are now coming greatly in use on the Madras line of rail. Exclusive of teak, which is found too expensive, the Railway Engineer Officers had most confidence in Saul, Ilupe or Bassia longifolia, Karra marda or Terminalia glabra, Vengé or Pterocarpus marsupium, and the Chella Wunge or Acacia odoratissima, but the Inga xylocarpa has seemed best of all. It has been well said that the most important applications of wood are in the building and repairing of houses and ships, and in the construction of machinery. For these purposes, the woods of the larger trees, which come under the denomination of timber, are chiefly employed. For all engineering purposes, it is desirable, not only that the wood should be strong and not liable to decay from mere exposure to the weather, but, also, that it should work freely, and be able to withstand the ravages of the various insects to which wood of all kinds is more or less exposed in tropical countries. It is true that even the most porous and spongy woods may be rendered to some extent capable of resisting all such influences, by being impregnated with various solutions, but it is obviously far better, when possible, to select such woods as are naturally saturated with resinous and aromatic substances, as in this latter case all cost of preparation is saved, besides that the preserving matter is far more perfectly disseminated throughout the whole of the wood than can possibly be effected by any artificial process after the tree is felled. In examining the comparative value of different sorts of wood, it is of the first importance to ascertain the nature of the encrusting matter deposited throughout the cells and tubes of the wood. For all practical purposes, those woods appear to be best in which the cells are lined with resinous matter; those filled with hygroscopic gummy matter are, for the most part, of less value; they are seasoned with difficulty, and are always more liable to decay. The best woods are those having a strong fibre protected from all external influences by a coat of resinous matter, or at least of a matter insoluble in water, and one which does not attract atmospheric moisture. It is probable also, that some of the ornamental and other woods of India will become articles of import into Britain when their properties and uses are better known and appreciated by that country's artizans.—*Jur. Rep. of* 1851.

In collecting specimens to exhibit the characters of wood, the points to which attention should be directed, have been thus laid down : viz.

a. The uses to which the several parts of the tree is applied, and those for which the experienced natives of the country consider it specially adapted.

b. Its distribution in the district, the localities where the best is procurable, with the nature of the subsoil, the distance from the nearest seaport, or town of any size, whether water carriage be available ?

c. The extent of supply, whether this is increasing by self-sown seedlings of fresh plantations, &c. or is decreasing ? the average size in height and circumference of the native tree, its character, whether straight or crooked, the average length, &c. of the logs or planks, the time required for seasoning, and the amount of seasoned timber generally procurable.

d. The age at which the tree reaches maturity, *i. e.* when increasing age brings no further increase of diameter. This is a point of great importance ; for, on it depends the relative value of trees for planting. Thus, supposing there are two species of trees, of equal value as regards timber, &c., but one attains maturity in 25, while the other requires 35 years, it is obvious that the first is much the more valuable of the two : its money value being realised ten years sooner.

The value of wood depends much on its age. The young tree possesses strength and elasticity in a greater degree than mature, *i. e.* when it would shortly cease to increase in diameter ; as it increases in age it acquires its maximum of stiffness and durability, and in its aged state, it would probably best suit the purposes of the cabinet maker. The grain of the wood depends greatly on the nature of the soil, being generally straight and open in a tree growing rapidly, in a rich, and the reverse in a poor soil. In some cases, the root affords wood of great resisting power for furniture, the root of a healthy oak, for instance, is preferred for spokes of wheels, and veneers from that of an aged specimen, often bear a high value for cabinet makers' purposes. But the value of wood and timber in India, is not to be measured by the estimation in which they are held, in England. In India, they are not only applied to those economic uses with which all in Britain, are familiar, but they also furnish fuel to all classes, supplying the place of that valuable mineral, coal. Besides this, the influence of trees on climate is very considerable, tending as they do, to prevent the too rapid withdrawal of moisture from the soil, a point of great importance in a country where the heat of the sun is intense and the supply of water is dependent only upon periodical falls of rain. It is impossible to ascertain the amount used in India. But there are some data which allows an idea to be formed of the quantities required. The quantity of firewood alone imported, by sea, into Madras during 5 years is given below, and that for 1849-50 was estimated by the Military Board to be equal to 12,000 tons.

Years.	Billets.	Value Rs.
1845-46	63,61,816	32,536
1846-47	42,77,013	22,746
1847-48	56,78,794	31,974
1848-49	104,75,590	58,026
1849-50	98,51,050	66,101

The above is exclusive of imports by Cochrane's Canal, and the trunk roads which that

Board estimated at upwards of 85,000 tons yearly.

The trade Reports of the Madras Presidency show that the exports of the following five woods alone, amounted in value to 3,84,000 Rs. in 1854, viz.:—

Sandalwood, cwt ....11,684.........137,944
Redwood, ,, ...47,431......... 59,570
Sappanwood, cwt .... 5,248......... 15,350
Ebonywood, ,, ... 4,859
Teak, ,, ...216,368

The imports of timber into Great Britain alone in 1850, amounted to ten millions of cubic feet.

The value of the Imports and Exports into Calcutta, Madras and Bombay, has been :—

Imports into Bengal

1854-55.	Fir.	Mahogany.	Masts and Spars.	Planks.	Sleepers.	Teak.
FROM	Rs.	Rs.	Rs.	Rs.	Rs.	Rs.
United Kingdom	...	3,110	1,224	18,136	1,76,349	...
North America	1,07,542	36,420	38,787	...	...	...
South America	...	...	...	...	165	...
Ceylon	...	...	...	266	5,461	...
France	...	...	...	463	...	...
Bourbon	...	...	...	...	...	61
Hamburg	...	...	933	...	...	44
Rangoon	...	...	...	...	1,188	3,82,820
New Zealand	...	...	2,429	...	...	...
Penang, Singapore & Malacca	...	...	65	3,381	...	886

In this year, the Exports and Re-exports from Bengal to Mauritius were respectively Rupees 550 of Saul timber and Rupees 80 of Teak.

Imports into Bengal

1855-56.	Mahogany.	Masts and Spars.	Planks.	Satin.	Sleepers.	Teak.	Timber Saul.
FROM	Rs.	Rs.	Rs.	Rs.	Rs.	Rs.	Rs.
United Kingdom	...	731	6,894	...	2,32,910	...	...
North America	50,008	47,788	21,354	...	...	...	...
Bourbon	...	...	...	104	...	...	...
Cape of Good Hope	...	...	50	...	...	...	...
Ceylon	...	...	...	3,899	2,186	...	...
France	...	165	415	...	...	...	...
Bombay	...	...	...	...	...	500	...
Rangoon	...	400	...	...	...	5,89,820	...
Persian Gulf	...	...	10,659	...	...	...	...
Exports from Bengal to							
Bourbon	...	...	...	...	...	...	220
France	...	...	...	...	...	...	13,247
Mauritius	...	...	...	...	...	...	2,269
Re-exports from Bengal to							
United Kingdom	...	...	...	...	...	545	...
Ceylon	...	...	...	...	...	571	...
Mauritius	...	1,175	...	...	...	...	...
Penang, Singapore and Malacca	...	250	...	...	...	...	...
New South Wales	...	125	...	...	...	...	...

Imports into Bengal

1856-57.	Mahogany.	Masts and Spars.	Planks.	Sleepers.	Teak.	Timber Saul.
FROM	Rs.	Rs.	Rs.	Rs.	Rs.	Rs.
United Kingdom	6,591	7,448	5,940	63,455	...	...
North America	...	51,878	52,935	...	...	...
Bourbon	...	...	206	...	...	...
China	...	650	...	...	...	...
France	...	...	1,431	...	...	...
Hamburg	...	...	1,120	...	...	...
Maldive Islands	...	100	...	...	...	...
Rangoon	...	...	...	...	1,19,115	...
Mauritius	...	...	350	...	...	...
Penang, Singapore & Malacca	...	...	1,730	...	1,125	...
Ceylon	...	...	84	...	...	...

The Exports this year, from Bengal to United Kingdom, were Rupees 80 of Teak: Re-exports none.

1857-58.........None.

1858-59.	Mahogany.	Masts and Spars.	Planks.	Sleepers.	Teak.	Other Sorts.
From	Rs.	Rs.	Rs.	Rs.	Rs.	Rs.
United Kingdom	...	845	7,971	16,509	...	...
North America	4,543	24,622	70,911	...	...	...
China, Hongkong	...	...	23,880	...	...	...
Other ports	...	...	500	...	...	...
France	...	2,590	...	...	...	...
Hamburg	...	2,257	3,278	...	...	...
New South Wales	...	...	...	400	...	...
Penang, Singapore and Malacca	...	...	...	3,005	...	...
Rangoon	...	...	100	...	5,20,466	...

In this year, there were no Exports from Bengal and the Re-exports were to Rangoon, Rupees 100, of Teak.

Imports into Bengal

1859-60.	Mahogany.	Masts and Spars.	Planks.	Sleepers.	Teak.
From	Rs.	Rs,	Rs.	Rs.	Rs.
United Kingdom	2,944	390	...	4,844	12,454
North America	...	16,109	...	...	100,968
France	...	600	2,800	...	...
Hamburg	...	...	...	...	3,850
Mauritius	...	...	...	...	200
Penang, Singapore and Malacca.	...	100	...	...	...
Bombay	1,713	...	...	...	...
Akyab	...	...	...	260	...
Rangoon	...	...	12,200	...	356,739
China	...	742	...	...	...
Moulmein	...	...	485,683	950	151,511

In this year there were no Exports from Bengal and the Re-exports were to the Mauritius, Rupees 1,250, of Teak.

Imports into Bombay

1858-59.	Masts and Spars.	Planks.	Other Sorts.	Teak.	Black Timber.
From	Rs.	Rs.	Rs.	Rs.	Rs.
United Kingdom	5,830	12,160	20,385	...	...
North America	249	230,007	...	...	...
Mauritius	...	65,040	...	...	...
France	...	...	208	...	...
Penang, Singapore	...	23,430	...	648	...
Siam	...	46,011	...	994	...
Calcutta	...	...	...	4,400	...
Moulmein	...	...	...	146,191	...
Rangoon	...	...	...	105,341	...
Concan	...	...	...	185	...
Guzerat	...	...	...	1,246	...
Exports from Bombay to					
Arabian Gulf	...	1,054	1,000	...	...
Persian Gulf	...	...	...	5,164	...
Cutch	...	...	3,289	680	...
Re-exports from Bombay to					
Aden	...	...	...	2,275	...
Persian Gulf	320	...	...	1,219	...
Guzerat	...	...	...	...	2,848

TIMBER, IMPORTS AND EXPORTS.

Imports into Bombay

1859-60.	Masts and Spars.	Planks.	Teak.	Other sorts.
FROM	Rs.	Rs.	Rs.	Rs.
United Kingdom	9,902	13,799	34,792	...
Aden	...	2,099	...	...
North America	270	20,731	...	...
Bourbon	...	25	...	...
China and other Ports	120	...	...	...
Penang, Singapore and Malacca	...	11,837	...	...
Siam	...	28,634	1,603	...
Calcutta	...	45	...	...
Moulmein	...	...	161,680	...
Rangoon	...	56,095	31,070	...
Guzerat	...	...	7,811	...

The only Export from Bombay was to Persian Gulf, Rupees 4,644, of Timber of sorts.

Re-exports from Bombay to

	Masts and Spars.	Planks.	Teak.	Other sorts.
Mauritius	...	300	...	...
Persian Gulf	...	...	1,675	...
Goa, Demaun and Diu	140	...	...	...

Imports into Bombay

1860-61.	Masts and Spars.	Planks.	Teak.	Other sorts.	Black Timber.
FROM	Rs.	Rs.	Rs.	Rs.	Rs.
United Kingdom	2,016	11,986	...	...	...
Africa	...	95	...	332	...
North America	...	4,780	...	...	...
China	...	...	...	600	...
Penang, Singapore and Malacca	525	...	8,678	...	11,575
Siam	...	1,207	6,780	...	...
Moulmein	...	18,900	107,641	...	...
Rangoon	...	...	43,404	...	...
Goa, Demaun and Diu	...	...	364	...	...
Guzerat	...	...	845	...	...

The only Export from Bombay was to Cutch, Rupees 419, of Black Timber.

Imports, into Madras Territories, for the last 10 *years, from*

	United Kingdom.	America.	Ceylon.	Pegu.	W. Coast of Sumatra.	W Indies.	Cape of Good Hope.	Bengal.	Bombay.	Sumatra.	Indian F. Ports.	Malacca Straits.	Travancore.
	Rs.	Rs.	Rs.	Rs.	Rs.	Rs.	Rs.	Rs.	Rs.	Rs.	Rs.	Rs.	Rs.
1851-52	80	2,434	1,00,851	1,81,294	244	10	...	17,206	...	...	74	2,820	18,263
1852-53	25	2,723	1,19,065	84,357	...	...	...	8,993	...	...	861	11,372	22,020
1853-54	645	2,373	1,45,380	2,32,523	...	...	...	8,536	800	...	516	9,195	40,802
1854-55	...	4,551	1,28,071	570	...	...	...	9,137	...	...	1,142	2,319	44,685
1855-56	3,215	1,028	1,36,525	50	...	...	...	20,240	...	...	632	4,279	89,599
1856-57 Teak	...	...	...	...	...	...	...	1,607	...	...	...	90	...
Mahogany	...	2,983	...	...	...	...	...	...	...	...	...	...	...
Timber and Plank	3,222	5,047	1,59,721	...	...	...	...	5,320	116	...	...	2,901	74,035
1857-58	...	2,763	1,33,882	...	...	...	690	10,198	...	...	3,002	7,456	96,870
1858-59 Poon Spars	...	1,412	...	...	...	...	...	2,445	...	...	...	...	...
Teak	...	...	326	...	...	...	...	3,788	...	...	...	40	1,046
Timber and Plank	...	14,681	1,78,797	...	...	...	...	175	...	122	...	3,912	1,21,695
1859-60	2,119	5,153	1,53,616	...	...	...	...	746	...	...	561	3,312	78,970
1860-61	20,869	6,747	1,48,667	...	...	...	...	...	671	75	2,877	5,608	51,486

	N. South Wales.	Chittagong.	Concan.	Balasore.	Mauritius.	China.	Bassein.	Moulmein.	Rangoon.	France.	Laccadive Islands.	Arracan.	Grand Total.
	Rs.	Rs.	Rs.	Rs.	Rs.	Rs.	Rs.	Rs.	Rs.	Rs.	Rs.	Rs.	Rs.
1851-52	...	...	...	...	...	...	...	...	...	...	...	...	3,23,276
1852-53	...	...	155	...	...	...	...	...	...	...	...	...	2,49,416
1853-54	7	...	...	...	100	...	...	...	...	...	...	...	4,41,032
1854-55	1,058	...	...	...	...	300	...	1,92,743	130	...	...	...	3,72,795
1855-56	...	...	...	...	150	...	...	5,95,593	31,033	...	213	...	8,82,557
1856-57 Teak	...	...	...	...	...	...	12,000	1,16,476	15,600	...	...	...	1,45,173
Mahogany	...	...	...	...	...	...	...	...	...	...	...	...	2,983
Timber and Plank	...	...	...	364	...	...	30	5,85,382	23,698	...	...	...	8,60,764
1857-58	...	...	...	...	...	...	...	12,47,912	39,863	...	...	...	15,42,636
1858-59 Poon Spars	...	...	...	...	...	...	...	...	...	...	...	...	3,857
Teak	...	...	...	...	...	...	...	4,09,949	39,227	...	...	...	4,54,376
Timber and Plank	...	...	...	...	...	...	...	32,578	8,941	...	...	...	3,63,967
1859-60	...	**5,552**	**45**	...	...	...	150	**4,89,790**	**40,905**	**3,046**	...	120	7,84,082
1860-61	...	**6,502**	**306**	...	...	...	...	**3,71,461**	**35,035**	...	...	...	6,50,345

Exports, from Madras Territories, for the last* 10 *years.

Year	Article	United Kingdom.	Arabia and Persian Gulf.	Persian Gulf.	Ceylon.	Maldive Islands.	Mauritius.	Bengal.	Bombay.	
		Rs.	Rs.	Rs.	Rs.	Rs.	Rs.	Rs.	Rs.	Rs.
1851-52		27	15,980	...	190	431	357	2,983	227,670	
1852-53	Poon Spars	...	4,799	...	...	...	...	...	8,711	
	Teak	...	13,398	...	...	69	...	...	275,456	
	Timber and Planks.	...	3,075	...	...	...	...	1,895	1,211	
1853-54	Bamboo	...	5	...	...	1	...	...	8,881	
	Timber and Planks.	...	5,185	...	...	...	389	...	...	
	Teak	...	7,985	...	...	52	...	...	150,214	
	Poon Spars	11	4,554	...	...	...	...	...	13,638	
1854-55		...	8,883	1,580	...	...	...	243	191,511	
1855-56	Poon	...	2,509	1,729	...	...	...	...	13,829	Co 's
	Teak	...	477	6,083	...	...	...	...	157,256	Acct.
	Timber and Planks.	...	3,141	6,009	...	...	...	...	3,330	44,345*
1856-57	Poon	...	1,468	107	...	...	...	...	14,140	
	Teak	...	5,171	729	72	...	...	...	210,727	36,770
	Timber and Planks.	...	...	...	110	...	...	13,685	2,244	
1857-58	Poon	...	2,303	...	...	...	...	...	26,887	
	Teak	...	8,505	23	587	...	67	...	250,912	23,983
	Timber and Planks.	...	1,554	...	427	...	136	...	92	
1858-59	Poon	...	2,100	1,705	...	...	...	...	16,928	
	Teak	...	60,714	30	...	5	66	...	184,653	26,016
	Timber and Planks.	...	...	...	220	...	...	1,412	...	
1859-60	Poon	...	4,300	3,061	...	...	...	...	7,126	
	Teak	...	28,179	18	...	...	...	11,065	177,702	
	Timber and Planks.	...	6,447	...	1,779	31	244	...	...	
1860-61	Poon	...	6,707	3,313	...	..	...	...	10,418	
	Teak	...	18,860	150	...	...	...	35	2,34,802	
	Timber and Planks or other Sorts	101	18,150	1,011	844	277	168	10	1,74,284	

Year	Article	Concan.	Cutch.	Goa.	Guzerat.	Indian F. Ports.	Sind.		Turkey
		Rs.	Rs.	Rs.	Rs.	Rs.	Rs.		Rs.
1851-52		92	12,728	253	138	1,854	3,097		...
1852-53	Poon Spars	...	1,942	...	...	...	111		...
	Teak	301	26,523	13	...	...	2,467		...
	Timber and Planks.	...	81	15	1	...	141		...
1853-54	Bamboo	31	3,715	...	26	12	2,776		...
	Timber and Planks.	...	...	...	...	...	...		...
	Teak	324	27,900	...	...	...	3,933		...
	Poon Spars	33	2,757	...	...	115	401		...
1854-55		...	21,067	3,845	105	922	1,344		...
1855-56	Poon	9	2,230	...	...	93	342		...
	Teak	52	19,101	6	...	...	5,974		...
	Timber and Planks.	...	273	641	...	70	297		...
1856-57	Poon	66	4,528	...	...	67	422		218
	Teak	...	17,504	...	...	...	8,389		78
	Timber and Planks.	...	...	...	...	1,230	...		...
1857-58	Poon	87	6,403	...	127	...	129		1,080
	Teak	393	29,134	46	40	...	2,726		75
	Timber and Planks.	...	83	5	...	3,425	1,572	Co.'s	1,435
1858-59	Poon	338	9,117	...	96	...	376	Acct.	1,827
	Teak	...	38,203	342	102	5,850	8,150	1,608	...
	Timber and Planks.	...	...	56	...	...	...		...
1859-60	Poon	421	5,943	...	...	31	818		1,654
	Teak	1,466	18,955	549	926	...	3,394		78
	Timber and Planks.	4,120	9,252	3,923	705	1,913	16,673		1,214
1860-61	Poon	219	4,183	75	...	...	1,788		1,448
	Teak	967	14,250	170	48	13	3,489		...
	Timber and Planks or other Sorts	5,820	11,803	330	114	3,896	42,000		3,323

Exports, from Madras Territories, for the last 10 *years.—(Continued.)*

	France.	Bour-bon.	New South Wales.	Aden.	Tra-van-core.	Lacca-dive Is-lands.	Bas-scin.	Ran-goon.	Grand Total.	
	Rs.	Rs.	Rs.	Rs.	Rs.	Rs.	Rs.	Rs.	Rs.	Rs.
1851-52	...	...	...	...	...	...	...	...	2,65,800	
1852-53 Poon Spars	...	...	...	...	...	...	...	...	15,563	
Teak	...	...	...	...	...	...	...	...	3,18,227	
Timber and Planks.	...	...	...	...	...	...	...	...	6,419	
1853-54 Bamboo	...	...	...	...	...	...	...	...	15,447	
Timber and Planks.	...	...	...	...	...	...	...	...	14,580	
Teak	172	...	3,186	...	...	...	...	...	1,90,580	
Poon Spars	...	...	...	...	...	...	...	...	21,511	
1854-55	100	...	...	512	...	113	750	1,125	2,32,105	
1855-56 Poon	...	...	...	...	212	...	...	...	20,953	Co.'s
Teak	...	...	...	...	...	136	...	...	1,89,175	Acct.
Timber and Planks.	...	...	...	...	...	...	...	...	13,761	44,345
1856-57 Poon	...	...	...	...	267	...	...	...	21,283	
Teak	...	...	...	...	...	...	...	...	2,42,670	36,770
Timber and Planks.	...	...	...	...	...	...	...	...	17,269	
1857-58 Poon	...	...	...	...	80	79	...	...	37,206	
Teak	...	...	...	...	...	...	...	...	2,92,522	23,983
Timber and Planks.	...	...	...	...	...	...	...	...	8,729	
1858-59 Poon	...	...	...	...	...	...	...	...	32,149	
Teak	...	...	...	...	...	...	...	...	2,98,453	27,624
Timber and Planks.	...	...	...	...	...	...	...	1,500	3,188	
1859-60 Poon	...	...	...	...	631	224	...	...	24,209	
Teak	...	...	...	...	...	173	...	...	2,37,505	
Timber and Planks.	...	642	...	...	6	310	...	...	47,259	
1860-61 Poon	...	...	...	120	...	207	...	...	28,471	
Teak	...	...	...	187	...	...	...	...	2,72,971	
Timber and Planks or other Sorts	...	...	...	3,496	...	1,794	...	...	2,67,512	

In addition to the timber trees in Eastern and Southern Asia, there are woods suited for engraving, furniture and ornamental purposes. The forests of Southern India contain a variety of such woods but only ebony, rosewood or blackwood, satinwood and sandalwood are exported. Occasionally, beautiful specimens of ornamental woods are seen, equal to anything ever made up into furniture in England. The wood of the margosa tree (Azaderachta and Melia) is often very beautiful, though seldom employed, possibly from the difficulty of seasoning it,—and some samples of teak are veined and waved with a beauty not inferior to the finest mahogany. The Chittagong-wood (Chickrassia tabularis) light, cheap and durable, is more used in Madras for furniture than any other. The Toon (Cedrela toona) resembles its congeners, Chittagong-wood and mahogany, and is in much request for chairs and other furniture all over the Madras Presidency. Jackwood (Artocarpus integrifolia) takes a polish little inferior to mahogany and, in England, is used for the backs of hair brushes. A favourite furniture wood in Madras, however, is the Rosewood or East Indian Blackwood, (Dalbergia latifolia) but the satinwood (Chloroxylon Swietenia) and sandalwood (Santalum album) are well known ornamental woods. The cedar, one of the longest known ornamental woods, used for internal decorations, is a native of the warmer temperate mountainous regions of Asia. The Himalayan "*deodar*," a tree very closely related to, indeed by some supposed identical with, the Cedar of Lebanon, really possesses all the good qualities, for which the latter has been so long celebrated. But, travellers in writing about cedars, often confound various kinds of arborescent juniper and other woods under that name. (See Cedar.)

In searching for ornamental woods, it is well to remember that the wood of roots is different in structure from the wood of stems, and that the same tree may furnish two very different kinds of ornamental wood, according as they are derived from its ascending or its descending axis. This is well exemplified in the Lingoa and Kyaboka or Amboyna woods of commerce, both obtained from the Pterospermum Indicum. As Mr. Tomlinson remarks, the wood of the inner portions of a stem may be of very different colour and quality from that of its outer parts. In the immediate neighbourhood of the origin of branches, it may exhibit varieties of pattern, such as to render it greatly more ornamental than elsewhere, and, in some cases, when under the influence of morbid growth, reveals additional beauties, so as to be prized for qualities which in nature are defects. If we compare a number of transverse sections of wood, one with another, it will be evident that there are two principal types or modifications of structure. If a cross cutting of teak or mango be viewed along with a like portion of Palmyra wood, the differences between them will be strongly contrasted. In the former, the layers of wood are ranged in concentric circles round the central pith, and are encased externally in a binding of bark, itself composed of distinct and differently organized portions. In the latter, there is an uniform appearance throughout the section, the substance not being disposed in concentric rings, but appearing as if a bed or ground of one kind was studded with specks of another order of tissue. These dissimilarities indicate differences of the greatest structural importance in the economy of the respective trees. Corresponding with them are peculiar modifications of every portion of the plant's organization. The external aspect of the plants of either type is altogether unlike that of the other. It is, also, necessary to remember, that the inner layers of wood, after the tree has become aged, often become compact, and frequently different in colour from the new wood. They are then styled the heart-wood. Botanists term them the duramen and apply the name alburnum to the outer layers or sap-wood. In the former, the tissues have become dry and dense, and charged with solidifying deposits, so as to prevent them aiding in the ascent of the sap. Often, too, they become more or less deeply coloured, so as conspicuously to contrast with the pale sap-wood. This difference is especially conspicuous in the ebony-tree, the black portion of which is the duramen, or heart-wood.

Several Indian woods have, from time to time, been tried for the purposes of the engraver; and we may instance those of the guava (Psidium pyriferum); the Mimusops hexandra: Wrightia antidysenterica; the jujube-tree (Zizyphus jujuba): the wood apple tree (Feronia elephantum) the satin-wood, and a species of box from the Himalaya.

Conservation.—The preservation of growing timber is an art of considerable importance, and can be said only to be fully in operation in countries where timber is comparatively scarce. Within the last twenty years, however, its necessity, for India, has been acknowledged, and, in the Punjab, Sind, Bombay, Madras and Pegu, scientific men of recognised attainments, are now employed as Conservators. They mostly have directed a knowledge of botany to the duties of their office; and, in a few years more, our acquaintance with the forests and their products ought to be very perfect. Plantations of Teak, Acacia Arabica, Thespesia populnea and of Australian trees have been formed in several parts, and their larger extension may be looked for. And the extension of this practice, with the preservation of the existing forest trees of India, producing timber, is of the utmost importance; for, everywhere, the forests are diminishing and, in numerous places, actually disappearing before the advancing population of the countries. Dr. Cleghorn, writing regarding the western parts of India and the disappearance of its forests, mentions, from authorities (Dr. Hove's Travels 1786, Buchanan 1801, Lord Valentia's Travels 1804), the fact that, in the beginning of the century, an immense, almost unbroken, forest covered the Western Ghauts on the Malabar Coast, from near the water shed to the most elevated ridges, then left to nature, thinly peopled, abounding in wild animals, and all the higher portions without exception, covered with timber; and, even now, the passing traveller, looking down from the higher peaks of Coorg or Malabar, conceives that an inexhaustible forest lies below him; but, as he descends the ghauts, he finds that the best timber has been cut away and that the wood contractor is felling in more remote localities. He speaks, he says, especially of teak, blackwood and poon spars, which are everywhere becoming more scarce in accessible situations. And he adds that the practice in India, has been the converse of that in Europe, where the soft wood is thinned out and the hard woods left. But, here, the valuable kinds are removed and the scrub left. By one of the authorities whom he quotes, burning the jungles was recommended as a sanatory measure and to diminish the number of wild animals, but circumstances have much changed since then. For, now, the axe of the coffee planter and of the koomree cultivator (see Koomri) have made extensive and often wanton havoc, devastating a large portion of the area of the primeval forest. And, though the former is encouraged, as endeavouring to rescue the soil for legitimate purposes (except when the timber is peculiarly valuable), the squatter who clears, without leave, in one year, the land which he abandons the next, is punished and repressed. Such profuse waste has been altogether prohibited in Mysore and the Bombay collectorates, and is checked to a great extent in Canara, but has not altogether ceased. The exertions of the Collector and Sub-Collector have, however, been very successful in keeping under the destruction, called koomree, caused by vagabond tribes burning wood with the view of raising from the ashes a crop of inferior grain. He specifies Palghaut, the Shevaroy Hills, and the North Arcot Hills, as instances where the old woods have every where fallen, to meet the urgent demand for timber. He quotes the official Road Book (published not many years ago) containing, opposite Walliar, this remark, "Dense jungle, beware of elephants," but, adds that, in looking from the staging bungalow, the traveller sees several tentative lines of Rail each 200 yards broad and so extensive a clearing of the neighbouring forest that no elephant could easily find a cover. The encircling hills, formerly crowned with timber, are now to a considerable degree laid bare. And these changes, so far as he could learn, have been the gradual result of unrestricted cutting, but much aggravated during the last few years. Lieutenant Beddome's report on the Pulney Hills, communicated by Government to the Madras Journal of Science, describes the devastation which has been committed there in the formation of plantain gardens. The green hills have been stripped of their woods, and much of their beauty has departed.—*Madras Conservator's Report.*

Dr. Gibson, writing of Sind, remarks that, with few exceptions, the whole number of middle Sind forests were mere skeletons of what they were under Major Scott in 1847, when they were all properly surveyed. Since then, a steady system of destruction had been carried on by the zemindars, and, whether from misrepresentation or ignorance of the extent of the injury, a stop had not been put to it by the Forest Department. Although Major Scott, Captain Crawford, and Dr. Stocks all foresaw, and had all placed on record their opinion that the system of giving up forest land to cultivators would end in the ruin of the forests, yet he believed that no one could have imagined the rapidity with which the utter ruin of nearly all the forests had been accomplished. He described the existing forests of Mid-Sind as the Nassree and Mudh forests; the Mehrabpoor forest which contains a very small quantity of timber in three detached moharees: the Marree forests, a large area, but a very poor straggling forest, with few large trees in it; the Rannah forest on the left bank of the Ghara creek. The Noorpoor Bootta forest is on the right bank of the river, opposite Rannah; and, on the same side of the river, is the Majenda forest, on the left bank is the Noor Kettee forest; in the Bhanote forest were a few good Babool trees, the rest being Kundee and Tamarisk; the Khanote forest, thirty-two miles above Hyderabad, had been a very fine forest, and there were still a few fine Babool and Bhawn trees in it; on the right bank is the Oonerpoor or Meysah Gote Baila. The Khebranee forest is also mentioned by him. In the Shekaot forest, he says, the timber trees were scattered about. The Jakree forest is mentioned as having very little timber—nothing to speak of. The Kettee or Muttaree Baila had some good young trees on the river bank. On the right bank, is the Gug or Pettara forest, divided into two parts by the cultivators. The Gullee forest, on the left bank of the river, had not much timber left. In the Goondee Baila forest, nothing was left but a few trees on the bank of a nulla, not worth cutting down. Meer Mahomed Khan's forest was reported to have been then closed for three years. The Katra forest, on the left bank of the Fullailee. He proposed strictly to enclose the following forests—Marree, left bank; Canote, left bank; Meeanee (two), left bank; Noorpoor Bootta, right bank; Oonerpoor, right bank; Gug or Pettara, right bank. The quantity of wood supplied for the Indus Flotilla in the last year of his report was 190,000 maunds.—*Surgeon Gibson's Bombay Forest Report,* 1849 to 1856, pp. 223 to 229.

In a report to Government, for 1859, Dr. Cleghorn mentions that the establishment of railways causes such an immense demand for timber, as entirely to change the features of the districts through which they pass. Each sleeper, he remarked, measures three cubic feet, and as one mile of single rails requires 1,760 sleepers, and these will not, on an average, last above eight years at the most, we have an annual demand of at least 220 sleepers per mile, or 22,000 for every hundred miles. He estimated the total length of lines in the Madras Presidency, either sanctioned or contemplated, at about 1,150 miles, so that, if the above estimate as to duration be correct, at least 2,53,000 sleepers, say 35,000 trees, will be required annually. A portion of these, he thought, would, no doubt, be procured from England, Ceylon, Burmah, the Andamans, and perhaps Australia, but he considered that there would still be a regular and heavy drain on the forests of the Madras Presidency. And, to meet this prospective demand, he recommended that immediate steps should be taken to raise large numbers of hard-wood trees suitable for sleepers, especially as sleepers of indigenous woods may be estimated at one-half the cost of those obtained from England. And he suggested that railway companies, irrigation companies, sugar factory proprietors and others, who consume large quantities of fuel, charcoal and timber, should plant, to some extent, for their own use, in station compounds, along railway embankments, on the banks of channels, &c.

On another occasion, he reports (1859-60) that there are many causes at work which are gradually thinning the ranks of the indigenous forests of the Madras Presidency. The first and by far the most formidable of these is *Railway requirements.* And he adds that it is scarcely credible the many thousands of large forest trees which have been felled in the neighbourhood of the various lines of railway within the last few years. He alludes to another source of diminution, but affecting only scrubby copse and minor forest, viz. the extension of cultivation, consequent upon the reduction of the land tax and increased facilities of communication.

He tells us that the forests of Malabar and Canara still abound in fuel, whilst the jungles of the East Coast are generally small and stunted, except the mangrove belts of the Godaveri and

Kistna deltas, and the woods of the moist climate of Orissa, where there is a more rapid growth of luxuriant vegetation. Dr. Cleghorn urges various means of checking this destruction. Amongst the foremost of these is planting, and in this some progress has been made by the late Mr. Conolly with teak, and, on the Neilgherries, with Australian trees. Dr. Gibson largely preserved and planted the Acacia Arabica and made some progress with the Thespesia populnea, and Mr. Rohde planted many seeds of the mangrove. Wherever salt water tidal creeks occur, with muddy banks, the seeds of the mangrove tribe might be sown; various species of Acacia might be grown in the interior, and the dirisana (Acacia speciosa) might be encouraged. The entire eastern coast of the peninsula might be planted with the Cocoanut and the Casuarina, and groves of the useful Palmyrah might be seen in every village. But, Dr. Cleghorn is of opinion that the preservation and increase of the Palmyrah should remain in connection with the Abkari department. It grows well on all the barren ground of the coast at present unproductive. The sandy soil is congenial to it. The seeds buried in drifting sand often take root, and make their way to the surface. This palm also grows well in the stiff black mould near the backwaters, where the seed should be planted eight inches deep, when the soil is moist.

In the process of conservation of forests and plantations, the practice of thinning them out, not only as affording a supply of wood, but, by admitting an increased supply of air and light to the remaining trees, promoting their growth, is one of much importance. In all forests, too, on the borders of which an active population reside, he thinks it essential that certain trees should be reserved, and amongst these, he recommends the following for the value of their timber.

1. Santalum album. Sandal.	8. Artocarpus integrifolia. Jack.
2. Pterocarpus santalinus or Red Saunders.	9. Hardwickia binata. Acha maram.
3. Diospyros melanoxylon. Ebony.	10. Terminalia coriacea. Marda.
4. Chloroxylon Swietenia. Satinwood.	11. Common Terminalia.
5. Tectona grandis. Teak.	12. Terminalia glabra. Glabrous Terminalia.
6. Dalbergia latifolia. Blackwood	13. Nauclea cadamba. Kadam
7. Borassus flabelliformis. Palmyra.	14. Acacia Arabica. Babul.
	15. Acacia speciosa. Sirissa.
	16. Acacia catechu. Catechu.

He adds the following as the trees or shrubs which should be reserved for the value of their products.

1. Custard apple.	8. Ventilago Maderaspatana. Surul Chaki.
2. Psidium pyriferum. Guava.	9. Acacia concinna. Si-kai-maram.
3. Soap-nut.	10. Calophyllum inophyllum. Pinné.
4. Rottlera tinctoria. Calipa	11. Tamarindus Indica. Tamarind.
5. Illupé.	
6. Cashew-nut.	
7. Strychnos potatorum. Tetaucotay.	

He particularizes Satinwood, Sandalwood, Redwood, Acacia leucophlea (the bark of which is used in distilleries), and the A. Catechu, as producing products, the collection of which require the destruction of the tree; those products also should be reserved in any agreements made with contractors to prevent extermination. Under native rule, the reserved trees comprised only Teak, Sandal, and Blackwood, but the Madras Government has extended the rule to others, highly valuable for building purposes, viz.

Jack, (Artocarpus integrifolia)	Palava, (Mimusops.)
Ayenee, (Artocarpus hirsuta.)	Muradhu (Terminalia coriacea)
Vengay, (Pterocarpus marsupium.)	Cedar, (Cedrela toona.)
	Erool, (Inga xylocarpa.)

And Dr. Cleghorn particularly directs attention to the preservation of the Teak, Dammer, (Shorea,) Yegis (Pterocarpus), Blackwood. Ebony, Conda Tungadoo (Inga xylocarpa), the varieties of Muddee (Terminalia), Nauclea (Daduga) and Cadamba, and Yepi (Bauhinia diphylla) as all valuable woods. But, in another report, he adds that, for the future one thing seems evident, viz. incorporated bodies must plant quick-growing trees for their own use, and amongst these he classes the

Acacia Arabica.	Cassia Florida.
Acacia leucophlea.	Cassia Javanica.
Acacia speciosa.	Inga dulcis.

In summing up the value of plantations, he says they create and improve the soil, and secure the permanency of the springs; they shelter from violent winds and modify the climate; they furnish material for house-building, furniture, &c.; they furnish fuel, fencing materials, &c.; and, they are ornamental.—*(Cleghorn's Forests and Gardens of South India*, p. 171.)

It has already been remarked that the preservation of growing timber is an art of considerable importance, and can only be said to be cultivated in countries where timber is comparatively scarce. The practice of thinning out plantations is of importance not only as affording a supply of wood, but, by admitting an increased supply of air and light to the remaining trees, their growth is greatly promoted. Forest trees are often planted on soil that is unfit for other purposes and by the annual fall of leaves they accumulate in time a certain depth of soil.

Seasoning.—The proper time for the felling of trees is described to be that in which the largest quantity of hard and durable wood can be obtained as free from sap as possible. It is a common fault to fell trees before they have attained their maturity. If suffered to complete their growth, they would have the heartwood of equal weight and strength throughout; whereas, in those cut down prematurely, the centre wood alone possesses this requisite, the outer concentric rings being considerably softer: such timber may be said to decrease in hardness and strength in arithmetical proportion as it approaches the sap wood. All trees should be felled when there is least sap. In deciduous plants, like teak, this is indicated by the nakedness of the trees, and in evergreens by the ripening and falling of the fruit. The proportion of heart to sap wood varies in different trees, according to the age at which they have been felled and the soil upon which they have grown. In mature trees, there is no sap wood, and it is one of the main objects of conservancy that these only should be cut. In cold countres, timber is felled during the cold months, when the natural juices are most inactive and the tree is in a measure dormant. With the Kurambars, who are employed in felling and squaring timber in the Sigur forests, the practice is to fell after full and in the waning moon, and to employ themselves in squaring, during the increasing moon. They also fell chiefly in the months of December, January and February while the trees are leafless. It is a wide-spread opinion that trees should be felled during the wane of the moon. This planetary influence is open to doubt, but the opinion prevails wherever there are large forests: the wood-cutters of South America act upon it, and the natives of this country believe that the timber is much more likely to decay if cut when the moon is on the increase. It has been stated that trees felled after ringing or girdling, have the heart-shake increased, and, if this be the fact, it is difficult to give an explanation. But, before the timber can be used, the juices must be got rid of from the capillary vessels, or the wood will remain moist or green for a considerable period, and the planks formed from it will, in a confined situation, become stained, and then subject to decay or dry rot: these effects are prevented by free exposure to dry air. It is described to be usual in the royal dockyards to cut out the timbers for ships of the required shape and dimensions about a year before they are framed together, and the skeleton frame is usually left another year to complete the seasoning. In some way or other, as will be seen, the natural juices of the tree must be got rid of, by seasoning, in order that the wood may become dry and hard. After the tree has been lopped, barked, and roughly squared, it is left for some time exposed to the weather, and may be soaked in fresh running water (as some think) with advantage, or boiled or steamed. This dilutes and washes out the juices, which, the more readily evaporate from the wood at a subsequent period, and the colour of white woods is said to be improved thereby. In this way, fir timber, on its arrival at the port of London, is commonly formed into floats on the Thames, and allowed to remain for some time. Teak, Sal, Blackwood, &c., improve by lying in water or in the soft black mud of an estuary, but the Nauclea cordifolia decidedly deteriorates from steeping. It has been suggested that desiccation may be expedited by first immersing timber in water and then drying it in a current of air; and, it is mentioned that, instead of immersing the logs in water, the practice is sometimes adopted of burying them in a dunghill which is regarded as a modification of the steaming process, by which the nitrogenous matter is dissolved out. When timber is removed from the water, it is left to dry thoroughly before it is taken to the pit to be sawn; usually, it is blocked up from the ground so as to have a free circulation of air; and, if it be cut into boards, they should be piled one on the other with billets of wood between them, or laid in a triangular form, with their ends alternating so as to allow the air to have free access to them. In cold countries, such as England, thin pieces will be seasoned in about a year, but thick wood requires two or three years before it is removed into the house to complete the drying. The warm air of a stove-heated room will then act upon it with benefit. In the stacking of timber for the purpose of seasoning, the pile should be so far raised from the ground as to allow the air to circulate below, as well as around and through it; and, if not sheltered from the rain, care should be taken to prevent the wet from lodging in any part. It is now usual in English dockyards to have elevated supports of iron or of stone for the stacking of timber, and all over Europe, ships are built under covered sheds. The drying of timber should be gradual, for, if rapid, it suffers a loss in toughness as well as in pliability: the pores at and near the surface become contracted and prevent the interior moisture from escaping. Plans for the more rapid drying of timber by means of kilns have, however, been tried, as in Price's patent, in which timber destined for building purposes is placed in a room, into the lower part of which hot and dry air is introduced, and this, charged with the moisture of the timber, is allowed to escape at the upper part. By this process, timber can be seasoned in one-third of the time required in the open air. Oak loses nearly two-fifths of its weight by proper seasoning. All timber should be dry before it is cut into planks, or they would be liable to warp and shrink. Amongst the advantages of seasoning, Dr. Cleghorn also mentions, in his reports, that seasoned logs of teak become lighter by 25 per cent. In India, as he tells us, in seasoning timber, it is of the utmost importance to protect it from heat and especially from the hot winds, to prevent splitting, which greatly detracts from its value. But logs should never be so enclosed that they cannot be exposed to a free current of air. The ends are most liable to split up, and then the cracks are generally radial, but occasionally concentric, and the harder the wood, the more likely is it to crack. The best modes of protection, he says, are dipping the ends of the log in a mixture of cow-dung and water, or covering them with grease, mud, petroleum or matting. Timber, if expected to last, must be thoroughly dried by exposure to sun and air, and ventilation is of the utmost importance. With all woods time is also a requisite, in seasoning: when required for naval purposes, two years are necessary to season Teak and Sal, and three years for Black-wood. Unseasoned wood, if used, very soon decays. But other mischiefs almost as fatal as decay also occur to unseasoned woods; round blocks, cut out of the entire circular stem of green wood, or the same pieces divided into quarterings, split in the direction of the medullary rays, or radially; also, though less frequently, upon the annual rings. Such of the round blocks as consist of the entire section contract pretty equally, and nearly retain their circular form, but those from the quarterings become oval from their unequal shrinking. In general, woods do not alter in any material degree in respect to length. Boards and flat pieces contract, however, in width; they warp and twist; and, when they are fitted as panels into loose grooves, they shrink away from that edge which happens to be the most slightly held; but, when restrained by mills, mortises, or other unyielding attachments, which do not allow them the power of contraction, they split with irresistible force, and the materials and labour thus improperly employed will render no useful service." Dr. Cleghorn deprecates applying a coat of paint over green unseasoned wood, the almost inevitable result of which is that the centre becomes decayed.

Decay.—The presence of air, light, and moisture seem to be necessary to the re-vegetation of timber or the growth of that fungus which leads to its destruction. Mr. Fincham of Her Majesty's dock-yard bored a hole in one of the timbers of an old ship built of oak, the wood being sound; and, in 24 hours, the admission of air caused the hole to be lined with a white mouldiness due to the growth of a peculiar fungus, which, some time after, became so compact as to admit of being withdrawn like a stick. Cracks or splits in timber would therefore predispose it to decay in damp situations by admitting the air. There are great differences in woods as to their power of resisting decay; some perish in a year or two, others are sound and even fragrant for centuries. Teak has been found to last six or seven times as long as oak when used in English green houses, as boxes for growing plants, the latter wood not existing more than two or three years; but the moist atmosphere, light and heat of a greenhouse form a severe trial for any wood. The various wood oils smeared on timbers tend to their preservation. In stacking, the logs should be piled, supported on bricks or stone, and the ground should be strewed with ashes to prevent the growth of grass or fungi.

Artificial preservatory processes.—In the process of seasoning, it is of the utmost importance to allow the sap freely to dissolve out, and any plan of seasoning which interferes with this, is imperfect. Mr. Boucherie's preserving process is on the principle of displacing the fermentable sap by the introduction of a fluid less liable to change, but it is known that only the softer woods can alone be thus penetrated, and that it cannot be made to pass into hard fully formed wood like oak: nevertheless the Permanent Way Company in London have adopted it for their sleepers. Sir William Burnett's process, which has been tested in the Royal Dock-yards, consists in charging the wood with a solution of chloride of zinc and is thought to be the most practicable and the best, timber thus treated being found to withstand not only the effects of moisture but the inroads of insects and fungi. Mr. Bethell uses creosote, with the object of coagulating the albumen and preventing putrefactive decomposition. His process has been tried on the Madras Railway, but creosoted sleepers have of late been found decayed in the centre, the interior portion scooped out, leaving nothing but a deceptive shell, in some instances not more than half an inch in thickness. It has also been observed by Mr. McMaster that, on the Madras line, decay of sleepers nearly always commences under the chairs, which hold water like a cup and gradually sink into the wood. This may, however, be partly owing to two materials of different density being together, as it is found that when applying two kinds of wood end to end, as for instance oak to Malabar teak, or Lignum vitæ, the harder of the two will decay at the point of juncture. Latterly, in the Madras Presidency, the practice, copied it is said from the experience in Bengal and Northern India, has been followed of not closing in the ends of the beams of roofs, but allowing their two sides and ends to be freely exposed to the air, and Dr. Cleghorn mentions that instances have occurred where the dry rot, which had assailed such beams, had been arrested by allowing a free current of air to act upon the wood. He mentions that in Southern India, no wood and no Railway sleepers have yet been found to resist white ants (Termites) and the exposure to heat and moisture. In the telegraph department, it was found that timber, sunk unprotected into the ground, was constantly damaged by white ants, but the ends are now protected by a metallic socket, and liquid dammar is poured into the sheaths so as to coat the enclosed part with resin. Of the insects which cause injury, the white ant, which attacks timber alike during its growth and after it has been felled, and the carpenter bee

(Xylocopa)* which confines itself to dead wood, are the most destructive. The carpenter bee makes long passages through beams and posts of buildings, and, if the colony be numerous, their ravages are dangerously destructive. Yellow arsenic (*Hartal*, HIND.) mixed with the paint, white-wash or masonry, has been recommended as a protection against white ants, and, for smearing timber, a composition of Gambier, dammar and oil has also been used with success. And, where the timber was exposed to the attacks of the teredo, black varnish or tar was substituted for dammar oil. Dr. Cleghorn adds that Colonel Scott of the Engineers at Bombay had obtained satisfactory results by boiling timber under pressure, in antiseptic solutions of sulphate of copper, arsenious acid and corrosive sublimate. But, he is of opinion that the process of Mr. Boucherie, which impregnates timber with metallic oxides, rendering the softer woods durable under ground and thus saving much valuable timber, would be of great importance to Indian railways, and should, therefore, be patronised. Great as is the importance of preserving the forests, the various means of preserving timber after it has been felled will thus be observed to be, in an economical point of view, a subject also of no less importance, for Dr. Cleghorn reports that Railway sleepers, which ought to have stood five or six years, at least, have been found useless after being laid down not more than one-third of that time; that, in fact, there are some parts of the Madras line where it was necessary that they should be taken up and replaced before the District itself was completed. He further reports the prevalence of a belief that iron will in the end be found the most economical material for sleepers. (*Report of Conservator of Forests* 1859-60, *p.* 3,) and iron sleepers are now, indeed, largely employed on some parts of the Madras line.

The Ordnance Departments use large quantities of the best timbers of the country. The following is a list of the quantities received at the Gun Carriage Manufactory, Madras.

	1855-56.	1856-57.	1857-58.	1858-59.	1859-60.	1860-61.	1861-62.
	Cubic feet.	Cubic feet.	Cubic feet.	Cubic feet.	Cubic feet.	Cubic feet.	Cubic feet.
Teak Annamullay.........	3,609	3,703	...	406	...	...	...
Teak Pegu..................	4,459	26,460	...	58,863	1,659	2,955	10,518
Peddowk	...	2,711	3,591	15,026	6,476	5,374	6,484
Peengandoo................	...	...	...	210	231	163	...
Peemah	...	1,353	1,709	41,275	6,552	...	...
Peemah white	...	...	...	55	...	...	...
Rose...........................	1,149	308	...	3,292	2,216	785	3,209
Saul............................	5,742	...	...	5,745	6,831	1,708	2,966
Trincomallie...............	2,418	1,505	7,215	7,036	...	...	...
Paula...........................	...	...	153	374	...	...	...
Thumbagum...............	...	797	...	...	...	...	...
Angelly	...	138	...	...	...	...	...
Malavemboo..............	..	96	...	...	...	...	...
Satin	157	...	...	2,689	1,485	...	...
Autcha........................	23	...	...	...	...	...	...

Of the following kinds of timber, in use in the Bombay Gun Carriage Department, the quantities used in the official year, 1859-60, were as follows:—

	Cub. Ft.	*Ins.*		*Cub. Ft.*	*Ins.*
Teakwood..	3,828	1,405¾	Heady	272	1,571
Blackwood.	1,097	1,225	Culbun	43	1,185
Baubool....	964	206¾	Jungle......	1,108	1,556
Bhendy.....	42	884	*Plank.*		
Eynee.......	796	697	Blackwood.	331	63
Cedar.......	129	794¼	Heavy......	679	1,164
Phunsey....	249	867½	Jungle teak.	176	54¾
Dealwood..	61	60¾	Teak.......	13,077	1,110¼

The quantity purchased during the official year 1860-61 has been Teakwood 4,648, 1,133 cubic feet in plank, numbering 621 only. The scantling is for round logs, length not less than 15 feet, and girth 80 inches upwards; for plank not under three inches thick, and of any breadth over eight inches and over ten feet in length;—sided logs are not generally purchased by the Bombay Department, not being procurable unless in Teakwood from Burmah, of which very little is obtained. The timber is usually supplied from the Conservator's Department partially seasoned, and that obtained from local sources unseasoned wood, free from knots and splits, of even grain and straight, is invariably selected when purchases are made from the market, and as near as possible to those qualities, in dealings with the Conservator of Forests, in 1860-61, in Bombay,

				R.	A.	P.
The rate per cubic foot of Teakwood was...				3	0	0
Ditto	ditto	ditto	Blackwood...	3	8	0
Ditto	ditto	ditto	Baubool wood	1	9	7

Dr. Wight, Mr. Rohde, Dr. Gibson. Holtzappfell: Dr. Cleghorn's Reports, Captain Beddome, Dr. Falconar, Proceedings of Madras Central Committee for the London Exhibition of 1851, *Proceedings, Catalogues and Juries Reports of London Exhibition* 1851 *and Madras Exhibitions of* 1855-57 *and* 59. *Simmond's Commercial Products. Tomlinson's Cyclopædia. Mr. C. Shubrick in Records of Madras Custom House. Colonel Maitland, Gun Carriage Manufactory.*

* NOTE. Karr wandu, கரிவண்டு TAM. Nalla bauka, TEL. Kala bora, کالا بھورا HIND.

AB-ENEY. TAM.? qu. Ebony? A large tree of the Palghat jungle: wood of a brown colour, used for furniture.—*Colonel Frith.*

ACACIA. This genus of plants contains about 360 species, which are found in the tropical parts of the Old and New worlds, and over all Australia. Many of them furnish strong useful woods and other economic products, as in their gums, fruits and extracts. Some of the trees have not yet been determined specifically. In the plains of India, there are several of value as timber trees, and five species remarkable for the strength and durability of their wood, grow in the forests of Pegu, namely, Acacia sundra, A. stipulata, A. alata, A. serissa, and A. Smithiana.—*Eng. Cyc. McClelland.*

ACACIA *species?*

Gouharea. TEL. URIA.

A tree of Ganjam and Gumsur. Extreme height 45 feet, circumference $4\frac{1}{2}$ feet and height from ground to the intersection of the first branch 15 feet. It is a wood of great strength and used, on that account, for sugar crushers, bandy wheels, ploughshares and rice pounders. The bark is used for tanning skins. The tree being tolerably common is burnt for firewood.—*Captain Macdonald.*

ACACIA *species*

Popiah. BURM.

Grows in Tavoy. Dr. Wallich describes this as a very large tree, used for posts and rollers.

ACACIA *species?*

Paingadu. BURM.

Grows in Tavoy. But the Burmese pyn-ka-do is a name for the Inga xylocarpa.

ACACIA *species.*

Kouk-koe. BURM.

A tree of Moulmein. Its wood is used for boats, carts, and other ordinary house-building material.—*Cal. Cat. Ex.* 1862.

ACACIA AMARA. *Willd.; W. & A.*

SYN. Mimosa amara, *Roxb.*

Bel Kambi. CAN.	Wunja maram. TAM.
Lallye. MAHR.	Nalla regu. TEL.

Grows in Coimbatore, and is common in the more inland jungles of the Bombay presidency, but less so on their coasts: Dr. Gibson says it grows above the ghats of Canara and Sunda, not inland and not north of the Gungawalli river. This is a tolerably large tree in Coimbatore, but of rather low stature. Its flower is very beautiful. In Coimbatore, the wood is dark coloured and hard. In the Bombay presidency, the wood is always very crooked, otherwise, when ripe, it is strong and tough, and might be applicable to domestic purposes. From its black colour, the natives of Cañara and Sunda deem it (wrongly) a species of ebony.—*Dr. Wight, Dr. Gibson.*

ACACIA ARABICA. *Willd.; Linn.; W. & A.*

SYN. Mimosa Arabica, *Roxb.*

Amghitan. AR.	Kurru-vaylam. MALEAL.
Sumug Arabi. AR.	Saugh-i-Arabi. PERS.
Babul. BENG. HIND. MAHR.	Kari-velam TAM.
Nan-lung-kyen. BURM.	Nalla-tumma. TEL.
Bab-bul. DUK.	Tumma chettu. TEL.
Kali-kikar. DUK.	Barburamu. TEL.
Babul tree. ENG.	Its gum is the Babul ka Gond, HIND. The vallam pisin; kar. velam pisin, TAM.
Indian Gum Arabic tree. ENG.	
Babula. HIND.	

This yellow flowered and rather ornamental tree is met with in varying abundance throughout Southern India. It is of rapid growth and requires no water, flourishing on dry arid plains and especially in black cotton soil, where other trees are rarely met with. In the western Dekhan of the Bombay Presidency, it is most frequent in the interior, less common on the sea coast and hardly known in its southern jungles. We do not find mention of it as occurring in Burmah, Pegu or Tenasserim. In Ganjam and Gumsur, it attains an extreme height of 25 feet with a circumference of 2 feet. In Nagpore, the maximum length of its timber is 14 feet, with $3\frac{1}{2}$ feet of girth, but 10 feet long and 3 feet in girth is the average, and it sells there at 6 annas per cubic foot. The height from the ground to the intersection of the first branch is about 8 feet. It can never be had of large size, and is generally crooked, but, it is a very hard tough wood, and is extensively employed for tent pegs, ploughshares, sugar-cane rollers, for the spokes, naves, and felloes of wheels, for the knees and ribs of country ships, and generally for all purposes to which a hard bent wood is applicable. It is not attacked by white ants. Although in great demand for ship-building, when so applied, it does not last above sixteen years. Amongst its other useful products, may be named its gum, bark and seeds, the latter being extensively used in the Dekhan for feeding sheep. The bark is very largely employed in the centre of the Peninsula, as a tanning material, and, when properly managed, makes a good leather, with a reddish tinge, though, in native hands, the leather is often porous, brittle, and ill-coloured. Dr. Buchanan mentions that, in Mysore, the bark was employed in the process of distilling rum; but, in this, he probably mistook another acacia. The ground bark mixed with the expressed seeds of the Sesamum orientale has been used as food in times of scarcity. A decoction of the bark makes a good substitute for soap, and is used in dyeing various shades of brown. It yields an abundance of transparent gum which flows out from incisions or fissures in the bark and hardens in lumps of various sizes and figures. This is used in India as a substitute for the true gum arabic, which is the product of A. vera. In the medicinal practice of the people, the bark is used internally as a tonic and astringent; in decoction, as a wash for ulcers, and finely powdered and mixed with gingelly oil, externally, in cancerous affections. Dr. Gibson has, for years, advocated extensive planting of this useful tree, in the Bombay side of India, and several forests of it at Khangaum, Kasoordee and other places have been preserved. He tells us that the Acacia arabica, Babool, is most common in the interior; less so on the coast, and hardly known in the southern jungles. As the vernacular term Babul is generic, and applied in the Mahratta, Guzerati and Hindi to various species, there are, he adds, two if not three varieties or species, Babool, Ram kanta and Eree babool. The first is the most common species, the second less so, and distinguished from the first by its straight stem, and general appearance, resembling that of a gigantic broom. The wood is quite equal to that of the common Babool. The third species is distinguishable from the first by its more horizontal mode of branching; the smaller branches long and stretched out, the side branches from them going off at right angles nearly. The bark also is much more reticulated, broken, and corky than that of the other. The wood is very inferior, as regards its use for agricultural implements, house material, &c. The distinction between the two should always be kept in view as practically important. The pod of this third species, also, is much broader-margined, and very partially moniliform, and can be at once distinguished from that of the first two species, which is so contracted between each seed as to be nearly severed. The pods and tender branches of all the three species form important articles of food for sheep, goats, and cattle, from February to the beginning of the rains. The flesh of lambs fed on the pods has a flavour equal to that of the best Europe lamb.—*Captain Sankey, Drs. Wight, Cleghorn, Gibson, Mr. Rohde, Reports of the Juries of the Madras Exhibition, Dr. Riddell, Useful Plants quoted in Cyclopædia of India and Supplements, Captain Macdonald.*

ACACIA CÆSIA. *W. & A.*

Mimosa cæsia. *L.*	Acacia arrar. *Buch.*
Acacia alliacea. *Buch.*	„ intsioides. *D.C.*
Tella Korinda. TEL.	Konda Korinda. TEL.

This scandent shrub grows in the Circars, Olipur, Monghyr and Saharunpore, wood said to be valueless.—*Voigt.*

ACACIA CATECHU. *Willd.; W. & A.*

A. polyacantha. *Willd.*	Mimosa catechu. *Linn.*
A. Wallichiana. *D.C.*	„ catechnoides. *Wall.*
Khair. BENG.	Khaira. HIND.
Khaira-ghach. BENG.	Kheir. MAHR.
Sha. BURM.	Khadiramu. SANS.
Sha-bin. „	Wodalé or Wothalé. TAM.
Catechu Tree. ENG.	Podala-mánu. TEL.
Khair. HIND.	Khadiramu. TEL.

This tree grows on the Malabar and Coromandel Coasts, in the Dekhan, the Northern Circars, is one of the most common trees of the Bombay coast and its ghat jungles,—grows at Serampore, Monghyr, Rajmahal, Delhi, Nepal, the Morung mountains and Assam. It is common all over the plains and scattered over the hills of British Burmah; in great quantities in the forests of the Prome and Tharawaddy districts. Immense numbers of these trees are annually cut down and made use of for the extraction of Catechu. There are several varieties differing in shade, specific weight and yield of Cutch. A cubic foot weighs from lbs. 56 to lbs. 70. In a full grown tree on good soil the average length of the trunk to the first branch is 20 feet and average girth measured at 6 feet from the ground is 6 feet. The wood possesses great strength and durability, and is considered more durable than teak. It resists the attacks of insects, and is employed for posts and uprights of houses,—for spear and sword handles, bows, &c. The Catechu, formerly known as Terra Japonica is extracted from the wood. The Burmese variety called "sha," is common all over the plains and scattered over the hills of British Burmah.—*Dr. McClelland, Major Drury, Drs. Gibson and Brandis.*

ACACIA CINERARIA. *Willd.; W. & A.*

Nela jami. TEL.	Chinna jami. TEL.

This tree is said to grow in the Circars. Character of wood not known.

ACACIA DEALBATA.

A handsome tree, from fifteen to thirty feet high, most abundant in Port Philip and Twofold Bay, forming luxuriant groves on the banks of streams, between the parallels of latitude 34 and 30 degrees. Its bark contains a greater per centage of tannin than any other, and pays to ship to England.—*Simmonds.*

ACACIA ELATA. *Graham.*

Mimosa elata. *Roxb.; Wall.*

Seet. BENG.	Chikul mara. CAN.
Thaeet-tha. BENG.	Tella sopara. TEL.

This is pretty common in Canara and Sunda, both above and below the ghats. It occurs in the Godavery forests, in Dehrah Doon, Assam, on the banks of the Irawadi and Ataran, and in Tavoy. Plentiful in the Pegu, Tounghoo and Prome districts, and very abundant all along the sea shore from Amherst to Mergui. Its maximum girth 4 cubits, and maximum length is 18 feet. When seasoned, it floats in water. Its timber is straight, lengthy and of large girth. The wood is red, and is hard and strong and very durable. It is much valued and useful for house buildings. It is used for posts for buildings. It is adapted for cabinet making, and of sufficient girth to be advantageously employed in Government buildings, and for packing cases.—*Voigt, Captain Beddome, Drs. Gibson and McClelland, Captain Dance, Madras Artillery.*

ACACIA FARNESIANA, *Willd.*

Acacia Indica, *Desv.*
Mimosa Farnesiana, *Willd*
" Indica, *Poir.*
Vachellia Farnesiana, *W. & A.*

Guya-babula. BENG.
Iri Babul. MAHR.
Vaday valli maram. TAM.
Kusturi, Peetuma. TEL.

Roxburgh says it is a native of every part of India, and is found in Assam, Bengal and the peninsula. It is a large shrub or small tree armed with thorns, but, in waste places in the western Dekhan, where it occurs also in garden hedges, it is only a scrubby shrub.

Dr. Gibson says its wood is only applicable for tent pegs and firewood, but Major Drury mentions that (in Travancore?) the wood is very hard and tough, and is much used for ship knees, tent pegs and similar work.

A delicious perfume is distilled from the flowers, and the tree exudes a considerable quantity of useful gum.— *Dr. Gibson, Major Dury.*

ACACIA FERRUGINEA, *D C.; W. & A.*

Mimosa ferruginea, *Roxb.*

Vel velam TAM.
Woani. TEL.
Vuni. "
Anasandra. TEL.
Anachandra. "

This tree grows in the Madras presidency, on the Coromandel Coast and Northern Circars, and is found at Courtallum, in the Bombay presidency. It attains a height of from 20 to 25 feet. The wood not known. The bark is very astringent and forms an ingredient in the manufacture of a kind of arrack.—*Voigt, Drury.*

ACACIA LATRONUM, *Willd.; D C.; W. & A.*

Mimosa latronum, *Koen.* | Mimosa coringera, *Linn.*

Buffalo thorn. ENG.

Common in the barren tracts of the Dekhan, and found on the Madras side of India.—*Voigt.*

ACACIA LEUCOPHLŒA, *Willd.; W. & A.; Roxb.; Corr.*

Acacia alba, *Willd.*
Mimosa leucophlæa, *Roxb.*
Mimosa alba, *Rottl.*
Mimosa tomentosa?

Panicled Acacia. ENG.
Kikar. HIND.
Safed kikar. HIND.
Hewar. MAHR.
Vel-velam. TAM.
Vellai-tumma. TAM.
Tella-tumma. TEL.
Its gum, Vel-velam pisin. TAM.

It grows in the Dekhan, in the woods and hills of peninsular India, in Coimbatore, in some parts of the Southern Mahratta country, and in the Sholapore districts between the Bheema and the Kistnah rivers. Its specific name and its Hindi, Tamul and Telugu names are given from the whitish or pale yellow colour of its bark, which in southern India, is one of the ingredients used in distilling arrack. In Coimbatore, the tree attains a medium size with a round head, but in the Dekhan, it is never of a size fit for anything beyond posts to small houses. The wood it furnishes, however, is strong, good and dark colored, though generally small. It is easily distinguished by its panicled globular inflorescence and stipulary thorns. A tough and strong fibre, in use for large fishing nets and coarse kinds of cordage, is prepared from the bark by maceration, after four or five days beating. The Acacia leucophlœa? under the Hindi name of *Rohnee,* is described as a tree of Jubbulpore, abundant in the Deinwah valley and Hoosingabad, yielding an excellent and tough wood, but which does not work smoothly.—*Cal. Cat. Ex.* 1862, *Dr. Wight, Dr. Cleghorn, Major Drury, Mr. Rohde, Voigt.*

ACACIA MYRIOPHYLLA, *Willd.; Grah.*

Mimosa myriophylla, *Roxb.*

Grows on the Khassia hills; wood unknown. The bark is used to make an intoxicating liquor with.—*Roxb. Voigt.*

ACACIA ODORATISSIMA, *Willd.; W. & A.*

Acacia lomatocarpa, *D C.*
Mimosa odoratissima, *Linn.*
Mimosa marginata, *Lam.*

Fragrant Acacia. ENG.
Chechua. GOND.
Sankæur. "
Sirsa. HIND.
Sirris. MAHR.
Ran Sirris. MAHR.
Karintha karra. MALEAL.
Karroo-vaga? TAM.
Karu vangai? "
Sela-wunja. "
Sælæ marum? "
Shinduga. TEL.
Telsu. "

This tree grows over all the peninsula of India, in any soil, on the coast or in the interior, and is found in Bengal, Assam, the eastern provinces of Burmah, Pegu and Tenasserim. In the Madras Presidency, about Coimbatore, it is of rapid growth and in considerable abundance, attaining the height of 30 to 40 feet. It often attains a good size in the Bombay presidency, but, in Nagpore, it is only in gardens that its dimensions are great, the timber it yields in other localities being, as a general rule, of small scantling. It is even there, however, obtainable in beams from 15 to 18 feet long and three feet in girth, at 5 annas per cubic foot. In Coimbatore, beams one foot square are procurable. The heart wood is dark colored, turning almost black with age; is strong and heavy and takes a good polish; the grain being ornamental, though rather open. In Nagpore, it is described as being distinguishable from the timber of the Pentaptera tomentosa, only by its much straighter grain and greater lightness. It has an outer ring of white wood, of from 2" to 3" in Nagpore, but which, Dr. Gibson says, is, in the western Dekhan, always 3-4ths of the whole.

This part alone is assailable by white ants: but, by being creosoted, could probably be made a useful railway timber. All accounts describe its heart wood as strong, hard and heavy; in Nagpore of sufficient size to form rafters, and excellently suited for naves and felloes of wheels, but there is an uncertainty as to its powers to bear moisture. A beam an inch and half square sustained a weight of 570 lbs. The oil manufacturers of Nagpore use it for their mills, and it is there generally employed to make carts. The wood is said to deserve being better known for the general purposes of carpentry.—*Voigt, Captain Beddome, Captain Sankey, Dr. Mason, Dr. Wight, Dr. Cleghorn, Major Drury, Dr. Gibson, Dr. McClelland, quoted in Balfour's Cyclopædia and 1st and 2nd Supplements.*

ACACIA RAMKANTA. Under this name, Drs. Gibson and Riddell describe an ornamental species of Acacia or a variety of A. Arabica, common in the Dekhan, though less abundant than A. Arabica, from which it is distinguishable by its straight, tall, erect stem and general cypress-like appearance, or resembling that of a gigantic broom, and the colour of its legumes. Its wood is quite equal to that of the Acacia Arabica, being hard and used for cart wheels, ploughs, &c., but the natives attach some superstitious notions to the tree.

ACACIA SPECIOSA, *Willd.; W. & A.*

Acacia serissa, *Buch.*	Mimosa serissa, *Roxb.*
Mimosa flexuosa, *Rottl.*	„ speciosa, *Jacq.*

Sirisha. BENG.	Vel-vanghai maram. TAM.
Seet. BURM.	Dirasana. TEL.
Sirris. HIND.	Dirasana chettu. TEL.
Sirissa tree. ENG.	Sinduva chettu. „
Kátúvagi. TAM.	Sirissee. URIA.

This, the Mimosa sirissa of Roxburgh, in the Madras Exhibition Juries' Reports, is stated to be the Acacia serissa which is extensively planted along the banks of the Ganges canal. Like the Seet of the Burmese, described by Dr. Mason and Dr. McClelland, it is a tree of large size and rapid growth, but the Seet is described as a red wood or of a dark colour, and that of the A. speciosa as white or light coloured. This large tree is plentiful in Pegu, particularly in the Toungboo district; it is found on the Irawaddy and may exist in the Tenasserim provinces. In Ganjam and Gumsur, it is very plentiful, and attains an extreme height of 30 feet and circumference 4½ feet, the height from the ground to the intersection of the first branch being 22 feet. It is used for sugar crushers, pestles, mortars, and ploughshares. It is common in the forests of the Bombay presidency, grows in Travancore, on the Coromandel coast, and is a common tree in Coimbatore where it is frequently seen growing by the road sides on account of the shade that its large head affords. The timber is easily procured in Madras, and is said to be a white or light coloured, durable and very hard and strong, for Dr. Wight found a 1½ inch bar to sustain 560 lbs. Dr. Gibson seems to refer A. speciosa to A. odoratissima, and to think that their Sirris and Ran Sirris are not different. Others describe it as a large, red or dark coloured timber, very hard, adapted to cabinet making and ship building.—*Dr. Mason, Captain Macdonald, Dr. McClelland, Dr. Cleghorn in M. E. J. R., Dr. Wight in M. E. P., and Dr. Gibson in Bomb. Geo. Soc. Journal.*

ACACIA SIRISSA ?

Tseek-tha. BURM. ?

A tree of Moulmein was sent to the London Exhibition of 1862 under these names. Wood reddish colored and used for furniture.—*Cal. Cat. Ex.* 1862.

ACACIA STIPULATA, *D C.*

Mimosa stipulata, *Roxb.*	Mimosa stipulacea, *Roxb.*

Amluki. BENG.	Seet. BURM.

This unarmed Acacia, with flowers of a pink colour, is one of the largest trees of the genus. And, is found in Dera Dhoon, in the mountains north of Bengal, in Travancore, Courtallum, in most parts of the peninsula, in Assam, in the forests from Rangoon to Toungboo, and on the banks of the Ataran river. Dr. Gibson does not mention its existence in the Bombay forests, nor is it known to be found in Tenasserim. It yields a large heavy timber, wood of a red colour, close grained and strong, and adapted to cabinet making, furniture and other purposes.—*Voigt, Dr. McClelland, Major Drury.*

ACACIA SUMA, *Buch.*

Mimosa suma, *Roxb.*

Shai kanta. BENG.	Tella chandra. TEL.

Grows in Bengal—uses not known.

ACACIA SUNDRA, *D C.*

Acacia chundra, *Willd.*	Mimosa sundra, *Roxb.*

Lall Kheir. HIND. MAHR.	Nalla chandra. TEL.
Karangally maram. TAM.	Sandra. „
Chandra. TEL.	

This tree grows in the peninsula and the Sunderbuns, but varies in size, in different localities. Dr. Gibson mentions that it is common in the jungles of Bombay, there always scrubby, small and crooked; and, though rather plentiful in the forests under the ghats, he had not seen it of a size capable of affording planks. It is somewhat abundant in the jungles and a rather large sized tree. At Guntoor Mr. Rohde mentions he had obtained planks one foot broad; that posts five feet long are procurable at 12 Rupees per 100, well suited for fencing, and that the natives regard it as the most durable wood for posts in house building, though, from its non-elastic nature it is unfavorable to the holding of nails driven into it. The wood is, however, not obtainable in the market generally in planks of any size. The wood is of a dark colour, very hard, heavy and very strong, a one inch bar sustaining a weight of 500 lbs. It is also used for rice pestles. A resin similar to that which exudes from the A. catechu, is procured from this tree. The two trees are nearly alike, the uncertainty of the prickles absent or present, being a distinguishing characteristic of this one.—*Mr. Rohde, Dr. Wight, Dr. Cleghorn's Reports, Useful Plants.*

ACACIA TOMENTOSA, *Willd.*

Mimosa tomentosa, *Roxb.* | Mimosa Kleinii, *Poir.*

Salsein-babula. Beng. | Jungle Nail Tree. Eng.
Elephant Thorn. Eng. | Ani mulla. Tam.

Grows on the Madras side of India, common near Sholapore, in the Kandeish jungles and the Bombay Dekhan, and is found in Bengal.—*Voigt.*

ACACIA VERA, *Bauh.*

Acacia nilotica. | Mimosa nilotica, *Linn.*

Αχαθος αιγυπτιχη. Gr.

The Acacia vera is a tree of the African desert, and its leaves yield the camel the sole forage it can meet in those arid regions. Under the Singhalese name of Andere, Mr Mendis describes this as a tree, growing in the eastern Ceylon provinces, the wood weighing 71 lbs. per cubic foot, and lasting 15 years, and used for cross bars of fishing dhonies and pins for wooden anchors, but, the Andere is probably some other Acacia. This tree affords two products, one natural, the other artificial, namely the acacia juice and gum arabic. The acacia juice (Akakia of Dioscorides and Eastern writers), is a solid, heavy, shining, brittle, dark coloured substance, inodorous, insipid at first, flavour astringent, powder brown, soluble in water which it colours red. Dioscorides, and before him Hippocrates, have described and highly lauded the properties of this juice. It is obtained by pounding the unripe fruit, and expressing the juice; this is thickened before the sun, and then placed in bladders in which drying gradually takes place. The little bladders of akakia found in Europe contain about 5 or 6 ounces each; it is sold in the bazars of Bengal in thin, very black cakes, about the size of a rupee.—*O'Shaughnessy, pp.* 299,300.—*Mendis.*

ACER, the Maple. Several species grow in the northern parts of India, in Nepaul, Sirmoor, Kumaon, Srinagur &c., of which the following are mentioned.

ACER CAUDATUM, *Wallich.* The Long-pointed Maple, is a native of the highest regions of Nepaul, of Sirmoor, Kumaon, and Srinaghur.—*Eng. Cyc.*

ACER CULTRATUM, *Wallich.* The Curve-keyed Maple, is a large tree, native of the regions towards the Himalayas, in Kumaon and Srinaghur.—*Eng. Cyc.*

ACER DOBINEA, the Maple of Norfolk Island, is a very handsome tree, and its wood is used for cabinet work.—*Keppel's Ind. Arch. Vol. II. p.* 282.

ACER LEVIGATUM. *Wallich.* The Polished Maple, is found in the woods of the higher mountains of Nepaul, and also in the Alps of Sirmoor, where it acquires a trunk thirty or forty feet high and from three to four feet thick. Its growth is slow; its timber is said by Dr. Wallich to be used by the inhabitants of Nepaul for rafters, beams, and similar building purposes.—*Eng. Cyc.*

ACER OBLONGUM, Oval-leafed Maple, an ever-green tree, of rapid growth, native of the northern parts of India, growing both in Nepaul and Kumaon. It is probably confined to the hot valleys of those regions, for it has been found incapable of supporting the climate of England.—*Eng. Cyc.*

ACER STERCULIACEUM, *Wallich.* The Shady Maple, is a large tree, with a trunk often three feet in diameter; found in Nepaul.—*Eng. Cyc.*

ACER VILLOSUM, *Wallich.* The Shaggy Maple, is a very large tree, found on the Himalaya mountains, approaching the limits of perpetual snow, in Sirmoor and Kumaon.—*Eng. Cyc.*

ACHRAS SAPOTA, *Linn.*

Bully or Bulli Tree. Eng. | Simi Elupai maram. Tam.
Sapota Plum Tree. „ | Sima ippa chettu. Tel.

This valuable fruit tree, which bears the Sapodilla plum, has been introduced into India from South America, and is found about Goa and the Dekhan, and in gardens in other parts of India. Its wood is hard and close grained, and in South America is reckoned of great value for the shingles for corn houses. The bark is said to be a good substitute for Cinchona. The seeds are aperient and diuretic: in over-doses they are dangerous. The Tamil name means the foreign Bassia longifolia.—*Mr. Jaffrey, Dr. Riddell.*

ACHOO is a tree of the forests of Ganjam and Gumsur, which attains an extreme height of 36 feet, with a circumference of 2½ feet. The height from the ground to the intersection of the first branch is 10 feet. It is supposed to be the Morinda tinctoria. It furnishes a light, hard wood, of which the stocks of all the Uria matchlocks are made. A pink dye is extracted from the root. It is not very common. *Captain Macdonald.*

ADANSONIA DIGITATA, *Linn.*

Adansonia baobab. *Gærtn.*

Baobab tree. Eng. | Lalo Plant. Eng.
Monkey Bread tree. Eng. | Papara pulia maram. Tam.
Ethiopian sour gourd. | Anai pulia maram. „

This plant has been naturalised in India, and may be seen at Madras, Negapatam, Samulcottah, Bombay and Guzerat. Its trunk is very short, but, in girth attains the largest size of any known tree. As a timber tree, it is useless, the wood being spongy and soft, but fishermen use its fruit as floats for their nets.—*Useful Plants, Dr. Riddell, Eng. Cyclop., Voigt.*

ADENANTHERA PAVONINA, *Linn.*

Rakto chandan. Beng.	Kámbhóji. Sans.
Ranguna. "	Manjadi. Tam.
Y-wai-gyi. Burm.	Ani Ganda-mani. Tam.
Red wood tree. Eng.	Ani kundamani. "
Ranjana. Hind.	Bandi Gurivenda. Tel.
Ku-chandana. Hind.	Manseni Kotta. "
Manjati. Maleal.	Bandi Guruvindza. "

This is a large and handsome tree, found in most of the forests of India. It is not very plentiful in Burmah, being widely dispersed; but it is met with in sufficient quantity in the Rangoon, Pegu and Tounghoo districts. It grows in both peninsulas of India, in Sylhet, Bengal, Assam, and the Moluccas. The inner wood of large trees, is deep red, hard, solid, and durable, suitable for the purposes of the cabinet maker. As, in old trees, the wood is of a red colour, from this, in upper India, it gets its name of Rakto chandan, or red Sandal wood; but the true Red Sandal or Red Sandars wood of commerce, is the Pterocarpus santalinus. The wood is not procurable in any quantity. The wood is said to yield a red dye; ground to a paste with water, it is used by hindus to make the sectarian marks on their foreheads. The seeds are of a shining scarlet colour, with a circular streak in their centre, and are used as weights by jewellers, and as ornaments in the form of beads, bracelets &c. Books represent these as usually weighing four grains, and they are in common use by the Burmese, as equivalent to that weight. The seeds, however, have to be selected for the purpose; many of them not weighing more than two or three grains each. A cement is made by beating them up with borax and water. The pulp of the seeds mixed with honey, is applied externally to hasten suppuration in boils and abscesses, the natives in Travancore have an idea that, taken internally, they are poisonous, especially when in a powdered state.—*McClelland, Mason, Useful Plants, Juries' Reports Madras Exhibition.*

ADHATODA VASICA, *Nees.; Roxb.*

Justicia adhatoda, *Linn. Roxb.*

Bakus. Beng.	Asganda. Hind,
Basoka. "	Urus or Utarosha. Sans.
Malabar Nut. Eng.	Adadodé. Tam.
Aris. Hind.	Addasaram. Tel.
Arus. "	

This shrub grows in Ceylon, in both the Indian peninsulas, in Bengal, Nepal, Sylhet, and Java. The wood is soft and considered very fit for making charcoal for gunpowder.—*Ainslie, Voigt.*

ÆGLE MARMELOS, *Corr.*

Cratava marmelos, *Linn.* | Feronia pelucida, *Roth.*

Bel. Beng.	Vilva maram. Tam.
Ouk-sheet. Burm.	Márédu chettu. Tel.
Bel. Hind.	Bilvamu chettu. Tel.
Bel. Mahr.	Vilva chettu. Tel.
Tanghai? or Tangul. Malay.	Malu-ramu chettu. Tel.
Kuvalam. Maleal.	

The Bel, Bengal quince, or larger Wood apple, is a large thorny tree with ternate leaves, growing throughout India, which flowers during the hot seasons, and its large spheroidal fruit ripens after the rains. The tree is common on the Bombay side, in waste places, inland forests, and old gardens. It is found in gardens in the South of India, and, about towns and villages throughout the Prome district and also about Tounghoo, more especially on the Shan side of the river, where the large spheroidal fruit may be had in great quantity from the end of February to the end of July. The wood is light coloured, variegated with veins, compact and hard, but is not used, partly perhaps from a religious feeling on the part of the hindus, with whom the tree is sacred to Siva and partly from the value of the tree from the great medicinal virtues of the fruit. It belongs to a family, the Aurantiaceæ or orange tribe, remarkable for the excellence of its timber, which is usually small. The wood is very strong, and, on the Godavery districts, the native dhol or drum, is often made of it. In Ganjam and Gumsur, it attains an extreme height of 30 feet and circumference of 3 feet. The height from the ground to the intersection of the first branch, being 10 feet. The wood is ground with water into a sort of oily paste, which is poured on the lingum in the temples dedicated to Siva. The leaves are offered to Siva and to the female divinities in the same way that the leaves of the Toolsee are offered to Vishnoo. The fruit is delicious to the taste and very fragrant. It is smooth, resembling an orange, with a yellow hard rind, which is astringent and used in dyeing yellow. The fruit has been long in use, in diarrhœa, and its aperient and detersive qualities and its efficacy in remedying habitual costiveness, have been proved by constant experience. It has lately been brought into repute when fresh and in conserve as a remedy in some kinds of dysentery. When dried before it is ripe, the fruit is used in decoction in diarrhœa and dysentery, and when ripe and mixed with juice of tamarinds, forms an agreeable drink. The mucus which surrounds the seeds is, for some purposes, a very good cement; Dr. Gibson says the beautiful ready made varnish which surrounds the seeds, will one day be turned to use in the arts. The roots, bark and leaves are reckoned refrigerant in Malabar. The bark of the former, especially is given, in decoction, in intermittent fever, and the leaves are applied as a poultice in ophthalmia. They abound in a volatile fragrant bitter exciting oil. In Ceylon, a fragrant perfume known as marmala water, is distilled from the flowers, and is much used by the natives as a perfume for sprinkling on visitors.

Lest the resemblance of the Wood apples, to the fruit of the Nux vomica might give rise to accidents, their strong aromatic smell like that of all other fruits of the orange family, to which they belong, will distinguish them easily from the Nux vomica, which is devoid of aroma.—*McClelland, Dr. A. Wight, Dr. Mason, Dr. Gibson, Useful Plants, Dr. Riddell, Dr. Waring, Mr. Elliot, Dr. O'Shaughnessy.*

ÆSCHYNOMENE ASPERA, *Linn.*

Æ. indica, *Wall.*	Æ. aquatica, *Roxb.*
Æ. lagenaria, *Lour.*	Hedysarum lagenarium, *Roxb.*

Phul-sola. Beng.	Attunette. Tam.
Shola. Hind.	Jilugu bendu. Tel.
Sola. Hind.	Jilugu. Tel.
Attukedasa. Maleal.	Niru jilugu. Tel.

This is not a tree, but a plant which grows in moist or marshy places in India. It is mentioned because its pith is much used for making hats, bottle covers, artificial flowers and models of temples.

AGATHIS AUSTRALIS, *Hort.*

Dammara Australis.

The Kawrie or New Zealand Pine, one of the Coniferæ, in its native forests, attains a considerable height, with a straight clean stem, which, from its lightness and toughness, has been found well calculated for the masts of ships. It was introduced into the Bombay Horticultural Society's Gardens.—*Dr. Riddell, Eng. Cyc.*

AGATHIS LORANTHIFOLIA, *Salisb.*

Dammara Loranthifolia.

The Dammar Pine or Pinus dammara of Linnæus, is a large tree, found on the very summits of the mountains of Amboyna, Ternate, and many of the Molucca Islands. When young, it has something the aspect of a young cedar, the wood of which it is said to resemble. Griffith mentions it as a member of the Tenasserim Flora, and Dr. Mason has seen the young plants of the tree, to which Griffith referred and which the Burmese call Theet-men or Tree Governor. The leaf is precisely that of the dammar pine, but the Tenasserim tree is not known to yield any dammar. The timber of the Archipelago tree is represented to be light and of inferior quality, wholly unfit for any situation exposed to wet, but answering tolerably well for in-door purposes. The wood of the Tenasserim tree is white, rather light, and bears a considerable resemblance to some kinds of pine. It is used by native carpenters for various purposes, and the Burmese have a superstition that the beams of balances of their scales, ought to be formed of this wood.—*Dr. Mason, Dr. Riddell, Eng. Cyc.*

AGATI GRANDIFLORUM, *Desv.*

Agati coccinea.	Coronilla grandiflora.
Æschynomene grandiflora. *Roxb.*	„ coccinea.

Buko. Beng.	Agati. Tam.
Agati. Maleal.	Agisi. Tel.
Buka. Sans.	Avisi. Tel.

This tree, which is easily recognised by its bright scarlet flowers, is seen in every town and village of the Tenasserim Provinces, and in the Betel gardens of Peninsular India, where it is much cultivated for shade, and as a trellis for the support and shelter of the Piper betel. It grows also in Bengal and Assam. Its wood, called in the circars, Auguste wood, is soft, is only fit for fuel, and of no use in carpentry or cabinet work, but the tree grows with great rapidity, and could be usefully planted to shelter young trees of slower growth. There are varieties of the Agati, some with variegated and some with red flowers, and the leaves and flowers of a white variety, known in Tamul as the Agati-kire-pu are used in soups, curries and as greens. On the Madras Coast, the legumes which are 12 to 18 inches long are not frequently eaten, but they are a favourite vegetable with the natives of Burmah. Medicinally, the bark is a powerful bitter tonic: and the leaves are used, in infusion in catarrh, as an aperient.—*Mr. Jaffrey, Dr. Riddell, Dr. Mason, Useful Plants, Mr. Elliot, Dr. O'Shaughnessy, Voigt.*

AGLAIA MIDNAPORENSIS, *Carey.*

A. grata, *Wall.*

This tree grows in the forests of Midnapore. Wood not known.—*Voigt.*

AGLAIA ODORATA, *Lour.*

Cammunium Sinense, *Rumph.*

This tree grows in Cochin-China and China. Wood not known.—*Voigt.*

AGLAIA SPECTABILIS. A large tree, met with along the banks of rivers in the Pegu and Tounghoo districts. It affords a light serviceable timber, somewhat stronger than the American Pine, and capable of being wrought with little labour. Wood, red-colored, strong and adapted for house-building.—*McClelland.*

AHGUIL. *Tam.?* A light, yellow coloured wood of Travancore; specific gravity 0·674. Very abundant; used for furniture.—*Col. Frith.*

AHLINE NGAI. *Burm.* A tree of Moulmein. Used for ordinary house-building purposes. Leaf is eaten boiled as greens.—*Cal. Cat. Ex.* 1862.

AH-NAN. *Burm.* A tree of Tavoy and Moulmein, probably the Fagræa fragrans, *Roxb.* Wall. Griff., (the Cyrtophyllum fragrans of *Falconar*). That of Moulmein, is described as a strong wood, good for building purposes. That of Tavoy, as a strong, hard, and very durable timber used in ship-building.—*Cal. Cat. Ex. of* 1862, *Captain Dance.*

AH SEE EHA. *Burm.* A tree of Moulmein. Wood hard, used for making musical instruments.—*Cal. Cat. Ex.* 1862.

AILANTHUS EXCELSUS, *Roxb.*

Maruk. MAHR.	Pedda man. TEL.
Peru mara. MALEAL.	Peru maram. TAM.
Pedda manu. TEL.	Pey yápa. TEL.

This tree grows in Coromandel, Surat, Baroach, and Baroda. It resembles the ash in its general appearance, and attains a larger size; flowering in January and February. It is common about old buildings and in raviny ground of the Dekhan and of Guzerat, about Baroach and Baroda. It is seldom found as a tree in the Bombay forests. It is common in the Northern Circars, and in the Godavery forests and is met with in Coimbatore.

Doubts seem to exist as to the value of the wood. Dr. Wight says it is described as hard, close-grained and heavy, and fit for gun-stocks, and he had been told that it is much used in Bombay, in cabinet making, but greatly doubted the correctness of the information, in which Dr. Gibson agrees. Dr. Cleghorn in the Madras Exhibition Jury Reports, describes the wood as light and white, and he and Graham say it is used for making sword handles &c. It is also employed to make sheaths for spears, catamarans, and is not durable. On the Godavery, the natives never use it.—*Dr. Wight, Dr. Cleghorn, Dr. Riddell, Useful Plants, Mr. Elliot, Mr. Jeffrey, M. E. Juries' Reports, Captain Beddome, Voigt.*

AILANTHUS MALABARICUS, *D C.*

Mudde doop. CAN.	Peru maram. TAM.
Peru mara. MALEAL.	

A large tree similar to the above, with very few points of difference, in its botanical character. It is common in Travancore and occurs in the Anamalai forests and Malabar, and has rather an ornamental appearance from its dark, shining pinnate leaves. In Canara and Sunda, it is common near the ghats above. According to Dr. Wight, the bark is rough, very thick, and studded with bright garnet looking grains, apparently of a resinous nature, which do not, however, dissolve either in spirit or water. The bark has a pleasant and slightly bitter taste, is considered a tonic and febrifuge, and is given in cases of dyspepsia. It yields a fragrant resinous juice, known as *matti pal*, which was first noticed by Buchanan. This, reduced to powder, mixed with milk and strained, is given, in small doses, in dysentery, and reputed to be an excellent remedy, owing chiefly to the balsamic properties of the resin. Wood said to be worthless. The fruit, triturated with mango and mixed with rice, is reckoned useful in cases of ophthalmia.—*Useful Plants, Dr. Gibson.*

ALANGIUM DECAPETALUM, *Lam.*

Alangium tomentosum, *Lam. D C.*	Alangium hexapetalum, *Roxb.*

Bagh-ankra. BENG.	Kara Angolam. MALEAL.
Ansaruli mara. CAN.	Ankolamu. SANS.
Sage leaved alangium. ENG.	Ankola. SANS.
Akola. HIND.	Nieo-chaka. SANS.
Akarkanta. HIND.	Alinji maram. TAM.
Ankulo. MAHR.	Ankolamu. TEL.
Ankul. „	Uduga. TEL.
Angolam. MALEAL.	Udugu. TEL.

This is a small tree found in Coimbatore in Cochin and throughout the Peninsula of India. It is common, on the Bombay side, both in the open country and in some of the jungles towards the coast, but, there, it is less a jungle tree than one found in hedges and village lanes. It grows in the Khassia hills, in Assam, up to the base of the Himalaya, and is found in the Malay Peninsula and in Cochin-China. The wood is said by Dr. Roxburgh to be beautiful, and in Dr. Wight's experiments, he found it sustain a weight of 310lbs., but neither Dr. Wight nor Dr. Gibson had ever seen a ten inch plank and Mr. Rohde says it wants size; Captain Beddome, however, describes it as an ornamental, beautiful wood, attaining a fair size in the forests of the Godavery and Circars. The root has a reputation in snake bites.—*Drs. Wight and Gibson, Mr. Elliot, Voigt, M. E. J. Rep. Mr. Rohde, Captain Beddome.*

ALANGIUM HEXAPETALUM, *Lam.*

Akola. HIND.	Unkotha. Nieochaka. SANS.
Ankulo. MAHR.	Unkola nieochaka. „
Kara-angolam. MALEAL	Wuduga or Uduga. TEL.

This tree grows in Malabar, Gumsur, Ganjam, Allahabad. It attains an extreme height of 30 feet, with a circumference of 2½ feet, the height from the ground to the intersection of the first branch being 12 feet. Little is known of the wood which, in the Useful Plants, is considered valuable. In Ganjam and Gumsur, the leading bull in a herd of buffaloes, has a wooden bell called "Lodoko" attached to its neck. This is heard at a great distance in the jungle, and is always made of this wood, which is said to be peculiarly sonorous. Excepting this, the wood appears to be used only for firewood. The root is used in snake bites.—*Captain Macdonald in M. E. Proceedings, Useful Plants.*

ALBIZZIA: *Species.*

Kokoh. *Burm.*

Grows in the Northern districts of Pegu, on and near the hills of British Burmah. The wood is valued by the natives as much as Padouk (Pterocarpus Wallichii) or even more so. It is used for cartwheels, oil presses and canoes. In the Prome district a special tax was levied on the felling of "Kokoh" and "Padouk" under the Burmese rule. Large trees are becoming very scarce in the Irrawaddy valley, but are not uncommon in the Tounhgoo district. A cubic foot weighs 48 lbs. In a full grown tree on good soil, the average length of the trunk to the first branch is 60 feet and average girth, measured at 6 feet from the ground. is 12 feet.—*Dr. Brandis, Cal. Ex. Cat. for* 1862.

ALBIZZIA ELATA.

Seet. BURM.

Abundant throughout the country in the plains of British Burmah, particularly near the banks of rivers. This wood may, at a future time, become an important article of trade. The heartwood is strong and durable, and less heavy than that of most trees of same family. The only drawback is, that the proportion of sapwood is large. Used by the Burmans for bridges and house posts. Breaking weight 250 lbs. A cubic foot weighs 42 to 55 lbs. In a full grown tree on good soil, the average length of the trunk to the first branch is 40 feet and average girth measured at 6 feet from the ground is 10 feet. It sells at 12 annas per cubic foot.—*Dr. Brandis. Cal. Ex. Cat. of* 1862.

ALBIZZIA STIPULATA, *Boiv.*

Boomayza. BURM.

Common throughout the forests on elevated ground of British Burmah, heartwood brown, beautifully streaked, but rather small, the sapwood being very large : much prized for cartwheels, also used for the bells of cattle. A cubic foot weighs 66 lbs. In a full grown tree on good soil, the average length of the trunk to the first branch is 30 feet and average girth measured at 6 feet from the ground is 9 feet. It sells at 12 annas per cubic foot.—*Dr. Brandis. Cal. Ex. Cat. of* 1862.

ALEURITES TRILOBA, *Forst.*
Camirium cordifolium. *Gært.*
Juglans camirium. *Lour.*

Akrot. BENG.	Kamiri. JAV.
Belgaum Walnut. ENG.	Akrot. MALAY.
Country Walnut. ENG.	Akrot. MALEAL.
Molucca tree. ENG.	Akrot. PERS. ? ?
Akrot. HIND.	Tiaily. TAHITI.
Mijli Badam. HIND.	

This tree is a native of the Society Islands, from which it was introduced into India, and a variety of it, the A. Moluccensis, is known to the Javanese under the name of Kamiri. A. Triloba is now indigenous in several parts of India, the Moluccas, the Malay Islands, Ceylon, plentiful near Hyderabad of the Dekhan, in the Southern Mahratta country, about Belgaum, in Bengal and Assam. Almost all parts of it, are covered with a farinaceous substance, and a gummy substance exudes from the seeds (as also, it is said, from the tree itself), which is chewed by the natives of Tahiti. The tree grows to a large size, but the quality of its wood is unknown. In Tahiti, tissues are made from the bark, but its most valuable product is its fruit, which is roundish, two celled, each containing a nut resembling in flavour the filbert or English walnut. They are considered aphrodisiac in the Moluccas, but are apt to purge and produce colic, unless roasted, or kept for a year. About 50 per cent. (or according to Simmonds 31½ gallons of the nut yield 10 gallons), of a useful, fine clear lamp oil, is expressed with very little difficulty and simple machinery, from the kernels of the nut, and the oil-cake is a good food for cattle and useful as manure. About 10,000 gallons of oil are yearly produced in the Sandwich Islands, and, in Ceylon, where it is manufactured, it is known as Kekuna oil. It is so bland as to be used for the table in Java, as well as for burning. In the Sandwich Islands the nuts are employed for candles. A number of them, strung upon a stick, will burn for hours, giving a clear and steady light. The tree grows readily from seed, and might be easily cultivated.—*Mr. Jaffrey, Dr. Riddell, Useful Plants, Madras Exhibition Jury Reports, Hogg's Vegetable Kingdom, Simmonds' Commercial Products, Voigt.*

ALHAGI MAURORUM, *Tourne ; W. & A.*

A. mannifera, *Desv.*	Manna Hebraica, *D. Don.*
,, Nepaulensium, *D C.*	Hedysarum alhagi, *Linn.*
Ononis spinosa, *Hasselq.*	

Juvasa or Juwassa. BENG.	Juwansa. HIND.
Camel's Thorn. ENG.	Giri karnika. SANS.
Shutur-khar. HIND.	Giri karnika. TEL.
Us-shutur-khar. ,, PERS. ? ?	Tella-giniya chettu. TEL.

This shrub grows in the deserts of Egypt, Syria, Mesopotamia, Beluchistan, Sind, in Guzerat, the Southern Mahratta country, at Monghir, Benares, Delhi. It sends forth leaves and flowers, in the hot season, when almost all the smaller plants die, and affords a grateful food for the camel, in desert places. The Hebrew manna exudes from its leaves and branches.—*Voigt.*

ALPHONSEA LUTEA, *H. F. & T.*
Uvaria lutea, *Roxb., Corr., W. & A.*

Muvi. TEL.	Chiri dudduga. TEL.
Muvvi. ,,	

See Uvaria.

ALSOPHILA EXCELSA. The Tree Fern of Norfolk Island, measures forty feet in height, and has a magnificent crest of frondes. The black portion of the trunk is used for stringing by cabinet makers.—*Keppel's Ind. Arch. Vol.* II. *p.* 184.

ALSTONIA SCHOLARIS, *R. Br.*

A. oleandrifolia, *Lodd.*	Echites scholaris, *Linn.*

Lutiana. ASSAM.	Ayugma chadda. SANS.
Chatinn. BENG.	Ir-elli-palai. TAM.
Let-htuk. BURM ?	Eda-kula-ariti. TEL.
Kori-kowan. MAHR.	,, ,, pala. ,,
Satwin. ,,	,, ,, ponna. ,,
Pala. MALEAL.	Pala garuda. ,,
Mukampala. ,,	Eda-kuta nati. ,,
Ayugma parma. SANS.	

This handsome looking tree grows in the Moluccas, Bengal, and to a very large size in

Ceylon, the South Konkan. In Canara and Sunda it is not very common; but found near the Ghats above and below of great size. It is found in the Travancore forests, in Burmah? and in Assam. It seems to be known to the Malay race, the excellent boards or thin planks it affords being used by Malay children and children in the Bombay presidency to write their lessons on, hence its name. Its existence in Magotna was not known, and it does not grow inland from Bombay, but grows freely enough in their Botanical Gardens, The whole plant abounds in a milky juice. Its wood is white and close grained but rather coarse, and in Assam is much prized for beams and light work, such as boxes, trunks, scabbards &c. It is valuable for the turning lathe and, in Ceylon, is used for coffins. It is as bitter as gentian, and is possessed, it is said, of similar virtues. The bark is a powerful tonic.—*Dr. Mason, Hogg's Vegetable Kingdom, Useful Plants, Dr. Gibson.*

ALSTONIA VENENATA, *R. Br.*

Echites venenata, *Roxb.*

Is figured by Dr. Wight in his Icones (436) but its properties are not known. Found on the Pulney Hills.

ALTINGIA EXCELSA.

Araucaria excelsa, *H. K.*

The Norfolk Island Pine, is seen 100 feet above the other forest trees, and resembles the Norway spruce, but its tiers are more distant. Its timber is not of good quality, as it soon rots when exposed to the weather, and the teredo, or auger worm, makes fearful ravages in the fences made of its timber, which seldom stand three years. It is generally used for building purposes, flooring, partitions, &c., and when kept dry and not exposed to the weather, it is more durable.—*Keppell's Voyage of the Meander, p.* 282.

AMBALETA. A small tree or shrub, attaining the extreme height of 12 feet with a circumference of 1½ feet, growing in the forests of Ganjam and Gumsur. The height from the ground to the intersection of the first branch is 3 feet. The character of its wood is not known. The juice of the leaves is mixed with preparations of mercury and taken internally for rheumatism and other diseases.

AMHERST PROVINCE furnished the following 90 woods to the Great Exhibition of 1851, which will be found described under their respective names.

1 Anan.
2 Ban-boay.
3 Ban-kha.
4 Bep-than.
5 Bhai-bya.
6 Bhyeng-tseng.
7 Bijion.
8 Daup-yat.
9 Dien-necung.
10 Eng.
11 Eng-gyeng.
12 Gan-gan.
13 Gyo.
14 Ka-theet-nee.
15 Kha-boung.
16 Kiep-dep.
17 Kiep-maup.
18 Kiep-yo.
19 Koup-ha.
20 Kya-nan.
21 Kya-zoo.
22 Kyway-thoay.
23 Kywon
24 Kywon-bo.
25 Kywon-gaung-noay.
26 Lammay.
27 La-phyan.
28 Lep-dwat.
29 Lieun.
30 Liep-yo.
31 Mala-ka.
32 Ma-thloa.
33 Maza-neng or Maga-neng.
34 Meet-gnyoo, or Neet-gnyoo.
35 Meng-ba, or Ming-ba.
36 Moma-kha, or Morna-kha.
37 Mou-tha-ma.
38 Myaup-loaut.
39 Myaun-ngo.
40 Mya-ya.
41 Na-kyeen.
42 Naoo.
43 Nga-soay.
44 Nyaung-lan.
45 Oun-thuay.
46 Pad-dan.
47 Pa-ngan.
48 Pa-ra-wa.
49 Peng-lay-oun.
50 Pinnai.
51 Povin-gunyet.
52 Pyeen-ma.
53 Raung-thmoo.
54 Seet-seen.
55 Tan-labet.
56 Taup-sha.
57 Teng-khat.
58 Thab-ban.
59 Tha-bwot-gyee.
60 Tha-byion.
61 Tha-khwot.
62 Thammai.
63 Than-kya.
64 Thanna-Dan.
65 Tha-nat.
66 Than-that.
67 Theet-phyion.
68 Theng-gan.
69 Theet-to.
70 Theet-ya.
71 Theim.
72 Thep-yeng.
73 Toung-bien.
74 Toung-tha-khwa.
75 Toung-tha-byiou.
76 Toung-thau-gyee.
77 Tseet.
78 Tsekka-doun.
79 Tshan-tshay.
80 Tshaup-yo.
81 Tshiet khyeen.
82 Tshwai-lwai.
83 Tsoay-dan.
84 Tswot-ba-lwot.
85 Yammandy.
86 Yeng-taip.
87 Yetha-byay.
88 Yoya-theet.
89 Zee-byion.
90 Yeng-bywom.

Captain Dance gives, from Amherst and Tavoy Provinces, and Mergui Archipelago, the following list of 113 woods which, also, will be found described under their several names.

1 Lagerstræmia Pymmah. Peema Nee.
2 Calophyllum Longifolium. Therapee.
3 Tee ka loung or Tha or Kadat-Ghee.
4 Sibia Glomerata. Thayt Pew Tha or White Thayat.
5 Artocarpus echinatus. Mountain Jack or Tong By-ne.
6 Xylocarpus Granatum, Penlaypyoung or Peng-lay-oun.
7 Heritiera Litoralis, Kouzozaloo or Kanazoe.
8 Heritiera Minor, Manazoe.
9 Kannan Tha or Crab Tree.
10 Kaya Nan in Tavoy, Kaiyah in Moulmein.
11 Parrawah.
12 Tha Byke or Tha-bay-Kya.
13 Gongoo or Gangaw.
14 Ancestrolobus Carnea; Toungala in Martaban Provinces, Zeengalay in Tavoy.
15 Bong long Tha.
16 Tha nat Khee.
17 Tay-tha.
18 Mai tai Yo.
19 Kya Mouk.
20 Pa-ka-than.
21 Dillenia Speciosa. Thee-Bew-Tha.
22 Kye-zai: Laurus, species
23 Myouk sho or Monkey tree, (also called Moulmein Lancewood, Dalbergia.
24 Careya aborea. Ban Bambbooai.
25 Kye yo Thoo.
26 Sow-yew.
27 Shorea Robusta. In-Jin or Enghyen.
28 Melanorrea usitata. Theetsee.
29 Fagrœa fragrans, Annan-Tha or Annan.
30 Hopea odorata. Thingan
31 Inga xylocarpa. Pyeng Khadoe.
32 Hopea odorata. Thingan Pew.
33 Acacia elata. Thacet-Tha
34 Pet-Than.
35 Mezzale.
36 Meenaban; Apocinaceæ.
37 Laurus (Sassafras). Carrawaytha, or Sassafras wood.

38 Pouk-Tha or Than-Yen.
39 Maikay ; Murraya, species.
40 Pterocarpus dalbergiodes.
41 Pinatha.
42 Ta-Kouk Tha in Tavoy, Yay Mine, Burm.
43 Tim Book Tha.
44 Them-Mai Tha.
45 Vateria lanceolata: Pantheya or Panthit-ya.
56 Kyaitha or Itchwood.
47 Chee Neb or Stinking Wood.
48 Kyet Thay or Theeay Kyay.
49 Dagoo Tha.
50 Kanyeen Tha or Wood Oil Tree.
51 Ka Meen Tha.
52 Young Tha.
53 Neen Tha.
54 Pew Bock.
55 The-La-Bay.
56 Mong-dayat nee or Red Mong dayat.
57 To Dooryan or Forest Dooryan.
58 Book Tha.
59 Tay Yo Tha.
60 Thay Yo Tha.
61 Maneeoga.
62 Mah yuh gah.
63 Thah Byay Nee.
64 Thee Khya Tha.
65 Dow Yat.
66 May-byoung.
67 Pee Ma Pew or White Peema.
68 Na Pew Gee or Let Thouk Gee.
69 Tha Yingee.
70 Tha Nat Thayt Pew Tha.
71 Kha Moung Tha.
72 Ka theet Tha.
73 In-Jin Pewoo, White Injin.
74 Thah yay Bew.
75 Thay kya Ba.
76 Thay Tha.
77 Thah Byay Ynet Ghee.
78 Tha Pyke Tha.
79 Kyai Yew.
80 Toung Bye Nay.
81 May Snoung.
82 Tha Bate Kee.
83 Mong-Dayat Pew, or White Mong-Dayat.
85 Kab-Ban-Tha.
86 Kyee Tha.
87 Tha Bong Pew.
88 Koung Moo.
89 Na Yoo-ya.
90 Khai Yah.
91 Dalbergia latifolia; Yendaik ; Black wood.
92 Phyoo.
93 Tye Yoo Tha or Lan Thah.
94 Phet Honway.
95 Ouk Guay.
96 Ngy-soung Tha.
97 Na Ghee.
98 Tayet Khyee.
99 Murrh Neen.
100 Yemmanee.
101 Soway Do.
102 Thayet Kya.
103 Chin Zooay.
104 Than That.
105 Yeen Ga.
106 Moketammatha.
107 Gyew.
108 Pinlay Jallat.
109 Bee-ew, not identical with Thee Bew Tha.
110 Kussoo.
111 Kyai tha.
112 Phangah.
113 Tunyeen or Tunyeen Dha.
114 Ebony. Diospyros, Tai.

AMBOYNA WOOD OR LINGOA WOOD.

A fragrant wood of various colours, used in cabinet work in England. There are several varieties of this very beautiful wood used in England ; they are probably all furnished by the same tree, *Pterospermum Indicum*. It is most beautifully mottled and curled, of various tints from light-red to dark-yellow, and always in small lumps, being evidently excrescences or burrs cut from the trees. The varieties of Amboyna wood are principally used for inlaying and by the makers of ornamental snuff boxes.—Localities, Ceram and Amboyna. At the Great Exhibition of 1851, it was sent from Singapore. See Lingoa wood, Kyaboca, Pterospermum Indicum.—*Archer, Faulkner, Lond. Ex. Juries' Reports.*

AMOORA ROHITUKA, *W. & A.*

Andersoniarohituka.*Roxb.*	Sphærosacme rohituka. *Wall.*
Meleacea Wightiana. *Wall.*	

Tiktha-raj. BENG.	Khana. HIND.
Chayau ka-yoe. BURM.	Chem-maram. MALEAL.
Hurin-hura. HIND.	

A native of the Peninsula of India, Travancore, Bengal, Moulmein, and found in the forests of Tounghoo though scarce. The wood is white coloured and adapted to every purpose of house building. The seeds yield an oil, which is used for many economic purposes.—*Voight, McClelland, Useful Plants.*

AMYGDALUS COMMUNIS, *Linn.*

Louz. AR.	Amygdalæ dulces. LAT.
Kataping. BALI.	Louzan. MALAY.
Badamsi ? BURM.	Badam. "
Badam. DUK.	Badam. PERS.
Amandelin. DUT.	Badam-i-Farsi. "
Almond. ENG.	Amendo. PORT.
Amandes. FR.	Mandel. RUS.
Mandelu. GER.	Inghurdi. SANS.
Badam. GUZ.	Walu luway. SINGH.
Badam. HIND.	Almendra. SP.
Badam-i-Farsi. HIND.	Parsi vadam maram. TAM.
Mandorli. IT.	Parsi badama chettu. TEL.
Kateping. JAV.	

The Almond Tree.

ANACARDIUM OCCIDENTALE, *Linn.*

Acajuba occidentalis, *Gærtn.*	Cassuvium pomiferum, *Lam. ; Rheede.*

Kaju. BENG.	Kola mavah. TAM.
Hijli badam. BENG.	Mundiri maram. "
The-ho-thayet. BURM.	Jidi mamidi. TEL.
Cashew nut tree. ENG.	Munta mamidi chettu. TEL.
Kaju. HIND.	Its Gum
Hijli badam. HIND.	Hijli badam ka gond. HIND.
Jambu-monat. MALAY.	Mundiri pisin. TAM.
Parunkimavah. MALEAL.	

This small tree, sixteen feet high, is very ornamental, when in leaf. It was introduced from the West Indies, and is now cultivated in Ceylon, all over India, in Burmah, in Pegu, the Tenasserim Provinces and in Tavoy. It sometimes grows to a large size, and in Pegu it is much cultivated about Phoungye houses, and in groves near towns.

The wood is dark brown, and is not, generally, deemed of value in carpentry, but, in Tavoy, Captain Dance says it is a large tree, used in boat building, and it forms a charcoal, which the iron-smiths there consider the best for their trade.

It bears sweet smelling flowers, succeeded by a pea-shaped fruit of a yellow or of a red color, very acrid and with an astringent juice highly recommended as a remedy in dropsical habits.

The nut hangs at the end of the fruit, outside, and is about an inch long, of a kidney shape, edible and wholesome when roasted, to be found in every bazar in India, and forming an article of trade and commerce. They are used for imparting a flavour to Madeira wine. Also, ground up and mixed with cocoa, they make a good chocolate and are said to yield a spirit by distillation, superior to rum or arrack, and described as a powerful diuretic. They also yield, by expression, an edible oil, equal if not superior to olive or almond oil.

The pericarp of the nut produces a black acrid oil, called Cardole or Cashew apple oil. It is a powerful vesicating agent, and, owing to its caustic properties is often applied to warts, corns, ulcers, &c. and to floors or wooden rafters of houses to prevent the attacks of white ants. It requires, however, to be used cautiously. Exposure to the vapour of the oil, when under preparation, will produce violent swelling and inflammation.

An astringent gum is exuded from the trunk of the tree to the extent of 5 to 12 lbs. annually, which should be collected when the sap is rising. It makes a fair substitute for gum arabic, forms a good varnish, and is particularly useful where the depredations of insects require to be guarded against. In S. America, bookbinders wash books with a solution of it, in order to keep away moths and ants. The juice which flows from an incision in the trunk of the tree imparts an indelible stain to linen. The bark of the tree is given internally in infusion, in syphilitic swellings. The fresh juice of the flower stalks is used in lemonade, and wine and vinegar are also made from it by fermentation.—*Voigt, Mr. Jaffrey, Dr. McClelland, Dr. Mason, Useful Plants, Vegetable Kingdom, Dr. Riddell, M. E. Jur. Report.*

ANCISTROLOBUS CARNEUS, *Wall.*

Hypericum carneum, *Wall., Cat.*

Soung-ga-læ. BURM. | Zin-ga-læ. TAVOY.
Toung-ga-la. MARTABAN.

This tree attains a maximum height of 30 feet, it rarely exceeds 3 feet in girth and its maximum is 3 cubits. It is plentiful in the Pegu and Tounghoo forests, where the timber grows very tall, and it is found, widely scattered, all over the Amherst, Tavoy and Mergui Provinces, but in none abundant. It is also a native of China. Its dark brown wood, when seasoned, floats in water. It has a long fibre, tenacity, durability and sufficient lightness, and is very free from knots.

It is used, by the Burmese, for building, for ploughs, and for utensils of all kinds, and is recommended for handles of chisels, hammers and tools generally.—*Captain Dance, Dr. McClelland, Dr. Mason, Voigt.*

ANCISTROLOBUS MOLLIS.

Yin-bya. BURM.

This tree is described by Dr. McClelland along with A. carneus, as plentiful in the Pegu and Tounghoo forests. The timber grows very tall, but seldom exceeds three feet in girth. Wood dark brown.—*McClelland.*

ANDGERI. *Can.*

Ind yern. MAHR. | Yern. MAHR.

The flower of this timber tree has not been seen, and its generic name remains undetermined, but it is supposed to be a species of Sapindus or Nephelium. It is found in the Canara and Sunda forests, above the Ghat, chiefly at Nilcoond and in the southern jungles.

The wood is serviceable in house building.—*Dr. Gibson.*

ANDRACHNE TRIFOLIATA, *Roxb.*

Stylodiscus trifoliatus, *Bennett.*
Psychodendron trifoliatum, *Wall.*

Uriam. ASSAMESE.

A tree of quick growth; found in Java, Ava, Peninsula of India, at Hurdwar, Chittagong, Nepal and Assam. Wood and bark red. Employed for masts and spars of small vessels.—*Voigt, Cal. Cat. Ex.* 1862.

ANGELY, OR ANGILICA, according to Edye, the Malayalam and Tamil name of a tree which grows to two and a half and three feet in diameter, and from fifty to sixty feet high. It is described by him, as used for large canoes and snake-boats, and, if kept oiled, as very durable. Also, as used for planks, for native vessels, in consequence of its being very tough, and well fitted to hold the yarns where the planks are sewed together, which is the case with all the flat bottomed boats on the coast, where there is a surf on the beach, as at Madras, for the Massula boat; at Mangalore and Calicut, for the manchee boats, &c.; and many of the pattamahs are fastened by paddings of coir on the joints of the planks, &c. Dr. Wallich names the Angelly wood, the Artocarpus hirsuta, and it is described in Useful Plants as A. hirsutus. —*Lam. Edye, Malabar and Canara.*

ANISOPHYLLUM ZEYLANICUM.

Welipiyanna. SINGH.

A tree of the western and northern parts of Ceylon, its timber is used for common house building purposes.—*Mendis.*

ANOGEISSUS ACUMINATUS, *Wall.*

Conocarpus acuminatus, *Roxb.*

Pachi manu. TEL. | Panchi. TEL.
Pashi. „

This tree is met with in several parts of India. Its timber is good and durable, and fit for house building purposes. On the Godavery, it is described as a very hard strong timber.—*Voigt, Captain Beddome.*

ANOGEISSUS LATIFOLIUS, *Wall.*

Conocarpus latifolius, *Roxb.*

Sheri manu. TEL.

This timber tree grows at Chillaune, Islamabad, in the Kennery Jungles, the valleys of the Concan rivers near their sources, the inland Dekhan hills, and in the Dehra Dhoon. The timber, if kept dry, is good and durable.—Near the Godavery, the wood is said to be one of the hardest in the forests. It grows to an enormous size. Axles of carts are generally made of this wood.—*Voigt, Captain Beddome.*

ANTIARIS. Of this genus of trees, there are six or seven species recognised, (1) the A. toxicaria, *Lesch.*, the genuine Upas tree of Java: (2) the A. innoxia, *Bl.:* and A. macrophylla, *R. Br.:* a fourth species to which no name has been applied (ramis foliis-que utrinque velutinis) is cultivated in the Kew Gardens: the A. saccidora, *Dalz.* of the Western coast of Peninsular India is a fifth: the sixth is the A. Zeylanica, *Thwaites*, of Ceylon, which like A. saccidora, yields sacks: and the seventh is A. Bennetti, *Seeman*, the Ma-mi or Ma-vu-ni-Toga, of the Tonga Islands—all trees of great height.—*No.* 53, *Vol.* 9, *Ann. Mag. Nat. Hist.*

ANTIARIS SACCIDORA, *Leschen.*

Lepurandra saccidora, *Nimmo.*

Jagguri. CAN.	Karwat. MAHR.
Karwat. „	Araya-angely. MALEAL.
Sack tree. ENG.	Riti-galia. SINGH.
Chandal. HIND.	Netavil maram. TAM.
Jagguri. MAHR.	

A stately forest tree indigenous on the West side of India, as in the ravines at Kandalla and in the jungles near Coorg. It is very common and the most gigantic of all the trees in the Wynaad Jungles. The wood is not much used, but the Cooramboor bags or sacks are made from the bark by a very simple process. A branch is cut, corresponding to the length and diameter of the sack wanted. It is soaked a little, and then beaten with clubs until the inner bark separates from the wood. This done, the sack, formed of the bark, is turned inside out and pulled down, until the wood is sawn off, with the exception of a small piece left to form the bottom of the sack, and which is carefully left untouched. These sacks are in general use among the villagers for carrying rice, and are sold for about six annas each. The Singhalese sew up one end of the bark for a sack.—*Royle, Fib. Pl. page* 343, *Mr. McIvor in M. E. J. R.*

ANTIARIS TOXICARIA. *Leschen.*

Ipo toxicaria, *Persoon.*

The Upas Tree of Java. ENG.	Anchar. MALAY.
Anchar. JAV.	

This tree is often over 100 feet in height, wood not known. The Upas antiar poison is prepared from the juice, which flows from incisions in the bark.—*O'Shaughnessy, Voigt.*

ANTIDESMA ALEXITERIA.

Noli tali maram. TAM.

A small tree and a very handsome one, common enough in the jungle at Coimbatore. It is not common in the Bombay forests, but in that side of India affects rather the skirts of cultivated land, and there never reaches a size sufficient to render it fit for purposes of carpentry. Bark made into cables. Leaves in decoction in snake bites. Fruit delicious.—*Vegetable Kingdom, Drs. Gibson and Wight.*

ANTIDESMA BUNIAS, *Spreng.*

A. alexiterium, *Spreng.* | Stilago bunias, *Linn.*

Ariya poriyam. MALAY.	Nolai Talai maram. TAM.
Noli Tali. MALEAL.	

A middle sized tree, growing on the Coromandel and Malabar sides of the peninsula of India, in Assam and in Nepaul. It grows to rather a large size in Assam with a girth of twelve or fourteen inches, but the wood by immersion in water, becomes heavy and black as iron. The bark is used for making ropes. Its leaves are acid and diaphoretic, are used as decoction in snake bites, and when young are boiled with pot herbs like sorrel, and employed in syphilitic cachexia.—*Useful Plants; Vegetable Kingdom.*

ANTIDESMA DIANDRUM, is found on the Travancore mountains, yields a tolerable timber, which is useful for various purposes.—*Roxb., Lindley &c. quoted in Useful Plants.*

ANTIDESMA PANICULATA.

By-it-zin. BURM.

A low tree found in the Rangoon, Pegu, Tounghoo and Tharawaddy forests. On the same plant are notched, rounded and pointed leaves and it bears a red sour fruit, resembling the barberry. It furnishes a small crooked timber, of a close grain, with the wood of a red colour and adapted to cabinet making.—*Dr. Mason, Dr. McClelland.*

ANTIDESMA PUBESCENS, *Roxb.*

Jeriam Kottam. MALEAL.	Pollari. TEL.
Jeram Kottam. „	Pollai. „
Jana palaseru. TEL.	

This tree grows in the Northern Circars, is similar to A. Bunias, and the bark is used for making ropes. The succulent drupes are eaten by the natives.—*Roxb. quoted in Useful Plants.*

AQUILARIA AGALLOCHA, *Roxb.*

Aqulugin. AR.	Ud-i Samudri. HIND. PERS.
Ugoor or Ag'r. BENG.	Agallochum. LAT.
Aloes wood tree. ENG.	Kalamba. MALAY.
Black Agallocha. „	Gahru. „
Eagle wood tree. „	Kaya gahru. „
Agila wood tree. „	Agaru. SANS.
Bois d' Aigle. FR.	Ag'ru ch'ka. TEL.
A'g'r. HIND.	Ag'ru. TEL.
Ud-i Hindi. HIND. PERS.	Krishna agaru. TEL.
Ud-i Kamari. „	

This is described by Roxburgh as an immense tree, a native of mountainous tracts E. and S. E. of Sylhet, in lat. 24° to 25° N. It is supposed to be one of the trees that furnish the Eagle wood of commerce.—*O'Shaughnessy, Voigt.*

AQUILARIA MALACCENSIS, *Lam.*

A. ovata of Botanists.

This tree has a whitish timber. It is a native of Malacca, China? and Ceylon?—*Voigt, Eng. Cyc.*

AQUILARIA SECUNDARIA.

This tree has a white and inodorous timber,

but, when diseased, secretes a resinous matter said to be the true Eagle wood.

ARANELLAH—? A wood collected by Colonel Frith in Travancore, where it is employed for building ordinary houses. It is of a dark brown colour with a specific gravity of 0·645. The tree is not determined. The Tamil name of Cicca disticha, is Aranclli.

ABRUS *species.*

Yong-tha-ngai. BURM.

A tree of Moulmein. Used in ordinary building materials.—*Cal. Cat. Ex.* 1862.

ARCHIPELAGO OF EASTERN ASIA. Extensive collections of woods from Borneo, New Guinea, and several other of the Archipelago islands, were contributed to the Exhibition of 1851, including sandal wood from Timor, and Lingoa or Amboyna wood, from Ceram, in the Moluccas.

ARECA CATECHU, *Linn.*

A. Faufel, *Gærtn.*

Fufil. AR.?	Adaka. MALEAL.
Banda. BALI.	Cavughu. „
Gua. BENG.	Puwak. SINGH.
Bonga. BISAYA.	Bonga. TAG.
Rapo. BUGIS.	Paku maram. TAM.
Kunthi? Kwun-ben. BURM.	Kamuga? „
Supeari. DUK.	Poka. TEL.
Areca Palm. ENG.	Poka chettu. „
Betel-nut Palm. „	Oka. „
Catechu Palm. „	Vakha. „
Supari. HIND.	Kunda-poka. „
Jombi. JAV.	Kola-poka. „
Pinang. MALAY.	The variety Kola-poka has long nuts.
Kachu. MALAY.	

This graceful palm grows in all tropical Asia and the islands, and often attains a height of 50 or 80 feet. The trunk is only a few inches in diameter and is used in Ceylon for pins and Pingo sticks,—in Travancore for spear handles and bows, and Dr. Cleghorn says for small objects in turnery. The nuts are chewed as a luxury, and are also used in turnery for small ornamental work.—*Voigt, Mendis, Dr. Cleghorn, Useful Plants, M. E. Juries' Reports, Ell.*

ARECA DICKSONII. *Roxb.* On the mountains of Travancore and Malabar, a wild species, the A. Dicksonii, is found in great abundance. Fruit used as betel. Wood unknown.—*Useful Plants., Voigt.*

ARECA OLERACEA, *Linn.*

Oreodoxa oleracea, *Endl.* | Enterpe caribæa, *Spring.*

Cabbage Palm. ENG.

A native of the West Indies, wood used the same as Areca catechu.

ARECA VESTIARIA, is so called from clothing being made of its fibres.

ARENGA SACCHARIFERA, *Labill.*

Borassus Gomutus, *Lour.*
Saguerus Rumphii, *Roxb.*

The Tree.	*The Sap.*
Nawa. AMB.	La-gen. JAP.
Nama. „	Barum or Baru?
Aren. JAV.	*The Gossamer.*
Monchons. MACASS.	Karvel. JAV.
Anao. MALAY.	Kawal. „
Anowe. „	*The Hair.*
Akel. PORT.	Makse. AMB.
Mandar. „	Duk or Dok. JAV.
Sagwan. SP.	Iju, Ejoo or Eju. JAV.
Sagwire. „	Gomuti. „
Scho. TER.	

A handsome tree of the Indian Archipelago, attains a height of 30 or 40 feet. Its commercial products are its wine, its Barum or Baru, and its horse-hair like Iju or Eju or Gomuti. It grows wild in dense shady forests.

This is one of five species of the genus "*Arenga*" which chiefly inhabit the islands of the Indian Archipelago, although they also grow on the continent of Asia. They are, all of them, handsome trees, their favorite localities being dense shady forests and in the neighbourhood of rivers and rivulets; it comes into bearing about the seventh year, and continues to flower from 2 to 5 years. It was so highly thought of by Dr. Roxburgh, that he introduced it largely into India, where the natives, it is said, took kindly to them, but they seem to have been lost again. Its commercial products are its wine, the "Barum" or "Baru," and its Eju or Gomuti. The Gomuti is the only one of this genus of any commercial importance. It occurs in abundance, in a wild state, throughout the islands of the Indian Archipelago, and yields its horse hair like substance, Javanese *Duk: Malay*, Iju or Eju or Gomuti, the last of which has given the name to the tree. Its leaves, when very young, are eaten like the American Cabbage palm, Oreodoxa oleracea, *Endl.* The fleshy outer covering of the fruit of the Gomuti, when macerated, affords a fiery liquor, appropriately denominated "hell-water," by the Dutch, and the seed, or rather the albumen when freed from its noxious covering, is made into a sweetmeat by the Chinese. It yields Sago, Palm wine, Gomuti Sugar and the Baru.—*Crawfurd's Dictionary Archipelago: Seeman on Palms, Dr. Royle's Fibrous Plants, Voigt.*

ARMOSIA DASYCARPA.

Thit-wa-jee. BURM.

This is found here and there widely scattered in the Swar and other Forests North of Toung-hoo, and in Pegu, Wood red; equivalent to mahogany.—*McClelland.*

ARREMENE, SINGH. A timber tree which grows in the Central province of Ceylon. It weighs 57 lbs. per cubic foot, and lasts to 50 years. It is employed there, for furniture and house building. It is said to be the Cassia Sumatrana.

ARAUCARIA CUNNINGHAMII, *G. Don.* Australian or Moreton Bay Pine. A remarkable but tender species, forming vast forests along the shores of Moreton Bay in lat. 14° to 29° S., and on the alluvial bank of the Brisbane Rive lat. 27° to 30° S. It attains from 100 to 130 feet in height, with a circumference of upwards of 14 feet, having a clear stem to 80 feet. Voigt, however, describes it as a shrub, perhaps a mistake of his.

ARAUCARIA EXCELSA, *R. By.*

Dombeya excelsa. *Lamb.* | Colymbeya excelsa. *Spreng.*

The Norfolk Island Pine, grows also in New Caledonia, Botany Island, and Isle of Pines. It is a majestic tree, growing to the height of from 60 to 228 feet, with a circumference of 30 feet. Its wood is useful for carpenters in-door work, but is too heavy for naval purposes as spars. Though Keppell says that this tree is not so lofty as the Altingia excelsa, but is of the same quality and is used for the same purposes, the two trees are supposed to be identical.—*Voight, Ind. Arch. Vol. II, p.* 282.

ARTOCARPUS, *Species.*

Myauk Sook. BURM.

A tree of Akyab, used in house-building. It grows to a large size, is very plentiful in the province, and the fruit is edible.—*Cal. Cat. Ex.* 1862.

ARTOCARPUS, *Species.*

Patta del. SINGH.

Grows in the Southern provinces of Ceylon, and is there used for boats and buildings; a cubic foot of the wood weighs 34 lbs and it is said to last 30 years. The fruit—9 × 2½ inches —is boiled and eaten as food.—*Mendis.*

ARTOCARPUS, *Species.*

Toun-pein-nai. BURM.

Wood yellow, a cubic foot weighs lbs. 39. In a full grown tree on good soil the average length of the trunk to the first branch is 80 feet and average girth measured at 6 feet from the ground is 12 feet.—*Dr. Brandis.*

ARTOCARPUS, *Species.*

Thoun-ben. BURM.

Dr. Wallich tells us that this species of the genus grows in Tavoy, and is a large tree, used in boat building. Perhaps identical with the last.

ARTOCARPUS, *Species.*

Py-nathe. BURM. | Tanna Ben. BURM.

Dr. Wallich describes this as growing in Tavoy but wood not used.

ARTOCARPUS, *Species.* Trap tree, of Singapore, furnishes the gutta used as bird-lime; and the fibres of its bark are used there for fishing lines, cordage and nets.—*Royle. Fib. Pl.*

ARTOCARPUS, *Species.* SMALL BREAD-FRUIT. This species is not scarce in the Tenasserim forests. It yields an orange colored fruit resembling in taste a custard apple, and in appearance a fig.—*Dr. Mason.*

ARTOCARPUS CHAPLASHA, *Roxb.*

Lesser Jack. ENG. | Chaplasha. HIND.
Thorny Jack. ENG.

This large, often immense tree, grows in Malabar, Bengal, Assam, Tipperah, and Chittagong, and in some places attains an immense size yielding a valuable timber, from which the canoes of the Fennec and Gomootee rivers are made. The wood is applied for other uses, and is said by Roxburgh to be particularly valuable for work which has to be immersed in water.—*Eng. Cyclopædia, Useful Plants, Voigt.*

ARTOCARPUS ECHINATA, *Roxb.*

Toung Ben. BURM. | Mountain Jack. ENG.
„ peing-nai. BURM. | Tampooni. MALAY.
Kanæ Kya-tha. CAN.?

This is a large tree with its leaves gashed like some species of oak. It is very common about the Balaghat and Wynaad, is found in Burmah, and, though not abundant, all over the Tenasserim and Martaban Provinces, in Amherst, Tavoy, and the Mergui Archipelago,—a large expanse of country. Its maximum girth is 5 cubits and maximum length 30 feet. The wood is not known to be used in Southern India, but, in Burmah, according to Dr. Mason, it is deemed a valuable timber by the natives, especially for canoes. Captain Dance however, tells us that though it floats in water when seasoned, the seasoned wood is too light and spongy, for durability, and should be regarded as a useless wood. Whether these conflicting opinions be the consequence of examining trees which have grown in different localities, subsequent enquiries must determine, but the wood possibly improves by immersion in water. It is said to produce an agreeably acid fruit, and Dr. Mason mentions Dr. Wallich as saying that "it produces a sort of caoutchouc, with which the Burmese pay their boats." But he imagines this to be a mistake, as the Burmese almost universally pay their boats with a substance that is produced by a bee, mixed sometimes with dammer.—*Dr. Mason, Mr. McIvor, Voigt.*

ARTOCARPUS HIRSUTA, *Lam.*

Artocarpus pubescens, *Willd.*

Helbulsoo. CAN. | Aini maram. MALEAL.
Hairy Bread-fruit tree. ENG. | Ansjeni. MALEAL.
Wild Bread-fruit tree. ENG. | Del. SINGH.
Pat Fannas. MAHR. | Aladel. „
Hebolsu. MAHR. | Anjili maram. TAM.

This large handsome tree, well adapted for affording shade, is not found in the northern jungles of the Bombay presidency: sparingly in those south of the Savitri to the bounds of Sawantwarri, after which it becomes more plentiful and continues abundant all down the Western coast of the Peninsula. Dr. Gibson says that it grows in Canara and Sunda, above, and in the ravines of the Ghats, but mostly in Honore and Bilgy talooks, and is there valuable for canoes and for planks. It is scarcely entitled to a place in the list of Coimbatore woods, being a native of the coast, and not extending so far inland. It is indigenous in Burmah, but abounds in the forests of Malabar whence, Mr. F. N. Maltby, in 1860, believed that ten thousand loads per annum, of this wood, for five years, could be supplied at the rate of twelve to fourteen rupees per candy. It grows on the Western, Southern and Eastern sides of Ceylon, and its timber, which is there used for fishing boats and in house building, weighs 40 to 51 lbs. the cubic foot, and is calculated to last from 25 to 70 years. The fruit (9 in. × 3 in.) is there boiled and eaten as food by the natives. It yields the Anjely wood of commerce, a wood esteemed particularly useful as a timber which bears exposure under water. The wood is valuable for canoes, ships' frame-work, and in house building, for which purposes it is largely used on the Western side of the peninsula of India, in Malabar and Canara, and is sought after for H. M. Dockyards. Its bark is occasionally used in Canara in the preparation of a brown dye.

The fruit is the size of a large orange, and abounds in a viscid juice which flows freely from the rough rind if touched. This is manufactured into bird-lime. The pulpy substance, which surrounds the seeds is much relished by the natives, being almost as good as the fruit of the Jack.—*Dr. Wight, Madras Exhibition Juries' Reports, Dr. Gibson, Dr. Mason, Mr. Jaffrey, Voigt, Useful Plants, Dr. Cleghorn in Conservator's Reports, Mr. Mendis.*

ARTOCARPUS INCISA, *Linn. fil.*

Rademachia incisa, *Thunb.*	Soccus granosus, *Rumph.*

Bread fruit tree. Eng.	Nang-ka. Malay.

This tree is a native of the South Sea Islands, and has been introduced into the various parts of South Eastern Asia—into Ceylon, in some parts of the Madras territories, where it is occasionally seen in gardens, in parts of the Bombay Presidency, in some parts of the Dekhan, and is cultivated in a few gardens in Tavoy and Moulmein and is extensively cultivated throughout the Malay Archipelago. It is a tree of slow growth, but it attains a tolerable large size in Bombay, where however it seldom ripens, the fruit which is muricated falling off in the cold season. In the Dekhan, its fruit is the size of a large orange, or small pumplemose with a muricated rind. The fruit is of that variety which is full of seeds and is of no value, bears well at Tavoy and Moulmein. The fruit of the useful variety, cut into slices and fried, has something of the flavour of the sweet potato, similarly dressed. Like the jack, Artocarpus integrifolia, it bears fruit on the branches, the trunk and the root. It will grow from cuttings, and requires a light soil, with care, and watering at first. The bark stripped, and then beaten and prepared, makes a kind of cloth with which the South Sea Islanders clothe themselves. At Tahiti, clothing made of it, and worn chiefly by the common people, was more common than that made from the paper mulberry, though inferior to it in softness and whiteness.—*Royle, p. 34, Crawfurd's Dictionary, Dr. Riddell, Dr. Mason, M. E. Jury Reports, p. 24, Voigt.*

ARTOCARPUS INCISA. *Variety* communis, *of Forst.*

Soccus lanosus, *Rumph.*
Seedless Bread Fruit.

This variety of the Bread-fruit tree attains a height of 30 to 40 feet, with a stem of a foot or a foot and a half of diameter. Of the two varieties one contains seeds and one without them, but both have been introduced into some parts of India, several years since into Penang and Ceylon, and more recently into Mergui, from the South Sea islands, of which it is a native. It is the seedless variety, that has given the name to the tree, and in some islands of the Pacific is much used.

The fruit which has an unpleasant smell is scarcely yet known in peninsular India. It is often larger than a man's head, and weighs sometimes as much as fifty pounds, is round, greenish, and covered with prominent papillæ, enclosing a white fibrous pulp, which becomes yellow and succulent at maturity. The pulp contains much starch, and in Polynesia, is used as food. The natives of these islands, before eating the unripe fruit cut it into quarters and roast it in the ashes. The ripe fruit requires no preparation.

The bark furnishes a fibrous tissue, of which the people of Tahiti make a large part of their clothing.

The true seedless bread-fruit tree is cultivated in Penang, and has been introduced into Ceylon. It has also been introduced into the Tenasserim Provinces, and Mergui, where it is said to flourish.—*Dr. Mason, Voigt.*

ARTOCARPUS INTEGRIFOLIA, *Linn.*

A. heterophylla, *Lam.*	Polyphema Jaca, *Lour.*
Rademachia integra, *Thunb.*	Sitodium cauliflorum, *Gært.*

Kantal. Beng.	Fannas. Mahr.
Peing-nai. Burm.	Sukun. Malay.
Pani Nai. Burm. ?	Kluwi. „
Alase gana mara. Can.	Tambul. „
Jack Tree. Eng.	Pilavuh. Maleal.
Indian Jack Tree. Eng.	Pila maram. Tam.
Entire leaved Bread-fruit. Eng.	Panasa chettu. Tel.
Pannas. Hind.	Veru panasa. „

This valuable fruit and timber tree is found all over India, more or less abundantly, growing rapidly to about 2½ feet in diameter. In the Bombay presidency, it is met with commonly about villages, rare in the North Konkan, but most common south of the Savitri creek. It is, there, always planted and often carefully manured, and when so treated it attains a great size.

It grows in the South Eastern and Western provinces of Ceylon, where its fruit. weighing from 5 to 60 lbs. is used in various ways for food, and its timber, which weighs 42 lbs. to the cubic foot, and is esteemed to last from 25 to 80 years, is in general use for building boats and for all kinds of furniture. Colonel Frith mentions that this wood, in Travancore, is of 0·554 sp. gr. and measures 2 to 4 feet in circumference. Dr. Gibson has seen pillars of it, in the interior of the buildings of the old forts at Severndroog, having four feet on each side. In Burmah, it occurs, and is a tree of Moulmein where its yellow wood is used to dye the yellow cloths that the Poongyes or Burmese Priests wear. It is there a large tree and affords a very dark grateful shade, and when the fruit, which is often larger than a man's head, is hanging all around its branches, it is a grand object. Malcolm says it is a very common tree in South Eastern Asia, but not thought to be indigenous, attaining a height of 80 to 100 feet, with thick alternate and spreading branches, and very dark green leaves.

It yields an excellent and valuable timber, at first yellow when cut, but afterwards changing to various shades of brown. When made into tables and well kept, it attains a polish little inferior to mahogany in colour and appearance. It is used for musical instruments and ornamental work. It is suitable for house carpentry in general, but it is a very brittle wood when dry and does not bear great alternations of dryness and moisture. It is well known in England as the Jack fruit tree wood, where it is used for cabinet and marquetry work, likewise for the backs of brushes. It affords an excellent fancy wood for tables, chairs, frames, &c., and the root of the older trees furnish a dark coloured wood admirably adapted for picture frames and carving work of all kinds. The wood is also valued for grain measures. Mr. Mason says that the yellow wood of the jack affords beautiful timber for furniture, and in some parts of India it is highly valued, but this does not seem applicable to the present day, though Mr. Faulkner tells us that Jackwood is imported into Bombay from the Malabar Coast, and was at one time in great request for making furniture. Of late years, however, it has been entirely superseded by blackwood for this purpose. It is imported into Britain in logs from 3 to 5 feet diameter, and also in planks; the grain is coarse and crooked, and often contains sand. The wood is yellow when first cut, but changes to a dull red or mahogany colour. It is still, however, used in India for almost every purpose of house carpentry and furniture, and in England for cabinet work, marquetry, and turning, and also for brush backs. The Jackwood is sometimes named Orange-wood from its colour and also Jack-wood, Jaack-wood and Kanthul.

In the south and west of Ceylon, where the trees are of rapid growth and very fruitful, it is in general use for building: beams, rafters, doors, and furniture are all made of it. It is not a common timber in the Circars, though some good trees are occasionally procurable from the hill zemindaries, resembling mahogany in colour and appearance. The full grown fruit weighs from 30 to 60 lbs., growing direct from the branches and the trunk, to which it hangs by a peduncle, and in aged trees, grows from the roots, where they are detected by the cracking of the soil. These last are said to be most prized. The fruit is covered with a very thick, rough green skin, has an unpleasant odour, and is full of white kernels, the size of a pullet's egg, the fleshy parts around which are eaten both green and ripe. It is not prized by Europeans, who, at most, have only tasted it, but it is said to be more relished by a continued use. Natives of India, however, highly prize the fruit, and to the natives of Burmah, where it is more abundant than any other fruit, except the plantain, it is invaluable. It is said to be very indigestible. The kernels of the ripe fruit, boiled or toasted, resemble the Spanish chesnuts in flavour, and when roasted are prized by the natives. The green fruit, after removing the outer rind, is used in curries, and, when ripe, the pulp and seeds are used similarly. As with all cultivated fruits, there are many varieties of the Jack. A bird-lime is manufactured from the juice. In Travancore, the entire fruit is planted, and when the various seeds germinate and grow up, the shoots are tied together with straw, and they unite into one stem, which bears fruit in about 6 or 7 years.—*Mr. Mendis, Dr. Wight, Dr. Cleghorn in M. E. J. Rep., Useful Plants, Crawfurd's Dictionary, Dr. Gibson, Dr. Mason, Dr. McClelland, Vegetable Kingdom, Voigt, Faulkner, Holtzapfel, See Baker's Papers.*

ARTOCARPUS LACOOCHA, *Roxb.; W. Ic.*

Dephal. BENG.	Small Jack. ENG.
Pain-nai? BURM.	Kamma-regu. TEL.
My-ouk-loke. „	Laku-chamma. „
My-ouk-louk. „	Nakka-renu. „
Lacoocha Bread-fruit. ENG.	

This tree is occasionally grown in gardens or near houses, in Bengal, Burmah and the Tenasserim Provinces, where it is usually called a kind of fig. Dr. Royle thinks it may be found to yield fibres. Its roots are used in dyeing yellow. Dr. Brandis tells us the wood is used for canoes. A cubic foot weighs 40 lbs. In a full grown tree on good soil the average length of the trunk to the first branch is 30 feet, and average girth measured at 6 feet from the ground is 6 feet.

The whole tree and unripe fruit contain much tenacious milky juice. The fruit is prized by the Burmese, and is eaten in Bengal. The male spadix is acid and astringent, and eaten by the natives in their curries.—*Voigt, Dr. Royle, Dr. McClelland, Useful Plants, Dr. Mason, Dr. Wight, Dr. Brandis, Flor. Andh.*

ARTOCARPUS MOLLIS, *Wall.*

Tounbein. BURM.

An immense tree in British Burmah, wood used for canoes and cart wheels. On the hills, large trees rather scarce. A cubic foot weighs 30 lbs. In a full grown tree on good soil the average length of the trunk to the first branch is 80 feet, and average girth measured at 6 feet from the ground is 12 feet.—*Dr. Brandis.*

ARTOCARPUS POLYPHEME, Champadah of Botanists, a tree of the same natural family with the jack and bread-fruit; fruit smaller than the first, but of more delicate flavour, is greatly esteemed by the Malays. It seems to be an indigenous plant of the Archipelago, and even there to be limited to the Western parts of it, such as Sumatra, the Malay Peninsula, and their adjacent islands.—*Crawfurd's Dictionary, page* 93.

ARTOCARPUS PUBESCENS, *Willde.*

White Bread-fruit. ENG.
Aludel. SINGH.
Del. SINGH.

A synonym of Artocarpus hirsuta.

ARTOCARPUS SYLVESTRIS.

Ran fannas. MAHR.

Character of wood not known.

ASH WOOD. A tree of Mehra Forest, near Abbottabad, Hazara. A species of Fraxinus different from that common in England.—*Cal. Cat. Ex.* 1862.

ASSAN. A tree of Cuttack sells at 6 annas per cubic foot. Light brown coloured wood and strong. Plentiful in the Santhal jungles from Raneebahal to Hasdiha. The wood is used by the natives for beams, planks and building purposes generally. The silk-worm from which Tussa cloth is made, feeds chiefly upon this tree. Several timber trees are procurable in abundance in the forests of the Sumbulpore district, and on the banks of the Mahanuddy, Brahminy, and Bytury rivers, and it is believed that their uses might be very much extended were a demand to spring up, and some experiments be made to test their properties and value.—*Cal. Engineer's Journal, July* 1860.

ATALANTIA MONOPHYLLA, *DC.; W. & A.*

Limonia monophylla, *Roxb., Rheede.*
Limonia pumila, *Burm.*
Turræa virens, *Koen.*
Trichilia? spinosa, *Willd.*

Wild-lime. ENG.
Makhur limbo. MAHR.
Malvaregam. MALEAL.
Kat-elle-michammaram, TAM.
Kat-elle-micha maram. TAM.
Adivi nimma. TEL.
Konda nimma. „

This small sized tree is found on the Malabar and Coromandel Coast, and is one of the most common trees in the greenwood jungles or "raaes" about the ghats of the Bombay Presidency. It is less common below and inland. Its hard heavy wood is white or pale yellow, and is very fine or close grained; but is not procurable in pieces which would square more than four inches, but for this, it would be suitable for cabinet purposes.—*Dr. Wight, Dr. Gibson quoted in Cyclop. of India, Voigt.*

ATTALI, the Tamil name of a tree in Ceylon which is of little value. It grows to about ten or twelve inches in diameter, and eighteen feet long. It produces a flower, and then a seed-pod, which is used as a medicent.—*Edye, Ceylon.*

ATTI. Hatey or Arti, is given by Edye as the Tamil name of a Ceylon tree which grows from two to three feet in diameter, and from twelve to twenty feet high. It is used for general purposes in small country vessels. He states that it produces the wild fig.—*Edye, Ceylon.*

ATTOO VUNJEE. An amber coloured, Travancore wood, specific gravity 0·480. Very cheap; used for firewood.—*Col. Frith.*

AUMLAH. HIND.? A whitish colored wood, not strong, plentiful in the Santhal jungles from Raneebahal to Hasdiha or about forty miles. Planks made from this wood are used by the natives in making boxes. The fruit when dried is used by them for washing and also eaten as a kind of preserve.—*Calc. Engineer's Journal* 1860.

AURA DOKA. HIND.?

A tree of Chota Nagpore, with a soft, white timber.—*Cal. Cat. Ex.* 1862.

AURANTIACEÆ, Citron Worts, or the Orange Tribe; the Orange, Lemon, Lime, Shaddock, Pompelmoose, Forbidden Fruit and Citron being the produce of this order. The Wampee, a fruit highly esteemed in China and the Indian Archipelago, is produced by Cookia punctata. The fruit of Glycosmis citrifolia is delicious; and that of Triphasia very agreeable. The Ægle marmelos is used in medicine and a perfume is made from its rind. The woods of the plants of this order are hard, but generally, small. The flowers are remarkable for their fragrance and beauty.—*Eng. Cyc.*

AVERRHOA BILIMBI, *Willde.*

Bilimbi. BENG.
Bilimbi. ENG.
Cucumber tree. ENG.
Kama-ranga. HIND.
Wilampi. MALEAL.
Blimbing basi. MALAY.
Blimbing bas. „

A small tree, about 8 feet high, with timber of doubtful value, growing generally in gardens in South Eastern Asia, and producing a beautiful green, smooth fleshy fruit, about the size of a small cucumber. In Burmah it bears profusely. The unripe fruit is intensely acid and cannot be eaten raw, but the acidity becomes less as it ripens. Amongst the Malays, it is used like the citron, the gooseberry, the cucumber and the caper in Europe, but can be candied or made into pickles or preserves, or preserved in sugar. Its acid juice is useful in removing iron mould.—*Dr. Mason. Mr. Jaffrey, Useful Plants, Vegetable Kingdom, Voigt.*

AVERRHOA CARAMBOLA, *Linn.; Willde.*

Kama-ranga. BENG.	Blim-bing manis. MALAY.
Zoung yah. BURM.	Tamara-tonga. MALEAL.
Mit-ha kama-ranga. DUK.	Carambola. PORT.
Coromandel Gooseberry Tree. ENG.	Tamartam maram. TAM.
Kam-ruk. HIND.	Tamarta Chettu. TEL.
Karmal. HIND.	Koro-monga. TEL. ?

a. Sweet variety, *dulcis*, mitha kamaranga.
b. Acid variety, *acida*, kamaranga.

This beautiful, but small tree, about 14 feet high, with a spreading head, is supposed to be a native of the Moluccas, from which it has been introduced into Ceylon, India, the Burmese provinces and South America, where it is now quite naturalized. In Burmah, Pegu and the Tenasserim Provinces it is not abundant, being often only found near towns, and, in India, in gardens. The tree is said to grow, but, to be scarce in Ganjam and Gumsur. It there attains an extreme height of 36 feet, but no use is made of the wood, though it attains a circumference of 3½ feet and a height of 9 feet from the ground to the intersection of the nearest branch.

The quality of its dark brown wood is not known. It bears, and in some places profusely, from three to fifty years and three times a year, a fruit about the size of a hen's egg, with five acute angles and a yellowish, thin, smooth rind. There are two varieties, a sweet and an acid. The latter contain an acid, watery pulp, and are candied, made into pickles or tarts. They make an agreeable dish when cut in pieces and cooked with sugar and wine or with skimmed milk. In Burmah, where the fruit is highly prized as a wholesome dish, it is used like other green fruits, in curries. The juice of the acid variety is useful in removing iron moulds from linen. The acid leaves are a good substitute for sorrell. Rheede tells us that the root, leaves and fruit are used medicinally, and the fruit in dyeing.—*Dr. Mason, Dr. McClelland, Vegetable Kingdom, Useful Plants, Elliot, Voigt.*

AVICENNIA TOMENTOSA, *Linn.; Roxb. W. Ic.*

A. resinifera, *Forst.*	Sceura marina, *Forst.*
A. oepata, *Buch., Herb.*	Mangium album, *Rumph.*
A. Africana, *Palisot.*	

Bina. BENG.	Nalla mada. TEL.
White Mangrove. ENG.	Mada chettu. „
Oepata. MALEAL.	

A small tree, grows within the tropics all over the world. It has small dingy yellow flowers. From its wood-ashes, the washermen make a preparation used in washing and cleaning cotton cloths, and which painters mix with their colors to cause them to adhere more firmly. The kernels are bitter but edible. The green fruit mixed with butter and boiled, is made into a plaster, which is employed for softening and maturing tumours and to induce granulation in ulcers resulting from small pox. In Rio Janeiro its bark is used for tanning.—*Flor. Andh., Useful Plants, Lindl., Voigt.*

AZADIRACHTA INDICA, *Ad. Juss.; W. & A.*

Melia azadirachta, *Linn., Roxb., Rheede.*

Nim. BENG.	Nimba. SANS.
Thembau-ka-makah. BURM.	Vepam maram. TAM.
Margosa tree. ENG.	Vepa. TEL.
Nim. HIND.	Nimba. „
„ MAHR.	Yepa chettu. „
Weppa. MALEAL.	Nimbamu. „
Aria Bepou. MALEAL.	

This beautiful tree is found in Ceylon, throughout India and Burmah, and in some localities attains a large size. It is to be seen every where, though more seldom as a forest tree than in waste places and in the villages of the people and gardens of Europeans, where it is grown for ornament and shade. In the south of India, it is in considerable abundance in most parts of the inland country, and in the Pegu province, is plentiful in the Prome district only.

The quality of its timber varies in these localities. Throughout the peninsula of India, it yields a compact, hard, heavy durable wood, when old—difficult to work but—beautifully mottled and deserving attention for ornamental purposes. It is well fitted for ship building and carts. Some samples exhibited by Mr. Rohde, at the Madras Exhibition, equalled the best fancy woods, and some of the finest furniture he had seen, was from an old margosa tree. It is used in Coimbatore for cart wheels, and in bare districts of the Bombay Presidency, it is of great importance for building and agricultural purposes. In the Prome district of Pegu, it is described as a large but soft timber only fit for flooring. In some beautiful specimens that we have seen, it is of a light reddish brown colour.

This is one of the trees which it would be of importance to increase throughout the country. It reaches a large size even in stony ground. It comes into full foliage in the very midst of the hot weather. Every part of the tree is bitter, and its leaves, bark, seeds and the oil from its seeds are largely used in native medicine. It is venerated by the Hindu people, who, regarding the small pox as a goddess, employ the leaves in that disease, and, like the shrew ash tree, in England, it is often resorted to by the friends of the insane, who pass the sick person through a cleft of the tree, or through a stem which, having parted and re-united, forms a circular opening.—*Dr. Wight, Mr. Rohde, Dr. Cornish, Dr. Gibson, Cyclop. of India and Supplement. Elliot, Voigt.*

BABOOL. A Hindi vernacular word, applied as a generic term to some species of Acacia: but, the Babul, proper, is the A. Arabica (which see). In Sinde, the Babool is very abundant and grows to a very large size. It is exceedingly hard and weighty. For agricultural implements and all native purposes, it is excellent. It was also much used by the Indus Flotilla, for paddle flats, rudders, stanchions and boats' knees—in fact for every purpose to which wood can be applied. Besides other parts, its bark is employed in tanning, its pods form a valuable food for cattle, its young branches are the favourite food of camels and goats, its bark yields gum and lac, and for all these articles, wood, bark, pods and lac, a sale is always found. Drs. Gibson and Cleghorn have strongly advocated the extension of this tree by plantations, Dr. Cleghorn (Report p. 7) suggested that this most useful tree should be conserved along the banks of the Tumbuddra, both in the Bellari district, and in the Nugger division of Mysore. The Babool springs up in the alluvial soil on both banks (in similar ground to the Shikargahs of Sinde), and, he adds, if three trees be planted when one is cut, there will be an increased supply of useful material in a few years. Dr. Gibson, continuously, for years, strove to form these preserves. He says (Report of 1857-60, p. 14) the several proposed Babul reserves in this eastern line should be kept in view, otherwise the want of tree reserves in a bare country may hereafter be felt. He tells us (pages 18 and 19) of Babool preserves on the Bheema and Moota Moola rivers, and adds that, the net profit of all these Babool preserves for the year, after deducting every expense, including Rs. 432 per annum for keepers, reached the figure of Rs. 1,068-9-8, being the best return yet had since the commencement of conservative measures in 1846. He mentions that there are Babool preserves on the Bheema river, in the Ahmednuggur Collectorate, and that the supply of wood from these Babool forests continues to increase, not only as regards firewood, but also in respect to large wood for the Gun Carriage Manufactory, and, to meet the increasing demand, every opportunity had been taken for extending the preserves. He informs us that the large Babool wood which used to be obtained from Kutch and Kattywar seems now to be not procurable, but adds that the roadside Babools, especially in the Sattarah Districts, will soon afford a large supply of Gun Carriage timber.

BAH-MAH-THOA, Burm. A useful timber of Tavoy.

BAIBGA.? A tree of Akyab, plentiful in the Sandoway district. Used for firewood.—*Cal. Cat. Ex.* 1862.

BAIRIYE, Singh. A tree of the northern and western provinces of Ceylon, found near the mouths of rivers. A cubic foot weighs 57 lbs., and the wood is used for anchors and in house building. It is said to last from 10 to 30 years.—*Mr. Mendis.*

BALANITES ÆGYPTIACA, *Delile.*

Balanites Ægyptiaca, var Indica, *W. Ill.*	Ximenea Americana, *Linn.*
Ximenia Ægyptiaca, *Roxb.*	

Hingon. Beng.	Nanjunda maram. Tam.
Hingun Bet. Dux.	Gara chettu. Tel.
Nanjunda wood tree. Anglo-Tam.	Gari „ „

This small, thorny tree has alternate, bifoliate leaves, with greenish-white flowers. It is found throughout India, grows in Coimbatore, and is common about Delhi, and in the Doab as far as Allahabad, and especially on the banks of the Jumna. It flourishes in black soil. The wood is said to be good only for fuel. Its leaves are slightly acrid and are said to possess anthelmintic properties. The fruit, when ripe, can be eaten without inconvenience, but Dr. Roxburgh describes the pulp as exceedingly bitter and having an offensive greasy smell. It is about the size of an egg and covered with a smooth dry cortex. It is used in native fireworks; the kernel being scooped out the shell is filled with gunpowder, and explodes with a very loud report. A fat oil, called zachun, *qu. zaitun?* is extracted from the seeds. The fruits are said to be mixed in commerce with myrobalans. —*Dr. Wight, Dr. Riddell, Mr. Jaffrey, Dr. O'Shaughnessy, Voigt.*

BALSAMODENDRON AGALLOCHA, *W. & A.*

Balsamodendron Roxburghii, *Arn., Wight Ill.*
Amyris commiphora, *Roxb.*
„ agallocha, *Roxb.*

Googgul. Beng.	Bódanki chettu. Tel.

This small tree grows in Assam and the Garrow hills. It produces the Gum Bdellium of commerce, and perhaps of Dioscorides. The whole plant, while growing, is considerably odoriferous, and when any part is bruised and broken it diffuses around, to a considerable distance, an agreeable fragrance like that of myrrh. Wood unknown.—*Voigt, Fl. Andhr.*

BAMAU. Burm.

A close-grained wood, of Pegu?—possibly a substitute for box-wood prized by Karens for bows. A cubic foot weighs lbs. 52. In a full grown tree on good soil the average length of the trunk to the first branch is 30 feet, and average girth measured at 6 feet from the ground, is 6 feet.—*Dr. Brandis, Cal. Ex. Cat.*

BAMAW. A tree of Akyab, but not very plentiful. Used by natives for bows, &c. This seems identical with the last.—*Cal. Cat. Ex.* 1862.

BAMBUSA, THE BAMBOO.

Bansh. BENG.	Mambu. MALAY.
Bamboo. ENG.	Buluh. ,,
Bambou. FR.	Kul-mulla. MALEAL.
Indianischer rohr. GER.	Mungal. TAM.
Bans. HIND.	Bongu veduru. TEL.
Bamba. ,,	Kichakai. ,,
Bambu. IT.	Penti veduru. ,,
Preng. JAV.	Potu ,, ,,
Bambu. MALAY.	

The Bamboo, the most gigantic of the grasses, consists of many species, which are applied to so many useful purposes, that it would be difficult to point out an object in which strength and elasticity are requisite, and for which lightness is no objection, to which the stems are not adapted in the countries where they grow,—hollow cases, bows, arrows, quivers, lance shafts, masts of vessels, bed posts, walking sticks, the poles of palanquins, the floors and supporters of rustic bridges, scaling ladders, durable water pipes, rafts for floating heavy timber, frameworks of houses, floorings of houses, scaffolding, planking, uprights in houses, roofing, bambooware,- fishing rods, walking sticks, handles of parasols, tent poles, books, musical instruments, paper, pencils, rules, cups, baskets, buckets, cages, crab-nets, fish poles, pipe sticks, sumpitan or blowing tube, chairs, seats, screens, couches, cots and tables, and, parts of it are used as pickles or candied. There are many species of Bamboo: and, in the Khassia Hills alone, there are fifteen.

1. Bambusa agrestis, *Poir.* On mountainous and dry desert places in all China, Cochin-China and the Malay islands. Joints crooked, often a foot thick, a foot and a half long and nearly solid.

2. Bambusa amahussana, grows in Amboyna and Manipa, has short joints and a thick wood.

3. Bambusa apus, *Schultes.* A gigantic species growing on Mount Salak in Java, stems 60 or 70 feet high, and as thick as a man's thigh.

4. Bambusa aristata, *Loddiges.* Slender stems.

5. Bambusa arundinacea, *Willde.; Roxb.*

Arundo bambos, *Linn.*	Bambos arundinacea, *Zet.*
Nastus arundinaceus, *Sm.*	

Stems grow in clusters of 10 to 100, and are straight for 18 or 20 feet.

6. Bambusa aspera, *Schultes,* Found at the foot of mountains in Amboyna with stems 60 to 70 feet high, and as thick as a man's thigh.

7. Bambusa balcooa, *Roxb.*

Dendrocalamus balcooa, *Voigt.*

The Balcooa bans and Dhooli balcooa of Bengal is of gigantic size and reckoned there the best for building purposes. Before using it, it is steeped in water for a considerable time.

8. Bambusa bitung, *Schultes.* Found in Java.

9. Bambusa Blumeana, *Schultes.* A native of Java, with stems as thick as a child's arm.

10. Bambusa maxima, *Poir.* Found wild in Cambodia, Bally, Java, and various islands of the Archipelago. It grows 60 to 70 feet high, and as thick as a man's body. Its wood is however very thin.

11. Bambusa mitis, *Poir.* Cultivated in Cochin-China, wild in Amboyna. Its stems are thin but sometimes as thick as a man's leg, and 30 feet long, and are said to be very strong.

12. Bambusa multiplex, *Lour. Qu.* B. Nana? Stems 12 feet long and an inch thick, cultivated for hedges in the north of Cochin-China.

13. Bambusa nana, *Roxb.* A native of China, makes beautiful close hedges and fences.

14. Bambusa nigra, *Loddiges;* of the neighbourhood of Canton, where its stems, not more than a man's height, are cut for walking sticks and handles of ladies' parasols.

15. Bambusa prava, forms large woods in Amboyna, which come down to the coast: its leaves are 18 inches long and 3 or 4 inches broad.

16. Bambusa picta, common in Ceram, Kelanga, Celebes and other islands of the Archipelago. Its joints are 4 feet long and 2 inches thick, and are used for light walking sticks.

17. Bambusa spinosa, *Roxb.* The *Behor bans,* spined. Common about Calcutta and in the south of India. It has a small cavity and is therefore strong. Its stems are from 30 to 50 feet long.

18. Bambusa spina.

Conta Banso, URIA.

Extreme height 80 feet. Circumference 1½ feet. Two species of Bamboo which abound in Ganjam and Gumsur.

19. Bambusa stricta, *Roxb.*

Dendrocalamus strictus, *Voigt.*	Nastus strictus, *Sm.*

Somewhat spiny. Its great strength, solidity and straightness render it fit for many purposes. Lance-shafts are made of it.

20. Bambusa tabacaria, *Poir.* Grows wild in Amboyna, Manipa and Java, its stems with nearly solid joints, 3 or 4 feet long but not thicker than the little finger, when polished, make the finest pipe sticks. The outside is so hard that it emits sparks of fire when struck with the hatchet.

21. Bambusa tulda, *Roxb.*

Dendrocalamus tulda, *Voigt.*

The Tulda or Pika bans of Bengal and India is common all over Bengal, and grows rapidly to 70 feet long and 12 inches in circumference, rising to their full height in 30 days. Improves in strength by steeping in water. The *Jowa bans* with long joints is one variety, and the *Basini bans* used to make baskets, is another.

22. Bambusa vulgaris, *Wendl.* Its stems are from 20 to 30 feet long, and as thick as a child's arm.

In one of his reports, Dr. Cleghorn mentions that immense quantities of fine Bamboos are floated down the various rivers of the Western Coast of India. They are one of the riches of those Provinces. They are ordinarily 60 feet long and five inches in diameter near the root, these are readily purchased standing at 5 Rupees per 1000, and small ones at 3½ Rupees per 1000. Millions are annually cut in the forests and taken away by water in rafts or by land in carts. From their great buoyancy, they are much used for floating the heavier woods as (Mutte) Terminalia tomentosa and (Biti) Dalbergia arborea, and piles of them are lashed to the sides of the pattimars going to Bombay. The larger ones are selected as outriggers for ferry boats, or studding-sail-booms for small craft. He tells us that in addition to the vast export by sea, it is estimated that two lacs are taken from the Soopah talook eastward. The Malabar bamboo is much smaller than that of Pegu (Bambusa gigantea) which is 8 inches in diameter. At another place he says that immersing in water or better still, in a solution of sulphate of iron or lime water, is attended with good results, as it extracts the sweet sap which would otherwise induce decay. But, when it is intended to split the bamboos for reepers, this should be done before steeping them in the metallic bath. The merchants on the western coast of India prefer the water-seasoned bamboos which have been months in the water attached to the rafts, that are floated down the Nelambur and Sedashegbur rivers to the sea. The bamboos, there, are often eighteen yards long, and are brought down in immense floats tied together in bundles of fifty by the root ends which are turned towards the forepart of the float.—*Roxb. Fl. Ind., Eng. Cyc., Dr. Mason's Tenasserim, Dr. Clegkorn's Reports, Dr. Hooker's Him. Journ.*

BAN-BOAY, Burm. In Amherst, a strong and useful wood, a kind of Mimosa, (*qu.* Acacia?) employed for house posts.—*Captain Dance.*

BAN-KHA, Burm. In Amherst, a peculiar kind of wood, colour grey, used for house posts, and other common purposes.—*Captain Dance.*

BARRINGTONIA, *Species.* There is a white flowered species of Barringtonia in the Tavoy and Mergui jungles with drooping spikes of white flowers three or four feet long; and which would be much admired if introduced into the cities. The leaves are very large and lyre-shaped, and both flowers and foliage would contrast well with the other trees around it. The character of the wood, not known.—*Dr. Mason.*

BARRINGTONIA ACUTANGULA, *Gærtn.*

Stravadium rubrum, *D. C.*	Eugenia racemosa, *Roxb.* In the Flora Indica, this is corrected.
Stravadium coccineum, *D. C.*	Meteorus coccineus, *Lour.*
Eugenia acutangula, *Linn.*	

Kyai-tha. Burm.	Radami. Tam.
Samandar phal. Hind.	Kanapa chettu. Tel.
Hijjul. "	Kanigi. "
Sjeria-samstravadi. Maleal.	

This is a large tree, with dark scarlet colored flowers. It grows in Saharunpore, the Morung hills, Bengal, Chittagong, in both the peninsulas of India, and is plentiful in the Tharawaddy district. The wood is of a red color, hard, and of a fine grain, is used in constructing carts, and is equivalent to mahogany. Dr. Mason says it is very abundant in the Tenasserim forests, of which it is a great ornament.—*Drs. O'Shaughnessy, McClelland, Mason, Voigt, Useful Plants, Elliot.*

BARRINGTONIA RACEMOSA, *Roxb.*

Eugenia racemosa, *Linn.*

Samudra pu. Maleal.	Samudra pallam. Tam.
Sam stravadi. Maleal.	

This stout timber tree is a native of the Moluccas, Penang, the delta of the Ganges and Malabar. Its root is slightly bitter, and considered by the hindus to be aperient, cooling, and febrifuge.—*Flora Andhrica, Voigt.*

BARRINGTONIA SPECIOSA, *Linn.*

Butonica speciosa, *Lam.* | Maumea Asiatica, *Linn.*

Kyai-gyee. Burm.

This large and beautiful tree is a native of Pegu, the Tenasserim Provinces, the Malay Archipelago, Singapore, the Moluccas, and the South Sea Islands. It is very plentiful in Pegu. Its wood is red, hard, of a fine grain, and equivalent to mahogany. It is used in the construction of carts. The fruit is mentioned by Ainslie as being used in Java for intoxicating fish.—*O'Shaughnessy, page* 337, *McClelland, Roxb., Voigt.*

BARU, *Malay;* Kawal, *Javanese:* is a gossamer-like substance, found at the base of the petioles of the Gomuti palm, the Arenga saccharifera. It is imported into China where it is applied like oakum, for caulking, and also for tinder.

BASSIA, a genus of plants belonging to the natural order *Sapotaceæ* found in the East Indies and in Africa, where they are of great economical importance on account of the abundance of a sweet buttery substance which is yielded by their seeds when boiled.—*Eng. Cyc. p.* 396.

BASSIA, *Species.* In the southern Provinces of Tenasserim, a Bassia tree is quite abundant in a few localities: and it is said to afford a timber in no way inferior to teak.—*Dr. Mason.*

BASSIA BUTYRACEA.

Indian Butter tree. Eng.	Phalwarra. Hind.
Falwa. Hind.	Yel-pote. Lepcha.

The trunk of this tree sometimes measures 50 feet in height and 5 or 6 feet in circumference. It is found wild in Sikkim, Nepal and on the Almora hills, but its timber is nearly as light as that of the Bombax heptaphyllum, the Semul or Cotton tree, and is of no value. A delicate white colored oil, solid at 95° is expressed from the bruised kernels, which is used in medicine and for unction.—*Eng. Cyc., Hooker, O'Shaughnessy.*

BASSIA ELLIPTICA, *Dalzell.*

Isonandra Cullenii, *Drury.* | Pachonta, *Can.*

This majestic tree has been traced from Coorg to Trevandrum. It yields a substance which, as was at one time thought, would be a substitute for Gutta Percha, but subsequent report is less favorable. The timber deserves attention.—*Dr. Cleghorn's Forests and Gardens, p.* 13.

BASSIA LATIFOLIA, *Roxb.*

Mohu. BENG.	Ipei ? TAM.
Mahwa Tree. ENG.	Illupa. „
Mahwa. HIND.	Kaat Illupa. „
Mula ? „	Epi ? TEL.
Moho. MAHR.	Ippa. „
Poounam. MALEAL.	Ippe chettu. „
Maduka. SANS.	

This tree grows in the mountainous parts of the Circars, in Bengal, in Malwa, Nagpore and Guzerat. In the Circars, it is never felled by the natives, and it is preserved in Nagpore on account of its large fleshy flowers which are eaten raw by the natives and used in distilling arrack. It is common all over the Bombay jungles, both on the coast and above the ghauts. The timber, in Nagpore, is from 15 to 20 feet long, and in girth 4 or 5 feet.

The character of its wood seems to vary in different localities. Captain Sankey says that in Nagpore it is of a pinkish color, and but a weak timber, while, from being invariably rotten at the heart, 4 to 6 inches square of really good sound timber is all that can be reckoned on. In the plains the tree is preserved for the flower, and consequently is very little used. In the Upper Provinces of India, he adds that the timber is more esteemed, and has been used for door and window frames. He does not class it as a building material, and it is eagerly devoured by white ants. Dr. Gibson however, says that the wood, particularly the large logs brought from the Barria forest and Kupperwunje hills, is extensively used for house and cart purposes in Guzerat, but seldom appears in the market in Bombay or elsewhere. It appears strong and tough. In the Upper Provinces of India, its wood is described as hard and strong and proper for the naves of wheels.—*Voigt, Captain Sankey, Dr. Gibson, M. E. J. Rep., Flora Andhrica.*

BASSIA LONGIFOLIA, *Linn,*

Wild Sapota Tree. ENG.	Ennai carrai maram ? TAM.
Mahwa. GUZ.	Yepa ? TEL.
Mohe-ka jhar. HIND.	Ippa. „
Ellupi. MALEAL.	Pinna. „
Mee. SINGH.	Ippa manu. TEL.
Illupa ? TAM.	Oodooga maram of Wynaad.
Elupa. „	

This tree grows in Ceylon, in Coimbatore, on the Malabar Coast, in the Wynaad and in the Bombay forests north of the Goa border. It is a large tree, a good deal like Bassia latifolia, but its leaves are narrower, and its flowers much more fleshy. It is a native of the Peninsula of India, and is found in plantations along the southern coast of Coromandel. Mr. Rohde says that the Ippi of the Teloogoo country is valued for keels of ships and for planking below the water line. Exposed to the wind and sun in the log, it rends into strips, but, it is considered a good wood for trenails and it is comparatively free from the attacks of the Teredo navalis. It is procurable among the logs brought down the Godavery. In the Wynaad, it is known as the Ooodagoo maram, and is there an ordinary sized tree: its wood being much used on the Malabar side for building. Dr. Wight says it is a light colored hard and durable wood nearly equal in these respects to teak, but much smaller. In Coimbatore it is much used in the construction of carts, where great strength is called for. In Malabar, where it attains a large size, it is used for spars. Dr. Cleghorn describes it as a good wood for trenails. It grows in the northern province of Ceylon, and its wood which is said to last from 25 to 80 years, weighs 61 lbs. to the cubic foot. It is there used as keels for dhonies, for bridges and in house building. The seeds contain about 30 per cent. of oil of a bright yellow color. 12½ lbs. of seed, in the ordinary native rude way of expressing, produce 2 English gallons of oil. The oil or its seed may form an important article of export as a putty oil. This oil makes excellent candles and soap. Its chief use is, however, for burning in lamps, and as a substitute for butter in native cookery. In medicine, the oil is used externally to cure the "Itch" and other cutaneous disorders; and the leaves, milk of the green fruit, and bark, are boiled in water as a remedy in rheumatic ailments.—*Mr. Mendis, Dr. Wight, Mr. Rohde, Mr. McIvor, Dr. Mason, Dr. Cleghorn, Flora Andhrica.*

BASTARD WOODS. An Anglo-Indian term applied to woods of India which have some outward resemblance to other woods: such as,

Bastard teak, Chiri Teku, TEL. applied to several kinds of trees with large leaves. On the Nagari hills the Yanadis apply it to Dillenia, now Wormia, bracteata. In Bombay it is applied to the Butea frondosa, the Ban-Teak or Ben-Teak being the Lagerstræmia microcarpa.

Bastard Ebony, in Ceylon, is their Kadem-Beriye, SINGH., and probably a species of Dalbergia.

Bastard Cedars, of Southern India, are the Soymeda febrifuga, and Guazuma tomentosa.

Bastard Sago-palm, of Southern India, is the Caryota urens.

BAUGLAN is the western talooka of Kandesh. Stretching north in Bauglan is a series of valleys separated by small chains of hills. These hills form, as in the Poona Mawuls, ground naturally formed for forest reserves.—*Gibson's Bombay Forest Reports of* 1857-60, *p.* 38.

BAUHINIA. A genus of plants, many of which afford valuable timber and useful woods, while others are but climbing plants. They grow in the plains of the south of India, but Dr. Hooker, at a thousand feet above Punkabaree in the outer Himalayas, found the prevailing gigantic timber, scaled by climbing Leguminosæ, as Bauhinias and Robinias, which sometimes sheathed the trunks or spanned the forests with huge cables joining tree to tree. Several of the species in India are as yet undetermined. The woods are often of a dark colour.

BAUHINIA, *Species.*

Ambhota. URIA.

A tree of Ganjam and Gumsur. Extreme height 20 feet, circumference 2 feet and height from ground to the intersection of the first branch, 7 feet. Useless except for firewood.—*Captain Macdonald.*

BAUHINIA, *Species?* A small timber tree, native of Tenasserim, bears a sour twin-formed leaf, and a pod containing sweet pulp like that of the honey locust of America.—*Dr. Mason.*

BAUHINIA ACUMINATA, *Linn.*

B. candida, *Ait. not Roxb.*

Chitka. BENG.
Kanchan. „
Kanchan chakta. BENG.
White Bauhinia. ENG.
Mountain Ebony. „
Cuchunar. HIND.
Duolo Kunchun. MAHR.
Velutta mandarum. MALEAL.
Mandareh. TAM.
Vellai Muntharai maram. TAM.
Deo-kanchana. TEL.
Kachana. „
Kasana. „

Grows in Mauritius, Ceylon, Assam, both peninsulas of India. Rare in Coimbatore, and does not seem to be indigenous in the Bombay side, where it is cultivated, as also in the Dekhan and Tenasserim. It is only a handsome shrub, with large pure white flowers.—*Drs. Riddell, Gibson, Wight, Mason, Flora Andhrica, Voigt.*

BAUHINIA ALBIDA.

B. candida, White, rose-scented Bauhinia.

Duolo Kunchun. MAHR. | Vellai-munthari-poo. TAM.

The flower buds of this pretty tree yield an excellent vegetable for curries,—the flowers of all the Bauhinia are eaten by the natives,—the flowers are very handsome when open, being almost pure white, with a sweet odour. Dr. Gibson says that this tree is found in the Bombay forests, but rarely; and is more common in the vicinity of villages. It reaches a fair size, and gives a wood of a good quality, but seldom of scantling sufficient for house purposes.—*Mr. Jaffrey, Dr. Gibson.*

BAUHINIA ANGUINA, *Roxb.*

Bauhinia piperifolia, *Roxb.*

Nang-put. HIND.

It grows in Assam and the Concans. Is an extensive and rambling shrub, with flexuous compressed stems and small white flowers. This Bauhinia is highly ornamental.—*Riddell, Voigt.*

BAUHINIA BRACHYCARPA, *Wall.*

Bwai-jin. BURM.

Attains to nearly three or four feet in the Tenasserim Provinces, its wood is white colored and adapted for fancy work and cabinet making. It is there of smaller size than the B. parviflora.—*McClelland, Voigt.*

BAUHINIA CANDIDA, *var.* of B. variegata, *Linn.*

Bauhinia candida, *Roxb. q. v.*

Kana-raj. BENG.
Kana-raja. „
White mountain Ebony. ENG.
Kana-raja. HIND.
Kuvidara. SANS.
Yuga purra. „

This grows in Prome, Assam, Bengal, Nepal and Oude. It is a small handsome tree with large white flowers, which appear at the commencement of the hot season.—*Roxb., Voigt.*

BAUHINIA DIPHYLLA, *Buch.*

Yepi. TEL. | Apa. TEL.

This tree grows in Burmah, on the banks of the Irawaddy and at Masulipatam, Cuddapah, Guntoor and Nellore, where it is called *Yepi* in Telugu.—*M. E. Jur. Rep., Voigt.*

BAUHINIA MALABARICA, *Roxb.*

Boay-gy-in. BURM.

This pretty large tree is a native of Malabar, where it blossoms in October and November. It also grows in Assam, at Prome and Malloon. Indeed, it is common in the plains of British Burmah, where its wood is used for the cross pieces of harrows, house posts, &c. &c. A cubic foot weighs lbs. 42. In a full grown tree on good soil the average length of the trunk to first branch is 15 feet, and average girth, measured at 6 feet from the ground, is 4 feet.—*Roxb., Dr. Brandis, Voigt.*

BAUHINIA NITIDA. WHITE BAUHINIA.

B. acuminata?

Kana raja. HIND.

Cultivated in gardens at Kotah. Wood not known.—*Irvine Gen. Med. Top. p.* 191.

BAUHINIA PURPURASCENS, *var.* of B. variegata, *Linn.; Roxb. Fl. Ind. II.* 319.

Bidal. BENG.
Rakta-kanchan. BENG.
Segapoo Munthari maram. TAM.

A small tree, with beautiful purple flowers: quality of wood unknown. It grows in the peninsula of India, in Serampore, Pateram, Monihari and Puraunya.—*Voigt, Mr. Jaffrey.*

BAUHINIA PURPUREA, *Linn.*

Bauhinia Coromandeliana, *D C.*

Deva Kanchun. BENG.	Shegapu Munthari maram. TAM.
Sarul mara. CAN.	Bodanta chettu. TEL.
Purple mountain Ebony. ENG.	Pedda aré. „
Kunchun. MAHR.	

A largish tree, with large, deep rose-colored fragrant flowers. Native of the Mauritius and Coromandel, grows, however, now, in Burmah, Assam and Oude. It grows to a large size in the mountains of India. In Canara and Sunda found both above and below: most common near the Gungawallee creek. Wood strong and good for agricultural implements; but seldom large enough for building.—*Dr. Gibson, Voigt, Dr. Riddell, Mr. Jaffrey, Flora Andhrica.*

BAUHINIA RACEMOSA, *Lam.* not *Vahl.*

Bauhinia parviflora, *Vahl.; D C.; Roxb.*
Bauhinia epicta, *Kön.*

Ban-raj. BENG.	Malu? TEL.
Bwai-jin. BURM.	Mali-jhun.? TEL.
Hpa-lan. BURM.	Patwa Mawal? „
Mawil Ghila. HIND.	Ada? „
Apta. MAHR.	Aré. „
Atcha maram? TAM.	Adavi avisa. „

This tree is described by Dr. Gibson as found throughout the Bombay forests, both on the coasts and inland and is very plentiful throughout the Toughoo and Prome forests, where it attains 3 feet in girth. Found also in Mysore, the hilly parts of the Concans, and ghats of the Bombay side, along the forests of the Sewalik Hills, in the hot valleys of the Himalayas, from the doons of the N. W. to the valleys of Assam, at Monghyr in Bengal and in British Burmah. The wood is small, but the heart wood is exceedingly hard and fine. In British Burmah a cubic foot of the wood weighs lbs. 44. In a full grown tree, there, on good soil the average length of the trunk to the first branch is 10 feet, and average girth, measured at 6 feet from the ground, is 3 feet. In Bombay, the wood is reckoned very strong, but is never found of a good size, and in British Burmah it is said to be of a white color and adapted for fancy work and cabinet making. Its outer bark makes good ropes.—*Drs. Gibson, McClelland, Wight, Brandis, and Mason, Voigt, Mr. Jaffrey, Madras Museum, Flora Andhrica.*

BAUHINIA RETUSA, *Roxb.*

Grown in the Calcutta Botanical Gardens; yields a brownish mild gum like that of the cherry tree.—*Roxb., Voigt.*

BAUHINIA RICHARDIANA, *Wall.*

Introduced from Madagascar. Of this wood we have no knowledge, the trees in this country being still young.—*Madras Hort. Gard.* 58, *Voigt.*

BAUHINIA SCANDENS, *Linn.; Willde.*

Bauhinia lingua, *DeCand.*

Rod Bauhinia. ENG.	Naja balli. MALEAL.
Esculapian do. „	

Grows in the Moluccas, Concans, Assam, is not uncommon about Gowhatti and is a common species at Sylhet. Mr. Mason mentions that the tree is remarkable for its contorted stem, and it is said by Loudon to have been the origin of Esculapius' snaken rod which he brought from India. Bauhinia scandens, in its properties and uses, is similar to the B. racemosa. Its fibre is used by the Nagas, and cloth made therefrom was sent to Major Jenkins by Major Hannay. A line made from the fibre sustained for forty-five minutes 168 lbs., having stretched six inches only in three feet, and therefore is almost of the same strength as the best Sunn Hemp of Bengal. But Captain Thompson reported that, whether from the nature of the material or the mode of preparation, he found the fibre so harsh and stubborn and to so stick together that the heckles tore it to pieces and injured its strength.—*Mason, page* 68, *Royle, page* 296, *Voigt.*

BAUHINIA TOMENTOSA, *Linn.*

Yellow Bauhinia. ENG.	Kát-atti. TAM.
Kanchana. MALEAL.	Triviat putrum. „
Usamaduga. SANS.	Theer-vala-counaie. „
Petan. SINGH.	

A native of the Eastern provinces of Ceylon, Coimbatore, the Concans, Patna, Oude, Nepal, Assam. This, like the atcha maram is a strong very dark coloured wood, hence the name Kaat Atti or Wild Ebony. Even the younger branches show the heart-wood very dark brown, the bark of this is employed as extemporary cordage. It is a tree of small size, the wood dark brown and very hard and not much in use, being too small to be of any commercial value, but in Ceylon it is said (seemingly erroneously) to be used for boxes, chests, walking sticks, cornice work, &c.—*Dr. Wight, Voigt, Dr. Cleghorn, Mr. Jaffrey, Mr. Mendis.*

BAUHINIA TRIANDRA, *Roxb.*

This is a native of Bengal and, when in flower, is one of the most beautiful of the Bauhinias. Its trunk is straight and of considerable size. Its flowers are large and white.—*Roxb.; Voigt.*

BAUHINIA VARIEGATA, *Linn.; W. & A.; Roxb.*

Bauhinia purpurascens.
„ candida, *Roxb.* not *Ait.*

Ructo-kanchan. BENG.	Sona. HIND.
Irkumbalitha mara. CAN.	Chovanna-mundari. MALEAL.
Mountain Ebony. ENG.	Kuvidara? SANS.
Kuchnar. HIND.	Borodhá. URIA.

An ornamental tree with variegated flowers, sparingly found in the Bombay forests, and, there, it never reaches a size for a 10 inch plank. The wood, however, is hard and good. In Ganjam and Gumsur its extreme height is 30 feet, circumference 2 feet, and height from the ground to the intersection of the first branch 8 feet, and is tolerably common and used for firewood. The flower pods are eaten as a sort of vegetable.—*Drs. Irvine, Mason, Gibson, Riddell, Cleghorn, Voigt, and Captain Macdonald.*

BAUHINIA VAHLII, *W. & A.*

B. racemosa, *Vahl.; Roxb., Fl. In.*
B. scandens *Roxb. in E. I. C. Mus.*

Chamboolee. DUK.	Adda. TEL.
Mahwal. HIND.?	Shyalee. URIA.

This is an immense scandent shrub, with a circumference of 1½ feet. It grows in the Thull ghats, ravines at Khandalla, Morung mountains, in the Darra Dhoon and Kamaon. In Ganjam and Gumsur it abounds in the jungles, and yields a fibre which is most extensively used. The leaves which are a foot in length with rounded lobes, are used for eating from and for making "tullaries"—small umbrellas worn on the head and for packing. The seeds are used medicinally. Dr. Riddell describes it as an immense scandent shrub; leaves about a foot in breadth, with rounded lobes; legumes pendulous, from twelve to twenty inches long, covered with a brown velvet down.—*Riddell, Voigt, Captain Macdonald, Fl. Andh., Useful Plants.*

BAUJHONOO, URIA? In Ganjam and Gumsur, a tree of extreme height 45 feet, circumference 5 feet, and height from ground to the intersection of the first branch, 22 feet. The wood is used for bandy wheels on account of its strength. It is rather scarce.—*Captain Macdonald.*

BAYGOONA, URIA? A tree in Ganjam and Gumsur of extreme height 24 feet, circumference 1 foot, and height from the ground to the intersection of the first branch, 5 feet. The wood is useless except for firewood. The leaves are used medicinally for fever. The tree is tolerably common.—*Captain Macdonald.*

BEAR WOOD. A tree of Meera Forest, near Abbottabad, Hazara. Natural order, *Coniferæ,* Pinus longifolia.?—*Cal. Cat. Ex.* 1862.

BEDEE. A taluk in the Belgaum Collectorate with forests; but Dr. Gibson says that neither teak, seesoo, nor honee *(Pterocarpus marsupium)*, the three most valuable woods in the forest, had been spared.—*Report,* 1849 *to* 1856, *p.* 8.

BEE-EW, BURM. A timber of Tenasserim not identical with *Thee Bew Tha.* Its maximum girth is 3 cubits, and maximum length 22 feet. Trees very abundant near the sea or the river's edge, all over the Tenasserim provinces. When seasoned, sinks in water. It is a very hard, strong wood; used in rice mills where great strength and durability are indispensably required: recommended for handles of tools.—*Captain Dance.*

BEHENTA, URIA? A timber tree of Ganjam and Gumsur, extreme height 30 feet, circumference 3 feet, and height from ground to the intersection of the first branch, 10 feet. It is used for axletrees, oil presses and rice pounders. It is also burnt for firewood the tree being very common. The bark and leaves are used medicinally.—*Captain Macdonald.*

BELOO, TEL. URIA.? A tree of Ganjam and Gumsur, extreme height 30 feet, circumference 3 feet, and height from the ground to the intersection of the first branch, 15 feet. Its wood is sometimes employed for making bandies, but it is chiefly used for firewood the tree being extremely common: the leaves are used for making a sort of umbrella which is worn on the head by the ryots and coolies in this part of the country.—*Captain MacDonald.*

BELUNNAN, HIND? A tree of Chota Nagpore, with hard brown timber.—*Cal. Cat. Ex.* 1862.

BEP-THAN.—? In Amherst, a timber used for making handles for spears and swords; it is a superior wood, and looks like white Jarrool.—*Captain Dance.*

BEP-THAN. In Tavoy, used for building.—*Captain Dance.*

BEP-WON. In Tavoy, used for building.—*Captain Dance.*

BERBERIS ARISTATA, *D C.*;

Var. *a.* NORMALIS.

Berberis tinctoria, *Lesch.*	Berberis angustifolia,
,, chitra, *Ham.*	*Roxb.*

Var. *β,* FLORIBUNDA.

Berberis floribunda, *Wall.*	Berberis affinis, *Don.*
,, petiolaris, ,,	,, ceratophylla, ,,
,, aristata, ,,	,, coriaria, *Royle.*
	,, umbellata, *Lindl.*

Var. *γ.* MICRANTHA, *Wall.; Hook. & Thom. Fl. Ind.*

This is a widely distributed plant over the mountains of India, and assumes many various forms, which has caused Botanists to give it a host of specific names. It is found on the Neilgherry and Pulney Hills at from 6 to 7,000 feet. It is generally known, from its yielding a dye, as Berberis tinctoria. The berries are much esteemed in the countries where they grow for their agreeable acid flavour.

BERBERIS NEPALENSIS, *Spr.*

Berberis miccia, *Ham.*	Berberis pinnata, *Roxb.*
,, acanthifolia, *Wall.*	Mahonia Nepalensis, *D C.*
,, Leschenaultii. *Wall.*	Ilex Japonica, *Thunb.*

This shrub is found on the Neilgherry, Pulney, and Travancore Hills, at an elevation of from 5 to 8,000 feet. It is also on the Himalaya, Bhotan, Garwhal, and Khassia mountains. The wood is small and of little use.

BERBERIS LYCIUM, *Royle.*

Huziz-Hindi. AR.	Chitra. HIND.
Raisin Berberry. ENG.	Kashmul. HIND.

Found on the Himalaya and other mountains in India. There are several other species found on the mountains of India, but none of them wood of any size.

BERGERA KONIGII, *Linn.; W. & A.; Roxb.*

Murraya Königii, *Spreng.*

Barsanga. BENG.	Kare-bepon. MALEAL.
Karripak ka jhar. DUK.	Kareyapela. MALEAL.
Curry leaf tree. ENG.	Kristna nimbu. SANS.
Karripak ka jhar. HIND.	Kari-vepelli maram. TAM.
Kudia nim. HIND.	Karivepa. TEL.
Barsanga. MALEAL.	Kariampaku chettu. TEL.

A small tree, a native of the mountainous parts of the coast and common throughout the country; of easy culture, cultivated generally in gardens for its leaves, which retain their fragrance when dry, and are used to flavour curries, mullagatawny, chatnies, &c. and are mixed in the curry pastes and powders prepared in India for transmission to England and other parts of the world; the mixture of these leaves not only imparts a peculiar flavour to these condiments but adds a zest to them. It grows to a tree of tolerable dimensions, with pinnate leaves strongly scented; flowers in February and March; fruit of a deep purple colour, wood hard and close grained; medicinally, the leaves are considered stomachic and tonic, used raw in dysentery and when roasted are administered in decoction to stop vomiting. The bark and root employed as stimulants.—*Royle Ill. are quoted by O'Shaughnessy, page* 232, *Voigt, Flora Andhrica, Useful Plants.*

BERRYA AMMONILLA, *Roxb.*

Trincomallie wood. ENG.	Tircanamalay maram. TAM.
Somendilla. SINGH.	" chettu. TEL.
Halmilile. "	Sarala devadaru. TEL.
Hameniel. "	

Introduced from Ceylon to the continent of India. In the Tamil of Ceylon, *Somendilla:* it is commonly called *Halmilile* and *Hameniel*, by the Dutch and Portuguese. The wood is annually imported from Trincomallee, by which appellation it is known in the Madras market. It is highly esteemed for its lightness and strength, is straight grained, slightly pliant, tough and little affected by the atmosphere, and is employed in the construction of the massoola boats of Madras. It is also used for the spokes of wheels, for helves, handles, planes, frames, poles and shafts of carriages, it is inferior to *Sal* for spokes, and to the babool for some other purposes, but it is comparatively light and easily worked. The Madras market is still dependent on importation from Ceylon.—Dr. Helfer mentions this tree, as growing on King's Island opposite Mergui, and as a light, strong, and valuable wood. The tree yields the best and most useful wood in Ceylon for naval purposes. It grows straight, from twenty to forty feet high, and from twelve to thirty inches in diameter. It and satin wood, were reported by Mr. Edye, in his time, to be the most plentiful and valuable found in Ceylon; and obtainable at a moderate rate to answer the demands of the navy in India. He said that this may be considered superior to any wood for capstan bars, cross and trussel-trees, cask-staves, battens for yards, fishes for masts, boat-building &c. And he states that, at Madras, it was highly valued for coach-work from the toughness and fineness of its grain.—It grows in the Northern and Southern side of Ceylon, a cubic foot weighs 48 lbs., and it lasts 10 to 80 years, and is there used for casks, tubs, carts, waggons and house building. It is the best wood for oil casks in the island.—*Drs. Wight, Cleghorn, Mr. Edye, Mr. Rohde, Mr. Mendis, Dr. Helfer, M. E. J. R.*

BERRYA MOLLIS, *Wall.*

Petwoon. BURM.

Found on elevated ground of British Burmah. Wood red, much prized for axles, the poles of carts and ploughs, also used for spear handles. A cubic foot weighs lbs. 60 to 62. In a full grown tree, on good soil, the average length of the trunk to the first branch is 50 feet, and average girth measured at 6 feet from the ground is 7 feet. It sells at 12 annas per cubic foot.—*Dr. Brandis.*

BETULA, THE BIRCH. Some species of this genus grow in the Himalayas, but nothing is known of their woods.

BETULA ACUMINATA, the Tapering-leaved-Birch, is found on many of the mountains of Nepal and in the great valley of that country, following the course of rivers.

BETULA BHOJPATRA, *Wall, Royle.*

Bhurjamu. SANS.	Bharjapatri chettu. TEL.
" TEL.	

The Indian paper Birch, was found by Dr. Wallich on the alps of Gharwal and Kumaon. It is the Bhurjamu of the Sanscrit and the Bharjapatri chettu of the Teling. Its inner bark was, till lately, used as paper, and is now brought to the plains for lining the tubes of hookahs and the leaves or bark are used to cover the baskets of Ganges water sold by itinerant pilgrims.—*Elliot's Fl. Andh., Eng. Cyc., Royle, p.* 383.

BETULA CYLINDROSTACHYA, Cylindrical spiked Birch, is found in Kumaon.—*Eng. Cyc. p.* 452.

BETULA NITIDA, the Shining Birch, grows in Kumaon.

BHAI-BYA, BURM.? In Amherst, a timber used for house posts, commonly called White Jarool.—*Captain Dance.*

BHAN, SINDI. The Bhan or Poplar, used in Sind for rafters and turning work. It is to be found nowhere else in the Bombay Presidency. (Its Botanical name required.)

BHAN-BHWAY, BURM. In Tavoy, used for house posts; like Sissoo. (*qu.* is this the Bhai Bya.)

BHA-TA-KA, BURM. In Tavoy, a wood used for common carpentry.—*Captain Dance.*

BHATKOORAL, HIND. A hard-grained, close wood, of a light grey color and not heavy. Rather scarce in the Santhal jungles from Raneebahal to Hasdiha about forty miles. Well adapted for timber bridges, where strength and toughness require to be combined with lightness.—*Calc. Engineers' Journal*, 1860.

BHA-WOON, BURM. A tree of Moulmein, converted into planks for building.—*Cal. Cat. Ex.* 1862.

BHOOT-THA.—A tree of Akyab. Not much in use. Grows to a large size, and is plentiful in Ramree and Sandoway districts.—*Cal. Cat. Ex.* 1862.

BHURKUNDA, HIND.? A tree of Chota Nagpore. Soft, white timber.—*Cal. Cat. Ex.* 1862.

BHURSO, HIND.? A tree of Chota Nagpore, Soft, white timber. *Cal. Cat. Ex.* 1862.

BHYENG-TSENG, BURM. In Amherst, a close-grained, compact, grey wood, fit for general purposes, and seems to be exempt from attacks of insects.—*Captain Dance.*

BIGNONIA, a genus of plants, which are usually climbing shrubs with flowers mostly in terminal or axillary panicles. There are betwixt 60 and 70 known species and varieties. In floriculture, they grow in any situation or soil; but do not succeed well in pots owing to their rapid growth. The leaves of Bignonia chica yield a red colouring matter. The bark and capsules of B. indica are astringent, and used in tanning and dyeing. The pleasant tasted and fragrant flowers of B. chelonoides (suaveolens?) are described as being used as a cooling drink in fevers.—*O'Shaughnessy, page* 489, *Eng. Cyc. page* 454.

BIGNONIA, *Species.* Dr. Mason tells us that the Karens often build their boats with the wood of a species of Bignonia, as the genus is defined by Roxburgh; and the timber which is sometimes large is frequently used in joinery.

BIGNONIA, *Species.*

Tha-thee. BURM.

A very large tree of Tavoy.—*Captain Dance.*

BIGNONIA, *Species.* (?)

Thuggainee. BURM.

A large tree of Tavoy, used in building.—*Captain Dance.*

BIGNONIA, *Species.*

Lainbha. BURM.

A middle-sized tree of Tavoy.—*Captain Dance.*

BIGNONIA, *Species.*

Than-day. BURM.

A light, loose-grained wood of British Burmah, not much used. Breaking weight 125 lbs. A cubic foot weighs lbs. 33 to 36. In a full grown tree on good soil, the average length of the trunk to the first branch is 30 feet, and average girth measured at 6 feet from the ground is 7 feet. It sells at 4 annas per cubic foot.—*Dr. Brandis.*

BIGNONIA, *Species.*

Kyoun-donk. BURM.

Wood of British Burmah, not used. A cubic foot weighs lbs. 23. In a full grown tree on good soil, the average length of the trunk to the first branch is 15 feet, and average girth, measured at 6 feet from the ground, is 2 feet.

BIGNONIA, *Species.*

Thau Thet Ngai. BURM.

A tree of Moulmein. Used in common purposes of building.—*Cal. Cat. Ex.* 1862.

BIGNONIA CHELONOIDES, *Linn.*

Stereospermum chelonoides, *D C.*

Keersel. MAHR.	Tagada. TEL.
Tuatuka „	Kaligoru. „
Padri maram. MALEAL.	Kalighutru. „
Pon-padria maram. TAM.	Kalugoru. „
Pathiri maram. „	Pamphoonea. URIA.
Kaligottu. TEL.	

Its wood is highly colored, hard and durable, and much used on the hills where it abounds. This tree is wrongly supposed to be identical with the B. suaveolens of Roxburgh. In Southern India, it is found in Coimbatore and various parts of the Madras Presidency; both above and below the ghats in Canara and Sunda, though not common there: in the Dekhan, abundant on the right bank of the Godavery and in Ganjam and Gumsur; also in the Bombay ghats, at Khandalla, and Parr, also in Sylhet and Assam. It attains an extreme height of 20 feet, with a circumference of 1 foot, and the height from the ground to the intersection of the first branch is 8 feet. The tree is held sacred by the hindus in consequence of which it is difficult to obtain the timber, but it is a good fancy wood, and suitable for buildings. The bark and fruit are used medicinally, and the pleasant tasted and fragrant flowers are used to make a cooling drink in fevers.—*Drs. Mason, Wight, and Gibson, Voigt, Captains Beddome and Macdonald, Flor. Andh.*

BIGNONIA CORONARIA, a large tree with white flowers, very plentiful in the Tharawaddy and Pegu districts; it and *Bignonia spathoidea*, found throughout the province, both afford from their inner bark material for rope employed for local purposes.—*McClelland.*

BIGNONIA INDICA, *Linn.*

Calosanthes Indica, *Blume.*
Bignonia pentandra, *Lour.*
Spathodea Indica, *Pers.*

Tetoo. MAHR.

In the Bombay side, this is common near water streams, chiefly below the ghats, but the wood is described by Dr. Gibson as of no value, neither does it, there ever reach any size. It grows in Behar, and immense pods hang from its branches in its leafless state. In the Tenasserim Provinces, its large terminal erect racemes, are often seen near the dwellings of the natives; and its seeds are frequently noticed on account of the large membranous wing with which they are surrounded. It grows luxuriantly in the cold regions of the Himalaya, and might probably grow in the open air of Europe also. At Lahore there was received from the hills a gigantic pod, not less than half a yard in length and four inches in breadth. The bark and capsules of this tree are astringent and used in tanning and dyeing.—*O'Shaughnessy, page* 480, *Hooker's Him. Jour. vol. I. p.* 86, *Mason, Honigberger, p.* 244.

BIGNONIA QUADRILOCULARIS, *Roxb.*

Spathodea Roxburghii, *Spreng.*

Wurrus. MAHR.

This tree is found in the higher hilly places of the Concan, and the higher valleys of the ghats, Circar mountains, Malabar Hill Bombay, Elephanta, the Ghats, and is very common in Paddashapore jungles, in the Southern Mahratta country. Its flower is very beautiful. Wood is reckoned strong, tough, durable and serviceabe, both for beams and for planks. It is much used as planking for carts. It is employed for many purposes by the natives?—*Roxb., Gibson.*

BIGNONIA SPATHOIDEA. This large tree is found throughout the Tenasserim Provinces. It is plentiful and its inner bark affords a material for rope.—*McClelland.*

BIGNONIA SPATHACEA, *Linn. fil.*

Spathodea Rheedii, *Spreng.*
„ longifolia, *Vent.*

BIGNONIA STIPULATA, *Roxb.*

Spathodea stipulata, *Wall.*

Pha bhan of Akyab.
Ka mhoung „
Ma shoay of Moulmein.

Stipuled trumpet flower tree. A common flowering tree throughout Tenasserim, with a long twisted pod. It is common at Maulmain: and the flowers are often seen in bazars where they are sold for food. The tree enters the native materia medica, as affording a cure for psora. The tree of Moulmein is said to afford a strong wood for any ordinary purposes, and, in Akyab, where the natives make a spirituous liquor from the bark, it is a small tree, and very plentiful, and wood used by natives for bows, &c.—*Cal. Cat. Ex.* 1862, *Dr. Mason.*

BIGNONIA SUAVEOLENS, *Roxb.*

Stereospermum suaveolens, *W. Ic.*
Tecoma suaveolens, *G. Don.*

Patulee. BENG.
Parool. „
Parul. MAHR.
Bhita padari? SANS.
Krishna vrinta. SANS.
Kuberakoshi. TEL.
Pádari. „
Patali. „
Kalagoru. „

This tree is quite different from B. chelonoides. It grows in the Dandelle forest above the ghats, in Canara and Sunda. It occurs, though not very common, in Ganjam and Gumsur, where it attains an extreme height of 20 feet, with a circumference of 1½ feet, and the height from the ground to the nearest branch is 12 feet. It also occurs in the Dekhan, Bengal, in Sukanuggur, Gorukpur, and the Kheree jungle. It has large, dark, dull crimson flowers. Its wood is very similar to B. chelonoides, but of a redder hue. The bark is employed medicinally.—*Voigt, Dr. Gibson, Captains Beddome and Macdonald.*

BIGNONIA SUBEROSA, *Roxb.*

Millingtonia hortensis, *Linn. fil.*

Indian Cork tree. ENG.
Neemi Chambeli. HIND.
Cork maram. ANGLO-TAM.

A very handsome tree, common in gardens of India, grows in Tanjore, in Madras, Segaon, between Ava and Taong Dong. The wood is soft and of little use. In January the tree is covered with beautiful and fragrant blossoms.—*Dr. Cleghorn in M. E. J. R., Voigt.*

BIGNONIA UNDULATA, *Roxb.*

Tecoma undulata, *G. Don.*

Wave-leaved Bignonia. ENG.
Bohira Reora. HIND.
Rukt Reora. MAHR.
Khew. SINDI.

A tree with drooping branches like the weeping willow. Dr. Gibson says it is rare in the Bombay forests, but is found in the northern parts of Baglan and in Kandesh; it is more common in Sind, in some of the valleys of the Pubb Hills, and at Shah Bilawul; yet Voigt says it is abundant in one locality of Kandesh, and that it occurs in Guzerat. It is very common in Marwar and other parts of Rajwarra, and when covered in the month of March with its immense quantities of orange-coloured blossoms, it is a most splendid object and would be highly ornamental in compounds; the wood is fine grained and valuable, having a scent like the walnut leaf. The wood is reckoned very strong and durable, but from its size, applicable only to small purposes.—*Dr. Irvine, Gen. Med. Top. p.* 200, *Dr. Gibson.*

BIGNONIA XYLOCARPA, *Roxb.*

Tecoma xylocarpa, *G. Don.*

Ghan seng. CAN.
Khurseng. MAHR.
Vadenkurni maram. TAM.

This large tree has been noticed by Dr. Wight as growing in Coimbatore. It is found, also, though rare, in the Godavery forests, but grows on the Neilgherries, in the Thullghaut, Jowar jungles, hills about Nagotnah, jungles about Ratnagherry and on the Parr ghat. Dr. Gibson says it is common in the forests both inland and on the coast, and that it may be easily distinguished by its peculiar rough pods, two feet or more in length. The wood is never large, is very hard and good if ripe; of a brownish yellow colour, rather close-grained, takes a good polish, is used in turnery and in cabinet making. It also affords an oil, obtained by a simple process of reverse distillation, and said to be of great efficacy in cutaneous affections.—*Drs. Wight, Gibson, Captain Beddome.*

BIJION, BURM. In Amherst, a timber used for house posts, rafters, and the like purposes; it is a heavy, compact, grey, close-grained wood. —*Captain Dance.*

BINTANGOR. A wood of the Malay Peninsula, in general use for planks, masts and spars, &c. It holds the same position in the Straits Settlements that the pine holds in America. It is in the greatest abundance around Singapore, and is exported in large quantities to the Mauritius, California, &c. In Singapore, "Bintangor" wood is the most used especially in ship building, serving for planks, masts, spars, &c.—*Exh. of* 1851.

BINTAGON? A large Penang tree; occasionally used for masts. This is probably the Bintangor, *q. v.*

BLACKBURNIA MONODELPHA, *Roxb.*

A large erect timber tree, a native of the mountainous parts of the Northern Circars. The wood is white, close-grained, and durable, and employed by the natives for a variety of purposes. It flowers at the beginning of the hot season.—*Roxb. Fl. Ind. vol. I. p.* 415.

BLACKBURNIA PIRMATA. A hard yellow wood of Norfolk Island, is much used for making household furniture.—*Keppel's Ind. Arch. vol. II. p.* 282.

BLACKWELLIA TOMENTOSA, *Vent.*

Myouk-kyau. BURM.

Wood tough, of a light yellow colour, produce of British Burmah; used for the teeth of harrows. A cubic foot weighs lbs. 56. In a full grown tree on good soil the average length of the trunk to the first branch is 70 feet, and average girth measured at 6 feet from the ground is 6 feet. It sells at 12 annas per cubic foot.—*Dr. Brandis.*

BLACK WOOD. ENG.

Biti. CAN.	Sisam. HIND.
Indian Blackwood. ENG.	Sit Sal. HIND.
Rosewood. "	Eru pottu. TAM.
Sisam. GUZ.	Irugudu chettu. TEL.

Holtzapfel mentions that East Indian Blackwood is from the *Dalbergia latifolia*, called Blackwood tree by the English and Sit Sal by the natives of India, on the Malabar coast, where it grows to an immense size. The wood of the trunk and large branches is extensively used for making furniture; it is heavy, sinking in water, close-grained, of a greenish black colour, with lighter coloured veins running in various directions, and takes a fine polish.—But, the Cassia Sumatrana also furnishes the Blackwood of Bombay. The wood called, in Bombay, Seesum in Guz. and Hind., is probably the timber of different species of *Diospyros* and probably of *Dalbergia*, which grow in various parts of India. Bombay Blackwood is brought to Bombay from the Malabar Coast, and is largely used in the manufacture of household furniture. Every locality has a wood which is known by this name. Dr. McClelland mentions that the Bombay Blackwood is the timber of the Cassia Sumatrana. Dr. Cleghorn in his reports recognises under this name only the Dalbergia latifolia.—*Dr. Cleghorn, Dr. McClelland, Mr. Faulkner, Holtzapfel.*

BLIGHIA. A genus of plants named after Captain William Bligh, R. N., master of the Bounty in the celebrated mutiny, belongs to the natural order *Sapindaceæ*.

BLIGHIA SAPIDA, *Kön.*

Cupania sapida, *Cambess.*

The Akee tree has been introduced from Guinea into India. The fruit has the size and shape of a pear, of a red colour, and is much esteemed in Guinea and the West Indies. Wood said to be very hard and durable.

BODOKA, URIA? In Ganjam and Gumsur, a timber tree, extreme height 35 feet, circumference 3 feet, and height from the ground to the intersection of the first branch, 15 feet. A light, white wood, used for scabbards, bazar measures, boxes, bullock yokes, the poles of palanquins and tonjons and for toys. It is tolerably common.—*Captain Macdonald.*

BODON. HIND? A tree of Chota Nagpore, with a hard, reddish, grey timber.—*Cal. Cat. Ex.* 1862.

BOECHEE, HIND? A red coloured wood, very hard and close-grained. The tree grows in the Santhal jungles from Raneebahal to Hasdiha or about forty miles, but scarce. Seemingly fit for any building purposes if it can be grown to any sufficient size, which it never has a chance of doing in its present condition in the jungles. Too heavy for use generally with reference to timber bridges.—*Cal. Engineers' Journal, July* 1860.

BOLUNGEE: BANSO, TEL.? URIA? Two bamboos of Ganjam and Gumsur, extreme height 25 feet, circumference ⅛ foot, which are not common.—*Captain Macdonald.*

BOMBACEÆ. A group of plants, usually large trees, with broad deep-green leaves, and flowers of considerable size, and containing some of the most majestic and beautiful trees that are known, but their wood is light and spongy; the long cottony substance found within the fruit of the Cotton trees, is too short in the staple and has too little cohesion between its fibres, to be manufactured into linen. The Baobab tree, *Adansonia*, is one of them, and is remarkable for the excessive thickness of its trunk as compared with its height. The genus *Eriodendron* is often defended by very large conical prickles, which do not fall off till they are exfoliated by the gradual distension of the trunk.—*Eng. Cyc. page* 553.

BOMBAX, *Species.*

That Pan. BURM.

A tree of Moulmein. Wood not known.—*Cal. Cat. Ex.* 1862.

BOMBAX, *Species.*

Burrul Mara. CAN.	Kanta Saeer. MAHR.

In Canara and Sunda, most common below, grows to a great size. Hollowed for canoes: planks sought after for light boxes.—*Dr. Gibson.*

BOMBAX CEIBA. This large "cotton tree," in South America and the West Indies, is used for canoes. It is common at Canton, and the fleshy petals of the flowers are sometimes prepared as food.—*Riddell, Williams' Middle Kingdom, p.* 284.

BOMBAX INSIGNE is a native of the Burman Empire, and is remarkable for its large red and very showy flowers.—*Eng. Cyc. p.* 554.

BOMBAX MALABARICUM, *D C.; W. & A.*

Bombax heptaphyllum, *Can.*	Salmalia Malabarica, *Schott. & Endl.*
	Gossampinus rubra, *Ham.*

Rakto-simal. BENG.	Mul-elavu. MALEAL.
Rakto-shimal. „	Mulu-elavu. „
Rakta-shimlu. „	Simbal. PERS.
Le-i. BURM.	Simal. SANS.
Lepan. „	Kattu imbal. SINGH.
Red Cotton Tree. ENG.	Mal-ailas marum. TAM.
Rakta-simal. HIND.	Mall elava marum. „
Simbal. „	Pula mula elavu. „
Sair. MAHR.	Buruga manu. TEL.
Sairi. „	Mula-buraka manu. „
Kanta Sair. „	Bouro. URIA.

This large and stately tree grows in most parts of Southern India; it reaches a great size in the Bombay Presidency, where, both on the coast and inland, it is one of the most common trees, and there the planks are extensively used in making the light packing boxes used in the export of bulky goods from Bombay and other places; also for fishermen's floats when the Adansonia is not at hand. The Red Cotton tree is common throughout Southern India, is abundant in the plains of British Burmah, and its light and loose grained wood is, there, used for coffins. A cubic foot weighs lbs. 28. The cotton is used for stuffing cushions and pillows. In a full grown tree on good soil the average length of the trunk to the first branch is 60 feet, and average girth measured at 6 feet from the ground is 15 feet. It yields the *Moochee-ras* resin, and its roots constitute the *Safed Moosli* of the bazars, which, powdered, forms a thick mucilage with cold water, and answers admirably as a nutritious demulcent for convalescent persons.—*Drs. Wight, Brandis, Gibson, O'Shaughnessy, Capt. Beddome.*

BOMBAX PENTANDRUM, *Linn.*

Eriodendron anfractuosum.
Ceiba pentandra, *Gœrtn.*
Gossampinus Rumphius, *Schott. & Endl.*

White Silk Cotton Tree. ENG.	Elavam marum. TAM.
Katan. HIND.	Burugu manu. TEL.

This produces a light wood, employed by the toy makers. It is likewise used for making rafts, Dr. McClelland mentions that, in the Tenasserim Provinces, Bombax pentandrum, B. heterophyllum and Cochlospermum gossypium, all afford a soft down, which is attached to the seeds and which the Burmese collect for stuffing pillows. It is in general use throughout the South of India for this purpose. At the Madras Exhibition of 1857, a very powerful bast was exhibited by Mr. Jaffrey, from the B. pentandrum.—*Dr. McClelland, Mr. Jaffrey, in M. E. J. R.*

BOMLE MARA, CAN.? Ind. Binteki? Dr. Gibson describes this as occurring below and near the ghats only in Canara and Sunda. Wood very serviceable for planks, and seems to be used only for this purpose.—*Dr. Gibson.*

BONG LONG THA, BURM. A timber tree of Amherst, Tavoy, and Mergui Archipelago, of maximum girth 3 cubits, maximum length 22 feet, and said to be abundant. Found all over the provinces, has not been easily obtained in Moulmein. When seasoned, floats in water. It is a durable yet light wood with a very straight grain; used for every purpose by the Burmese, and much recommended for helves.—*Captain Dance.*

BONO KONIAREE, TEL.? URIA? Extreme height 50 feet. Circumference 3 feet. Height from ground to the intersection of the first branch, 10 feet. Used for planks, boxes, and walking sticks. It is carce.—*Captain Macdonald.*

BON SONE, BURM.? A tree of Moulmein. Wood used for house building purposes.—*Cal. Cat. Ex.* 1862.

BOOK THA, BURM. A tree of Amherst, Tavoy and Mergui, of maximum girth 1½ to 2 cubits, and maximum length 11 feet. Scarce but found on the sea coast from Amherst to Mergui. When seasoned it floats in water. It is used by the Burmese for helves, but rots quickly, and therefore not recommended.—*Captain Dance.*

BORASSUS, *Species?* Dr. Mason says that the Tenasserim Provinces yield an indigenous palm, which the natives call the wild palmyra. It has the fruit of the palmyra, but the leaf differs from it sufficiently to constitute it another species. Wood not known.—*Dr. Mason's Tenasserim.*

BORASSUS FLABELLIFORMIS.

BORASSUS FLABELLIFORMIS, *Linn.; Rheede; Roxb.*

Lontarus domestica, *Rumph.*

The tree is named,

Tal-gach'h. BENG.	Tala. SANS.
Palmyra Tree. ENG.	Tal. SINGH.
Brab Tree. „	Panam maram. TAM.
Tar ka jhar. HIND.	Tatti chettu. TEL.
Rontal. JAV.	Penti-tati chettu. „
Lontar. MALAY.	Karata-lamu. „
Pana. MALEAL.	Potu tadi. „

The wood is called

Palmyra wood. ENG.	Panam maram kattai. TAM.
Porcupine wood. „	Tatti chettu karra. TEL.
Tar ke jhar ki lakri. HIND.	

The palm wine or toddy is known as

Tari. DUK.	Tuwak. MALAY.
Palmyra Toddy. ENG.	Pannang kallu. TEL.
Nera. MALAY.	Tati kallu. „

The sugar is

Tar-ka-gur. DUK.	Pannam vellam. TAM.
Jaggery of Palmyra Toddy. ENG.	Tati bellam. TEL.

The edible part is called

Geunghul. DUK.	Pannam kelangu. TEL.
Young Palmyra Plant. ENG.	Tati-gadda. TEL.
Tala. SANS.	

The fibres of the palmyra leaf are called

Pannam nar. TAM.	Tati nara. TEL.

Its fruit is the

Tar phal. DUK.	Tata. SANS.
Palmyra Fruit. ENG.	Pannam pallam. TAM.
Bua Lontar. MALAY.	Tati pandu. TEL.

To Eastern nations, the Palmyra tree is only inferior in usefulness to the date tree and the cocoanut palm. It grows to a height of 70 feet with a circumference of 5½ feet at bottom and 2½ at top. A Tamil poem, of Ceylon, the Tala Vilásam, enumerates 801 purposes to which the Palmyra may be applied. The trees have to attain a considerable age before they become fit for timber, as their wood becomes harder and blacker by age, and the harder and blacker it is the better. The wood, near the circumference of old trees, is very hard, black, heavy, and durable. A cubic foot weighs 65 lbs. and it is calculated to last 80 years. In some parts of the Ceylon and Madras coasts, this tree is very abundant, especially in sandy tracts near the sea, though it is to be seen in most parts of India, and occasionally so far north as 30°. It is used chiefly for rafters, joists and reapers. When of good age, the timber is very valuable for this purpose, the trunk is split into 4 for rafters, into 8 for reapers; these are dressed with an adze. Those of the Jaffna Palmyras are famous, and were largely exported in former times. From the structure of the wood it splits easily in the direction of its length, yet supports a greater cross strain than any other wood. Old black Palmyra wood, was, next to the Casuarina, the strongest wood that Dr. Wight tried, one specimen bore upwards of 700 lbs., and five of them gave an average of 648 lbs., though he found some very bad. Mr. Rohde remarks that it is the strongest wood he tried, retaining for a length of time the position it assumed when loaded, without increase of deflexion: iron nails soon rust in this wood. He procured it of excellent quality in the Circars. The thickness of rafters when trimmed up rarely exceeds two inches four feet from the ground and one inch at twenty or twenty-four feet from it. The fruit and the fusiform roots of the young trees are used as an article of food by the poorer classes. The leaves are used for thatching and coarse fibre. Jaggery and Toddy are extracted from the tree, the former being extensively used in the manufacture of sugar in Vizianagrum and Rajahmundry. Very neat baskets of Palmyra leaf are made in Tinnevelly. Some clean but brittle fibres were exhibited at the Madras Exhibition of 1855, by the Tinnevelly, Madura and Travancore local committees; and well twisted rope accompanied most of the samples, but the material is said to be stiff, brittle, and liable to rot when wet. This substance did not appear to have undergone any preparation, and it contained so much woody fibre that it is questionable whether it would ever be suited for manufacturing purposes. Its chief uses are for securing thatch and tying bamboos, in building native huts. The dried leaves of this plant are used for writing upon with an iron style, also in thatching, making fans, and light baskets for irrigation. Next to *Caryota urens*, it is the largest palm on the Madras coast, and it seems to thrive equally well in all soils and situations. The seeds when young are eaten by the natives, being jelly-like and palatable. The tree, during the first part of the season, yields a pretty large quantity of toddy or palm wine. This is either drank fresh drawn from the tree, or boiled down into a coarse kind of syrup called jaggery, or it is fermented for distillation. The leaves are universally used for writing upon, with an iron style. They are also employed for thatching houses, for making small baskets, mats, &c., and some also formed into large fans, called vissaries in Tam. The fibres of the petioles of the leaves *(Palmyra nar)* are employed on the Madras side for making twine and small rope. They are about two feet in length and strong. Trees tapped for toddy do not form wood. The large carpenter beetle "Xylocopa" delights in boring this hard wood, though the *Cumboo* is still more attractive to it. Small canoes are formed of this tree, two of which lashed to a couple of spars form the usual mode of crossing lakes and rivers in the Circars—the root forms the head of the canoe, the smaller end is either elevated out of water by the form, or some six inches of the pith is left at that end. As this decays, a lump of clay supplies its place. Formerly sea-going vessels were planked with this wood, but the iron fastenings were soon destroyed. Boats planked with it were lately common on the Godavery, being built probably where sawyers are not procurable. The peculiar structure of the wood of the Palms deserves attention, it appears formed of a series of hard stiff longitudinal fibres not interlaced or twisted but crossed at considerable intervals at various angles by similar fibres which proceed from the soft heart of the tree, to the outer part, probably to the leaf stem—a radial section of Palmyra rafter shows this, the interstices are filled up with pith the proportion of which increases with the distance from the outer part. The wood is much used in house-building, for rafters, joists, and reapers. In England for veneers and inlaying. It is exported in large quantities from Ceylon, where it is used for rafters, pillars, and posts of native houses. In the sandy parts of Jaffna in Ceylon, a hollow palmyra is inserted to form a well. The dark outside wood of very old trees, is used to some extent in Europe for umbrella handles, walking canes, paper rulers, fancy boxes, wafer stamps and other articles. The timber of the female tree is the hardest and best, and that of the male trees is never used, unless the tree be very old. It is too heavy to make ships of. At certain seasons of the year, thousands are employed in felling and dressing it. Each tree has from twenty-five to forty fresh green leaves upon it at a time, of which the natives cut off twelve or fifteen annually to be employed as thatch, fences, manure, mats, and mat baskets, bags, irrigation baskets, winnows, hats, caps, fans, umbrellas &c ; books and olays, tatakoo or puttays, for writing on. In the Bombay side, it is common only on the Northern Konkan, where it is in some parts so abundant, that it might be termed a forest. It is a rare tree in the southern jungles of the Bombay Presidency. The wood, when protected from moisture, is very durable, and may be used with advantage for terraces, &c. when the upper covering is complete. It is also used for canoes. Its leaves, prepared, furnish (" Ola" Tamil) the leaf on which the Tamuls write. Its palm wine is largely used, or converted into arrack or sugar. The germinating seeds (Ponatoo, *Singh,*) are boiled and eaten in Ceylon as a vegetable.—*Seeman, Simmonds, Drs. Wight, Cleghorn, Gibson, Mr. Rohde.*

BORO-KOLEE, TEL. URIA. This tree, supposed to be a species of Zizyphus, has an extreme height of 30 feet, circumference 3 feet, height from ground to the intersection of the first branch 8 feet. Planks, doors, boxes, matchlock stocks, and palanquins are made of this wood. The leaves pounded and mixed with turmeric are supposed to be efficacious in curing rheumatism. The seeds are also used medicinally in diseases of infants. The tree yields a lac. The large trees are scarce but young trees very common.—*Captain Macdonald.*

BOSWELLIA. A genus of plants, of which the B. glabra, B. serrata, syn. of B. thurifera occur in India, they yield a fragrant gum resin, called Luban *Arab.* also Kundur *Arab.*, supposed to be the Λιβανος of Theophrastus, and the Thurea virgo of the Romans. It seems to be the olibanum and identical with the frankincense that was used by the ancients in their religious ceremonies.—*Eng. Cyc.*

BOSWELLIA GLABRA, *Roxb. ; W. & A.*

Canarium balsamiferum, *Willd.*

Salai. HIND.	Andugu chettu. TEL.
Kunthrekum. MALEAL.	Gugalapu chettu. „
Moroeda. TAM.	Guggilapu chettu. „
Kundrikam. „	

A small tree ; flowers small, white, with a red nectary, yields the gum salai. Nothing is known of its wood.

BOSWELLIA THURIFERA, *Roxb.*

Boswellia serrata, *Stackh.*

Kundur Zuchir. AR.	Awul kandur. HIND. VERN.
Luban. BENG.	Dup-salai. HIND.
Salai ? „	Ganda Baroza. „
Luban. DUK.	Awal kundur. PERS.
Luban. HIND.	Luban. „

A tall tree with pinnate leaves, which yields the Olibanum, grows on the hills of the Deccan. In the Konkan jungles, above Rajoor, in the hill of Shendoor, in the Belgaum collectorate, in Bundlekund, it is a native of the mountainous tracts of Central India, and very common in the Shahabad country. Dr. Hooker remarks of this plant, that, in ascending from Belcuppee in Behar to the height of 1,360 feet, he came upon a small forest of the Indian Olibanum *Boswellia thurifera,* conspicuous from its pale bark and spreading curved branches, leafy at their tips ; its general appearance being a good deal like that of the mountain ash. The gum, celebrated throughout the East, was flowing abundantly from the trunk, very fragrant and transparent.—The *Salai* or *Salar* tree, *Boswellia thurifera,* remarks Dr. Irvine, is plentiful in the Ajmeer hills : the gunda birosa is the prepared gum resin of this tree, and is similar in appearance and qualities to Venice turpentine. It is brought from Mewar, Haraotee and the Shekhawattee hills : and is considered stimulating : an oil is distilled from it, said to cure gonorrhœa. It is used also in ointments : much used in painting and by the lakheries, one maund costing twelve rupees From the Shahabad country, Dr. O'Shaughnessy obtained fine specimens of the resinous products there called *sale gond or sale lassa.* At Chandalgur it is termed *gunda biroza,* and in the dry state *sukha biroza.* Dr. Hamilton however thought the English olibanum to be the produce of an Amyris, partly because he could not find that the sale resin was used as incense by the hindoos. The B. glabra and B. thurifera both furnish the male frankincense of Dioscorides. The resin olibanum occurs in reddish or pale yellow tears, oval, oblong, and obtuse, sometimes in dense, opaque brittle masses. The gunda barosa of the bazars is soft, ductile, opaque, greenish and white. The odour is balsamic and resinous, especially while the resin is burning; the flavour balsamic, and rather bitter. The powder, is citron yellow. It is frequently adulterated by dammer, sandarach, and other cheaper resins; when chewed the hard variety softens, and dissolves partially in the saliva, which it renders white and emulsive.—*O'Shaughnessy, Hooker Him. Jour. p.* 29, *Med. Top. of Ajmeer.*

BOTANY BAY HE OAK. The wood of this tree is used in making brush backs for veneers and in the manufacture of Tunbridge ware. (The She Oak is Casuarina quadrivalvis, may this also not be a species of Casuarina ?)

BOWSA, HIND.? A tree of Chota Nagpore. Soft, white timber.—*Cal. Cat. Ex.* 1862.

BOX WOOD.

Palm-hout. DUT.	Busso. IT.
Buis. FR.	Bosso. „
Buchsbaum. GER.	Bossolo. „

This is a valuable wood of a yellowish colour, close grained, very hard, and heavy, it cuts better than any other wood, and is susceptible of a very fine polish. It is chiefly used by engravers, turners, mathematical, and musical instrument makers, and also in the manufacture of combs, knife-handles, button-moulds, &c. It grows in the South of Europe, and West of Asia. But, a species of Box-wood has been introduced into Britain from the Himalayas; it is the Buxus emarginatus of Dr. Wallich. This is found of considerable size and thickness, and the wood appears as good and compact as that of the box-wood in use in Europe. On actual comparison the Himalayan box-wood is found to be softer than the common kinds, but is like them in other respects, and wood-cuts have been engraved upon it.—*Faulkner, Royle, Illust. Himal. Bot. p.* 327, *see* Buxus.

BRANTEY—? In Penang, a light brown coloured inferior, weak, wood; used for building.

BRAS-BRAS. A tree of the Malay Peninsula called by Europeans the Glam tree, furnishes a paper-like bark much used in caulking the seams of vessels. Wood used as floats for fishing nets.

BRIEDELIA, *Species.*

Undooroo Wood. ANG-TEL.	Undooroo Karra. TEL.

A wood of the Northern Circars.

BRIEDELIA LANCÆFOLIA, *Roxb.*

A tree of considerable size, a native of Bengal.

BRIEDELIA MONTANA.

Goonjun Mara. CAN.	Asanna. MAHR.

Found in Canara, common in Dandelee, where it reaches a great size. Many fine logs have been exported by merchants, since the cutting of teak trees was interdicted. Hardly inferior to teak and stands water equally well. If it has not been already tried for naval purposes, it seems well worthy a trial.—*Dr. Gibson.*

BRIEDELIA SPINOSA, *Willde.; Roxb.*

Cluytia spinosa, *Roxb.*

Asanna. CAN.	Mullu vangay. MALEAL.
Asun. CAN.	Mulla vengay maram. TAM.
Asun. DUK.	Kora manu. TEL.
Sun ? DUK.	Kora man. TEL.
Asun. MAHR.	Duria madde ? TEL.
Asanna. MAHR.	

This large tree is a native of several parts of Southern India. It is not uncommon in the alpine jungles of Coimbatore where it attains a considerable size. It is found in the Godavery forests, where its wood is esteemed as very strong and good. It is rather a common tree in the Bombay forests, both coast and inland. The wood is strong and tough and stands the action of water well: hence it is often used for the frames of wells, whereon the superstructure of masonry is erected. It is also used as beams for houses. This wood deserves, in Dr. Gibson's opinion, to be more extensively known than it is. Cattle eat the leaves voraciously. They are said to destroy worms in their bowels.—*Roxb., Drs. O'Shaughnessy, Gibson, Wight, and Cleghorn, Captain Beddome, Flor. Andh.*

BROUSSONETIA PAPYRIFERA, *Vent.*

Morus papyrifera, *Linn.*	Papyrius Japonica, *Lam.*
Kilia of Celebes.	Gluga. JAV.
Paper Mulberry. ENG.	

Is a shrub which has long been famous for its fibrous bark, as this is made into a kind of cloth as well as into paper. It is a native of the isles of the Southern Ocean, as well as of China and of Japan, but has been introduced into the Madras Gardens. In Taiti, or Otaheite, and other islands, they make cloth of its bark; and it is said that the finest and whitest cloth and mantles worn by the principal people at Otaheite and in the Sandwich Islands were made of the bark of this shrub, and this when dyed red takes a good colour. It is from the inner bark of this plant that the Japanese and the Chinese manufacture a kind of paper. It forms a small tree with soft brittle woolly branches, and large hairy rough leaves, either heart-shaped and undivided, or cut into deep irregular lobes.

BRUGUIERA PARVIFLORA, *W. & A.*

Rhizophora parviflora, *Roxb.*
„ cylindrica, *Roxb. H. B.*

Uravada. TEL.	Varavada. TEL.

This mangrove grows in the Moluccas, Sumatra, Cochin-China, in the Malay Islands, in both the Indian peninsulas, the Khassia mountains, Nepaul, Orissa, Jellasore. Character of wood not known. Berries dye black.—*Voigt, Elliot, Fl. Andhrica.*

BRUGUIERA RHEEDII, *L'Herit.*

Bruguiera gymnorrhiza, *Lam.*
Rhizophora gymnorrhiza, *Linn.*

Kankra. BENG.	Mangrove, ENG.

This species of mangrove is most abundant along the Tenasserim shores and furnishes a hard and durable timber. The tree is easily distinguished from its associates, for it drops no roots from its branches, but the trunk is divided into numerous roots for half its height, like a small bamboo pavilion. It grows in Cochin-China, the Moluccas, Java, Tenasserim, Penang, the Sunderbuns and in Malabar. The wood is yellowish, and hard and durable.—*Voigt, Mason.*

BUCHANANIA ANGUSTIFOLIA, *Roxb.*

Spondias simplicifolia, *Rottl.*
Mangifera axillaris, *Lam.*
Cambessedia, *Kunth.*

This tree grows in the hills of the south of India, in the Adjunta jungles and is seen about Rangoon. Wood not known.—*Voigt, McClelland.*

BUCHANANIA LATIFOLIA, *Roxb.*; *W. & A.*

Chirongia sapida, *Buch.?*
Spondias elliptica, *Rottl.*

Piyala? BENG.	Chara. SANS.
Thit-sai? BURM.	Kaat mango. TAM.
Lumbo. ,,	Moreda. ,,
Noas kool. CAN.	Chara-chettu. TEL.
Pia-Sal. GUZ.	Chara pappu ,, ,,
Pujal? HIND.	Charu-mamidi. ,,
Piar cheronji. HIND.	China moralli. ,,
Chironji. ,,	Jaru-mamidi. ,,
Charooli. ,,	Sara-puppoo. ,,
Char. MAHR.	Charo. URIA.

This straight growing handsome forest tree, with fragrant flowers, in the Bombay Presidency, is found more inland than in the coast jungles. In Canara and Sunda, it is most frequent above the ghats, particularly north of Dandellee, and Dr. Gibson describes the wood as rather strong and tough, but seldom found squaring above four inches, or of thickness more than sufficient for posts. The tree abounds in Mysore and Cuddapah, and occurs in Cuttack where its useful wood is worked up generally into furniture, house doors and windows, presses, tables, &c. It requires to be polished, otherwise it stains, of a burnt sienna colour, any cloth brought into contact with it. In Ganjam and Gumsur it has an extreme height of 36 feet and a circumference of 3 feet, and the height from the ground to the intersection of the first branch is 15 feet. There, bullock yokes are sometimes made of the wood, though it is chiefly used for firewood. It grows in Ajmeer. From these accounts, it would seem to be, in peninsular India, a rather hard, tough, strong and durable wood; but Dr. Brandis tells us that in Burmah it is a soft, light wood and not used: that a cubic foot weighs lbs. 36, that in a full grown tree on good soil the average length of the trunk is 20 feet and average girth measured at 6 feet from the ground is 6 feet and that it sells at 4 annas per cubic foot.

It bears fruit about the size of a small cherry, in long bunches, colour of a darkish purple: the kernels, or seeds, which are covered with a double shell, after being prepared by the natives, are sold in the bazars of India, four or five pounds for a rupee; they possess the flavor of almonds, and are used as such by the native confectioners, the fruit is agreeable, and the seed, called Chironji *Hind.* Charapuppoo, *Tam.*, has a very pleasant rich flavour. The method of preparing them by the Bheels is this: the fruit when ripe in May is gathered, then soaked in water to soften the outer pulp, when it is washed and rubbed off by the hands: the little nut is then dried in the sun, and afterwards broken between a common chuckee or stone hand-mill, such as is used for grinding wheat: the kernels are then sifted and winnowed. This kernel of the Buchanania latifolia is much used in native confectionary, for which purpose it is brought to Madras from Cuddapah, &c. The oily kernel is roasted and eaten by the Brahmins with milk, and is considered a great delicacy. The kernels of this tree are eaten by the natives, to promote fatness, they abound in a straw-colored, sweet tasted and limpid oil which is seldom extracted though a very fine oil might be expressed from the seed.—*Madras Exhibition, Dr. Irvine, Eng. Cyc., Drs. Gibson, Brandis, and Mason, Cal. Cat. of* 1862, *Voigt, Useful Plants, Flor. Andh.*

BUCHANANIA VARIEGATA?

Kachnar. HIND.

A tree of Chota Nagpore, with hard, white yellow timber.—*Cal. Cat. Ex.* 1862.

BUCKLALL. HIND.? A close straight-grained wood, light, tough and strong; grows in the Santhal jungles from Raneebahal to Hasdiha or about forty miles, but not very plentiful. Is suitable for timber bridges.—*Cal. Engineer's Journal,* 1860.

BUCKLANDIA, *Species.*

A magnificent tree of the Sikkim Himalayas. One seen by Dr. Hooker had a trunk twenty-one feet seven inches in girth at 5 feet from the ground. Its wood is brown, but, he adds, not valuable as timber.—*Dr. Hooker.*

BUCLANDIA POPULNEA, *R. Brown.*

A large tree of the Khassia mountains from Cherra Poonjee to Sarureem.—*Voigt.*

BUMBOO? TAM.? A Palghat wood, of a yellow colour, from a large tree. It is used for building and for furniture.—*Col. Frith.*

BUNHO. A Penang wood, from a large tree; occasionally used for building.—*Col. Frith.*

BURDUR—? A tree of Cuttack, an excellent wood for carriage poles, shafts, and wheels, and in all coach-builders' work.—*Cal. Cat. Ex.* 1862.

BURHAL—? A light yellowish coloured wood, not strong. Plentiful in the Santhal jungles from Sooree to Hasdiha; or about sixty miles. Used for doors, venetians, furniture, &c. by the natives.—*Cal. Engineers' Journal*, 1860.

BURMAH. The woods of Burmah, Pegu, and the Tenasserim Provinces southwards to Amherst, Tavoy and Mergui, have received the attention both of scientific and practical men. Amongst these, may be named Drs. Wallich, Falconer, McClelland, Mason and Brandis, of Colonel Simpson and Captain Dance of the Artillery, and Major Benson of the Madras Infantry. In all that tract, and perhaps also up to the southern mountains of the valley of Assam, the same trees,—furnishing timber, ornamental and fancy woods, seem frequently to recur. At the Great Exhibition of 1851, ninety specimens of woods were exhibited from Province Amherst: Captain Dance sent, to the Madras Military Board, notes on 114 trees from Amherst, Tavoy and Mergui; and of Pegu or British Burmah, Dr. McClelland noticed

White woods	...85	species,	soft and useless, fit only for fuel.
Red colored ,,	...25	,,	suited for timber, ornamental and fancy woods.
Yellow ,,	... 3	,,	hard and fine grained, suited to fancy purposes.
Dark brown ,,	...12	,,	suited for house and ship building.
Black woods	... 4	,,	all valuable for strength and hardness.
Light brown ,,	... 7	,,	embracing all the timbers of most value in these Provinces.

Dr. Mason, in his Tenasserim and again in his Burmah, gave valuable remarks on 63 timber trees. Dr. Wallich notices 89 trees of Tavoy, and Mr. Blundell sent 69 woods from the same place, to the Great Exhibition of 1851. Recently, the Calcutta Central Committee for the London Exhibition of 1862, sent valuable collections from those regions, 112 woods of British Burmah from Dr. Brandis—60 specimens of woods from Assam: 44 from Akyab: and 86 from Moulmein. Notices of all these will be found in their alphabetical places; but, it may be necessary to mention, that, in all that range, when the practical botanist shall have leisure further to identify trees, now undetermined and which as yet are only known by their vernacular names, and shall have again brought together species which, from some local peculiarity of structure or appearance, have been deemed worthy of a distinct specific name, the seeming numbers of wood and timber trees of those regions will probably be brought within a hundred and fifty species, many of which, too, are found, in more or less abundance, in other parts of South-Eastern Asia. Dr. Brandis' list, repeated in the Calcutta Catalogue for the Exhibition of 1862, contained the following series of woods of British Burmah, which, as being the most recent, is here given, in the mere names, as the more detailed notices will be found in the alphabetical arrangement.

Acacia catechu, L. var. a
,, catechu, L. var. b
Albizzia, sp.
,, stipulata, Boiv.
,, elata.
Artocarpus sp.
,, mollis, Wall.
,, lacoocha, Roxb.

Bauhinia Malabarica, Roxb.
,, racemosa, Lam.
Bamau, *Burm.*
Berrya mollis, Wall.
Bignonia, sp.
,, ,,
Blackwellia tomentosa, Vent.
Bombax Malabaricum, D.C.
Buchanania latifolia.

Calophyllum, sp.
,, sp.
Carallia integerima, D. C.
Careya arborea, Roxb. var. a (dark)
Careya arborea, Roxb. var. b (light)
Cassia, sp.
,, florida.
Cathartocarpus fistula, L.
Cedrela toona, Roxb.
Chikrassia tabularis, Juss.?
Conocarpus acuminatus.
Cordia myxa, L.

Dalbergia, sp.
Dillenia aurea, Sm.
,, pentagyna, Roxb.
,, speciosa, Thunb.
Diospyros, sp.
,, sp.
Dipterocarpus, sp.
,, sp.
Dipterocarpus alata, Wall.
,, grandiflora, Wall.
Duabanga grandiflora, Wall.

Eriolœna, sp.
,, sp.?
Eugenia sp.
,, obtusifolia, Roxb.
,, cerasoides, Roxb.
,, caryophyllæ-folia, Roxb.

Ficus lanceolata, Roxb.

Garcinia cowa, Roxb.
Gardenia lucida, Roxb.
Garuga pinnata, Roxb.
Gmelina arborea, Roxb.
Grewia microcos, L.

Henslowia paniculata Miqu.
Heritiera, sp.
Hopea sp.
,, odorata, Roxb.
,, suava.

Inga xylocarpa, L.

Katsitka, *Burm.*
Koo-than, *Burm.*

Lagerstrœmia, sp.
Lagerstrœmia pubescens, Wall.
Lagerstrœmia reginæ, Roxb. var. a, wood light red.
Lagerstrœmia reginæ, var. b, wood dark red.
Lagerstrœmia parviflora, Wall.
Leguminosæ. Thit-pouk, *Burm.*
,, Pouk-then-myek kouk, *Burm.*

Melanorhœa usitatissima, Wall.
Meliusa velutina, Hf. and Th.
Mesua ferrea, L.
Moondein, *Burm.*

Nattamin, *Burm.*
Nauclea sp.
,, cordifolia, Roxb.
,, diversifolia, Wall.
,, cadamba, Wall.
,, undulata, Wall.
,, parviflora, Roxb.
,,

Odina wodier.

Palawa, *Burm.*
Phyllanthus, sp.
Pierardia sapida.
Pinus Massoniana, Lamb.
,, Khasyana.
Podocarpus neriifolia.
Pongamia, sp.
,, sp.
Pouk-then-myek kouk.
Premna pyramidata, Wall.
Pterocarpus dalbergioides.

Quercus semiserrata, Roxb.

Rottlera, sp.

Salix lepto-sperma, Roxb.
Sapindus, sp.
Schleichera trijuga, Willd.
Shorea obtusa, Wall.
Spathodea sp.
,, stipulata, Wall.
,, Rheedii, Spreng.
Sterculia sp.
,, fœtida, L.
,, suava, Wall.
Stereospermum chelonioides
Strychnos nux vomica, L.

Terminalia bellerica, Roxb.
,, chebula, Retz.
,, bialata, Roxb.
,, macrocarpa.
Tectona grandis, L.
Thitnee, *Burm.*
Thit-pouk, *Burm.*
Toun-kat-seet.

Vitex, sp.
,, leucoxylon, Roxb.

Wrightia, sp.

Xylocarpus granatum, Koen.

Major Benson gives the following trials of Burmese woods.

Number.	BURMESE NAMES.	Breaking Weight.	Specific Gravity.		Deflection.	Girth of Timber.	REMARKS.
		lbs.	lbs.	oz.	Inches.	Feet.	
1	Seet, Acacia stipulata........ 1	997	48	13	2·12	5 to 6	Fractured specimens good.
11	Koko, Acasia species......... 2	758	38	9	1·2	5 to 6	
23	Seet, No. 2, do. do......... 3	600	56	3	1·25	5 to 6	
2	Yendaik, Dalbergia *sp.*....... 4	1,000	83	0	1·7	2 to 3	The average of 4 specimens fractured.
2½	Kyœ, Syndesmis Tavoyana. 5	646	not taken.		1	2 to 3½	Do. of 2 specimens fractured.
3½	Theetsee, Melanorrhæa usitatissima.................. 6	509	61	8	2·12	5 to 8	Do. 3 do.
15	Aeng, Dipterocarpus turbinatus...................... 7	758	40	0	1·5	6 to 8	
24	Aengdah, ,, lœvis.. 8	747	52	0	1·5	6 to 8	Do. 9 do.
46	Kanyeen-nee, ,, elatus. 9	702	46	0	1·5	6 to 9	
17	Thubuyew, Dillenia ornata...10	808	44	5	1·75	6 to 9	Do. do.
56	Kyet Zinbuin, do. scabrella.11	*691	44	5	1·5	6 to 8	* These were inferior specimens, 800 lbs. would be the real breaking weight.
58	Zinbuin, do. speciosa..12	930	58	0	1·5	6 to 8	
20	Meenaban, Pavetta Indica..13	1,000	60	0	1	1 to 2½	3 good specimens.
25	Maneoga......................14	772	44	5	1	3 to 4½	Do. do.
27	Bamboa, Careya arborea....15	900	47	0	2	3 to 5	Do. do.
33	Nubbay.........................16	795	60	0	1.5	0 0	Do. do.
35	Pethan, Bignonia stipulata.17	1,678	73	0	2·33	5 to 6	Do. do.
40	Yeng(k)at, Gardenia coronaria......... 18	906	60	0	1·75	4 to 5½	Do. do.
53	Pangah, Terminalia bellerica19	1,000	58	2	1·75	4 to 6	Do. do.
60	Toukian, Pentaptera *sp.*......20	969	71	5	1·5	4 to 6	Do. do.
100	Therapee, Calophyllum longifolium.....................21	590	53	0	1·62	5 to 7	Average of 4 good specimens.
101	Parawah, Garcinia *sp.*.......22	927	71	0	1·75	3 to 4½	Do. 3 moderate do.
102	Pedouk, Pterocarpus Indica.23	1,000	71	0	2·25	5 to 10	Do. 4 good do.
105	Peemah.........................24	822	38	0	1·5	6 to 12	The specimens broken seemed dry.
103	Pyenkado, Inga xylocarpa..25	1,153	83	0	2	5 to 7	Good specimens.
104	Pawoon, (*G*) Bytneria *sp*...26	1,351	72	0	3·5	5 to 7	These 3 specimens were not quite seasoned.
106	Engyeen, Shorea robusta...27	1,043	72	0	2·75	6 to 9	Good.
107	Letouk.........................28	785	37	0	1·25	4 to 6	Do.
108	Nuggee, (*G*) Pterospermum lancifolium.................29	925	not taken.		1·75	4 to 6	These specimens were too green to take out the specific gravity.
109	Gnew Yew, (*G*) Cassia fistula.30	1,151	do.		2	3 to 5	
110	Kyee Tha, Barringtonia acutangula.................31	628	do.		1·77	4 to 6	Do. do.

With the exception of the three specimens marked (*G*) the remaining 27 were selected from logs which had been exposed to two dry seasons and one monsoon, and may therefore be considered as nearly seasoned, but not completely so; hence, the specific gravity given cannot be taken as the true or constant quantity, though doubtless sufficiently accurate for the general purposes to which the timber will be applied.

The size of the specimens tested was (3 feet × 1 inch $\frac{4}{10}$ square,) three feet long by one inch and $\frac{4}{10}$ square, they were intended to be 1$\frac{1}{2}$ inch square, but the testing apparatus having only at the bearings a space of 1$\frac{1}{2}$ inch square, it became necessary to reduce $\frac{1}{10}$ of an inch to admit the specimens being fixed.

These 31 specimens were chosen from about 100, as being suitable for the different purposes of ship-building and house carpentry, of cabinet and ornamental work, and the construction of gun carriages, where great strength and elasticity are required.

In addition to these, the wood of Hopea odorata "Thingan," is used extensively by the Burmese in the construction of boats; and boats, carrying 3 or 4 tons, are formed from the trunks of these magnificent trees. The trunk is scooped or burnt out and stretched in the centre, whilst warm, by means of cross pieces of wood. When the required breadth is obtained, the sides are built up to obtain a greater capacity, these tree boats, if they may be so called, are from 7 to 8 feet beam. The Thingan trees grow to a height of 250 feet; they are found near Moulmein in laterite and sandstone chiefly. The breaking weight of Hopea odorata may be stated at 800 lbs. with a specific gravity of 45 to 46 lbs.

Quercus fenestra, Quercus turbinata, Quercus velutina.—These oaks produce good durable, timber, resembling that of the Dillenias in density and elasticity, the trees do not grow of that size to make the timber of the same value as the Dillenias, "Zinbuin." The Dillenias are not only valuable as timber trees, but for ornamental purposes. In March and April, the forests are really dazzling from the bright yellow flowers which are crowded on their leafless trees. Generally growing in a laterite soil. These trees would be worth cultivation in England.

The Fagrea fragrans, Anan, bears a breaking weight of 400 to 500 lbs., its chief value as a timber is its imperishability when exposed to water or damp. The phoongies or Burmese priests look on it as a sacred tree: it is scattered thickly over the alluvial plains together with Strychnos nux-vomica.

Of the Leguminosæ, the first 3 specimens No. 1 Acacia stipulata, Nos. 11 and 23, two species of Acacia not named, are used by the Burmese for naves and spokes of wheels. Acacia stipulata is a valuable wood for general purposes, its middling girth and scarcity would, however, render it useless except in small quantities and scantling. No. 2 Dalbergia, (species, resembling Bombay blackwood), 109 Cassia fistula—103 Inga xylocarpa and 102 Pterocarpus Indica are of this order. 109 is a beautiful ornamental tree, wood useful for furniture, naves and spokes of wheels and tool handles; No. 103 is a dense wood, resembling cassia fistula used for windlasses, block sheaves and for parts of the Gun Carriage; was found too brittle to resist concussion—Pterocarpus Indica is therefore preferred and generally adopted.

Of the Anacardiaceæ, No. 2½ Syndesmus Tavoyana is a beautifully variegated wood, well adapted for furniture and ornamental purposes, is said to contain a dye, it is in great abundance in the islands on the coast and near Moulmein. No. 3½ Theetsee, Melanorrhea usitatissima, a dark red wood, brittle, useful as above, it is from this tree that the famous theetsee varnish is obtained which is impervious to wet—33 Nbubay one of the Anarcadiaceæ has a dense wood, and brittle. The above woods are abundant.

Of the Combretaceæ, No. 53 Terminalia bellerica, a strong good serviceable wood, where elasticity and strength are required.

No. 60 Pentaptera *species* is similar to the above, a valuable wood, abundant.

Of the Cinchonaceæ, No. 20, Meenaban, Pavetta Indica? is called Moulmein Lancewood, but it is not equal to lancewood in elasticity, and beyond being useful for handles of tools, and such purposes. Major Benson thinks its qualities have been generally overrated, besides, it is susceptible to the attacks of insects.

No. 25 Maneoga, one of the Cinchonaceæ, its peculiarity of grain, which resembles oak, would make it useful for decorative purposes, very brittle.

No. 40. "Gardenia coronaria," this wood has a fragrant smell, and would be useful for boxes, but unfortunately when cut into planks there are so many flaws and cracks, that it is difficult to procure a piece of any size, it is a strong tough wood and would be useful for turning.

No. 27. Careya arborea, a good serviceable wood having a good tenacity of fibre and durable. No. 110 Barringtonia acutangula, a tolerably good wood but tough to work, not recommended, being short grained.

DIPTEROCARPACEÆ. No. 24, Dipterocarpus lævis, 15, D. turbinatus and 46, D. elatus? are nearly identical and are useful for planking when not exposed to wet, extensively used in the Straits for this purpose in house-building, the wood oil is obtained from Kanyeenee, D. elatus, they are magnificent forest trees growing straight to the height of 250 feet and more; an incision in the form of a cup is cut into the lower part of the trunk of the tree, which acting as a natural reservoir, collects the oil as it descends.

No. 106. Shorea robusta, a wood of dense structure and elasticity, well adapted for the manufacture of Gun Carriages, this wood stronger and less brittle than Pedouk.

BYTTNERIACEÆ. No. 104. Byttneria *Species*, a wood of great elasticity and strength, the deflection with 1351 lbs., being 3½ inches, the specimen was drawn through the supports, having only a bearing on each end of 1 inch; an invaluable wood for Gun Carriages.

No. 108. Pterospermum lancifolium, a dense strong wood, but not equal to the above.

GARCINIACEÆ. No. 101. Garcinia "parawah," a strong wood with a pretty variegated grain, the tree is of too small size to render the timber available for general purposes. No. 100 Calophyllum longifolium a wood of no great strength, useful for planking and such like purposes, plentiful.

BIGNONIACEÆ. No. 35. Bignonia stipulata, the strongest and most dense wood of the collection, a most valuable wood for purposes requiring strength, elasticity and density, it is pretty plentiful.

DILLENIACEÆ. Nos. 17, 56, 58 three species of Dillenia "ornata," D. "scabrella" and D. "speciosa," strong good timber, the trees are very plentiful and of large girth, useful for general purposes, as house and ship building.—R. BENSON, Captain, *Deputy Assistant Commissary General.*

The AKYAB woods, sent to the Exhibition of 1862, were as under;

Artocarpus.	Inhayon.
Baibga.	Iron wood or Pyeng.
Bamaw.	,, ,, Pya.
Bhoot-tha.	Kalat nothee.
Bignonia stipulata.	Ka-moung.
Champac.	Ka-ngan.
Chahoong.	Khoongho.
Cheuebroon.	Khouk ciah.
Crandoop.	Kran-dao.
Crawudow or kyoung-thya.	Kupoop.
Dipterocarpus, *sp.*	Ky-oung-thya.
Eleocarpus.	Mootsomah.
Erythina Indica.	Pa-bhan.
,, *sp.*	Pa-ran-yan.
Garcinia *sp.* parawah.	Proonbajah.

Rajaw.	Thoonghun.
Rambabha.	Thoungthalaz.
Taboot.	Tonuggaugaw.
Taiaboukbha.	Thing.
Talaz.	Thy.
Thabra king.	Thykado.
Tha-bya.	Thynan.
Thadoop.	Thyzauhoong.
Theuganet (Tilsa).	

The ASSAM woods sent to the Exhibition of 1862, were as follows :

Acacia *sp.* Koroi. Assam.	Koida.
„ Haulluk „	Kotorah.
„ Mota kuli „	Lagerstrœmia regina.
„ Jarool. „	Laurus sassafras.
„ Soom. „	Lookhoori.
Andrachne trifoliata.	Mageli.
Artocarpus, *species.*	Mangifera Indica.
„ integrifolius.	Mesua ferrea.
Bandar.	Michelia champaca.
Bon soom.	Modhoorullum.
Bowlah.	Mosai shalee.
Cedrela toona.	Neem.
Chickrassia tabularis.	Nopahi.
Dackuree.	Nota rohi.
Dalbergia.	Nauclea cadamba.
Dhoomkoorah.	Parli.
Dingari,	Patee hoondie.
„ red.	Pegai.
Doodkooru.	Peni, ? Wohi.
Ehretia serrata.	Quercus.
Gmelina arborea.	Salix tetrasperma.
Gohora.	Shaldoona.
Goondoree.	Sham.
Holow.	Sheedha.
Jam.	Soteeana.
Kajorkulla.	Syzygium jambolanum.
Kanda.	Terminalia citrina.
Ketamaya.	„ 2 *spec.*
Khoira.	Tetachopa.
Kohir.	Wohi.

BUROONGI— ? Quercus *species.*

Quercus flexuosa ?

A tree of Mehra forest, near Abbottabad. An ever-green oak, bearing acorns, leaves of young plant like those of the holly.—*Cal. Cat. Ex.* 1862.

BUTEA FRONDOSA, *Roxb.; W. & A.*

Erythrinum monosperma, *Lam.*

Pulasa. BENG.	Palasi. MALEAL.
Kinaka. „	Dhak. SANS.
Pouk-pin. BURM.	Palasa. „
Pouk.	Calu-keale. SINGH.
Mootr mara. CAN.	Porasa maram. TAM.
Thorus mara. „	Moduga chettu. TEL.
Pulas Tree. ENG.	Kimsukamu. „
Dhak kino tree. „	Palasamu. „
Bastard Teak. ENG.	Tella moduga. TEL.
Parasa. HIND.	Togaru moduga. „
Dhak. „	Polaso. URIA.
Pullus. MAHR.	

Its seed,

Porasum seed. ENG.	Porasam verré. TAM.
Palasha. SANS.	Moduga vittulu. TEL.

Its flowers,

Pulaspapare ke phul. DUK.	Pallas. MAHR.
Tesu. „	Palasha. SANS.
Kisu. „	Porasam-pu. TAM.
Porasum flowers. ENG.	Moduga-puvu. TEL.

This small tree occurs in most parts of India. That of the Central province of Ceylon is used for common house-building purposes, and a cubic foot weighs 38 lbs., and is there said to last 30 years. In Canara and Sunda, it is found most commonly below the ghats and in Dandelee forest. It, there, grows large, but always gnarled ; the wood is hardly distinguishable from teak, and is of similar qualities. Elsewhere, Dr. Gibson mentions that the tree is common in forests, more so in those inland than on the coast. In the former localities, especially in Guzerat, it may be seen covering almost the whole of the uncultivated country. The wood appears to be little used in the Concan and other southern countries : but, in Guzerat (where it is called Bastard Teak), it is extensively employed for house purposes : and from what he had seen of it, he deems it both durable and strong-grained. The roots afford a strong rope, and the beautiful red exudation forms one of the gum kinos of commerce. The flowers give a bright yellow dye. Polaso, *Uria,* is a common creeper of Ganjam and Gumsur, *supposed* to be the Butea frondosa, and described as having a circumference of 1½ feet. The flowers and gum of Butea frondosa are valuable in the arts, and the latter in native medicine.—*Mr. Mendis, Dr. Gibson, Captain Macdonald.*

BUTEA GIBSONII ?

Dhamin. HIND.	Dhamin. MAHR.

Under this name, Captain Sankey describes a Nagpore tree, with a wood of a light colour, possessing a fine clear grain, and with many of the properties of lancewood. It is procurable from 15 to 17 feet long and 2½ feet in girth at 6 annas per cubic foot. He says that, from the facility with which it bends, this wood is held in great esteem for buggy shafts. The natives use it exclusively for the bent ribs of hackerry poles. From the extensive use made of it, few, if any, trees attain their proper growth. Were it obtainable of proper size it would rival the finest timber, but, under the circumstances, he places it among the list of rafter woods, and even here the small quantity obtainable, will limit its application.—*Captain Sankey.*

BUTEA PARVIFLORA. A scandent shrub, flowers small and white.

BUTEA SUPERBA, *Roxb.; W. & A.*

Tige moduga. TEL.	Baranki Chettu. TEL.
Tivva moduga. TEL.	

This is an immense creeper with flowers resembling the Butea frondosa. It has glabrous branches ; roundish ovate obtuse leaflets, velvety beneath ; the corolla four times the length of the calyx ; calyx-teeth acute. It grows on the mountains of Coromandel, and is not uncommon in the provinces of Tavoy and Mergui. It yields the same kind of gum as Butea frondosa. —*Eng. Cyc. page* 703.

BUXUS.

Palm-hout. DUT.	Busso. IT.
Box Wood. ENG.	Bosso. IT.
Buis. FR.	Bossolo. IT.
Buchsbaum. GER.	

The species of this genus of plants afford the valuable hard wood called Box. Of the two European species, *B. sempervirens* and *B. balearica*, the former, or common Box, forms a large evergreen bush or small tree, common all over the south of Europe from Spain to Constantinople, and reaching even so far as the north of Persia. The chief supply of Box-wood is derived from the southern parts of Europe, and from Asia Minor. A distinction is drawn between "Turkey" and "European" Box-wood. The latter is more curly, softer, and paler than the former. Dr. Royle has called attention to Buxus emarginatus, a native of the Himalayas.

Note.—Several Asiatic woods have been discovered with much of the appearance of the common box wood, and, amongst others, the Karens sometimes furnished Dr. Mason with specimens of a wood that can scarcely be distinguished from the box-wood of Europe, but he had never seen the tree, though he named it a Murraya. Dr. Wallich found *Nauclea cordifolia* on the banks of the Irrawaddy, which has "wood coloured like that of the box tree, but much lighter, and at the same time very close grained." It may possibly be the same tree, as Dr. Mason's Murraya, although the Tenasserim wood is not light; or it may be a Tavoy tree, which he says has a strong tough wood, in grain like box.—*Dr. Mason, Eng. Cyc., Royle's Illust. Himl. Bot. p.* 327, *see* ENGRAVING, also *page* 17.

BUXUS CHINENSIS, *Lk.* The China box tree.—*Voigt.*

BUXUS EMARGINATUS, *Wallich.*

This Box-wood was introduced into Britain from the Himalayas; the wood appears as good and compact as that of the box-wood in use in Europe. But, on actual comparison, is found to be softer than the common kinds, though like them in other respects. Wood cuts have been engraved upon the wood of Buxus emarginatus, which has the advantage of being of considerable size and thickness.

C.

CADJANS—?

Jowli. GUZ.	Tennam olé. TAM.
Jowli. HIND.	Tati aku. TEL.
Pannam olé. TAM.	Cobaré aku. TEL.

A commercial word, used by the English in India, origin unknown, for the dried leaves of the cocoanut and palmyra palms, largely used in India for thatching.

CÆSALPINIA. A genus of plants, the species of which are trees or shrubs, yielding useful products. Of the Indian species, the C. bonducella and C. digyna are climbing plants, of which their seeds and oils are used in medicine. The pods of C. coriaria or sumach, a small tree, are used as a tanning material; C. paniculata, is a magnificent climber of the Himalayas, and C. sappan yields one of the Brazil woods of commerce.

CÆSALPINIA CORIARIA, *Willde.*

Poinciania coriaria, *Jacq.*

Libi Libi. ENG.	Dibi Dibi. ENG.
Divi Divi. „	American sumach. „

This small tree, met with in gardens in Madras, is now growing plentifully about Salem, Bangalore, Hoonsoor and at Chicacole. It is a native of South America, but was introduced into India by Dr. Wallich about 1830, and is cultivated for the seed pods, as a tanning material. The wood is not known, but deserves attention.—*Voigt, M. E. J. R., Dr. Cleghorn's Reports.*

CÆSALPINIA SAPPAN, *Linn.; Roxb.; W. & A.*

Lolan. AMBOYN.	Sachang. JAV.
Bakam. ARAB.	Pattang. MAHR.
Bakkam. BENG.	Sapang. MALAY.
Tein n'gyet. BURM.	Kaya sappan. „
Pattang. DUK.	T'sia-pangan. MALEAL.
Brasilienhout. DUT.	Samya. MANIL.
Sappan wood. ENG.	Pao Brasil. PORT.
Brazil wood. „	Patanga. SANS.
Red wood. „	Madera del Brezil. SP.
Brasiletto wood. „	Sibukas. TAG.
Bois de Brésil. FR.	Tsiapangam. TAM.
Brasilienholz. GER.	Vattanghy. „
Bakam. GUZ.	Pattungh. „
Bakam. HIND.	Pattanga chakka. TEL.
Pattangay. „	Bakkapu chettu. „
Legno del Brasile. IT.	Bakamu chakka. „
Verzino. „	Bokmo. URIA.

This tree, as the various names will show, grows widely over South-eastern Asia, but its great value as a dye wood, prevents its being used as timber. It is a very important article of commerce. It grows in the North Arcot forests, in the Nallamallai of Cuddapah: in the Kotah jungles. It is a native of Siam and Amboyna. It is found in the immediate vicinity of Prome, growing in the small hills of the place, but except near Thoungzai, in the northern part of the Rangoon district, where it is also seen in small quantity. Dr. McClelland had not found it in the interior of the province or in the larger forests, so that it is perhaps scarcely entitled to a place amongst the natural productions of Pegu. It is cultivated in Palghaut for the purpose of dyeing the straw used in mat making and from its high price for this purpose, it is not used for carpentry. It grows to a larger size in China than India. It grows with great luxuriance in South Malabar where it is cultivated rather extensively by the Moplahs who plant a number of the seeds at the birth of a daughter. The trees require 14 or 15 years to come to maturity and then become the girl's dowry. Dr. Cleghorn saw more on the banks of the Nellumboor River than any where else ; but he did not ascertain the cause of this. The quantity raised is not great, and why it should be there in particular was not obvious to him, as Malabar is generally uniform in its character. He says that a better system of cutting and cultivating the Sappan, there, is desirable, and thinks the dye-wood is damaged by being allowed to float in salt water. It grows there without any care. The tree is not indigenous in the Bombay forests, but the wood is imported in quantity from the Palghaut jungles (?) for dyeing purposes. It grows freely in their cultivated places without any care, but the heart-wood is dingy, and wants that fine pinkish red which the imports from the southern forest have. Its extreme height in Ganjam and Gumsur is 36 feet, circumference 2 feet, and height from ground to the intersection of the first branch, is 8 feet. The common powder used at the Holee festival is extracted from the wood of this tree. The seeds are used for colouring milk, and the wood as a red dye.—*Voigt, Captain Macdonald, Drs. Wight, McClelland, Gibson, and Cleghorn.*

CÆSALPINIA SEPIARIA, *Roxb.*

Reichardia ? decapetala, *Rottl.*

Mysore thorn. Eng.	Kilgatch. Hind.

Grows in Kemaon, Nepaul, Bengal, Ava, Tavoy, Mysore, Ajmire. It is not a timber tree, but is noticed as a scandent strong armed shrub, generally used to fence round fields, and forming a splendid impenetrable hedge, covered with bright green leaves and large yellow spikes of flowers. Hyder Ali surrounded fortified places with it.—*Voigt, Dr. Irvine.*

CAHAMILILE, Singh. In Ceylon, a very hard, fine, close, even-grained, heavy wood.

CAILLEA CINEREA, *G. & P.*

Dichrostachys cinerea, *W. & A.*	Desmanthus cinereus, *Willde.*
Mimosa cinerea, *Linn.*	Acacia dalea, *D C.*

Mavalinga maram, Tam.	Venuturu, Tel.

Wood not known. This small tree grows in Ceylon, in the Madras Presidency, and is common on sterile plains of the Dekhan, Delhi, Patna, and Paghamew.—*Voigt.*

CALAMANDER WOOD. Diospyros hirsuta.

Koulou-midvie. Singh.	Kalumederiye. Singh.
Koulmedvie. „	Calamander maram ? Tam.

See Diospyros hirsuta.

CALAMBUCO. The name of one of the best timber trees of the Philippine Islands, the wood of which is largely employed by the natives in the fabrication of domestic utensils and agricultural implements.—*Crawfurd's Dict. p.* 79.

CALAMUS. This genus of palm trees is indigenous to Asia, and Dr. Griffiths enumerates 58 species ; they abound in Southern Asia, in the Madras territories, along the foot of the Himalayas from Dehra Dhoon to Sylhet, in Assam, Chittagong, in the Malay peninsula, in Siam, Cochin-China, Sumatra, and in the Archipelago. The species of the genus Calamus are mostly spreading shrubs or small trees, erect, or climbing to a considerable height, or trailing their weak stems several hundred feet along. Some of the species are formed into walking sticks : some, as the C. rotang and others, form the canes or rattans of commerce, of which the people of the Khassia hills make bridges 300 feet long. Those of the Annamallai hills form long looped ladders of them. When split, canes are much used in caning chairs or the framing of light carriages. But, it is not possible to say from what particular species the canes of the shops are obtained, it being probable that many are gathered indiscriminately ; C. rotang has, however, been said to furnish the stouter, and C. scipionum the more slender sorts. But, the C. tenuis of Assam, C. gracilis, C. extensus and others, all furnish the canes of commerce. The flesh that surrounds the seeds of this genus is a delicate article of food ; limpid water flows from the stems when cut through ; and the young shoots of some of them, while still tender, are fritted or boiled, chopped small, and, being fried with pepper and gravy, are said to furnish a very delicate dish. One of the kinds of Dragon's Blood or Jurnang, is the produce of species of Calamus. Those which chiefly yield it are the C. petræus (Lour.) C. rudentum (Lour.), C. verus (Lour.), and C. draco (Willd.), of which the last three were by Linnæus reckoned mere varieties of the C. rotang (Linn.)—*Seeman, Voigt, Eng. Cyc.*

CALAMUS DRACO, of Sumatra and the Malay islands, is said to be one of the species which yield the Dragon's Blood of commerce.

CALAMUS PETRÆUS, *Lour.* One of the sources of the rattan cane.

CALAMUS ROTANG, *Linn. ; Roxb.*

C. Roxburghii, *Griff., Royle.*

Bet. Beng.	Perambu. Tam.
Beta. „	Betamu. Tel.
Rattan. Eng.	Bettapu chettu. „
Rattan Cane. „	Niru Prabba. „
Cane. „	Pemu. „
Rattan Cane Palm. Eng.	Pepu. „
Bet. Hind.	Prabba chettu. „
Rotan. Malay.	Prabbali „ „
Bed. Pers.	

This is said to furnish the stouter of the Rattan Canes of commerce. The hard flinty coating of their stems, which are readily split into strips, are extensively used for the caning in the backs and bottoms of chairs, sofas, and light carriages. In Java, canes are made into matting, and throughout the eastern islands of the Archipelago and about Malacca, vessels are furnished with cables formed of cane twisted or platted. They are likewise formed into ropes by the people of the forests, to drag heavy weights and to bind wild elephants.

C. rudentum, *Lour.*; C. verus, *Lour.*; and C. draco, *Willde.*; are regarded by Linnæus as varieties of C. rotang, and are said to yield the Dragon's Blood of commerce.

CALAMUS ROYLEANUS, *Griffith*. The most northern of the canes, being found in the Dehra Dhoon.

CALAMUS SCIPIONUM is said to furnish the more slender of the rattan canes of commerce; it is also supposed to produce the Malacca canes, brought from Siak: but this latter is doubtful.

CALUVERE, SINGH. Ebony, ENG.?? Under these names Mr. Mendis mentions a tree of the northern and eastern part of Ceylon, as furnishing a fine black wood, used largely for buildings and furniture. A cubic foot weighs 71 lbs., and it lasts 80 years.

CALLICARPA ARBOREA, *Roxb.* A small tree of Nepaul, Kemaon, Oude, the Morung mountains, Goalpara, Chittagong and Moulmein. Wood not known.—*Voigt.*

CALOPHYLLUM. A genus of plants distinguished by the beauty of their leaves, and named from καλος beautiful, φυλλον leaf. Several of these trees, in Southern India, have not, as yet, been specifically determined, and possibly they may all be one or two species. They furnish useful timber; C. angustifolium yielding the Poon spars of commerce, or one of them; and C. calaba, the East Indian Tacamahaca, though C. Inophyllum is also quoted as the Tacamahaca tree.

CALOPHYLLUM, *Species.*

Oondie. MAHR.

Common on the Bombay coast, growing on sandy sheltered spots close to the sea on the coast south of the Savitree. North of that river, it is rare. The wood never reaches any size, and is always crooked. A good bitter oil is furnished by the seeds.—*Dr. Gibson.*

CALOPHYLLUM, a *Species* of Tenasserim. House carpenters often use its timber and the tree also furnishes spars.

CALOPHYLLUM, *Species.*

Poonyet. BURM.

Firewood? of British Burmah. A cubic foot weighs 39 lbs. In a full grown tree on good soil the average length of the trunk to the first branch is 60 feet, and average girth measured at 6 feet from the ground is 12 feet. It sells at 12 annas per cubic foot.—*Dr. Brandis, Cal. Cat. Ex. of* 1862.

CALOPHYLLUM, *Species.*

Tha-ra-phee. BURM.

A wood of British Burmah, (Martaban? and Tavoy?) used for carving images, occasionally for canoes. A cubic foot of it weighs 57 lbs. In a full grown tree on good soil the average length of the trunk to the first branch is 20 feet, and average girth measured at 6 feet from the ground is 4 feet.—*Dr. Brandis.*

CALOPHYLLUM, *Species.*

Thurappe. BURM.

A large tree, used for masts and spars in Martaban.

CALOPHYLLUM, *Species.*

Turra-phee. BURM.

Used for masts, &c. in Tavoy. (These two seem identical with the above of Dr. Brandis.)

CALOPHYLLUM ACUMINATUM.

Waldombe. SINGH.

A tree of the western parts of Ceylon, the timber of which is used for common house building purposes. A cubic foot weighs 39 lbs. It lasts 20 years.—*Mr. Mendis.*

CALOPHYLLUM ANGUSTIFOLIUM, *Roxburgh.* This is the Piney Tree of Penang, where it grows. It occurs also in Coorg, Mysore, Canara, and along the Ghats northwards to Sawuntwarree, but rarely of any great size, beyond the line of the Neelgoond ghat. It is a magnificent tree when growing in the ravines of the southern ghats of Canara. According to Dr. Gibson and Dr. Cleghorn, the Poon spars are obtained from this tree, but the trees are becoming scarce, and are perhaps more valuable than teak. Dr. Gibson says that, to the best of his knowledge, the Poon spars are furnished by Calophyllum angustifolium, which is a magnificient tree in the ravines of the southern ghats. In habit and appearance, it is totally distinct from C. inophyllum. These spars are found along the ghats, from the Sawuntwarree border southward, but rarely of any great size till the line of the Neelcoond Ghat is passed. At another place he says that the poon spars of the first class were not procurable in the jungles nearest to the coast, and probably, owing to the continued extension of cultivation. It is rather from the inland forests of Canara, backed as these are by those of Coorg to the east, that the supply of Poon spars is principally drawn. On his way from the Mysore border to Sircee, he saw, in more than one place, immense spars of Poon standing as trees, but scorched, burned up, and rendered useless. Dr. Cleghorn tells us that Poon spars are becoming very scarce and consequently are perhaps more valuable than teak. Young trees, especially such as are in accessible places, are most carefully preserved. Strict orders on this subject have been given in Coorg, Mysore and Canara. In one case which came within his observation, several valuable spars were found in a bridge, the total estimate of which was 250 Rupees, and, he adds, several instances of the same kind have occurred. But Poon spars, although highly prized for ship building, are ill suited for making bridges. This incident he remarks, illustrates the importance of officers in the Department of Public Works, Telegraph, &c., making themselves acquainted with the description of timber available and suitable for their wants. He also mentions that the Superintendent of Coorg had received several tenders for the supply of Poon spars and other timber at the distance of at least 3 miles from the Soolia river, showing the scarcity of such wood and the readiness of the Mangalore contractors to carry it several miles to the nearest water carriage. These opinions of Drs. Gibson and Cleghorn, that the *Poon* spars of commerce, are obtained from the Calophyllum angustifolium are of great value. But, in 1850 in the Proceedings of the Madras Central Committee for the Exhibition of 1851, the poon of commerce, was supposed by Dr. Wight to be from the Dillenia pentagynia, "Rowadan" TEL., a large timber tree. The wood of Dillenia pentagynia is said to be exceedingly strong and very durable, even when buried under ground, and, it is a stately forest tree, common on the face of the W. Ghats. It is also a native of the Northern Circars and flowers in March and April.—The similarity of native names between this and Calophyllum inophyllum led Dr. Wight to suspect some confusion. Dr. Wight was satisfied that D. pentagynia is the tree which furnishes the Poon spars being a tall and Calophyllum inophyllum a short stunted tree. Dr. Cleghorn commends the strict conserving of C. angustifolium, in Coorg and Canara.—*Drs. Gibson, Cleghorn and Wight, Mr. Rohde's MSS. Dr. Roxburgh, Tredgold.* *See* POON.

CALOPHYLLUM CALABA, *Linn.*

Calophyllum spurium, *Choisy.*
Calophyllum calabioides, *G. Don.*
Calophyllum apetalum, *Willd.*
Calophyllum calaba, *Linn.*
C. Wightiana, *Wall.*

Bubbe mara. CAN.	Gorrukeenee. SINGH.
Calaba Tree. ENG.	Cheru Pinnai. TAM.
Tsira panna. MALEAL.	

This is a native of the western province of Ceylon, and of Travancore, and produces the true East Indian Tacamahaca resin. It grows to a height of 60 feet, and its timber is used for bullock carts, staves, cask headings and house buildings. In Canara and Sunda, it grows on the banks of rivers and streams, chiefly above the ghats. The wood is used for canoes. Sir J. Herschel seems to think the East Indian Tacamahaca to be the produce of C. inophyllum, for, he says, specimens obtained from Calophyllum inophyllum, the Tacamahaca of Ceylon, are desirable, in order to aid pharmacologists in accurately determining the Tacamahaca of European commerce.—*Herschel's Manual of Scientific Enquiry, p.* 414, *Dr. O'Shaughnessy, Mr. Mendis, Dr. Gibson, W. & A. p.* 103.

CALOPHYLLUM INOPHYLLUM, *Linn.; Roxb.*

Calophyllum bintagor, *Roxb.*
Balsamaria inophyllum, *Lour.*

Sultana champa. BENG.	Ponna. MALEAL.
Wuma mara. CAN.	Dombe. SINGH.
Undi. DUK.	Pinné maram. TAM.
Alexandrian Laurel. ENG.	Ponna chettu. TEL.
Undi. HIND.	Punnaga. „ „
Sultana champa. HIND.	Punnagamu. „ „
Oundi ? MAHR.	

The flower,

Surpun ka phul. HIND.	Pinne-pu. TAM.
Punaga. SANS.	Ponna-pu. TEL.

The oil,

Poon-seed Oil. ENG.	Pinnay yennai. TAM.
Surpun ka tel. HIND.	Pinnay nuna. TEL.
Pinne-cotte yennai. TAM.	

This beautiful tree grows in the western part of Ceylon where it is employed for masts and cross sticks of Yettra dhonies and fishing boats and poles of bullock carts. A cubic foot weighs 40 lbs. Dr. Wight says, as to Coimbatore, that the tree is rare at that distance from the coast, the wood is coarse grained, but very strong and durable, and on the coast is used in ship building. In the alpine forests, it attains a great size and furnishes the *poon* spars so valuable for shipping; so far as he could learn, there are two or three species of Calophyllum used for the same purpose under the general name of poon. This is a beautiful tree with an appropriate name and very common, and a good lamp oil is obtained from the seeds; wood coarse grained, strong, durable and ornamental. The tree he says is worthy of attention, as it grows well in sandy tracts close to the sea, where few others thrive. —*Drs. Wight, Cleghorn, Mr. Mendis, Voigt.*

CALOPHYLLUM LONGIFOLIUM.

The-ra-pi. BURM.	Tha-ra-bi. BURM.

In Pegu this is found near towns, together with two other species of the same genus, which are of smaller growth. It has a red wood adapted to cabinet making. It is abundant in Mergui, Tavoy, and in lesser quantities near the Attaran River and its branches. Maximum girth 3 cubits. Maximum length 22½ feet. When seasoned, it sinks in water. It is there used for masts and yards of junks; it is excellent for helves, but not procurable at Maulmein in sufficient abundance. Strongly recommended to make models.—*Dr. McClelland, Captain Dance.*

CALOSANTHES INDICA, *Blainv.*

Bignonia Indica, *Linn.*	Spathodea Indica, *Pers.*
,, pentandra, *Lour.*	

Pana wood. ANGLO-TAM.	Achi maram. TAM.

This tree has been noticed under its synonym, Bignonia Indica. It grows in Coimbatore, throughout the Konkans, in Mahim, and the jungles of Khandesh. Dr. Wight mentions that it is said to be a very soft and juicy wood, of no value.—*Dr. Wight, Voigt. See* BIGNONIA INDICA.

CALOTROPIS, *R. Brown.* Of this genus, three species are met with all over Southern Asia, viz.

C. GIGANTEA, *R. Br.*

Asclepias gigantea, *Willde.*

Ashur. ARAB.	Madar. HIND.
Gigantic swallow wort. ENG.	Arka. SANS.
Akund. HIND.	Yercum. TAM.
Ak. ,,	Jilladu chettu. TEL.

also

C. PROCERA, *R. Br.*

Asclepias procera. *Ait.*
Calotropis gigantea. *Andr.*

Beidelsar. HIND.

and

C. HERBACEA, *Carey,* Asclepias herbacea of Roxburgh.

Chota Akunda. HIND.

Their roots are employed to make gunpowder charcoal. The stem yields useful strong fibres, and the white silk-like materials of the pods, has been successfully tried to mix with silk. —*Voigt. M. E. Proceedings.*

CALYPTRANTHES CARYOPHYLLIFOLIA, *Willd. Swartz.*

The tree,

Jamoon. HIND.	Nawel maram. TAM.
Nawel wood tree. ANGLO-TAM.	Neredi chettu. TEL.

The fruit,

Jamoon ka phal. DUK.	Batte dombe. SINGH.
Nawel fruit. ENG.	Nawel pallam. TAM.
Kaka jemboo. SANS.	Neredi pandoo. TEL.

A large growing timber tree. The wood is light, and chiefly used for making grain measures, but is also made into carriage frames, cots &c., and, in Ceylon, for common house building: a cubic foot weighs 45 lbs. and lasts 20 years. The bark is astringent, and is used in decoction by the natives for dysentery. The fruit when ripe, is of a very dark purple colour, and about the size of a large cherry. In taste, it somewhat resembles the aloe, but is much sweeter. A variety of this tree,

Oojla jamoon ka phal. DUK.	Vullay nawel pallam. TAM.
Sweta jemboo. SANS.	Tella neredi pandu. TEL.

has a fruit nearly similar to it in natural qualities and has got its names from being of a different colour (white).—*Dr. Riddell, Mr. Mendis, Ainslie.*

CALYPTRANTHES CUMINI. ?

Mahadan. SINGH.

Grows in the northern and western provinces of Ceylon, where it is used for common house building purposes, wheels, &c. A cubic foot weighs 36 lbs., and it lasts 20 years. The berries are eaten when fully ripe.—*Mr. Ad. Mendis.*

CALYPTRANTHES JAMBOLANA.

Jamoon. HIND.	Turkolum. TAM.
Alubo. SINGH.	

This large and handsome tree, flowers in February and March, and thrives in any good soil. It occurs in the central province of Ceylon, and is met with in gardens all over the peninsula of India. It is employed, in Ceylon, for common house building. The fruit of the best sort is as large as a common blue plum, which it resembles in appearance; it has a rough astringent flavour, and should be soaked in salt and water before it is eaten. The fresh stone, if planted, grows immediately.—*Dr. Riddell, Mr. Mendis.*

CALYSACCION ANGUSTIFOLIA.

Soorpunni. CAN.	Koolmarar. CAN.

Grows in Canara and Sunda, in ravines of the Ghats and below in sheltered valleys; but is not common in North Canara and Sunda. The tree is used there for one of the "*Poon*" spars. It produces an excellent edible fruit. It is a tree which ought to be conserved everywhere and largely increased.—*Dr. Gibson.*

CALYSACCION LONGIFOLIA, *Roxb., Wight, Ill. I.* 130 *and Icon.* 1999.

Male Tree, Punag. CAN.	Taringi. CAN.
Female Tree, Wundi. ,,	Sura ponna. TEL.

A large tree which grows in the Northern Circars, Konkans, the Kennari jungles and in western Mysore. The flower buds are used for dyeing silk, and for their violet perfume.—*Useful Plants, Elliot's Flora Andhrica.*

CAMBESSEDEA OPPOSITIFOLIA, *W. & A.*

Mangifera oppositifolia, *Roxb.*

Opposite-leaved Mango. ENG.

This indigenous tree of Tenasserim has a reddish coloured, hard, and close-grained wood, said to be durable. It produces a fruit much like a plum. There are two varieties, one bearing an intensely sour fruit, and the other one as insipidly sweet.—*Mason, Voigt.*

CAMOOGA-WOOD, Kumooga maram. A wood of the Northern Circars.

CAMPHOR-WOOD. The camphor-wood of Sumatra is from the Dryobalanops camphora, of which the wood is hard, compact and brownish-coloured. The fragrant light-coloured, soft, wood of which the trunks and boxes from China are made, is supposed to be that of the Camphor tree of Japan, Laurus camphora, or Camphora officinalis. The Martaban Camphor-wood, Laurus (Sassafras) is a very large tree, scattered sparsely throughout the Tenasserim provinces. Wallich wrote that it was very like Laurus glandulifera, which furnishes the sassafras, and camphor-wood of Nepaul. The Karens call it the "tree galanga" from its fragrance.—*Holtz.*, *Mason.*

CANARA, NORTH AND SOUTH. The forests of N. Canara continue to furnish large quantities of the best timber produced in Southern India, but, till lately, the government authorities directed their attention principally to preserving the Teak, Sandalwood, Blackwood, Jackwood, Wild Jack and Poon trees—to the comparative neglect of other valuable woods. In the years 1843-44 to 1851-52 inclusive, the teak supplied from the Canara forests to the Bombay Dockyards and remaining in store amounted to 7,831 logs, equal to 26,714 candies, and the expenses incurred in delivering the same amounted to Rs. 1,47,277-1-8 or about six rupees per candy. There was, also, in addition, 784 logs, equal to 2,783 Bombay candies of Jungle wood. In the Fusly years 1251 to 1260 inclusive there was exported from Canara, by sea, of Teak 18,187 candies, Poon spars 6,918 in number: of Sandalwood 86 candies and Blackwood 352 candies. In 1837, Col. Frith gave a list of 29 woods of Canara. In 1844, Dr. Gibson gave another of 32 woods; both of these lists were merely in their native names, but, some years later, in 1845-46, the latter gentleman gave a list of 164 timber trees and fancy woods with scientific, Canarese and Mahratta names, which he had found in the forests of Canara and Soonda. It is as follows, and the descriptions will be found alphabetically arranged.

Acacia arabica.
" amara.
" catechu.
" Farnesiana.
" leucophlœa.
" odoratissima.
" odoratissima.
" speciosa.
" sundra.
Ægle marmelos.
Ailanthus excelsa.
Alangium decapetalum.
Alstonia scholaris.
Antidesma alexiteria.
Artocarpus hirsuta.
" integrifolia.
Atalantia monophylla.
Azadirachta Indica.
Balanites Ægyptiaca.
Bassia latifolia.
" longifolia.
Bauhinia acuminata.
" parviflora.
" variegata.
Bignonia Indica.
" quadrilocularis.
" undulata.
" xylocarpa.
Bombax Malabaricum.
Borassus flabelliformis.
Briedelia spinosa.
Buchanania latifolia.
Butea frondosa.
Cæsalpinia sappan.
Calophyllum inophyllum.
Canthium nitens.
" parviflorum.
Capparis divaricata.
" grandis.
Carallia integrifolia.
Careya arborea.
Caryota urens.
Casearia elliptica.
Cassia fistula.
Celastrus montana.
Cedrela toona.
Cluytea collina.
Chickrassia tabularis.
Chloroxylon Swietenia.
Chrysophyllum acuminatum.
Cinnamomum iners.
Conocarpus latifolia.
Cordia Rothii.
Cratæva Roxburghii.
Capania canescens.
Cullenia excelsa.
Dalbergia latifolia.
" Oojenensis.
" paniculata.
" sissoides.
Dichrostachys cinerea.
Dillenia pentagyna.
Diospyros cordifolia.
" melanoxylon.
" montana.
Ehretia ovalifolia.
Elædendron Roxburghii
Eriodendron anfractuosum.
Erythrina Indica, Pangara.
Erythrina suberosa.
Eugenia caryophyllata.
" jambolana.
Euphorbia tirucalli.
Euonymus garcinifolia.
Feronia elephantum.
Ficus t'siela.
Flacourtia montana.
Gardenia turgida.
Gardenia montana.
Garcinia glutinifera.
Garuga pinnata.
Givottia Rottleriformis.
Gmelina arborea.
" Asiatica.
Grewia tiliæfolia.
Guatteria cerasoides.
Hardwickia binata.
Holarrhena.
Hydnocarpus inebrians.
Hymenodyction obovatum.
Hymenodyction utile.
Inga xylocarpa.
Ixora parviflora.
Jambosa salicifolia.
Lagerstræmia microcarpa.
Lagerstræmia reginæ.
Limonia alata.
Mangifera Indica.
Melia azadirachta.
" bukayun.
" superba.
Memecylon tinctorium.
Mesua ferrea.
Michelia Nilgirica.
Michelia champaca.
Mimsops elengi.
" hexandra.
Morinda citrifolia.
Myristica cinerea.
Nauclea cordifolia.
" parviflora.
Nephelium longanum.
Nerium antidysentericum.
Odina woodier.
Olea dioica.
Pentaptera arjuna.
Phyllanthus emblica.
Pongamia glabra.
Premna integrifolia.
" tomentosa.
Prosopis spicigera.
Pterocarpus marsupium.
Pterocarpus santalinus.
Putranjiva Roxburghii.
Randia dumetorum.
Rhus buckiamela.
Rottlera tinctoria.
Salvadora Persica.
Santalum album.
Sapindus emarginatus.
Schleichera trijuga.
Semecarpus anacardium.
Sethia Indica.
Soymida febrifuga.
Spondias acuminata.
Spathodea arcuata,
Sterculia balanghas.
" fœtida.
" urens.
Stereospermum chelonoides.
Stereospermum suaveolens.
Strychnos nux vomica.
" potatorum.
Symplocos racemosa.
Swietenia febrifuga.
Tamarindus Indica.
Tectona grandis.
Terminalia alata.
" belerica.
" "
" catapa.
" Berryi.
" chebula.
" glabra.
Thespesia populnea.
Trophis aspera.
Ulmus integrifolia.
Vitex altissima.
Wrightia tinctoria.
Zizyphus glabrata.
" jujuba.
" œnoplia.
" xylocarpa.

In South Canara, the jungles bear no comparison to those of Malabar or North Canara where there are large tracts of forest uninhabited, and where, by making a single road, some three or four thousand trees could be got out. In South Canara, the jungles are thickly populated, not by wild or wandering tribes, but by farmers, who carry on cultivation to a considerable extent, Each farmer is allowed the space of 100 yards all round his fields, on which he can cut timber and bamboos for his own use, free of all charge, there are however several lines of good forests which are called Merch wurgs (Pepper wurgs) and the ryot pays a Beriz on the wurg of five pie per pepper vine. When the koomki land and merchi wurgs are separated there is but little of Government jungles left, and on this little, ripe trees are few and scattered. In 1861-62, the conservator was engaged in girdling 1,500 trees of restricted timber, in the jungles in the Uppenangadi taluq, but scattered over a tract of jungle some thirty miles long, by five miles average width. Young trees are found in abundance, and with care there may be a considerable quantity of timber got in this part some years hence.

From South Canara, Mr. V. Pedro Coelho sent the following 50 woods to the Exhibition of 1862.

Sandal wood.	Cadippila ,, (Dyeing.)
Teak wood or Sagavani.	Manjutty ,, (Medicine)
Jack wood or Halsu.	Purrally wood.
Wild Jack wood or Hebalsu.	Nalikai ,, (Building.)
Bengha wood.	Santamary ,, (GunStocks.)
Bou ,, (Building purposes.)	Renje ,,
	Page or Gargass (Polishing.)
Bannapoo ,, ,,	Ardall or Gamboge tree.
Terruvah ,, ,,	Cinnamon.
Marava ,, ,,	Mannadike wood.
Jembu Nerlu wood.	JungleGéru Kai (Medicine.)
Votte Hully wood.	Cashew tree wood.
Tamarind tree wood.	Hállay ,,
Michelia champaca or Uru sampige wood.	Tálly ,, (Building)
	Cocoanut tree ,,
Kaddu sampige wood.	Kunttal ,,
Daddalla ,,	Karmara ,,
Toreuha, or Pumbilo wood.	Dhuppa ,,
Kalu bóghe wood.	Lonkatty ,,
Pattu báge ,,	Tarrolly ,,
Shere Houe (Ship building.)	Arecanut tree ,,
Uru Honc (Ship building.)	Black ,,
Mango ,,	Ebony ,,
Járrige ,,	Jummi Kai ,,
Nánne ,,	Takote Kai ,,
Andippu naru ,,	Pith.

—*Dr. Gibson, Mad. Cat. Ex. of* 1862; *Rep. Con. For. of* 1862, *p.* 30.

CANARIUM, *Species.* Under the names of Dhoop, CAN., Dhoop and Googul, MAHR., Dr. Gibson mentions two species of Canarium, in Canara and Sunda, one on the Ghats above, and the second species seems to be cultivated near Bilgil; and also at Siddapore, and of great size. The choice gum resin afforded by these trees is extensively used in the arts and exported both inland and to the coast. Wood very good.—*Dr. Gibson.*

CANARIUM BENGALENSE, *Roxb. Fl. Ind.* vol. iii, p. 136. An immense forest tree, a native of Assam and Sylhet and the adjacent mountainous countries, and flowering in May and June. From fissures or wounds in the bark, a large quantity of very pure, clear, amber-coloured resin exudes, which soon becomes hard and brittle, and is not unlike copal; yet the natives set little or no value on it. In the Calcutta bazar it is only valued at from 2 to 3 Rs. for seven maunds of eighty pounds each. Roxburgh does not mention the native name of this resin. Wood not known.—*O'Shaughnessy, page* 285.—*Voigt.*

CANARIUM COMMUNE, *Linn.; DC.; W. & A.; Kœn.; Roxb.*

Canarium mehenbethene, *Gært.*
Amyris Zeylanica, *Retz.*
Balsamodendron Zeylanicum, *Kunth.*
Colophonia Mauritiana, *DC.*
Bursera paniculata, *Lam., Rumph.*

Java Almond. ENG. | Jungli Badam. HIND.
Bois de Colophane. FR.

Grows in the Mauritius, the Moluccas, Ceylon, the Peninsula of India, and the Indian Archipelago. Character of its wood is not known; but the bark yields an abundance of limpid oil with a pungent turpentine smell, congealing into a buttery camphoraceous mass. It has the same properties as balsam of copaiba; and is said to yield East Indian elemi.—*Dr. O'Shaughnessy, page* 288, *Voigt.*

CANARIUM GENICULATUM. A large and valuable timber tree found in the Pegu valley, but it is scarce. Wood, white colored, adapted to every purpose of house-building.—*McClelland.*

CANARIUM STRICTUM, *Roxb.*

Black dammer tree. ENG. | Kongilam maram. TAM.
Thelli. MALEAL.

Common in the alpine forests about Courtallum, and, in the Tinnevelly district, is regularly rented for the sake of its dammer. Character of wood not known. While adhering to the tree, the resin has a bright shining black appearance, but when held between the eye and the light it is translucent and has a deep brownish yellow, or amber colour.—*Voigt, quoting Wight, Useful Plants.*

CANES. Species of the Calamus palms.

Nathur. GUZ. | Bed. PERS.
Bet. HIND. | Perambugal. TAM.
Rotan. MALAY. | Bettamulu. TEL.

See CALAMUS.

CANGOO, TAM. A Tinnevelly wood of a whitish brown colour. Used for handspikes and wheelwright's work.—*Col. Frith.*

CANIS. ? In Penang, a large tree; used for door frames.—*Col. Frith.*

CANTHIUM DIDYMUM.

Nalla regoo. TEL.

A tree of the Godavery forests, centre wood mottled and of a dark colour like old seasoned oak.

CANTHIUM NITENS—?

Malai caurai. TAM.

Dr. Wight said that he had not seen the timber nor the tree itself, but that it had been described to him in Coimbatore, as a small tree. Dr. Gibson seems to consider Dr. Wight's Canthium nitens identical with C. didymum (the Canthium umbellatum (Wight) and adds, that if right in this conjecture, the tree is a common one on the Bombay Ghats, and, from its flowers and shining leaves, well worthy a place in gardens. The wood is small and, is said, not put to any use.—*Wight, Gibson.*

CANTHIUM PARVIFLORUM, *Lam.; Roxb.; DC.; G. Don.; W. & A.*

Webera tetrandra, *Willd.; Rheede.*

Kirni. CAN.	Karai-cheddi. TAM.
Burra munga. HIND.? ? ?	Sengarary maram. TAM.
Kandan karra. MALEAL.	Nalla balusu. TEL.
Naga valli. SANS.	Balusu kura. TEL.

Found as a small shrub, on many of the barren wastes of the Deccan, and on hill ridges and Dr. Gibson had never seen it of a size sufficient for any economical purpose. Captain Beddome describes it, on the Godavery, as a dark colored hard and pretty wood; good for turning small objects. This corresponds with Dr. Wight's experience at Coimbatore where he says it occurs as a small tree or rather moderate size shrub wood, close grained and hard, well fitted for turning small objects. *Drs. Wight & Gibson, Captain Beddome.*

CAPPARIS DIVARICATA, *Lam. W. & A*

Pachoonda, MAHR.	Bûdarèni. TEL.
Toaratti maram. TAM.	

A small tree, growing in Coimbatore, and not uncommon on the more arid wastes and in the dry hedges of the interior of the Bombay Presidency. Wood said to be only fit for fuel.—*Wight, Gibson.*

CAPPARIS GRANDIS. *Linn. W. & A. W. Ic.* 21.

C. Maxima, *Heyne in Roth.: Roxb. E. I. M.*
C. Bisperma, *Roxb.*
C. Grandis, *Klein.*
C. Brevispina ? *Gibson.*

Waghutty. MALAY.	Gullem chettu. TEL.
Vellai toaratti maram. TAM.	Regutti. TEL.
Guli. TEL.	

A small tree growing in Coimbatore, and common in waste places inland of the Bombay Presidency, wood close grained, hard and good, too small for general use, but good for turning.—*Wight, Gibson, Elliot, Flor. Andhrica, Useful Plants.*

CAPPARIS HORRIDA, *Linn.; W. & A. Ic.*

Capparis zeylanica, *Roxb.*

Ardanda. DUK.	Katallikai. TAM.
Thorny caper-bush. ENG.	Atanday. „
Ardanda. HIND.	Adonda. TEL.
Hunkara. SANS.	Arudonda. „

CARALLIA LANCEÆFOLIA, *Roxb.* A tree of Sumatra.—*Voigt.*

CARALLIA LUCIDA, *Roxb.*

Carallia integerrima, *DC.*
Carallia integrifolia, *Grah.*

Kierpa. BENG.	Phansi. CAN.
Maneioga. BURM.	

This tree grows on the Malabar side of India, in the Konkans, in the Circars, Kemaon, Silhet, Chittagong, Pegu and Mergui. On the Bombay side, it is a handsome tree, pretty frequent in the forests of the South Konkan; not seen elsewhere. Wood hard, close-grained, and might be used in turning. It is seldom large enough for any other purpose. It is a large tree, common north of Rangoon and throughout Pegu. Wood of a peculiar structure, thick medullar rays going through from the centre to the circumference, colour red, used for planks and rice pounders, and may possibly be found useful for cigar boxes A cubic foot weighs lbs. 60. In a full grown tree on good soil the average length of the trunk to the first branch is 50 feet, and average girth measured at 6 feet from the ground is 10 feet. It sells at 8 annas per cubic foot. In the southern forests of Pegu it is a plentiful tree, of large girth, and, in Calcutta, is employed in house-building under the name of *Kierpa.—Drs. Gibson, McClelland and Brandis, Voigt.*

CARALLIA ZEYLANICA.

Davette. SINGH.

Grows in the western parts of Ceylon. The wood is used as roofings for common house-buildings. A cubic foot weighs 42 lbs., and it is calculated to last 25 years.—*Mr. Adrian Mendis.*

CARAPA.

Taila-oon. BURM.

A Tavoy wood, used in building.—*Col. Frith.*

CAREEMARADOO. TAM.? A Travancore wood, of dark brown colour, 2 to 6 feet in circumference; used for carts and building. (This is probably a species of Pterocarpus.)—*Colonel Frith.*

CAREYA, *Species.*

Kaga. BURM.

A large timber tree of Tavoy.—*Col. Frith.*

CAREYA, *Species.*

Zaza. BURM.

A Martaban wood, used for posts, &c.—*Col. Frith.*

CAREYA ARBOREA, *Roxb.; Corr.; Rheede; W. & A.*

Ban-bambhooai. BENG.	Kahatta. SINGH.
Bambouai. BURM.	Ave-mavo. TAM.
Baubwai. „	Puta-tanni maram. TAM.
Cumbia. CAN.	Pailæ maram ? „
Careystree. ENG.	Kumbhi. TEL.
Kamba. HIND.	Budada-nedi ? TEL.
Koombha. MAHR.	Cumbi. „
Wae koombha. „	Koombee. URIA.
Peloa. MALEAL.	

This tree grows in most parts of India, of good size, and in many places abundant; and, except Drs. Riddell, Wight and Cleghorn, its timber is praised by all who have noticed it, as a good serviceable wood, having a good tenacity of fibre and durable. It occurs in the south and west of Ceylon, in Coimbatore, is very common in the inland and coast jungles of Bombay, is found in the Dekhan, in Ganjam and Gumsur, is one of the most numerous trees throughout the province of

Pegu, and is abundant in Tenasserim, Amherst, Tavoy, and Mergui. Dr. McClelland says that in Pegu the timber is large, the wood red and equivalent to mahogany, and there forms the chief material of which the carts of the country are made, Dr. Mason adding that it is a useful timber for house building, and Dr. Brandis mentions that it is used for gun-stocks, house posts, planks, &c. A cubic foot of the Pegu wood weighs 55 lbs. In a full grown tree on good soil the average length of the trunk to the first branch is 20 feet, and average girth, measured at 6 feet from the ground, is 9 feet. It sells, in Pegu, at 12 annas per cubic foot. Captain Dance says it is abundant in Amherst, Tavoy and Mergui, with a maximum length of 15 feet and maximum girth of 3 cubits : that its timber, when seasoned, floats in water, is useful, durable, and tough, and for ordnance purposes he recommends it for helves. Dr. Gibson tells us that it is not much used on the Bombay side, but that the timber stands the action of water well. As it is generally crooked, he thinks it merits trial for the crooks of boats, corners of carriages, &c. In Ceylon, it is used for the axles of bullock carts and in buildings. Its fibrous bark is used as matches for matchlocks, guns, &c., and in Ganjam, according to Capt. Macdonald, the scanty clothing of the Byragi and other hindus affecting peculiar sanctity, is made of the fibrous bark of this tree. In Ceylon, a cubic foot of its wood weighs 35 lbs. and it lasts 10 to 20 years. In Ganjam and Gumsur, according to Captain Macdonald, its extreme height is 36 feet, circumference 3 feet, and height from the ground to the intersection of the first branch is 6 feet.—*Drs. Wight, Cleghorn, Brandis, Mason, McClelland, Gibson, and Riddell, Captains Macdonald and Dance, Major Benson.*

CAREYA SPHÆRICA.

Bambouai. BURM.

This tree which is almost identical with C. arborea, grows in the Northern Circars and at Moulmein. Its bark serves as cordage and is used as a slow match for guns.—*Dr. Wight, Colonel Frith, Dr. McClelland.*

CARRIMARRIDDI. TAM. ? A timber of Travancore, of dark colour, 1 to 4 feet in circumference ; used by wheel-wrights.—*Colonel Frith.* *See* CARREEMARADOO.

CARISSA CARANDAS.

Gotho in Ganjam and Gumsur.

Described by Captain Macdonald as of extreme height 20 feet, circumference 2½ feet, height from ground to the intersection of the first branch, 7 feet. But, useless except for firewood.

CARYOTA HORRIDA, *Gardn. ; Moon's Cat.*

Areca horrida, *Thwaites, Hooker.*
Katu kittul. SING.

A tree of Caracas, introduced into Ceylon, and into the Calcutta gardens.—*Voigt.*

CARYOTA URENS, *Linn.*

Ban khajur. BENG.	Shunda pana. MALEAL.
Ramguoah ? „	Nepera. SINGH.
Bon khejur. „	Kittul. „
Burra flawan ? „	Ootali panna. TAM.
Yels kae ? CAN.	Bherli-mahar. „
Bhyni. „	Cundal panai maram. TAM.
Mear ? „	Konda panna. „
Malabar Sago palm. ENG.	Evim-pannah. „
Ghat palm. „	Erim pannah. „
Bastard Sago palm. „	Chirugu. TEL.
Ram-guoah ? HIND.	Konda jiligu. „
Mare ? „	Jirugu. „
Bara flawan ? „	Marre. „
Berli. MAHR.	Salopa. URIA.
Nibong. MALAY.	

This very ornamental palm grows in Ceylon and Malabar, in Canara, Sunda, on the Godavery, in Ganjam, Gumsur, Assam, Sumatra, and Borneo. It grows to a height of forty feet with a ringed, tall and slender stem, of more than a foot in diameter. It is found on the sea-shore and ascends the mountains of Sikkim to the height of 5,000 feet. Its outer wood (outside the pith) is nearly as hard as flint, of which, like all the grasses and palms, it contains a considerable quantity. Where it grows in abundance, it is one of the most useful of trees. The root is hollowed for the buckets used in irrigation, and the trunk, when hollowed, by freeing it from the inner pith, forms a convenient and economical water conduit. In Ceylon, Sumatra and Borneo, it is used for rafters, reepers, window bars, posts, &c., but is little durable, rarely lasting above 3 or 4 years. Its pith or farinaceous part is filled with starch granules equal to the best sago, which are extracted by the people and made into bread or pottage. Its spathes yield a toddy or palm wine, *Koondel panai kallu*, TAM., and, during the hot season, a single tree will yield at the rate of a hundred pints in the 24 hours. This is used as an intoxicating liquor, as yeast in baking bread, is converted into the spirit called Bhyni Arrack, and into sugar or the jaggery called *Koondel panei vellum*, TAM. Its cabbage is preferred to that of the cocoanut. Its leaves are very large, measuring eighteen or twenty feet in length, and from ten to twelve across ; from their fibre, the "kittul fibre" of commerce, ropes of great strength, brushes, brooms, caps, and similar articles are manufactured ; the kernel is used for buttons and beads : the woolly material found on the petioles is used as oakum for caulking ships. In a recent account of the 'Vegetable Products of Ceylon,' by Mr. Ondatjee, it is said that the *black fibre* from the leaf-stalks, manufactured into rope, of great strength and durability, is used for tying wild elephants. The Rodyahs, a forest race among the Kandyans, make this rope generally with considerable skill, as it is both regular and compact. At the Madras Exhibition of 1855, the nar or fibre of this, the Indian Sago palm, was exhibited from Cocanada, Nellore, Masulipatam and Travancore. It is much used by the natives for making fishing lines and bow-strings, is very strong and resists water for some time, but is liable to snap if suddenly bent or knotted. It resembles black horse hair and might be employed similarly. In Borneo, the outer part is split into the form of lathes which are used as the rafters to which the roof covering and the open flooring are tied. These are two inches apart, but kept together by rattans, interwoven amongst them. Dr. Gibson says it is one of the most useful trees in the country, and he had heard that the farm of this tree, throughout the single district of Yellapore in Soopah, yielded Rs. 30,000 per annum.—*Drs. Wight, Gibson, Royle, Hooker, Marsden, Low and Ainslie, Mr. Mendis, Captain Macdonald, M. E. J. R., Seeman.*

CASEARIA, *Species.*

Peda-kal-mesura. TEL.

A large tree of the Godavery, leaves ovate, oblong, glabrous, serratulate, flowers 8 anthers, capsule 3 valved with 3 ridges on the outside of fruit. Wood of a light yellow colour, hard, does not warp, and is worthy of attention. Fruit used to poison fish.—*Captain Beddome.*

CASEARIA, *Species.*

Dr. Gibson says, a species of Casearia, not elliptica, may be seen growing at Darebae Wurgaum, on the horse road from Jooneer to Nuggur, and which he had not seen elsewhere. It is of a size fit for house building.—*Dr. Gibson.*

CASEARIA, *Species.*

Peda-kal-mesura. TEL.

A large tree, with ovate leaves of the Godavery forests, wood of a light yellow colour, hard and does not warp. It is worthy of attention. Fruit used to poison fish.—*Captain Macdonald.*

CASEARIA CAUZIALA, *Wall.*

Samyda cauziala, *Buch.*

Ana vinga. MALEAL.

A large tree growing in Assam and Bengal, very bitter. Its leaves are used in baths, and the pulp of its fruit as a diuretic.

CASEARIA ELLIPTICA.

Bhogara. MAHR. | Klaare maram. TAM.

This, in Coimbatore, is a large shrub rather than a tree. On the Bombay side, it occurs as a small tree, not uncommon near the Ghats but much less so elsewhere. The wood is smooth, fine grained and yellow coloured, but from its small size is unfit for timber purposes, and can only serve as an ornamental wood.—*Drs. Wight and Gibson.*

CASEARIA PENTANDRA.

Thabyaiywet-kya. BURM.

Found in the Pegu district, but, scarce. Timber strong and close-grained. Adapted for fancy work and cabinet making.—*Dr. McClelland.*

CASSIA, a genus of plants belonging to the natural order *Leguminosæ*. It consists of a large number of species, chiefly inhabiting the tropical or temperate parts of the world, and including among them the plants that produce the senna leaves so commonly employed as a purgative.

CASSIA, *Species.*

Ngoo-tha. BURM.

A tree of Moulmein, made into house posts, Fruit and bark used medicinally.—*Cal. Cat. Ex.* 1862.

CASSIA, *Species.*

Gnoo-gyee. BURM.

Common in the plains and on the hills of Pegu, wood used for bows, axles of carts, &c., &c. A cubic foot weighs 57 lbs. In a full grown tree on good soil the average length of the trunk to the first branch is 15 feet, and average girth measured at 6 feet from the ground is 4 feet.—*Dr. Brandis.*

CASSIA, *Species.*

Tanghani. URIA.

A tree of Gumsur and Ganjam; extreme height 40 feet, circumference 3 feet, height from ground to the intersection of the first branch 18 feet. Used in Ganjam for posts and rafters, and burnt for firewood. It is tolerably common in Bodogoda, but seems to be scarce in Gumsur. —*Captain Macdonald.*

CASSIA AURICULATA.

Turwer. HIND. | Avarai maram. TAM.
Mayharie. SANS. | Tanghedoo. TEL.
Talopodo. SANS.

Its wood is known as the Tangada wood, Tangada karra, *Tel.* and its bark as Avaraipattai, *Tam.* One of the commonest shrubs in the Madras Presidency, grows abundantly in the sterile tracts and, in all parts of the Deccan. The bark is used for tanning, and the stems to make native tooth-brushes; with the bark a soft and durable leather may be turned out. On the whole, it is perhaps the best of the indigenous astringents of Southern India for this purpose. All parts of the plant have much astringency, and seem to possess no other property.—*O'Shaughnessy, p.* 309, *Ainslie, M. E. J. R.*

CASSIA CINNAMOMUM.

Dawol kurundo. SINGH.

Under these names, Mr. Mendis describes a wood, used for common house building purposes. The tree grows in the central province of Ceylon A cubic foot weighs 39 lbs., and it is esteemed to last 20 years.—*Mr. Adrian Mendis.*

CASSIA FLORIDA.

May-za-lee. BURM.

Cultivated in British Burmah, heartwood almost black, used for helves, walking sticks, mallets, &c., &c. A cubic foot weighs lbs. 58.

In a full grown tree, on good soil, the average length of the trunk, to the first branch, is 15 feet and average girth, measured at 6 feet from the ground is 6 feet. Dr. Mason tells us that the Cassia florida in Tenasserim has wood "not inferior to ebony."—*Drs. Brandis and Mason.*

CASSIA SUMATRANA.

Mazalee. BURM.	Kyee. BURM. of Moulmein ?
Bombay Black wood. ENG.	Arremenc. SINGH.

This tree grows in the central province of Ceylon, where a cubic foot of its wood weighs 57 lbs., and it is said to last 50 years. It is there used for furniture and house building. It is plentiful throughout the Hlaine, Pegu and Tounghoo forests, and is very plentiful, especially on the Mazalee Choung, the name of which is derived from this tree. It affords a very strong wood like ebony.—*Dr. McClelland, Mr. Mendis.*

Under the names of Cassia Sumatrana ? Kyee BURM. ? there was sent to the Exhibition of 1862, specimens from a tree of Moulmein, of which the wood is said to be used in ordinary house building. (Are these two identical ?)—*Cal. Cat. Ex.* 1862.

CASTANEA INDICA.

Theet-khya. BURM.

Is a large tree, plentiful in the Rangoon, Pegu and Tounghoo districts. Wood red; equivalent to mahogany.—*Dr. McClelland.*

CASTANEA MARTABANICA.

Thit nya. BURM.	Zi-tha. BURM. ? of Tavoy.
Norne. „ of Tavoy.	

A tree of Moulmein and Tavoy. The fruit eaten exactly like chesnuts.—*Cal. Cat. Ex.* 1862.

CASTANOSPERMUM AUSTRALE.

Moreton Bay Chesnut. ENG.

This tree grows to a height of thirty or forty feet, and has been introduced into India from Australia.

CASUARIA POMANDRA.

Thabyaiywetkya. BURM.

This is found in the Pegu districts, but scarce. Timber strong and close-grained. Wood, white coloured, adapted for fancy work and cabinet making.—*McClelland.*

CASUARINA EQUISITIFOLIA.

Sarv (Cypress) ka jhar. DEKHANI.	Filaof of Mauritius.
Arroo tree of the Archipelago	Iron wood of the South Sea Islands.
Fir tree of the English.	Chouk maram. TAM.
Filaof of Madagascar.	Serva chettu. TEL.

This tree was introduced into India about the beginning of this century, and is now well established, growing freely and ripening seed in great abundance. In general appearance, it much resembles the Larch Fir,—it grows in 10 years to the height of about 30 feet. It generally grows very straight, and, where the main shoot is broken or lopped off, throws out secondary shoots readily which are usually straight and erect. It thrives best in sandy tracts along the sea shore, and it would be desirable to plant it largely on the sand hills, North and South of Madras where some numbers have already been grown. The wood is reddish in colour: in density and appearance it somewhat resembles Trincomallee. It bears a great strain, is well adapted for posts, and is said to bear submersion in water very well. The bark contains tannin, and a brown dye has lately been extracted from it by M. Jules L'Epine of Pondicherry. On the whole, this tree well deserves extensive cultivation on sandy tracts, where it grows so readily. It is a favourite avenue tree; and, kept stunted, forms a beautiful hedge. Much of the sandy coast of the eastern side of the Peninsula of India might be planted with it.—*M. E. J. R.*

CASUARINA MURICATA, *Roxb.*

Fir Tree of the English in India.	Beef wood.
Tinian Pine.	Club wood of Tahiti.
	Huri. HIND. ?

This is grown in all parts of the Dekhan, where it was introduced about 1830. It is a native of Chittagong, is the only species indigenous to the Tenasserim coast, and has been diffused over Bengal. In Tenasserim, it is found only in the loose sandy soil of the sea board and never inland. In general outline, it resembles the pine, but it is of a more slender figure, and more elegant in appearance. Dr. Mason tells us that, in Tenasserim, it is a remarkable tree, growing eighty feet high and spreading out without a leaf of covering; but its numerous fine knotted branchlets, mantled with brilliant green, and hanging in drooping bunches, or floating out lightly upon the breeze like long skeins of green silk, adorn it with the most graceful drapery and make it one of the most desirable trees for embellishing a Tenasserim park. It grows 60 to 80 feet high, with trunks 3½ feet in circumference four feet above the ground. The wood is very hard and durable, and the Tahitians in their war-days chose it for the manufacture of their ingeniously carved war-clubs; hence they termed it the club-wood. They also fashioned valuable fishing hooks from its roots. Dr. Mason further informs us that the Casuarina muricata or Beef-wood, is imported into the United States in considerable quantities, for various purposes where a hard heavy wood is required, and the Casuarina on the Tenasserim Coast can furnish almost any quantity of this timber, but it is very little used. Roxburgh says it resembles toon in appearance. The natives of Tenasserim call it by the same name as the pine.—*Drs. Roxb.*, (vol. iii, p. 59) *Riddell and Mason.*

CATHARTOCARPUS FISTULA, *Pers.*

Cassia fistula, *Linn.*
The tree and its product.

Bukbur. AR.	Dranguli. JAV.
Kyyar-chember ? „	Tung-guli. „
Banur lati-gach'h. BENG.	Its product Cassia pulpa. LAT.
Sondali. „	Bawa. MAHR.
Sonalu. „	Baya. „
Guoo-shwoay-ngu-bin. BURM.	Gurmala. „
Kukae. CAN.	Chuné. MALEAL.
Cakay. „	Mentus. „
Amultas. DUK.	Khyar-i-Chembir. PERS.
Pykassie. DUT.	Cassia purgante. PORT.
Pudding pipe tree. ENG.	Suvarnam. SANS.
Purging Cassia. „	Suvarnuka. „
Casse fistulense. FR.	Ahilla. SINGH.
Purgir cassie. GER.	Konné maram. TAM.
Gurmalla. GUZ.	Sarakonnué maram. „
Amltas. HIND.	Suvarnam. TEL.
Gurmalla. „	Réyla. „
Its product Polpa di cassia. IT.	Soonaree. URIA.

A tree from 20 to 40 feet high, met with all over Southern Asia, with a girth of 3 or 4 feet, and the height to the first branch 10 to 15 feet. It is uncommonly beautiful when in flower: few trees surpassing it in the elegance of its numerous, long, pendulous racemes of large, bright yellow flowers, intermixed with the young lively green foliage. It bears a striking resemblance to the laburnum. It varies in size, in different localities; in Coimbatore, being too small for useful timber, but in Malabar it attains sufficient size to be adapted for the spars of native vessels. The wood weighs lbs. 66 to the cubic foot, is close grained and of moderate strength; in Coimbatore, used for tom-toms. In Ganjam and Gumsur, where it is tolerably common, it is made into plough-shares and rice-pounders. It is common on the hills and plains of Pegu, where it is used for bows, axles of carts, &c. It has long cylindrical pods, from 9 inches to 2 feet in length, internally, divided into partitions, each with a flat seed, surrounded by a soft pulp. Two pounds weight of the fruit yield eight ounces of the concrete pulp: which forms an article of commerce. Its bark is used in tanning. The bark of the root is a strong purge. —*Drs. Wight, Gibson, Irvine, and Brandis, Mr. Rohde, Roxb.*, vol. ii., p. 333.

CATHARTOCARPUS JAVANICUS, *Pers.*

Cassia Javanica.
Horse cassia. ENG.

A native of Java and the Moluccas, with legumes above two feet in length, containing a black cathartic pulp used in India, as a horse medicine.—*Eng. Cyc.*

CATHARTOCARPUS NODOSUS, *Voigt.*

Cassia nodosa.
Knotted cassia. ENG.

Remarkable for its large pink coloured flowers. It is highly esteemed in Bengal, and is found in the Tavoy forests.—*Dr. Mason.*

CATHARTOCARPUS ROXBURGHII, *DC.*

Cathartocarpus marginatus, *G. Don.*
Cassia marginata, *Roxb. (not Willd.)*
Roxburgh's cassia. ENG.

A highly ornamental tree, in form much resembling the weeping ash. It is a native of Ceylon, and of the south of India, frequent in the jungle between Trichinopoly and Dindigul, and to be found in Indian gardens. The wood is hard and handsomely marked, and may hereafter prove a valuable addition to the timbers of India.—*Roxb.*, vol. ii., p. 338.

CAUTOVANGA, a dark coloured, very strong wood of Palghat, used for wheelwright's work.—*Col. Frith.*

CAWA-ARANG, a light brown or pale brown coloured wood of Penang, from a very large tree; used for furniture and ornamental work.

CEDAR.

Ceder. DUT.	Cedrus. LAT.
Cedre. FR.	Kedr. RUS.
Zeder. GER.	Cedro. SP.
Cedro. IT.	

A commercial term given to the woods of several distinct kinds of forest trees, the timbers of which are distinguished as Red and White Cedar; Barbadoes, and Bermuda cedar: Cedar of Lebanon, Pencil cedar, Bastard cedar, &c., some of them growing in America, some in Europe and some in Asia. The cedar of Lebanon so famous in Scripture, was, in ancient times, much employed in the construction of temples, and for other religious buildings and purposes. It is usually called Pinus cedrus, but sometimes Cedrus Libanus. The lofty Deodara, a native of the Himalayas, with fragrant and almost imperishable wood, and often called the Indian cedar, is sometimes referred to the genus Pinus, and sometimes to that of Cedrus or Larix, with the specific name of deodara. But, Dr. Hooker is of opinion that the Deodar and the cedar of Lebanon are identical. The woods of several of the Conifera are called cedars. But, in India, the term Bastard cedar, is applied to the Guazuma tomentosa, while, in New South Wales, the term white cedar is applied to Melia azaderach, and red cedar to that of Flindersia Australis, and the name is also given to the woods of the Cedrela toona and Chickrassia tabularis. In China, a kind of cedar, probably a cypress, called Nan Mah, or Southern Wood, which resists time and insects, is considered peculiarly valuable and is especially reserved for imperial use and buildings, and the cedar-wood of Japan, according to Thunberg, is a species of cypress. The cedar of Guiana is the wood of Icica altissima. The white wood or white cedar of Jamaica is Bignonia leucoxylon. The word "cedar," in the United States, is applied to various genera of the pine family. The red cedar (J. virginiana) is a juniper; the white cedar of the southern swamps is a cypress; the wood of Juniperus virginiana is called Red or Pencil cedar, that of J. Bermudiana is called Bermuda cedar, and, that of J. Barbadensis, is called Barbadoes cedar; while the Juniper of the North of Spain, and South of France, and of the Levant, is from J. oxycedrus. The White Cedar of North America, a less valuable wood than the Red Cedar, is yielded by Cupressus thyoides. Under the term Cedar, Col. Frith describes a reddish coloured wood of Palghat, specific gravity 0·507, as a large tree, wood aromatic and used for furniture. And under the name of Cedar-root, a very aromatic wood, used for ornamental furniture, in Palghat. These two are possibly from the Cedrela toona. The wood of the Cedar of Lebanon, as now met with, is not in much esteem, but that of the Cedrus deodara, of the Himalayas, really possesses all the good qualities for which those of Lebanon were praised. Specimens of the wood of the Indian cedar, Cedrus deodara, and of the cypress, "Cupressus torulosa," from the Himalayas, were shown by Dr. Royle at the Exhibition of 1851: the former has been introduced into England as a beautiful ornamental tree and appears to promise well as a useful timber tree, as the wood works well and freely.—*Faulkner, Dr. Hooker, Holtzappfel, McCulloch, Williams, Burton's City of the Salt Lake.* *See* CHICKRASSIA TABULARIS.

CEDRELA TOONA, *Roxb.*
C. hexandra, *Wall.*

Tunna. BENG.	Toona. HIND.
Thit-ka-do BURM.	Toon. MAHR.
Tundu. CAN.	Kooruk. „
Suola mara. „	Loodh ? SANS.
Toon tree. ENG.	Toon maram. TAM.
Bastard cedar. „	Wunjooli maram ? „
„ mahogany. ENG.	Maha limbo. URIA.

This large and valuable tree grows at the foot of the Himalayas and to the south, in Bengal and both Peninsulas of India, in varying abundance. It is said to be abundant in Travancore. A specimen of wood sent by General Cullen, as of this tree, showed the grain and polish remarkably well: it was however of a brighter colour, and apparently of a denser quality than any met with in the market, inducing a doubt as to its being of the same species. It was stated to be abundant, 25 miles North East of Trevandrum. It is found in the Mysore and Salem jungles in large quantities, also along the crest of the ghats from Tranvancore to Goa. In Coimbatore, it is a valuable timber tree of large size, and its reddish coloured wood is used for cabinet-making purposes. It or an allied species is known also in Coimbatore under the name of Wunjooli maram; but, as this is a very heavy and strong hard wood, said to be admirably fitted for pestles and mortars and other purposes demanding great strength, but not for cabinet purposes, Dr. Wight suspected Roxburgh's toona and the Wunjooli to be different trees. Dr Gibson reports that he had found this choice tree in one situation, viz., inland of Koorsulee; but adds, it probably exists all along close below the ghats; and, at another place, he says that it is not a common tree in our forests, but found in some of the greenwood jungles about the ghats, and also in the hill range abutting on the Rajpooree Creek to the south. The wood is a choice one for cabinet purposes, but is not used for any others, except for house beams, when it is procurable in sufficient quantity. In the races of the south Konkun and lower Canara the tree is more common. It is, in as far as he was aware, never found inland. And, again, he says it grows abundantly in some of the deep ravines in western Kandeish, and it grows in the ravines of the Concan. In Ganjam and Gumsur, where it is known as Mahalimbo, its extreme height is 70 feet, circumference 5 feet, and height from the ground to the intersection of the first branch, 22 feet. Under this tree's name, Captain Sankey describes a Nagpore timber as averaging 10 to 12 feet long and $3\frac{1}{2}$ to $4\frac{1}{2}$ feet in girth, and selling at 16 annas the cubic foot. At the Tambur river, in East Nepal, the vegetation in some spots is exceedingly fine, and several large trees occurred. Dr. Hooker measured a Toon tree *(Cedrela)* thirty feet in girth at five feet above the ground. Southwards, Lieut. Nuthall, as quoted by Captain Munro, mentions toon as one of the woods of Arracan, under the name of "thit-kado." A tree is found, also, Dr. Brandis tells us, on the hills and on the plains of British Burmah, plentiful in some districts and if not identical with the Toon of Bengal certainly nearly related to it. A cubic foot of the Burmah wood weighs lbs. 28. In a full grown tree on good soil the average length of the trunk to the first branch is 40 feet and average girth, measured at 6 feet from the ground, is 8 feet. It sells in Burmah at 8 annas per cubic foot. It will be seen from the above, that it has a wide range throughout India and takes its name from a beautiful wood, common in the northern provinces, where it is made into furniture of all kinds, and is much admired for its close grain and beautiful colour, resembling, though lighter than and not so close grained as, Mahogany, to which it is deemed equivalent. It is called Bastard Cedar from an aromatic resin, exuding from it, resembling that of the American Cedar. It is often sold in Madras under the general name of "Chittagong wood" and is the most valuable of the woods known by that commercial name. It has an erect trunk of great height and size, with smooth gray bark. The flowers are very numerous, small, white, and fragrant, like honey. The seeds are numerous, imbricated, winged. It seems probable that the trees known "commercially," as Toon are, at least, different species; but, the woods sold under this name, are red coloured, of varying hues. It is used all over India by cabinet makers for furniture. The Gumsur "*Mahalimbo*" wood, said to be this tree, and to be tolerably common, is described as not liable to be attacked by insects, and is, on that account, used for making boxes, &c. The fruit and bark are used medicinally for fever and rheumatism. The bark is powerfully astringent, but not bitter. The native physicians use it in conjunction with the powdered nut of the Cæsalpinia bonducella, an intense bitter. M. Nees Von Essenbeck has published an account of some experiments on the bark, which indicated the existence of a resinous astringent matter, a brown astringent gum, and a gummy brown extractive matter, resembling *ulmine*. The bark was used in Java by Blume in epidemic fevers, diarrhœa, and other complaints. Horsfield gave it in dysentery, but only in the last stage, when inflammatory symptoms had disappeared. Its flowers, in conjunction with safflower (Koosumba) are used by the inhabitants of Mysore, for dyeing the beautiful red colour called there Gul-i-nari.—*Drs. Wight, Hooker, Mason, Gibson, Cleghorn, M. E. J. R., Drs. Ainslie, O'Shaughnessy, and McClelland, Captain Macdonald, Captain Sankey.*

CEDRUS DEODARA.

Pinus deodara.
Larix deodara.

Deodar. ENG. | Indian Cedar. ENG.

The lofty deodara, a native of the Himalayas, has a fragrant and almost imperishable wood. Dr. Hooker is of opinion that it is identical with the cedar of Lebanon.

CELASTRINEÆ. Spindle trees. ENG.

The English name is derived from the use made of its very compact wood.—*John's Forest Trees of Britain, Vol. I., p. 34.*

CELASTRUS EMARGINATA, *Willde.*

This shrub, which grows on the Coromandel Coast, makes good fences and fuel.—*Voigt.*

CELASTRUS MONTANA, *Roxb.; W. & A.; W. Ic.*

Kangunee. MAHR. | Gaja Chinno. TEL.
Mal „ Kangunee „ | Gi-changi. „
Danti Chettu. TEL. | Pedda danti. „

A scrubby, crooked shrub, found on the Coromandel Coast and in barren hills, chiefly of the Deccan. The wood, hard and durable, is sought after as a choice dunnage for roof tiles, said to last for forty years,—a duration greatly exceeding that of any other dunnage material. —*Gibson, Voigt.*

CERBERA MANGHAS, *Linn.*

C. lactaria, *Buch.*
C. quaternifolia, *Roxb.*

Kulloon. BURM.

This tree grows in Pegu, Tenasserim, Tavoy, Penang, Singapore, Java, Moluccas and the adjacent islands in wet situations. The wood is said not to be used. Its fruit is used very extensively by the Burmese, to make an oil which they burn in their lamps and use to anoint their heads. The kernels are described as emetic and purgative. The leaves are said to be used in Java, as a substitute for senna, and the bark is said to possess similar properties.—*Voigt, Dr. Mason, Eng. Cyclop.*

CERESE. HIND? A reddish coloured, hard and close grained strong wood, found in the Santhal jungles from Sooree to Hasdihal, but scarce. Used by the natives for buildings, furniture, cart-wheels, &c. Suitable for the construction of timber bridges.—*Cal. Engineers' Journal, July 4, 1860, p. 155.*

CEYLON WOODS. The late Sir George Anderson sent to me, for the Madras Museum, the following specimens of the principal timber trees of Ceylon, collected by Mr. Adrian Mendis, Mohandiram of Moorrotto, and Master Carpenter, Royal Engineer's Department.

Acacia vera. Andere.
Adenanthera pavonina. Madetiye.
Agimea. ? obliqua Kebelle.
Almond. Cottamba.
Aniso phyllum zeylanicum. Welipiyanna. ? ? ?
Areca nut. Puwak.
Artocarpus, sps. Patta Del.
„ integrifolia. Cos. Jack.
Artocarpus pubescens. Del.
„ „ Aludel.
Bairiye.
Bassia longifolia. Mee.
Bauhinia tomentosa. Petan.
Bead tree. Common; Lunu Midelle.
Berrya ammonilla. Hal Milile.
Borassus flabelliformis. Tal. Palmira.
Butea frondosa. Calukeale.
Calophyllum acuminatum. Waldombe.
Calophyllum calaba. Gorrukeenee.
Calophyllum, Sweet scented; Dombe.
Calyptranthes cumini. Mahadan.
Calyptranthes, Clove-tree leaved. Battedombe.
Calyptranthes. Jambolana. Alubo.
Careya arborea. Kahatte.
Carullia zeylanica. Davette.
Caryota urens. Kittool. Nepera.
Cassia cinnamomum. Dawol kurendoo.
Cassia Sumatrana Arremene.
Choecarpus pungens. Hedde woke.
Chloroxylon. Satin. Burute.
Chloroxylon. Flowered Satin Mal burute.
Cicca distica. Nelly.
Cocatiye.
Cocos nucifera. Cocoanut.
Cratæva religiosa. Wea warene.
Cynometra, Branch flowered Hal mendora.
Cynometar, Branch flowered. Gal mendora.
Dalbergia lanceolaria. Nendoon.
Daminne.
Dillenia, Toothed. Gode parre.
Diospyros hirsuta Calamander. Calu Mediriye.
Dipterocarpus, Turbaned Horre.
Dipterocarpus, sp. Doon.
Dive parre.
Ebony. Caluvere.
Ebony, Bastard. Kadoembeiriye.
Echites, Lance leaved Kiri walla.
Echites scholaris. Book attene.
Embryopteris glutinifera. Timbery.
Eugenia laurina. Walboamboo.
Ficus Indica. Indian fig tree. Kiripelle.
Grewia paniculata. Hunukirille.
Hibiscus, Tilia leaved. Beligobel.
Illicebrum latrum. Nerreloo.
Iron wood. Naw.
Jonesia asoca. Dive ratembela.
Katie kale.
Lagerstrœmia regina. Murute.
Limonia citrifolia. Pamburoo.
Melia, sp. Hulanhick.
Millingtonia, sp. Ramenecidelle.
Michelia champa. Sappoo.
Mimosa. Sooriva mara.
Mimusops elengi. Moone mal.
Mimusops hexandra. Paloo.
Morre, Eye ball.
Murraya, Ash leaved Etteiriye.
Nauclea parviflora. Helembe.
Nebede.
Nephelium, sp. Gal morre.
Oak. Ceylon Koang.
Olax zeylanica. Melle.
Patkeale.
Penebarroo.
Persian. Sooriya.
Pterospermum ruberifolium. Velenge.
Rhizophora, sp. Hirikaddol.
Rhizophora. Leafy mangrove Cadol.
Rhus decipium. Pehimbive.

Rottleria, sp. Otte.	"Taikke Molmine. Maulmein Teak."
Sapota, sp. Lawoloo.	Ukbeiriye.
Spathodea. Long flowered Daanga.	Vateria Indica. Hal.
Sterculia fœtida. Telemboo.	Vitex trifoliata. Caha milile.
Suvande.	„ „ Meean „
Tamarindus Indicus. Siyembela.	Vitextrifoliata. Sappoomilile
Tectona grandis. Taikke ceylemey. Ceylon Teak.	Vitmannia trifoliata. Samedera.
"Taikke Cotchiye. Cochin Teak."	Walukeene.
	Webera cerifera. Tarrene.

In the above list, are several Botanical names evidently incorrect, in so far as they can possibly be timber trees; and others cannot be traced to other authority, but the woods sent with them, were all valuable and many of them very beautiful.—*Mr. Adrian Mendis.*

CHADACHEY. TAM? A small tree of Palghat, wood of a light brown colour, used for buildings and carts.—*Colonel Frith.*

CHAHOONG.? A tree of Akyab, grows to a moderate size, and is plentiful in Ramree and Sandoway districts. Used in house building. (Qu. Is this Chakoong—or the Cordia myxa?) —*Cal. Cat. Ex.* 1862.

CHAILE. HIND.? A tree of Chota Nagpore, furnishing a hard, white, grey timber.—*Cal. Cat. Ex.* 1862.

CHAKOLTI. HIND.? A light, pale yellow coloured wood, not strong. Plentiful in the Santhal jungles from Raneebahal to Nonihaut or over a distance of about thirty-five miles. Native furniture, tables, palkees, venetians and doors are made from this wood.—*Cal. Engineers' Journal, July* 1860.

CHANNEE. TAM? A tree of Travancore; wood of a brown colour, used for oil-mills, &c.—*Col. Frith.*

CHANNY MARAM. TAM? A tree of Travancore: wood of a brown colour, used for building common houses.—*Col. Frith.*

CHANNY VENGAH. TAM? Travancore; wood of a light yellow colour, one to six feet in circumference, used in house building.—*Colonel Frith,*

CHAMÆROPS, a genus of Asiatic palms, some species of which furnish useful products, but no timber.

CHAMÆROPS EXCELSA, a palm of Northern China, the brown fibre surrounding its trunk is employed for many domestic purposes, and for ropes and cables.—*Seeman.*

CHAMÆROPS RITCHIANA, *Griffiths.*

Maizurrye. PUSHTOO.
Pfees. SINDI.

Grows in masses on the barren hills and passes, below five thousand feet, leading up into the table land of Beloochistan and Affghanistan. Its leaf bud or cabbage is eaten. Its scurf with saltpetre, used as match for the matchlock. Its wood for fuel, and its leaves "*phurra*,' are fabricated into baskets, fans, brushes, sieves, sandals, pouches, platters, and ropes for waterwheels.—*Seeman.*

CHANGAL. HIND.? CHAMPAC. HIND.? A moderate sized tree of Akyab, not plentiful. Wood used for making boats.—*Cal. Cat. Ex.* 1862.

CHARCOAL.

Zugal. AR.	Kolsa. HIND.
Fahm-chobi. AR.??	Carbone de legna. IT.
Mi-thwa. BURM.	Carbonium. LAT.
Koela. DUK.	Carbo-ligni. „
Carbon also Charcoal. ENG.	Arang-bara. MALAY.
Wood charcoal. „	Zeghal-i-chobi. PERS.
Charbon. FR.	Lippe-anghoru. SINGH.
Charbon de bois. FR.	Carbon de lena. SP.
Kohlenstoff. GER.	Adapu carri. TAM.
Reine kohle. „	Karri. „
Ku-e-la. GUZ.	Bogu. TEL.
Koela. HIND.	Poibogulu. TEL.

In the south and east coast of Asia, where coal is found only in a few localities and the cost of carriage is great, charcoals are in great request, and attention to the modes of preparing them is of much consequence. In the peninsula of India, the common native mode is to set on fire a heap of small wood and, after allowing it to burn for some time, to quench it either by water or by heaping earth upon it; but charcoal so prepared is of little value in reducing iron ore, and the process is wasteful. In various parts of the country, there are slight differences in the mode of preparation, but all are faulty and objectionable in an economical point of view. It is therefore, of great importance to this country that more economical modes of preparing charcoal should come into general use, the destruction of firewood in the neighbourhood of iron works being grossly wasteful. Indeed, between the loss in preparing the charcoal and the loss of heat in preparing the iron, the consumption of the fuel is probably, at least, ten times as great as it ought to be, inducing great loss and in many cases rendering useless extensive beds of most valuable ore. Native iron smelters only employ fuel from one to three inches in diameter; and, to procure this, they take saplings, or the tops and branches of the largest hard wood trees, allowing the trunks to decay. For, large trees are not adapted for fuel for native smelting, as the cost of splitting them adds greatly to the expense; and, unless the logs are split, the inner wood is not carbonised. Charcoal, to be good, should be of wood burned with as little exposure to the action of the air as possible and be black, brittle, easily pulverised, perfectly insipid, solid, and inodorous. Charcoal is mostly used as a fuel, and in the manufacture of gunpowder. For the forge, the best is that prepared from bamboos and from stems of palmyra leaves (Tel. Tati komaloo). The Tamarind yields a good charcoal for the same purpose, as do most hard woods. But the charcoal of the Acacia sundra is said to be amongst the best for this purpose. For gunpowder, the root of the milk hedge, Euphorbia neriifolia, and of the Calotropis gigantea is preferred. At the Government Powder Mills, Madras, that of the gram bush, Dolichos uniflorus, and, in that of Bengal, the Cajanus indicus or pigeon pea, is used. Charcoal used for gunpowder manufacture is generally made from small shrubs or herbs as the Vitex and Cajanus, also from the mudar, Calotropis gigantea and Parkinsonia aculeata, the Parkinsonia being said to yield a very good charcoal for gunpowder, though the charcoal for gunpowder considered the best, is manufactured from the Sesbania Ægyptiaca. The gunpowder charcoal used at the Damoodah coal works is made from an *Acacia*: the Sikhs, employ *Justicia adhatoda*, which is also in use all over India: at Aden the Arabs prefer the *Calotropis*, probably, because it is most easily procured. The grain of all these plants is open, whereas, in England, closer-grained and more woody trees, especially willows, are preferred.

The best charcoal for a dentrifice, is that of the Betel-nut. Charcoal possesses remarkable antiseptic properties, as it resists the putrefaction of animal matter, and destroys the smell and colour of many substances.—*Mr. Faulkner, Mr. Rohde, Dr. Cleghorn, McCulloch's Dict., p.* 266, *Mr. Wall's Report in G. O.* 17*th July, No.* 1040 *of* 1859, *Hooker's Him. Jour. Vol.* 1, *page* 9.

CHARLOMBI, the Tamil name of a Ceylon tree which grows to about fifty feet high, and twenty inches in diameter. It is very close-grained and light, and resembles some kinds of mahogany. It is used in house-work, &c.; the fruit which it produces is of little value.—*Edye, Ceylon.*

CHAULMOOGRA ODORATA.

Taliennoe. BURM.	Fetarcura. HIND.
Chaolmugra. HIND.	

This is a native of Sylhet, but, there are a few trees about Rangoon, and it is also met with on the banks of streams in the Toungoo Forests, though it must be considered scarce. Its wood is adapted for fancy work and cabinet making. Its seeds are medicinal, being beaten up with ghee into a soft mass and applied three times a day, to cutaneous diseases. They yield 10 per cent. of oil by expression and it has been similarly used. The seeds have been recommended for tapeworm, and an ointment, prepared from the seeds, is a favorite application among native practitioners for the treatment of several cutaneous diseases, especially herpes and tinea.—*O'Shaughnessy, Beng. Phar. p.* 382, *Dr. McClelland, Honigberger.*

CHAURIOCHO. HIND? A tree of Chota Nagpore, yielding a hard wood.—*Cal. Cat. Ex.* 1862.

CHENA; in Ceylon, the destructive form of cultivation, known as Kumari, on the western coast of India, *see* Kumari.—*Dr. Cleghorn.*

CHEE NEB. BURM. STINKING WOOD. ENG. This wood, of maximum girth 4 cubits and maximum length 22½ feet, is abundant in Tavoy and Mergui. When seasoned, it sinks in water. The flowers of this wood have an intolerably fetid sickening smell, hence its name; it is used, by the Burmese, for boxes, tables, &c., and is long fibred tough wood when new, but rots so readily that, with a whole tree in Captain Dance's possession, he could not cut out a decent specimen.—*Captain Dance.*

CHENEBROON. A tree of Akyab used in house building. Grows to a large size, and is plentiful in the Ramree and Sandoway districts.—*Cal. Cat. Ex.* 1862.

CHENNAT NAIR, a forest near Palghat, which furnished a large supply of well grown Terminalia glabra, Pterocarpus marsupium, and Inga xylocarpa.

CHERRO CANNY. TAM.? A light brown coloured wood of Travancore, only used for firewood.—*Col. Frith.*

CHERRO NALAMPELLA. TAM.? A light brown coloured wood of Travancore, specific gravity 0·483, used for making canoes.—*Col. Frith.*

CHERROPOONA. TAM.? A dark coloured wood of Travancore, used for building houses.—*Col. Frith.*

CHEROTANNY. TAM.? A light colour of Travancore, used for firewood.

CHERROTIMBA. TAM.? A dark coloured wood of Travancore, specific gravity 0·843. About 3 feet in circumference, used for house building, tools, &c.—*Col. Frith.*

CHERRO VUNJEE. TAM.? A Travancore wood of a brown colour, specific gravity 0·644. Used for firewood.—*Col. Frith.*

CHERRY TREE of Norfolk Island. The bark of this tree is used for tanning, and it furnishes one of the most useful woods. It is decreasing rapidly by being stripped of its bark, and so left to perish.—*Keppel's Ind. Arch. Vol. II. p.* 282.

CHICACOLE. The sea face of the mountains, in this district, does not contain any tree vegetation which can be denominated timber.—*Dr. Cleghorn's Report.*

CHICKRASSIA TABULARIS, *Ad. Juss.*

Swietenia chickrassa, *Roxb.*

Chikrassi. BENG.	Cedar. ENG.
Yimma. BURM.	Deodar. „
Zimma. „	Pubha. MAHR.
Dul mara. CAN.	Pabba. „
Dal mara. „	Agle maram. TAM.
Bastard cedar. ENG.	Chittigong chettu. TEL.
Chittagong wood. „	„ karra. „

This tree occurs in the mountainous countries to the East of Bengal. It was discovered by Mr. Nimmo on the Toongur Hills, in 1838. It occurs also in Coimbatore, where, in common with one or two other light red coloured woods, it currently passes under the general name of cedar and bastard cedar, and all are extensively employed in cabinet making. This has quite a cedar-like smell. The wood is well known in Madras and easily procured, and is extensively used in cabinet making, coming under the denomination of "Chittagong wood," being imported from that province, though it is abundant in the mountainous parts of the Peninsula. It makes beautiful and light furniture, but is apt to warp during the season of hot land winds. According to Dr. Gibson, it is a fine straight-growing tree, rather common in the southern jungles of the Bombay Presidency, but much less so in the northern. Its wood could be creosoted easily. It is valuable for cabinet and house purposes, and is used in the Madras gun carriage manufactory to make plane tables and for furniture work. It furnishes one of the Deodars of Malabar. It is found, also, in Canara and Sunda, in the tall jungles near and on the Ghats, particularly at Gunesh Good. Wood, there, whiter, but tough and close grained; and, from its general situation, it is hardly known to the carpenter. Dr. Brandis tells us that, there is scattered throughout the forests on elevated ground, in British Burmah (large trees are scarce) a tree either identical with "Chittagong wood" or nearly related to it. A cubic foot of it weighs lbs. 24, and in a full grown tree on good soil, the average length of the trunk to the first branch is 80 feet and average girth measured at 6 feet from the ground is 8 feet. This wood was not known to Mr. Rohde as a product of the Northern Circars, but as imported there among the "Chittagong woods." Beautifully veined and mottled pieces, he says, are occasionally met with, but its complaints during the season of the hot winds and dry northerly winds of November and December, in the Northern Circars, render articles made of it, containing wide planks and framing, as armouries, very disagreeable bed-room companions. The Chittagongwood, he adds, is used at Madras for all purposes for which ordinary mahogany would be used in Britain, as furniture, panels of carriages, &c ; and one variety is sufficiently tough to be employed for felloes of wheels. Mr. Rohde concludes that all the wood imported under the name of "chittagong" is not the produce of the same tree, the only wood of the Circars at all resembling it is the "pinna ayeinpa" of Ganjam and northern parts of the Vizagapatam districts. Indeed, it would be difficult, so far as his recollection enables him to state, to distinguish one from the other, though he believes it to be from a species of neem, *Melia azaderachta*. These remarks will show that the wood of the Chickrassia tabularis, enters the market indiscriminately, as one of the cedars, bastard cedars, deodars, and Chittagong woods, and that several woods are known in the market under the name of Chittagong wood though seemingly all possessing a similarity of character which prevents them being distinguished, but allows of them all being used for one another—*Mr. Rohde, Drs. Gibson, Wight, Cleghorn, Brandis.*

CHINA RED WOOD. A Penang wood, of a red colour. Only used for furniture.

CHINJERITT. A Penang wood, of a brown colour, specific gravity 2·165. A small tree ; used for furniture.

CHIN ZOOAY. Burm ? Meaning Elephants-teeth. A wood of maximum girth 1½ to 2 cubits, maximum length 10 feet, abundant on the hills, inland, always on rocky barren hard ground, in mountainous or hill districts all over the Tenasserim provinces. When seasoned, sinks in water. This wood is believed by Captain Dance to be the hardest and strongest known in these latitudes, perhaps anywhere in the world. It is however only procurable in such rocky spots as no other tree will grow in, so must be sent for on purpose. It cuts up, as yendaik and other hard woods do, with huge cracks through it ; in fact this is the most wasteful of all known valuable timber in this respect and the original scantling is but small, so that it is not available for general purposes, but it is invaluable for the edges of Phillester planes, for spoke shaves, and for such purposes in which much scantling is not required.—*Captain Dance.*

CHINNY. Tam ? A Travancore wood, of a rather dark colour, specific gravity 0·515. From 8 to 16 feet in circumference ; used for building canoes.—*Col. Frith.*

CHITTA LINNY. Tam ? A Travancore wood, of a red colour, specific gravity 0·847, 1 to 1½ feet in circumference ; used for furniture.—*Col. Frith.*

CHITTAGONG. From this province, on the north eastern coast of the Bay of Bengal, only the names of a few woods have been obtained. Captain Marquart, sent five woods to the Exhibition of 1851, and the Calcutta Catalogue for the Exhibition of 1862, contains the names of 10 woods. Captain Marquart's woods are,

Acacia, *sp.*, koom koyre.
Conocarpus, *sp.*, buthna.
Diospyros melanoxylon.
Dipterocarpus, *sp.*, Sargotiah.
Swietenia chickrassa.

The list for the 1862 Exhibition is,—

Chaplasha,	Jarool,
Chickrassi,	Kandeb,
Chuckwa,	Loehah,
Gamar,	Tazeboil,
Gout gootia,	Toon.

See Burmah, Akyab and Assam.

CHIURACY. ? A Penang wood, of a brown colour, specific gravity 1·081. Used for beams; does not work kindly.

CHLORIDE OF ZINC. Captain Keppell believes Sir William Barnett's solution of chloride of zinc, properly applied, the only composition yet known that will preserve anything from the white ants.—*Keppel's Ind. Arch., Vol. II., p.* 189.

CHLOROXYLON SWIETENIA, *Roxb.; W. & A.; D C.*

Swietenia chloroxylon, *Roxb.*

Satin wood. ENG.	Porasham. TAM.
Dhoura. HIND.	Kodawah porasham. TAM.
Halda. MAHR.	Billuda. TEL.
Mal burute or flowered satin	Billu chettu. TEL.
Burute. SINGH.	Bilugu? URIA.
Mududa. TAM.	Bhayroo. „
Vum-maai. „	

The Satin wood tree grows in Ceylon, in the northern and southern but chiefly in the eastern districts, where it attains a large size and is esteemed next to Calamander in value. It grows in Coimbatore, in the Anamallai hills, where, latterly, Dr. Wight got planks 15 inches broad. Indeed, some of the finest Satinwood to be any where seen is to be met with near the foot of the Anamallais; though, even there, this valuable wood is rapidly disappearing, under the cultivator's axe. Dr. Gibson, writing from the Bombay Presidency, says he had never seen it reach beyond the size of a small tree, which, when straight (seldom the case), would afford a log squaring three inches. It is a rare tree, also, being, in so far as he had seen, found only in the Padshapoor jungles, and in those of the upper Mool, in the Ahmednuggur Collectorate. In the coast forests, he had never seen it. Dr. Cleghorn, in the M. E. J. Reports, says the tree grows abundantly in the mountainous districts of the Madras Presidency, but seldom attains a large size, though occasionally planks of 10 to 15 inches in breadth may be procured. In Ganjam and Gumsur, its extreme height is 40 feet, circumference 3 feet and height from the ground to the intersection of the first branch, 20 feet. The tree is not so common in Gumsur as in Bodo godo, and it is said to be still more plentiful in Mohery and other talooks to the South. The Billu Karra of the Circars, says Mr. Rohde, is a most serviceable hard wood well suited for naves of wheels and, were it procurable in any quantity, for all frame work requiring strength and durability. The Peradenia bridge, a single arch of 205 feet on the road to Kandy, was designed and principally executed in this wood. The wood is very close grained, hard and durable, of a light orange colour, takes a fine polish, and is suited for all kinds of ornamental purposes, but is somewhat apt to split. For picture frames, it is nearly equal to American maple. The timber bears submersion well, in some instances it is beautifully feathered. The flowered or feathered satin wood when first polished is one of the most beautiful woods in the world. Mr. Rohde has seen specimens surpassingly beautiful, but, the logs are not distinguishable from ordinary satin wood till sawn, and twenty or forty may be cut without one of any beauty being found—the feathered satin wood seems very liable to sever when dry and old: articles of satin wood get darker and lose much of their beauty by age, unless protracted by a coat of fine varnish. A cubic foot weighs 55 to 57 lbs. It is used for axletrees, oil presses, posts, bed posts, rafters and the handles of axes and, in the Madras Gun Carriage manufactory, for naves of wheels; also, for fuses. The leaves are applied to wounds. The wood is heavy and strong, and reckoned very excellent for pieces of agricultural implements. Latterly it has been much employed as fuses, in Madras. Dr. Gibson had not seen it used in cabinet work in the Bombay territory.—*Drs. Gibson, Wight, Cleghorn, Mr. Rohde, Mr. Mendis.*

CHOCHENA. URIA.? A tree of Ganjam and Gumsur. Extreme height 60 feet, circumference 5 feet and height from ground to the intersection of the first branch, 9 feet. Chiefly used for firewood, the tree being tolerably common. The bark is used medicinally in fever. The milk is given medicinally to children in a disease, there called "Doobellee."—*Captain Macdonald.*

CHOECARPUS PUNGENS. ? ? ?

Hedde woke. SINGH.

Under these names, is mentioned a tree of the Western province of Ceylon. Its wood weighs lbs. 58 to the square foot and lasts 50 years. It is used for common house building purposes.—*Mendis.*

CHOCHHI. HIND? A tree of Chota Nagpore, yielding a hard, red grey timber.—*Cal. Cat. Ex.* 1862.

CHOMONDRI, or Chalembry, the Tamil name of a Ceylon tree, the wood of which is of a very dark colour, and durable. It grows to between twelve and twenty inches in diameter, and twenty feet in height. It is used by the native carpenters for general purposes. It produces a fruit which is used as medicine. (Qu. is this the Calamander wood, the Singhalese Kalu Medirye?)—*Edye, Ceylon.*

CHOONOKOLEE. URIA.? A tree of Ganjam and Gumsur. Extreme height 10 feet, circumference 1 foot and height from ground to the intersection of the first branch, 5 feet: said to be a common useless tree. The fruit is eaten.—*Captain Macdonald.*

CHORAYEGODEE. URIA.? A tree of Ganjam and Gumsur. Extreme height 22 feet, circumference 1½ feet and height from the ground to the intersection of the first branch, 6 feet. Used for firewood.—*Captain Macdonald.*

CHOROCADAMBOO. ? TAM. A Travancore wood, of a yellow colour, specific gravity 0·529, used for packing cases.

CHOUREEONA. URIA.? A tree of Ganjam and Gumsur, extreme height 30 feet, circumference 3 feet, height from the ground to the intersection of the first branch, 8 feet. Tolerably common and burnt for firewood. The bark is used medicinally for rheumatism. The flowers are worn.—*Captain Macdonald.*

CHRYSOPHYLLUM ACUMINATUM.

Hali mara. CAN.	Tursee phul. MAHR.
Star apple. ENG.	Tarsee ,,
Pita-kara. HIND.	

This tree, one of the Sapotaceæ, grows to a large size, 30 feet or more. In Canara and Sunda, it is very common in the jungles near the ghats above, particularly to the south, and reaches a great height. Dr. Gibson heard of it as existing in some of the ghat jungles of the Southern Konkun, but had never seen it except in the Upper Canara and Sunda forests, where it is rather common. There are some trees in the Residency garden, at Hyderabad. The wood seems straight and good, but the tree is chiefly noticeable from the Gutta Percha-like incrustation common on the fruit. Fruit, about the size of a large crab-apple, ripens in October, and is edible.—*Dr. Gibson, Dr. Riddell.*

CINCHONA. A South American genus, species of which, C. Succiruba and C. Calisaya, have been introduced into India, since the beginning of 1861. The sites selected have been near Ootacamund and Neddiwattam on the Neilgherry hills, at an elevation of 5,400 feet and C. Lucumœfolia and C. Pahudiana, to the number of 500,000 plants, had previously been planted by the Dutch in Java. The following are the species and their numbers, planted, on the Neilgherries.

Botanical Names.	Commercial Names.	No. of Plants.	Value in the London market per lb. of dry Bark. (s. d. s. d.)
1. Cinchona Succirubra	Red bark	14,450	2 0 8 9
2. ,, Calisaya	Yellow bark	237	2 10 to 7 0
3. ,, Condaminea var. Uritusinga	Original Loxa bark	1	2 10 to 7 0
4. ,, ,, var. Chahuarguera	Rusty crown bark	8,000	2 10 to 7 0
5. ,, ,, var. Crespilla	Fine crown bark	105	2 10 to 6 0
6. ,, Lancifolia from Java	Crown bark	1	1 8 to 2 10
7. ,, Nitida	Genuine grey bark	2,922	1 8 to 2 9
8. ,, Species without name	Fine grey bark	1,211	1 8 to 2 10
9. ,, Micrantha	Grey bark	3,780	1 8 to 2 9
10. ,, Peruviana	Finest grey bark	357	1 8 to 2 10
11. ,, Pahudiana from Java	Unknown	425	Worthless.
	Total No. of plants	31,402	

CINNAMOMUM AROMATICUM, *Nees v. Esen.*

Cinnamomum cassia, *Blume.*
Laurus cassia, *Nees t.* 3.
,, cinnamomum, *Andrew's Report.*

A tree of considerable size, is said to grow in the dry sandy districts lying N. W. of the town of Fai-foe, between *Lat.* 15 and 16 N. It is said to produce the cinnamon of China and Cochin-China, as also cassia bark and the aromatic fruits called Cassia buds.

CINNAMOMUM CULILAWAN, *Nees.*

Laurus culilawan, *Roxb.*
,, caryophyllus, *Lour.*
Cortex caryophylloides, *Rumph.*

A native of Amboyna, especially in Leitimoo near the villages of Saya Rutton and Ema. Its pungent astringent bark is used medicinally.

CINNAMOMUM INERS, *Nees.*

Ran dal-chini. MAHR.	Pooli pilla. TAM.
Sembela. TAM.	

The tree is found in the Bombay Ghat forests, chiefly to the south. It grows in the forests of the western coast of the peninsula of India, and in the Coimbatore district. Dr. Gibson says, the wood is rather strong, but is little used in house building, or for implements. Dr. Wight says, it is a tall tree in Coimbatore, rather slender in proportion to its height; the wood is fine, even grained and supposed very good, but apparently has never been used by the carpenters there, as none of them are acquainted with it.—*Drs. Gibson and Wight.*

CINNAMOMUM EUCALYPTOIDES, *Nees.*

Laurus malabarathrica, *Sol. & Roxb. Hort. Cal.*

CINNAMOMUM JAVANICUM, is a tree with a trunk 20 feet to 30 feet high, growing in Java and Borneo. The bark is a deep cinnamon-brown colour, and deserves attention on account of its powerful antispasmodic properties.—*Eng. Cyc. page* 1089.

CINNAMOMUM LOUREIRII, grows on the lofty mountains of Cochin China, to the west towards Laos, Japan. The flowers of Cassia are produced by this species.—*Eng. Cyc. page* 1089.

CINNAMOMUM RUBRUM, grows in Cochin China, and contains an essential oil.—*Eng. Cyc. page* 1089.

CINNAMOMUM SINTOC, grows on the Neilgherry mountains, in Hindustan, and the higher mountains of Java. It is a tree 80 feet high. The bark is bitter and dry.—*Eng. Cyc. page* 1089.

CINNAMOMUM TAMALA, is a native of India, wild in Derwanee and Gongachora, cultivated in the gardens of Rungpoor. The taste of the leaves when dried is aromatic; they are sold in the shops under the name of folia Malabathri Tamalapathri or Indica of India.—*Eng. Cyc. page* 1089.

CINNAMOMUM XANTHONEURON, is a tree growing on the Papuan Islands and the Moluccas. The bark has great fragrance when fresh, but loses this quality in time.—*Eng. Cyc. page* 1089.

CINNAMOMUM ZEYLANICUM, *Nees.* Laurus Cinnamomum. Cinnamon tree.

Its product

Darsini. ARAB.	Cinnamomum. LAT.
Kurundu. CYNG.	Cauella. „
Kancel. DUT.	Kaimanis. MALAY.
Cinnamon. ENG.	Dalchenee. PERS.
Cannelle. FR.	Canella. PORT.
Zimmet, Kanchl. GER.	Canela. SP.
Κιναμον. GR.	Carruwa puttay. TAM.
Tuj. GUZ.	Sanalinga putta. TEL.
Dalcheence. HIND.	Darasita. SANS.
Canella. IT.	

Cinnamon is the bark of Cinnamomum Zeylanicum, *Nees von Esenbeck, (Laurus Cinnamomum,* Linn.), and *True Cinnamon* of the shops. Cinnamon is the *Kinnemon* of Exod. xxx. 23, (see Bible. Cycl. ii. p. 210), and the *κινυμάωμον* of Herodotus, a name which he states the Greeks learned from the Phœnicians. The name seems derived from the Cingalese. This is a native of Ceylon and Java, and is cultivated in various parts of the world. Trunk 15 to 20 feet high, by 1½ feet in diameter. This is the source of the true cinnamon, and indeed nearly all parts of the tree are of value and importance. In addition to the aromatic oil contained in its bark, the root of the cinnamon tree yields camphor; the liber, oil of cinnamon; the leaves, oil of cloves; and the fruit a peculiar terebintaceous ethereal oil. When the branches are peeled, the finest sticks of Cinnamon are said to be obtained from the liber of the middle sized branches, an inferior sort from the youngest shoots, and that which is produced by the thickest branches, is considered of very little value.—*Royle, McCulloch's Dict. p.* 277.

CIRCAR WOODS: Northern Circars and Godavery.

The forests on the Godavery and on the mountainous tracts which run parallel with the coast in the north-eastern parts of the peninsula, furnish a great variety of useful timbers and fancy woods, of which perhaps only a small portion have been determined and made known. The following lists from the Reports of the London Exhibition of 1851, of 31 woods, and from that of Madras of 1857, of 108 woods, enumerate many of value, the larger list, being from Captain Beddome. This tract of country was well examined, in the close of the last, and beginning of the present century, by Dr. Roxburgh, whose valuable Coromandel plants were published in 1797 by the East India Company.

Woods sent to the Exhibition of 1851.

Odina wodier, Goompana wood. Goompana kurra.
Ganara wood. Ganara kurra.
Feronia elephantum, Wood-apple wood; Valaga kurra, Koweet, Vella maram.
Pentaptera tomentosa, Nulla muddi wood, Nulla muddi kurra: Caroomaroodum.
Pentaptera glabra, Tella muddi wood, Tella muddi kurra Vel maroodum maram.
Cassia auriculata, Tangada wood, Tangadu kurra, Auvarai maram.
Paya wood. Paya kurra.
Annen wood, Annen kurra.
Morinda citrifolia, Togara wood. Togara kurra.
Red dye wood, Vizianagrum Zemindary.
Bombax Malabaricum or *heptaphyllum,* Boorooga wood, Buruga kurra.
Strychnos potatorum, Induga wood, Induga kurra.
Thse than maram.
Cordia myxa, Muckaroo wood, Mukkera kurra.
Tobica wood, Tobica kurra
Tella oolemara wood. Telloo oolemara kurra.
Diospyros chloroxylon, Nulla Ulemara wood Nulla-Uloomara kurra.
Mimosa cinerea. Vulture wood, Vulture kurra.
Ficus racemosa, Bodda wood, Bodda kurra.
Voodaga wood.
Pterospermum Heynei, Lolooga wood Lolooga kurra
Thespesia populnea, Gungarane wood, Gungarane kurra. Poovarasa murum.
Æschynomene grandiflora Aguste wood.
Erythrina Indica, Bandita wood, Bandita kurra.
Sapindus emarginatus Soapnut, or Koonkoodoo wood, Koonkoodoo kurra.
Camooga wood. Kumoogamuram.
Doduga wood.
Cumba wood, Cumba kurra.
Gmelina.?
Goomoodoo wood, Goomoodoo kurra.
Unkoodoo wood, Unkoodoo kurra.
Undooroo wood, Undooroo kurra. Briedelia.?
Iscarasee wood, Iscarasee kurra.
Gantha wood, Gantha kurra.

Timber trees of the Godavery and of the Circars, between Bhadrachellum and Condapilly by Lieutenant (now Captain) Beddome.

Acacia Arabica.
Acacia elata.
Acacia ferruginea.
Acacia kalkora.
Acacia leucophlœa.
Acacia odoratissima.
Acacia speciosa.
Acacia suma.
Acacia sundra.
Ailanthus excelsa.
Alangium decapetalum.
Anogeissus acuminatus.
Anogeissus latifolius.
Azadirachta Indica.
Ægle marmelos.
Bassia latifolia.
Bauhinia, sp.
Bignonia chelonoides.
Bignonia suaveolens.
Bignonia xylocarpa.
Briedelia spinosa.
Canthium didymum.
Canthium parviflorum.
Cappparis grandis.
Caryota urens.
Casearia, sp.
Chloroxylon Swietenia.
Cluytia collina.
Cordia angustifolia.
Cordia myxa.
Cordia, new species.
Cordia polygama.
Crataeva Roxburghii.
Dalbergia frondosa.
Dalbergia latifolia.
Dalbergia Oojeinensis.
Dalbergia paniculata.
Dillenia pentagyna.
Dillenia speciosa.
Diospyros chloroxylon.
Diospyros melanoxylon.
Diospyros, sp.
Diospyros, sp., D. Syhrtica.??
Emblica officinalis.
Ehretia lœvis.
Eriochlena Hookeriana.
Euphorbia tirucalli.
Flacourtia sapida.
Ficus Indica.
Gardenia gummifera.
Gardenia latifolia.
Gardenia lucida.
Gardenia, sp.
Givotia Rottleriformis.
Gmelina arborea.
Grewia Rothii.
Grewia tiliæfolia.
Guatteria cerasoides.
Gyrocarpus Jacquini.
Hardwickia binata.
Hymenodyction, sp.
Inga xylocarpa.
Ixora parviflora.
Lagerstrœmia parviflora.
Limonia acidissima.
Maba buxifolia.
Mangifera Indica.
Mimusops hexandra.
Morinda exserta.
Nauclea cordifolia.
Nauclea parviflora.
Nycthanthes arbor tristis.
Pavetta tomentosa.
Pongamia glabra.
Premna tomentosa.
Prosopis spicigera.
Pterospermum Heynei.
Pterocarpus marsupium.

Pterocarpus santalinus.
Randia. sp.
Sapindus emarginatus.
Schleichera trijuga.
Schrebera Swietenoides.
Sclerostylis atalantioides.
Shorea robusta.
Soymida febrifuga.
Spathodea Roxburghii.
Spathodea Rheedii, (Bignonia spathacea, Roxburgh.)
Sponia, sp.
Sterculia colorata.
Sterculia urens.
Strychnos nux vomica.
Strychnos potatorum.
Stylocoryne Webra.
Syzygium jambolanum.
Tamarindus Indica.
Tectona grandis.
Terminalia catappa.
Terminalia chebula.
Terminalia glabra.
Terminalia tomentosa.
Uvaria tomentosa.
Vitex arborea.
Wrightia tomentosa.
Wrightia tinctoria.
Ximenia Americana.
Zyziphus jujuba.

CITRUS AURANTIUM, *Linn.*
C. nobilis, *Lour.*

Naranj. ARAB.
Narang. „
Kumla-nebu. BENG.
Lieng-mau. BURM.
Orangen. DUK.
Orange tree. ENG.
Common orange. „
Sweet orange. „
Oranges. FR.
Pomeranzen. GER.
Naringi. HIND.
Melarance. IT.
Jerooc. MALAY.
Simao-manis. MALAY.
Naranj. PERS.
Pomeranezu. RUS.
Nagranga. SANS.
Naranjas. SP.
Naranja. SPAN.
Kolinji maram. TAM.
Kitchili „ „
Kichidi. TEL.

The well known orange tree has a hard wood, but is not available of any size, and seldom of any quantity. The orange is not mentioned, either by the ancients or by the Arab authors, and is supposed to have been introduced into Europe after the middle ages. Dr. Royle states, that the orange and lemon are natives of India, the orange being found on the Neilgherries, on the borders of the Sal forests of Sylhet and, perhaps, also in China. Mr. W. Elliot states that a very small variety of the orange ("Ida chettu, TEL." "Chota kichili, HIND;" Kiri kittali, CAN;" which is the C. variatro of Heyne, 57 Musk orange) grows both cultivated and wild in all the hilly country of the Circars; and, he asks, if it be the original of the cultivated Citrus aurantium.—*Voigt, Mr. Elliot, Royle.*

CITRUS BERGAMIA, *Risso & Poit.* The Lime.
„ DECUMANA, *R. Linn.* The Shaddock or Pumplemose.
„ LIMONUM, *Risso & Poit.* The Lemon.
„ MEDICA, *Linn.* The Citron.

These are small trees producing hard close grained wood, all natives of India.

CITRUS MEDICA ? ? ?
Ambele Toba. URIA.

Under these names, Captain Macdonald describes a tree of Ganjam and Gumsur. Extreme height 30 feet. Circumference 1 foot. Height from the ground to the intersection of the first branch, 6 feet. Wood useless except for firewood. The bark is used medicinally for colic and diseases of the stomach. The fruit is pickled. The tree is not common.

CLUYTIA COLLINA, *Roxb.*

Woadugu maram. TAM.
Wodisha. TEL.
Kadishen. „
Vodisa. TEL.
Kurscea. „
Kursee. „

A small tree, frequent in the Walliar jungles of Coimbatore, not found by Dr. Gibson, on the Bombay side. Flowers in hot season, seeds ripen in December and January. Bark or outer crust of capsule said to be exceedingly poisonous. Wood red coloured, exceedingly hard and durable but of small size. Notwithstanding its hardness, being very even grained, it is easily worked and is, from its fine close grain, a pretty wood.—*Mr. Rohde's MSS. Dr. Wight, O'Shaughnessy, p.* 552.

CLUYTIA PATULA, *Roxb.*

Pala ? TAM. | Jegura. TEL.

A tree of Southern India, furnishing a very fine close grained heavy chocolate coloured wood. It grows to a large size, and logs measuring 4 to 5 feet in girth, are purchased in the market. The wood is hard, very brittle, of specific gravity 75·8, and, when broken, the fracture seldom shows any fibre. It is used for rulers, knobs, handles for tools, such as chisels, &c., and in turning. Mr. Rohde says, it is a much larger tree than C. collina a native of moist valleys amongst the Circar mountains. It flowers during the hot season. Roxburgh says, the wood of this tree is of the colour of dried rose leaves, also hard and durable.—*Mr. Rohde's MSS., Voigt.*

CLUYTIA SPINOSA ? ? ?
Korada. URIA.

A tree of Ganjam and Gumsur, extreme height 30 feet, circumference 3 feet and height from ground to the intersection of the first branch, 8 feet. A light wood, used for rafters, spinning wheels and door frames. It is also burnt for fire wood, the tree being very common. The leaf is used medicinally for itch. The bark of this tree is poisonous and a preparation of it is often used for the purpose of destroying life, particularly by Oriya widows among whom suicide is a frequent occurrence.—*Captain Macdonald.*

COCHLOSPERMUM GOSSYPIUM. *DC. W. & A.*
Bombax gossypium. *Linn., Roxb.*

Chima-punji. MALEAL.
Tanaku. TAM.
Konda gogu. TEL.

This tree grows in Travancore, on the Coromandel coast and at Hurdwar. It yields the katira, which in the N. W. Provinces of India is substituted for Tragacanth; wood soft, and only used as firewood.—*Voigt.*

COCOS NUCIFERA, *Linn.*
Palma indica major, *Rumph.*
Calappas, *Rumph.*
Cocoa-nut palm tree.

Narikel. BENG.
Kinghena. CAN.
Coconnut tree. ENG.
Narel-ka jhar. HIND.
Kalapa. JAV.
Cocas nucifera. LAT.
Kalapa. MALEAL.
Klapa. „
Kalambir. „
Nur. MALEAL.
Nari-kera. SANS.
Nali „ „
Tenna maram. TAM.
Tenkaia chettu. TEL.
Erra bondala kobbari chettu. TIB.
Kobbari chettu. TIB.
Gujju narikedam. „

The nut.

Jouz-i-hindi. ARAB.	Nur. MALAY.
Naril. "	Calapa. "
Narel. DUK.	Kalambir. "
Kokosnuten. DUT.	Tangha? "
Cocos. FR.	Jouz-i-hind. PERS.
Kokonusse. GER.	Nargil. "
Narul. GUZ.	Kokos. RUS.
Naril. "	Narikela. SANS.
Narul. HIND.	Narikayla. "
Naril. "	Cocos. SP.
Cocchi. IT.	Tengai. TAM.
	Tenkaia. TEL.

The palm wine.

Nargilli. AR.	Tennam kallu. TAM.
Narilli. DUK.	Tenkaia " TEL.
Cocoanut toddy. ENG.	

Its cabbage.

Naril ka krute. DUK.	Tennam kurtu. TAM.
Cocoanut cabbage. ENG.	Tenkaia gurtu. TEL.

Its sugar or jaggery.

Naril ka gur. DUK.	Tennam vellam. TAM.
Jaggery of cocoanut toddy. ENG.	Tenkaia bellam. TEL.

Its oil.

Cobri. CAN.	Kalapa minak. MALAY.
Naril ka tel. DUK.	Narikaylum. SANS.
Cocoanut oil. ENG.	Tengai yenne. TAM.
Nur minak. MALAY.	Tenkaia nuna. TEL.

Its water or albumen.

Yel nir ka pani. DUK.	Yella-nir. TAM.
Cocoanut water. ENG.	Yella-niru. TEL.

Its fibre.

Coir. HIND.	Tenkaia nara. TEL.
Tennam nar. TAM.	

The cocoanut palm does not seem to have been known to the ancients, though it is indigenous in the East, from which they received Ambassadors. It grows in great abundance in the Maldive and Laccadive islands: on the Malabar Coast, in Ceylon: on the Eastern side of the Bay of Bengal, whence it ascends both the Burrampooter and Ganges rivers to a considerable distance. It grows in most of the islands of the Eastern Archipelago, from the Sunda Islands to Molucca, and in those of the Pacific Ocean, and is now cultivated in various tropical parts of the New World. It is self propagating. Its keel shaped nut, protected from the salt water by its tough and thick, though light covering, sails on the ocean to barren spots where it germinates and causes even the smallest islets to become covered with clumps of the cocoanut palm. The cylindrical stems, with a diameter of about two feet, attain an elevation of from sixty to one hundred feet. They are surmounted by numerous wavy leaves, called fronds, by botanists, and their foot stalks are often called branches, by travellers. The leaves are gigantic in size—being about 20 feet in length, with a strong tough stalk, which forms the midrip, and has a number of narrow and long leaflets ranged along the two sides. This tree thrives best on the sea coast, and its wood is used for reepers, for which purpose it is, however, inferior to the palmyra, though, in Ceylon, and on the Western Coast hard and durable rafters are procurable. It furnishes a strong and durable wood, a cubic foot weighs 70 lbs., and its timber is esteemed to last for 20 to 50 years. It is used for ridge poles, for temporary roofs, aqueducts, &c. for small boats, for the beams, posts and rafters of houses, for spear handles, paling, and walking sticks: for fancy boxes, and furniture; for boat's frames, bridges, ramparts, water butts, conduits, gutturs and drums, it forms one of the porcupine woods of commerce and is used for fancy articles: and, a farinaceous substance is contained in the stem which forms a good substitute for sago. Each tree produces annually from 50 to 60 cocoanuts. These are enclosed in a thick fibrous husk from which the coir of commerce is obtained by maceration and beating. The husk is employed as a scrubbing brush and polishing brush, it is converted into cordage of various kinds, employed for the rigging of ships, fishing nets, matting, and brushes; and, in India, in its loose state, it is the usual material with which mattresses, pillows and sofas are stuffed. Within the fibrous husk, is the shell, which is very brittle, though its structure is somewhat fibrous. Cut in various ways, it is formed into cups and drinking vessels, into pitchers, funnels, and lamps. It is susceptible of a high polish, and admits of being turned in an agreeable manner. Those shells which are tolerably circular are used for the bodies of cups and vases, the feet and covers being made of wood and ivory. Common buttons are also made of the cocoanut shell, and are considered better than those of horn as they do not, like that material, absorb the moisture which causes horn buttons to swell and burst. The shell forms a valuable charcoal. In its young and green state, the cocoanut contains a clear albuminous fluid, with a sweetish taste and a slight degree of astringency which makes it a very agreeable refreshing beverage, and it is also used by house plasterers as an ingredient in their white washes made of pure lime. But, as the nut advances to its full maturity, the fluid disappears and the hollow is filled by the almond like dried albumen which is the germinating organ. This pulp or kernel, when young, can be easily removed by a spoon: when cut in pieces and dried in the sun, this is called copra, which forms an extensive article of commerce throughout the South and East of Asia. It is used grated in curries throughout the East, or its milk is expressed from it; and, from copra, a valuable oil is expressed, which is employed in annointing the body, is used in lamps, is largely converted into the stearine candles of England, and forms an invaluable substitute for cod liver oil. The refuse oil cake "Poonac" forms an excellent manure. The white and solid albumen is often cut into ornaments of flowers and fruits, meant to represent the garlands given to visitors of distinction. They are worn by Tanjore ladies at particular festivals. The very young or heart leaves of this palm, are called the cabbage, and form an excellent vegetable either cooked or dressed in stews, hashes or ragouts. In the Laccadive islands, the heart leaves of the tree, just before they unfold, are cut out and plaited into mats of fine quality which are there used as sails for the smaller boats and are much esteemed when exported. In India, the leaves dried, and called cadjans, are plaited and used as thatch, and for the outer and inner linings of walls of houses: the leaves are also made into mats, baskets, both fancy and plain, into fans, combs, brooms, screens, buckets and lanterns, into articles of dress, and into leaf books, torches and fuel. The midrips of the leaves or frouds are fibrous but brittle and are used as brooms. The roots of the tree are chewed as a substitute for betel nut.

The beverage known to Europeans as palm wine or toddy is obtained from the flower spathes. Before the flowers have expanded, the spathes—and these are themselves astringent and used medicinally—are tied with the young leaves and then cut transversely from the top downwards, and beaten daily with the handle of the knife or a piece of hard wood, and the toddy, after a few days, exudes into a calabash or earthen pot. In the early morning, this is a pleasant, refrigerating drink, but it ferments towards night and becomes an intoxicating fluid, which is largely drank and is used as a ferment. It is to a great extent artificially brought to the vinous and acetous fermentations, and, in the former state, an alcoholic spirit is distilled from it, which forms one of the arracks of commerce; one hundred gallons of toddy produce, it is said, by distillation, twenty-five gallons of arrack: eight gallons of sweet toddy boiled over a slow fire, yield two gallons of a luscious syrup, from which, by further boiling, a coarse brown sugar is produced, known in commerce as jaggery.—*Simmond's Commercial Products, Royle's Fibrous Plants, Madras Exh. Jury Reports, Seeman on Palms, Ainslie's Materia Medica, Madras Lit. Soc. Journ., English Cyclopædia, Elliot's Flora Andhrica.*

COIMBATORE WOODS. The district of Coimbatore, in the south of the Indian peninsula, has a general elevation of about 800 feet above the sea, but several Alpine forest tracts occur in it. Dr. Wight, while residing there in 1850, sent to the Exhibition of 1851, a collection of 133 woods, with valuable notes as to their abundance. These notes, with additions by Mr. Rohde, formed the first concentrated information regarding the timber trees and woods of the Madras Presidency. Dr. Wight's 133 specimens were as under—

Acacia Arabica.
Acacia amara.
Acacia catechu.
Acacia sundra.
Acacia odoratissima.
Acacia odoratissima?
Acacia speciosa, or flectuosa.
Alangium decapetalum.
Artocarpus hirsuta.
Antidesma alexiteria.
Atalantia monophylla.
Artocarpus integrifolia.
Ailanthus excelsa.
Azadirachta Indica.
Ægle marmelos.
Balanites Ægyptiaca.
Bassia longifolia.
Bauhinia acuminata.
Bauhinia racemosa.
Bauhinia tomentosa.
Bignonia xylocarpa.
Borassus flabelliformis.
Bombax malabaricum.
Briedelia spinosa?
Butea frondosa.
Calosanthes Indica.
Calophyllum inophyllum.
Canthium nitens?
Careya arborea.
Cinnamomum iners.
Canthium parviflorum.
Casearia elliptica.
Cassia fistula.
Capparis divaricata.
Capparis grandis.
Cedrela toona.
Chickrassa tabularis.
Chloroxylon swietenia.
Cratæva Roxburghii.
Cordea Rothii.
Cedrela toona.
Cœsalpinia sappan.
Conocarpus latifolia.
Cluytia collina.
Cullenea excelsa.
Dalbergia sissoides.
Dalbergia latifolia.
Dalbergia paniculata.
Dichrostachys cinerea.
Diospyros cordifolia.
Diospyros ebenaster.
Diospyros melanoxylon.
Dillenia pentagyna.
Ehretia ovalifolia.
Elæodendron Roxburghii.
Eugenia caryophyllifolia.
Eriodendron anfractuosum.
Erythrina Indica.
Euphorbia tirucalli.
Eugenia jambolanum.
Feronia elephantum.
Ficus t'siela.
Garcinia? glutinifera.
Gardenia turgida?
Garuga pinnata.
Givotia Rottleriformis.
Grewia tiliæfolia.
Gmelina arborea.
Gmelina asiatica.
Guatteria cerasoides.
Holarrhena codaga.
Hydnocarpus inebreans.
Hymenodyction utile.
Hymenodyction obovatum.
Inga xylocarpa.
Lagerstrœmia reginæ.
Lagerstrœmia microcarpa?
Lagerstrœmia microcarpa.
Limonia alata.
Mangifera Indica.
Melia azadirachta.
Michelia Nilagirica.
Mimusops elengi.
Morinda citrifolia.
Morinda citrifolia?
Myristica cinerea?
Nauclea cordifolia.
Nauclea parviflora.
Nephelium longanum.
Nerium antidysentericum.
Odina woodier.
Premna tomentosa.
Premna integrifolia.
Pongamia glabra.
Prosopis spicigera.
Pterocarpus santalinus.
Prosopis spicigera?
Pterocarpus marsupium.
Putranjiva Roxburghii.
Randea dumetorum.
Rhus?—Sp?
Santalum album.
Sapindus emarginatus.
Schleichera trijuga.
Semecarpus anacardium.
Sethia Indica.
Soymida febrifuga.
Stereospermum suaveolens.
Spathodea arcuata.
Soymida febrifuga.
Strychnos potatorum.
Strychnos nux vomica.
Stereospermum chelonoides.
Sterculia urens.
Tamarindus Indica.
Tectona?
Tectona grandis.
Terminalia belerica.
Terminalia Berryi.
Terminalia glabra.
Terminalia alata.
Terminalia catappa.
Terminalia chebula.
Terminalia belerica?
Thespesia populnea.
Ulmus integrifolia.
Vachellia farnesiana.
Vitex altissima.
Wrightia tinctoria.
Zizyphus œnoplia.
Zizyphus glabrata.
Zizyphus jujuba.

COLUBRINA ASIATICA, *R. Br.*

Ceanothus Asiaticus, *Linn.*
,, capsularis, *Roxb.*
Asiatic Red wood. Eng.

A large shrub with pale greenish flowers. Voigt notices other two shrubs of this genus, C. Nepaulensis of Nepaul and C. macrophylla, of Martaban.—*Mr. R. Brown.*

COMMIPHORA MADAGASCARENSIS, *Lindl; Fl. Med.* 173.

Amyris commiphora, *Roxb.*
,, aggalocha, *Roxb. W. A.*

Balsamodendron Roxburghii, *Arn. W: Ill.*
Balsamodendron agallocha, *W. & A.*

Daracht-i Muql. Pers.

Its resin.

Aflatoon. Arab.	Googul. Hind.
East Indian Myrrh. Eng.	Muql. Pers.
Bdellium. Eng.	Googula. Singh.
βδελλιον. Greek.	Kookool. Tam.
Μαδελχον of Dioscorides	Googooloo. Tel.

A small tree, a native of Sylhet, Assam, the Garrow hills and Madagascar: wood not known. It produces a valuable gum resin, of which the above are given as synonyms.—*Elliott's Flora Andh. O'Shaughnessy, p.* 287, *Voigt.*

CONGO. A wood used in Madras for fuzes.

CON-MOO. Burm.? A tree of Tavoy, furnishing a good timber, used for building houses and boats.

CONJEE MARAM. Tam? A light red coloured wood, of Travancore, specific gravity 0·650, used for furniture, &c.

CONNARUS PANICULATUS, *Roxb.*

A large timber tree of Chittagong.—*Voigt.*

CONNARUS NITIDUS, *Roxb.*

This is described by Voigt as a tree of Sylhet. Dr. McClelland says that, in British Burmah, it is a shrub about ten feet high, very plentiful, especially in the Rangoon districts, and affords an oil seed of small size, but rich in a sweet oil. —*McClelland.*

CONNARUS SPECIOSA.

Gwai-douk. Burm.	Kadon kadet. Burm.

A large tree, very plentiful throughout the Rangoon, Pegu and Tounghoo districts, where it is known under the name of *Kadon kadet.* It is plentiful in all the forests, growing scattered with Teak in the Tounghoo district and in the forests of Pegu. It is a large, heavy and strong timber. Wood, white-coloured, adapted to every purpose of house building, remarkable for the quantity of its seed, which are of large size, abounding in sweet oil.—*Dr. McClelland.*

CONOCARPUS ACUMINATUS, *Roxb. Royle.*

Andersonia acuminata, *Roxb.*
„ lanceolata, *Rottler.*
Anogeissus acuminatus, *Wall.*

Yoong. Burm.	Pashi. Tel.
Pachiman. Tel ?	Panchi. „
Pachcha manu ? Tel.	

This large timber tree has already been noticed, briefly, under its other generic name, Anogeissus. It grows in the Northern Circars, in the forests of the peninsula of India, and is found, along with the Conocarpus latifolius. It is a large very valuable and plentiful timber tree throughout the Southern forests. In British Burmah, it is almost equal to the Terminalia microcarpa in size and the regular growth of its stem. Its wood is reddish brown, hard and strong, its breaking weight being 262 lbs. A cubic foot weighs lbs. 50 to lbs. 57 and, in a full grown tree on good soil the average length of the trunk to the first branch is 80 feet and average girth measured at 6 feet from the ground is 12 feet. It sells there at 12 annas per cubic foot. It flowers during the cold season. This tree is valuable on account of its wood, which is exceedingly like, and fully as strong, and as durable, if kept dry, as the C. latifolia, but exposed to the water, it soon decays. Of course it is thus unfit for the marine yard, but equally fit for house building when it can be obtained straight, which is seldom the case. But for its weight, it would be most excellent timber.—*Drs. McClelland and Brandis, Mr. Rohde's MSS., Voigt,* see Anogeissus acuminatus.

CONOCARPUS LATIFOLIA, *Roxb.; W. & A.; W. Ic.*

Andersonia altissima, *Roxb.*
Anogeissus latifolius, *Wall.*

Thoura. Hind.	Chiri manu. Tel.
Dawura. Mahr.	Siri manu. „
Thoura. „	Dhoboo. Uria. ?
Velle naga maram. Tam.	Nongoliah. „ ?
Duca. Tel. ?	Pooroo. „ ?
Tella neredu chettu. Tel.	

This large timber tree has already been noticed under its other generic name Anogeissus. It grows in the Dahra Dhoon,—in the Kenneri jungles, valleys of the Konkan rivers, on the inland Dekhan hills, at Chillaime and Chittagong. This is one of the largest timber trees that are found amongst that chain of mountains, on the peninsula of India, which separates the Circars from the Mahratta dominions, where it is a native. It flowers during the cold season, in January and February. Its trunk is erect, straight, varying in length and thickness, the largest being thirty-five feet to the branches, and about six feet in circumference. Dr. Wight, writing from Coimbatore, says it is a tall handsome tree, furnishing an excellent and very strong timber. The specimens tried there, though not the best, sustained 500 lbs. Dr. Roxburgh speaks of it in very high terms. But Mr. Rohde could not learn that its timber was to be of any size or value found in Rajahmundry or the Masulipatam Circar, these being the only localities in which he had met with it in common use. And he thinks its wood is over estimated. He had seen many instances in which it has, though sound when put out, given way in buildings, and he had never seen it above a foot in diameter. On another occasion, Mr. Rohde says, "if this be the wood known by the name of *Seriman,* given by Roxburgh, I must say I never met with any worthy of the character he gives it—it is the common timber of Masulipatam, where I never saw a log of a size exceeding 12 inches diameter. The Tamil name given by Dr. Wight is that of the white Eugenia." Other notes in our possession describe this as a large tree, in some cases, but the stem is often so deeply furrowed as to prevent it yielding a good plank. There is a fine specimen of this tree in the neighbourhood of Sydapet, near Madras. It is found about the sources of the Concan rivers; Kennery jungles; and on the inland Deckan hills, where it has a stunted and gnarled form. Dr. Gibson also says that, in the Bombay forests, it varies in size from a scrubby shrub to a great tree, according to soil and situation, and it seems to be as common in the inland forests as it is in those of the coast. The wood is well described by Dr. Wight as very strong. It is also tough, and hence is much in use for the wooden axles of carts. It is much used in agriculture and house building. This, also, is one of the trees which should be largely increased. Its timber is universally esteemed for almost every economical purpose. House building, shafts and yokes, and general use for Railway purposes, but makes very good cabinet furniture. Towards the centre, it is of a chocolate colour and is exceedingly durable. For house and ship building the natives reckon it superior to every other sort—Pentaptera tomentosa, and teak excepted. Captain Sankey writing from Nagpore says, it is a white wood with a heart of a dark colour, and somewhat like rosewood. Its average length, there, is 12 feet and girth 7 feet. It is so much prized by the natives of Nagpore for axletrees, that but few trees are permitted to attain their proper growth. By all accounts, in Nagpore, about 20,000 axletrees are made from this wood yearly. It is attacked by white ants. Though not obtainable in very large quantities it ranks high as a rafter timber.—*Drs. Roxburgh, Gibson and Wight, Mr. Rohde, Captain Sankey, Voigt. See* ANOGEISSUS LATIFOLIUS.

CONOCARPUS MYSTIFOLIUM ?

Kardahee. HIND ?

Under these names was sent to the Exhibition of 1862, as a tree of Jubbulpore, a tough wood, but difficult to work; tolerably abundant, (similar to Dowrah), grows along the banks of the Nerbudda.—*Cal. Cat. Ex.* 1862.

CONOCARPUS ROBUSTUS.

Baibyah. BURM.

A very large and strong timber tree, growing plentifully in the Pegu, Tounghoo and Prome forests along with teak. Adapted for fancy work and cabinet making.—*Dr. McClelland.*

CONIFERÆ, a natural order of gymnospermous exogens (called by Dr. Lindley *Pinaceæ*), consisting of resinous, mostly ever-green, hard-leaved trees or shrubs, inhabiting all those parts of the world in which aborescent plants can exist. In Sikkim and Bhootan, there are twelve Coniferæ, viz., 3 Juniper, Yew; Cupressus funebris, Abies Webbiana, Brunnoniana, and Smithiana; Larch; Pinus excelsa and longifolia, and Podocarpus neriifolia. Four of these, viz., Larch, Cupressus funebris, Podocarpus neriifolia and Abies Brunoniana, are not common to the North-west Himmalaya, west of Nepal, and the other eight are common. Of the 13 natives of the North-west Provinces again, only the following five, Juniperus communis; the Deodar, Pinus Gerardina, Pinus excelsa and Cupressus torulosa are not found in Sikkim. Dr. Mason, mentions the Pinus Latteri, as growing in Tenasserim and Dr. Brandis adds Pinus Massoniana, *Lamb.*, and Pinus Khassiana. Thunberg mentions many pines in Japan and they are numerous in China.—*Eng. Cyc. p.* 123, *Hooker, Vol.* 1, *p.* 256, *Cal. Cat. Ex. of* 1862, *Drs. Brandis and Mason.*

COOKIA PUNCTATA, *Retz.*

Quinaria lansium, *Lour.*

Whong-pi. CHIN. | Wham-pi. CHIN.

The yellow and very agreeable fruit of this small Chinese tree has a white pulp, rather acrid but sweet, and which is much esteemed as an article of diet in China and the Archipelago.—*Voigt.*

CORDIA, a genus of plants belonging to the natural order *Cordiaceæ*. In the southern part of the Peninsula, the Tamil name, Narvilli maram, seems to be applied indiscriminately to three or four species, viz., Cordia Rothii, C. obliqua and C. fulvosa, so that it is impossible to say which is the one meant by it. Dr. Wight believes that the wood of all is very inferior, the trees being usually small. Dr. Wight gives, in his Icones, Cordia cuneata, 1379; domestica, 1378; fulvosa, 1380; Leschenaultii, 1380; myxa, 1378; obliqua, 1578; Perrottettii, 1381; Rothii, 1379; serrata, 466; tomentosa, 1378, trichostemon, 1380; and Wallichii, 1378.—*Dr. Wight, Eng. Cyclop.*

COORAN—? A light brown coloured Penang wood, used for planks for building.

CORDIA ANGUSTIFOLIA, *Roth.*

Cordia reticulata, *Roxb.*

Narrow leaved Sepistan. ENG. | Naruvalli. TAM.
Gund. HIND. | Chinna botuku. TEL.
Gundni. „ | Nukkeru. „

This tree is from 30 to 40 feet high, the wood is very tough, and is used for carriage poles, posts and in house building. It is common about villages in the Circars, but never seen in the jungles. Fruit the size of a large pea, round and smooth, the pulp yellow, and gelatinous, the tree is common throughout the Deccan. Its fruit is esculent, but tasteless.—*Royle, Fib. Pl. page* 11, *Dr. Riddell, Captain Beddome.*

CORDIA LATIFOLIA, *Roxb.*

Buhuari. BENG. | Barra lesura. HIND.
Broad leaved Sepistan. ENG. | Kicha virigi chettu. TEL.
Bhokur. HIND.

The tree is common at Ajmeer, is found in Hindostan, but mostly confined to the southern parts of India. It has numerous spreading branches and the young shoots are angular and smooth. The general height of trees, ten or twelve years old, about 20 feet. The fruit is eaten: "phaleetas" or slow matches are made of the bark. This tree is hardy and ornamental, and would do well in compounds along with other trees. The wood is very inferior, and of small size. Under the name of sebesten plums, sebestans, or sepistans, two sorts of Indian fruit have been employed as pectoral medicines, for which their mucilaginous qualities, combined with some astringency, have recommended them. They are believed to have been the *Persea* of Dioscorces. This tree furnishes one of them. Linnæus applied the name of Sebesten to an American species of this genus which is not known in medicine.—*Eng. Cyc. p.* 146, *Drs. Irvine, O'Shaughnessy, Wight, Royle and Mr. Elliot in Fl. Andh.*

CORDIA MACLEODII ? (*qu.* monoica ?)

Dhengun. HIND ?

Under these names, of a tree of Jubbulpore, there was sent to the Exhibition of 1862, specimens of a remarkably beautiful wood, found in Mundlah and Seonee.—*Cal. Cat. Ex.* 1862.

CORDIA MYXA, *Linn.; Roxb., Fl. Ind. p.* 500. ? ?

Lebuck of Avicenna.	Sebestana domestica, *Lam. and Commel. and Pr. Alp.*
Mochayet, of Forskal.	Sebestana myxa, *Commel.*
Prunus sebestana, *Pluk.*	„ officinalis, *Gærtn.*
Cornus sanguinea, *Forsk.*	
Cordia officinalis, *Lam.*	
„ domestica, *Roth.*	

Lebuk ? AR.	Bukampadaruka. SANS.
Buhuari. BENG.	Lolu. SINGH.
Tha-nat. BURM.	Vidi maram. TAM.
Sepistan plum tree. ENG.	Nakkera. TEL.
Nakkeru wood tree. ANGLO-TEL.	Nakeru. „
Muckeru ? „ „ „	Iriki. „
Lusora. HIND.	Banka nakkera. TEL.
Lesura. „	Ura nakeru. „
Kendal. JAV.	Pedda botuku. „
Vidi mara. MALEAL.	Mookooroo karra. „

A native of Egypt, Persia, Arabia, of Hindostan, Nepaul, and the forests of the Godavery. It is common throughout the Konkan, Pegu and the Malay Peninsula. The trunk is from 8 to 12 or 15 feet high, generally crooked, but as thick or thicker than a man's body, with numerous spreading branches bent in every possible direction and forming a dense shady head with a grey cracked bark. The wood is soft, and of little use except for fuel. In British Burmah, its soft wood is not used. A cubic foot weighs lbs 33. In a full grown tree on good soil the average length of the trunk to the first branch is 15 feet and average girth measured at 6 feet from the ground is 4 feet. The leaves are collected extensively and sold for cover leaves for cegars. It is reckoned one of the best kinds of wood for kindling fire by friction, and is thought to have furnished the wood from which the Egyptians constructed their mummy cases. The wood and bark are said by Dr. Royle to be accounted a mild tonic. Its fruit is the smaller sebestans or lobestens of European medicine, and its seeds are the chakoon ki binj, *Hind.*, used in powder mixed with oil as an application in ringworm.—*Dr. O'Shaughnessy, p.* 498, *Dr. Royle, Eng. Cyclop., Flor. Andh, Voigt, Dr. Brandis.*

CORDIA OBLIQUA. *Willd.*

Cordia tomentosa, *Wall.*
„ Wallichii, *G. Don.; W. C.*
„ Domestica ? *Roth.*

Gondni. DUK.	Selu. SANS.
Lasora. HIND.	Naruvalli pallam. TAM.

This is a large handsome tree, common in the lower provinces of India, with a small, round, reddish coloured, pleasant tasted, but glutinous, fruit.—*Ainslie, page* 228.

CORDIA POLYGAMA, *Roxb.*

Bottu kuru chettu. TEL.	Pach-cha botuku. TEL.

A strong close grained wood, small and crooked, found in the Circars.

CORDIA ROTHII. *Ræm. & Sch.*

Cordia cuniata, *Heyne.*

Bokur. MAHR.	Narvillic marum. TAM.

Dr. Wight says the Tamil name seems to be applied indiscriminately to three or four species of the genus, so that it is impossible to say which is the one meant. Cordia obliqua, C. Rothii and C. fulvosa had all been brought to him under this name. He believes the wood of all is very inferior, the trees being usually small. Dr. Gibson says that none of the different species or varieties of C. Rothii, C. fulvosa and C. obliqua give a timber fit for any thing but firewood. They are not uncommon in the Bombay forests, but are more generally met with near cultivated lands and villages.—*Drs. Wight & Gibson.*

CORDIA SERRATA.

Gab. HIND.	Gad Gondori. HIND.

CORNUS.

Bhumowra. HIND.

This genus of plants consists of large trees and shrubs. Several species have been found in the Himalayas, in Sylhet, and Nepaul, by Drs. Wallich and Royle; the Cornus oblonga occurs in the Deyra Doon; C. macrophylla, and C. nervosa, Mussoorie; and Cornus capitata, Wall., (Benthamia fragifera Lindl.) at a still higher elevation. The fruit of *Benthamia* is eaten in the hills, and from the seeds of some species an oil is expressed. Wight, in Icones, gives figure of Cornuus altera, 1211, Sylvestris, 1211, and Zeylanica, 1210-11.—*Drs. Riddell, O'Shaughnessy, and Wight.*

CORONILLA SESBAN ? ? CORONILLA PICTA ? ?

Sohn. URIA ?

Under these doubtful botanical names, Captain Macdonald notices a principal tree, (it is one of the Terebintheæ,) growing in Ganjam and Gumsur, leaves pinnate, 4 pinnæ. Extreme height 50 feet. Circumference 6 feet. Height from ground to the intersection of the first branch, 12 feet. It yields a very heavy wood and of great strength. It is almost exclusively reserved for making posts for pagodas and sacred edifices, the use of it in ordinary house building being, it is said, forbidden in the shastras. The tree is very common, but owing to this superstition very little use is made of it, the only purposes to which the wood is applied being for making rice pounders and the wooden stands on which the large grain baskets used in that part of the country, are placed. The bark is used for tanning skins and also medicinally by women after childbirth, a sort of fungus or excresence from this tree is applied externally to wounds and sores and is also taken internally in colic and affections of the stomach.—*Captain Macdonald.* (The botanical names given are those of the Sesbania Ægyptica, *Pers.;* but according to the description it must be some other tree.)

CORYLUS, a genus of plants of which *C. lacera* and *C. ferox* are two species found in the Himalaya Mountains, the former, gathered in Kumaon, is hardly different from *C. coturna;* the other, from Mount Sheopore, has narrow taper-pointed leaves, and excessively hard nuts inclosed in a husk, with divaricating narrow spiny divisions.—*Eng. Cyc. p.* 166.

CORYLUS AVELLANA. The (HAZEL), Abundant in the Himalayas, nuts called *Bendick* and *Finduck* in bazars, are grouped in clusters together. By expression the kernel yields a very agreeable oil, nearly in the proportion of half its weight. The wood of the hazel was the material of the divining rods of the magicians and snake enchanters.—*Dr. O'Shaughnessy, page* 609.

CORYPHA, a genus of Palms, which are valued for different products and employed to supply the place of cordage plants.

CORYPHA ELATA, *Roxb.*

Taliera elata, *Wall.*
Bujoon. BENG.

Grows in Bengal and, according to Mr. Mason, in the Tenasserim Provinces.

CORYPHA GEBANGA is one of the most useful of all the palms of Eastern Asia. Its pith furnishes a sort of sago; its leaves are plaited into bags and baskets and used for thatch and broad-brimmed hats; fishing-nets and linen shirts are woven from its fibres, and ropes from its twisted leaf-stalks; the root is both emollient and slightly astringent; sliced, it is used in slight diarrhœas, and Waitz says that it is a most valuable remedy for the periodical diarrhœas which in the East Indies attack Europeans.—*Eng. Cyc. page* 167.

CORYPHA TALIERA, *Roxb.*

Taliera Bengalensis, *Spreng.*

Tara. BENG.	Taliera. HIND.
Taliera. „	Sri talam. SANS.
Tariat. „	Sri talam. TEL.

The *Tara* of Bengal and *Talipat* of the peninsula of India, is an elegant species inhabiting Bengal, and much employed for making leaf hats and leaf umbrellas. The leaves, moreover, when smoothed, are much used for writing on, and also for tying the rafters of their houses, as they are strong and durable. Its trunk is about 30 feet high, and as nearly as possible of equal thickness throughout. The leaves are in about 80 divisions, each 6 feet long by 4 inches broad, radiating from the point of a leaf-stalk from 5 to 10 feet long, and covered with strong pines at its edge. Roxburgh describes the spadix as decompound, issuing in the month of February from the apex of the tree and centre of the leaves, forming an immense diffuse ovate panicle of about 20 or more feet in height. The fruit is the size of a crab-apple, wrinked, dark-olive, or greenish-yellow. The leaves are used by the natives of India to write upon with their steel styles, and for other purposes. In Tenasserim, it is known as the book palm and specimens of this palm, the leaves of which are commonly used to write on instead of paper, are not unfrequent in the neighbourhood of religious edifices. The leaves of Corypha talliera are said to be greatly employed in the Tenasserim Provinces. —*Eng. Cyc., page* 167, *Dr. Mason.*

CORYPHA UMBRACULIFERA, *Linn.*

Tali. BENG.	Koda pana. MALEAL.
Fan palm. ENG.	Konda panna maram. TEL.
Talipat palm. „	Sidalam. TEL.

The Tala, or Talipat palm, is a native of Ceylon, and similar in appearance; but its leaves are not so round as those of the Talliera, the divisions in the centre being shorter than those at the sides. The trunk grows 60 or 70 feet high; the leaves are 14 feet broad and 18 feet long, exclusive of the stalk, and they form a head about 40 feet in diameter. Fans of enormous size are manufactured from this plant in Ceylon; the bole of this palm is wholly pith which furnishes a sort of flour from which bread is made; the leaves make excellent thatch, and are also used for writing on, like those of the Talliera. Griffith met with trees in flower at Mergui, which he thought belonged to this species, but "not having access to a complete copy of Martius' Palm," he could not speak with certainty. For the same reason, other trees that Dr. Mason saw in Tavoy, he regarded as probably talipat palms. The dark coloured roundish seeds of these trees are used as beads by the Taders, (religious fanatics of the sect of Vishnoo) which people the Telingas call Dasaries. *C. umbraculifera*, the *Codda-panna* of Madras and the *Talipat* of Ceylon, and very like the former, is common in Ceylon, and found also on the Malabar Coast. Of this, the leaf, being dried, is very strong and limber—and, according to Knox "most wonderfully made for men's convenience to carry along with them; for though this leaf be thus broad enough to cover fifteen or twenty men when it is open, yet it will fold close like a lady's fan, and then it is no bigger than a man's arm; it is wonderfully light." "This tree is, within, a pith only; they beat it in mortars to flour, and bake cakes of it, which taste much like to whiten bread; it serves them instead of corn before their harvest is ripe." The Burmese books are all made of the leaf of a species of Corypha.—*Knox's Ceylon, quoted in Royle's Fib. Pl., Seeman, Eng. Cyc. page* 176, *Ains. Mat. Med. page* 143, *Dr. Mason.*

CRATÆVA, a genus of plants belonging to the natural order *Capparidaceæ*. The *C. religiosa* is common in India. The *Æ. marmelos* (Bilva or Mahura,) formerly considered a species of this genus, is now referred to the order Aurantiaceæ, and call *Ægle marmelos*. C. Roxburghii grows in India as also does C. nurvala.—*Eng. Cyc. Dr. O'Shaughnessy.*

CRATÆVA NURVALA, *Ham.*

Cratæva tapia, *Burm.*
,, inermis, *Linn.*

Tapia. HIND.
Birmi. ,,
Nir vala. MALEAL.
Mavalingum. TAM.
Maridu. TEL.

A small tree, 15 to 20 feet high, which grows in Malabar and Mysore.—*Voigt.*

CRATÆVA RELIGIOSA, *Linn.*

Ægle marmelos, *q. v.*

Bel ka jhar. DUK.
Bilva. SANS.
Wea warene. SINGH.
Vilva maram. TAM.
Bilva chettu. TEL.

Its leaf.

Bel ka pat. DUK.
Vilvei ellei. TAM.
Bilva akoo. TEL.

This has been already noticed under its synonym Ægle marmelos. It grows, under cultivation, all over India, and in the central province of Ceylon; its wood is used for pestles, and in house building. A cubic foot weighs 62 lbs., and it is calculated to last 60 years.

In the Deccan, this tree is generally found near tombs and temples. The leaves are somewhat aromatic, in a slight degree bitter, and are considered by the native practitioners as stomachic. The root, as it appears in the bazars, has a singular sub-aromatic and bitterish taste, and is supposed to possess alterative properties. An infusion of Bel is slightly bitter and aromatic, and much used by the natives of Bengal. Its dose is two to four ounces thrice daily.—*Mr. Mendis, Riddell, Ains. Mat. Med. p.* 124, *Beng. Phar. p.* 298. *See* ÆGLE MARMELOS.

CRATÆVA ROXBURGHII, *R. Br.; W. & A.*

Cratæva tapia, *Vahl.*
,, odora, *Ham.*
Capparis trifoliata, *Roxb.*

Tikto-shak. BENG.
Narvala. CAN.
Birmi-ki-jhar. DUK.
Three leaved Caper tree. ENG.
Garlic pear. ENG.
Kurwan. MAHR.
Koomla. ,,
Tapia. SANS.
Varana. ,,
Narvala. TAM.
Mavilinga maram. TAM.
Tella ulimarra chettu. TEL.
Tella ulimide. ,,
Ulimido. TEL.
Urimidi. ,,
Uru mutti. ,,
Usiki manu. ,,

A tree of both the Indian peninsulas, of the Circars, and growing in Bengal, at Saharunpore. Wood very hard. The native dhol is often made of it, and Ainslie states it is used for many common purposes. Dr. Gibson says the wood is white, and in use by the turners, that it is not a common tree on the Bombay side, and he had not seen it in the forests. The juice and a decoction of its astringent bark is given in intermittent fevers and typhus.—*Voigt, Flor. Andh. Drs. Ainslie, Wight and Gibson, Useful Plants.*

CRATÆVA, *Species ? ?*

Boroana. URIA.

A tree of Ganjam and Gumsur, which has not been determined. Its extreme height is 40 feet, circumference 5 feet, height from the ground to the intersection of the first branch, 9 feet. It is tolerably common and burnt for firewood. The bark is used medicinally for wounds.—*Captain Macdonald.*

CROTON SANGUISFLUINA. The Blood-Wood of Norfolk Island. Is said to be of little value except for firewood; on an incision being made in the bark, a fluid exudes which is used for marking the convict's slopes, staining furniture, &c., and it is a good tonic and astringent.—*Keppel's Ind. Arch. Vol. II, page* 282.

CRYPTOMERIA JAPONICA, *D. Don.*

Cupressus Japonica, *Thunb.*

The Japan Cedar, a tree which is greatly admired. It is a species of pine, not unlike the Araucarias of Norfolk Islands and Brazil. When growing luxuriantly, it is highly ornamental, rising from the ground as straight as a larch, and sending out numerous side branches almost horizontally from the main stem, which again droop towards the ground in a graceful and "weeping" manner. The wood of the tree has a kind of twisted grain, and possesses great strength and durability. It is highly valued by the Chinese and, from its beauty and straightness, is often used by the Mandarins and priests for those long poles which are generally seen in front of their houses and temples. It is also well known and highly prized by the natives of Japan. The beautiful *Cryptomeria*, or Japan Cedar, is a most conspicuous tree. It is evidently in high favour with the priests of Buddha, and well deserves to be so." It has been introduced into England.—*Fortune's Wanderings, page* 128, *Fortune's Tea District, page* 212 *and* 304.

CUDDAPAH AND KURNOOL WOOOS.

Cuddapah is a Madras collectorate, about 150 miles N. W. of Madras, and the collectorate of Kurnool, is on its north and west. The Nalla Mallaiis a mountain range bordering these two collectorates on the east. The hills are covered with dense forests, to their highest peaks, with beautiful timber trees, from 30 to 60 feet in height, without a branch, principally, Mad dhi, (Pentaptera), Yegis (Pterocarpus marsupium), and Ippa (Bassia longifolia) with a great deal of teak, though much of it is young. Mr. Latham, Resident Engineer, in a letter to Mr. Pinson, dated 12th January 1861, gave the following notices of the woods found on these mountains. The Botanical names seem to have been traced out from the vernacular names given in the Cyclopædia of India and from those in Mr. Elliot's Flora Andhrica, but his notices of the woods, from his professional knowledge, must be regarded as of great value. I have placed notes of interrogation where further information seems necessary. I have been indebted for this report to Captain Prendergast, Royal Engineers.

Acacia Arabica, *Tuma*, Tel. *Kurvalum*, Tam. *Babool*, Hind. A well known and useful timber, used generally.

Acacia leucophlœa, *Tella tuma*, Tel. *Velvaila*, Tam. A hard light colored wood, streaked with brown ; used for various purposes. The bark is used as an ingredient in arrack distillation.

Acacia odoratissima, *Telsoo*, Tel. *Shinduga*, Tel. *Caroovangah*, Tam. A well known and valuable wood of a light brown color, straight fibre, medium weight ; used in large beams, and for general purposes.

Acacia speciosa or flexuosa, *Tella dirasana*, Tel. *Dirasana chettu*, Tel. *Velvengah maram*, Tam. A common tree : color of wood light brown, and it is exceedingly strong and durable.

Acacia suma, *Tella sundra*, Tel. A very good, strong dark red wood, weighty : used for agricultural implements and generally.

Ægle marmelos, *Maradu chettu*, Tel. *Vilva maram*, Tam. This tree is of the orange tribe, and furnishes a close, smooth grained wood : it does not attain to a large size.

Alangium decapetalum, *Udaga*, Tel. *Alingie maram*, Tam. A very fine wood, though white, it is equal to beech and sustains a weight of 310 lbs. ; it is highly spoken of by Roxburgh : it does not attain a very large size.

Alangium hexapetalum, *Nalla udaga*, Tel. Extreme height 30 feet ; the wood is of use, it is said to be peculiarly adapted for producing sounds. The root is used for snake bites, it has a great resemblance to beech : it is a yellow color and slightly cross grained.

Anisomeles Malabarica, *Magabira*, Tel. *Mogabira*, Tel. A light wood, useful for temporary purposes.

Anogeissus latifolius, *Sheriman*, Tel. A light colored compact wood, said to be the hardest and toughest found ; wooden axles for carts are generally made from it, it is also used as posts, beams &c.

Auckwthee ? Tel. Wood sienna color, much used in bandy work.

Azadirachta Indica, *Yepa*, Tel. *Yapa*, Tel. *Vaypum maram*, Tam. The margosa tree : a very useful wood, used generally in house work by natives.

Bassia longifolia, *Ippee*, Tel. *Elloopi maram*, Tam. A light colored hard and durable wood, nearly equal to teak. It grows to a large size in Malabar where it is used for spars.

Bauhinia racemosa, *Arree*, Tel. A dark reddish brown close grained wood called at Kurnool *Koa Arree*. Used in beams &c.

Boswellia glabra, *Andagu chettu*, Tel. A soft spongy wood, of little use.

Briedelia spinosa, *Woramen*, Tel. *Moolloo vengay maram*, Tam. A white, close grained, strong and useful wood ; this tree attains a great size in alpine forests.

Butea frondosa, *Moduga chettu*, Tel. This tree is found in Pegu, is called *Poukpin*. The Tamil name is *Porasum* ; *Palas* in Sans, *Dhak* in Hind. *Thorus mara* in Can. It is a common tree, thrives every where, but the wood is of little value except for gunpowder charcoal, flower deep red, used as a dye, which is also used for the sectarian marks of the worshippers of Vishnoo and is mixed with kino ? ? to produce the red powder used at the Holee festivals.

Cavallium urens, *Tobisa kurra* or *Tabasa* or *Tunkumanu* Tel. Its whitish wood is of little use, and is much attacked by the worm.

Chloroxylon swietenia, *Bilugu*, Tel. and *Bilu* at Kurnool. It is a poor sort of satinwood, used for common purposes.

Cluytia collina, *Vadisa chettu*, Tel. *Wodesha*, Tel. *Woadoogoo maram*, Tam. A small tree ; wood red colored, exceedingly hard and durable, with a fine close grain and is easily worked.

Canthium parviflorum, *Balsu*, Tel. called *Beer Chinapah*, at Kurnool. A dark and good wood, of serviceable character.

Capparis grandis, *Keygutti*, Tel. A light sienna colored wood, close grained and hard ; of medium weight. Is a very useful timber.

Careya arborea, *Buda darinee*, Tel. A very useful wood, dark red in the centre of the tree and yellow outside : used for large beams.

Cassia fistula, *Rela chettu*, Tel. *Koanny maram*, Tam. A good wood of medium hardness. It is a tree of great beauty when in flower but on the eastern side of the Ghats, is small ; it however attains a sufficient size in the forest to provide a good and useful wood. Spars for native vessels are made from it (? ?)

Cathartocarpus Roxburghii, *Uskiamen*, Tel. or *Urimiddee*, Tel. A light strong hard wood, very useful.

Dalbergia frondosa, *Yerra-patseroo*, Tel. *Tella-patseroo*, of the Circars, and the *Peda Sopara* of the Godavery forests. Is a yellowish wood, strong, close, and hard. It is a useful timber.

Dalbergia latifolia, *Jitigee*, Tel. *Yerru Gudu*, Tel. *Erroopootoo*, Tam. The rose wood of India, a dark mottled wood, very useful but heavy.

Dichrostachys cinerea, *Vellatura*, Tel. *Vadatala maram*, Tam. Dr. Wight says it is a small tree or large shrub, wood very hard and strong. It grows to some size in the Nalla Mallas, and is a very useful timber : it is in common use.

Diospyros choloroxylon, *Ullinda*, Tel. *Yellinda*, Tel. A straight grained, compact hard wood, of a light brown color : appears a very useful timber.

Diospyros melanoxylon, *Timkee*, Tel. *Tookee*, Tel. A very good close wood, white on the outside, the centre generally black and heavy : when large a very serviceable timber, the Tamil name is *Toombie maram* (ebony.) This tree grows to a large size, the centre being black : the white portion is however useful.

Emblica officinalis, *Usrika*, Tel. *Nelly maram*, Tam. *Emblic Myrabolan*, Eng. *Aoula*, Hind. The wood is close-grained and straight, and is useful for common purposes : it is a fruit bearing tree.

Erythrina Indica, *Barchanapa*, Tel. *Barjupu chettu*, Tel. A common close grained light colored wood, used in building native houses. It is also called Moochy wood, also in Brown's Dictionary Bastard teak, a translation of the Telugu term *Chiri teku* ; this term is applied to several kinds of trees with large leaves. On the Nagary hills the Yanadis give it to Dillenia (now Wormia) bracteata.

Ficus t'siela, *Juvi*, Tel. *Eichie maram*, Tam. A light wood, but like others of the Ficus genus, of little use.

Feronia elephantum, *Vullaga chettu*, Tel. *Vaila maram*, Tam. The wood apple tree, attains a large size, the wood is rather heavy, light colored, hard and durable. It sustained a weight of 860 lbs. (? ?)

Ficus glomerata, *Medi chettu*, Tel. *Kulla Kith mara*, Can. It grows to a height of 40 feet with a circumference of 4½ feet; bandy wheels are made from it. It is straight grained, strong, and appears useful; it is considered sacred, and is burnt when libations are offered: the fruit is eaten and a medicinal extract is obtained from the root.

Ficus Indica, *Mari chettu*, Tel *Banyan* tree, Eng. *Ala maram*, Tam. The wood is of little use; the drops or aerial roots yield a heavy hard timber.

Gardenia latifolia, *Bikkee*, Tel. A light wood of little use. Native combs are made from it.

Givotia Rottleriformis, *Tella Poonkee*, Tel. *Boolallie maram*, Tam. A very common tree in Southern India. A light soft wood, like mango wood; useful for temporary purposes.

Gmelina arborea, *Goomer tek* or *Gumudu teken*, Tel. A hard durable wood called at Kurnool *Ghooteky*.

Gmelina Asiatica, *Gumudu chettu*, Tel. A hardish wood of yellow color; useful.

Grewia Rothii, *Jana*, Tel. A light, ash colored wood, with a straight grain, hard and strong, is much used and very serviceable.

Guatteria cerasoides, *Chilka dudugu*, Tel. *Mooleely maram*, Tam. A white tolerably hard wood. The natives use it but little, but it is a useful wood.

Hardwickia binata, *Nar yepa*, Tel. A very dark red heavy wood, used in large beams: it is often hollow through the heart.

Kodara chettu, Tel. Mr. Elliott describes this "as a kind of tree." It appears to be of little use.

Lagerstrœmia parviflora, *Chimna nagee*, Tel. A light brown, compact, hard, serviceable wood, used generally.

Lookkee, Tel. A fine grained wood, of a greyish color; found in small quantity.

Maba buxifolia, *Nalla maddee*, Tel. A hard sepia colored wood, used by the natives for all purposes.

Midudu, Tel. An ash colored timber, sound and useful.

Miliusa velutina, *Nulla daduga*, Tel. A pale light yellow soft wood, used for (small) brams; is useful.

Morinda citrifolia, *Maddi chettu*, Tel. *Munjee pavala maram*, Tam. The wood is of a deep brownish yellow, is easily worked, and is used for common purposes. The roots are used in dyeing.

Mangifera Indica, *Mamadi chettu*. Tel. *Mango tree*, Eng. Its wood useful for temporary purposes, is not plentiful in Nalla Mallai.

Nauclea parviflora, *Bute karamee*, Tel. A hard, tough wood, light red in color; used as yokes, posts and small beams.

Nella poleeki, Tel. A light wood, of coarse grain, unserviceable except for temporary purposes.

Nera, Tel? This name is probably incorrect and is used for Nerar the Syzigium jambolana. Balfour calls a నేరేడు Engenia, (Syzigium) jambolana.

Odina wodier, *Goompinee*, Tel. *Gumpena chettu*, Tel. A soft light reddish wood, useful for general purposes.

Palavaraynee, Tel. Wood light, yellow, hard, and is, Mr. Latham thinks, the *Peda kalmesura* of the Northern Circars.

Pentaptera glabra, *Tella maddee*, Tel. *Velmarrodum maram*, Tam. A light yellow wood.

Pongamia glabra, *Kanuga chettu*, Tel. *Poonga maram*, Tam. This large tree attains a great height, flourishes equally well on the arid plains of the Carnatic or on the sub-alpine tracts of Mysore. Roxburgh recommends the wood, which is light, of a whitish color, and fit for a variety of purposes.

Premna tomentosa, *Nagaru chettu*, Tel. *Navooru* or *Nagool*, Tel. *Kolcutty teak maram*, Tam. The tree is rather small, the wood, hard and close-grained, of a brownish yellow color; it is more a fancy wood, than a timber and is rather scarce; the natives use the sap in some of their ceremonies.

Prosopis spicigera, *Janum chettu*, Tel. *Purrembay maram*, Tam. This thorny tree attains to a considerable size; the wood is strong, straight grained, and easily worked, a specimen sustained a weight of 592 lbs. Dr. Wight asks if it is the same as the *Venny maram* Dr. Cleghorn states that the foliage of the tree and character of the wood closely resembles that of its congener "Acacia sundra."

Pterocarpus marsupium, *Yegis?* Tel. A darkish, coarse grained serviceable timber.

Pterocarpus santalinus, *Chandun*, Tel. Red sanders wood.

Pulsundra, Tel. This wood is of a reddish color, strong and useful.

Roodra ganapa, Tel. A light porous wood of little use.

Sarra or *Sarrah*, Tel. This wood is of a dark grey color and appears to be readily attacked by the worm.

Schriebera swietenoides, *Makkan*, Tel. A hard yellowish wood, is very useful.

Seecuranee, Tel. This is a white colored, light, straight grained wood, would be useful for temporary purposes.

Soymida febrifuga, *Somee*, Tel. *Shem maram*, Tam. *Choar kullie*, Tam. A reddish wood, strong and durable, much used in buildings.

Spathodia Rheedii? *Wodee*, Tel. *Vodi*, Tel. (Is this the Spathodea arcuata, the Tamil name of which is *Kanpillay maram*, as mentioned by Wight?) a white wood, much cut by natives and used in carts and for small beams.

Spathodia Rheedii? *Ganoru karra*, Tel. A soft wood of little use.

Sphœranthus hirtus, *Butta ganapoo*, Tel. *Boda tarupu*, Tel. A wood of light yellow colour, of medium weight, useful for general purposes.

Striychnos nux vomica, *Musidi*, Tel. *Mushtee*, Tel. *Yetti maram*, Tel. The wood is very hard and strong and white ants will not touch it. It is used for ploughshares; the poisonous fruits are the favorite food of the Malabar hornbill, Buceros Malabaricus.

Strychnos potatorum, *Chilla*, Tel. *Taita maram*, Tam. The fruit is the well known clearing nut. The wood is white, close grained, and hard, and is used for implements and rafters.

Syzigium jambolanum, *Nerar*, Tel. Mr. Latham thinks this is the Tamil *Nawel maram*. It is called *Neradee* in Kurnool, and is a very useful wood, of a light sepia color, of medium hardness, and used generally as planks.

Tamarindus Indica, *Chinta chettu*, Tel. *Polia maram*, Tam. *Onara mara*, Can. The large well known handsome Tamarind tree. The wood is hard, durable, and fine veined, but apt to be hollow and decayed in the centre, it is the best timber in India for brick burning, 1½ lbs. for each brick, in large kilns, being sufficient. It is also used in the manufacture of oil (?) and is valuable for its fruit and the shade it affords.

Tectona grandis, *Tek*, Tel. *Teak maram*, Tam. The Teak tree; the most useful wood in India. There are very large trees in the interior of the jungle. It is not so good or so heavy as the Malabar teak, but it is superior to Moulmein or Rangoon teak.

Terminalia belerica, *Thanddee*, Tel. A serviceable wood chiefly used as posts. Its color is yellowish brown and it has a close grain.

Terminalia chebula, *Karaku chettu*, Tel. *Pilla murdah maram*, Tam. It grows to a gigantic size, and furnishes planks 30 feet long: it is a dark colored, heavy and hard wood, but very cross grained. It sustained about 400 lbs.;

the seeds of this tree are used as galls and as an astringent, also as a mordaunt in dyeing.

Terminalia glabra, *Tella muddee*, Tel. *Currai murda maram*, Tam. The tree grows to a large size, and the wood is of a dark red color. A dye is obtained from it ? it is hard, heavy and strong, 1 inch bars sustaining a weight from 430 to 450 lbs.

Thandraikya, Tel. An ash colored wood, resembles hickory in fibre, is close and tough and would be a very useful wood.

Ulmus integrifolius, *Namille*, Tel. *Nowlee*, Tel. A light colored, close grained wood, used for general purposes.

Wrightia antidysenterica, *Kola mukki chaka*, Tel. *Kodisa chettu*, Tel. A very white wood, used as beams, planks, &c.

Yellaree, Tel. This is used in small quantities but it appears a useful wood: it is of a light brown color with a good grain.

Yerra poleeki, Tel. A hardish wood of a red color and very useful.

Zyziphus jujuba, *Renga*, Tel. *Yellanday maram*, Tam. A very good strong wood. The tree never attains a large size, but the wood is much used for cultivating implements.

CULLENEA EXCELSA.

Malai konji maram. TAM.

A very large and tall tree, trunk straight, from 60 to 80 feet high. Wood white, rather open grained, apparently not very good, but the outside sap-wood only was examined. Under the microscope, its longitudinal section is very peculiar; altogether such as Dr. Wight had not elsewhere observed. Dr. Gibson had not met with this tree within the Bombay bounds.—*Drs. Wight and Gibson.*

CUMPAS—? a light brown coloured wood of Penang, a large tree; used only for planks.

CUNDA LAH PALLAH—? a Bamboo coloured wood of Travancore; used for making sandals.

CUPANIA CANESCENS.

Amba curb. MAHR.

Tree common in the upper Ghat jungles. Wood of average quality, but does not bear exposure. Dr. Gibson had not seen it elsewhere. —*Gibson.*

CUPRESSUS. The Cypress, a forest tree, a native of the south-eastern parts of Europe, particularly of Italy; but it grows in Mexico, and the southern parts of N. America. The wood of the cypress is hard, elastic, and strong. It resists worms, and its odour repels insects from whatever may be contained in a cabinet or chest made of it. Its duration is very considerable, but the precise period or the age to which the tree lives have not been clearly ascertained. In some countries this tree is planted over the graves of the dead as an emblem of immortality. There are several species of this class of evergreen trees.

CUPRESSUS FUNEBRIS. The funeral cypress, ENG. Grows in the Himalayas, and in China, and is a species of weeping cypress. It is a most beautiful tree. Fortune says, "It was during one of my daily rambles that I saw the first specimen. About half a mile distant from where I was, I observed a noble-looking fir-tree, about sixty feet in height, having a stem as straight as the Norfolk Island pine, and weeping branches like the willow of St. Helena. Its branches grew at first at right angles to the main stem, then described a graceful curve upwards, and bent again at their points. From these main branches others long and slender hung down perpendicularly, and gave the whole tree a weeping and graceful form. It reminded me of some of those large and gorgeous chandeliers, sometimes seen in theatres and public halls in Europe. Its stem was perfectly straight, like *Cryptomeria*, and its leaves were formed like those of the well known arbor-vitæ, only much more slender and graceful.—*Fortune's Tea Districts, p.* 61 *and* 62.

CUPRESSUS GLAUCA.

Surus. DUK.

This is a tall, elegant, and graceful tree, well adapted for border walks in a garden, being always green, and a favorite with the natives of India. It grows easily, and is generally planted alternately with Areca. Slips, if taken off before the commencement of the rains, and planted in beds shaded from the sun, take root; each slip should be six inches apart, and if common care is used, one-fourth of the plants will strike and grow. After that, they may be put out in nursery beds, at the distance of one foot from each other, until required for transplanting to where they are to remain.—*Riddell.*

CUPRESSUS HORIZONTALIS, the Spreading cypress, is a handsome species.—*Eng. Cyc. p.* 258.

CUPRESSUS LUSITANICA, the Cedar of Goa, has a free mode of growth, its leaves have a singularly glaucous colour.—*Eng. Cyc. p.* 258.

CUPRESSUS PENDULA? Drooping cypress, *Goa cedar*. South of Europe, the oriental physicians used to send their patients labouring under lung diseases to breathe the air of Candia, where the cypress was abundant, in the persuasion that the emanations were particularly wholesome.—*O'Shaughnessy, page* 621.

CUPRESSUS SEMPERVIRENS.

Shajr ul Hyat. ARAB.	Cypress. ENG.
Saras. DUK.	Sarv. HIND. PERS.
Evergreen cypress. ENG.	Saro. „ „

Its berries and leaves are popularly deemed a panacea for all diseases. It is found in gardens at Ajmeer and Kotah, but is a native of the warmer parts of Europe, though it has long been transferred to gardens for the sake of its deep evergreen branches and leaves. Among the ancient inhabitants of the Grecian Archipelago, it was customary, upon the birth of a daughter, to plant a *Cupressetum*, or grove of Cypress trees, to be given her for a portion; hence every plantation of this kind was called *dos filiæ*, or a daughter's dower. According to Evelyn, the timber of the Cypress was of infinite esteem among the ancients. It is supposed that the durable bridge built over the Euphrates by Semiramis, was made of this material, and it is reported that Plato chose it to write his laws on, before brass itself. It is certain that it never rifts or cleaves but with great violence; and the bitterness of its juice preserves it from worms or putrefaction. The gates of Constantinople, famous for having stood from the time of Constantine to that of Pope Eugene IV., a period of eleven hundred years, were of Cypress.—*Dr. O'Shaughnessy, p.* 621, *Dr. Irvine, p.* 208, *Eng. Cyc. p.* 258, *Book of Trees, p.* 200.

CUPRESSUS TORULOSA, *D. Don.* Grows in the Himalayas.

CURCUMBARRY, a valley once filled with forest trees, 90 miles west of Madras near Nagery in the N. Arcot collectorate. Lately, from 20 to 30 bandy loads of timber daily passed through it, of different descriptions of timber, chiefly the red sanders. The Conservator reports that the valley is being deforested with great rapidity, and that, if strict vigilance be not exercised, the already impoverished forest will disappear, and the ryots will not only suffer from want of fuel, but the climatic effect may be disastrous.

CYATHEA ARBOREA, Tree fern. Wood quite worthless as timber, but the section of this tree fern displays well the structure of an acrogenous stem, hollow in the centre, marked on the outside by the scars of the fallen leaves, and showing the elongation of the axis by junction of the petioles.

CYATHEA MEDULLARIS. The tree Fern of Norfolk Island, is about twenty feet in length, and presents a beautiful appearance.

CUTTACK WOODS. The timber trees of this province have only received a partial attention. There were sent 13 specimens of its woods to the Exhibition of 1862, which were furnished by T. W. Armstrong, Esq., Superintending Engineer of the Division, who also gave the following table of their specific gravity, &c. and who mentions that, for logs over 18 feet, the rates rise.

	Specific gravity, water being 1·000.	Price per cubic foot in the log.
Black Sissoo, Dalbergia *sp.?*	875	8 Annas.
Red Sissoo, Do.?	1,000	Ditto.
Koossoom. URIA?	1,286	5 Annas.
Teak, Tectona grandis	875	10 „
Kooroom. URIA? or Koossoom. URIA	714	4 „
Geeringa. URIA? or Guringa, URIA?	714	6 „
Sal, Shorea robusta	1,000	8 „
Jack, Artocarpus integrifolia	750	8 „
Peasal, Buchanania latifolia	875	6 „
Bondhun. URIA? or Burdur. URIA	1,000	8 „
Keehur. URIA?	1,250	6 „
Abloos or Kandoo		
Aman		

The two *Sissoo woods*, it is mentioned, are used for every description of furniture, both by Natives and Europeans, in grain and color somewhat resembling rosewood. The heart of this timber is generally unsound.

Large quantities of Sal, Shorea robusta, are floated down the Mahanuddy to Cuttack. But, in mature trees, the heart is always unsound.

Burdur is described as an excellent wood for carriage poles, shafts and wheels, and in all coach-builders' work..

Keehur, is a hard useful wood, for mallets, pestles, rammers and the like, and likely to be useful in furniture.

Gumbari is plentiful in Sumbulpore and the Tributary Mahals.

Dhamna, hard but pliable and makes good felloes.

Kangra, a hard wood.

Abloos or *Kandoo*, Ebony, a very handsome fancy wood, costing 12 annas the cubic foot. The heart wood is of the darkest shade. *See* ASSAN, BURDUR, GUMBARI, GURINGA, KOOSSOOM, KOOROOM.

CYCAS. The Cycads or Cycadeaceæ, a tribe of plants containing about 50 species, some of which grow in India, and in the islands of the Eastern Archipelago.

CYCAS CIRCINALIS, *Linn.*

Cycas inermis, *Lour.*

Todda-pana. MAL.	Vara guna. TEL.
Wara gudu. TEL.	Rana guvva. „

Chiefly occurs in India and the Moluccas; said to yield a sago, also a gum like tragacanth. It is a very handsome tree, in appearance resembling the Palm tribe, and is common from Tellicherry to the foot of the ghats. It is also common, in the Karen forests of Tenasserim.—*O'Shaughnessy, page* 622, *Mason.*

CYCAS PECTINATA, is a sago palm which grows in Sikkim, on the flats by the streams. Its stem is ten feet high, with a beautiful crown of foliage.—*Hooker, Vol.* i. *p.* 151.

CYCAS REVOLUTA, *Thunb.* A native of Japan; a kind of sago is said to be obtained from the cellular substance. The whole plant yields a copious mucilage, which hardens into a transparent gum.—*O'Shaughnessy, page* 682.

CYNOMETRA *Species.*

Maingga of Martaban.

A small tree of Martaban.

CYNOMETRA RAMIFLORA, *Linn.*

Cynometra cauliflora, *Wall.*

Branch flowered cynometra. ENG.	Gal mendora SINGH.
Iripa. MALEAL.	Hal „ ? „

A tree which attains a height of 60 feet in Malabar, in Java, the Moluccas, Sumatra, and in the western, eastern and southern provinces of Ceylon, at Batticaloa and Trincomalee. A cubic foot weighs 56 lbs., and it is said to last from 15 to 60 years. It is used for bridges and buildings, and is the best kind of wood for under-ground purposes. Its roots, leaves and an oil from the seeds are used medicinally.—*Mr. Mendis, Useful Plants, Voigt, Thwaites.*

CYRTOPHYLLUM FRAGRANS.

Anan. BURM.

Grows in Moulmein. Is one of the nux vomica tribe and one of the hardest, most compact, and heaviest woods known.—*Cal. Cat. Ex.* 1851.

CYTISUS CAJAN, *Linn.* Cajanus Indicus, *Spr.*

Toovaray. CAN. TAM.	Shakhool. PERS.
Tooar. DUK. MAHR.	Adaki. SANS.
Pigeon Pea. ENG.	Kandaloo. TEL.
Urhur. HIND.	

One of the plants employed in the Bengal Powder works at Eshapore, in the manufacture of gunpowder charcoal. It might probably be employed in the manufacture of pyroligneous acetic acid.—*Beng. Phar. p.* 235.

D.

DAGOO THA, BURM.? meaning Crooked Timber, Maximum girth 3 cubits, maximum length 30 feet. Found abundant in Tavoy and Mergui. When seasoned, floats in water. It is used for building boats, for planks of houses, ladders, &c., but is liable to attacks of worms and dry rot.—*Captain Dance.*

DALBERGIA, *Species?* Chisel-handle tree. A common forest tree of Tenasserim, produces a hard, fine-grained wood which the Karens call the egg tree, and Burmese the chisel-handle tree, its wood being much used for chisel handles. Dr. Mason had not seen the flower he says, but the fruit he identified with Roxburgh's genus Dalbergia.—*Dr. Mason.*

DALBERGIA, *Species?* There is a large timber tree found throughout the Tenasserim Provinces, sometimes wrought into canoes, which Dr. Mason thinks is a species of Dalbergia, but he had never seen it in flower. It is the tree of which, according to Burman geography, there is an immense specimen growing on the Great Eastern Island.—*Dr. Mason.*

DALBERGIA, *Species?* Myouk-sho, BURM. Called Moulmein Lancewood, also Monkey tree, so called because its bole is so straight, so slippery, and to so great a height free from branches that no monkey was ever seen to climb it. Maximum girth 4 cubits, maximum length 40 feet. Found very abundant in Tavoy and Mergui: also somewhat abundant all over the provinces inland. When seasoned, floats in water. The wood is much praised in Tavoy, as resembling lancewood in properties but found to split when seasoned, perhaps good specimens have not been obtained. At any rate, other woods of unquestionable value are abundant in Amherst. The Karens make bows of it, but prefer Cassia fistula. Dr. Mason never met with the tree in flower, but thinks it a species of Dalbergia, though it may possibly be a Cassia.—*Captain Dance, Dr. Mason.*

DALBERGIA, *Species?* Myouk-shaw, BURM. A tree of Moulmein. Wood used in ordinary house building.—*Cal. Cat. Ex.* 1862. (NOTE.—Is this identical with the preceding).

DALBERGIA, *Species.*

Thapya. BURM.	Water Dalbergia. ENG.

A tree of Moulmein. Wood used in ordinary house building.—*Cal. Cat. Ex.* 1862.

DALBERGIA, *Species.*

Youdine. BURM.

A tree of Moulmein. A hard heavy black wood, useful for furniture.—*Cal. Cat. Ex.* 1862.

DALBERGIA, *Species.*

Yen-dike. BURM.

Common in the plains and on the hills of British Burmah, particularly at Yendike which takes its name from this tree. Yields a kind of blackwood well worth notice. The sap wood of this tree decays rapidly, but the heartwood is extremely durable, it is black, sometimes with white and red streaks, elastic, but full of natural cracks. Used for ploughs, bows, handles of dahs and spears. There are probably two kinds in the country. A cubic foot weighs lbs. 64. In a full grown tree on good soil the average length of the trunk to the first branch is 35 feet and average girth, measured at 6 feet from the ground is 9 feet. It sells at 12 annas per cubic foot. Dr. McClelland says there are four kinds of Dalbergia, all yielding a heavy timber, which will not float, similar to Sissoo. These trees are very plentiful in the Tharawaddy and Hlaine districts, also in the lower parts of the Tounghoo district. The timber seldom attains a very large size and is generally found of a girth of three or four feet, taller and straighter than Sissoo.—*Drs. Brandis and McClelland, Cal. Cat. Ex. of* 1862.

DALBERGIA, *Species?*

Yendike. BURM.	Blackwood. ENG.

Under these names Captain Dance describes a timber of maximum girth 2 cubits, maximum length 10 or 12 feet. Found abundant all over the provinces, but mostly in Tavoy and Mergui. When it is seasoned, it sinks in water. This, he says, unlike the Blackwood of India, has a fœtid smell like that of new Corduroy and a white grain interspersed amongst the black and red. It is not so handsome a wood as Indian blackwood, but is far tougher, is not brittle, and is excellent for spokes, halves, for handles of screw drivers, augers, gimlets. Used by the Chinese carpenters for planes, and is excellent for that purpose though heavy; but they use smaller planes than we do. Like others of the hardest woods of Burmah, it is so full of natural cracks, that two feet of timber are wasted for one foot made up after being sawn; but, when made up, this wood cracks no more and resists sun or rain admirably. The "Tai" he says is not Yendaik but Ebony, and is brittle and devoid of smell. Dr. Mason tell us that, under the Burman name of yendaik, the wood of two different trees is sometimes seen. One, a species of ebony, and the other a leguminous tree which, according to the descriptions of the Karens, is a species of dalbergia, and the wood resembles the blackwood of Hindostan.—*Dr. Mason, Captain Dance.*

DALBERGIA, *Species ?*

Thevus. HIND.	Thevis. MAHR.

In Nagpore, a light colored wood merging into a light reddish brown. Its strength is considerable, and by the natives the wood is highly prized for bandies. White ants attack it. Only a small supply is obtainable. Its average length is 15 feet and average girth 3½ feet. It sells at 6 annas the cubic foot.—*Captain Sankey.* (NOTE. Is this D. Oojeinensis, Roxb. Fl. Ind. 3, p. 220.

DALBERGIA ACUMINATA, *Ains.*

Sissa. CAN.	Sesso. HIND.
Sessu tree. ANGLO-HIND.	

Dr. Ainslie describes this as growing in Oude, Bahar and Canara, as furnishing a valuable wood, employed for the knees and frames of ships.—*Mat. Med. p.* 210.

DALBERGIA ALATA ?

Tsouk-yoa. BURM.

A tree of Moulmein. Used for tool handles. —*Cal. Cat. Ex.* 1862.

DALBERGIA ARBOREA, *Willde.*

Robinia mitis, *Linn.*	Galedupa Indica, *Lam.*
Pongamia glabra, *Vent.*	

Canaga. CAN.	Karrunjie. SANS.
Kurrunje ki jhar. DUK.	Punga maram ? TAM.
Poongum tree. ENG.	Kanuga manu. TEL.
Kurinj jhar. HIND.	

Described as a large tree, with light green foliage, deciduous at the close of the cold season. The wood is light and firm, and serves for common purposes. The seeds yield a useful oil.—*Ains. Mat. Med. p.* 103. *See* PONGAMIA.

DALBERGIA FRONDOSA, *Roxb.; W. & A.; W. Ic.*

Dalbergia arborea, *Heyne.*

Erra pachchari. TEL.	Pedda sopara. TEL.

In Ceylon, not uncommon in the central provinces and elsewhere up to an elevation of 3,000 feet. Grows in the Godavery forests and in the Circars; also in Pegu where it attains a girth of four feet and upwards, and is taller and straighter than the Sissoo, and furnishes a strong useful timber.—*Fl. Andh., Captain Beddome, Dr. McClelland, p.* 10, *Thw.*

DALBERGIA LANCEOLARIA, *Linn. fil.*

Nedun. SING.	Nendoon. SING.

Described as growing in the western and southern provinces of Ceylon, and its wood as employed in buildings and for furniture. A cubic foot weighs 56 lbs, and it lasts from 60 to 80 years.—*Mendis.*

DALBERGIA LATIFOLIA, *Roxb.; W. & A.*

Shwet Sal. BENG.	Iti. MALEAL.
Sit Sal. "	Eruputtu maram. TAM.
Yendike? BURM.	Iti. "
Bitti. CAN.	Korin-toware. "
Todigate. " ?	Virugaduchava. TEL.
Vriksha. " ?	Iruvudu. "
Sweta-shala. DUK. ? ?	Irugudu. "
Rosewood Tree. ENG.	Jittegi. "
Blackwood Tree. "	Nalla Irugudu. "
MalabarBlackwoodTree. ENG	Tella " "
Sweta Sal. HIND.	

This tree grows in the peninsula and northern parts of India, in more or less abundance; in the Godavery forests, the Circar mountains, in Coimbatore, Malabar, Canara and Sunda, the S. Konkun, on the banks of the Kali Naddi river, in the Southern Mahratta Country, the N. W. Provinces, in Bengal, the Khassia hills, and in Assam: and, on the Coromandel and Malabar Coasts. It grows to an immense size, the trunk sometimes measuring 15 feet in circumference, exclusive of the bark. In Coimbatore, it is less abundant than the eatty maram, perhaps from being more sought after as yielding more valuable timber; it is, there, a very dark, heavy and strong wood, sustaining a weight of 515 lbs. Everywhere, in Southern India, this valuable wood has risen much in price, the two indents from the Madras and Bombay Gun Carriage Manufactories amounting, in 1858, to 5,000 cubic feet. In Canara, this tree was formerly given to applicants at 3 Rupees each; but that practice has been disallowed. There is not much blackwood remaining in the Anamallai Forest, but there is a considerable quantity in the escheated forest of Chennat Nair, and it is abundant in Wynaad and Coorg. In consequence of its increasing value instructions were given, in 1858, for an experimental sowing at Nellumboor, with what result is not known. In Canara and Sunda, it is abundant and large at north end of Dandelee forest; scanty elsewhere. It is rather common in most of the Bombay coast forests, particularly in ravines of the hills and under the Ghats, also on the Ghats; but, there, it never reaches the great size which it attains in Malabar. It is also often crooked. The wood is extensively used for cabinet work, knees of vessels, agricultural implements, combs, &c. It appears, in density of grain and endurance, to be much superior to the Sissoo of Hindostan. The wood of the centre of the trunk and large branches, is greenish or greenish black, often mottled, or with light coloured veins running in various directions. It is close grained, admitting of the finest polish, and is employed for furniture of every description, and, in the Madras Gun Carriage Manufactory, for light field beams, cheeks, axle cases, braces, perches, poles, splinter bars, waggon perches and framing, light field spokes and felloes. For gun-carriages it is so valuable that large plantations have been formed in waste places of the North-western provinces of Hindostan. In Malabar, it is the magnificent tree from which the well known Malabar blackwood is obtained, and planks 4 feet broad are often procurable, after all the external white wood has been removed: it is heavy and close grained, admitting of fine polish very much used for furniture. It is one of the most valuable woods of the Madras Presidency.—*Drs. Roxburgh, Wight, Gibson and Cleghorn, Voigt, Flor. Andhr., Captain Beddome.*

DALBERGIA OOATA ??

Tsouk yo. BURM.

A tree of Moulmein. A tough wood: much used for tool handles.—*Cal. Cat. Ex.* 1862.

DALBERGIA MOONIANA, *Thw.: Moon's Cat. p.* 51; *folios* 5-8,

D. Lanceolaria, *Linn. fil.*

Nadoong-gass. SINGH.

A great tree, which grows in the southern and central parts of Ceylon, at no great elevation.—*Thwaites' Enumeratio Plantarum Zeylanicæ, Part II. p.* 93. *See* D. LANCEOLARIA.

DALBERGIA OOJEINENSIS, *Roxb. W. Ic.*

Tevus. MAHR.
Tennus. „
Tunnus. „
Ati muktamu. TEL.
Manda motuku. TEL.
Nemmi chettu. „
Tella motuku. „

A tree 30 feet high, grows in the valleys of the Himalayas, the Kheree jungle, Dehra Dhoon, Kamaon, Sirmore, in Oude and the Godavery forests. Found both in the Konkun and inland Bombay forests, especially common in some parts of Kolwan, Khandeish, and the Satpoora Hills. It is a wood of great strength and toughness, especially applicable for cart building, ploughs, &c., seldom reaches a size sufficient to give a plank of 9 inches. The wood of that which grows on the Godavery is valuable, but the tree is rather rare there.—*Voigt, Fl. Andh., Useful Plants, Dr. Gibson, Captain Beddome.* (NOTE.—Is this the "Thevus" of Nagpore? See above).

DALBERGIA PANICULATA, *Roxb.; W. & A.*

Putchalay wood. ANGLO-TAM.
Phassie. MAHR.
Putchalai maram. TAM.
Pachchari. TEL.
Porilla sapara. TEL.
Tella pachchari. „
Tella patsaroo. „

This tree grows in Moulmein, Assam, Oude, in the Northern Circars, in the Godavery Forests, Coimbatore, at Courtallum, in the Mawul districts, and above the Ghats. In Coimbatore, it attains a considerable size, and the timber is said to be strong, and fit for many purposes. It is rather common in most of the Bombay forests, both of the coast and inland. The wood there is light yellow, strong, compact, and fit for many purposes in house building, agriculture, &c. But, Captain Beddome tells us of Porilla sopara, (Godavery) Tella patsaroo (Circars) *Tel.* Dalbergia paniculata, that the wood is perfectly useless—it is arranged in rings with softer substance in between the layers. Voigt tells us that it is white and firm but less useful than some of the other species. The character of the wood would thus seem to vary according to locality.—*Drs. Wight and Gibson, Voigt, Captain Beddome.*

DALBERGIA ROBUSTA, *Roxb.; W. Ic.*

Dalbergia Krowree, *Roxb.*
„ latifolia, *Gibson.*

This tree grows in Nepaul, Assam and Pegu, where it is very abundant, and attains a girth of four feet and upwards, and is taller and straighter than Sissoo.—*Voigt, Dr. McClelland, p.* 10.

DALBERGIA SISSOIDES, *Grah.*

Rose wood. ENG.
Black wood. „
Eatty maram. TAM.
Biti maram. TAM.
Vitty maram. „
Kar-itti. „

Dr. Wight says that this is perhaps the best known, in the Coimbatore jungles, of the trees yielding blackwood, but there are several others as good or perhaps better. It abounds in the Palghaut forests, but, in 1850, was rarely to be met with of great size; when it and its congener Dalbergia latifolia are carried to Madras it becomes one of the rose woods of the furniture shops. It is a smaller tree than D. latifolia, but more common in the forests. Both yield a black wood, and in Madras are indiscriminately called "Rose wood." The wood contains much oil, which unfits it for receiving paint. Mr. Rohde says that this, the blackwood or East India Rose wood, is one of our best woods for plain furniture, though at Madras it is said to cast about a good deal; by experiment he found it to be one of the strongest timbers we have in the Circars, he is inclined to believe that the wood imported from the Western Coast is not equal in strength to the smaller but closer grained wood of the Circars, and the appearance of the latter is more veined and he thinks closer in the grain than that of the Western Coast—the wood contains much oil which renders it unfit for receiving paint—logs are almost invariably faulty in the centre: as a tough strong wood it will be found useful whether curved or straight. Dr. Gibson does not recognise this as a species distinct from Dalbergia latifolia.—*Dr. Gibson, Mr. Rohde and Dr. Wight in Cat. of Ex. of* 1851, *Dr. Cleghorn in Madras E. J. R.*

DALBERGIA SISSOO, *Roxb.*

Pterocarpus sissu, *Roxb.*

Sissoo wood. ENG.
Sissu. HIND.
Yerra-chava kurra. TEL.
Sissoo. TEL.
Sissowa. URIA ?

This tree grows in Bengal, Nagpore, Guzerat, in the hills about Nagotnah, and Kennery jungles. It is a native of Bengal and the adjoining provinces to the northward where the timber is much prized. Sissoo is scarce in the hills of Ajmeer, but more abundant in Kotah. In Nagpore, logs of it are procurable from 10 to 15 feet long, and 3 to 2½ feet in girth at 6 annas the cubic foot. But it is said to attain a great size in Chandah. It is there employed in ornamental work, domes of gharries, &c. It was introduced into the Madras Presidency from Bengal at the recommendation of Dr. Wallich, and has been planted on the banks of the Toomboodra, where it is said to be thriving wonderfully; it is growing extensively in the cantonment of Masulipatam, as an avenue tree, and has been planted in some places on the banks of the Kistnah annicut. The trees thrive well at Masulipatam, and from their appearance, Mr. Rohde thinks it would thrive well in the Madras provinces. Its rapid growth recommends it for avenues, for the tree attains perfection in 28 years, it is propagated and reared with facility, and early attains a good working condition of timber. The wood is greyish brown with darker coloured veins, very strong, but said to be not very durable. It is used in Bengal for gun carriages, and furnishes the Bengal ship-builders with their crooked timbers and knees, being remarkably strong, but not so durable as could be wished; it answers well for various other economical purposes. Captain Macdonald tells us that, in Ganjam and Gumsur, it has a circumference of 4½ feet, and height from the ground to the intersection of the first branch 15 feet, and furnishes the material of which tables, chairs, couches, book-stands and other articles of furniture are usually made in that part of the country. It is not so plentiful as it was, being in great request. In the Dekhan, the wood is used principally, from its strength and natural bend, for native hackeries: when it can be procured long and straight, it makes good shafts for buggies. The wood of the Ajmeer tree is very dark and beautifully veined, like rosewood. Upon the whole there is scarcely a tree which deserves more attention; for, when its rapid growth in almost every soil, its beauty and uses are taken into account, few trees can be compared with it. Major Campbell's estimate of the value in practice, of this wood, is 96, being higher than that of the best specimens of teak. Wood hard, strong, tenacious, and compact, whilst its great durability combines to render it one of the most valuable timbers known. Dr. Wallich and others have recommended it for plantations, showing the probable return. Flowering time, the beginning of the hot season: the seed ripens about the close of the year.—*Voigt, Captain Macdonald, Mr. Rohde's MSS., Dr. Irvine's Gen. Med. Top. of Ajmeer, p.* 203, *Drs. Riddell, Cleghorn, and Roxburgh, Captain Sankey.*

DAL BULLOO GEERA. CAN. Grows in Canara and Sunda, on the elevated plateau between Gungawalee and Black rivers, does not reach a great size. Wood very strong and tough, sought after for agricultural implements.—*Dr. Gibson.*

DALECHAMPIA POMIFERA.

Douk-ya mah. BURM.

Scarce, but met with on the banks of streams in the Pegu Valley, particularly in the Pymmah Choung. The trees are from three to four feet in girth. Wood, red or dark brown, and adapted for cabinet making.—*Dr. McClelland.*

DALOSINGHA OR TALOOSINGHEE, URIA? A tree of Ganjam and Gumsur, extreme height 25 feet, circumference 1½ feet and height from the ground to the intersection of the first branch, 6 feet. Abounds, and is burnt for firewood and charcoal. Ploughshares are sometimes made of the wood.—*Captain Macdonald.*

DAMARLOUT—? A wood of Penang of a brown colour. Used for building and general purposes.—*Col. Frith.*

DAMINNE. SINGH. A tree of the Eastern provinces of Ceylon. A cubic foot weighs 44 feet and it is calculated to last 40 years. It is used for gun-stocks and common house buildings.—*Mendis.*

DAUP-YAN. A Tavoy wood, used for building.—*Col. Frith.*

DAUP-YAT. In Amherst, a timber employed for rafters; it is a beautiful yellowish-white compact wood, but has a tendency to split. The leaves are used as a dye.—*Captain Dance.*

DEALS.

Dœler. DAN.
Deelen. DUT
Deal boards. ENG.
Sawn wood. „
Planches minces. FR.
Dielen. GER.
Tavole. IT.
Piane. „
Tarcice. POL.
Doski. RUS.
Tiljor. SW.

See page 8.

DASYAULUS, *Thwaites.*

Several species occur in Ceylon, middle sized trees, viz., D. fulvus, at Hewessee in the Pasdoon Corle: D. microphyllus, in the south, but rare: D. Moonii, at Caltura near Ratnapoora: and D. neriifolia, "Gang mee," *Singh.*, common on the banks of rivers and streams in the warmer parts of the island. The last is the Bassia neriifolia of Moon's Cat.—*Thwaites.*

DELIMA SARMENTOSA, *Linn.*

Grows in Ceylon, in the southern parts of the island, up to an elevation of 1,000 feet.—*Thwaite's En. Pl. Zeyl., p.* 21.

DENDROCALAMUS. A genus of bamboos. D. balcooa, prized for its solidity and strength grows in Bengal. D. strictus, of the peninsula is used for spear shafts, and D. tulda is the common bamboo of Bengal.—*See* BAMBUSA.

DENKENACOTTA. A forest, the finest in the Salem collectorate of the Madras Presidency. It contains sandal wood, acha wood.—*Cons. Rep.*

DEREAH. HIND.

Dareah. HIND,	Bhera. MAHR.

A wood of the Nagpore forests: though of great strength, it cannot, from the small size the tree attains, rank as a building material: the average logs are from 6½ to 10½ feet long and from 3 feet to 2 feet in girth. It has a winding and,as it were, netted grain, from which, as well as the extraordinary toughness of its fibres, butchers invariably use it for chopping blocks; the sharp edge of the knife apparently having no effect on it.—*Captain Sankey.*

DHAMNA, URIA? A tree of Cuttack which makes good cart wheel felloes, and is hard, but pliable —*Cal. Cat. Ex. of* 1862.

DHAMNA, HIND.? A reddish coloured wood, strong, very plentiful in the Santhal jungles from Raneebahal to Hasdiha or about forty miles. Used chiefly for cart wheels.—*Calcutta Engineers' Journal, July* 1860. (NOTE. These two seem identical as to quality of timber: are they the Grewia tiliæfolia?)

DHAN DHAUTA, HIND.? A tree of Chota Nagpore with hard, white timber.—*Cal. Cat. Ex.* 1862.

DHANNEE, TAM. A dark coloured wood of Travancore, specific gravity 0·733. Very strong, but knotty, used for common buildings. —*Col. Frith.*

DHARINJO, URIA. A tree of Ganjam and Gumsur, extreme height 60 feet, circumference 4 feet, and height from the ground to the intersection of the first branch, 8 feet. Tolerably common. No use seems to be made of the wood. The bark is used medicinally by women after child-birth; the juice of the leaves is supposed to cure itch.—*Captain Macdonald.*

DHELA KATA, HIND? A tree of Chota Nagpore, with hard, yellow timber.—*Cal. Cat. Ex.* 1862.

DHEWUS, HIND.

Dhaves. HIND.	Dhivus. MAHR.

A timber of Nagpore, of a light colour. It is devoured by white ants, and is only procurable of a small scantling, from 12 to 15 feet long and two feet in girth. Its strength, however, is considerable, and, if found of a proper size, would doubtless be valuable. The young trees are all cut down for bandy poles. It sells at 8 annas the cubic foot.—*Captain Sankey.*

DHIMEREE, URIA? A tree of Gamjam and Gumsur, extreme height 40 feet, circumference 4½ feet, and height from the ground to the intersection of the first branch, 8 feet. Bandy wheels are sometimes made of the wood, but it is chiefly used for firewood, being tolerably plentiful. It is considered sacred and is burnt when libations are offered. The fruit is eaten: a juice extracted from the root is used in rheumatism.—*Captain Macdonald.*

DHOBOO, URIA? A tree of Ganjam and Gumsur, extreme height 36 feet, circumference 3 feet and height from ground to the intersection of the first branch, 15 feet. There are two kinds of this tree, the "Nongoliah" and the "Pooro," both of which are very common. It seems to be only used for firewood.—*Captain Macdonald.*

DHOBO KHOIRO, URIA? A tree of Ganjam and Gumsur, extreme height 25 feet, circumference 2 feet, height from the ground to the intersection of the first branch, 6 feet. A white variety of the same species occurs. Both trees are very common.—*Captain Macdonald.*

DHOO, URIA? A tree of Ganjam and Gumsur, extreme height 45 feet, circumference 4½ feet, height from ground to the intersection of the first branch 22 feet. This tree abounds and is extensively used for fuel. The wood is of little value.—*Captain Macdonald.*

DHOSORA KHENDOO, URIA? A tree of Ganjam and Gumsur, extreme height 60 feet, circumference 5 feet, and height from the ground to the intersection of the first branch 18 feet. The wood is used for ploughshares and bandies, is tolerably common and is burnt for firewood. The fruit is eaten.—*Captain Macdonald.*

DHOWA, HIND.? A whitish colored wood, close-grained and hard. Plentiful in the Santhal jungles and hills from Raneebahal to Hasdiha, a distance of about forty miles. The wood of it is chiefly used for cart wheels, beams, and door posts, by the natives, also for mallets and tent pegs.—*Calcutta Engineers' Journal, July* 1860.

DICHROSTACHYS CINEREA, *W. & A.*

Mimosa cinerea, *Linn.; Roxb.*
Desmanthus cinereus, *Willd.*
Acacia cinerea, *Spreng.*
,, dalea. *Desv.*

Vurtuli. HIND.	Veluturu. TEL.
Andara.gass. SINGH.	Yel-tur. ,,
Wara-tara. TAM.	Velliturn. ,,
Veda-tara. ,,	Venuturu. ,,
Vadatala maram. TAM.	

Abundant in the hot and drier parts of Ceylon. It is a small scrubby tree or large shrub in Coimbatore and common in waste places of the inland country, in the Bombay Presidency. Dr. Gibson had not seen it near to the coast. The wood is very hard, strong and good for pegs, but too small for any other purpose.—*Drs. Wight, Gibson, Flor. Andh., Thwaite's En. Pl. Zeyl.*

DIEN-NEEUNG. — ? In Amherst, a timber used for rice-pounders; it is a close-grained, strong, compact, brown, hard wood.

DILLENIA, a genus of plants, several species of which, yielding useful and valuable timbers, grow in Ceylon, in the two peninsulas, and in the northern provinces of India. Some, of which the timbers are described, are not yet specifically determined.

DILLENIA, *Species*.

Zin Pyun Ngan. BURM.

A tree of Moulmein. A strong wood for any ordinary purposes. Fruit edible.—*Cal. Cat. Ex.* 1862.

DILLENIA *Species*.

Zimboon. BURM.

A timber of Tavoy, used in building.—*Capt. Dance*.

DILLENIA AUGUSTA, *Roxb.*

Zin-byewn. BURM.

Grows in the Garrow hills, and is plentiful in the forests of the Pegu district but becomes scarce to the north of it. Its wood is of a light brown colour, and it yields a large and good timber for house building.—*Dr. McClelland, Voigt*.

DILLENIA AUREA, *Sm.*

Zimbyoon. BURM.

Abundant in the plains and hills and on the forests of British Burmah but more scarce to the north of it. Wood of a light brown colour occasionally used in house building, but mostly for firewood. Breaking weight lbs. 198. A cubic foot weighs 48 lbs. In a full grown tree on good soil the average length of the trunk, to the first branch is 20 feet, and average girth, measured at 6 feet from the ground, is 9 feet. It sells at 12 annas per cubic foot.—*Dr. Brandis, Cal. Ex. Cat. of* 1862.

DILLENIA DENTATA ? ?

Gode para. SINGH

Grows in the western parts of Ceylon, where its wood is used for roofs of houses. A cubic foot weighs 51 lbs. and it is said to last 40 years. —*Mr. Mendis*.

DILLENIA INTEGRA, *Thunb.*

Wormia integra, H. f. et T., I. c. p. 68 cum syn.

Said to grow in Ceylon, but Mr. Thwaites suspects some error as to four species of the large Dilleniaceous trees growing in Ceylon.—*Thw. p.* 5.

DILLENIA RETUSA, *Thunb.*

Wormia retusa, *H. f. et T.*

Goda para. SINGH.

A moderate sized tree, growing in Ceylon, to an elevation of 2,000 feet, but not abundant. —*Thw.*

DILLENIA PENTAGYNA, *Roxb.*

Colbertia coromandeliana, *D C.*
Wormia coromandeliana, *Spreng.*

Bjoo-ben. BURM.	Rawa-dara. TEL.
Poon spar tree. ENG.	Rowadan. „
Kurmul. MAHR.	Chinna kalinga. „
Kanagaln. „	Ravudana. „
Pinnay maram. TAM.	

This is a stately forest tree, of great value, being one of those which yield the Poon Spars of commerce. It is common on the face of the Western Ghauts. In Coimbatore, it is a tall tree. It is a great tree, common in the Konkun and Ghat jungles of Bombay, but never found inland. As a treeof British Burmah, it is abundant in the Eng Forest (the Forest of Dipterocarpus grandiflora) where its wood is hard and strong, and used for rice mills. A cubic foot weighs 69 lbs. In a full grown tree on good soil the average length of the trunk, to the first branch, is 20 feet and average girth measured at 6 feet from the ground is 6 feet. It is a large timber tree in Assam where it is used for canoes, its wood there being close grained. Captain Beddome says it is a very strong, hard wood, abundant on the Indrawatty and in jungles on the left bank of the Godavery but not known on the right bank. Dr. Cleghorn says "this is believed to be the tree, which furnishes the *Poon* spars, so valuable for shipping, though *Calophyllum inophyllum* has hitherto been so considered." Dr. Wight says, in Coimbatore "the similarity of native names between this and Calophyllum inophyllum leads me to suspect some mistake here. The wood of Dillenia pentagyna is said to be exceedingly strong and very durable even when buried under ground, Since this paper was written, adds Dr. Wight, I have been informed that this is the tree that furnishes the Poon Spars, and judging from the manner of growth, I feel satisfied that this information is correct. This is a tall, the other, a short stunted tree." "I do not find" says Dr. Gibson, "that the wood is used for any purpose more important than for the loose planks used in the decks of native boats. It is not employed in house purposes. This tree is in great request by the merchants of Bombay, from the wood splitting well. It has, thus, seemed advisable to give all recent information regarding a tree, which is supposed to yield a timber so valuable as the Poon Spars.—*Drs. Wight, Cleghorn, Gibson, Brandis, Voigt, Captain Beddome, Cal. Cat. Ex. of* 1862, *Useful Plants*.

DILLENIA ORNATA—?

Grows in Pegu and Moulmein. The trees are plentiful and of large girth, and furnish a strong good timber, useful for general purposes in house and ship building. It has large gaudy yellow flowers.—*Dr. Mason, Captain Benson*.

DILLENIA PILOSA, *Roxb.*

Grows in Assam near Goalpara, on the banks of the Megna, and furnishes a hard tough wood, much used for canoes.—*Voigt*.

DILLENIA SCABRELLA, *Roxb.*

Byew. BURM.	Kurmul. MAHR.
Kulgul. CAN.	

Grows in Chittagong and in Canara and Sunda where it is most common below the Ghat. Grows large, long, and straight. Wood seems to be used for boat planks in Canara, but it is not reckoned a choice wood in the Bombay Presidency. It is plentiful in the Pegu province, but becomes scarce to the north of it, and it is, there, of large girth, furnishes a large good timber and is useful for general purposes, as house and ship building.—*Drs. Gibson and McClelland, Captain Benson.*

DILLENIA SPECIOSA, *Thunb.; Rheede; W. & A.; W. Ic.*

Dillenia Indica, *Linn.*
„ elliptica, *Thunb.*

Chalita. BENG.	Syalita. MALEAL.
Chalta. „	Honda-para. SINGH.
Thab Yew. BURM.	Uva maram. TAM.
Thab-yoo. „	Pedda Kalinga. TEL.
Thee-bew-tha. „	Kalinga. „
Muta Kurmul. DUK.	Uvvachettu. „
Girnar. HIND.	

This large and ornamental tree, is hardy and thrives well in compounds. It grows in Ceylon, in the two Indian peninsulas, in Bengal, Assam, Chittagong, and in Java and the Moluccas. It is abundant at Kotah in Ajmere and is a native of the valleys in the Circar mountains. Mr. Thwaites says it is common in the warmer parts of the island of Ceylon, up to an elevation of 2,000 feet, and is most frequent on the banks of streams. Captain Beddome says it grows in the jungles of the Godavery, and furnishes a very hard wood. Dr. Brandis mentions that it grows on the banks of the mountain streams of British Burmah, but the wood is not used. A cubic foot he says weighs 41 lbs. In a full grown tree on good soil the average length of the trunk to the first branch is 15 feet, and average girth measured at 6 feet from the ground is 5 feet. Dr. Brandis is the most recent writer, but, if the same tree, his opinion does not correspond with that of Dr. McClelland who describes it "Thabyew" as scarce in Pegu, but as affording a large and good timber for house building, and for wood of a light brown colour. And Captain Dance describes the "Thee-bew-tha" as growing in Amherst, Tavoy and Mergui. Maximum girth 3 cubits, maximum length 22 feet and the trees abundant, but widely scattered all over the provinces, here and there, inland. When seasoned, it floats in water. It yields a durable, tough, light wood, seeming very good for helves. It is used by Burmese for building houses and for sundry other purposes. —*Thwaites, Voigt, Drs. Brandis and McClelland, Captains Beddome and Benson, Drs. Riddell and Irvine.*

DINDUGA TREE, ANGLO-CAN.

Dinduga. CAN.	Bayla Nava maram. TAM.

According to Dr. Roxburgh, a species of Andersonia. A large and valuable tree of the Wynaad.—*Ains.*

DIOSPYROS. A genus of plants, belonging to the natural order Ebenaceæ. The species form large trees with alternate, thick, and, often, leathery leaves. They are found in the Mauritius, Ceylon, in every part of India, and are remarkable for the woods and fruits they afford. The Karens have distinct names for four different species of Tenasserim ebony trees. The salt water swamp ebony, the water ebony, the yellow ebony, and the true ebony. Dr. Mason never met with the trees in flower, so as to be able to distinguish the species of Diospyros; but has seen specimens of the wood in the southern provinces, not inferior to the ebony of commerce. Some of the species of these countries, the woods of which have been noticed are, as yet, not described specifically.—*Eng. Cyc. Dr. Mason.*

DIOSPYROS, *Species.*

Kurwul. CAN.

Grows in Canara and Sunda in the great jungles in the Ghats above, chiefly to the south. Ripe wood particularly good, as it has the ebony heart.—*Dr. Gibson.*

DIOSPYROS, *Species.* Nulla kaka mushti, *Tel.* of (Circars only.) D. Syhrtica? Wood whitish and very hard.—*Captain Beddome.*

DIOSPYROS, *Species.* Muchi twikee of the (Godavery forests) Warungul. *Tel.* A very hard light colored wood.—*Captain Beddome.*

DIOSPYROS, *Species.*

Ouk-khyin-za. BURM.

A beautiful wood of British Burmah, white and black mottled, used for house posts. A cubic foot weighs lbs. 41. In a full grown tree on good soil the average length of the trunk to the first branch is 30 feet, and average girth measured at 6 feet from the ground is 9 feet. It sells at 8 annas per cubic foot.—*Dr. Brandis.*

DIOSPYROS, *Species.*

Ghoot. BURM.

In British Burmah, a wood similar to that of the foregoing but a much smaller tree: small quantities of black heart wood (Ebony) are occasionally found near the centre of very old trees of this and another kind nearly related to it (Tayben.) A cubic foot weighs lbs. 49. In a full grown tree on good soil the average length is 15 feet and the average girth measured at 6 feet from the ground is 3 feet.—*Dr. Brandis.*

DIOSPYROS, *Species.* Moulmein ebony. There is an inferior kind of ebony often seen at Moulmein, which the natives do not call by the same name that they do the trees which produce the good ebony, though evidently a product of the same genus. A similar wood at Tavoy is often denominated iron wood.—*Dr. Mason's Tenasserim.*

DIOSPYROS (?) *Species ?* Ryamucha? Used in house building at Martaban.

DIOSPYROS, *Species.*

Ebony. Eng.	Tai. Burm.

Maximum girth ½ to 1 cubit, maximum length 8 feet. Found, very scarce, from the forest in the direction of Shuay Gheen. When seasoned it sinks in water. This wood was much sought for, by Captain Dance, but could not be procured in Moulmein in sufficient abundance for it to be made suitable for any ordnance purpose. —*Captain Dance.*

DIOSPYROS, *Species.*

Kendhoo. Uria?

A tree of Ganjam and Gumsur, extreme height 60 feet, circumference 4½ feet, height from ground to the intersection of the first branch, 30 feet. A hard wood blacker than the Sisoowa. Boxes &c. are made of it. It is tolerably common. The fruit is eaten. —*Captain Macdonald.*

DIOSPYROS ACUTA, *Thwaites.* A middle sized tree of Pasdoon Corle, in Ceylon.—*Thw. En. Pl. Zeyl. p.* 182.

DIOSPYROS AFFINIS, *Thwaites.* A middle sized tree growing at Ooma Oya, on the lower road from Kandy to Badulla, in Ceylon. The timber is suitable for building purposes.—*Thw. En. Pl. Zeyl.* III, *p.* 179.

DIOSPYROS ATTENUATA, *Thwaites.* A middle sized tree of Pasdoon Corle, in Ceylon. *Thw. En. Pl. Zeyl. p.* 182.

DIOSPYROS CHLOROXYLON ? *Roxb.*

Nullaulemara wood. Anglo-Tel.	Peddi illinda. Tel.
Ullinda. Tel.	Nella ulimera. „
Nellarulemara kurra. Tel.	Illinda. „
	Pedda ulimera. „

Grows to a large tree on the Circar mountains, and gives a very hard useful wood, whereas it is generally a shrub about the Godavery forests. The fruit is edible.—*Voigt, Captain Beddome.*

DIOSPYROS CORDIFOLIA, *Roxb.*

Diospyros montana, *Wight* ? ?

Ban-gab. Beng.	Nalla ulimera. Tel.
Goundhan. Mahr.	Kaka ulimera. „
Vuckana maram. Tam.	Nalla urimida. „

Grows in Ceylon near Jaffna, in the peninsula of India, in Coimbatore, in the Bombay forests, and in Bengal. It yields a hard, heavy, strong wood, of a dark brown colour and difficult to work. Not uncommon in the Bombay side of India, but more in ravines and waste places than in forests. Dr. Gibson had never seen a tree that would turn out a log 4′ inches square. The wood is strong and durable.—*Drs. Wight and Gibson, Thwaites, Voigt.*

DIOSPYROS CRUMENATA, *Thw.*

A tree of the Central Province of Ceylon growing at an elevation of 2,000 to 4,000 feet. —*Thwaite's En. Pl. Zeyl. III. p.* 179. *See* D. QUÆSITA. D. OOCARPA.

DIOSPYROS EBENUM, *Linn.; Retz.; W. Ic.* 188.

Diospyros ebenaster, *Retz.*

„ Hebenaster, *Rumph.*

Abnoos. Ar.	Kal oowara gass. Singh.
Kurre mara. Can.	Kal woora gass. „
Ebony. Eng.	Kadu beriya? „
Εβενος. Gr.	Tai maram. Tam.
Abnoos, the Ebony. Hind.	Acha maram. „
Tendu, the white wood. „	Kaka-tati. „
Tendua. „ „ „ „	Tumbi maram. „
Ebenus. Lat.	Tuki. Tel.
Abnoos. Pers.	Kendhoo. Uria?

This great tree, which, in Ceylon, yields the best kind of Ebony wood, is not uncommon there up to an elevation of 5,000 feet. It is said to grow in the Denkencottah forest, in the Salem collectorate, and, writing in 1850, from the Coimbatore collectorate, Dr. Wight says of the Diospyros ebenaster, Ainsl. (*Ebenaceæ* Icon. 188. Acha maram, *Tam.*) that this name was copied by him from Ainslie but "that he was still uncertain whether this is the species that yields the ebony of the Palghaut jungles, as there is reason to believe more than one species contributes wood black enough to pass current for ebony. The plant produced to him, under that Tamool name, was Bauhinia tomentosa, a widely different tree but having a very dark or black heart-wood." Dr. Gibson says that Kuree murra, Ebnoos, *Hind.* Diospyros ebenum, is not common in Canara and Sunda though found near Oopenputam in Canara; also below the Woolwee Ghat. Dr. Cleghorn, writing in the Jury Reports of the M. E. of 1855, says of Diospyros ebenaster, Acha maram, *Tam.* that Ebony of very superior quality is procurable in Madras districts as well as in the Northern Circars, and that Mr. Rohde had received 16 inch planks of a fine uniform black. Captain Sankey says that, in Nagpore, this tree, which yields a very fine ebony, has very little of the blackwood. When young, as it advances in age the blackwood increases, and eventually nothing but blackwood is found. From the ease with which the white wood bends, natives employ it in the manufacture of buggies, carriages, &c. &c., but, as it soon loses its essential oil, the unseasoned timber is preferred for such purposes. White ants attack the white wood readily, and it is nearly always beetle bored. In strength it excels teak, yet from the above circumstances, as well as from the fact that it is very seldom obtainable of more than 6 inches square, he rejected it as a building material. It grows in the Dekhan and in the Kotah jungles of Ajmeer. Ebony is much affected by the weather, on which account European cabinet makers seldom use it except in veneer, and its use is restricted to delicate and costly cabinet work. The Atcha maram, which yields one of the ebonies of Madras, is the Bauhinia tomentosa.—*Drs. Gibson, Wight, Cleghorn, Riddell and Irvine, Voigt, Thwaites, Mr. Rohde, Capt. Sankey, Tredgold, Holtzappfel. See* Ebony.

DIOSPYROS EMBRYOPTERIS, *Persoon; W. Ic.* 843, 844.

Diospyros glutinosa, *Kön., Roxb., Rheede.*
Embryopteris glutinosa, *W. Ic., Rheede.*

Tumika? Beng.	Timberee-gass. Singh.
Gaub. „	Panichi maram? Tam.
Gab Tree. Eng.	Tumbikai. „
Gaub. Hind.	Tubiki. Tel.
Gab? Sans.	Tinduki. „
Sindica. „	Tumiki. „

Grows in Ceylon, in damp forests, towards the South of the island; also, in peninsular India, in the Circars, at Hurdwar, in the Dehra Dhoon, and all along the foot of the Himalayas, to Silhet and Assam. Wood of an indifferent quality and not much used. The astringent viscid mucus of the fruit is used for paying boats' bottoms, and, as they contain much tannin, an infusion is used to steep fishing nets.—*Roxb., Mr. Rohde's MSS., Thwaites, Voigt.*

DIOSPYROS CANDOLLEANA, *Wight. Ic. tt.* 1,221, 1,222.—*c. p.* 3,394.

Homedereya-gass. Singh.

In Ceylon, a middle sized tree, in the Saffragam district and Hinidoon corle.—*Thw. En. Pl. Zeyl. p.* 181.

DIOSPYROS GARDENERI, *Thw.*

Kadoombaireya-gass. Singh.

A middle sized tree of Ceylon, at Saffragam and Kornegalle districts, and less commonly near Kandy.—*Thw. En. Pl. Zeyl. p* 181. *See* Ebony.

DIOSPYROS HIRSUTA, *Linn. fil.*

Calamander wood tree. Eng.	Koul-midvies. Singh.
Calu midiriya. Singh.	Calamander maram. Tam.

A middle sized tree of the forests of Ceylon in the Saffragam and Galle districts which furnishes one of the Calamander woods of commerce. Its density is nearly 60 lbs. to the cubic foot. Tredgold mentions that the figure is between that of rose-wood and zebra-wood; the colour of the ground is usually of a red hazel brown, described also as chocolate brown, with black stripes and marks. It is said to be so hard as almost to require grinding rather than cutting; but, this is not strictly accurate, as the veneer saws cut it without particular difficulty: it is a very handsome furniture wood and turns well; Mr. Layard says that there are three varieties of it;—the Calamander or Coromandel, which is the darkest, and the most commonly seen in England; the Calemberri, which is lighter coloured and striped, and the Omander, the ground of which is as light as English yew, but of a redder cast, with a few slight veins and marks of darker tints. He says, the wood is scarce and almost or quite limited to Ceylon; that it grows between the clefts of rocks, this renders it difficult to extract the roots, which are the most beautiful parts of the trees. A cubic foot weighs lbs. 57, and it lasts 80 years: even in Ceylon, it is a scarce though beautiful wood, close-grained, and the most valuable for ornamental purposes in that island. It is exceedingly hard, and finely veined, with different shades of black and brown. Thunberg was inclined to believe that this was the true Ebony, but Koenig afterwards discovered that to be from a different tree.—*Ain's. Mat. Med. p.* 211, *Th. p.* 181, *Tredgold, Holtzappfel. Mr. Faulkner. See* Calamander; Diospyros quæsita; D. oocarpa.

DIOSPYROS INSIGNIS, *Thw.*

Gona-gass. Singh.

A large tree of the damp forests of Ceylon, growing up to an elevation of 2000 feet.—*Thw. En. Pl. Zeyl. p.* 180.

DIOSPYROS MABOLA, *Roxb.*

Diospyros discolor, *Willd.*
Embryopteris discolor, *G. Don.*
Cavamillea Philippensis, *Desrouss.*

Often called "Mangosteen" under which name it is cultivated extensively in gardens at Vizagapatam. A small tree, native of the Phillippine Islands, wood black, very compact. The fruit, called *Mabola,* is brown, with a pink-colored, fleshy rind, about the size of a quince; its flavour is said to be agreeable.—*G. Don's Mill. Dict.* 4, *p.* 40.

DIOSPYROS KAKI, *Linn.*

Diospyros chinensis, *Bl.*
Embryopteros kaki, *G. Don.*

A tree of Nepal, Cochin-China, China and Japan.—*Voigt.*

DIOSPYROS MELANOXYLON, *Roxb.*

Kendu. Beng.	Tumbai maram (ebony.) Tam.
Kiu. „	Tumbali maram. „
Ouk-chin-ya. Burm.	Tumma chettu. Tel.
Balai? Can.	Tumida. „
Coromandel Ebony tree. Eng.	Tummeda. „
Ebony tree. „	Tummika. „
Godavery ebony. „	Tunki chettu. „
Tendu. Hind.	Tuniki chettu. „

Grows in Coimbatore, north Canara, in Malabar and Orissa, is the Toonkee of the Godavery and the Tookee of the Circars, and in Pegu it is found very plentiful throughout the forests, seldom however of greater girth than three or four feet. It is a very large tree, in Coimbatore, the outer wood being white like that of other species of Diospyros, and the inner black and heavy. The white wood is, however, used for common purposes. Dr. Gibson says that he has not seen it in any of the Bombay forests, but that it is found sparingly in those of North Canara, as below the Woolwa Ghat, and near Meerjan inland. It occurs plentifully, in the Southern forests of Pegu, from fifteen to eighteen inches in diameter and fifty to seventy feet in length and might afford spars for naval purposes. (The authority for the last point is Dr. McClelland's Report, but Dr. Brandis does not mention this as a Pegu wood.)—*Drs. Wight, Gibson, McClelland, p.* 10, *Voigt, Captain Beddome.*

DIOSPYROS MONTANA, *Roxb.* ; *W. Ic.*

Teemroo. MAHR. | Erra gadda. TEL.
Teemboorni. „

A middle sized tree of the Circar mountains, in the hills eastward from Panwell, extending northwards to Ruenka Lake, near Nahu. The tree is very common in the larger Bombay jungles, both near the coast and elsewhere, and it would be one of the most common of their mountain trees if allowed to grow ; but it is generally cut off for burning material, or such like worthless purposes. Wood dark and strong. Fitted for agricultural implements, in-door work, &c. Does not bear exposure, and could not be creosoted. Dr. Roxburgh says it is hard and durable, and is variegated with dark and white colored veins.—*Ainslie, Voigt, Gibson.*

DIOSPYROS MOONII, *Thw.*

A middle sized Ceylon tree near Cultura, and Pasdoom corle.—*Thw. En. Pl. Zeyl., p.* 182.

DIOSPYROS OOCARPA, *Thw.*

Kalookadoombaireya-gass. SINGH.

A middle sized Ceylon tree of the Kornegalle district, and at Haragam, near Kandy at no great elevation. It furnishes one of the Calamander woods.—*Thw. En. Pl. Zeyl. p.* 180. *See* D. HIRSUTA and D. QUÆSITA.

DIOSPYROS OPPOSITIFOLIA, *Thw.*

Kaloomidereya-gass. SINGH.

A middle sized tree of Ceylon at Hinidoon corle, up to an elevation of 1000 feet.—*Thw. En. Pl. Zeyl. p.* 181.

DIOSPYROS OVALIFOLIA, *Wight Ic. t.* 1,227.

A middle sized Ceylon tree at Jaffna, in the Central province, at Hewahette and below Hapootelle, at an elevation of 2,000 to 4,000 feet. —*Thw. En. Pl. Zeyl. p.* 181.

DIOSPYROS QUÆSITA, *Thwaites.*

Kaloomidereya-gass. SINGH.

A great tree of Ceylon, at Singherajah and other forests between Ratnapoora and Galle. This species produces the most valuable of the timber known as Calamander wood so much esteemed for ornamental cabinet work. This plant is nearly allied to D. crumenata, but its larger leaves and fruit, and its pentamerous flowers, well distinguish it.—*Thw. En. Pl. Zeyl. III, p.* 180. *See* D. HIRSUTA and D. OOCARPA.

DIOSPYROS STRICTA, *Roxb.*

A tree of Tipperah.—*Voigt.*

DIOSPYROS SYLVATICA, *Roxb.*, Pl. Cor. I. p. 38 to 47.

Soondoo Kadoombaireya-gass. SINGH.

A tree of Ceylon, in the damp forests in the Hantani district and near Ratnapoora, up to an elevation of 4,000 feet.—*Thw. En. Pl. Zeyl. III. p.* 178.

DIOSPYROS TOMENTOSA, *Roxb.* ; *W. Ic.*

Tumal. BENG. | Kaka tanduka. SANS.
Kiu. „ | Chitta tumiki. TEL.
Tumal. HIND.

A tall elegant tree of the northern part of Bengal, extending to Kheree jungle and furnishing a hard and heavy black wood.—*Voigt.*

DIOSPYROS TOMPOSIA, *Ham.*

D. racemosa, *Roxb. Fl. Ind.* II. *p.* 536 ; *Wight, Ic. t.* 416, *c. p.* 1911.
Embryopteris racemosa, *G. Don.*

Kaha-kaala-gass. SINGH.

A tree of Ceylon, not uncommon in damp forests, up to an elevation of 4,000 feet.—*Thw. En. Pl. Zeyl.* III, *p.* 179.

DIPTEROCARPUS, a genus of enormous trees with erect trunks, in Eastern and Southern Asia, occurring in Ceylon, Assam, Tipperah, Burmah, Pegu and Tenasserim. They abound with resinous juices, called wood oils, which dissolve caoutchouc, and have medicinal properties similar to Copaiba.—*Eng. Cyc.*

DIPTEROCARPUS, *Species.*

Doon. SINGH.

Grows in the central province of Ceylon, and its timber is used in house buildings. A cubic foot weighs 29 lbs., and it lasts 50 years.—*Mr. Mendis.*

DIPTEROCARPUS, *Species.*

Kaungmhoo. BURM.

Trees of an immense size in British Burmah, used for canoes. In a full grown tree on good soil the average length of the trunk to the first branch is 100 feet and average girth measured at 6 feet from the ground is 12 feet. It sells at 8 annas per cubic foot.—*Dr. Brandis.*

DIPTEROCARPUS, *Species.*

Kyau-thoo. BURM.

A large tree found in the hills of British Burmah, wood used for canoes and cart wheels. A cubic foot weighs lbs. 43. In a full grown tree on good soil the average length of the trunk to the first branch is 80 feet and average girth measured at 6 feet from the ground is 20 feet. —*Dr. Brandis.*

DIPTEROCARPUS, *Species.*

Kanyoung. BURM. ?

A tree of Akyab. Used in house building, and sometimes for posts. This tree grows to a large size, and is not very plentiful.—*Cal. Cat. Ex.* 1862.

DIPTEROCARPUS, *Species.* Sour wood oil tree. This large tree grows on the Karen mountains, but it produces comparatively very little wood oil.—*Dr. Mason.*

DIPTEROCARPUS ALATUS, *Roxb.*

Battee Sal. BENG | Aing ? BURM.
Ka-Nyin. BURM. | Wood oil tree of Burmah. ENG.

A magnificent forest tree of Pegu and the

Mascal islands, rising 250 feet in height. It is found chiefly to grow on laterite in the Tounghoo and Prome districts. Its wood is of a light brown colour. A cubic foot weighs lbs. 38. In a full grown tree on good soil the average length of the trunk to the first branch is 100 feet and average girth measured at 6 feet from the ground is 25 feet. It sells at 4 annas per cubic foot. This timber is excellent for every purpose of house building, especially for posts. It is useful for planking when not exposed to wet and is extensively used in the Straits, for house building: when exposed to wet, however, it rapidly decays, and canoes made of it do not last 3 or 4 years. To obtain the wood oil, an incision in the form of a cup is cut into the lower part of the trunk of the tree, which, acting as a natural reservoir, collects the oil as it descends.—*Drs. McClelland, Brandis, Voigt, Captain Benson.*

DIPTEROCARPUS ANGUSTIFOLIUS, *W. & A.*

Dipterocarpus costatus, *Roxb.*

Tilia garjan. Rakh.

A large tree of Chittagong, furnishing a wood oil in the largest quantity.—*Voigt.*

DIPTEROCARPUS GLANDULOSUS, *Thw.*

Dorana. Singh.

A large, Ceylon tree, in the Saffragam and Ambagamowa districts, at no great elevation. —*Thw.*

DIPTEROCARPUS GRANDIFLORA, *Wall.*

Eng. Burm.
Ain? "
Ain tha. Burm.
Large flowered Dipterocarpus. Eng.

An immense tree of Burmah and Pegu, which grows on the sandy plains near the sea-shore, and on a similar soil in the interior. This tree, in company with a few other kinds, forms extensive forests which cover upwards of 2,000 square miles in the province of Pegu. The wood is somewhat more durable than that of "Kanyin" D. alatus, and is used for canoes, house posts, planking, &c. A cubic foot weighs 55 lbs. In a full grown tree on good soil the average length of the trunk to the first branch is 60 feet and average girth measured at 6 feet from the ground is 10 feet. It sells at 8 annas per cubic foot. It grows also in Tavoy.—*Drs. Brandis and Mason, Col. Frith.*

DIPTEROCARPUS GRANDIS— ?

Tng-tha. Burm.

A tree of Moulmein, the wood of which is converted into planks for building.—*Cal. Cat. Ex.* 1862.

DIPTEROCARPUS HISPIDUS, *Thw.*

Boohora-gass. Singh.

An immense tree of Ceylon, in the Saffragam district, at no great elevation.—*Thwaites.*

DIPTEROCARPUS INSIGNIS, *Thw.*

An immense tree of the Saffragam district, in Ceylon.—*Thwaites.*

DIPTEROCARPUS LÆVIS, *Buch.*

Dipterocarpus turbinatus, *Roxb.*

Tilea gurjun. Beng.
Ka nyeen tha? Burm.
Wood oil tree. Eng.
Horre, Singh.?

This majestic tree grows to a height of 250 feet. It is met with in Assam, Tipperah, Chittagong, Burmah? and Pegu? Found very abundant all over the provinces of Amherst, Tavoy and Mergui, where its wood is used similarly to D. alatus. Dr. Mason says it is a very useful timber, which is sawn into boards at Tavoy and Mergui, and used in house building. Where not exposed to the wet, they answer as well as teak, and are sold at half the price; they are, however, not impervious to white ants. But Captain Dance, who tells us that it is used for rafters and planks, adds that it is an inferior wood, by no means durable as it rots as soon as it is exposed to water and shrinks readily. He says that Dr. McClelland speaks of this wood more favourably, but thinks he must mean some other wood, as this is decidedly bad, very porous, and, when kept, the oil oozes out and stands in globules over it, it warps to a great extent, and though used for cases does not last for more than about two years. (Vide No. 81, page 135 of Dr. McClelland's Report, where this tree is described as Dipterocarpus turbinatus.) Maximum girth 6 cubits. Maximum length 70 feet. When seasoned, floats in water.—*Dr. Mason, Voigt, Captains Dance and Benson.*

DIPTEROCARPUS OBLONGIFOLIUS, *Thw.* A great tree near Ratnapoora, in Ceylon. —*Thwaites.*

DIPTEROCARPUS SCABRIDUS, *Thw.*

A great tree near Ratnapoora, in Ceylon.—*Thwaites.*

DIPTEROCARPUS ZEYLANICUS, *Thw.*

Hora-gass. Singh.

A great tree, in Ceylon, abundant up to an elevation of 3,000 feet. A cubic foot weighs 45 lbs, and its timber, which is used for the roofs of common buildings, lasts 15 years.—*Thwaites, Mr. Mendis.*

DIVE PARRE, Singh. A wood of the western province of Ceylon, used in common house buildings. A cubic foot weighs 44 lbs. and the timber lasts 20 years.—*Mr. Mendis.*

DODDA GODDA, Can.? A wood of Mysore.

DODUGA, Tel.? A wood of the Northern Circars.

DOHEE. Hind.? A tree of Chota Nagpore, with a soft, white wood.—*Cal. Cat. Ex.* 1862.

DOKA. HIND.? A tree of Chota Nagpore, with a hard red timber.—*Cal. Cat. Ex.* 1862.

DOONA, *Thwaites.*

A genus of great trees of Ceylon, D. affinis occurs between Ratnapoora and Galle, at no great elevation. D. congestiflora, "Tinneya gass, *Singh.*, at Hinidoon and Pasdoon Corles, D. cordifolia, at no great elevation at Pasdoon Corle and Ambagamowma : D. Gardneri, in the central province at an elevation of from 3,000 to 5,000 feet. D. nervosa at Eknalagodde near Ratnapoora.—*Thwaites, En. Pl. Zeyl.*

DOONA TRAPEZIFOLIA, *Thwaites.*

Tuccahaaloo-gass. SINGH.

Grows as a common forest tree, in the central and southern parts of the island of Ceylon up to an elevation of 1,500 feet.—*Thw. p.* 55.

DOONA ZEYLANICA, *Thwaites.*

Doon-gass. SINGH.

Grows in the central province of Ceylon, up to an elevation of 4,000 feet. A large quantity of colourless gum-resin exudes from the trunk and branches of this fine tree, which, when dissolved in spirits of wine or turpentine, makes an excellent varnish.—*Thw. p.* 34.

DOR-KHAIR, HIND.? A tree of Chota Nagpore, with hard, yellowish red timber.—*Cal. Cat Ex.* 1862.

DORDONEA ORIENTALIS. Hop wood of Norfolk Island, does not attain to more than a foot in diameter, and is principally used for veneering and in turning ornaments.—*Keppel's Ind. Arch. vol. II. p.* 282.

DOW YAT, BURM. Maximum girth 3 cubits. Maximum length 18 feet. Found abundant, but, always inland all over the country, at Amherst, Tavoy and Mergui. When seasoned, floats in water. A soft bad wood, useless except for elephant bells.

DRUM? A Penang wood, light brown colour, used for ornamental furniture. A very small tree.

DUABANGA GRANDIFLORA, *Wall.*

Myoukgnau. BURM.

A wood of British Burmah, used in house building. A cubic foot weighs lbs. 30. In a full grown tree on good soil the average length of the trunk to the first branch is 80 feet and average girth, measured at 6 feet from the ground is 12 feet. It sells at 8 annas per cubic foot.—*Dr. Brandis, Cal. Cat. Ex.* 1862.

DUDHHI. HIND.? A tree of Chota Nagpore with a soft white timber.—*Cal. Cat. Ex.* 1862.

DULCHIRRAM. TEL. Acacia kalkora. On the Godavery an enormous tree. Wood hard and reddish.

DUNORHUNG. A Penang wood, of a brown colour, specific gravity 1·235. Used by the Chinese for carving images.

DUP-MARAM, MALEAL.? TAM. According to Edye, a tree of Malabar and Canara, also named Nademara, and to be found in the forests of the coast from north to south. It grows from sixty to eighty feet high, and from two to three feet in diameter. It is a light sort of wood, similar to the white American fir of New England. This is the tree which produces the best description of country damar, (damar is a resin used as a substitute for pitch for the seams of ships after caulking, &c. It is prepared with oils, but it is not so valuable as the damar from the island of Sumatra.) The natives use the large trees as rafters, and as catamarans, and for house building, and the small spars to make sheds and yards for the native vessels. So long as the moisture of the wood remains, it may be considered to answer these purposes; but, when it becomes dry, it is very brittle and of no use. At Cochin, he formed the rafters and uprights of the roofs over the ships of war at that port of this wood, with the purlings of split bamboo over them, and cadjans (cocoanut leaves platted), all of which were lashed together by coir yarns. The amount of expense for a roof with sheds was about 350 rupees, or 44*l.* sterling.—*Edye, Timber of Malabar.* (*Note*—Edye here seems to describe the Vateria Indica?)

DURIA MADDEE also kora maddee and koraman, *Tel.* Briedelia spinosa. On the Godavery, wood appears to be very strong and good. Cattle eat the leaves most voraciously.—*Captain Beddome.*

DYSOXYLON CHAMPIONII. A great tree of Central province of Ceylon, found up to an elevation of 4,000 feet.—*Thw. En. Pl. Zeyl. p.* 61.

DYSOXYLON MACROCARPUM, *Blume.*

Guarea binectarifera, *Roxb. Cat.*
Amoora ficiformis, *Wight Illust. I.* 147.

A great tree of Ceylon, found in the Central province, up to an elevation of 3,000 feet, and at Batticaloa.—*Thw. En. Pl. Zeyl. I. p.* 60.

EAGLE WOOD.

Agalugen. AR.	Ud-i Samudri. HIND. PERS.
Ugoor. BENG.	Aggur. " "
Ag'r. "	Kalambak. JAV.
Ag'r. DUK.	Agallochum. LAT.
Agel-hout. DUT.	Al-camericum. "
Lign aloes. ENG.	Lignum aloes. "
Aloes wood. "	Xylo-aloe. "
Eagle wood. "	Tarum of Pliny. "
Incense wood. "	Agila gahru. MALAY.
Agalocha. "	Garu. "
Black agalocha. "	Kayu gahru. "
Bois d' aigle. FR.	Pao d' agila. PORT.
Agallochee. GR. ?	Pao d' aguila. "
Agallochum " of Dioscorides	Pao d' aquila. "
Ahel. HEB.	Agara. SANS.
Ahelim. "	Agarhu. "
Ahiloth. "	Kisna. SIAM.
Ud-i Chini. HIND. PERS.	Agaru. TAM.
" " Hindi. " "	Agaru. TEL.
" " Kimari. " "	Krishna agaru. "
" " Bukhoor. " "	Haud and Ud of Garcias.

A highly fragrant wood, much esteemed by Asiatics for burning as incense. It is made into the pastilles, called Ud batti, in Hindi. There are several kinds in commerce, and supposed to be obtained from the Aloexylon agallochum, *Lour.*, Aquillaria agallocha, *Roxb.*, the Aq. Malaccensis, *Lam.* and the Aquilaria secundaria, q. v. The Eagle wood seems to be a resinous deposit in the interior of the tree. A good specimen of it is in the Government Central Museum, Madras. It is mentioned in *Num.* xxiv, 6 ; *Prov.* vii, 17 ; *Cant.* iv, 14.—*Drs. O'Shaughnessy and Roxburgh, Eng. Cyc., Voigt.*

EBONY.

Kendu. BENG.	Kaya-arang. MALAY.
Yendike. BURM.	Abnus. PERS.
Tai. "	Ebenowoederewo. RUS.
Ebben-hout. DUT.	Kalu vere. SINGH.
Ebene. FR.	Kaka tatee. TAM.
Ebenholz. GER.	Atcha maram. "
Abnus. GUZ.	Atcha manu. TEL.
Hobnem. HEB.	Tookee. "
Tendua. HIND.	Nalla toomi karra. "
Abnus. "	Toombi kara. "
Ebeno. IT.	Toomi-chava karra. "
Kaya-arang. JAV.	Toombika. "
Ebenus. LAT.	Abnus. URIA.
Tendua. MAHR	Tendua. "
Abnus. "	

A black wood, exceedingly hard, and heavy, of great durability and susceptible of a high polish. It is exported from Upper Egypt, Abyssinia, Zanzibar, Madagascar, Mauritius, Ceylon, India, and Jamaica. The ebonies of South Eastern Asia, are obtained from several species of Diospyros, Dalbergia, and Bauhinia, from trees growing in the Mauritius, Ceylon, in several parts of the Peninsula of India, in Coimbatore, Malabar, Canara, the Dekhan, in the Circars, Ganjam, Cuttack and Gumsur, also in Assam, the Malay peninsula, in Penang, Siam, and eastwards through the Asiatic Archipelago to the Philippine Islands. The true ebony is so deep a black, as to be used to personify blackness. But, woods sold under this name have also reddish, greenish or yellowish hues, and are distinguished in commerce as red, green and yellow ebonies, though these are in much less esteem than the ebonies which are jet black, free from veins, and close-grained. The jet black kinds are solely employed for ornamental furniture, cabinet and turnery work, rulers, and for handles for doors, knives, piano-forte keys, philosophical, musical and surgical instruments, mosaic work and inlaying, though cheaper woods, dyed black, are frequently substituted : but it is much affected by the weather, on which account it is seldom used in the plank solid. It is first mentioned in Ezekiel xxvii, 15 : but in the plural, when the men of Dedan are described as bringing horns of ivory and ebony. Herodotus (iii, 97) mentions ebony as part of the presents brought in considerable quantities to the king of Persia by the people of Ethiopia, and Dioscorides describes two kinds, one Ethiopian which was considered the best and the other Indian which was intermixed with whitish stripes and spotted. But there are ebonies in the Mauritius, Ceylon and the south and east of Asia, equal to those of any other part of the world. The ebony in the south of the peninsula of India, is chiefly obtained from Coorg and Canara, from various species of Diospyros and is of a superior description, being perfectly black in colour. Smaller pieces are procured from Cuddapah, Salem, Nuggur, &c., but there is no steady demand, though, for ornamental cabinet work, it is peculiarly fine veined. That of Ceylon, from the Diospyros ebenaster, is of great value. And another heart wood, that of the Kadoem beriye or Bastard ebony of western Ceylon, also from species of Diospyros, is occasionally met with of extraordinary beauty. The ebonies of the Palghat and Coimbatore districts, are supposed to be from species of Diospyros (ebenaster,) and Bauhinia. In none of the trees, is the entire bole black, only the heart wood, the outer and white wood being the Tendua of the Mahrattas. The ebony tree of the Malabar forests, Diospyros melanoxylon, is also found sparingly in those of N. Canara below the Woolwa Ghat and near Meerjan inland. It is procurable, of a very superior quality, in the hill Zemindaries of the Northern Circars, particularly in the Ganjam district : also, inland from Ellore in the Masulipatam district, logs of Diospyros ebenaster yield an ebony richly variegated with bright brown stripes and mottled, similar in appearance to Calamander wood, which, also, is from species of Diospyros. The Karens have distinctive names for four different species of Tenasserim ebony trees—the salt water swamp ebony, the water ebony, the yellow ebony, and the true ebony. Dr. Mason never met with the trees in flower, so as to be able to distinguish the species of Diospyros to which they belong, but had seen specimens of the wood in the southern provinces, not inferior to the ebony of commerce. Also, under the Burmese name of "yendaik," the wood of two different trees is sometimes seen. One, a species of ebony, and the other a leguminous tree which, according to the descriptions of the Karens, is a species of dalbergia, and the wood resembles the blackwood of Hindostan. There is an inferior kind of ebony often seen at Moulmein, which the natives do not call by the same name that they do the trees which produce the good ebony, though evidently a product of the same genus. It, also, is from a species of *Diospyros*, Moulmein ebony. A similar wood at Tavoy is often denominated "iron wood." The Burmese ebony, known as "Tai" is found in the direction of Shooay Geen, but is very scarce. Ebony sells in England at £5 to £10 a ton.—*Drs. Gibson, Wight, Mason, Tredgold, Holtzappfel, Faulkner, Crawford, Thwaites, Voigt, Captain Dance, Mr. Rohde, Eng. Cyc.*

EDANAH. The Tamil name of a Malabar tree that grows to about forty feet in height, and two feet and a half in diameter. It is very soft, and not durable: it produces a sort of gum, or resin, like the Payani. The wood is used for catamarans, rafts for heavy timber, canoes, spars for sheds, and other purposes.—*Edye, Forests of Malabar and Canara.*

EDDELLAH. The Malayala name of a Malabar tree which grows to about thirty feet high, and twelve inches in diameter. It is used in boats and country vessels; and is designated jungle wood. In consequence of its scarcity it is not much known or used.—*Edye, Forests of Malabar and Canara.*

EHRETIA LÆVIS, *Roxb.*

Beurreria lævis, *G. Don.*

Pal-dantam, Godavery TEL.	Seregada. TEL.
Peda pulmera, Circar ,,	

A pretty large tree, common in the drier parts of Ceylon, in the peninsula of India, is a native of the Circar mountains, grows in Hindostan, in the Dhera Doon, the Kheree pass and in Bengal. It furnishes a hard valuable wood, though not of great size, which in the Circars is used by the hill people for many purposes.—*Dr. Ainslie, Voigt, Thwailes, Dr. Cleghorn, Captain Beddome.*

EHRETIA OVALIFOLIA, *Wight's Ic.* 1383.

Gundnn. MAHR.	Naraga maram. TAM.

In the Coimbatore district, a common but generally small tree and found about towns on the Bombay side, never in forests. The wood is said to be of no account.—*Drs. Wight, Gibson.*

EHRETIA SERRATA, *Roxb.*

Ehretia pyrifolia, *D. Don.*

Kala aja. BENG.	Nulshima. NEP.

A tree growing in Bengal, Chittagong, the Khassia mountains, Nepal, Bhootan, and the Dehra Dhoon, and furnishes a tough light wood easily worked and durable, made into sword handles.—*Voigt.*

EIN WIN. BURM. A tree of Moulmein. Used for all ordinary purposes of building.—*Cal. Cat. Ex.* 1862.

ELAVUM. The Tamil name of the wild cotton tree of Malabar, which grows to sixty or eighty feet high, and from four to six feet in diameter. It is a very soft, light wood, and used by the natives for catamarans and canoes; and also for rafting the heavy timber from the forests: it is not durable or of much value.—*Edye, Forests of Malabar and Canara. (Note.*—This seems the Eriodendron anfractuosum.)

ELATE SYLVESTRIS, *Linn.*

Phœnix sylvestris, *Roxb.*

Wild date,

Eajata. CAN.	Itcham maram. TAM.*
Sendi ka jhar. DUK.	Ita chettu. TEL.

The leaf.

Itcham elle. TAM.	Ita-aku. TEL.

Its fruit.

Sandulay ka phall. DUK.	Itcham palliam. TAM.
Parushaka. SANS.	Ita pandu. TEL.

Has the general characteristics of the family, but is inferior to the Palmyrah, Cocoanut, &c. In India, the fruit, when ripe, is small, oval shaped, dark coloured, and sweetish; but, though it is now believed that this tree is identical with the date palm of Arabia, the fruit is not esteemed, being unimproved by cultivation. The leaves and stalks are made into baskets, boxes and hats, the leaves are twisted into rope, and used for thatching and in the manufacture of light mats for building huts. The inner wood furnishes, by boiling, a kind of catechu, which contains much tannin.—*Ains. pp.* 153, 224, *Simmonds.*

ELÆOCARPUS, *Species.*

Poeechandia. URIA.

A tree of Ganjam and Gumsur, of extreme height 48 feet, circumference 5 feet and height from the ground to the intersection of the first branch, 9 feet. Ploughshares are occasionally made of this wood, but it is chiefly used for firewood. The rosaries worn by Byragees and Vishnoos are made of the seeds of this tree.—*Captain Macdonald.*

ELÆOCARPUS, *Species.*

Mhaghai. BURM ?

A moderate sized tree of Akyab, plentiful in Ramree and Cheduba; wood used for knife handles, rules, &c., and the fruit and leaves are used by the natives for food.—*Cal. Cat. Ex.* 1862.

ELÆOCARPUS, *Species.* A very large timber tree of Martaban, used for masts and house posts.

ELÆOCARPUS, *Species.* A hard valuable timber tree, very abundant in the neighbourhood of Rangoon, and not uncommon in some parts of the Tenasserim Provinces. Carts are sometimes constructed of it, and it is used in house and boat building.—*Dr. Mason's Tenasserim.*

ELÆOCARPUS, *Species.* Salwen, *Burm.* The river Salwen derives its name from a tree that grows on its banks of that name. From the character of the genus, it would probably yield useful wood.—*Dr. Mason's Tenasserim.*

ELÆOCARPUS AMŒNUS, *Thw.*

A middle sized tree of the central province of Ceylon, grows up to an elevation of 4,000 feet.—*Thw. En. Pl. Zeyl. p.* 32.

ELÆOCARPUS GANITRUS, *Roxb.*

Ganitrus sphæricus, *Gaertn.*

Rudrakaya. DUK. ?	Rudra-chai. TAM.
Utrasum Bead tree. ANG.TEL.	Rudra challu. TEL.
Rudrakaya. TAM.	

A tree of Java. The seeds are used for necklaces, rosaries, &c.

ELÆOCARPUS LANCEÆFOLIUS, *Roxb.*

Ootradi ke munke. DUK. | Utrasum ? TAM.

A tree of the Khassya hills, Assam, Moulmein and Java. The seeds are used similarly to those of the Ganitrus sphæricus, Royle.—*Drs. Royle, Ainslie, Mason and Voigt.*

ELÆOCARPUS LONGIFOLIUS, *Bl.*

A tree growing on the banks of the Salwen, and in Java.—*Voigt.*

ELÆOCARPUS LUCIDUS, *Roxb.*

A tree of Chittagong.—*Voigt.*

ELÆOCARPUS MONTANUS, *Thw.*

A middle sized tree of Ceylon.

ELÆOCARPUS OBOVATUS, *Ain.*

E. coriaceus, *Hook.*

This tree grows at Newera Ellia and other elevated parts of the island of Ceylon, at an elevation of from 6,000 to 8,000 feet.—*Thwaites.*

ELÆOCARPUS OBLONGUS.

Kassow. DUK.

A handsome Dekhan tree.—*Dr. Riddell.*

ELÆOCARPUS SERRATUS, *Linn.*

Grows in the warmer parts of Ceylon, up to an elevation of 2,000 feet.—*Thwaites.*

ELÆOCARPUS TUBERCALATUS, *Roxb.*

Rudrachai. TAM.	Rudracha. TEL.
Badrachai. "	Badracha. "

A tree of the Travancore forests. The seeds are used by Vaishnava brahmins as rosaries.—*Mr. Rohde's MSS.*

ELÆODENDRON GLAUCUM, PERS.

Schrebera albens, *Retz.*	Senacia glauca, *Lam.*
Mangifera glauca, *Rottl.*	Ceylon tea tree. ENG.

This tree is a native of Ceylon, with small green flowers.—*Voigt.*

ELÆODENDRON INTEGRIFOLIA.

Jouk-bin. BURM.

This is a very plentiful, strong, fine timber, found throughout the forests of the Tounghoo and Pegu districts, as well as about Rangoon. It is adapted for fancy work and cabinet making.—*Dr. McClelland.*

ELÆODENDRON ROXBURGHII, *W. & A.*

Elæodendron glaucum, *Wall.*
Nerija dichotoma, *Roxb.*
Rhamnus nerija, *Spreng.*

Boot-kus. MAHR.	Nerasi. TEL.
Selupa maram. TAM.	Nirija. "
Bira. TEL.	

This tree is a native of the mountainous parts of India. In Coimbatore, this tree is more remarkable for its fine form than the length and thickness of its bole, but the wood, if good, can only be fit for cabinet making and small sized objects. Dr. Gibson says this tree is more common in the inland than in the coast forests of Bombay, but he had never seen it of a size fit for timber. The wood is however strong and compact.—*Drs. Wight and Gibson.*

ELLAHNEEL. TAM ? In Travancore, a small tree, with a light red coloured wood, specific gravity 0·779, used for temples, pagodas, and furniture.

ELLANDE. The Malayala name of a Malabar tree which the natives use for general purposes. It produces a fruit from which they extract a sweet scented oil, which is used medicinally; and also for the hair of the women in days of ceremony.—*Edye, Forests of Malabar and Canara.*

ELOOPAY, TAM, in Tinnevelly, a wood of a red colour, used for building in general.

ELUPE MARAM, The Malayala name of a Malabar tree, which grows to fifty feet in height, and two and half feet in diameter. It is said to be a useful timber, and is found to be durable in native vessels for planks, beams, &c. It produces a fruit from which an oil is extracted, which is used for lamps and other purposes.—*Edye, Forests of Malabar and Canara.* (*Note.*—This seems to be Bassia latifolia or B. longifolia.)

EMBLICA OFFICINALIS, *Gærtn.*

Phyllanthus emblica, *Linn. Roxb. W. Ic. Rheede.*
Myrobalanus emblica, *Bauhin.*

Aonla. BENG.	Anola. HIND.
Anola. „	Malaca. MALAY.
Nelli mara. CAN.	Kadondong. „
Nilika-mara. „	Nelli. MALEAL.
Emblic myrobalan. ENG.	Amlaki. SANS.
Μυραβαλανος εμβλικα. GREEK.	Umriti. „
Amliki. HIND.	Amalaca. „
Amlika. „	Amusada nelli. SINGH.
Aruli. „	Nellikai. TAM.
Aungra. „	Nelli maram. „
Aonla. „	Usirika manu. TEL.
	Amla kamu. „

A crooked tree, almost the thickness of a man's body. It grows in the south of the Peninsula, in Canara, the southern Mahratta country, the Konkan, the Dekhan, in the forests of the Godavery and Circars, in Bengal, on the banks of the Jumna, and eastwards in the Moluccas. The valuable wood of this tree is hard and durable, is used for boxes, and for veneering : is good for well rings, does not decay under water, is well adapted for turning. The strongly astringent bark is used as a tanning material, and in dysentery and diarrhœa. The Myrobalan fruit, can be pickled or preserved in sugar,—*Voigt, Captain Beddome, Mr. Rohde, Dr. Cleghorn.*

EMBRYOPTERIS GLUTINIFERA, *Roxb.*

Diospyros glutinosa. *Koen.*
„ embryopteris. *Pers.*

Gab. BENG.	Timberri. SINGH.
Kusharta mara. CAN.	Tumbika. TAM.
Cusharatha mara. „	Pani-chika. „
Wild mangosteen. ENG.	Tumei. TEL.
Gab. HIND.	Tumika. „
Pani-jika. MALEAL.	

This tree has already been described under its synonym of Diospyros glutinosa. In the northern province of Ceylon, its timber is used for common house buildings, and the juice of the fruit is used to rub over fishing lines for the purpose of hardening and preserving them, also for paying the bottoms of boats. Remention of it, here, is to notice that a cubic foot weighs 45 lbs. and that it is esteemed to last 20 years.—*Mr. Mendis, Dr. Cleghorn.*

ENG. BURM. In Amherst, a wood used for boat-building, and produces oil. It is a strong, heavy, useful, grey wood, suited for beams, piles, and the like.

ENG-BENG. BURM. In Tavoy, a strong wood ; used for common carpentry.

ENG-GYENG. BURM. In Amherst, a timber used for posts of religious buildings. A useful wood, but liable to split.

ERAMBOO. TAM.? A Travancore wood of a dark brown colour : used for common houses.—*Col. Frith.*

ERINOCARPUS NIMMONII.

Jungle Bendy. ANGLO-TAM.

A middle sized tree.—*Mr. Jaffrey.*

ERIOBOTRYA JAPONICA, *Lindl.*

Mespilus Japonicus, *Thunb.*

Young-mai. CHIN.	Loquat. VERNAC.
Yang ma. „	

This small tree of Japan and China, is now introduced all over the Deccan, and bears fruit twice in the year. It is highly esteemed both for deserts and preserves. It also grows in great perfection in New South Wales. The finest fruit is produced at the second crop, at the end of the cold season, and requires protection day and night ; from birds in the former, and flying foxes in the latter. The fruit is a yellow colour, with thin skin, a sweet acid pulp, one or two seeds in the centre—sometimes more. The seeds grow easily, and it appears to be capable of great improvement. In Ajmere, it is cultivated in gardens but does not thrive well. It is very common in China and is often mentioned by Fortune, who found it growing at one place, along with peaches, plums, and oranges, and at another, the Chinese gooseberry (*Averrhoa carambola*), the wanghee (*Cookia punctata,*) and the longan and leechee.—*Tea Districts, page* 7, 30, *Drs. Riddell, Irvine, Med. Top. p.* 195, *Voigt.*

ERIODENDRON ANFRACTUOSUM, *D C. W & A. W. Ic.*

Bombax pentandrum. *Linn. Rheede. Roxb.*
Gossampinus Rumphii *Sch. & End.*
Ceiba pentandra *Gærtn.*

Shwet Shimool. BENG.	Pulim. SINGH.
White Cotton tree. ENG.	Imbool. „
Hattian. HIND.	Imbool gass. „
Safed Simal. „	Elavum maram. TAM.
Shamicula. MAHR.	Elava maram. „
Paniala. MALEAL.	Pur. TEL.
Pania. „	Buruga. „

There are 6 species of this genus of plants, 5 of which are natives of America but all known by the name of Wool or Cotton Trees. They are large trees, with a spongy wood which is used for little besides making canoes in the districts where they grow and only this one grows in Asia and Africa. It attains a height of 150 feet or more, but there are two varieties described, the one growing in the East Indies and the other in Guinea, which differ chiefly in the colour of their flowers. The Indian variety *E. a. Indicum,* has flowers yellowish inside and white outside ; whilst that of Guinea *E. b. Africanum,* has large crimson flowers. The Guinea tree is one of the largest and tallest of the forest-trees and the trunk is employed for making the largest-sized canoes. In Ceylon, this is very common, up to an elevation of 2,000 feet. It is an elegant tree, common on the Coromandel Coast ; the leaves fall during the cold season, and the blossoms appear in February before the leaves. It grows in many parts of the Deccan, but is not common on the Bombay side save in some parts of Khandeish. The trunk is perfectly straight. It is a light wood, is employed by the toy-makers or moochis. It is likewise used for making rafts and floats. The seeds are numerous, smooth, black, and enveloped in a very fine soft silky wool. The gum is termed *Huttian ke gond*, and is given in solution with spices in bowel complaints.—*O'Shaughnessy, p.* 227, *Ainslie's Mat. Med. p.* 208, *Drs. Gibson, Wight, Riddell and Cleghorn, Voigt, Thwaites.*

ERIOLÆNA, *Species.*

Dwa-nee, BURMESE.

This tree is not uncommon in British Burmah but not very large: wood of a beautiful brick red color, tough and elastic, used for gun stocks, paddles and rice pounders, and is a wood well worth attention, the weight being moderate, a cubic foot weighing lbs. 47. In a full grown tree on good soil the average length of the trunk to the first branch is 50 feet and average girth measured at 6 feet from the ground is 7 feet. It sells at 12 annas per cubic foot.—*Dr. Brandis.*

ERIOLÆNA, *Species.*

Chlo aini, BURM.

A tree of British Burmah. A red light wood, used like Dwa-nee, Eriolæna *sp.*, for gun stocks paddles, and rice pounders, sells at 12 annas per cubic foot.—*Dr. Brandis, Cal. Cat. Ex.*

ERIOLÆNA CANDOLLI, *Wall.*

A tree of the Prome mountains. *Voigt.*

ERIOLÆNA HOOKERIANA.

Nara botku. TEL.

A strong hard Godavery wood—(something like the Botku, a new species of Cordia)—*Capt. Beddome.*

ERIOLÆNA TILIIFOLIA.

Let pan, BURM.

Grows plentifully throughout the Pegu and Tounghoo districts, attaining a height of fifty feet, with a girth of seven or eight feet sometimes, but usually about six feet. It is a strong tough timber, similar in its properties to Kydia. Wood white-colored, adapted to every purpose of house-building—*McClelland.*

EROOPOOTTOO-IRVOLLY. TAM.? A Palghat wood of a brown color, specific gravity 0·861. Used for buildings and bullock-yokes. —*Colonel Frith.*

ERUPUNA, TAM. Tremburapan, MALEAL. The timber of this Malabar and Canara tree, is of a dark brown colour, with a yellow tinge, and in texture resembles the marda; it is heavy and strong, grows to about fifteen to eighteen feet long. It produces a small black fruit which is of no use. The natives prefer it to other woods for rice-beaters, from its weight and texture.—*Edye, Forests of Malabar and Canara.*

ERYTHRINA, a genus of tropical trees and tuberous herbs with clusters of very large long flowers, which are usually of the brightest-red; whence their name of Coral-Trees. Frequently their stem is defended by stiff prickles.—*Eng. Cyc.*

ERYTHRINA, *Species.*

Thykadah. BURM.?

A tree which grows to a large size, and is procurable throughout the province of Akyab. Its wood is used for making banghies, also for boxes.—*Cal. Cat. Ex.* 1862.

ERYTHRINA, *Sp.* The Mountain coral tree. A fine looking timber tree of this genus producing a reddish wood, is not uncommon in the interior of Tenasserim. The Karens select this tree in preference to all others on which to train their betel vines.—*Dr. Mason.*

ERYTHRINA INDICA, *Lam.; Roxb.; W. & A.*

Erythrina corallodendron, *β Linn.*

Palita mandar, BENG.
Moduga vriksha, CAN.
Coral tree ENG.
Indian Coral tree, „
Bastard teak, „
Moochy wood tree, „
Furrud, HIND.
Pangra, „
Panjirah, „
Pangara, MAHR.
Panjirah, „
Erabadoo gass, SINGH.
Kaliana murukai. TAM.
Murukka maram. „
Muluku murukku. „
Moochoo maram. „
Badida chettu? TEL.
Badapu chettu. „
Badidapu chettu. „
Barijamu. „
Barjapu chettu. „
Mahameda. „
Bandita chettu. „
Chalo-dhona. URIA?

A large tree of Ceylon, of the peninsula of India, also growing in the Konkans, Bengal, Assam, Tenasserim, Martaban and Amherst, and in the islands of the Archipelago: everywhere, a pretty large tree, and in India, flowering at the beginning of the hot season, its seeds ripening in June and July. In Ceylon, it grows in the hot drier parts of the island. In Ganjam and Gumsur, where it abounds, it attains an extreme height of 30 feet, circumference 2 feet, and from the ground to the intersection of the first branch, is 6 feet. It is a common tree in all parts of the Bombay country, but most so on the coast. Its place in the forests is generally taken by Erythrina suberosa. It supplies, in Tenasserim, a soft, white wood, as easily worked as the pine, which might be made valuable for many economical purposes. It is the wood commonly used by the Moochie men, for making light boxes, scabbards, children's toys &c. It is likewise employed in making rafts, and fishermen's floats, and is hollowed out and made into canoes. The wood used for the purpose in upper Hindostan is the Bombax ceiba. It is the "Moochee" wood of Madras, and is there, also, used for toys, light boxes and trays, and the varnished toys from the Northern Circars are made of it. For sword scabbards, it is a first rate material, and may be exported to Europe so soon as the eyes of the military public shall have been sufficiently opened to the necessity of sacrificing clank and shine to utility in the matter of sword-scabbards. The wood is exactly ⅓rd the weight of water, and of necessity very weak. It is particularly applicable to many purposes for which deal is employed at home, such as in making packing cases, &c., &c. The natives of Nagpore use it exclusively for sword cases. It is eaten by white ants eagerly. The timber, in Nagpore varies from 14 to 17 feet in length, and from 3 to 2½ feet in circumference, and sells at 3 annas the cubic foot. This tree is employed in many parts of India to support the black pepper vine. What seems to render these trees very proper for this purpose is their quick growth (from cuttings), their firm, permanent, though smooth bark, which never peels off and gives firm hold to the roots of the vine, and lastly, they are full of leaves and very shady during the hottest months of the year which shelters the vine from the intense heat of the sun and keeps the ground moist. As soon as the hottest weather is over, the leaves drop and expose the vines to the sun and weather during the cool season.—*Drs. Ainslie, Wight, Mason, O'Shaughnessy, Cleghorn, and Gibson, Mr. Rohde, Capts. Sankey and Macdonald, M. E. J. Reports, Voigt, Thwaites.*

ERYTHRINA OVALIFOLIA, *Roxb.*

Huri kankra. BENG.	Yak erra baddoo gass. SINGH.

A tree of the hot drier parts of Ceylon, and grows in Bengal.—*Voigt, Thwaites.*

ERYTHRINA SUBEROSA, *Roxb.*

Muni. TAM.	Muni? TEL.
Motaga. „	Moduga. „

A small tree of Guzerat, Khandesh, of the Mahal districts east of the ghats, and a native of the Circars, growing in every soil and situation: leaves deciduous during the cold season. Flowers in February and March, soon after which the leaves appear; the trunk is generally erect and from eight to twelve feet to the branches. It is less common than the E. Indica, and the trunk is covered with deeply cracked corky bark, deciduous in the cold season—*Roxb., Voigt.*

ERYTHRINA SUBLOBATA, *Roxb.; W. & A.*

Erythrina maxima, *Roxb. in E. I. C. Mus. t.* 105.

Badadumu? TAM.	Badedam? TEL.
Mullu moduga. TEL.	

This tree is a native of the inland mountains of the Circars, and is frequently of great size, with branches spreading and numerous, and trunk without prickles. The wood, like that of all these species is remarkably light, soft and spongy, and is much employed by the moochies who make trunks, toys, and other things that are to be varnished, the wood retaining its priming or under coat of paint better almost than any other wood; and it is not liable to warp, contract or split. The moochies at Condapilly and Nursapore are famed for their art in forming and varnishing this wood for toys &c. It is planted by the Tamil people about their temples. In Bengal, the leaves fall during the cold season in February, when destitute of foliage, the blossoms appear and soon afterwards the leaves: the seed ripens in May, the trunk is perfectly straight in large trees, five or six feet in circumference, tapering regularly, and the seeds are enveloped in fine, soft, or silky wool, adhering slightly to them.—*Mr. Rohde's MSS., Mr. Jaffrey.*

ERYTHROSPERMUM PHYTOLACCOIDES, *Gard.*

A middle sized tree of the Ambagamowa and Ratnapoora districts in Ceylon; growing up to an elevation of 1,500 feet.—*Thw. p.* 18.

ERYTHROXYLON AREOLATUM?

Shajr-ul-jin. AR.	Devadara. SANS.
Dawadar. DUK.	Devatharam. TAM.
Deo dhari. HIND.	Devadari. TEL.

The flowers of this small tree are very small and of a yellowish green colour. The wood is so fragrant that the inhabitants of Mysore use it in lieu of sandal wood. Its leaves, Devadarum kirai, *Tam.*, are used by the people as greens: and bruised and mixed with gingelli oil, are used as a refreshing application to the head.—*Ainslie.*

EUCALYPTUS. This genus, consisting of lofty trees, is found in the Malay peninsula, but it is chiefly Australian, where the species occur in great profusion, and, with the leafless acacias, give a most remarkable character to the scenery. E. calophyllum, attains a height of 150 feet; and a girth of 25 to 30 feet is not an uncommon dimension of these trees:—Several of them have been introduced into India and are growing on the Neilgherry hills. E. resinifera yields the Botany Bay kino. Large cavities occur in the stem of Eucalyptus robusta, between the annual concentric circles of wood, filled with a most beautiful red or rich vermilion-coloured gum, which flows out as soon as the saw affords an opening. Eucalyptus rostrata of western Australia, is the mahogany of the colonists, also the Jarrah or Yarrah and has been recommended for the railway sleepers of India.

EUCALYPTUS PERFOLIATA, is now growing abundantly, both on the Neilgherry and Pulney Hills, and also at Bangalore, in Mysore. It is one of the most hardy of the genus and the best suited to the hills.

EUGEISSONIA TRISTIS, *Griff.*

Bartam. MALAY.

A palm growing on the hills about Ching, Malacca and Penang. The leaves are used in Penang in making mats for the sides of houses, also for thatch, and for all the purposes to which those of the *Nipa fruticans* are applied.—*Griffith's Palms.*

EUGENIA, a genus of plants named in honour of Prince Eugene of Savoy. It contains nearly 200 species, though numbers have been removed to the genera *Nelitris, Jossinia, Myrcia, Sizygium,*

Caryophyllus, and *Jambosa*, in which are now contained the Clove-Tree, the Rose-Apple, and Jamoon of India, formerly included in *Eugenia*. This genus is confined to the hot and tropical parts of the world, as Brazil, the West India Islands, and Sierria Leone, and extends from the Moluccas and Ceylon to Silhet and the foot of the Himalayas in Asia. Some of the species secrete a warm volatile oil in their herbaceous parts ; abound in tannin : yield good wood : and a few have fruits which are edible, though not very agreeable, from being impregnated with the aroma of the oil. Dr. Wight gives, in Icones, the following species of Eugenia :

(E) angustifolia,
,, cymosa,
(N) acuminata,
,, bracteolata,
,, claviflora,
,, grata,
,, inophylla,
,, lanceolata,
,, leplantha,
,, Wightiana,
(R) Mooniana.
,, Willdenowii,
(J) alba,
,, amplexicaulis,
,, aquea,
,, cylindrica,
,, hemispherica,
,, lanceolaria,
,, laurifolia,
,, macrocarpa,
,, Malaccensis,
,, Munroii,
(J) pauciflora,
,, polypetala,
,, purpurea,
,, ternifolia.
(S) alternifolia,
,, Arnottiana,
,, brachiata,
,, calophyllifolia,
,, caryophyllifolia,
,, caryophyllœa,
,, cerasoides,
,, cordifolia,
,, corymbosa,
,, cymosa,
,, ferruginéa,
,, fruticosa,
,, glandulifera,
,, grandis,
,, jambolana,
,, jambolana, var. microcarpa,
,, lanceæfolia,
(S) montana,
,, myrtifolia,
,, Neesiana,
,, oblata,
,, obtusifolia,
,, operculata,
,, Paniala,
,, polyantha,
,, Praecox,
,, pulchella,
,, reticulata,
,, revoluta,
,, Rottleriana,
,, rubens.
,, rubicunda.
,, salicifolia,
,, sylvestris,
,, Thumra,
,, toddalioides,
,, venusta,
,, Wallichii,
,, Zeylanica,

Mr. Thwaites mentions as growing at no great elevation in Ceylon, the Eugenia decora, *Thw.*, a small tree near Galle. Eugenia floccifera, *Thw.*, a small tree at Reigam Corle ; Eugenia fulva, *Thw.*, a small tree at Pasdoon Corle ; Eugenia rivulorum, *Thw.*, a small tree, on the banks of streams, in the Singherajah forest, between Galle and Ratnapoora, and Eugenia terpnophylla, *Thw.*, a middle sized tree of Ambagamowa and Ratnapoora Districts, and Reigam Corle, Eugenia mabæoides, *(Wight Illust.)* grows in the central province, at an elevation of 4,000 to 7,000 feet. Eugenia Mooniana, *Wight, Ill.* is abundant in the central province, up to an elevation of 4,000 feet, and Eugenia Willdenovii, *D C.* Tambaleyagass, *Singh.*, is common in the hotter parts of the island. Dr. McClelland names seven species of Pegu, viz,

Eugenia nervosa, E. pulchella, E. myrtifolia, Tha-bai-jeen, *Burm*, *E. jambosa*, of the Southern parts of Pegu, affording dark strong wood.

Eugenia pulchella, Khway-tha-byai is very plentiful in the Pegu and Tounghoo districts.

E. vulgaris, Thabyai-tha phan, *Burm.*

E. ternifolia, Thab-yew-tha-byai, and *E. jambolana* also occur, but less plentifully than *E. pulchella*. These all afford excellent close grained strong timber, but subject to the attack of white ants. Wood red colour, strong and adapted for house-building.—*Drs. Wight and McClelland, Voigt, Thwaites, Eng. Cyc.*

EUGENIA, *Species.*

Thab-yeh-tha-pan. BURM.

The different kinds of Thabyeh, of British Burmah, have a hard red coloured wood, close, but not straight grained, and supposed to be brittle. The wood is subject to the attacks of white ants. The stems are occasionally used for canoes. This is also used for house building. Breaking weight of the "Thabyehgah" E. caryophyllifolia, 254 lbs. A cubic foot weighs 50 lbs. In a full grown tree on good soil the average length of the trunk to the first branch is 30 feet and average girth measured at 6 feet from the ground is 9 feet. It sells at 8 annas per cubic foot. (*Note.*—This seems to be Dr. McClelland's E. vulgaris).—*Drs. McClelland and Brandis.*

EUGENIA, *Species.*

Tha bya. BURM.

A tree of Moulmein.—*Cal. Cat. Ex.* 1862.

EUGENIA, *Species.*

Tha-bya-gyiu. BURM.

A tree of Moulmein. Wood soft, used in the ordinary purposes of a building material.—*Cal. Cat. Ex.* 1862.

EUGENIA ACRIS, *W. & A.*

Eugenia pimenta, *D C. var.* ovalifolia.
Myrtus pimenta, *Linn. var.* latifolia, *Roxb.*
,, acris, *Sw.*
Myrcia acris, *D C.*
,, pimentoides, *D C.*

Wild Cinnamon-Tree. ENG. | Sung. HIND.
,, Clove ,, ,,

A small tree, grows in Bombay, the leaves have a pleasant smell when bruised. Timber hard, red and heavy, capable of being polished and used for mill cogs and other purposes, where much friction is to be sustained.—*Dr. Riddell, Voigt.*

EUGENIA ACUTANGULA. ?

Hinjolo. URIA.

Under these names, Captain Macdonald describes a tree of Ganjam and Gumsur, of extreme height 30 feet, circumference 4½ feet and height from ground to the intersection of the first branch, 6 feet. Grows in abundance on the banks of rivers. The wood is not affected by damp, and is therefore generally used for the wooden framework at the bottom of wells. Rice pounders are also made of it. The bark is given medicinally to women after childbirth.—*Captain Macdonald.* (*Note.*—Is this the Barringtonia acutangula ? See page 44.)

EUGENIA ALTERNIFOLIA, *Roxb.* ; *W. Ill.* ; *W. Ic.*

Movi chettu. TEL. | Moyi chettu. TEL.

Very common on the Nagari hills.—*Flora Andhr.*

EUGENIA AMŒNA, *Thwaites.* A small tree of Ceylon, at Kokool Corle and Dolosbage district, up to an elevation of 1,500 feet.—*Thw.*

EUGENIA BRACTEATA, *Roxb.; W. & A.*

Eugenia Roxburghii, *D C.*
„ Zeylanica, *Roxb.*
„ læta, *Ham.*
Myrtus bracteata, *Willde.*
„ littoralis, *Roxb. in E. I. C. Mus.*
„ Coromandeliana, *Köen.*
„ ruscifolia, *Willde.*
„ latifolia, *Heyne.*
„ Heynei, *Spreng.*

Aramanda. TEL. | Goragamudi. TEL.
Arivita. „

A shrub, frequent in low jungles near the sea on the Coromandel coast, and in the Northern Circars. It is only used for firewood. It, likewise grows at Jaffna in Ceylon.—*Flora Andh., Thwaites.*

EUGENIA CARYOPHYLLIFOLIA, *Roxb.; W. Ic.*, 553.

Calyptranthes caryophyllifolia. *Ains.*

Choto jam. BENG. | Naurei. TAM.
Thab-yeh-gah. BURM. | Nawel maram. „
Naradidi Vriksha. CAN. | Neredu manu. TEL.
Nawel wood tree. ANG.-TAM. | „ chettu. „
Koata naga? TAM.

Grows in Coimbatore, in the Northern Circars, in Bengal and British Burmah. It is a native of various parts of India growing luxuriantly in almost every soil and situation. Flowering time the hot season; bears a round berry, black when ripe, the size of a pea. Ainslie gives a favorable account of the timber, and the wood is very strong, close grained, hard and durable. The different kinds of Eugenia, called Thab-yeh in British Burmah, have a hard, red colored wood, but not straight grained, and supposed to be brittle. The stems are occasionally used for canoes, especially those of Thab-yeh-gah, the breaking weight of which is 254 lbs. A cubic foot weighs 56 lbs. In a full grown tree on good soil, the average length of the trunk to the first branch is 20 feet, and average girth measured at 6 feet from the ground is 6 feet. It sells at 8 annas per cubic foot.—*Drs. Roxburgh, Wight and Brandis, Mr. Rohde's MSS. Voigt, Cal. Cat. Ex.* 1862.

EUGENIA CARYOPHYLLATA, *Thun.*

Caryophyllus aromaticus, *Linn.*
Myrtus caryophyllus, *Spreng.*

Lavunga. BENG. | Ran jambool. MAHR.
Clove tree. ENG.

A tree of the Moluccas, but cultivated in Ceylon, the Malay Peninsula, in the south of India, in Travancore, also in Mauritius and Bourbon. The cloves of commerce are the unopened flowers, the flower buds. It is hardly found on the Bombay side, north of the Savitree. South of that river it is found only in Raees or greenwood jungles, and about temples. The wood appears quite equal to that of the common Jambool the Eugenia jambolana.—*Dr. Gibson, Voigt, M. E. J. R.*

EUGENIA CERASOIDES, *Roxb.*

Thabyehgyin. BURM.

The different kinds of Thabyeh of British Burmah have a hard red coloured wood, but not straight grained and supposed to be brittle. The stems are occasionally used for canoes. A cubic foot weighs 51 lbs. In a full grown tree on good soil the average length of the trunk to the first branch is 40 feet and average girth measured at 6 feet from the ground is 9 feet. It sells at 8 annas per cubic foot.—*Dr. Brandis, Cal. Cat. Ex.* 1862.

EUGENIA JAMBOLANA, *Lam.; Roxb.*

Syzigium jambolanum, *D C.; W. Ic. W. Ill. W. & A.*
„ caryophillifolium, *D C.*
Eugenia jambolana. *Lam.*
„ jambolifera, *Roxb. in E. I. C. Mus.*
„ obtusifolia, *Roxb. Fl. Ind.* 2, *p.* 485.
„ caryophyllifolia, *Lam.*
Calyptranthes jambolana, *Willde.*
„ caryophyllifolia, *Willde,*
Myrtus cumini, *Linn.*

Kalo jam. BENG. | Sirru naga. TAM.
Burra jamon. HIND. | Kotti naga maram. TAM.
Rai jamun. „ | Pedda neredu. TEL.
Jambool. MAHR. | Sanna neredu. „
Koatti naga maram? TAM. | Jamo. URIA?
Nirarlay? TAM. | Bodo jamo. „
Peru nagal. „ | Coojee jamo. „
Sina naga. „

Mr. Robert Brown of the Madras Agri-Horticultural Gardens considers that this is the Calyptranthes caryophyllifolia and Jambolana mentioned at page 67; he sent for specimens according to the Tamil names, Nawel maram and Naga maram, and they were both the same plants: and, as far as he can make them out, the following are one species:

Syzigium jambolanum.
Eugenia caryophyllifolia.
„ jambolana.
Calyptranthes caryophyllifolia.
„ jambolana.

About Madras, this tree is generally much destroyed by the Carpenter Bee. It, likewise, grows in the Bombay side of India, in Coimbatore, in Ganjam and Gumsur, in Bengal and Kemaon. It is found in all the Bombay ghat and coast forests; also pretty extensively near villages, where it has been planted. The tree is not very common either in Bodogoda or lower Goomsur, but is said to be rather plentiful in the Chokapaud forests. There are two kinds there termed respectively the "Bodo" and "Coojee" Jamo. Dr. Wight, writing in Coimbatore, says "of this wood I have no knowledge, it is said to be brittle and bad, but is described by Ainslie as fit for house building purposes." But Dr. Gibson thinks that Dr. Wight underrates the quality of the wood and he says that it makes excellent beams, but on account, probably, of its brittleness, is never cut up for cabinet purposes. The bark affords a large supply of kino extract.—*Drs. Wight and Gibson, Captain Macdonald, Voigt.*

EUGENIA JAMBOS, *Linn.*

Jambosa vulgaris, *D C.*

Gulab jam. Beng.	Gulab-jamun. Pers.
Gulabijam. Duk.	Raja jembu. Sans.
Rose apple. Eng.	Jambo. Singh.
Jamb. Hind.	Jambu-nawel maram. Tam.
Jam. Maleal.	Jembu-neredi manu. Tel.

Grows in both the Indian peninsulas, in Bengal and Sirmore. This tree bears a light whitish yellow fruit, pear shaped, with smooth skin, having a rose flavor: whence its English name. It is commonly cultivated in gardens on the coasts and in Hyderabad. It is easily propagated by seed, and grows luxuriantly in a good garden soil. The red coloured species, having the same flavor, is called the Jambo Malacca. The fruit is not much esteemed. In Tenasserim, the rose apple is cultivated to a small extent in European gardens.—*Drs. Ainslie, p.* 228, *Mason and Riddell.*

EUGENIA LAURINA, —?

Wal boamboo. Singh.

Under these names, Mr. Mendis mentions a timber tree of the central province of Ceylon, used in house buildings. A cubic foot weighs 36 lbs, and it lasts 15 years.

EUGENIA MALACCENSIS, *Linn.*

Jambosa Malaccensis, *D C.*
„ purpurascens, *D C.*
„ domestica, „

Malaka amrool. Beng.	Jambu Malacca maram. Tam.
Namball paio. Maleal.	

This tree was brought to India from Malacca. The fruit somewhat resembles a pear in shape, is pleasant to the taste, is reckoned very wholesome, and bears some resemblance in taste to a juicy apple, but it is a very indifferent fruit.—*Drs. Ainslie and Mason.*

EUGENIA OBTUSIFOLIA, *Roxb.*

Thabyehgjo. Burm.

The different kinds of Thabyeh of British Burmah have a hard, red colored wood, but not straight grained and supposed to be brittle. The stems are occasionally used for canoes. A cubic foot weighs 48 lbs. In a full grown tree on good soil the average length of the trunk to the first branch is 20 feet, and average girth measured at 6 feet from the ground is 9 feet. It sells at 8 annas per cubic foot.—*Dr. Brandis, Cal. Cat. Ex. of* 1862.

EUONYMUS GARCINIFOLIA (?)

A small tree, growing near the Bombay ghats in the upper country to the south. It seems to be often cultivated in Canara, on account of its straightness, as applicable for house rafters. It does not reach a size sufficient to fit it for general purposes.—*Dr. Gibson.*

EUONYMUS REVOLUTUS, *Wight Ill.* 178.

A middle sized tree of Newera and other very elevated parts of Ceylon.—*Thw. En. Pl. Zeyl. p.* 73.

EUPHORBIA TIRUCALLI. *Linn.*

Lanka sij. Beng.	Kulli. Tam.
Unarmed milk bush. Eng.	Manchee jamudu. Tel.
Milk hedge. „	Lodhoka sijhoo. Uria.?
Seyr Teg. Mahr.	

The wood, when mature, is reckoned very strong and durable when not exposed to wet. On the Bombay side, it is extensively used, whenever procurable, as a dunnage material for the flat roofs of houses. It is sufficiently close-grained to be useful to turners. Could be readily creosoted, but is very seldom of scantling sufficient for sleepers. Wood light colored, the root of old shrubs is understood to be well adapted for gun stocks, but plants of sufficient age are seldom met with. Dr. Wight had often heard it spoken of as excellent for gun stocks, but it seems too light colored. On the Godavery it grows to a large tree and the wood seems hard but is not used. In Gumsur and Ganjam it is not common, but extreme height 20 feet, circumference 2 feet, and the height from the ground to the intersection of the first branch, 6 feet.—*Drs. Wight, Gibson and Cleghorn, Captain Beddome, Captain Macdonald.*

EUPHORBIA, *Species.*

Yamula. Burm.

Used for frames of lacquered ware.

EUPHORIA LITCHI, *Desf.* A fruit tree, introduced from China, the Litchi attains a height of 25 to 30 feet but does not ripen its fruit at Madras. It grows well in the Mauritius and in Bengal.

EURYA, *Species.*

Thaun. Burm.

Used in Tavoy for fuel only.

EURYA JAPONICA, *Thunb.*

Neyadasse-gass. Singh.

Var. α. E. Thunbergii.	Var. γ. E. Chinensis.
Var. β. E. acuminata.	Var. δ. E. parviflora.

Vars. α, β, and δ in the more elevated parts of Ceylon island, up to 8,000 feet; δ in exposed situations; var. β from a little above the sea-level, up to an elevation of 5,000 feet, very abundant.—*Thw. En. Pl. Zeyl. I. p.* 41.

EXCŒCARIA, *Species*? Thurrotha, Burm. A Tavoy wood.

EXCŒCARIA AGALLOCHA, *Linn.*; *Roxb*; *W. Ic.*

Uguru, Sunderbuns, Beng.	Tella keeriya gass. Singh.
Boue-bayaza. Burm.	Tella chettu. Tel.

In Ceylon, very common near the sea, grows in the Sunderbuns, and is plentiful in the Rangoon and Toungoo districts. Wood white coloured and adapted for every purpose of house building.

EXCŒCARIA JAMETTIA, *Spreng.*

Tiger's milk tree. ENG. | Kametti. MALEAL.

Grows on the western coast of India. It abounds in an acrid juice, from which a good kind of caoutchouc may be prepared.—*Useful Plants.*

EXCŒCARIA OPPOSITIFOLIA, *Jack* in Cal. Journ. of Nat. Hist. IV, p. 386.

Common in the Central Province of Ceylon, at an elevation of 4,000 to 6,000 feet.—*Thw. En. Pl. Zeyl. p.* 269.

F.

FAGRÆA FRAGRANS, *Roxb.*

Annah-beng. BURM? of Martaban.
Annan. BURM? of Amherst, Tavoy and Mergui.
Annan-tha. BURM? of do. do. do.

This useful tree grows in Martaban, Tenasserim, inland, particularly up the Attaran river: is very abundant in Amherst, Tavoy and Mergui, and in the islands of the Tenasserim Coast. Its maximum girth 4 cubits, and maximum length 20-25 feet, but of so slow growth that the Burmese refer to it in a proverb. When seasoned, it sinks in water. In Martaban, it is described a compact, hard, yellow and very beautiful wood. In Tenasserim, also, as a very hard and excellent timber. In Amherst, Tavoy and Mergui, though almost imperishable, it is not found capable of bearing so heavy a strain as some of the other valuable woods of the province. It bears a breaking weight of 400 to 500 lbs. and its chief value as a timber is its imperishability when exposed to water or damp. Mr. Riley and Captain Dance say that the teredo navalis will not attack it, and Captain Dance mentions that neither heat nor moisture will warp or rot it, that it is impervious to the attacks of ants, and that the posts of a wharf at Tavoy, which for several years had daily, as the tides flowed and ebbed, been partly dry and partly wet, continued untouched by the worms. It is used for building houses, kyoungs, zyats, &c. posts for buddhist edifices, piles for bridges, wharves, &c., but for lay purposes only by the English, as the Burmese regard it as too good for the laity and say it ought to be confined to sacred purposes. Hence the phoongies or Burmese priests look on it as a sacred tree. Annan wood has been more preserved in the forests of Amherst, Tavoy and Mergui than any other valuable wood: it is scattered thickly over the alluvial plains together with Strychnos nux vomica. It has been recommended for railway sleepers. Dr. Wight in Icones figures three species of this genus, viz., F. Coromandeliana; Malabarica and Zeylanica, the properties of which are not known.—*Rev. Mr. Mason's Tenasserim, Captain Dance's Report, Dr. McClelland's Report.*

FERONIA ELEPHANTUM, *Corr.*

Cratæva vullahga, *Kon.*

Kat bel. BENG.
Bilvar titha mara. CAN.
Cavita vriksa. „
Wood apple tree. ENG.
Elephant apple tree. „
Koit ka jhar. HIND.
Koit. MAHR.
Kowta. „
Velaga. MALEAL.
Vella maram. TAM.
Vellanga maram. „
Valaga chettu. TEL.

The large and tall wood apple tree, one of the aurantiaceæ or orange tribe, is well known south of the Nerbudda. It is widely diffused in India, being met with in the Northern Circars, generally through the Madras Presidency, in Coimbatore, is very common in the inland jungles of the Bombay Presidency, where it grows well every where; and, in Guzerat, it attains a good size. In the Nalla Mallai hills the wood apple tree attains a large size, and the wood is rather heavy, light colored, hard and durable. In Coimbatore the tree attains a large size, and its wood is white, hard and pronounced durable. A specimen which was tried bore 360 lbs. In Vizagapatam, it yields a hard, strong, heavy wood, and is there much used in house building, but said not to be very durable. In Guzerat, it is used in building and could possibly be creosoted so as to withstand exposure. Its spheroidal fruit, when ripe contains a dark brown, agreeable subacid pulp. When an incision is made in the trunk, a transparent oily fluid exudes which is used by painters for mixing their colours. Both leaves and flowers have a strong odour of anise, and the young leaves are given in the bowel complaints of children as a stomachic stimulant. It yields a large quantity of a clear white gum (Koit ka gond, *Hind.*), much resembling gum Arabic in its sensible properties. It is very abundant, and forms the well known "East India Gum Arabic;" and, from its ready solubility without residue it gives the best mucilage for making black ink.—*Mr. Rohde, M. E. J. R. Dr. Gibson's Report, M. E. Jur. Rep., Dr. O'Shaughnessy, Dr. Wight's Report, English Cyclopædia.*

FERREOLA BUXIFOLIA, *Roxb.*

Maba buxifolia, *Pers.*

Eroombala. ANGLO-TAM.
Illumbilli maram. TAM.
Eroombala maram. TAM.

This plant grows among the Circar mountains to the size of a small tree, but, in the low countries, it is only a shrub. The wood is dark colored, remarkably hard and durable; when its size will admit, it is employed for such uses as require the most durable heavy wood. Its small red fruit, containing one seed when ripe, is pleasant to the taste and is well known over all the lower provinces of India.—*Ainslie, p.* 254, *Mr. Rohde's MSS.*

FICUS, a genus of tropical plants, many of which occur in South Eastern Asia,—Dr. Wight in Icones gives 54 species. Amongst those which attain the height of a tree, are several remarkable for throwing out aerial roots, from their branches, which grow into the ground and again throw out branches. Some are valuable as fruit trees, and yield viscid and useful juices, but few of them are of value, for timber. Amongst those for which a mere notice will suffice, are the Ficus carica, the common fig tree, cultivated in many parts of India. Ficus Benjaminoides, the Tenasserim Banyan tree, which drops aerial roots like the Indian fig tree, grows amidst mangroves and near tidal streams. Ficus cinerascens, *Thw.*, the Walgoona-gass of Ceylon, is a large tree of the warmer parts of that island. F. Citrifolia, *Willde.* grows in Ceylon and on the western side of India, where some parts of it are employed in medicine. Ficus distichа, *Blume*, grows in the Central province of Ceylon, at an elevation of 3,000 to 5,000 feet, and F. diversiformis, *Miq.*, is very common in Ceylon, up to an elevation of 2,000 feet. The root of Ficus excelsa, *Vahl.*, of peninsular India and the Moluccas, is given, in decoction, as a purgative. A soft, grey, timber is obtained from the F. Gooleeria, *Roxb.*, which grows in Hindostan and Chota Nagpore. F. heterophylla, *Roxb.* Wal-ahatoo, *Singh.*, is common in Ceylon, in damp shady places. F. infectoria, *Willde*, is of Ceylon and India, and its bark is chewed with betel, in lieu of the Areca nut. Ficus laccifera, *Roxb.* Nooga-gass, *Singh.*, is not uncommon, in the Central province of Ceylon. F. lanceolata, *Roxb.* Thapan, *Burm.*, of Pegu, yields a soft useless wood. F. lucida, *Ait.*, the Kappootoo-bo-gass, of Ceylon, occurs in the drier parts of that island. F. nitida, *Thunb.*, which grows in the south of China and in many parts of India, is a valuable ornamental tree and good for shade. The F. racemosa, *Linn.*, of India, produces a fruit of little value. Ficus religiosa, *Linn.*, the Pipul of India, and Bo tree of Ceylon, is a graceful and ornamental plant. F. t'siela, *Roxb.*, is common, but its timber of no value.—*Drs. Wight and Gibson, Thwaites, Voigt.*

FICUS, *Species.*

Baee dhimeree. URIA ?

A tree of Ganjam and Gumsur, extreme height 30 feet, circumference 2½ feet, and height from ground to the intersection of the first branch, 8 feet. It is burnt for firewood being tolerably common. The leaves are used for eating from; the fruit is eaten.—*Captain Macdonald.*

FICUS, *Species.*

Kulli kae. CAN.

Generally a climber. Abounds in Canara and Sunda, in the country from Bilgy to the Ghats. Juice peculiarly abundant and viscid and used as a bird-lime. Well merits a further examination.—*Dr. Gibson.*

FICUS, *Species.*

Thubboo. BURM.

A Tavoy tree, used in house carpentry.

FICUS, *Species.*

Thuppan. BURM.

In Tavoy, a large tree; wood not used.

FICUS ASPERRIMA, *Roxb.*

Ficus ampelos, *Burm.*
„ pohloria, *Moon.*

Wana maddiya-gass. SINGH.
Pindi chettu. TEL.
Karasa. „
Tella barranki. TEL.
Barranki chettu. „

A large tree, a native of the peninsula of India, and grows in Ceylon, up to an elevation of 2,000 feet. The trunk is remarkably short, but very thick and sometimes so completely covered with small very leafy branchlets, as to be entirely hidden. The leaves are used to polish ivory, horn, &c., and, in Ceylon, are in general use amongst native cabinet makers as a substitute for fine sand-paper, similarly to those of the Trophis aspera.—*Voigt, Thwaites, Mr. Rohde's MSS.*

FICUS BENJAMINA, *Linn.*

Kamrup. BENG.
Oval leaved fig tree. ENG.
Warangan. MALAY ?
Itti alu. MALEAL.
Tella barranki. TEL.

Grows in peninsular India, also in the Archipelago. Is a valuable avenue tree, as it does not throw down aerial roots.

FICUS CORDIFOLIA ?

Nga thingyee. BURM.
Heart leaved fig tree. ENG.

A tree of Moulmein and the Tenasserim Provinces. In Tenasserim, this tree usually supplies the place of the peepul in the public places, and in the neighbourhood of religious edifices. It approaches nearest to *F. religiosa*, yet is easily distinguished from it by the leaves being narrower in proportion to the length, with much shorter points, and the fruit being perfectly round and not, as in *religiosa*, vertically compressed. It yields a strong wood, fit for any ordinary purpose.—*Dr. Mason, Cal. Cat. Ex.* 1862.

FICUS ELASTICA, *Roxb.*

Kusnir. BENG.
Elastic fig tree. ENG.
Caoutchouc tree. ENG.

The Indian Caoutchouc tree inhabits the Pundua and the Juntipoor mountains, which bound the province of Silhet on the north, where it grows to the size of a European sycamore, and is called (Kasmeer or) Kusnir. It is chiefly found in the chasms of rocks and over the declivities of mountains among decomposed rocky and vegetable matter. It produces when wounded a great abundance of milk, which yields about one-third of its weight of caoutchouc. It grows with great rapidity; a tree is described as being 25 feet high, with the trunk a foot in diameter when only four years old. Its juice is used by the natives of Sylhet to smear the inside of split rattan baskets, which are thus rendered water-tight. Old trees yield a richer juice than young ones. The milk is extracted by incisions made across the bark, down to the wood, at a distance of about a foot from each other, all round the trunk or branch up to the top of the tree, and the higher the more abundant is the fluid said to be. After one operation the tree requires a fortnight's rest, when it may be again repeated. When the juice is exposed to the air it separates spontaneously into a firm elastic substance, and a whey fetid coloured liquid. Fifty ounces of pure milky juice taken from the trees in August yielded exactly 15½ ounces of clean-washed caoutchouc. This substance is of the finest quality, and may be obtained in large quantities. It is perfectly soluble in the essential oil of cajeput. This tree abounds in Assam, but the outer Himalaya at Punkabarree, is its western limit. It penetrates amongst the mountains, as far as the Teesta valley in Sikkim, but is of small size.—*Roxb., Fl. Ind., III.* 545, *Hooker, Him. Jour. Vol. I. page* 102, *and II. p.* 13, *Voigt.*

FICUS GLOMERATA, *Roxb.; Willde, Rheede; W. Ic.*

Ficus cunia, *Buch.*
„ racemosa, *Willde.*
Covellia glomerata, *Miq.*

Jaguga doomoor. BENG.
Rulla? kith mara. CAN.
Kulla kith mara. „
Oombur. DUK.
Glomerous fig tree. ENG.
Gooler. HIND.
Perena teregram. MALEAL.
Atteekka-gass. SINGH.
Atti maram. TAM.
Medi chettu. TEL.
Atti chettu. „
Bodda chettu. „
Paidi chettu. „

A large tree, thrives best near a watercourse, or on the banks of rivers, fruit like the common fig, which grows in clusters along the branches, flavour insipid, but eaten by the poorer classes. In Ceylon, it is common on the banks of rivers, up to an elevation of 2,000 feet: grows also in the peninsula of India, the Konkans, at Taong Doug, Moulmein, Nepaul and all over Oudh. The wood is used there for furniture, and some of the lac of commerce is gathered from this tree. Mr. Latham says that in the Nalla Mallai, it grows to a height of 40 feet with a circumference of 4½ feet; bandy wheels are made from it. It is straight grained, strong, and appears useful; it is considered sacred, and is burnt when libations are offered: a medicinal extract is obtained from the root.—*Cal. Cat. Ex. of* 1862, *Mr. Latham, Voigt, Thwaites, Mr. Rohde's MSS. Fl. Andh.*

FICUS INDICA, *Linn.; Roxb.*

Ficus Benghalense, *Linn.*
Urostigma Benghalense, *Miq.; Gasp.; Rheede: W. Ic.*

But. BENG.
Bat. „
Bar. „
Ahlada mara. CAN.
Indian fig tree. ENG.
Banyan tree. „
Bengal fig tree. „
Bar ka jhar. HIND.
Vata vriksha. SANS.
Maha nooga-gass. SINGH.
Kiripelle. „
Ala maram. TAM.
Marri chettu. TEL.

The Indian Fig tree grows in most parts of the mainland and islands of India and in the hotter parts of Ceylon, where, however, it seems to have been introduced. It is found in great perfection and beauty about the villages on the skirts of the Circar mountains. Its fruit, the figs, grow in pairs, and, when ripe, are about the size and colour of a middle-sized red cherry. If the seeds drop into the axils of the leaves of the palmyra-tree, the roots grow downwards, embracing the palmyra trunk in their descent; by degrees, they envelop every part except the top, whence, in very old specimens, the leaves and head of the palmyra are seen emerging from the trunk of the Banyan Tree, as if they grew from it. The hindoos regard such cases with reverence, and call them a holy marriage instituted by Providence. Some of these trees cover an immense space even when comparatively young. In the Botanical Gardens at Calcutta, Dr. Falconer ascertained the great Banyan tree, which is still the pride and ornament of the garden, to be only seventy-five years old; for, people were alive a few years ago who remembered well its site being occupied, in 1782, by a Date-palm, out of whose crown the Banyan sprouted, and beneath which a devotee sat. I write from memory after a lapse of 28 years; but when, in 1834, I paced, at noon, the outer shadow of its branches, the circumference was near 360 paces, and Dr. Hooker writing more recently mentions that this tree was eighty feet high, and throws an area, 300 feet in diameter, into a dark cool shade. Large banyans are common in India; but few are so symmetrical in shape and height, as that in the Calcutta gardens. Dr. Roxburgh had seen such trees full 500 yards round the circumference of the branches, and 100 feet high, the principal trunk being more than 25 feet to the branches, and 8 or 9 feet in diameter. Marsden mentions a remarkable banyan or burr tree, near Manjee, twenty miles west of Patna in Bengal, diameter 363 to 375 feet, circumference of shadow at noon 1,116 feet, circumference of the several stems, in number fifty or sixty, 921 feet. Under this tree sat a naked devotee, who had occupied that situation for twenty-five years; but he did not continue there the whole year through, for his vow obliged him to lie, during the four cold months, up to his neck in the waters of the river Ganges. A remarkably large Banyan tree grows, or grew, on an island in the river Nerbudda, ten miles from the city of Baroach, in the province of

Guzerat, and was described by Colonel Sykes. It is called the Kabir Bar, a name said to have been given to it in honour of a saint, but more probably the Arabic adjective for great. It was once much larger than at present, but high floods have carried away the banks of the island on which it grows, and with it a portion of the tree. Indian armies, when in that neighbourhood, have encamped around it, and at stated seasons hindoo festivals are held there, to which thousands of votaries repair. This is the tree, alluded to in Paradise Lost when Adam and Eve

* * * * * * * both together went
Into the thickest wood : when soon they choose
The Fig-tree ; not that kind for fruit renowned,
But such as, at this day, to Indians known
In Malabar and Deccan, spreads her arms,
Branching so broad and long, that, in the ground,
The bended twigs take root, and daughters grow
About the mother tree, a pillared shade
High overarched and echoing walls between.
There, oft, the Indian herdsman shunning heat,
Shelters in cool, and tends his pasturing herds
At loop-holes cut through thickest shade : those leaves
They gathered, broad as Amazonian targe,
And, with what skill they had, together sewed,
To gird their waist.

The tree, however, is not, as Milton sang, remarkable for the broadness of its leaf. The branches spread to a great extent, dropping their roots here and there, which, as soon as they reach the ground, rapidly increase in size till they become as large as, and similar to, the parent trunk. As the Banyan tree gets old, it breaks up into separate masses, the original trunk decaying, and the props becoming separate trunks of the different portions. The banyan hardly ever vegetates on the ground ; but its figs are eaten by birds, and the seeds deposited in the crowns of palms, where they grow, sending down roots that embrace and eventually kill the palm, which decays away ; the drops or aerial roots yield a heavy hard timber and, when well prepared by water seasoning, oiling &c., are valued for tent poles, spars of small vessels &c. The timber of the tree is not employed in India, but Mr. Rohde had used planks, sawn from large drops after they had been seasoned in water with advantage : for knife boards it is excellent. In Ceylon, Mr. Mendis says, it is used for common furniture and house buildings. A white glutinous juice is extracted by incision, from which birdlime is prepared and it is applied to the mouth to relieve tooth-ache ; it is also considered a valuable application to the soles of the feet when cracked and inflamed. The bark is supposed by the Hindoos to be a powerful tonic. The leaves are pinned together, to form platters, off which brahmins and hindoos eat. Much lac is often to be collected from this tree.—*Drs. Riddell, O'Shaughnessy, Dr. Hooker's Him. Journ. Vol. II. p.* 246, *Marsden's Hist. of Sumatra, p.* 160, *Mr. Mendis, Milton, Book of Trees, Voigt, Thwaites, Mr. Rohde's MSS., Eng. Cyc.*

FICUS VIRENS.

Juvi manu. TEL.

The people use the wood for common purposes. It is well adapted for avenues, being a very ornamental tree constantly in leaf. There are many varieties, the smaller leafed seem to stand better than the banyan in exposed situations.—*Mr. Rohde's MSS.*

FINOKI, JAP. A cypress tree, of Japan, which yields a light whitish wood, of a good substance, and does not absorb water.—*Thunb., Hist. Jap. Vol. I. p.* 118.

FLACOURTIA CATAPHRACTA, *Roxb.*

Panayala. BENG.	Paniala. HIND.
Talisputri. „	Talishputri. MALEAL.
Paneeyala. „	Talisha. SANS.
Panayala. DUK.	Talishapatri. TAM.
Talisputri. HIND.	Talisapatri. TEL.

A tree of Assam, Monghyr and Nepal. Fruit palatable and reckoned wholesome.—*Voigt.*

FLACOURTIA MONTANA.

Ram tambut. MAHR.	Uttuck. MAHR.

A tree common in forests above and below the Bombay ghats, but does not, in as far as Dr. Gibson had seen, extend inland. The wood is rather strong and close-grained, but the girth is never such as to render it sufficient for general purposes of carpentry or building.—*Dr. Gibson.*

FLACOURTIA SAPIDA, *Roxb.; W. & A.; W. Ic.*

Booinch. BENG.	Pedda kanaregu. TEL.
Bincha. DUK.	Pedda canrew. „
Oogoorassa. SINGH.	Nakka neredu. „

A small sized tree growing to an elevation of 1,500 to 3,000 feet in the central province of Ceylon, grows, also, in Peninsular India, on the Godavery, in Ganjam and Gumsur, extreme height 15 feet, circumference 1 foot, and height from ground to the intersection of the first branch, 5 feet, also in Bengal and northwards to Dehra Dhoon. It yields a very hard close grained wood which does not warp, and is worthy of attention. This wood is burnt when libations are offered for a person who has died on an inauspicious day.—*Captains Beddome and Macdonald, Voigt.*

FOTHERGILLIA INVOLUCRATA, *Falc.*

Chob-i-pao. KASH.

Forms whole tracts of low jungles in Kashmir, and Mr. Vigne tells us that it grows, also, in Ladak, and is very common in the straths and mountain sides at the western end of Kashmir, growing at an elevation from 4,400 to 5,000 feet. In general form, it resembles a ground ash or gigantic hazel, ten or twelve feet high, with branches about $2\frac{1}{2}$ inches in diameter and its fruit in clusters of small nuts. Its wood is very hard, resembling, but darker than, box. Messrs. Rudall and Rose formed the portion taken to England by Mr. Vigne, into a finely toned flute. It makes excellent tent pegs.—*Vigne.*

GALEDUPA ARBOREA.

Karunga ? HIND. ?	Kenja. HIND. ?
Kurmeja ? „ ?	

A very common tree in Tenasserim and Pegu, more especially in the Prome district. The seed may be collected in any quantity, it is a large seed and an oil. "Karunga ka tel" is expressed from it, which is used in Bengal for burning, and medicinally as a liniment.—*Dr. McClelland.* (*Note*—This and the next seem the same.)

GALEDUPA INDICA, *Lam.*

Pongamia glabra, *Vent.*

(Qu. ? Dalechampa arborea, p. 95 ?

Kurmeja. HIND.	Gannga. TEL.
Kenja. „	

A very large timber tree, from 40 to 50 feet high, common all over the Indian peninsula, in Bengal, &c. It flowers during the hot season, and the seeds ripen towards the close of the year. They yield a useful oil. Its wood is light, white, and firm, and serves for a variety of economic purposes. Branches stuck in the ground grow readily, grass and every thing else grows well under its shade.—*Mr. Rohde's MSS.* See PONGAMIA.

GALEDUPA TETRAPETALA. A common tree of Tenasserim and Burmah, more especially in the Prome district. Its seeds yield an oil for burning and the flowers a fine red dye. —*Dr. McClelland.*

GALEX, *Species.*

Mohmagah. BURM.

A tree of Moulmein. Used in common purposes of building.—*Cal. Cat. Ex.* 1862.

GAMBIER is extracted from the leaves of the Uncaria gambir, in Siak, Malacca, and Bittang, inspissating by decoction, strained, suffered to cool and harden, and then cut into cakes of sizes or formed into balls. A composition of this extract is valuable as a preservative for timber. Dissolve three parts of gambier in twelve of dammar oil, over a slow fire. Then, stir in one part of lime, sprinkling it over the top, to prevent its coagulating and settling in a mass at the bottom. It must be well and quickly stirred. It should then be taken out of the cauldron and ground down like paint on a muller till it is smooth, and afterwards returned to the pot and heated. A little oil should be added to make it tractable, and the composition can then be laid over the material, with a common brush. As a protection against the teredo, black varnish or tar are substituted for dammar oil, omitting the grinding down which would not answer with tar. —*Journ. Ind. Arch., also Dr. Cleghorn's Report,* 1859-60, *para.* 13, *page* 7.

GANDHI, HIND. ? A tree of Chota Nagpore. Soft, white wood.—*Cal. Cat. Ex.* 1862.

GANARA WOOD. Ganara kurra. A timber of the Northern Circars.

GAN-GAN, BURM. In Amherst, a very strong, tough, hard, crooked grained, fibrous, red wood, which would be suitable for machinery or any purpose requiring the above properties.

GANJAM, Goomsur, and Kimedy Forests. The most recent and valuable list of their trees is from Lieutenant (now Major) Macdonald from Ganjam and Lieut. (now Captain) Philipps sent a note on those of Kimedy.

The Kimedy forests cover an area of 400 square miles, those of chief consequence and most accessible, lying on both banks of the Vumshadara river, above and below "Buttely," "Barsinghy," and Jeranghee; Jeranghee, Giba, Cothoor, Jadoupully and indeed the whole of the hilly tracts abound with fine trees, the only difficulty being their removal when cut. He particularly notices a tree, the "Dhamono," or "*Kurkurra.*" Its extreme height is 39 feet. The circumference of its trunk is $3\frac{1}{2}$ feet, and height from the ground to nearest branch 18 feet. It furnishes a very long grained tough wood, pliant and light. It is used for dhoolies, cots, buggy shafts, bandy wheels, and poles, spear and axe handles, fishing rods and lance handles and other purposes where strength and elasticity are required.

In Capt. Macdonald's list of Ganjam and Goomsur woods, he mentioned that the forests in the northern portion of that district, although not to be compared in size or importance with those in some other parts of the Madras Presidency, are nevertheless somewhat extensive and contain many useful trees. The most important and accessible are situated in the talook of Goomsur and the Zemindary of Bodogoda, both of which are watered by rivers which afford facilities for floating the timber down to the coast during the freshes. The jungles change their names every two or three miles, and a list of them would be so long that it seems sufficient to indicate in general terms the localities in which the largest and finest timber is procurable. In Goomsur, these are the Kookoo-loobah, Gullery, Ootoro-godoloto, Poorwa-goodoloto, Juggurnauthprasaud, Kurcholy, Bhootapilly and Beerecota Mootahs. In Bodogoda there are three Mootahs below the Ghauts, the Coradakonna, Godo and Jagiree, all three of which are well wooded, but the first contains the largest forests. Above the ghauts, are the Mootahs of Jorraow, Gowdo-gotho, Morihano, Gokalopoor, Meerecote, Woddobah and Loha-gooddee, all abounding in timber, which remains uncut chiefly on account of the difficulty of transporting it. The same remark applies to the forests of Chokapaud and Poomaghur, two hill dependencies of Goomsur. In the former, the Cottarikiah, Woolingiah, Mettribiah and Koondopottro Mootahs contain forests which are of little use to any one except the inhabitants of the country—of these forests the largest are the Dodo-soroo, Dehenko-soroo, Jhoonda-soroo and Suboolodeyee. In the Hill tracts under Poomaghur, for the same reason, but little use is made of any of the forests with the exception of those in the Punchagodotolo Mootah which lies at the foot of the ghauts. Captain (now Major) Macdonald adds, "I am not in possession of any returns from Soorada, but I know from personal observation that this small talook is most extensively wooded and that it supplies large quantities of fire-wood to the Aska factory, the sum paid for this single item being, I have been given to understand, equal to one-third of the revenue collected from the Talook. It was till lately noted for its extensive tamarind topes and orange groves but in other respects probably differs but little from the neighbouring talooks. Bodogoda is a Zemindary, and the forests belong to the Zemindar, in whose name a variety of small taxes are levied on the products of the jungle. Their amount is however very insignificant and the privilege of collecting them is farmed out to a renter who is styled "Ghoto Bissoye," "Bono Bissoye" and "Bono borilla," (Jungle-ranger), which last name is expressive of the nature of his ordinary duty. He paid this year Rupees 84 for his farm and levies a small sum varying from 4 Annas to a Rupee from each village for the general privilege of cutting fire-wood, a tax of 2 annas on every new bandy, of one Rupee on every new boat, of Rs. 1-8 on every tree cut down for a mast, half an anna on every bandy load of fire-wood, 1 anna on every bandy load of bamboos, 2 annas and 6 pice on every bandy load of plank wood, and similar small sums for wood required for ploughshares, oil press &c. There is also a Zemindary tax termed Pohondee Ghuttum, levied on all sales of honey, rosin, Arrow root, Moholo flowers, Moholo seeds, and Korunjo seeds, but in Bodogoda this tax has apparently merged in the farm of the forest renter. In Goomsur and the other tracts alluded to, which are all Government talooks, no such taxes are known, and although the forests are, almost without exception, Government property, no revenue whatever is derived from them. In the time of the Goomsur Rajahs, it is said that a tax called Bono Cowry of 2 annas was levied on each plough, and that, altogether, the forests yielded a revenue of about Rupees 2000 a year, but these taxes have been abolished. Throughout the whole of this part of the District, there is far more timber than is required for the local consumption, but there is no doubt that, with the exception of the Hill Tracts, the jungles are all rapidly diminishing—partly owing to the increase of cultivation and partly to meet the demand for timber at Aska, Berhampore, Ganjam and other places. In the time of the Rajahs, the felling of timber was systematically discouraged from motives of policy with a view to render the country less accessible to troops. With the exception of an order recently issued by the Collector forbidding the indiscriminate cutting of timber there is at present no system of any kind regarding the felling, cutting or the reproduction of trees. Timber is cut at all times of the year, but most of it seems to be felled between January and May, these being the months during which the Ryots are less occupied with their cultivation. Bamboos and other trees which have little or no heart wood, are cut during the wane of the moon being, otherwise, it is said, liable to be attacked by insects, but there is no such belief with regard to the larger kinds of timber. There are however five days in each Hindoo month, which are supposed to be inauspicious and on these no trees are felled. Large patches of jungle are constantly cleared for the purpose of being brought under cultivation and the destruction of the trees is often, and on the hills it may be said always, effected by fire. This destruction is however not altogether indiscriminate, certain trees being always carefully preserved. Among these are the Mango and date tree, the koeto, the Bovadah (*Bauhinia*) and Soondorogoodee, (*Rottleria*) to which, if the cultivators are Khonds, may be added the Solopo palm (*Caryota*) and the Mohollo (*Bassia*) which are especially reserved from destruction on account of the intoxicating liquors which they yield, and which are largely drunk. Annexed is a list of the forest trees in this part of the country with their dimensions and remarks on the use to which they are generally applied. None of these seem to be subject to any kind of regulation, and it has not been possible to ascertain the extent of traffic which is carried on in them. No exotic trees of any kind have as yet been introduced.—R. M. MACDONALD, *Asst. Agent.*, Asst. Agent's Office, Russellcondah, 4th Dec. 1854.

Since these remarks were written, Dr. Cleghorn visited that tract of country, and, in Gumsur, he says, the principal jungles are Kukuluba, Gulleri, Jaggarnatprasad &c., and the Sal is their most useful and most abundant tree. The Khonds in their destruction of the forests, carefully preserve fruit trees such as the mango, the date, Caryota urens or salopo, Bassia latifolia, (Mohollo) wood apple, bastard sago, elupi, Bauhinia (Bovada) and Rottleria tinctoria, (Sundosa gunda.) The jungles are rapidly diminishing, the clearance being effected by fire. In his rapid journey, he was able further to identify, and note in the first edition of this work, the names of several trees of which only the vernacular terms had been given, and he obligingly allowed me to correct my own copy, from his corrected one. Captain Macdonald's valuable list of timber trees &c. with the names, thus modified, are given here, and merit further attention.

Acacia arabica. Babolo.
Acacia catechu. Khoiro.
Acacia. Gouharea.
Acacia serissa. Sirisee
Alangium hexapetalum. Ankolo.
Ambaleta.
Averrhoa carambola? Koromonga.
Ægle marmelos. Bello.
Bambusa spinosa. Conta banso.
Bassia latifolia. Mohoollo.
Bauhinia. Ambhota.
Bauhinia vahlii. Shyolee.
Bauhinia variegata. Borodha.
Baujhonoo.
Baygoona.
Bodoka.
Behenta.
Beloo.
Bignonea suaveolens.? Patolee.
Bignonia chelonoides.? Pamphoonea.
Bolungee banso.
Bombax heptaphyllum. Bouro.
Bono koniaree.
Boroana.
Buchanania latifolia. Charo. Bhalleah.
Butea frondosa. Polaso.
Caryota urens. Solopo.
Careya arborea. Koombee.
Cassia, *sp.* Tanghany.
Cassia fistula. Soonaree.
Cæsalpinia sappan. Bokmo.
Cedrela toona. Mahalimbo.
Chochena.
Choonokolee.
Chorayegodee.
Choureeona.
Citrus aurantium. Naringhee.
Citrus medica? Ambelee toba.
Conocarpus latifolius. Dhoboo.
Cluytia spinosa. Korada.
Carissa carandas. Gotho.
Dalbergia sissoo. Sisoowa.
Dalosingha or Taloosinghee.
Dharoujo.
Dhimeree.
Dhobo Khoiro.
Dhoon.
Dhosora khendhoo.
Diospyros ebenum. Ebony, Kendhoo.
Elæocarpus. Poecchandea.
Erythrina Indica. Chalodhoua.
Eugenia jambolana. Jamo.
Eugenia acutangula.? Hinjolo.
Euphorbia tirucalli.? Lodhoka sijhoo.
Feronia elephantum. Koeto.
Ficus, *sp.* Bace dhimeree.
Ficus Indica. Boro.
Ficus t'siela. Joree.
Flacourtia sapida. Boincho.
Gardenia. Bahmonea.
Gardenia. Patauwa.
Gardenia. Pendra.
Garuga pinnata. Moee.
Ghoralanjea or Tentara.
Ghunteoh Patoolee.
Gmelina, *sp.* Gombhare, Gomidi.
Gondo-polaso.
Gongosheolee Dondeepoholo.
Gooroohado.
Gooroobolee.
Grewia tiliæfolia. Dhamouo.
Grouhonee Kubatee.
Hadakoukalee.
Ixora. Tillakooroowan.
Jhoontiah.
Jonesia asoca.? Oshoko.
Jundamaree.
Kaloochia.
Khakodha.
Khookoondea.
Kodoro.
Kola sahajo.
Kolee Kouradea.
Kontabaolo.
Kopassea.
Kossaye.
Mangifera Indica. Ambo.
Melia azadirachta? Limbo.
Meresingha.
Mesua ferrea.? Nagishvoro.
Michelia champaca.? Konchona.
Mimusops kaki? Kheerokolee.
Minjharee or Paloodhona.
Moddoro goodee.
Modoroo toba.
Morinda tinctoria. Achoo.
Mosanea.
Nauclea cordifolia. Holondho.
Nauclea cadamba.? Kodumbo.
Nauclea parviflora. Moondomonde.
Neraso.
Nerium odoratum.? Goonaieho.
Nooniaree, Looniaree or Noononoaea.
Oshrosto.
Paneeollo.
Pentaptera glabra. Sahajo.
Phasee.
Phyllanthus emblica? Emblic myrobalan. Olla awla.
Phyllanthus emblica.? Gondhona.
Pichoolee.
Pitta Kaloochia.
Pitolo.
Pochoboro.
Ponaso.
Pongamia glabra. Korunjo.
Ponposo Komaree.
Porto koorwan.
Potoobaolo.
Pterocarpus marsupium. Piasalo.
Rahana.
Rayee.
Rooradea.
Rottleria tinctoria. Soondoro-goondee, Koomalagoondee or Bosonto-goondee.
Salora.
Schleicheria trijuga. Koossoomo.
Semecarpus anacardium.
Shalimbo-banso.
Shorea robusta. Salwa or Sorunghee.
Siddha.
Sohn, one of the Terebinthaceæ.
Soogondhee.
Sohojo Maree.
Soondorogoyan banso.
Soroopottree Moee.
Spondias mangifera. Ambodha.
Sterculia sp. (not fœtida.) Kodalo.
Strychnos nux vomica. Korra.
Strychnos potatorum. Kotoko.
Swietenia chloroxylon. Satinwood, Bhayroo.
Tentoollee or Koyan.
Terminalia. Kosee.
Terminalia alata. T. glabra. Orjoono.
Terminalia belerica. Bahadha.
Terminalia chebula. Koredha.
Trophis aspera. Sahadha.
Vangueria spinosa.? Mohonea.
Woon.
Wrightia. Beejee Kooroowan.
Zizyphus. Borokolee.
Zizyphus. Contayecoollee.

GARANIA SPECIOSA?

Balawa. BURM.?

A tree of Moulmein. Used in common purposes of building.—*Cal. Cat. Ex.* 1862.

GARCINIA. A genus of plants, trees of considerable size, consisting of about 21 species, growing in Ceylon, Travancore, Malabar, and other parts of the peninsula of India, in Sylhet, Assam, the Malay peninsula, and the southern parts of China. Several of them yield edible fruits, and one of them is the Mangosteen fruit tree, *G. Mangostana*, L, a tree of the Malay peninsula and islands of the Moluccas: *G. Kydia*, Roxb., of the Andaman islands, is a tree, with a sharp but agreeably acid fruit, similar to the large fruit of *G. pedunculata*, Roxb., which grows in Rungpore: *G. paniculata*, Roxb., a tree of Sylhet, has a palatable fruit something like the mangosteen: *G. Roxburghii*, Wight, a tree of Travancore, Malabar and Chittagong, has an edible but very acid fruit: *G. purpurea*, Roxb., grows on the western coast of peninsular India. Useful timbers are obtained from others, but the species are not defined.—*Ainslie, Voigt, Thwaites, Dr. Mason, Useful Plants, Eng. Cyc.*

GARCINIA, *Species.*

Young zalai. BURM.

A tree of Moulmein. Its wood is made use of for ordinary house building purposes. Fruit edible.—*Cal. Cat. Ex.* 1862.

GARCINIA, *Species.* Parawah. BURM?? A tree of Akyab, but not plentiful. A large wood, used to make bows and in house building.—*Cal. Cat. Ex.* 1862.

GARCINIA, *Species.*

Parawah. BURM.

In Pegu, a strong wood with a pretty variegated grain, the tree is of too small size to render the timber available for general purposes. —*Major Benson.*

GARCINIA, *Species.* A timber tree of Tenasserim, the largest that Dr. Mason had seen of the genus. In frequent demand for house posts in Tavoy.—*Dr. Mason.*

GARCINIA, *Species.*

Pulloua. BURM.

A large tree of Tavoy, used for posts, &c.—(*Note*, are these all one species ?)

GARCINIA CAMBOGIA, *Desrous.*, not *Roxb.*

Garcinia Kydia, *W. & A.* ?
" Indica, *Choisy.*

Wontay. CAN.	Gorakah-gass. SINGH.
Valaitie amlie. DUK.	Karka-pulie maram ? TAM.
Kurka pulie. MALEAL.	Woda chinta chettu ? TEL.
Racta shrava. SANS.	

A tall tree, growing in Ceylon up to 1,500 feet, grows in Travancore and in the forests of Malabar, is very abundant in Tenasserim, and very common in Siam and Cambodia. It yields a pleasant tasted acid fruit.—*Eng. Cyc., Drs. Ainslie, Mason, Thwaites.*

GARCINIA CORNEA, *Linn.*

A tree of Moulmein, Penang, and Amboyna, with a tall though not very thick trunk. The wood is heavy though not very hard, like horn, and is used for the handles of tools. The young trees are used also for house building purposes, but the timber of old trees is too hard to work. The fruit has a resinous smell.—*Dr. O'Shaughnessy, Eng. Cyc.*

GARCINIA ? GLUTINIFERA, *Ainslie.*

Panichekai maram. TAM.

Dr. Wight says this is one of the very few trees admitted into his list, that he had not himself seen and verified, and it was introduced in the hope that some resident on the Malabar Coast, would favour him with specimens to determine its name and botanical relations. Dr. Gibson believes that a Diospyros must be here meant, but thinks it may be that the Bombay Garcinia sylvestris is alluded to. If so, the tree he says is common in the southern Konkun, Malabar and Canara; always planted; affording a good wood and palatable fruit, from the kernel whereof is extracted by boiling the vegetable concrete oil "kokum." The dried fruit is a common ingredient in native cookery, having an agreeable acid.—*Drs. Wight and Gibson.*

GARCINIA GUTTA, *R. W.*

Cambogia gutta, *Linn.*
Hebradendron cambojioides, *Graham.*

A tree, native of Ceylon, not uncommon about Colombo, and generally on the South West Coast of the Island. Produces a kind of gamboge.—*Wight's Illustrs.* i. 126.

GARCINIA ROXBURGHII, *R. W.*

G. Cambogia, *Roxb.*, not *Desr.*
G. Zeylanica, *Roxb.*
G. Affinis, *W. & A.*
G. Cowa, *Roxb.*

Toung-tha-lay. BURM.	Cowa. HIND.

A tree of Ceylon, Travancore, Malabar, Chittagong, and scattered over the hills of British Burmah but scarce. Wood not used, but is yellow and fit for a fancy wood. A cubic foot weighs lbs. 42. In a full grown tree on good soil the average length of the trunk to the first branch is 20 feet and average girth measured at 6 feet from the ground is 6 feet. Fruit eatable, but very acid.—*Drs. Brandis & McClelland, Cal. Cat. Ex. of* 1862, *Voigt, Wight's Illust.* i. *p.* 125.

GARDENIA, *Species.*

Telega? TEL.

A tree of the Godavery forests and Dekhan, furnishes a very hard wood which would be very good for turning.

GARDENIA CORONARIA, *Buch.*

G. costata, *Roxb.*

Yin-gat. BURM.

A tree of Chittagong and Moulmein. Wood used for building purposes. This wood has a fragrant smell, and would be useful for boxes, but, unfortunately, when cut into planks there are so many flaws and cracks, that it is difficult to procure a piece of any size; it is a strong tough wood and useful for turning. Fruit edible.—*Voigt, Cal. Cat. Ex.* 1862, *Major Benson.*

GARDENIA FLORIBUNDA—?

Thet-ya. BURM.

A tree of Moulmein. This wood is made use of for ordinary house building purposes.—*Cal. Cat. Ex.* 1862.

GARDENIA ENNEANDRA, *Kön.; W. & A.*

Gardenia latifolia, *Roxb.; Cor. pl.*

Bikki. TEL.

A small tree of peninsular India, growing in the Carnatic, the Nalla Mallai, the Circars, Khandesh and Guzerat. It furnishes a light wood of little use. Native combs are made of it.—*Voigt, Mr. Latham.*

GARDENIA GUMMIFERA, *Linn.; Roxb.; W. & A.; W. Ic.*

Gardenia arborea, *Roxb.*

Chiri bikki. TEL.	Garaga. TEL.
Chatta matta. "	

A large shrub or small tree, with large fragrant flowers, which, in the morning, are white and become yellow by the evening. The wood is hard. The natives eat the fruit. It grows in Ceylon, in the Gingi hills, on the Godavery and in the Circars, and is very common about Duddi, on the Gutpurba river.—*Voigt, Captain Beddome, Mr. R. Brown.*

GARDENIA LATIFOLIA, *Ait.*

Papura. HIND.	Kokkita. TEL.
Bikki. TEL.	Kurukiti. "
Konda manga. TEL.	Kumbay maram. TAM.
Kakkiti chettu. "	Peda karinga. TEL.
Kariuguva. "	

A small tree in the south of the peninsula of India; also a Godavery wood, close grained, and promises well for turning.—*Captain Beddome.*

GARDENIA LUCIDA, *Roxb.; W. & A.*

Gardenia resinifera, *Roth.*

Tsay-tham-by-ah. BURM.	Cumbi. TAM.
Dikamalli. DUK.	China karinguva. TEL.
Dikamalli. GUZ.	Tella manga. "
Dikamalli. HIND.	

Grows in the southern Mahratta country, Circars, on the Godavery, and Chittagong, and gives a close grained wood, well adapted for the lathe. In British Burmah, it is a white close grained wood apparently well adapted for turning. This wood like that of several other species of Gardenia and Randia is used for making combs. A cubic foot weighs lbs. 49. In a full grown tree on good soil the average length of the trunk to the first branch is 15 feet and average girth, measured at 6 feet from the ground is 3 feet. Its resin, Cumbi-pisin, *Tam.*, is a strong disagreeable smelling gum-resin; procurable in most Indian bazars. It is much used by native doctors as an external application, when dissolved in spirits, for cleaning foul ulcers. It is now used by some European practitioners in cases of worms in children.—*Faulkner, Voigt, Dr. Brandis, Captain Beddome.*

GARDENIA TURGIDA, *Roxb.*

Nunjoonda maram. TAM.

Dr. Wight says, he only knew this from small specimens, and was unable to say whether it is a tree or shrub, but believed the former; the wood which is hard and close grained, is useful in cases where small timber will serve. Dr. Gibson asks if Wight's Gardenia turgida be not G. montana (?) and adds "I do not recognise this species or variety; neither do I find it noticed in Dr. Wight's Prodromus. If it be our Gardenia montana, the tree is rather common in the coast and inland jungles. It may be recognised by its straight stem, long stout thorns, and general absence of leaves. The wood is hard, but always small, never squaring to more than 3 inches." The Gardenia turgida of Roxburgh is a tree of Bhootan, both it and G. montana are in Wight's Icones, ii. t. 577 & 579.—*Drs. Wight and Gibson.*

GARUGA PINNATA, *Roxb.*

Khyong-youk. BURM.	Carri vembu maram. TAM.
Kuruk. HIND.	Garuga chettu. TEL.
Kooruk. MAHR.	

In Coimbatore, a considerable sized tree with a round umbrageous head. It is common in the Bombay jungles, where the wood appears of little value; but might be creosoted. The tree is rather common in the plains and on the hills of British Burmah, but the wood is not much used. A cubic foot weighs lbs. 52. In a full grown tree on good soil the average length of the trunk to the first branch is 40 feet and average girth measured at 6 feet from the ground is 9 feet. It sells, in Pegu, at 8 annas per cubic foot.—*Drs. Wight, Gibson and Brandis, Cal. Cat. Ex.* 1862.

GELONIUM BIFARIUM, *Roxb.*

Hsai than bayah. BURM.

Is found in the Rangoon district, it seldom exceeds three feet in girth, and is only fit for house posts. Wood white colour, and adapted for every purpose of house-building.

GHANTHA WOOD. ANGLO-TEL. Gantha karra, *Tel.* A wood of the Northern Circars.

GHATNA, HIND.? A tree of Chota Nagpore. Hard, yellow timber.—*Cal. Cat. Ex.* 1862.

GHORALANJEA. URIA? TENTARA. URIA? A tree of Ganjam and Gumsur, extreme height 30 feet. Circumference 3 feet and height from the ground to the intersection of the first branch, 10 feet. Used for spinning wheels, sugar presses and ploughshares, and burnt for firewood, being tolerably common.—*Captain Macdonald.*

GHUNTEOH PATOOLEE, URIA? A tree of Ganjam and Gumsur, extreme height 22 feet. Circumference 1½ feet, and height from ground to the intersection of the first branch, 10 feet. Used occasionally for axletrees and rafters but chiefly for firewood, the tree being rather common.—*Captain Macdonald.*

GIVOTTIA ROTTLERIFORMIS, *Griff.; W. Ic.*

Putalli maram. TAM.	Tella ponuku. TEL.
Batalli. "	" Poonkee. "

One of the Euphorbiaceæ, common in Southern India. Dr. Wight had not learned anything regarding the timber, one carpenter in Coimbatore spoke disparagingly of it, but he did not consider him a trustworthy authority. It is found in the Circar hills and is, there, a very light soft wood. Found also in a very few of the Bombay jungles, but in these only inland above the ghats. Not seen in Guzerat. The wood is light, and is used only for making the figures and models manufactured at Gokak, in the Southern Mahratta Country.—*Drs. Wight and Gibson, Captain Beddome.*

GLOCHIDION, *Thwaites.* A genus of small trees, in Ceylon, of which Thwaites mentions G. coriaceum; G. Gardneri; G. Jussieuianum; G. montanum; F. nemorale; and G. Zeylanicum.

GLAM.—? A tree of Singapore, supposed to be a species of Artocarpus: furnishes a paper-like bark, used in caulking the seams of vessels.

GMELINA, *Species.*

Cumba wood. ANGLO-TEL.	Cumba karra. TEL.

A tree of the Northern Circars.

GMELINA, *Species.*

Gombharee. URIA.

A tree of Ganjam and Gumsur, extreme height 50 feet: circumference 4½ feet: height from the ground to the intersection of the first branch, 18 feet. A white light wood. Boxes, chairs, bed-posts, lamp stands, bullock yokes, bazar measures, toys and other articles are made of it. It is said to be rather scarce and expensive. The bark is said to be used medicinally.—*Captain Macdonald.*

GMELINA ARBOREA, *Roxb.; Cor. Pl. W. Ic.*

Gmelina Rheedii, *Hooker, Bot. Mag.*

Gumar. Beng.	Kumbulu. Maleal.
Gumber. "	At-demmata. Singh.
Gumbari. "	Cummi maram ? Tam.
Yemaneh. Burm.	Gumudi maram. "
Kyunboe ? "	Teggu muda. Tel.
Yamana. "	Gummudi chettu. "
Sewun. Duk.	Gumudu-teku. "
Jugani-chukur. Hind.	Pedda gumudu. "
Seevum. "	Goomer tek. "
Seevun. "	Gombhari ? "
Shewun. Mahr.	Ghooteky. "
Seevun.	

This large tree grows in Ceylon, where it is common up to an elevation of 5,000 feet. It grows in Coimbatore, is rather frequent on the Malabar Coast, grows on the Godavery forests: is not very common on the Bombay side, where it is found more in the forests below the ghats than inland. It grows in Burmah and is plentiful in the Pegu and Toungboo forests. In British Burmah it is a large tree with white, light wood, used for house posts, planks and for carving images. Recommended for planking and furniture. A cubic foot weighs 35 lbs. In a full grown tree, there, on good soil, the average length of the trunk to the first branch is 50 feet, and average girth measured at 6 feet from the ground is 12 feet. Dr. McClelland calls "Kyoonboe," *Burm.*, a yellow wood, says it is plentiful in the Pegu and Toungboo forests, is a large and remarkably strong tough timber, and fit for fancy wood. In Moulmein, it is used in ordinary building material. Fruit used as medicine. On the Bombay side, the wood is in much esteem for carriage panels, and other purposes. According to Dr. Roxburgh, it also stands exposure to weather and water well. From its great size, straightness, and general spaciousness in appearance (being a beautiful flowering tree), this is one of the most desirable for propagation throughout the country. Dr. Cleghorn in the Jury reports says it is a large timber tree, growing in mountainous districts: that the wood is light, of a pale yellow colour, easily worked, and does not shrink or warp; used for picture frames, decking small boats, for making venetian blinds, sounding boards, palankeen panels, gram measures, &c. It is very commonly used, in the Vizagapatam district, for the foundation of wells and other purposes, which require it to be submerged in water, where it is remarkably durable. On the Godavery, the large trees of this yield a very hard durable wood and the yokes for bullocks are made from it. In Nagpore, the "Seevum" is of a very light colour, has a sort of netted grain, is free from faults, and altogether may be considered a very excellent timber, although unfortunately not procurable in large quantities. Its length, there, is from 13 to 18 feet and from 4½ to 3½ feet in girth. The Commissariat there, supply it to the Ordnance Department for making packing cases, &c., and the natives employ it in the construction of palkies. It takes varnish well, and works up nicely into furniture, but is attacked readily by white ants. From the small scantling of which it is there obtained, it must be classed merely as a rafter wood.—*Drs. Wight, Gibson, Brandis, Cleghorn, Captains Sankey and Beddome, Cal. Cat. Ex. of* 1862, *Thwaites.*

GNEMIUM GNETUM, *Linn.*

Wagoo. Jav.	Bagu. Malay.

This tree abounds on the southern coast of the island of Sumatra where its bark is beaten, like hemp, and the twine manufactured from it is employed in the construction of large fishing nets. The coarse cordage from the bark is in extensive use throughout the Archipelago. The leaves are dressed in curries.—*Crawfurd's Dictionary, p.* 26, *Marsden's Hist. of Sumatra, p.* 91.

GOAY-PIN-GYEE, Burm. A tree of Moulmein. Used in common purposes of building: its seed is used for weights in weighing gold.—*Cal. Cat. Ex.* 1862.

GOAY THA, Burm. A tree of Moulmein. Used in common purposes of building.—*Cal. Cat. Ex.* 1862.

GODDA, Can.? A Mysore wood, one of Cedrelaceæ, a wood that polishes well, and is good for turning.—*Captain Puckle in Mad. Cat. Ex.* 1862.

GOMPHIA ANGUSTIFOLIA, *Vahl.; W. & A.; Prod. I.* 152.

Walkera serrata, *Willd.; D C. Prod.*
Gomphia Zeylanica, *D C.*
" Malabarica, *D C.*
Ochna Zeylanica, *Lam.*

Bokaara-gass. Singh.

Grows in Ceylon where it is common up to an elevation of 3,000 feet. The wood of this tree, which grows to the height of thirty feet, is useful for building purposes.—*Thw. En. Pl. Zeyl. I. p.* 71.

GOMUTO, Malay.

Makse, Amb.	Si ji. Malay.
Gomuti. Eng.	Sagwire. Port.
Duke. Jav.	Anow. Sum.
Dok. "	Cabo negro. Sp.
Iju. Malay.	Seho. Ter.
Eju. "	

A fibrous product of the Arenga saccharifera, which see. Since printing the notice of that palm, Mr. New of the Bangalore gardens, has informed me that the Arenga grows in Bangalore and to some extent in the Nuggur division of Mysore.

GONDOPOLA, Uria? A tree of Ganjam and Gumsur, extreme height 45 feet, circumference 2¼ feet and height from the ground to the intersection of the first branch, 8 feet. Bandy wheels and ploughshares are occasionally made of this wood, but it is chiefly burnt for firewood, being tolerably common.—*Captain Macdonald.*

GONGOO or GANGAW, Burm. A tree of Amherst, Tavoy and Mergui, maximum girth 3 cubits, maximum length 32 feet. Found very abundant; near Mergui, also thence along coast as far as Amherst. When seasoned, it floats in water. It is used for tables, chairs and miscellaneous articles by the Burmese; a good, hard, tough wood, durable and recommended for helves, also for handles of all kinds of tools. (Vide Major (now Colonel) Simpson's Report.)—*Captain Dance.*

GONGOSHEOLEE, Uria.? Dondeepoholo. Uria? A tree of Ganjam and Gumsur, extreme height 25 feet, circumference 3 feet and height from ground to the intersection of the first branch 7 feet. No use seems to be made of the wood. The flower which has a powerful perfume is offered in all the pagodas to the presiding divinity.—*Captain Macdonald.*

GONIOTHALAMUS HOOKERI, *Thw.* A middle sized tree of Ceylon at Hinidoon and Reigam Corles, at an elevation of about 1,000 feet.—*Thw. En. Pl. Zeyl. p.* 6.

GOOROOHADO, Uria? A tree of Ganjam and Gumsur, extreme height 22 feet, circumference 2 feet, height from ground to the intersection of the first branch, 10 feet. Chiefly used for firewood though rafters are occasionally made of this wood.—*Captain Macdonald.*

GORDONIA, *Species.*

Anan pho, Burm.

A tree of Moulmein. A strong wood, good for building purposes.—*Cal. Cat. Ex.* 1862.

GORDONIA, *Species.*

Zaza. Burm.

A large common timber tree of Martaban.

GORDONIA FLORIBUNDA and G. integrifolia: the former is called "itch wood" by the Tavoyers, from the itching that its chip or bark occasions when brought in contact with the skin. Dr. Mason had often seen its compact timber used for house posts, and for rice mortars.—*Dr. Mason's Tenasserim.*

GORDONIA SPECIOSA, *Thw.*

Carria speciosa, *Gardn.*

A large tree, 40 to 50 feet high, rather uncommon, in damp forests of the central province of Ceylon at an elevation of 5,000 feet and upwards.—*Thw. En. Pl. Zeyl. I. p.* 40.

GORDONIA ZEYLANICA, *Wight.*

Var. *a.* lanceolata. | Var. *b.* elliptica.

Grows in forests of the central province of Ceylon, at an elevation of 4,000 to 7,000 feet.—*Thw. En. Pl. Zeyl. I. p.* 40.

GREWIA, a genus of plants belonging to the natural order Tiliaceæ, of which many species grow in South Eastern Asia; they are mostly shrubs or small trees, the fruits, fibres and timbers of which are applicable for economic purposes. The inner bark of *G. oppositifolia*, Buch., a small tree, is used in the Himalayas, for coarse cloth and cordage. The acid berries of *G. sclerophylla*, Roxb., a shrub, are used for making sherbet, as are, also, the berries of *G. Asiatica*, Linn. *G. ulmifolia* is a tree of Assam and China.—*Eng. Cyc., Voigt.*

GREWIA, *Species.* At Tavoy, when vessels require spars they are usually furnished from a small tree which grows on the sea board, belonging to this genus.—*Dr. Mason's Tenasserim.*

GREWIA, *Species.*

Maiva. Burm.

A Tavoy wood.

GREWIA, *Species.*

Tha-ran. Burm.

A tree of Moulmein. Wood used to make dancing dolls.—*Cal. Cat. Ex.* 1862.

GREWIA ASIATICA, *Linn.*

Fulsa. Hind. | Fulsa maram. Tam.

Grows in the peninsula of India, in Bengal, and is a large tree of Pegu, like *G. floribunda*, but not so plentiful. Wood white colour and adapted for every purpose of house building.—*Dr. McClelland.*

GREWIA ELASTICA, *Royle.*

Dhamnoo. Hind.

Is figured in Royle's Himalayan Botany. It is valued for the strength and elasticity of its wood.—*Eng. Cyc.* (*Note*—Is this the Dhamnoo of Kimedy and of Ganjam and Gumsur? *q. v.*)

GREWIA FLORIBUNDA, *Wall.*

Myat ya. Burm. | Mya ya gyee. Burm.

A very common tree, throughout the Rangoon, Pegu and Tounghoo districts, but scarce in the Prome and Tharawaddy districts. It is a good serviceable timber for all ordinary purposes of house building. The bark affords a coarse strong fibre, not much employed, however, by the Burmese.—*Dr. McClelland, Cal. Cat. Ex.* 1862.

GREWIA HOOKERII, *McClelland.*

Phet woon. Burm.

Very plentiful in Pegu. It attains a girth of about 3 to 4 feet, and grows up tall and remarkably straight. It is found with teak in the forests of Pegu and Tounghoo. Wood white coloured and adapted for every purpose of house building.—*Dr. McClelland.*

GREWIA MICROCOS, *Linn.*

Mya ya. Burm.

Found on elevated ground of British Burmah. Wood not used. A cubic foot weighs lbs. 51. In a full grown tree on good soil the average length of the trunk to the first branch is 10 feet and average girth measured at 6 feet from the ground is 4 feet.—*Dr. Brandis, Cal. Cat. Ex.* 1862.

GREWIA OBLIQUA.

Darsook mara. CAN. | Damun. MAHR.

A tree of Canara and Sunda, found mostly below, seldom grows large. Wood used in agriculture, house posts, &c.—*Dr. Gibson.*

GREWIA ROTHII?

Jana. TEL.

A tree of the Cuddapah Nalla Mallai. A light, ash-colored wood, with a straight grain, hard and strong, is much used and very serviceable. Wood very hard and much used in the Circars.—*Captain Beddome, Mr. Latham.*

GREWIA SALVIFOLIA —? Of the Madras provinces, its wood makes good walking sticks.—*M. E. J. R.*

GREWIA SPECTABILIS.?

Phet-woon. BURM.

Very plentiful; attains a girth of about three to four feet and grows up tall and remarkably straight. They are found with teak in the forests of Pegu and Tounghoo. Wood white color and adapted for every purpose of house building.—*Dr. McClelland.*

GREWIA TILIÆFOLIA, *Vahl., W. Ic.*

G. arborea, *Roxb. in E. I. C. Mus.*
G. variabilis, *Wall.*

Damun. MAHR.	Tharra. TEL.
Chadachy maram. TAM.	Dhamono. URIA?
Sadachoo „ „	Dhamono. „
Talathi „ „	Karkana. „ ?

In Coimbatore, a considerable tree and the wood is soft and easily worked: It is useful for inferior building and common purposes: but is said to be unfit for cabinet purposes, for which in appearance it seems well adapted, on account of its hygrometric properties, which causes it to contract and expand, however well seasoned, with every change of the weather. It is a common forest tree in the Bombay coast jungles; rare inland, and there the wood is not deemed of any value for household purposes, agricultural instruments, or cabinet work. It grows very large on the mountains of the Circars, and is there a valuable timber, much used for handles of axles, pellet bows, cowars, and walking sticks. In Ganjam and Gumsur, the Dhamono (Grewia tiliæfolia) is of extreme height 35 feet, circumference 3 feet, height from ground to the intersection of the first branch, 20 feet. It is used for cot frames and bandy wheels; the handles of axes, knives, spears, mamoties, pickaxes, and carpenters' tools are made of this wood, which is also burnt for firewood, being tolerably plentiful. Grewia tiliæfolia (or Grewia elastica) is said to yield the Damonu or Karkana of the Parla Kimedy jungles, from which many hundred poles could be obtained. It closely resembles lancewood or hickory. It is procurable in the bazars eight inches broad, and is used for house posts, gig shafts, dhooli poles, spear handles and fishing rods. It seems eminently suited for purposes where strength lightness and elasticity are required. The bark should be allowed to remain, and the poles should be steeped in water and then rubbed with oil. The bark gives a strong rope. (*Note*—It would seem from these remarks either that the quality of the timber of this tree varies in different localities, or that the timbers of two trees have been brought for examination.)—*Drs. Wight and Gibson, Captains Beddome and Macdonald.*

GREWIA PANICULATA, *Roxb.*?

Microcos tomentosa, *Sm.?*

Hunu-kirille. SINGH.

A tree, according to Mr. Mendis, of the southern province of Ceylon, where its wood is used in house building. A cubic foot weighs 44 lbs. and it is esteemed to last 25 years. But Voigt calls it a shrub, and it is possible that Mr. Mendis' botanical name requires attention.

GROUHONEE, URIA? KUBATEE, URIA.? A tree of Ganjam and Gumsur, extreme height 80 feet, circumference 6 feet, and height from ground to the intersection of the first branch, 12 feet. The platform of the cars used at the Juggurnauth festival is often made of this wood, but it is chiefly used for firewood being tolerably common. The bark is said to be used medicinally in diarrhœa.—*Captain Macdonald.*

GUATTERIA CERASOIDES, *Duval. Cor.; W. & A.; Hook. & Thom. Fl. Ind.*

Uvaria cerasoides, *Roxb., Cor.*

Hoom. MAHR.	Dudduka. TEL.
Nulœli? maram. TAM.	Chitta duduka. „
Mulili? maram. „	Chilka? dudugu. „
Duddaga. TEL.	

This tree grows in the Bengal, Madras and Bombay Presidencies. In Coimbatore, it is a moderate sized tree. Its wood, as seen in a three or four years old branch, is white and close grained. It is a tree common in the Bombay coast and ghat forests; less so inland and may be easily recognised by its great straightness, and handsome appearance. Its reddish and close grained wood is there useful in carpentry, as well as for naval purposes, as boat-masts, small spars, &c. On the Godavery it appears to be a tolerably hard wood and does not seem to warp. The natives, on the Godavery, do not however, use it, and say that it is soft. Mr. Latham writes of it as occuring in the Nalla Mallai, as a white tolerably hard wood. The natives he says use it little, but he considers it a useful wood.—*Voigt, Drs. Wight and Gibson, Captain Beddome, Mr. Latham.*

GUATTERIA LONGIFOLIA, *Wall.; W. & A.*

Uvaria longifolia, *Roxb.*
Unona „ *Dun.*

Mast tree. ENG.	Thevatharu. TAM.
Asok maram. TAM.	Asoka chettu. TEL.
Deva-daru. „	Asokam. „

A very handsome erect growing large tree, but wood soft and useless. It is much grown in Madras for ornament.

GUAZUMA TOMENTOSA, *H. B.; Kanth. W. & A.; W. Ill.*

Guazuma ulmifolia, *Wall.*
Bubroma guazuma, *Willde, Spreng.*

Bastard cedar. ENG.	Rudraksha chettu. TEL.

A tree introduced by Dr. Anderson about 70 years ago from South America, common in the Dekhan, pretty common about Madras, evidently planted, the fruit is tubercled, about the size of a cherry. It grows at Jaffna in Ceylon. Its young bark abounds in mucilage and is used in the Mauritius to clarify sugar.—*Dr. Cleghorn in M.E.J.R; Thw., Voigt, Dr. Riddell, Dr. O'Shaughnessy.*

GULONCHI, HIND.? A tree of Chota Nagpore, with hard, white timber.—*Cal. Cat. Ex.* 1862.

GUMBHAR. HIND.? A light coloured wood, close grained and light, grows in the Santhal jungles, but scarce. It is used for planks and in constructing palkees. It is this wood with which the beautiful lac ornaments are made, such as work boxes, envelope cases, pen trays, &c. for which Sooree is celebrated.—*Cal. Engineers' Journal, July* 1860.

GUMBAREE. HIND.? A tree of Cuttack, found more or less plentifully throughout the forest jungles of the Sumbulpore district and the Tributary mahals.—*Cal. Exhib.*

GUND, it is chiefly from this plateau on the Malabar Coast, that the demands of H. M. naval department are intended to be met.—*Dr. Cleghorn.*

GYEW, BURM.? A tree, maximum girth 2 cubits, maximum length 15 feet. Found abundant in the jungles round Moulmein and all over the provinces. When seasoned it floats in water. Stated by the Burmese to be equal to chisel handle tree, Dalbergia, *species*, but if so, Captain Dance had not seen a favorable specimen.—*Captain Dance.*

GYO, BURM.? A wood of Amherst used for house posts, ploughs, handspikes, &c.; it is a close grained, compact fine wood.—*Capt. Dance.*

GYROCARPUS JACQUINI, *Roxb.; Cor. pl.*

Gyrocarpus Asiaticus, *Willde.*
„ Americanus, *Grah.*

A tree of the Coromandel mountains; grows on the banks of the Kistnah at Nilatwar and not uncommon in the hot and drier parts of Ceylon. Wood white and very light: when procurable, it is used for catamarans, in preference to all others.—*Thwaites, Voigt, Roxb.*

H.

HADIWICKE, SINGH. A moderately hard, fine and close grained, rather heavy Ceylon wood. —*Edye?*

HÆMATOXYLON CAMPECHIANUM, Logwood. This tree has been introduced into India. It grows readily and seeds abundantly, but it remains to be seen whether it will attain a large size in this country. It is used only as a dye, and the bark is astringent in a considerable degree. It is a promising tree and deserves attention. It is a low spreading tree, seldom thicker than a man's thigh.—*Eng. Cyc., Dr. Cleghorn in Madras E. J. R.*

HAL, the Tamil name of a Ceylon tree which grows to about 2 feet in diameter, and 12 feet high. It is used in native vessels, palanquins, &c. and produces a fruit which the natives eat. —*Edye on the Timber of Ceylon.*

HAMA RAJA? A very small Penang tree, little used.

HANDRO, HIND.? A tree of Chota Nagpore. Hard, red timber.—*Cal. Cat. Ex.* 1862.

HARDWICKIA BINATA, *Roxb.; W. & A.*

Anjun. MAHR.	Epe. TEL.
Acha maram. TAM.	Nara épe. „
Atti maram. „	Nar yepa. „

This large leguminous tree grows in the forests of the Godavery; in the Nalla Mallai, on the mountains of the Coromandel coast, in some parts of Khandeish, and in the Padshapoor jungles, in the Guzelhete pass, common in Lulling pass between Malligaum and Dhoolea and on the hills of the Sone valley. It is a most elegant tree, tall and erect, with an elongated coma and the branches pendulous. On the Godavery, it is often hollow in the centre. Yields a timber of an excellent quality for beams and a variety of uses. The wood is red or dark coloured, very hard, very strong and heavy. As the shoots grow up very striaght, it is also valuable for rafters. The bark yields a strong fibre and the people of the island of Siva Samudram use it without further preparation.—*Voigt, Mr. Rohde's MSS., Hooker's Him. Journ. Vol. I. p.* 50, *Mr. Latham, Captain Beddome, Dr. Gibson.*

HAUDIGA, CAN.? A Mysore wood used for furniture; polishes and turns well, useful for the cabinet maker; and would do for veneering. *Mad. Cat. Ex.* 1862.

HAVUN. A yellow coloured and strong wood of the Santhal jungles from Rancebahal to Hasdiha or about forty miles, but scarce. It is used for building purposes by the natives and also for cart wheels.—*Cal. Engineers' Journal, July* 1860.

HEADIE, the Malayala name of a tree in the forests of Canara. It grows from eighteen inches to two feet in diameter, and from thirty to fifty feet high. It is a close grained wood, and is said to be durable; but it is rather scarce.—*Edye, Forests of Malabar and Canara.*

HEBRADENDRON GAMBOGIOIDES, *Graham.*

Cambogia gutta, *Linn.*
Mangostana morella, *Desrouss.*

Gokatu. SINGH. | Kana goraka. SINGH.

A moderate sized tree of Ceylon. The gamboge of commerce oozes out of the bark of this tree.

HEBRADENDRON PICTORIUM, *Lindley.* A tall tree of the Malabar coast, yields a gamboge.—*Royle's Mat. Medica.*

HEDERA EXALTATA, *Thw.*

A large tree growing in the central province of Ceylon, at an elevation of 4,000 to 6,000 feet.—*Thw. En. Pl. Zeyl. p.* 132.

HEMICYCLIA, a genus of moderate sized trees of Ceylon. H. Gardneri, *Thw.*, not very abundant: H. lanceolata, *Thw.*, grows at Caltura, Ceylon, and H. sepiaria, *W. & A.*, "Weera-gass," *Singh.*, is abundant in the hot drier parts of the island.—*Thw., p.* 287.

HEMIGYMMA MACLEODII, *Griff.?*

Cordia, *species. Beddome.*

Botku. TEL. | Deyn gan. HIND.? of Jubbulpore.

This tree is abundant in the Godavery forests. near Mahadeopore: it does not extend down to the Circars. It is found near Warungul. It is also indigenous to the Jubbulpore forests, where it is called "Deyngan." It is, Captain Beddome feels certain the tree described by Dr. Griffiths as "Hemigymna Macleodii." He described it from dried specimens and thought that the leaves were opposite (instead of alternate) otherwise his description and native name agree. A very beautiful wood. It would answer as a substitute for maple for picture frames, &c. —*Captain Beddome.*

HEBALSU. CAN.?

Wild Jack wood. ENG.

Sent to the Exhibition of 1862 from South Canara.—*Mad. Cat. Ex. of* 1862.

HENSLOWIA PANICULATA, *Miqu.*

Anambo. BURM.

A reddish colored wood of British Burmah, not straight grained, used occasionally for cart wheels, mostly for firewood. In a full grown tree on good soil the average length of the trunk to the first branch is 50 feet and average girth measured at 6 feet from the ground is 9 feet.—*Dr. Brandis, Cal. Cat. Ex.* 1862.

HERITIERA, *Species.*

Pinlay kanazoe. BURM.

Common in the Delta of the Irrawaddy, in British Burmah, wood used for house posts and rafters, and for firewood for the manufacture of salt. The tree is nearly related to the "Soondree" of Bengal. A cubic foot weighs lbs. 66. In a full grown tree on good soil the average length of the trunk to the first branch is 30 feet and average girth, measured at 6 feet from the ground, is 6 feet.—*Dr. Brandis, Cal. Cat. Ex.* 1862.

HERITIERA MINOR, *Lam.; D C.; Roxb.*

Heritiera fomes, *Willde, Buch., D C.*
Balanopteris minor, *Gærtn.*

Soondree. BENG. | Kun-na-zoo. BURM.
Ka-na-zo. BURM. | Kon-nay-zow.

A gloomy looking tree that may be distinguished from all others for many miles distant. It is remarkably characteristic of a peculiar soil. Wherever the tides occasionally rise and inundate the land, this tree is sure to be found throughout the whole Tenasserim coast, but it is never found at home, either on the high dry lands on the one hand, nor in the wet mangrove swamps on the other. It is the tree which was described by Dr. Buchanan Hamilton, who accompanied Symes' embassy, as *Heritiera fomes.* It grows in the Sunderbunds, and is used in Calcutta for firewood. Both the *Heritiera minor* and *H. littoralis* are common in the Rangoon district, along the creeks, and *H. minor* furnishes the Soondree wood so well known in Bengal for its strength and durable qualities. Although so common on the Bengal coast, as to give name, as Captain Munro thinks, to the Soonderbunds, yet the tree grows much larger in the Tenasserim Provinces, and affords finer timber. It is indigenous in the Mayagee forests and on the Choungs Kayoo, Thabyeed and Thuuat, and in some sections is quite abundant. In Tavoy, it is a large tree furnishing very hard and durable wood. In Amherst, Tavoy and Mergui its maximum girth is 2 cubits and maximum length 15 feet. It is very abundant, but straggling; found in Martaban, and on both sides of the Moulmein river, and all along the sea coast; an unlimited supply of it is procurable. When seasoned, it floats in water, and is tough, light and durable. Indeed, it is the toughest wood that has been tested in India. When Rangoon teak broke with a weight of 870 lbs. Soondree sustained 1312 lbs. It is not an equally durable wood, but stands without a rival in strength. It is used for boats, also piles of bridges, boxes? and many other purposes. It is recommended for helves, but should be killed a twelvemonth before being cut down, or otherwise should be seasoned by keeping after it has been cut down. Dr. Wallich says it stands unrivalled for elasticity, hardness, and durability, and adds that "if not extensively employed for the construction of naves and felloes of gun carriages, it is solely because pieces of adequate dimensions are not procurable." But Dr. McClelland's informants asserted, that immense quantities, sufficient for such purposes, are obtainable here. Dr. Wallich adds that the charcoal made from it is better than any other sort for the manufacture of gunpowder.—*Dr. McClelland in Selec. Records Government of India, Foreign Dept. No. IX., p.* 43, *Dr. Mason, Captain Dance, Voigt.*

HERITIERA LITTORALIS, *Ait.; D C.; Roxb.*

Balanopteris Tothila, *Gærtn.*

Ka-na-zoe. BURM. | Kon-zo-za-loo. BURM.

Grows in the Mauritius, the peninsula of India, in the Sunderbunds? common in the Rangoon district, and along the sea-shore in Amherst, and Tavoy. Very abundant on the Islands; found on Pannat Island and all the Mergui Archipelago, also all along the coast of Amherst province. When seasoned, it floats in water. Maximum girth four cubits, maximum length thirty feet. It is used for boats, boxes, planks of houses, &c., is a very light wood, scented, durable and tough. And is recommended for fuzes beyond any other wood from Amherst, Tavoy or Mergui, also for helves, and for gunstocks. Strongly recommended for packing cases of all descriptions.—*Voigt, Dr. McClelland, Captain Dance.*

HERNANDIA SONORA, *Linn.*

Hernandia Guianensis, *Aub.*

Bong-ko. JAVAN.

A tall, erect tree of the West Indies, of the Moluccas and the Fiji islands, in the last, forming one of the sacred groves—a complete bower. The wood is so very light and takes fire so readily from a flint and steel, that it may be used as tinder. The bark, seed and young leaves are cathartic. The juice is an effectual depilatory, removing the hair without any pain. —*Ains., O'Shaughnessy, Voigt, Seeman's Fiji Islands, Eng. Cyc.*

HIBISCUS LAMPAS, *Cav.* A small tree of Hindostan, Bengal, and both peninsulas of India.—*Voigt, M. E. J. R., Wight's Ic.*

HIBISCUS MACROPHYLLA — ? is very plentiful in the forests of the Pegu and Tounghoo districts, also in Tavoy: it is a tall slender timber, of three or four feet girth, and would do for boards and house posts. Wood white colour and adapted for every purpose of house building.—*Dr. McClelland.*

HISBICUS PATERSONII, *D C.; Prod. I. p.* 454, *Ait.*

Lagunæa Patersonia, *B. M.*

White oak of Norfolk Island, a shady tree forty feet high. Its leaves are a whitish green, sepals green and petals pink, fading to white and the size of a small wine glass. It is the largest of the mallow tribe, and attains sixteen feet in circumference. In an economic sense it is said to be valueless, except for firewood.—*Keppel's Ind. Arch. Vol. II, p.* 283, *Voigt.*

HIBISCUS TILIÆFOLIA—??

Belygobel. SINGH.

Under these names, Mr. Mendis gives a wood of the western province of Ceylon, a cubic foot of which weighs 38 lbs. and is esteemed to last 20 years. It is used for carriages, palanqueens and hackeries—found near rivers.—*Mr. Adrian Mendis.*

HLAINE, an elongated valley of Pegu, extending north and south with the Yomah range, at a distance of ten to thirty miles from its east bank; the hills at intervals advancing and then receding from the river, but always leaving a broad plain on its bank. The lower part of the plain has been cultivated: the higher parts are covered with forest. The *Phoungyee* valley, which lies to the eastward of Hlaine, from which it is separated by a branch of the Yomah, is an amphitheatre, open to the south and surrounded on all other sides by hills. Its breadth from east to west is probably about ten or fifteen miles, and its length from north to south thirty. The *Pegu* or *Zamayee* valley lies to the east of Phoungye, from which it is separated by another branch of the Yomah. This valley is enclosed on all sides by hills; it is about forty or fifty miles in length from S. S. E. to N. N. W., which is the direction in which it lies, and twenty miles in breadth from E. to W. The Zamayee river is large and navigable for small craft in the rains, for a distance of sixty or eighty miles above Pegu, to the extremity of the valley; and although only about knee deep in the dry season, it rises forty feet in the rains: its bed is sandy and unimpeded by rocks. The mountains extending along the N. W. side of the valley, separating it from Phoungyee, the Hlaine and Tharawaddy, are of considerable extent and elevation and form a part of the Yomah range. On the east side it is separated from the plains of Tounghoo and Shoay Gyeen by a lower branch of the same chain, and finally it is enclosed to the south by a low hilly tract through which the river passes by a series of small defiles to Pegu. Dr. McClelland ascended the Thounzai valley in the Hlaine district to its head, and descended through the Oakkan valley, and, having traversed the forests from thence to Mazalee, ascended the Choung. This Hlaine forms a part of the valley of the Irrawaddy with which the Hlaine river is connected by means of creeks. *Dr. McClelland in Selec. Records Govt. of India Foreign Dept. No. IX. p.* 8.

HOCOMLIA MONTANA ?

Sampga. CAN. | Kudkee. MAHR.
Tambut. MAHR.

In Canara and Sunda, on and close to the head of the Ghats; wood seldom runs large, is white, hard and tough; used for agricultural implements.—*Dr. Gibson.*

HOLARRHENA ANTIDYSENTERICA, *Wall.*

Echites antidysenterica, *Roxb.*
Chonemorpha „ *G. Don.*

A small tree of Nepal, Sylhet and Chittagong. —*Voigt.*

HOLARRHENA CODAGA. *Apocynaceæ*, Wight's Icon.

Kooda pallei maram. TAM.

In Coimbatore, a white small sized, but very fine grained wood, employed in cabinet-making.—*Dr. Wight.*

HOLARRHENA MITIS, *R. Br. A. D C.* Prod.

Kirri-walla-gass. SINGH.

A moderate sized tree of Ceylon, not uncommon, up to an elevation of 1,500 feet.—*Thw. En. Pl. Zeyl. p.* 194.

HOLIGARNA LONGIFOLIA, *Roxb. Fl. Ind.* ii. p. 80.

Holgeree. CAN. | Holgeree. MAHR.

One of the trees yielding the well known black lacquer varnish. It grows in Travancore, in Malabar, in Canara and Sunda, mostly above the ghats, at Nilgoond, in the Konkan, Assam, Chittagong, and in the forests of Tenasserim. Its exudation is used by the natives to varnish shields, and for other purposes. Juice dangerously acrid. A fine black varnish from its fruit is brought from Munnipore. This turns of a beautiful black colour, when applied to a surface, owing, according to Sir D. Brewster, to the fresh varnish consisting of a congeries of minute organised particles, which disperse the rays of light in all directions; the organic structure is destroyed when the varnish dries, and the rays of light are consequently transmitted. There also come from Munnipore, a varnish, made from *Semecarpus anacardium* (marking nut), and a remarkable black pigment resembling that from *Melanorrhæa usitatissima*, which is white when fresh, and requires to be kept under water. Wood good for houses and beams.—*Voigt, Drs. Gibson, O'Shaughnessy and Mason, Hooker's Him. Jour. Vol. II. p.* 331.

HOLONG, HIND. ? A tree of Chota Nagpore, furnishing a hard, red timber.—*Cal. Cat. Ex.* 1862.

HOMALIUM TOMENTOSUM— ?

Myouk-kyan. BURM.

A tree of Moulmein. A strong wood for any ordinary purpose.—*Cal. Cat. Ex.* 1862.

HONAGUL, CAN. A Mysore wood.—*Mad. Cat. Ex.* 1862.

HOONSOOR COMMISSARIAT TEAK FOREST is large, exclusively under the Madras Commissariat, and worked by them; but arrangements have been made to place it under the Forest Department. It has been much neglected, and requires to be conserved, for there has been wasteful exhaustion of teak. The cooroobura revel in this forest, and have done immense damage, and it is still going on. It is supposed that this forest alone if worked under a systematic plan would give a regular supply of good timber to the state and the public. It has better means of communication than any in the belt of teak, and contains about one hundred and thirty square miles of timber trees.—*Madras Conservator's Report.*

HONGE. CAN.

Honge. CAN. | Moha. HIND. MAHR.
Hip-pe. CAN. | Nella Kalavalu. TEL.
Kuranj. HIND. MAHR.

Under these names are known two different trees growing in the woods of Mysore. Oil is obtained from both of their seeds and sold, but the oil of the former is very smoky and bad though clear to look at; that of the Hippay, is as white and good as the cocoanut oil. The Hip-pe trees are extensively planted in topes in front of villages, for the purpose of obtaining oil.—*M. Ex. of* 1857. (*Note*—They seem to be species of Bassia.)

HOONSAY. CAN. A Mysore wood.

HOPEA. *Sp.*

Thingadoe. BURM.

This large tree abounds in the same localities of British Burmah as H. odorata, but the wood is not equally valued. A cubic foot weighs lbs. 52. In a full grown tree on good soil, the average length of the trunk to the first branch is 100 feet and average girth measured at 6 feet from the ground is 20 feet. It sells at 12 annas per cubic foot.—*Dr. Brandis, Cal. Cat. Ex.* 1862.

HOPEA DECANDRA, *Buch.*

Ooroopa. MAL.

Ooroopa is the Malayala name of a tree which the natives of that country prefer to teak for building ships, being more durable and close grained.—*Ain's. Mat. Med. p.* 207.

HOPEA DISCOLOR, *Thw.* A large tree of Ceylon in the Saffragam and Ambagamowa districts, at no great elevation. The under side of the leaves are of a rich brown colour.—*Thw. En. Pl. Zeyl. I. p.* 36.

HOPEA FLORIBUNDA ?

Tantheya. Burm.

A very large tree of Tavoy.

HOPEA ODORATA, *Roxb.*

Thingan. Burm.

It grows in Chittagong, Dr. McClelland says it is scarce in Pegu, and that a few trees are to be found about the vicinity of Rangoon ; Dr. Brandis mentions that it is one of the finest timber trees of British Burmah, being found near mountain streams and in the evergreen forest, and that large specimens of this valuable tree are common east of the Sittang river, but it is rather scarce in the greater part of Pegu. The trees are found near Moulmein in laterite and sandstone chiefly ; it is a light brown wood, and at Moulmein is a very strong but coarse-grained timber, used extensively by the Burmese in the construction of boats and canoes,—which are formed from the trunks of these magnificent trees of a size fit for carrying 3 or 4 tons. The trunk is scooped or burnt out and stretched in the centre, whilst warm, by means of cross pieces of wood. When the required breadth is obtained, the sides are built up to obtain a greater capacity, these tree boats, if they may be so called, are from 7 to 8 feet beam. The Thingan trees grow to a height of 250 feet, and are considered the most valuable indigenous timber trees in the southern provinces of Tenasserim ; at Tavoy and Mergui it is sawn up for building purposes. The breaking weight may be stated at 800 lbs. with a specific gravity of 45 to 46 lbs. ; the wood is much prized for cart wheels and boats made of it are said to last for more than twenty years. A cubic foot weighs lbs. 64. In a full grown tree on good soil, the average length of the trunk to the first branch is 80 feet, and average girth measured at 6 feet from the ground is 12 feet. Capt. Dance gives, under this name, two descriptions of timber, which it seems advisable to record, viz.

Hopea odorata. Thingan, Burm.

Maximum girth 6 cubits. Maximum length 60 feet. Scattered but abundant in the provinces of Yea on the coast beyond Amherst, also at Mergui, and in lesser quantity near Moulmein. When seasoned, floats in water.—Formerly considered the most valuable indigenous timber in the southern Provinces and used at Tavoy and Mergui for building houses. Used also for canoes, junks, &c. A very durable excellent wood when kept under water as in the planks of a boat or under cover on land ; but often liable to split when exposed to the sun in a dry state. Recommended for helves.

Hopea odorata. Thingan Pew, or White Tingan, in Amherst, Tavoy and Mergui, maximum girth 4 cubits, maximum length 30 or 40, scattered but abundant. Found in the same localities as the red Thingan. When seasoned, floats in water. It is a lighter variety of the red Thingan. This is a tolerable wood for durability, and would do for helves, but more suitable woods are in the list of those recommended.—*Drs. Mason, McClelland Brandis, Cal. Cat. Ex. of* 1862, *Captain Dance, Major Benson.*

HOPEA SUAVA, *Wall.*

Engyin. Burm.

This valuable tree is found in the English forests of British Burmah, but large trees are not common in Pegu. Wood tough and hard but heavy, used in house building, for bows and a variety of other purposes, and said to be as durable as teak. A cubic foot weighs 55 lbs. In a full grown tree, on good soil, the average length of the trunk to the first branch is 60 feet and average girth measured at 6 feet from the ground is 7 feet.—*Dr. Brandis, Cal. Cat. Ex.* 1862.

HUNDA PALE, a Malabar and Canara tree, which produces a fruit. It grows to about 18 inches in diameter, and 20 feet high. It is not of much use except for its fruit which is eaten by the natives and by wild animals.—*Edye's Forests, Malabar and Canara.*

HURA CREPITANS, *Linn.*

Sand box tree. A middle sized tree of rapid growth, native of tropical America. The trunk is strongly armed, the wood light and useless. The seeds are poisonous.—*M. E. J. R., Voigt.*

HYDNOCARPUS INEBRIANS, *Vahl. ; Gærtn.*

Kowtee. Mahr. | Murra vuttay maram. Tam.
Makooloo. Singh.

A large tree, growing in Ceylon on the banks of rivers up to an elevation of 2,000 feet. It is a common tree on the west coast, not so in the Coimbatore jungles. The tree is hardly found in the Bombay northern jungles on the coast ; more frequently in those south of the Savitree river. The wood is not used for any purpose. The seeds of the fruit afford an oil.—*Voigt, Thwaites, Drs. Gibson and Wight.*

HYMENÆA COURBARIL, *Linn.*

Locust tree. Eng. | Courbaril Locust tree. Eng.
Gum Anime tree. Eng.

It is a fine lofty spreading tree, and grows in the tropical parts of America, in Jamaica, and in Tenasserim. The timber of the old trees is very hard and tough, and is in great request for wheelwork, particularly for cogs. The wood is very hard and is so heavy that a cubic foot is said to weigh a hundred pounds : it takes a fine polish and is used by cabinet makers. The trunk acquires an immense height. When in a sickly state, it furnishes the resin called *Western Anime.* It was introduced into Tenasserim, by Major Macfarquhar, and is easily propagated. The resin exudes from between the principal roots. It is fine and transparent, of a red or yellowish-red colour, and in large lumps. It resembles amber, is very hard, and sometimes contains leaves, insects, or other objects imbedded in it. It burns readily, emitting a very fragrant smell. Dissolved in rectified spirits of wine it makes one of the finest kinds of varnish.—*Eng. Cyc., Drs. O'Shaughnessy, p.* 314, *Dr. Mason's Tenasserim, p.* 156, *Voigt, p.* 252.

HYMENODYCTION, *Species.*

Dudippa (Godavery Forests,) Tel.	Chetippa (Circars). Tel.

A large tree of the Godavery. Wood not used in the Godavery forests.—*Captain Beddome.*

HYMENODYCTION EXCELSUM, *Wall. in Fl. Ind.; W. & A.; W. Ic.*

Cinchona excelsa, *Roxb.*

Kala bachnak. Duk.	Bundaru. Hind.
Cedar wood. Eng.	Kala buchnak. Hind.
Kandaru.? Hind.	Sagapu maram. Tam.
Burja. Tel.	Bandara. Tel.
Burija. „	Pundaroo? „
Chetippa. „	

A very large tree, common all round the foot of the Neilgherries, and in the mountainous parts of the Circars, but chiefly in the valleys. The wood is firm, close-grained, of a pale mahogany colour, and very useful for many purposes. The bitter astringent bark is used by tanners, also medicinally, but it contains no alkaloid.—*Drs. Roxburgh, O'Shaughnessy, p.* 394, *Mr. McIvor, Ains. Mat. Med.*

HYMENODYCTION. Of this genus of plants, belonging to one of the Cinchonaceæ, *H. obovatum*, W. Icon., "Yella mala kai maram" Tam., "Kurwye" Mahr., *H. utile*, W. Ic., "Peronjoli maram" Tam., and "Kurwye" Mahr., grow in Coimbatore and in Canara, but wood only fit for fuel. *H. thyrsiflorum*, Wall., grows at Rajmahal, Chittagong, and at Rangoon.—*Drs. Wight and Gibson, Voigt.*

I.

IARVINI. Tam.?

Yarviney. Tam.	Crawn. Dut. & Port.

This Ceylon tree grows tall and straight, from twenty to forty five feet high, and from twelve to thirty inches in diameter. It may be obtained in great quantities, and answers many purposes in ship and house work.—*Edye, on the Timber of Ceylon.*

ICICA INDICA, *W. & A.*

Bursera serrata, *Wall.*	Schinus Saheria, *H. B.*
Schinus Bengalensis, *H. B.*	„ Niara. „

A tree of Assam and Chittagong, its timber is close grained and hard, as tough as oak, but heavier, and used for furniture by the natives.—*Voigt.*

ILEX. A genus of plants of which Dr. Wight mentions I. Gardneriana and I. Wightiana, Mr. Thwaites mentions, as growing in Ceylon, I. denticulata, a large, and I. Walkeri, a small tree. Mr. Hodgson, in his "Nagasaki" mentions eight species: woods not known.—*Wight's Icones, Thw. En. Pl. Zeyl.* *See* Japan.

INDIGOFERA, *Species.*

Doun-daloun. Burm.

This tree is four or five feet in girth, found both in the Rangoon and Tounghoo districts though it is scarce. Wood white colour and adapted for every purpose of house building.—*Dr. McClelland.*

INDIKE, Burm. Ebony of Moulmein.

INGA BIGEMINA, *Willde.*

Mimosa bigemina, *Linn.*
„ lucida, *Roxb. Fl. Ind.*

Ta-nyen. Burm.	Iron wood. Eng. of Burmah?
Katur konna.	

This tree grows in the Konkans, Nepaul, Assam and Pegu. It is of smaller girth than the I. xylocarpa, but grows to a great height, and has a black wood. Like the I. xylocarpa, it is called Iron wood by the English in Pegu and Tenasserim. In native gardens it is an ornamental tree, with sweet scented blossoms and affording a thick beautiful shade. Its seeds are poisonous when taken internally, notwithstanding which they are sold at a high price in the bazar, and are used by Burmese and Karens as a condiment to their preserved fish.—*Drs. McClelland and Mason, Voigt.*

INGA DULCIS, *Willde.*

Mimosa dulcis, *Roxb., Cor. Pl.*

Sweet Inga. Eng.	Koorkapuli maram. Tam.
Manilla Tamarind. Eng.	Sima chinta. Tel.

This small tree of the Philippines, isolated specimens of which are occasionally found from 12 to 18 inches in diameter, resembles the hawthorn in general appearance. It is cultivated in India. It was introduced from Manilla into the Circars, but was a Mexican tree, which the Spaniards introduced into the Eastern Archipelago. It furnishes a hard wood. It is a most valuable hedge plant, and is now sparingly used along some of the railway lines of the peninsula. The pulp of the fruit is edible.—*Voigt, Dr. Cleghorn in M. E. J. R.*

INGA XYLOCARPA, *D C.; W. & A.; W. Ic.; J. Graham.*

Mimosa xylocarpa, *Roxb. Cor. Pl.*
Xylia dolabriformis, *Berich.*
Acacia xylocarpa, *Willde.*

Pyangadeau ? BURM.
Pyu-kado. „
Pyeng-khadoe. „
Pingadoe. „
Yerool. CAN. ?
Jambay. „
Jamba mara. CAN.
Betada swamamki vriksha. CAN. ? ?
Iron wood of Arracan. ENG.
Partridge wood of London? ENG.
Jamboo. HIND.
Jamba. MAHR.
Erool of MALABAR.
Eruvalu maram. TAM.
Malei averei. „ ? ?
Tangedu. TEL.
Konda Tangedu. Circars, TEL.
Boja of the Godavery.

This valuable timber tree is remarkable for its thick woody legume; it grows to a large size, is a stately tree which blossoms during the hot season, at which period it is nearly destitute of foliage, and is met with in many parts of Southern India, in varying abundance. It is abundant in the Walliar forests of Coimbatore, it is also abundant in North Canara, particularly between Sircee and Yellapore, and is not uncommon in the sea board forests of the Bombay Presidency, south of Panwell. In Canara and Sunda, it grows chiefly above the ghats in Soopeh and Dandelee, where it grows large; and, there, its tough and strong wood is very useful in house building. It is met with in the Godavery forests where it grows very large on the mountains, and there is much of it in the Vizagapatam district. Dr. McClelland says that, in the Southern forests of Pegu, it is a plentiful large tree, fifteen to eighteen inches in diameter, very lofty and straight, and would afford excellent spars for naval purposes, if not too heavy. It is most plentiful in Prome, especially near the forks of the Tenasserim, and very abundant in Amherst, Mergui and Tavoy. In the Prome forests, it is usually about 6 feet in girth, but in all the other branches of the Tenasserim, it attains a larger size, frequently 8 or 9 feet. Dr. Brandis says it is abundant throughout the forests on and near the hills of British Burmah, and is, there, a magnificent tree, It is the *Ironwood* of Pegu. The sap wood is attacked by white ants and decays easily, but it is very limited in large trees. The heart wood of full grown trees is said to last as long as teak. This wood would be invaluable if it were not for its weight. It is used, he says, for house and bridge posts, ploughs, boat anchors, in the construction of carts and for other purposes. A cubic foot weighs lbs. 60 to 66. In a full grown tree on good soil, the average length of the trunk to the first branch is 50 feet and average girth, measured at 6 feet from the ground is 9 feet. It sells, there, at 12 annas per cubic foot. This wood is of a very superior quality, every where; is dark coloured, very hard, and dense, strong and durable—but, in the Bombay Presidency, the tree does not grow straight to any size, and, there, it is not available for house or ship building. An inch bar, of the Coimbatore wood, sustained lbs. 550. It is one of the Iron woods of the Arracan provinces, the other being the I. bijemina. It resists nails, which cannot be driven into it. It is excellent for naves of wheels and for all purposes demanding great strength, such as crooks for ships—knees and bends, posts, piles, and bridges: and it is excellent for railway sleepers and recommended for handles of chisels, gauges, &c., but is too heavy for other ordnance purposes. The hard wood is as impervious to white ants as teak and is even more durable in the ground. Natives assured Dr. Mason that they had seen house posts of this wood taken up after having stood forty years, and that the part which had been buried was as sound as new timber. That of the Godavery forests is described as yielding a valuable timber, and according to Dr. Roxburgh, the timber is remarkably strong and durable, but Mr. Rohde did not meet with it in the Circars exceeding a foot or 14 inches in diameter, and, then, always faulty in the centre, and he says that, in the Vizagapatam district, this wood is used for common purposes, but it is generally faulty in the centre, it is not a bad wood for furniture, is well adopted for handles of tools &c., the average size at Vizagapatam is 12 inches in diameter and fifteen feet long; on the Godavery it is seldom obtained exceeding 8 inches in diameter and generally is faulty in the centre; it is used for posts. He thinks it a good wood for screens, framing of furniture, linings of drawers, tool handles, and generally for all purposes, for which a moderately hard, strong wood, not liable to split or cast about, is required. It would, thus, seem to be in general use in the various countries of British India and in the adjacent Island of Ceylon. In the Madras Gun Carriage Manufactory, it is used for poles, axle cases, and braces for transport limbers, poles and yokes for water carts, cheeks, axle cases for transport carriages, light mortar carts. Captain Puckle, writing from Mysore, says it is used for furniture, shafts, plough heads and knees, and crooked timbers in ship building, and railway sleepers. It has been largely used on the Madras Railway. In a letter dated 1st September 1862, to Mr. R. B. Elwin, Agent and Manager, the Acting Chief Engineer, says, "From all I can gather, from the statistics furnished by the Engineers of the South West Line, it appears that, as far as can be ascertained, the sleepers of Erool employed in the Railway exhibited a very fair durability. Those that were laid down on the Western Division, two years ago, do not now appear to show the least symptom of decay. If judiciously selected and thoroughly seasoned, there can be little doubt of their continuing serviceable for at least 6 years, and further experience may prove sleepers of this wood to possess still greater durability. It has been employed extensively for different purposes, among others, for piles, transoms and walling pieces. The piles of the temporary bridge over the Kuddlehoondy river, completed in the commencement of 1859, are of this timber, and appear to have stood well; and, though the sea-worm has perforated them on all sides, the damage done does not appear to extend below the sap wood. In small scantlings, it is liable to split and warp under exposure to the weather. As an experiment, Mr. Lovell drove a small pile, 2 inches in section and which was purposely selected free of sap, into the river at the site of the Kuddlehoondy bridge, and after an exposure of 18 months when cut up, it was found to be destroyed to a depth only of a ¼ of an inch. The horizontal timbers in this bridge which are also of Erool are perfectly sound, they were however coated with Tar and appear to have been well seasoned previous to use. I have no doubt that, of all the timbers from the Indian forests, Erool will be found to hold a high place in respect of durability and general usefulness."—*Drs. Wight, McClelland, Mason, Gibson and Cleghorn, in Conservator's Report, Captain Dance, Mr. Rohde, Calcutta & Madras Catalogues of the Exhibition of* 1862, *Dr. Brandis, Captain Puckle & Colonel Maitland: Report of Acting Chief Engineer, Madras Railway, and Records of the Consulting Engineer, favoured through Mr. Elwin & Captain Prendergast.*

INHAYON—? A tree of Akyab, furnishing a moderate sized wood. It is plentiful, but not much used.—*Cal. Cat. Ex.* 1862.

INJIN PEWOO, Burm.

White Injin. Anglo-Burm.

Found in abundance all over the provinces of Amherst, Tavoy and Mergui, of a maximum length of 22 feet and maximum girth of 2 cubits. It is very light and perishable, and only fit for firewood.—*Captain Dance.*

IRGULI, Tam., also Ear-gulie, Tam. The name of a Ceylon tree, which is about fourteen inches in diameter, and eight feet in height. It is not a useful wood.—*Edye, on the Timber of Ceylon.*

IRON WOOD.

Pya of Akyab.	Eisenholz. Ger.
Pieng "	Legno di ferro. It.
Yserhout. Dut.	Lignum ferreum. Lat.
Iron wood. Eng.	Naw. Singh.
Bois de fer. Fr.	Plohierro. Sp.

Iron wood is a commercial term, applied to a great variety of woods, in consequence of their hardness, and almost every country has an iron-wood of its own. The product of an evergreen tree, *Sideroxylon*, remarkable for the hardness and weight of its timber, which sinks in water, receives this name: it is of a reddish cast, and corrodes like iron. This tree grows chiefly in the West India islands, and is likewise very common in South America. *Mesua ferrea*, a tree furnishing one of the iron woods, and which, also, has received its specific name from the hardness of its wood, is a native of Ceylon and of the peninsulas of India, of Northern India, Malacca and of the islands, and perhaps M. pedunculata, likewise, furnishes part of the timber known under this name. The timber of the *Metrosideros vera* of China, is called true iron-wood: the Chinese are said to make their rudders and anchors of it, and, among the Japanese, it is so scarce and valuable, that it is only allowed to be manufactured for the service of their king. The iron-wood of southern China, however, is *Baryxylum rufum*; of the island of Bourbon, *Stadmannia sideroxylon*, and of the Cape of Good Hope, *Sideroxylon milonophlæum*, which latter is very hard, close grained, and sinks in water. The Ceylonese have also an iron-wood tree, known under the name of "Naw," of the western provinces of Ceylon, perhaps the M. ferrea. It is described as used for bridges and buildings. That of the Canara forests is from two species of Memecylon, and, on the Coromandel coast, the term is occasionally applied to the wood of the Casuarina equisitifolia: in Tenasserim, the term is applied to the woods of Inga xylocarpa and I. biemina; and to that of a species of Diospyros. The iron wood of Australia is from a species of Eucalyptus, and that of Norfolk island from the Notolæa longifolia. The iron-wood of Guiana is from the *Robinia panacoca* (of Aublet), that of Jamaica is the *Tagara plerota*, and *Erythroxylon æreolatum*, which is also called red-wood. *Ægiphilæ Martinicensis* and *Cocaloba latifolia*, are other West Indian trees, to the timbers of which the name of iron-wood has been applied, *Ostrya virginica*, called American hop horn beam, has wood exceedingly hard and heavy, whence it is generally called iron-wood in America, and in some places lever-wood. Under the name of Iron wood, two specimens were sent by the Calcutta Committee to the Exhibition of 1862. One of them Pya, *Vern.*, a tree of Akyab, grows to a moderate size, and is plentiful in the Sandoway and Ramree districts. The other Iron wood, Pieng, *Vern.*, also, a tree of Akyab, grows to a large size, and is very plentiful in Arrakan, its wood is very hard, and used for posts. Like the commercial terms, Cedar, Ebony, Rose-wood, &c., &c., &c., this notice of the many trees, the timbers from which are termed "Iron woods" will show the necessity for careful discrimination.—*Holtzappfel, Mr. Faulkner, Mr. McGillivray, Dr. Bennett, Mr. Mendis, Dr. Mason, Cal. Cat. Ex. of* 1862.

IPPEE, Tel., of the Godavery, Bassia latifolia. A strong wood, but never felled by the natives, the flowers yield a toddy, and an oil is extracted from the seeds.—*Captain Beddome.*

ISCARASI KARRA, Tel., Iscarasi wood, Anglo-Tel. of the Northern Circars, is probably from the Sapindus rubiginosus.

ISONANDRA. A genus of large trees, growing in Ceylon, and in the two peninsulas of India. Dr. Wight, in Icones, has, I. Candolleana, 1220; lanceolata, 359; percha, 1589;

Perottetiana, 1219; polyandra. 1589, and villosa, 360. Thwaites mentions, in Ceylon, I. canalieulata, *Thw.*, a middle sized tree in the Caltura district; I. grandis, *Thw.*, a large tree of the central province and Saffragam districts, from the seeds of which an oil is extracted and which is used similarly to that of the Bassia longifolia. He also names I. lœvifolia; pauciflora; rubiginosa and Wightiana, as trees of moderate and large size.—*Dr. Wight, Thw. En. Pl. Zeyl.*

ISONANDRA GUTTA, *Hook.*

Mazer wood tree. Eng.	Niato. Malay.

The Gutta-percha tree is a native of the Malayan Archipelago, to which it is almost confined, and produces the Pertsha which is as indestructible by chemical agents as caoutchouc. I have no knowledge that the timber of this large tree has yet been usefully employed.

ITTI, Arali, Porrel, Attu, or Itti, according to Edye, the Malayala names of a Malabar and Canara tree which grows to about forty feet in height, and two feet in diameter; it is used by the native carpenters for the planks in vessels, and is said by them to be a valuable wood. This tree, the hindu people worship and respect, and consider of great importance and value.—*Edye, Forests of Malabar and Canara.*

IXORA, *Species.*

Tella kooroowan. Tel.

A tree of Ganjam and Gumsur, extreme height 20 feet, circumference 1 foot, height from ground to the intersection of the first branch, 6 feet. The fire sticks used by the shikarees for night hunting are taken from this tree. It also yields an oil which is applied to the sores of cattle. The tree is common.—*Captain Macdonald, Dr. Cleghorn.*

IXORA PARVIFLORA, *Vahl.*

Ixora alba, *Roxb.*	Webera corymbosa, *Sm. herb.*
„ pavetta, *Andr.*	
„ decipiens, *D C.*	

Gundhal Rungun. Beng.	Karang cottay. Tam.
Henna gorivi. Can.	Koree. Godavery Tel.
Torch Tree. Eng.	Korimi pala? „
Gandhul.? Hind.	Korivi pala. Circars Tel.
Runghun.? „	Komma chettu. „
Jilpai. „	Putta pala. „
Koora. Mahr.	Tedda „ „
Soowndee cottay. Tam.	

A small tree, not uncommon in many parts of India. It is common in the jungles and on the ghats of the Bombay coast; but is, there, seldom sufficiently long or straight for household purposes. It is met with in the Godavery forests and in the Circars. It grows at Nagpore and in Bengal, and on the banks and near talaos at Kotah, the flowers are very sweetly scented and it blossoms in the hot weather; it would form a very fit ornament for gardens and pleasure grounds. It furnishes a hard but very small wood, rather of good quality, which is sometimes used for beams and posts in the houses of the poor of the Madras presidency; but, throughout India, it is more used for torches than for any other purpose, as it burns very readily and clearly, and on that account its branches are often made into torches by people travelling at night.—*Voigt, Gibson, Ainslie, Irvine, M. E. J. R., Captain Beddome.—Flor. Andh.*

J.

JACK WOOD, Eng.

Phunsi. Guz.	Artocarpus integrifolia. Lat.
Funsi. „	Nangka. Malay.
Phannas. Hind.	Uram Pila. Maleal.
Fanas.? Hind.	Pilla maram. Tam.

Mr. Edye says, Viram Pila is the Tamil and Malayala name of the Artocarpus integrifolia, which grows in cultivated grounds, and is of value for its fruit. In Ceylon it supports the pepper vine. In many places it is found two feet and a half in diameter, and from thirty to thirty-five feet high. In Canara, this wood was preferred by Tipu sultan for the Grab vessels built at Onnoor, the naval depot. In Ceylon, at Point de Galle, it is used by the furniture makers for chairs, couches, &c., for which purpose it answers well; and, if polished with care, its brilliant colour is superior to that of mahogany. When worked and cut down, it is yellow, but turns dark and improves by age.—*Edye, Forests of Malabar and Canara.* *See* Artocarpus integrifolia.

JAMBAU, the name of a tree in Canara which grows from two to four feet in diameter, and from twenty-five to forty feet in height. This wood, as also the Kulbagi, is very scarce. It very much resembles mahogany, and is generally used for house furniture.—*Edye, Forests of Malabar and Canara.*

JAMBOSA AQUEA, *D C.* (W. et A. Prod. I. 332, *Roxb.*; Wight, Icones.

Eugenia (J.) aquea, Wight, Illustr.
Eugenia sylvestris, Moon's Cat.

Jambo. Beng.	Wal-jambo-gass. Singh.

Abundant in the Central Province of Ceylon, up to an elevation of 5,000 feet.—*Thw. En. Pl. Zeyl. p.* 115. *See* Eugenia aquea.

JAMBOSA CYLINDRICA.—?

Eugenia (J.) cylindrica, Wight, Icones.
Eugenia (J.) pauciflora, Wight, Icones.

A moderate sized tree of the Ambagamowa district, in Ceylon, up to an elevation of 3,000 feet.—*Thw. En. Pl. Zeyl.* ii. *p.* 115.

JAMBOSA SALICEFOLIA — ?

Pan Jambool. MAHR.

A crooked species of jambool, growing much on the rivers of the Bombay Deccan country. The stem is generally useless for house purposes, on account of its crookedness, but the straight shoots are eagerly sought after as rafters. —*Dr. Gibson.*

JAMBOSA VULGARIS, *DeCandolle.*

Eugenia Jambos.

Golab Jam. BENG. | Jambu Nawel maram. TAM.
Rose Apple Tree. ENG. | Jembu Niridi. TEL.

See EUGENIA JAMBOS.

JAPAN TIMBER TREES, many of the timber trees of Japan were noticed by Thunberg during his residence, there, nearly a hundred years ago. The most recent notice of the plants of that island is in *Hodgson's Nagasaki, p.* 342—43 and their names, alphabetically arranged, are as under :—

Abies tsuga, *S. & Z.*
,, (Picea firma) *S. & Z.*
,, (Picea) homolepis, *S. & Z.*
,, microsperma, *Lindl.*
,, Veitchii, *Lindl.*
,, Alcoquiana, *Lindl.*
,, bifida, *S. & Z.*
,, jezoensis, *S. & Z.*
,, Smithiana, *Loud.* (*polita, S. & Z.*)
Acer distylum, *S. & Z.*
,, palmatum, *Thunb.*
,, carpinifolium, *S. & Z.*
,, cratægifolium, *S. & Z*
,, rufinerve, *S. & Z.*
,, micranthum, *S. & Z.*
,, japonicum, *Thbg.*
,, pictum, *Thbg.*
,, polymorphum, *S. & Z*
,, sessilifolium, *S. & Z.*
,, dissectum, *Thunb.*
,, *two species undescribed.*
Aceranthus diphyllus, *Dcne.*
,, sagittatus, *S. & Z.*
Ægle sepiaria, *L.* (*Citrus* trifolia, *Thbg.*)
Æsculus chinensis, *Bunge*
,, turbinata, *Blume.*
,, dissimilis, *A. Gray*
Alnus firma, *S. & Z.*
,, japonica, *S. & Z.*
,, viridis, *D. C.*
Antidesma japonicum, *S. & Z.*
Ardisia crispa, *A. Dl.*
,, glabra, *A. Dl.*
,, japonica, *Bl.*
,, pusilla, *A. Dl.*

Berberis Thunbergii, *D. C.*
,, vulgaris, *Thbg.*
,, japonica, *S. & Z.*
Betula grossa, *S. & Z.*
,, carpinifolia, *S. & Z.*
,, ulmifolia, *S. & Z.*
,, japonica, *Sieb.*
Boymia rutæcarpa, A. *Juss*
Broussonetia papyrifera, *Vent.*
,, Kampferi, *Sieb.*
,, Sieboldii, *Bl.* (*kazinoki, Sieb.*)
Carpinus erosa, *Bl.*
,, cordata, *Bl.*
Castanea vesca, *Gærtn. var*
,, japonica, *Blume.*
,, crenata, *S. & Z.* (*japonica, var. crenata, Bl.*)
,, stricta, *S. & Z.* (*japonica, var. stricta, Bl.*)
,, chinensis, *Spr.* (*cult.*)
Calophyllum thalictroides (*Mich.*)
Celastrus articulatus, *Thb.*
,, punctata, *Thbg.*
,, Orixa, *S. & Z.*
,, striatus, *Thbg.*
Celtis Willdenowiana, *Roem.*
,, sinensis, *Pers.*
,, Muku, *Sieb.*
Cephalotaxus umbraculifera, *Sieb.*
,, drupacea, *S. & Z.*
,, pedunculata, *S. & Z.*

Cephalotaxus Fortunei, *Hook.*
Citrus japonicus, *Thbg.*
,, aurantium, *L.*
,, Decumana, *L.*
Ceraseidos apetala, *S. & Z.*
Cordia thyrsiflora, *S. & Z.*
Corylus heterophylla, *Fisch.*
,, Sieboldiana, *Bl.*
Cryptomeria japonica, *Don*
Cunninghamia sinensis, *R. Br.*
Cycas revoluta, *L. Thbg.*
β. prolifera, *S. & Z.*
Diospyros Kaki, *L.*
,, japonica, *S. & Z.*
Diphylleia cymosa, *Mich.*
Distegocarpus carpinus, *S. & Z.* (*Carpinus japonica, Bl.*)
,, laxiflora, *S. & Z.* (*Carpinus, Bl.*)
Elæagnus macrophylla, *Thbg.*
,, umbellata, *Thbg.*
,, pungens, *Thbg.*
,, longipes *A. Gray*
,, reflexa, *Moer. & Dcne.*
,, glabra, *Thbg.*
,, crispa, *Thbg.*
,, multiflora, *Thbg.*
Elæocarpus photiniæfolius, *Hook.*
,, japonicus, *S. & Z.*
Elæodendron, *Sp.*
Epimedium Muschianum, *D. C.*
,, macranthum, *Dcne.*
,, violaceum, *Dcne.*
,, Ikariso, *Sieb.*
Euonymus japonicus, *Thb.*
,, Sieboldianus, *Blume.*
,, Thunbergianus, *Bl.* (*Celastrus alatus, Thbg*
,, *Melanocarya. alata, Turcz.*
,, subtriflorus, *Blume.*
,, Hamiltonianus, *Wall.*
,, latifolius, *Mill?*
Eupteleapolyandra, *S. & Z.*
Euscaphis staphyleoides, *S. & Z.*
,, simplicifolia, *S. & Z.*
Evodia ramiflora, A. *Gray.*
Fagus sylvatica, *L.*
,, crenata, *Blume.*
Fatoua aspera, *Gaud.*
,, pilosa, *Gaud.*
Gardneria nutans, *S. & Z.*
Glyptostrolius pendulus, *Endl.?*
Homoioceltis aspera, *Bl.*
Ilex crenata, *Thbg.*

Ilex microphylla, *Bl.*
,, integra, *Thbg.*
,, latifolia, *Thbg.*
,, rotunda, *Thbg.*
,, serrata, *Thbg.*
,, aquifolium, *L.*
,, *var.* heterophylla.
Juglans, 3 sp.
Juniperus rigida, *S. & Z.*
,, taxifolia, *Hook.*
,, chinensis, *L.*
,, procumbens, *Sieb*
Koelreuteria paniculata, *Laxm.*
Larix leptolepis, *Sieb.*
Maclura gerontogœa, *S. & Z.*
Mæsa Doræne, *Bl.* (*Doræna japonica, Thbg.*)
Melia Azederach, *L.*
,, Toosendau, *S. & Z.*
,, japonica, *Don.*
Metrosideros, *Sp. S. & Z.*
Morus alba, *L. Thbg.*
,, Indica, *L. Thbg.*
,, japonica, *Sieb.*
Myrica rubra, *S. & Z.*
Myrsine neriifolia, *S. & Z.*
Nandina domestica, *Thbg.*
Pinus densiflora, *S. & Z.*
,, Massoniana, *Lamb.*
,, parviflora, *S. & Z.*
,, koraiensis, *S. & Z.*
,, sinensis, *Lamb.*
,, pinaster, *Ait.* (*cult.?*)
Piptosacca hypophyllantha, *Turcz.*
Platycarya strobilacea, *S. & Z.* (*Fortunea Chinensis, Lindl.*
Podocarpus macrophylla, *Wall.*
,, *Maki, S. & Z.* (*Chinensis, Wall.*)
,, Koraiana, *Sieb.*
,, nageia, *R. Br.*
,, japonica, *Sieb.*
,, cuspidata, *Endl*
,, grandifolia, *Endl.*
Populus, *Sp.*
Prunus Persica, *L.*
,, Padus, *L.*
,, paniculata, *Thunb.*
,, Mume, *S. & Z.*
,, japonica, *Thbg.*
,, tomentosa, *Thbg.*
,, spinulosa, *S. & Z.*
,, macrophylla, *S. & Z.*
,, Pseudo cerasus, *Lindl.*
Pterocarpa sorbifolia, *S. & Z.*
,, rhoifolia, *S. & Z.*
Pterostyrax corymbosum, *S. & Z.*
,, micranthum, *S. & Z.*
,, hispidum, *S. & Z.*

Punica granatum, *L.*
Quercus glabra, *Thbg.*
,, acuta, *Thbg.*
,, glauca, *Thbg.*
,, cuspidata, *Thbg.*
,, serrata, *Thbg.*
,, glandulifera, *Blume.*
,, dentata, *Thbg.*
,, phyllyraoides, A. *Gray.*
,, Sieboldiana, *Bl.*
,, urticæfolia, *Bl.*
,, canescens, *Bl.*
,, variabilis, *Bl.*
,, aliena, *Bl.*
,, crispula, *Bl.*
,, Burgerii, *Bl.*
,, sessifolia, *Bl.*
,, salicina, *Bl.*
,, myrsinæfolia, *Bl.*
,, gilva, *Bl.*
,, gross-eserrata, *Bl.*
,, lacera, *Bl.*
,, marginata, *Bl.*
,, lavigata, *Bl.*
Retinispora obtusa, *S. & Z.*
,, ericoides, *Zucc*
,, pisifera, *S. & Z.*
,, squarrosa, *S. & Z.*
Rhodomyrtus tomentosa, *D. C.*
Rhus semialata, *Murr.*
,, Javanica, L. *(cult.)*
,, succedanea, *L.*
,, sylvestris, *S. & Z.*
,, vernicifera, *D. C.*
,, toxicedendron, *L. var.*
Salisburia adiantifolia, *S. & Z.*
Sapindus Mukorossi, *Gærtn.*
Salix japonica, *Thbg.*
,, alba, *L.*
,, subfragilis, *Anders.*
,, purpurea, *L.*
,, padifolia, *L.*
,, viridula, *Anders.*
,, vulpina, *Anders.*
,, acutifolia, *W.*
Salix Sieboldiana, *Blume.*
,, integra, *Thbg.*
,, Babylonica, *L.*
Sciadopitys verticillata, *S. & Z.*
Skimmia japonica, *Thbg.*
Spiræa callosa, *Thbg.*
,, chamaedrys, *Thbg* (S. *Revesii.*)
,, Thunbergii, *S. & Z.*
,, prunifolia, *S. & Z.*
,, chamædryfolia, *L.*
,, japonica, *Sieb.*
,, betulæfolia, *Pall.*
,, palmata, *Thbg.*
,, Aruncus, *L.*
,, salicifolia, *L.*
Sponia nudiflora, *S. & Z.*
Staphylea Bumalda, *S. & Z.*
Sterculia japonica.
Styrax japonicum, *S. & Z.*
,, obassia, *S. & Z.*
Symplocos japonica, *D. C.*
,, prunifolia, *S. & Z.*
,, myrtacea, *S. & Z.*
,, lancifolia, *S. & Z.*
,, leptostachys, *S. & Z.*
,, theophrastæfolia, *S. & Z.*
,, neriifolia, *S. & Z.*
Taxus cuspidata, *S. & Z.*
,, adpussa, *Knight.*
Tecoma grandiflora, *D C.*
Thuja orientalis, *L.*
,, excelsa, *Bong.*
,, pendula, *Lamb.*
Thujopsis dolabrata, *S. & Z.*
Torreya nucifera, *S. & Z.*
Ulmus parvifolia, *Jacq.*
Xanthoxylum piperitum, *D C.*
,, schinifolium, *S. & Z.*
,, ailanthoides, *S. & Z.*
,, planispinum, *S. & Z.*
Zanthoxylum serrulatum, *Bl.*

JATI, MALAY. A wood of the Archipelago, much used in making prahus and in house building at Bawean. (*Note*—Is it the teak, Tectona grandis.)

JAVA TIMBER. In the time of Sir S. Raffles, notwithstanding the extent to which cultivation had been carried on in many districts of the island, large portions of its surface were still covered with primeval forests, affording excellent timber of various descriptions.

"*Jati*," extensive forests of the *Jati*, or teak of India, are found in almost all the eastern provinces. The teak tree in Java grows at a moderate elevation above the level of the ocean.

Besides the teak, there are several kinds of wood or timber employed for various domestic purposes, as

"*Suren*," the tuna of Bengal, of which the wood is very light, stronger, and more durable than all other kinds of similar weight produced on the island: as the grain is not fine, it is not employed in making furniture, but it is useful for chests, trunks, carriages, &c.; its colour is red, and its odour somewhat resembling that of the cedar. Its weight is probably inferior to that of the larch. (*Qu.* Is this the Cedrela tuna.)

"*Wungu*" or "*Ketangi*" wood is often used instead of teak: the grain is somewhat finer: when in full blossom, it is perhaps the most beautiful tree existing.

"*Wadang*" or "*bayur*" wood, a light and tolerably durable wood, is employed for masts and spars of small vessels; but the surface must be well covered with resinous substances to prevent it splitting.

"*Gintungan*" wood is employed in the same manner as "Wadang" but grows to a larger size; the colour of the wood and bark is red.

"*Lampean*" or "*laban*" wood is light but durable, and affords materials for the handles of the spears or pikes borne by the natives.

"*Nangka*" trees abound in several districts where teak is not found, and is almost exclusively used in the construction of houses, and other domestic purposes: the wood is more close and ponderous than the *suren*, which it otherwise resembles; it takes a tolerable polish, and is sometimes employed for furniture. The colour is yellow; but it is made to receive a brownish hue, by the application of the young teak leaves in polishing: its bark is used as a yellow dye.

"*Luren*" wood resembles the *nangka*, but is generally of rare occurrence, though in some tracts it furnishes the only timber: its use in the neighbouring islands, particularly in Sumatra, is well known.

"*Kusambi*" wood is uncommonly heavy, hard, and close: it supplies anchors for small vessels, blocks, pestles, and numerous similar utensils.

"*Sawur*" is a very beautiful and useful wood: the colour resembles that of mahogany, but the grain is closer, and it is more ponderous: its chief use is for handles of tools for carpenters and other artificers, for machinery, especially for the teeth of the wheels of mills, and other purposes where a hard and durable wood is required. On account of its scarcity, it is uniformly cut down in Java before it arrives at the necessary size for cabinet work. Forests of it grow on the hills of *Bali*, opposite the Javan shore, whence it is brought over by boat loads for sale.

"*Pilang*" is a very hard wood, and employed in the eastern districts, instead of lignum-vita, for the construction of ships' blocks, &c.

"*Pung*" is equally hard with *pilang*, and uniformly employed by the natives for pegs in constructing their prahus.

"*Wali kukun*" wood is equal to the kusambi in weight, and exceeds it in hardness: it is employed for anchors, naves of wheels, machinery, &c.

"*Tang gulun*" is a hard wood of a close grain, and employed by turners for various small works.

"*Kelumpit*" is a very large tree: sections are employed by the natives for cart wheels.

"*Jaran*" is a white wood taking the tool easily: the natives prefer it to all others for the construction of their saddles, which consist principally of wood.

"*Demole*" tree affords a light wood, which is made into planks, and employed where durability is not much required.

"*Kedawung*" wood is whitish and moderately hard.

"*Laban*" is a yellowish and hard wood, employed for the handles of axes and various utensils.

"*Janglot*" wood is considered by the natives as the toughest wood produced in the island, and is always employed for bows when procurable: the tree is of a moderate size.

"*Bendo*" is a light wood, useful for canoes.

"*Sentul*" is a light close grained wood, and easily worked: it resembles the *suren*.

For household furniture, cabinet-ware &c. are employed,

"*Sono kling*" of the *Malayas*, the colour of which is a deep brown, inclining to black.

"*Sono kombang*," which has some resemblance to the *lingaa* wood of the Moluccas.

"*Warm-lot*," dark brown; and

"*Pronosodo*," resembling the walnut, both scarce.

"*Wern*," of a brown colour, of a close substance and light, abundant in some districts.

"*Mentaus*" and "*Jumberit*," the wood of which is white and fine grained, uniformly used for inlaying.

"*Krandu kuning*," yellowish and close grained.

"*Ingas*," of a brownish red colour, and very brittle.

For the hilts and sheaths of krises, the natives make use of the "*timoko*," of which the black and white variegated fragments are called "*pelet*." There are various kinds.

"*Aruman*," variegated white and black, is also employed for canes, handles, and spears, &c. and is very heavy.

"*Ttike*," yellowish close and marbled.

"*Mangu*," the *ati ati*, the "*kraminan*," the *purwo-kuning* and several others, are employed for the same purposes.

"*Kamuning*" is of a brownish colour and very fine grain.

"*Tayuman*" resembles the last and is very much esteemed:—the *wuni stelago* affords a reddish wood.—*Raffles' History of Java, Vol. I., page from* 40 *to* 42.

JIOMRASSEE. Botanical name not known. A tree of Jubbulpore, with a beautiful close grained wood, the leaf oblong, and serrated edge; it is found in the more hilly tracts but does not attain any great size.—*Cal. Cat. Ex.* 1862.

JOGHY. CAN. A wood of Mysore.

JONESIA ASOKA, *Roxb. (W. et A. Prod. I.* 284; *Wight, Icon. t.* 206; *Walp. Ann. iv.* 608.)—*c. p.* 653.

Jonesia pinnata, *Willde.*
Saraca arborescens, *Burm.*
„ Indica, *Linn.; Rh.*

Ushok, BENG.	Dive ratembela. SINGH.
Deya ratmal. SINGH.	Oshoko. URIA.

Met with in Ceylon, on the sides of streams, under the shade of larger trees, up to an elevation of 3,000 feet, and is very abundant in the Bintenne district. It is a highly ornamental tree, is found on the Coromandel coast, at the Ramghat, on the Khassia hills, Assam and Martaban. According to Mr. Mendis, the timber of Diveratembela, in the northern parts of Ceylon is used for common house building purposes, its weight per cubic foot is 58 lbs. and it is esteemed to last 25 years. In Madras its timber is not available.—*Voigt, Thw., Dr. Cleghorn in M. E. J. R.*

JUGLANS REGIA.

Thit kya. BURM. ?	Persicon. GREEK.
Royal Walnut tree. ENG.	Akrot. HIND.
Walnut tree. „	Jaoz. PERS.
Common Walnut tree. „	Charmagz. „
Basilicon. GREEK.	Akrot. „
Caryon. „	

This noble tree, though not a native of Europe, was extensively cultivated in Greece and Italy, at a very early period. Its most ancient names were Persicon (Persian tree), and Basilicon (Kingly tree), both indicating its eastern origin. The Greeks also called it Caryon, from *kara* a head, because its powerful odour was supposed to cause headache, or from some fancied resemblance between the nut and the human head. The Romans, to mark the estimation in which they held it, gave it the name of Juglans, or Jupiter's mast, from its being as much superior to other kinds of mast, as their false god was supposed to be superior to men. It grows in Ghilan and in the north of China, and three species of this genus grow in Japan. It grows wild in Tartary, where a single tree is said to produce as many as from forty to sixty thousand nuts yearly. A sample of the Walnut tree wood was sent to the Exhibition of 1862 from the Mehra Forest, near Abbottabad, Hazara. As a timber tree, the Walnut holds a high rank: in young trees the wood is white and comparatively soft; but in full grown trees it becomes compact, and of a dark brown colour, beautifully veined and shaded with light brown and black. Before the discovery of mahogany it was much used for furniture, and many a curiously wrought cabinet or book-case is still to be found in old fashioned houses; its principal use, however, at the present time, is for gunstocks, for which it is admirably adapted, combining the necessary qualities of lightness and strength, and being at the same time not liable to warp.—*John's Forest trees of Britain, Vol. I. p.* 162.

JUGLANS TRICOCCA.

Ta-soung-let-wah. BURM.

Scarce, but found on the banks of the streams in the Pegu district. It is a hard strong timber. Wood white colour and adapted for every purpose of house-building.

JULOSTYLIS ANGUSTIFOLIA, *Thw.*

Kydia angustifolia, *Arn.*

A middle sized tree of the south of Ceylon, not uncommon.—*Thw., En. Pl. Zeyl. Part I. p.* 30.

JOREE. URIA? A tree of Ganjam and Gumsur. Extreme height 60 feet, circumference 5 feet and height from ground to the intersection of the first branch, 8 feet. Bandy wheels are occasionally made of this wood, which is also burnt for firewood. The seeds are eaten by the Khonds. The tree is tolerably common.—*Captain Macdonald.*

JEMBU NERLU. CAN.? A wood of South Canara.—*Mad. Cat. Ex. of* 1862.

JHOONTIAH. URIA? A tree of Ganjam and Gumsur. Extreme height 45 feet, circumference 4½ feet and height from ground to the intersection of the first branch, 15 feet. A hard, white wood, used chiefly for making hair combs and small boxes. It is tolerably common.—*Captain Macdonald.*

JUBBULPORE WOODS. The following are the names put on specimens of woods from Jubbulpore, which were sent to the Exhibition of 1862: viz.

Tectona grandis.
Vaticarobusta. Surrye. HIND.
Jiomrassee. ,,
Cordia Macleodii. Dhengun. HIND.
Terminalia arjuna. Saj.; Kowah. HIND.
Pterocarpus—Beejah. HIND.
Zizyphus xylopyra or glabra. Ghattoo. HIND.
Trosum. ,,
Conocarpus latifolia. Dhowrah. HIND.
Boswellia thurifera. Serlee. HIND.
Zyziphus jujuba. Bher. ,,
Mimosa Arabica. Babul. ,,
Khumee. HIND.
Gunjah. ,,
Acacia sirisa. Siris. HIND.
Nauclea cordifolia. Hurdoo. ,,
Nauclea parvifolia. Kaim. HIND.
Nauclea orientalis. Pindra. HIND.
Jymungul. ,,
Acacia leucophlœa? Rohnee. HIND.
Londya. ,,
Conocarpus mysetifolium. Kardahee. HIND.
Eugenia jambolana. Taman. ,,
Dalbergia sissoo. Tin or Sisso. HIND.
Pandur. ,,
Careyaarborea. Kumbee. ,,
Hurrah. ,,
Bassia longifolia. Mowah. HIND.
Diospyros ebenum.
Asclepias rosea. Doodhee. HIND.
Uvaria, *sp.* Karee. ,,
Grewia tiliæfolia. Damin. ,,
Dalbergia latifolia. Sissoo. HIND.
Acacia procera. Gurraree. HIND.
Cedrela tuna. Toon. ,,
Hardwickia binata. Unjun. HIND.

It will be observed that many of the botanical names and synonyms are incompatible.—*Cal. Cat. Ex. of* 1862.

JUNDAMAREE. Extreme height 30 feet, circumference 2½ feet and height from the ground to the intersection of the first branch, 6 feet. Used for ploughshares, and burnt for fire-wood, being very common.—*Captain Macdonald.*

K.

KAANTHA, BURM. A small but valuable wood of Tavoy.

KAB-BAN-THA, BURM. A timber tree of a maximum girth 6 cubits, and maximum length 30 feet, found inland in Amherst and Tavoy Provinces, but scarce. When seasoned, it floats in water. It makes beautiful furniture, and when long buried in ferruginous mud, turns of a *very dark* red. It is found to make excellent planes; and is used in Tavoy jail with great success, for all tool handles, and much recommended for such as do not receive direct percussion, as screw drivers, augers, hammers, handles —in fact for all tools except chisel handles, which are to be struck with a hammer, for which the chisel-handle tree, a species of "Dalbergia" is the best. It makes excellent planes. It is stated by Dr. McClelland to be most plentiful in Tharawaddy district, and to be hard, of fine grain, and used in constructing carts. Captain Dance says a quantity of this sold in August 1857, for export to Holland as a furniture wood.—*Captain Dance.*

KACHNAR, HIND. A tree of Chota Nagpore, with a soft, white wood.—*Cal. Cat. Ex.* 1862.

KADOEMBEIRIYE. Bastard Ebony, a generic name for several species of Diospyros, of the Western Province of Ceylon, weight per cubic foot 45 lbs., durability 40 years, used for furniture. The heart of this wood is occasionally met with of extraordinary beauty.—*Mr. Mendis.* *See* DIOSPYROS.

KADUKAI MARAM, TAM. A Coimbatore wood. *See* PILLAY MURDAH.

KAD-WOT-NU, BURM. Cedrela *sp.*? A Tavoy wood, used for house and ship building; a large timber, 40 to 70 feet, specific gravity 1·060.

KADDA PILOW, TAM. According to Edye, name of a tree, which is the river side Jack-wood. It is inferior to the wood of that name: the natives use it for inferior purposes in small pattamahs and coasting vessels. It is not of much value.—*Edye, Forests of Malabar and Canara.*

KAHLARU, the Malayala name of one of the jungle trees. It grows to about seventeen feet in height, and seven inches in diameter; is very hard, close grained, and strong; and is used by the natives in boats and for timbers and knees in vessels.—*Edye, Forests of Malabar and Canara.*

KAI-HU-YUD, COCH.-CHIN. Sandalwood.

KAJAW, the Malayala name of a tree which grows to about eight feet in height, and ten inches in diameter; it is very strong, and the crooks of it are used by the carpenters for boat work.—*Edye, Forests of Malabar and Canara.*

KAJOM MARA, which is the Malayala name for Cashew nut tree. This tree grows to about 10 inches in diameter, and covers a large surface. It is considered the best sort of wood for charcoal, and is fitted for this purpose only. With this, as a substitute for coals, the assistance of a sheep skin for bellows, and a hole in the ground for a forge, the native smiths produce any piece of iron work that may be required for ship work; iron knees and channel work for large vessels; and the brass founder, any piece of metal, such as the pintles and braces for ships of 700 tons burden.—*Eyde, Forests of Malabar and Canara.*

KALA-NATH, HIND? Cerasus, *Species.* A tree of Mehra forest, near Abbottabad, Hazara. It is a species of wild cherry. Natural order, *Rosacedæa*; genus, *Cerasus.*—*Cal. Cat. Ex.* 1862.

KALAT NOTHEE—? A tree of Akyab, grows to a large size, and is plentiful in the Akyab and Ramree districts. Wood used in house building.—*Cal. Cat. Ex.* 1862.

KALAYUM in Tamil, and Condle in Malayalam. This tree grows from ten to fifteen feet in length, and from twelve to eighteen inches in diameter; its branches at the top are very thick; the wood is of a reddish cast, and much like the pencil cedar; it grows on the banks of rivers, but is not of much value for any purpose. The tree produces a fruit which Mr. Edye could not find was of use either to man or beast.—*Edye, Forests of Malabar and Canara.*

KALLOW MOW, the Malayala name of a tree which grows to about sixteen inches in diameter, and twenty feet in height. It produces a nut which is food for monkeys and other animals of the forest: the wood is used for various purposes, but is of little value.—*Edye, Forests of Malabar and Canara.*

KALOOCHIA, URIA? A tree of Ganjam and Gumsur, of extreme height 25 feet, circumference 2⅓ feet, and height from ground to the intersection of the first branch, 12 feet. It is used for posts and ploughshares and burnt for firewood. It is not a common tree.—*Captain Macdonald.*

KALUDUMUM, the Tamil name of a tree which is remarkably heavy and very close grained, and much resembles the English pear tree wood; it grows to about eighteen inches in diameter, and from twelve to fifteen feet long: it is used for purposes where strength is required. Edye imagined it is not very durable, or that it is not to be procured in any quantity, as it is but little known.—*Edye, Forests of Malabar and Canara.*

KAMALAH, the Tamil name of a tree which very much resembles the wood in Ceylon named Halmilile and Somendille; its growth is about thirty feet long, and two feet in diameter; it is used for much the same purposes as the other jungle woods, in vessels and house work; and the crooks are similar to the last named.—*Edye, Forests of Malabar and Canara.*

KA MEEN THA, BURM. A tree of Amherst, Tavoy and Mergui, maximum girth 2 cubits, maximum length 25 feet. Abundant all along the sea coast near Tavoy and Mergui. When seasoned it sinks in water. It is used for posts and planks of houses; is very heavy and durable, but too easily split to be recommended.—*Captain Dance.*

KARNENE-WAEH, the Tamil name of a tree which is very close grained and heavy. It is used for the frames of native vessels, and is considered a good strong wood. It grows to eighteen inches in diameter, and twelve to fourteen feet in height.—*Edye, on the Timber of Ceylon.*

KA-MOUNG—? A tree of Akyab, grows to a large size, and is plentiful. Wood used for planks, posts, &c.—*Cal. Cat. Ex.* 1862.

KANARI, a tree of the Indian Archipelago, a native of the same country as the sago palm, and found to the westward, though it has been introduced to Celebes and Java. It is a large handsome tree and one of the most useful productions of the Archipelago. Its wood is not known. It bears a nut of an oblong shape nearly the size of a walnut, the kernel of which is as delicate as that of a filbert, and abounds with oil. The nuts are either smoked and dried for use or the oil is expressed from them in their recent state. It is used for all culinary purposes and is purer and more palatable than that of the cocoanut. The kernels mixed up with a little sago-meal are made into cakes and eaten as bread.—*Crawfurd, Simmond's Comml. Products, page* 546.

KA NAT THA, BURM. A tree of Moulmein, the wood of which is made use of for ordinary house-building purposes.—*Cal. Cat. Ex.* 1862.

KANDESH, the Kokurmundah Pehta jungles occupy a considerable area and are flanked on the north and west sides by the Sagbarah, Gorwallee, and Mutwar Forests. The three latter are independent states, all the produce of which passes through the Kokurmundah Pehta jungles, Zillah Candeish, *via* Tulloda and Shejda. These latter forests contain large quantities of jungle wood and some teak, which Dr. Gibson thought should be turned to account in the shape of revenue. The Sagbarah jungles have been extensively worked for several years: the timber is small but of good quality. Many of these jungle varieties of wood must and will be used for sleepers in the construction of the railway though the province of Candeish, and the nearest jungle, Kokurmundah, will be the first cut down. Under these circumstances, he recommends that the Nakas should be re-established. Writing in 1849 of some of the Kandesh forests, he remarked there is a sprinkling of older Teak and Sissoo trees, but the active burnings annually carried on by the Bheel population, for the purposes of the chase and of cultivation, effectually stop the shooting up of any seedling trees, while the practice of baring the valley heads, from whence the rivers of Bauglan take their rise close to the edge of the ghats, has the visible effect (long ago pointed out by Mr. G. Inverarity, when First Assistant Collector of Kandesh) of lessening the supply of water in the streams which feed the rich garden grounds of Bauglan.—*Surgeon Gibson's Bombay Forest Report,* 1849 *to* 1856, *p.* 68, ALSO *Report of* 1857-58-59-60, *p.* 24.

KANDLE, the Tamil name of a Ceylon tree which grows to about fourteen inches in diameter, and twenty-four feet high. It is used at times in house work.—*Edye, on the Timber of Ceylon.*

KANDOO of Cuttack, wood known as "*Abloos*" or ebony, the tree being called the "*Kandoo.*" The darkest shade of the wood of this kind is the heart of the tree, and specimens are not easy to procure there. The Kandoo is a very handsome fancy wood; and its price per cubic foot is 12 annas or 1*s.* 6*d.*—*Cal. Cat. Ex. of* 1862.

KANGA, a hard wood of Cuttack.

KANGA VITTEE, the Malayala name of a tree which grows to about sixteen feet high, and eight inches in diameter. It is one of the jungle trees of the coast.—*Edye, Forests of Malabar and Canara.*

KANJARA, the Tamil and Malayala name of a Malabar and Canara tree which grows to about two feet and a half in diameter, and from twenty-five to thirty, in height, of little use or durability. The natives value its fruit, which is very intoxicating, and is used by them as a medicine.—*Edye, Forests of Malabar and Canara.*

KANJAROM. An ash coloured wood of Travancore, used for common building.—*Col. Frith.*

KANJUREA, the Tamil name of a Ceylon tree which grows to about sixteen inches in diameter, and ten or fifteen feet high. The natives use it at times in house work. It produces a fruit which is used as a medicine.—*Edye, on the Timber of Ceylon.*

KANNAN THA, BURM., or Crab Tree. A tree of maximum girth, 4 cubits, and maximum length 30 feet. Abundant on an island called Pielo Island near Mergui, but scarcely procurable in Moulmein. When seasoned, the red variety sinks and the white floats. The wood is used for houses, zyats, &c., is a very durable wood of handsome grain. Of this wood, there are two kinds, red and white; the latter lighter than the former, likely to answer for helves; the former too heavy for that purpose. Both woods very good for turning purposes.—*Captain Dance.*

KANNA-TSO, BURM. A very tough close-grained wood of Tavoy.

KA-NYENG KYAUNG KHYAY, BURM. In Tavoy, used for boat, ship, and house building; not attacked by insects; yields an oil.

KA-NYENG PYAN, BURM. A heavy, grey wood of Tavoy, used for handspikes.

KARA KUNDLE, the name of a tree that grows in the Malabar and Travancore forests to about sixty feet in height, and two feet in diameter. It is used by Arabs for masts of dowes, budgerows, dhonies, and pattamahs. It is very strong, and is said to be durable; but must be considered heavy for the purposes to which it is applied.—*Edye, Forests of Malabar and Canara.*

KARAM, HIND.? A tree of Chota Nagpore furnishing a hard, yellow timber.—*Cal. Cat. Ex.* 1862.

KARANCHILLY, a Travancore wood, of a dark colour, specific gravity 0·519. Used for buildings and small boats.—*Col. Frith.*

KARANGALI, the Tamil name of a Ceylon tree which is more generally known to the English by that of "Ebony." It may be procured at Trincomalee in great quantities, but that which is near the water-side is very small. The largest may be about nine inches in diameter, and from ten to twelve feet high: it is used for chairs and house furniture. On the Malabar coast this tree is named Charu maram. It grows to about ten inches in diameter, and from fifteen to twenty feet high, but the black heart of it does not exceed seven inches in diameter. In the north part of Malabar, in Canara, it is named Acha maram, and, by some of the Kanatakas, Nugagha. The natives use the young buds, leaves, and flowers of this tree in cases of flux and in inflammation of the liver, for the cure of which it is said to be most useful. At Point de Galle, a great deal of the Ebony and Coromandel wood is exported to England.—*Edye, Ceylon.* (*Note*—Edye seems, here, to describe ebonies from quite distinct trees.)

KARANGELY in Tamil, and Karakili in Malayalam. This Malabar and Canara wood is very tough and of a whitish colour, and used by the natives for general purposes; many of the planks of the native boats are of this wood, and the edges are sewed together with coir, with wadding on the seams, and yarns crossing the joints, for the purpose of making the boats pliable in the surf, as it would be useless to fasten them with nails, &c. for the services for which they are required.—*Edye, Forests of Malabar and Canara.*

KAREOVAM, the Malayala name of a Malabar and Canara tree which grows to about eight inches in diameter, and twelve feet long. It is generally curved, and used for the frames of native vessels, and for agricultural purposes. It is known as a jungle wood.—*Edye, Forests of Malabar and Canara.*

KARI. HIND.? A tree of Chota Nagpore, furnishing a hard, yellow timber.—*Cal. Cat. Ex.* 1862.

KARINDAGARAH, the Tamil name of a Malabar and Canara tree which grows to about forty feet in height; and eighteen inches in diameter. It is used by the native carpenters in house and ship building, and for various purposes. It is not found in any quantity, and consequently it is not much known.—*Edye, Forests of Malabar and Canara.*

KARINCOLU in Tamil, and Karinjurah in Malayalam. This Malabar and Canara tree grows to twelve or fourteen feet long, and twelve inches in diameter; it is of a whitish cast, and not of much use or durability. It produces a fruit which the natives eat in a raw state.—*Edye, Forests of Malabar and Canara.*

KARINGA, TEL., of Godavery Forests, Tella Manga, Circars, TEL., Gardenia lucida. Wood not used on the Godavery but it is so in the Circars. It seems to be very hard and close grained and adapted for turning.—*Captain Beddome.*

KARINGATTA, the Malayalam name of a soft, light wood of Malabar and Canara, which is preferred by the natives for the soles of sandals, &c. It grows to about twelve feet high, and eight inches in diameter. It produces a fruit from which oil is extracted. This, with the leaves of the tree, is used in gout and rheumatic pains. —*Edye, Forests of Malabar and Canara.*

KARITY, TAM., or Black Wood of Travancore, black colour, specific gravity 0·948; 2 to 4 feet in circumference, a strong wood: used for furniture.—*Colonel Frith.*

KARKUTA, HIND.? A tree of Chota Nagpore, yielding a hard, red timber.—*Cal. Cat. Ex.* 1862.

KARTUMA, the Tamil name of a Ceylon tree which is considered to be the wild mango. This tree grows to about two and a half or three feet in diameter, and twenty-four feet high. It is used for canoes, native boats, &c. The fruit is very acid, and is sometimes made use of by the lower class of natives in cookery.—*Edye, Ceylon.*

KARNARA VETTE, the name of a Malabar and Canara wood which the native carpenters use for boat work, and small vessels. It ranks amongst the numerous jungle woods, and grows only to twelve inches in diameter, and about fifteen feet high. It is not of much consideration as to quality, quantity, or durability.—*Edye, Forests of Malabar and Canara.*

KAROOTAULEY, TAM.? A Tinnevelly wood of a black colour, used for fancy work.

KARTU NEDENARI, the Tamil name of a Ceylon tree which grows to about fourteen inches in diameter, and fifteen feet high. It is used by the natives for their huts. It is not very durable, and is of little value.—*Edye, Ceylon.*

KARTU TANGI, the Tamil name, in Ceylon, of the jungle cocoanut, it grows to about twenty inches in diameter, and twenty-five feet in height. The fruit of this tree is of no use, and the trunk is of little value.—*Edye, on the Timber of Ceylon.* (Qu? what is this).

KARUCUE WAEH, the Tamil name of a Ceylon tree the wood of which is very close grained and heavy. It is used for the frames of native vessels, and is considered a good strong wood. It grows to eighteen inches in diameter, and twelve to fourteen feet in height.—*Edye, Ceylon.*

KARUDU, the Tamil name of a Ceylon tree which the natives use in boat-work. It is not durable, and is of little value.—*Edye, Ceylon.*

KARUATAGARAH, in Tamil and Malayala. This Malabar and Canara tree has a close grained firm wood, when old it resembles the "Vitte maram," or black wood of Malabar, known in England by the name of Bombay Black or Rose wood. It grows from twenty-five to thirty-five feet long, and two feet in diameter, it is used for furniture and house building: it grows straight, and is found in patches on the ghats east of Cochin.—*Edye, Forests of Malabar and Canara.*

KASAWHA, in Malayala. This is a Malabar and Canara tree which grows to about eighteen inches in diameter, and twelve feet long; it is heavy and close grained, it produces a small berry much like pepper, which, as well as the wood, is not of much use.—*Edye, Forests of Malabar and Canara.*

KATAMANAK.

Katamanak. TAM.	Miniley. PORT.

This Ceylon tree grows to about thirty feet in height, and two feet and a half in diameter. It can be obtained in great quantities. It is used by the natives for planks in vessels, and is considered valuable; but from what Edye had seen of the stock in a store at the Trincomalee yard, he was of opinion that it is only applicable to inferior purposes in the dockyard and ships.—*Edye, Ceylon.*

KATEEMOOL, HIND.? A yellowish coloured wood, heavy, but not strong, found in the Santhal jungles from Raneebahal to Hasdiha, about forty miles, but not very plentiful. It is used by the natives for building purposes.—*Cal. Engineers' Journal, July,* 1860.

KA-THEET-NEE, BURM. In Amherst, a timber employed for house posts, boats, and carts. It is a heavy, hard, grey wood, rather liable to injury from insects.—*Captain Dance.*

KA-THEE-THA, BURM. This tree is found in abundance all over the provinces of Amherst, Tavoy and Mergui. Its bark is used by the Karens in lieu of betel, and could probably be put to use in turnery.

KA-THEET-THA, BURM. A timber in Amherst, Tavoy and Mergui, of maximum girth 4 cubits, maximum length 22 feet. Not very abundant.—*Captain Dance.* (Qu? are these identical.)

KATHMAHLI, HIND.? A tree of Chota Nagpore, with a hard, red timber.—*Cal. Cat. Ex.* 1862.

KATHU-KEVI. The Tamil name of a Malabar and Canara tree which grows in Travancore. The wood is very buoyant, and is generally used for rafting the heavy timber from the forests; and also for catamarans and canoes, as it is easily worked, and obtained without much trouble, and of all dimensions. It is not very durable.—*Edye, Forests of Malabar and Canara.*

KATIE KALE, SINGH. A tree of the eastern province of Ceylon, a cubic foot weighs 42 lbs. and it is said to last 25 to 50 years. It is used for common house building and in the construction of vettra dhonies.—*Mendis.*

KATSITKA, BURM. A red wood, abundant in the forests of British Burmah, north of Rangoon, used for boats, said to last from 5 to 6 years. In a full grown tree on good soil, the average length of the trunk to the first branch is 30 feet and average girth measured at 6 feet from the ground is 6 feet.—*Dr. Brandis, Cal. Cat. Ex. of* 1862.

KATSO, BURM. In Tavoy, a wood like toon; used in building, &c.

KATTU-KENDE, HIND? In Ajmeer, a hard, fine, rather close-grained, heavy wood.—*Gen. Med. Top., page* 142.

KA-UGAN—? A tree of Akyab, which grows to a great length, and is plentiful in Ramree and Sandoway districts. The wood is used for planking.—*Cal. Cat. Ex.* 1862.

KAURIE TREE of New Zealand, the Norfolk Island Pine *(Araucaria excelsa)* attains the height of 200 feet, and yields an invaluable, light, compact wood, free from knots, from which the finest masts in the navy are now prepared.—*John's Forest trees of Britain, Vol. I., page* lxxiii.

KAUNA, the Tamil name of a Ceylon tree, which is used for boat crooks, knees, &c. This tree grows to about fourteen inches in diameter, and six to ten feet in height. It is strong and durable, and produces a fruit which is similar to the cocoanut, and is used by the poorer natives as food.—*Edye, Ceylon.*

KAYA, MALAY, also spelled Kaia, MALAY. Wood: Timber.

KAYA AMBALLO, MALAY. A timber tree of the Archipelago, in Bawean.

KAYA-ARANG, MALAY AND JAVANESE. Ebony.

KAYA BALIAN, MALAY. The Iron Wood of Borneo. This wood, the most esteemed amongst the natives of Borneo, on account of its hardness and durability, is called by them 'balean' or kaya balean, the term kaya, which means wood, being always prefixed to the names of timber trees. The balean is a fine timber tree of the largest size; and, although its wood is so hard as to be almost incorruptible, the tree is of quick and vigorous growth: it is found most abundantly in the low damp forests in the neighbourhood of the sea and of large rivers. It is much used by the natives for posts of their houses, which, amongst the Dyaks, are handed down from father to son, for many generations. Many specimens which must have been in the river for ages, are as hard when cut as those fresh taken from the forests, and this timber is rarely seen in a state of decay; the water worm (Teredo) alone attacks it when in the water; and though its channelling of the wood must necessarily much weaken the post, the water being admitted into it does not cause it to rot. On land or under ground it equally resists the effects of the atmosphere and the attacks of white ants, so destructive in tropical countries to most other kinds of wood. This valuable timber was formerly sought after by the Chinese; as an article of export, and in those ports which they still frequent, continues a source of considerable trade.—*Low's Sarawak.*

KAYA BIDARRU, MALAY. A yellow wood of Borneo, of a very agreeable odour, is most plentiful, and being of a very hard and durable nature, is much esteemed for posts of houses and other purposes under ground: its perfume will ultimately rescue this beautiful wood from its present degradation.—*Low's Sarawak.*

KAYA BIN, MALAY. Terminalia chebula.

KAYA BINTANGUR. Several kinds of the "poon" of India grow in Borneo to perfection, they are called by the natives 'bintangur,' and are well known for their value in ship building.—*Low's Sarawak.* (Qu.—Is this a species of Calophyllum.) *See* BINTANGUR, also CALOPHYLLUM INOPHYLLUM.

KAYA BOKA, MALAY. This valued ornamental wood and another, the Lingoa wood of commerce, are the produce of the same tree, the Pterospermum Indicum. The tree throws out knotty excrescences or burrs, which are sawn off in slabs, 2 to 4 feet long and 2 to 8 inches thick, which are much esteemed for such fancy articles, as small boxes, writing desks, and other ornamental work. Of late years, its estimation seems to have decreased in Europe, but it is still much valued by the Chinese. It is brought from Ceram, New Guinea, Arru and other islands of the Moluccas. It resembles the hue of the yew, is very hard and full of curls, the colour being reddish brown, varying to orange. In Singapore it is sold by weight.

The Lingoa wood is also known in commerce as Amboyna wood and very large slabs are obtainable from the lower part of the tree by taking advantage of the spurs or lateral growths. They can thus sometimes be had as large as nine feet in diameter. It is very durable, takes a considerable polish, is very abundant and may be had in any quantity.—*Great Exhibition of* 1851, *and M. E. Juries' Report.*

KAYA DUNGUN, MALAY. Grows on the banks of rivers, and, though the timber is soft, the large buttress-like supports at the base of the tree are very hard, and are valuable for gun carriages, and other purposes: they would doubtless be useful in turnery.—*Low's Sarawak.*

KAYA BUNG NGAT? COCHIN.-CHIN. Emblic myrobalan.

KAYA GAHRU. MALAY. Eagle wood.

KAYA-JELU-TONG. MALAY. Is a large growing tree of Borneo, with verticillate leaves, and a bark which, on being wounded, emits plentifully a white milk, which is inspissated by boiling, but has not yet been discovered to be of any use. The timber it produces, though large, is not esteemed by the natives, on account of its early decay when exposed to the rain and sun; it is white, and being very soft, easily worked; and it is much used by the poorer Malays for the sides of their houses, which are protected from the rain by the overhanging roofs.—*Low's Sarawak.*

KAYA KAPUR. MALAY. A close grained and durable timber of Borneo, much valued by the natives, for boat-building purposes.—*Low's Sarawak.*

KAYA KAPUR BARUS. The timber of the Kapur barus, or true camphor tree, is also highly esteemed: excepting when charged with the valuable drug, it does not emit the camphor smell, as does the timber of the Laurus camphora, of which the Chinese manufacture trunks and boxes, which, from the odour emitted by the wood, preserve whatever is put into them, from the attacks of insects of all kinds, particularly of the small ants, which are so troublesome in hot countries.—*Low's Sarawak.*

KAYA-LEGI, MALAY.? Cassia lignea.

KAYA MANIS, MALAY. Syn. of bark of Cassia lignea.

KAYA MANIS, JAV. Cassia lignea.

KAYA MARAM, TAM. properly Koia maram. Psdium pyriferum.

KAYA MARAKA, SANS, also KAYA MARKA, SANS. Nerium tinctorium.

KAYA MARANTI, MALAY, also a quick growing timber tree of Borneo, is held in some esteem. In grain it resembles cedar, and like it is of a reddish colour, and it is much valued for making packing-cases, planks for the sides of houses, &c., when protected from the weather it is a good and useful timber. The kaya 'dungun' also belongs to this class: it grows on the banks of rivers, and though the timber is soft, the large buttress-like supports at the base of the tree are very hard and are valuable for gun carriages, and other purposes: they would doubtless be useful in turnery.—*Low's Sarawak.*

KAYA MENCABANG, MALAY, or MENCA BANG PINANG, MALAY., is one of the trees which produce the vegetable tallow: it is plentiful in the Borneo forests, but would be more profitable for its fruit (which is small, and produces good oil) better than its timber, though for this also it is held in high esteem. The wood is close-grained, hard, of a reddish colour, easily worked, and very durable. This tree differs from the others which produce the vegetable oil, in growing to a much greater height.—*Low's Sarawak.*

KAYA MERBAN, is a fine durable timber, very useful in ship and house-building, being easily worked and very durable.—*Low's Sarawak.*

KAYA MUNGRIS, is, while fresh, nearly as hard as the Kaya Balean iron wood, and more difficult to be worked, though it is very durable, but not so much so as the balean, or iron wood, but is a large timber and a very fine tree.—*Low's Sarawak.*

KAYAN— ? A tree of Mehra forest, Abbottabad, Hazarah.—*Cal. Cat. Ex.* 1862.

KAYA NAN in Tavoy, KAIYAH in Moulmein. The wood called Kyanan in Moulmein and, by Dr. Mason, Kyanan, is Tavoy red wood, Syndesmus Tavoyana. In Amherst, Tavoy and Mergui Archipelago, kaya nan is of maximum girth 20 cubits, maximum length 15 feet. Very abundant on the sea coast, from Amherst to Mergui: also on banks of rivers in the province of Martaban near the sea. When seasoned it floats in water. It is one of the best woods in the country for helves; tough, light, very durable, plentiful: long in the fibre, neither liable to split nor to warp nor to break readily. Used by Burmese for planes, spears, boats, stocks of guns and all kinds of purposes. This wood is of a most beautiful color, a combination of pink, cream color and red, and takes a very high polish. Recommended for helves, handles of tools, hand spikes and spokes of gun carriages, and timber wheels; also for gun stocks and planes.—*Captain Dance.*—*See* KYANAN.

KAYANN, the Tamil name of a Ceylon tree which is about ten inches in diameter, and fourteen feet in height, it produces a fruit which is of no value.—*Edye, on the Timber of Ceylon.*

KAYA 'NERI,' is a very hard Borneo wood, growing with the mangrove in salt swamps, its timber, which has a reddish appearance, is not large but very abundant.—*Low's Sarawak.*

KAYAN-YANG, MALAY. A shrub at Bawean, the fruit of which sells at Java, at 30 florins per picul.

KAYPHAL, GUZ. and HIND. Nutmegs.

KAYA-PUTEH, MALAY. White wood, Arbor alba of Van Rumph, the Cajaput tree.

KAYA RUNGAS, a red wood of Borneo, handsomely veined, which takes a fine polish, and is much used at Singapore for the purposes of furniture making; like the ebony, it is only the old wood in the centre of the tree which is of a useful colour.—*Low's Sarawak, p.* 61.

KAYAH RASACK, of Borneo; a wood which resembles the bintangur, is close grained, strong, and tough, and is used for rudders, masts, and oars for the trading boats.—*Low's Sarawak.*

KAYA SONA, MALAY. A timber tree of the Archipelago, much used in prahus and housebuilding, at Bawean.

KAYEA STYLOSA, *Thw.*

Soovanda-gass. SINGH.

A large tree of the Island of Ceylon, growing in the south of the island, at no great elevation.—*Thw. En. Pl. Zeyl. I. p.* 50.

KAYU-API-API, MALAY. Rhizophora gymnorhiza.

KAY YOOB, BURM. A tree of Moulmein. Its wood is used as an ordinary building material. —*Cal. Cat. Ex.* 1862.

KEEAHNAUN, BURM. In Tavoy, a strong crooked wood, used for stocks.

KEEHAR ? URIA. ? A tree of Cuttack. Is a hard useful wood for mallets, pounders, rammers, and such like articles, and would, perhaps, make up strong furniture.—*Cal. Cat. Ex.* 1862.

KEONJJI, HIND.? A tree of Chota Nagpore with a soft red wood.—*Cal. Cat. Ex.* 1862.

KENDH. A close grained, hard wood of light red colour. The heart wood is quite black and hard, like ebony, which it somewhat resembles in every respect: it is plentiful in the Santhal jungles from Raneebahal to Hasdiha or over a space of about forty miles in length. Used by the natives for beams, &c. the fruit of the tree is also eaten by them.—*Cal. Engineers' Journal, July* 1860.

KENGTHEP-GUYUNG-YWEPT, BURM. A light inferior wood; used in building, at Tavoy.

KENGTHEP-PHEOOT-KYAY, BURM. A sound small wood; used in building at Tavoy.

KHA-BOUNG. BURM. In Amherst, a strong wood small, but as strong as oak. The fruit is said to be used for rubbing on buffaloes to keep off flies.

KHAI YAH, BURM. A tree of Tenasserim, maximum girth 2½ cubits, maximum length 22 feet. Scarce all over the Province. When seasoned it floats in water. It is a tolerably good wood, but like the "Na-yoo-ya" it is very scarce.—*Captain Dance.*

KHAKODHA, URIA. A tree of Ganjam and Gumsur, extreme height 30 feet. Circumference 2 feet. Height from ground to the intersection of the first branch, 9 feet. A common tree only used for firewood.—*Captain Macdonald.*

KHAMOUNG-NEE, BURM. In Tavoy, a heavy wood, not attacked by insects.

KHAMOUNG-PY-ON. BURM. A small sized, compact, yellowish-grey wood of Tavoy.

KHAMOUNG THA, BURM. Very abundant in Amherst, Tavoy and Mergui, of maximum girth 2 cubits, maximum length 22 feet.

KHANDAR. In the Peepree and Garvee Dangs, a term used by the Bheel and Kunbee cultivators, signifying lopping the trees of their tops and branches for cultivation. Khandar is a destructive system by which acres of young trees are mowed down by the kunbi cultivators; the parts of the forest in which this system of khandar mostly obtains are Dangs Rambaj and Peepree. At a late annual meeting of the Bheel chieftains, two of the Rajas, Kairal Sing and Trimbuk, were fined respectively in the sums of Rupees 100 and Rupees 25.—*Surgeon Gibson's Bombay Forest Report*, 1849 *to* 1856, *pp.* 41 *and* 79.

KHARAWAY-NU, Burm. A porous, heavy, strong wood of Tavoy, not attacked by insects.

KHEEROKOLEE, Uria.

Mimusops Kauki ?

A tree in Ganjam and Gumsur. Extreme height 30 feet, circumference 3 feet, and height from the ground to the intersection of the first branch, 6 feet. A hard wood, used for ploughs and mallets. It is not common.—*Captain Macdonald.*

KHOIRA, Uria. ?

Acacia catechu ?

A tree of Ganjam and Gumsur. Extreme height 25 feet, circumference 2 feet, and height from the ground to the intersection of the first branch, 6 feet. Used on account of its strength for sugar presses, and rice pounders. The wood is burnt when libations are offered. The gum (qu? extract) is mixed with betel nut and gives a red colour to the spittle. This is generally known under the name of catechu.—*Captain Macdonald.*

KHOOKOONDEAH, Uria ? A tree in Ganjam and Gumsur. Extreme height 30 feet, circumference 2 feet, and height from ground to the intersection of the first branch, 9 feet. A common tree only used for firewood.—*Captain Macdonald.*

KHOONGHO — ? A tree of Akyab, which grows to a large size, and is plentiful in the Sandoway district. The wood is used for making oars for boats, and sometimes in house building.—*Cal. Cat. Ex.* 1862.

KHOOTAN, Burm. A tree of British Burmah, a loose grained light wood, recommended for packing cases: used for black boards in Burmese schools. Br. weight, 114 lbs.—*Cal. Cat. Ex.* 1862. (Qu ? Koothan of v.)

KHOUNAY in Tamil, Kakay in Malayala and Canataka. This Malabar and Canara tree produces the pod known by the name of Cassia fistula, or Banda lotte, which is considered an excellent purgative in cases of habitual constipation, both by Natives and Europeans.—It grows to thirty feet long, and from twelve to eighteen inches in diameter, it is curved in growth; is rather close grained and heavy; and very much resembles the Maragosa in Ceylon; but it is rather scarce on the coast of Malabar. *Edye, Forests of Malabar and Canara.*

KHUMEE—? A tree of Jubbulpore, yields a light, strong, and easily worked wood, much in request by natives.—*Cal. Cat. Ex.* of 1862.

KHUUR. Hind. A tree of Chota Nagpore, with a hard, yellow timber.—*Cal. Cat. Ex.* 1862. (Qu.–Is this the Kheir—the Acacia catechu ?)

KIEP-DEP. In Amherst, a strong wood, resembling Kha boung, a kind of Saul.

KIEP-MAUP. In Amherst, a timber employed for cart wheel spokes. Superior wood, free from attacks of insects; the tree is said to have an edible fruit.

KIEP-YO. In Amherst, a heavy, good wood, but small; used for house posts and rafters.

KINDLE BELLEROM is the Tamil name of the wood, which is called Kindle in Malabar and Canara. It resembles the wood named Angely at Cochin and in Ceylon. The Company's cruiser, Aurora, was built, by way of experiment, of this wood, it was procured from the forests in the north of Malabar; and it appeared to answer its purpose.—*Edye, Forests of Malabar and Canara.*

KIREEMULA, Can. Grows in Canara and Sunda in the jungles between Bilgil and Nilcoond; said to be choice wood for masts of boats, &c. Worthy of further inquiry.—*Dr. Gibson.*

KIRE PALLE. A very soft, coarse, open grained, light, Ceylon wood.—*Edye, Ceylon.*

KIRI WALLA, Singh. Lance leaved Echites. According to Mr. Mendis, a tree of the northern province of Ceylon, a cubic foot weighs 35 lbs., and it is esteemed to last 30 years. The wood is used principally for making ornamental furniture and cabinet work.—*Mr. Mendis.*

KOAN, a very hard, fine, close grained, heavy, Ceylon wood.—*Edye, Ceylon.*

KOANG, Singh. Ceylon oak of the English in Ceylon. Grows in the southern parts of Ceylon, a cubic foot weighs 42 lbs., but its durability is only from 5 to 10 years. It is used for native oil-presses and wooden anchors, its berries are eaten by the natives.—*Mr. Mendis.* (Qu. Is this and Koan identical ?)

KODARA CHETTU, Tel. Grows in the Nalla Mallai. Mr. Elliott notes this "as a kind of tree." It appears to be of little use.—*Mr. Latham.*

KODORO, Uria ? A tree of Ganjam and Gumsur, extreme height 30 feet, circumference 2½ feet, and height from the ground to the intersection of the first branch, 12 feet. It is said only to be used for firewood.—*Capt. Macdonald.*

KOENAR, Hind. ? A tree of Chota Nagpore with a soft, white wood.—*Cal. Cat. Ex.* 1862.

KOES ? or JACK ? According to Edye, a moderately hard, but rather coarse and open grained, though heavy, Ceylon wood, of a beautiful saffron yellow colour, emits a peculiar, but by no means unpleasant odour.—*Edye, Timber of Ceylon.* (Qu. Artocarpus integrifolia ?)

KOIR-PAH, the Malayala name of a Malabar and Canara tree which answers the purpose of small spars for native vessels: it is said to be strong and durable for such purposes.—*Edye, Forests of Malabar and Canara.*

KOKOONA ZEYLANICA, *Thw.*

Kokoon-gass. SINGH.

This tree is not uncommon on the banks of streams in the Saffragam and Ambagamowa districts, at an elevation of 2,000 to 4,000 feet. The inner yellow bark is employed by the natives medicinally as a sternutatory, and an oil is expressed from the seeds, which is used for burningin lamps. Wood unknown—*Thw. En. Pl. Zeyl. p.* 52.

KOLA MURDAH, TAM. A Coimbatore wood. *See* VILLAY MURDAH. (*Qu.* Vellai murdah?)

KOLA SAHAJO, URIA.? A tree of Ganjam and Gumsur, extreme height 50 feet, circumference 4 feet and height from the ground to the intersection of the first branch, 18 feet. Abounds and is burnt for firewood and potash. The bark is used in tanning.—*Captain Macdonald.*

KOLEE KOURADEA, URIA.? A tree of Ganjam and Gumsur, extreme height 25 feet, circumference 1½ feet, height from the ground to the intersection of the first branch, 8 feet. Tolerably common and burnt for firewood, the leaves are applied to wounds. The fruit is eaten.—*Captain Macdonald.*

KONTABAOLO, URIA. A tree of Ganjam and Gumsur, extreme height 30 feet, circumference 2 feet, and height from the ground to the intersection of the first branch, 7 feet. The tree abounds and is chiefly used for firewood, though ploughshares are occasionally made of the wood. The bark is used medicinally.—*Captain Macdonald.*

KOONGHEELYARA, TAM. A Tinnevelly wood, of a light brown colour, used for building purposes; yields dammer.

KOOSSOOM, URIA? A tree of Cuttack, its wood is used for the handles of tools, and native cart axles; and might be applied to other purposes.—*Cal. Cat. Ex.* 1862.

KOOSUMBH, HIND.? A tree of Chota Nagpore with a hard, whitish red timber.—*Cal. Cat. Ex.* 1862. (*Qu.* Are the last two identical and what are their botanical names? I observe frequent notices of useful woods so named.)

KOOTHAN, BURM. Qu? khootan q.v. A loose grained light wood, recommended for packing cases, used for black boards in Burmese schools. Breaking weight 114 lbs. A cubic foot weighs 28 lbs., in a full grown tree on good soil the average length of the trunk to the first branch is 40 feet and average girth measured at 6 feet from the ground is 6 feet. It sells at 4 annas per cubic foot.—*Dr. Brandis, Cal. Cat. Ex. of* 1862.

KOPASSEA, URIA. A tree of Ganjam and Gumsur, extreme height 20 feet, circumference 2 feet, height from the ground to the intersection of the first branch, 7 feet. Useless except for firewood.—*Captain Macdonald.*

KOSSAYE, URIA? A tree of Ganjam and Gumsur, extreme height 22 feet, circumference 1 foot, height from the ground to the intersection of the first branch, 7 feet. Useless except for firewood.—*Captain Macdonald.*

KOTA MARAM, TAM. A tree of Tinnevelly, wood of a brown colour; specific gravity 0·723, used for building in general.—*Colonel Frith.*

KOUK-KO, BURM. A Tavoy wood, employed for bottoms of boats.

KOUNG MOO, BURM. A tree of maximum girth 5 cubits, maximum length 30 feet. Scarce, but found near Moulmein, near Tavoy and Mergui, on the sea coast and on the banks of rivers. When seasoned it floats in water. It is not a good wood, being perishable and liable to rot readily.—*Captain Dance.*

KRANDOOP—? A tree of Akyab which grows to a great length, and is very plentiful. Wood used for masts and native boats.—*Cal. Cat. Ex.* 1862.

KRAWNDOW—? OR KY-OUNG-THYA—? A tree of Akyab, very plentiful. A small wood used for firewood.—*Cal. Cat. Ex.* 1862.

KULA, the Portuguese name of a Ceylon tree, called in Tamil "Kanugha." It is very heavy and close grained, grows to about twenty-four inches in diameter, and eight feet high. The natives use it for general purposes, and for houses and vessels. It produces a fruit which they eat, and from which they extract an oil which is used as a medicine.—*Edye, Ceylon.*

KULBAGI, the name of a tree in Canara, which grows to fifteen or twenty-five feet in height, and from twenty four to thirty-six inches in diameter. It yields a close grained, hard, and durable wood, and is used by the natives at Mangalore and Onnor for the keels and beams of vessels. It is of a dark colour, and is considered valuable.—*Edye, Forests of Malabar and Canara.*

KUDDAR. A whitish coloured wood, not good, found from Sooree to Hasdiha in the Santhal jungles. Planks are sawn from this wood, but it is not fit for any thing else.—*Engineer's Journal, July* 1860, *p.* 156.

KUDDOOT ALAIN, BURM. A large tree of Tavoy, used in house and ship building.

KUDDOOT-NU, BURM. An inferior wood of Tavoy, used in boat building.

KUEVEA, the Tamil name of a Ceylon tree which grows to about eighteen inches in diameter, and fourteen feet long. It is used by the natives in boats and house work.—*Edye, on the Timber of Ceylon.*

KUHUA, HIND. A tree of Chota Nagpore, with a soft, brown wood.—*Cal. Cat. Ex.* 1862.

KUMARI, CAN., of Mysore and Canara, this is the Pounam of Malabar, the Punakad of

Salem, the Chena of Ceylon, and the Tung-ya of Burmah, and is a rude system of culture followed in all these countries, wherein secluded tribes and others clear parts of the forest. The kumari cultivators earn a cheap, but wretched subsistence and live in miserable huts, the Irulars and Kurumbars on the Neilgherries, the Malai, also, on the Shevaroys, the Punam cultivators in Malabar, the kumari cultivators of Canara, and the Karens in Burmah, all endeavour to obtain a precarious subsistence by scattering grain after burning the jungle, and thus avoid, to them, the irksome restraints of civilized life. A hill side, is always selected and at the close of the year, a space is cleared. The wood is left to dry till the following March or April and then burned. The ground is then sown with Italian millet, Panicum Italicum, as also with rice, Oryza sativa. In Canara, the seed is generally sown in the ashes on the fall of the first rain, without the soil being touched by a plough. It is fenced and weeded, and the crop gathered towards the end of the year. A small crop is taken off the ground in the second year and sometimes in the third, after which the spot is deserted, for 7, 10, or 12 years until the jungle grows sufficiently high to tempt the tribe to renew the process. In Ceylon, the Chena lasts two years, and includes the culture of chillies, yams, sweet potatoes, cotton, hemp, &c. A few years ago, in Bekal, the most southern taluk of Canara, 25,746, or one-sixth of the rural population were engaged in it, but north of that taluk, it is carried on by the jungle tribes of Malai kaders and Mahratais to the number of 59,500. Kumari is now prohibited in Mysore and under great restriction in the Bombay Presidency and the Madras Government, in 1860, prohibited it in Government forests, without special permission, which they commanded to be given sparingly, and never in timber spots. Mr. Cannan, a coffee planter of Wynaad, says that in a spot thus treated, only wood re-grows, unfit for any building purposes, and he had never been able to get coffee to grow on it.—*Dr. Cleghorn in Reports to the Madras Government*, 1858 *&c., quoted in Forests and Gardens of India, p.* 126.

KUMHIR, HIND.? A tree of Chota Nagpore with a hard, green timber.—*Cal. Cat. Ex.* 1862.

KUMMI, BURM. A Tavoy wood.

KU-POOP —? A tree of Akyab. Grows to a large size, and is plentiful; wood used for making boats.—*Cal. Cat. Ex.* 1862.

KURKATA. HIND.? A tree of Chota Nagpore with a hard, white timber.—*Cal. Cat. Ex* 1862.

KUROTU-PALAH, the Malayala name of a tree in Malabar and Canara, which grows to about eighteen feet long, and eight inches in diameter. It is very close in its grain, and remarkably hard and strong. It produces a fruit which is eaten medicinally; but the wood is not much used in consequence of the labour required in working it.—*Edye, Forests of Malabar and Canara.*

KURRIMIA CEYLANICA, *Arn.*

Palang. SINGH. | Alareya-gass. SINGH.
Hoorakandoo. „

A large tree of Ceylon, one variety, α. grows in the warm, moister parts of the island, variety β. in the central province, up to an elevation of 5,000 feet.—*Thw. En. Pl. Zeyl. I. p.* 72.

KURROOMARDOO, TAM. In Palghat, a dark coloured strong wood; used for wheelwright's work.—*Col. Frith.*

KUROONGAULEE, TAM. In Palghat, a dark coloured heavy and hard wood used for furniture.—*Col. Frith.*

KURROOVALAGOM, TAM. In Palghat, a small tree, of a light brown colour, specific gravity 0·704; used for naves of wheels.—*Col. Frith.*

KURUMBOLE is the Malayala name of a wood from the forests in Canara. It grows to about twelve or eighteen inches in diameter, and from fifteen to thirty feet high: it is used by the natives for house work, and is considered a useful and durable wood.—*Edye, Forests of Malabar and Canara.*

KURVAH TANGA MARAM, TAM. Cinnamomum iners, which is the wild cinnamon wood of the jungle. It grows to about twenty or thirty feet high, and from twelve to fifteen inches in diameter: it is very scarce, and consequently not much known or used.—*Edye, Forests of Malabar and Canara.*

KUSSOO, BURM., not identical with Kye-zai, *Burm.* A tree of Tenasserim, maximum girth 2 cubits, maximum length 15 feet. Abundant near the sea or the rivers edge, all over the province. When seasoned it sinks in water. It is a very tough wood, durable, and as good as Kyazai, for helves. The Kya-zai is a wood of the colour of oak with a yellowish tinge. The Kussoo is nearly white. This is not the soondree wood, of which latter the Burmese name is nearly the same, and the soondree wood Captain Dance had failed to procure.—*Captain Dance.*

KUTH JAMUN, HIND.? A tree of Chota Nagpore with a soft, red wood.—*Cal. Cat. Ex.* 1862.

KUVEAMA, the Tamil name of a Ceylon tree which is remarkably heavy and strong. It grows to about two and a half or three feet in diameter, and is curved in its growth. It is used in the frames of native vessels: it produces a fruit which is of no use.—*Edye, Ceylon.*

KYAI THA, BURM. A Tenasserim tree, maximum girth $1\frac{1}{2}$ to 2 cubits, maximum length 7 feet. Scarce, but found widely scattered on low marshy grounds in the provinces. When seasoned it sinks in water. The wood is excellent for planes, or for any other purpose, for which a straight grain, great toughness and strength are required.—*Captain Dance.*

KYAITHA OR ITCHWOOD, BURM. A tree of maximum girth 4 cubits, maximum length 18 feet. Found abundant, but scattered up the Attaran, Gyne, and Thoungween rivers near Moulmein and near Tavoy and Mergui. When seasoned, it floats in water. It furnishes a very compact hard timber, used for posts of houses, zyats, &c. The fibre is liable to start with repeated percussion, and the wood itself is subject to dry rot. This is called Itchwood because the fruit, chips, or bark produce, when touched, an itching like that caused by Cowhage.—*Captain Dance.*

KYAI YEW, BURM. A tree of Amherst, Tavoy and Mergui, of maximum girth 3 cubits, maximum length 22 feet. Rather scarce, but found all along the banks of rivers all over the provinces. When seasoned it floats in water. Its wood is used by the Burmese to make charcoal, also sometimes for posts of small huts: but is brittle.—*Captain Dance.*

KYA MOUK, BURM.? A kind of oak in Amherst, Tavoy and Mergui, maximum girth 4 cubits, maximum length 22½ feet. Abundant but widely scattered, all over the provinces inland. When seasoned it floats in water. It is an excellent tough wood, durable and sufficiently light; used for all purposes by the Burmese. Strongly recommended for helves, hammer handles, handspikes, staves of casks, and many other purposes, but too widely scattered to be easily obtained, unless a large quantity be ordered which should repay a search in the forests: much used by Burmese as a pole for cavady baskets.—*Captain Dance.*

KYANAN, BURM. On the low lands near the sea-coast of Tenasserim, there is a large tree of which canoes are occasionally made, that is much used for sandals. The wood is red; but turns black on being anointed with petroleum. The tree has pinnate leaves, with two pairs of oval leathery leaflets, and is a leguminous tree.—*Dr. Mason.* *See* KAYANAN.

KYA-NAN, BURM. In Amherst, a very close grained, ebenaceous wood, of a dark red colour; used for house posts, musket-stocks, and spear-handles.—*Captain Dance.*

KYA NAN, BURM. A red wood of Moulmein, used generally by carpenters.—*Cal. Cat. Ex.* 1862. (*Qu.* are Kayanan and these three identical?)

KYAN-PHO, BURM. A tree of Moulmein. A strong wood, good for building purposes.—*Cal. Cat. Ex.* 1862.

KYAY-TSAY-GYU-KHY-AY, BURM. In Tavoy, a heavy, compact, dark wood; suitable for gunstocks.

KYAY-TSAY-BAYOUN, BURM. A Tavoy wood, useful for common carpentry.

KYA-ZOO, BURM. In Amherst, a very heavy wood, like Saul.

KYA-ZO, BURM. A tree of Moulmein. Used for building material.—*Cal. Cat. Ex.* 1862.

KYDIA AXILLARIS, *Thw.*; A middle sized tree near Badulla in Ceylon, growing at an elevation of about 2,000 feet.—*Thwaites.*

KYDIA CALYCINA, *Roxb. Cor.*; *W. & A.*

Kydia fraterna, *Roxb.*

Bokemaiza. BURM. | Potari. TEL.
Pandiki. TEL.

This is a middle sized tree, pretty common along the western ghats. It also grows in the vallies of the Circar mountains, in Mysore, and on the slopes of the Niligiris. The bark is mucilaginous and employed in northern India to clarify sugar. It is plentiful throughout the Pegu forests, more especially in the Pegu and Toungho districts. The small saplings are used, from their great strength and elasticity, by the natives, for making banghy sticks, but it is large enough to afford timber of three or four feet girth. Wood white coloured and adapted for every purpose of house building.—*Captain Drury's Useful Plants, Madras Hort. Gard. Cat., Dr. McClelland.*

KYEATTEE, TAM.? In Travancore, a wood of an ash colour, specific gravity 0·972. Used for carts and buildings.—*Col. Frith.*

KYEM, HIND.? MAHR.? In Nagpore, a light colored wood inferior to teak in strength, and greedily eaten by white ants. Its length is from 16 to 28 feet and girth from 4 to 3 feet. It sells at 5 annas the cubic foot and it would answer for rafters.—*Captain Sankey.*

KYE YO THOO, BURM. A tree, maximum girth 2½ cubits, and maximum length 15 feet. Very abundant at Mergui, but not procurable at Moulmein. Found inland up the rivers all over the Provinces. When seasoned it floats in water. It is an uncommonly smooth grained, tough, close, yet not heavy wood. Durable and with but one fault,—the smallness of its girth,—which unfits it for gun carriages. It is strongly recommended for helves and handles of tools of all sorts, also for handspikes and for spokes. This wood, on careful examination, appears to be identical with Trincomallee wood, though this cannot be positively stated till the flowers of the tree can be procured.—*Captain Dance.*

KYEN-YO, BURM. In Tavoy a kind of teak.

KYEE THA, BURM. The name, according to Dr. Mason, of *Syndesmus Tavoyana*; and also called *Kyay Mishoung*, according to Dr. McClelland *Barringtonia acutangula.* This tree is of maximum length 10 or 12 feet, it is very scarce in Moulmein, but sufficiently abundant at Tavoy.

When seasoned, it sinks in water. It is the same as Kab-ban-tha.—*Captain Dance.*

KYET THAY OR THEEAY KYAY, BURM. A tree found on the sea coast from Amherst to Mergui. When seasoned it floats in water. Dimensions and extent of supply not known. It is used for posts of houses, very durable but not recommended as liable to split.—*Captain Dance.*

KYWAY-THOAY, BURM. In Amherst, a strong, solid wood, probably a kind of Acacia. Used for house posts and rafters.—*Captain Dance.*

KYWON, BURM. In Amherst, a kind of teak wood.

KYWON-BO. BURM. In Tavoy, a soft wood like that of the Nauclea.

KYWON-BO, BURM. In Amherst, a timber used for house posts, rafters, and oars ; it is probably a sort of teak.

KYWON-MA, BURM. In Tavoy, a soft wood like the nauclea ; a variety of Kywon-Bo.

KYWON-GAUNG-NOAY, BURM. In Amherst, a close, heavy, compact, tough, yellowish-white wood, of which house posts, rafters, &c. are made.

KYUND, HIND ? A tree of Chota Nagpore. —*Cal. Cat. Ex.* 1862.

KYUNI, HIND. ? A tree of Chota Nagpore with a soft, white wood.—*Cal. Cat. Ex.* 1862.

L.

LABUAN TIMBER AND FANCY-WOODS.

	Feet in height.	Feet in diameter.
Dadarru,	30	2
Gabar Buto, about	60	3
Jatichina,	60	$1\frac{1}{2}$
Kalim pupa tandok,	12 to 15	$1\frac{1}{2}$
Kaya Aru, about	60	3
do. Arang, grows to a large size in Borneo.		
do. Arru,	30	2
do. Benatore bukit	70	3
do. Bencoola, about	60	3
do. Badak utan. A fruit tree.		
do. Bidarru, a scented tree,	30	2
do. Impas,	40	$2\frac{1}{2}$
do. Gading,	25 to 30	1
do. Jamber,	30	2
do. Jampalore,	60	$1\frac{1}{2}$
do. Kandis Dahan, a fruit tree	30	2
do. Kalam pappa,	30	2
do. Karye,	20	$1\frac{1}{2}$
do. Kapur Rangin,	90 to 100	4 to 5
do. Kuing ? Uing ?	70	3
do. Kapur,	90 to 120	5
do. Kring utan,	40	$2\frac{1}{2}$
do. Kamuning,		$0\frac{1}{2}$
do. Limau, liman,		$0\frac{1}{2}$
do. Laoh, small tree.		
do. Leda Karbau, about	60	3
do. Malam,		3
do. Madang sisik,	50	$2\frac{1}{2}$
do. Madang Iada,	30	2
do. Nibong binar,	90	A species of palm.
do. do. sabarane,	90	" "
do. Nasi nasi,	40	2
do. Oobah,	40	$1\frac{1}{2}$
Bark used to dye red silk.		
do. Plye,		
do. Palah palawan,	30	$1\frac{1}{2}$
do. Petong,	30	$1\frac{1}{2}$
do. Rask ? Sak ? Rassak ?	40	$2\frac{1}{2}$
do. Rangas,	30	$1\frac{1}{2}$
Used for common furniture.		
do. Sampilou,	60	$1\frac{1}{2}$
do. Senang annun bukit,	90	4
The fruit yields an oil.		
Kaya Samuck,	30	2
Used for dyeing.		
do. Sabadia,	90	
do. Samala,	50	$2\frac{1}{2}$
do. Saryiah,	30	3
do. Senang awan,	90 to 120	5 to 6
do. Sarogan,	25	1
do. Tampui pyah. A fruit tree.		
do. Tioro,	30 to 35	3
do. Tobah tobah utan,	30	3
do. Taratang,	20 to 30	2
do. Urat mata,	90 to 100	3 to 4

LAGERSTRŒMIA, a genus of plants of the natural family of *Lythraceæ*, which is found in the Peninsula of India, extends along the foot of the Himalaya mountains to the northern parts of India and from the Malaya-Archipelago into China and Japan. The species are few in number, but most of them highly ornamental in nature. Speaking of this genus, as they occur in China, Mr. Williams remarks that few trees in any country present a more elegant appearance, ; when in full flower, by far the most beautiful plants met with on the low ground, are the different species of Lagerstrœmia. There are two or three varieties, having red, white, and purple flowers, and in the summer months, when they are in bloom, they are quite hawthorns of China ; surpassing in their gorgeous flowers even that beautiful family. He generally met with them in a wild state, very near the sea shore.—The whole of the species may be propagated by seed or cuttings in any garden soil.—*Eng. Cyc., Fortune's Wanderings, page* 20, *Williams' Middle Kingdom, Riddell.*

LAGERSTRŒMIA, *Species.*

Kuen-mou-nee or Puma. BURM.

A Tavoy wood used in building.

LAGERSTRŒMIA, *Species.*

Pyimma. BURM.

A splendid tree, abundant throughout British Burmah, wood used more extensively than any other, except teak, and used generally for the fittings of boats, sometimes for the hulls of canoes, for house posts, planking, beams, scantling for roofs, carts, and a variety of other purposes. Large quantities are now employed for ordnance purposes. The wood of the light colored variety is less heavy and is said to be less durable. A cubic foot weighs 37 lbs. In a full grown tree on good soil, the average length of the trunk to the first branch is 30 feet, and average girth measured at 6 feet from the ground is 12 feet. It sells at 8 annas per cubic foot.—*Dr. Brandis, Cal. Cat. Ex. of* 1862.

LAGERSTRŒMIA, *Species.*

Pyen-ma-phoo. BURM.

A tree of Moulmein, wood used for making oars and for rough house building.—*Cal. Cat. Ex. of* 1862.

LAGERSTRŒMIA, *Species.*

Pyen-ma-zoat-gyee. BURM.

A tree of Moulmein, with a soft wood, used in the ordinary purposes of a building material. —*Cal. Cat. Ex. of* 1862.

LAGERSTRŒMIA, *Species.*

Thitpyoo. BURM.

A light, but comparatively strong wood of British Burmah, color white and pinkish, probably a valuable wood for furniture. Used for planking, breaking weight 153 to 179 lbs. A cubic foot weighs 30 to 38 lbs. In a full grown tree on good soil the average length of the trunk to the first branch is 80 feet and average girth measured at 6 feet from the ground is 12 feet. It sells at 4 annas per cubic foot.—*Dr. Brandis, Cal. Cat. Ex. of* 1862.

LAGERSTRŒMIA LANCEOLATA.

Bodah or Bondaga. HIND.

An erect Dekhan tree with oblong lanceolate leaves, flowers small, white, appearing in April and May.—*Dr. Riddell.*

LAGERSTRŒMIA MACROCARPA, *Roxb.; W. Ic. Ill., Wall.*

Pyen-ma? BURM?
Ben-teak, Anglo. CAN.
Ven-bugum. CAN.
Ben-teak. ENG.
Ven-teak. „
Bondarah. MAHR.
Nanah. „
Cutchay cuttay maram. TAM.
Ven-taku maram. „
Chinnangi. TEL.

This tree of the western side of India is common in Wynaad and on the Western ghats. It is very common in the Bombay forests, but less so to the north of the Savitree than to the south of that river. It is a tree of large size with a long straight stem, and, Dr. Wight says, for common purposes, where timber of inferior quality is sufficient, is very useful, being easily worked. Tested by the scale, it only bore 290 lbs., on a second trial, however, it sustained 374 lbs. Were it, he adds, stronger and more durable, the length and straightness of the stem would adapt it for spars. But, Dr. Gibson thinks that Dr. Wight underrates the quality of this wood which, he says, is very fit for many household purposes, and for the decks of ships, &c .and is much used in the, Bombay dockyards, which forms a good presumptive proof that the wood cannot be very inferior. In the Madras Gun Carriage Manufactory, it is said to be made use of for a variety of purposes. It has great "stiffness," and wooden bridges have been built of it. In Wynaad, it is prized for making coffee cases. It is said to be a tree of Moulmein, commonly known under the name of jarrool, but this is doubtful.—*Drs. Wight, Gibson and Cleghorn, Mr. McIvor, Madras Cat. Exs. of* 1851 *and* 1862, *Col. Maitland in Madras Cat. Ex.* 1862, *Madras Exhibition Jury Report* 1855.

LAGERSTRŒMIA PARVIFLORA, *Roxb.; W. Ic.*

Lagerstrœmia microcarpa, *Wight.*

Tsam-be-lay. BURM.
Belli nundi. MAHR.
Nundi muna. „
Bondara. MAHR.
Muna? „
Chinna nagi. TEL.

This tree grows in the Circars, in the Godavery forests, at Courtallum, and on the Neilgherries, in the Dehra Dhoon, and in the Tavoy forests. Dr. Gibson says it is most common in the Dandelee forest above; also not uncommon below, and reaches a large size. Its wood is tough and valued for its qualities in standing water. It is greatly in use for beams, rafters and boat timber. In the Nalla Mallai it is a light brown, compact, hard, serviceable, wood, and used generally. As a wood of British Burmah, it is not much used. A cubic foot weighs 40 lbs. In a full grown tree on good soil the average length of the trunk to the first branch is 15 feet, and average girth measured at 6 feet from the ground is 5 feet. It sells, there, at 8 annas per cubic foot.—*Voigt, Drs. Gibson, Wight, Brandis and Mason, Captain Beddome, Mr. Latham.*

LAGERSTRŒMIA PUBESCENS, *Wall.*

La-izah. BURM.

A very large tree of British Burmah, stem not always perfectly round, and inclined to form buttresses; timber valued for bows and spear handles, also used for canoes and cart wheels. A cubic foot weighs 53 lbs. In a full grown tree on good soil the average length of the trunk to the first branch is 100 feet, and average girth measured at 6 feet from the ground is 12 feet. It sells at 8 annas per cubic foot.—*Dr. Brandis, Cal. Cat. Ex.* 1862.

LAGERSTRŒMIA PYMMAH, *McClelland.*

Pymmah-nee. BURM.
Pymmah. „
Red Pymmah. ANGLO-BURM.

Dr. McClelland tells us that this is a common and valuable timber, found generally all over the Pegu country. It ceases, however, a little below

Toughoo and Prome, so that at those places it cannot be made available for building purposes; but, at all the lower stations from Prome and Tounghoo downwards, it ought to supersede the use of teak. It is a red-colored wood, strong and adapted for house building. At page 10 of his report, he says *Lagerstrœmia pymmah,* next to teak, is in greater request than any other description of timber, as it is not injured by white ants. The Burmese gun carriages are made of this wood: its fault is its liability to shakes. It is not, as supposed, *Lagerstrœmia reginæ*, but a different species. But, at page 42 of the same report he remarks that the Lagerstræmia regina or pymmah is found in the Mayagie forests of Pegu and on the Choungs Kayoo, Thabyeed and Thenat in abundance, it stands without a rival in strength; "for," says Mr. Mason the posts of an old wharf at Tavoy, which were of this wood (Pymmah) stood erect for twenty or thirty years; and, he seems, however, to consider that house posts often decay in the ground in a much shorter period. It is considered a valuable timberin ship building. This seems the tree described by Captain Dance as Pymmah Nee or Red Pymmah; as very abundant all over the Tenasserim and Martaban provinces, and found of maximum girth 6 cubits and maximum length 30 feet. When seasoned it floats in water, and is a tough wood, very good for helves, and already used for such, and for other ordnance purposes. He says that the great fault of pymmah is its liability to shrink and warp when exposed to the heat and sun, but it has not been killed and left standing as teak has been, otherwise the tendency to warp might disappear.—*Dr. McClelland, Capt. Dance, Selec. Records Govt. of India Foreign Dept. No. IX. pp.* 10 *and* 42. (*Note*—Does Dr. McClelland regard the white wood tree as L. reginæ, and the red wood as L. pymmah, which Dr. Brandis treats as two varieties of L. reginæ. Is this the species noticed at the bottom of p. 150 and top of p. 151, or are the white and red woods only from trees of different ages ?)

LAGERSTRŒMIA REGINÆ, *Roxb.*

Flos reginæ, *Retz.*

Adambea glabra, *Lam.*; *Rheede.*

Jarul. BENG.	Tannana. MAHR.
Jarool. „	Nanna. MAHR.
Arjuno. „	Jarul. MALAY.
Pym-mah. BURM.	Adamboe MALEAL.
Peemah. „	Jarul. „
Halee dasul. CAN.	Stotulari. SANS.
Queen Lagerstrœmia. ENG.	Muruta-gass. SINGH.
Jarul. HIND.	Muruta. „
Mota bondara. MAHR.	Cadali pua. TAM.

This large tree grows in Ceylon, in the Peninsula of India, at Coimbatore, in Canara and Sunda, in the mountains north east of Bengal, in the Jynteah hills, in Pegu and Tenasserim, Amherst, Tavoy and the Mergui Archipelago. Dr. Mason tells us that the queen Lagerstrœmia in its native soil is a large timber tree, and when in flower is one of the most conspicuous in the Tenasserim provinces. In full blossom, in the morning, a tree looks as if mantled with roses, but the flowers change through the day to a beautiful purple, making it appear at evening, if seen from a short distance, like a bower of English lilacs. It is not uncommon in the warm, moister parts of the western and southern parts of Ceylon, up to an elevation of 1,500 feet. In Canara and Sunda, it grows near the banks of rivers below, and reaches a large size. It is common in the jungles, below the ghats, south of the Savitree river; but is hardly found north of that and never in the inland Bombay jungles. In Ceylon it is used for water casks and buildings. Dr. Wight, writing in Coimbatore, says this tree, is more celebrated there, for its large handsome flowers than for its timber, which last, however, is used for common purposes, and Dr. Riddell, in the Hyderabad Dekhan, repeats that opinion: also, Dr. Gibson mentions that the timber of the Bombay forests, is reckoned rather good, and is used, being generally crooked, for the knees &c. of native boats. At another place he says the wood is of the same quality as L. parviflora; and is used in houses and boats. About 70 miles up the river Soormah, the mountains on the north, which are east of Jyntea, rise 4000 feet high, in forested ranges like those of Sikkim. Swamps extend from the river to their base, and penetrate their valleys, which are extremely malarious: these forests are frequented by timber-cutters, who fell the jarool "Lagerstrœmia reginæ," a magnificent tree with red wood, which, though soft, is durable under water, and therefore in universal use for boat building. Dr. Brandis tells us that it is a splendid tree throughout British Burmah. Its wood is used there more extensively than any other except teak, is used generally for the fittings of boats, sometimes for the hulls of canoes, for house posts, planking, beams, scantling for roofs, carts, and a variety of other purposes. Large quantities are now employed for ordnance purposes. There are, he says, two varieties of the wood, a red and white, but the light colored variety is less heavy and is said to be less durable. A cubic foot weighs lbs. 42 to lbs. 44. In a full grown tree on good soil the average length of the trunk to the first branch is 30 feet and average girth measured at 6 feet from the ground is 12 feet. It sells, in Pegu, at 8 annas per cubic foot. In Ceylon the wood is esteemed to last 30 to 40 years and, Dr. Mason tells us, that the posts of an old wharf at Tavoy which were of this wood, stood erect for twenty or thirty years; but house posts often decay in the ground in a much shorter period. In Tenasserim, it is considered a valuable timber in ship building. He adds that there is a smaller species of lagerstrœmia in the Pegu jungles whose wood is inferior, but it is sometimes confounded with the other. In the Madras Gun Carriage Manufactory it is used for light field cheeks, felloes, and cart naves, framing and boards of waggons, limbers, and platform carts, and ammunition box boards and heavy field cheeks.—*Voigt, Thwaites, Drs. McClelland, Riddell, Wight, Brandis, Mason and Gibson, Mr. Mendis, Captain Dance, Major Benson, Colonel Maitland in Madras Cat. Ex. of* 1862, *Dr. Hooker's Him. Jour. Vol. II. p.* 327. *(Note*—It will be observed that Drs. McClelland and Brandis and Captain Dance all recognise a red and a white wood from a tree of this genus.)

LAMMAY, BURM. In Amherst, a timber used for house posts; it is a red, light, but useful timber, like sandal wood, and is free from attacks of insects.—*Captain Dance.*

LA-PHYAN, BURM. In Amherst, a heavy, solid, large-sized timber, but rather liable to injury from a peculiar insect, not the white ant.—*Captain Dance.*

LANCE-WOOD. Tenasserim lance-wood. A tree which produces a timber possessing the properties of lance-wood, is not uncommon in the Tenasserim provinces, but it belongs to the dogbane tribe, and is not at all related to *Guatteria virgata*, the lance-wood of commerce.—*Dr. Mason.*

LARIX DEODARA ?

Cedrus deodara.

Deodar. ANGLO-HIND. | Kelon. HIND.

Its turpentine is the Kelon ka tel, *Hind.*

See CEDAR. CEDRUS. DEODAR.

LATOOR. A reddish coloured wood, but light and weak. Plentiful in the Santhal jungles from Raneebahal to Hasdiha. Light articles of furniture are manufactured from this wood by the natives, but it is too weak to be used by them for building purposes.—*Cal. Engineers' Journal, July* 1860.

LAURUS. A genus of plants some of which furnish useful products, though the woods of others are not in use. Of these last, we may notice the cinnamon tree of Ceylon "Laurus cinnamomum" the L. culilawan of Amboyna; the L. malabathrum of several parts of India, and L. nitida of Pegu and Tenasserim.

LAURUS, *Species.*

Panatha. BURM.

A Tavoy wood, used in house carpentry.

LAURUS, *Species.*

Kye-zai. BURM.

A tree of Amherst, Tavoy and Mergui, of maximum girth 2 cubits, and maximum length 15 feet. It is not obtainable at Moulmein, but is found along the coasts from Amherst to Mergui; also on the banks of the Tavoy river. When seasoned, it floats in water. It yields a very tough wood which has been often used for helves with great success and has been proved to possess extraordinary strength and tenacity. Very durable and not too heavy for helves, for which it is recommended as, also, for handles of tools of all kinds. Dr. Mason says that it is, in Tavoy, a hard wood used in carpentry.—*Dr. Mason, Captain Dance.*

LAURUS, *Species.*

Kullowa. BURM. | Kurrowa. BURM.

A Tavoy wood.

LAURUS, *Species.*

Thitya. BURM.

In Tavoy a very large tree, timber used in building, *&c.*

LAURUS, *Species.*

Thuggoo. BURM.

A wood of Tavoy, used for oars, &c.

LAURUS.

Keemna. BURM.

In Tavoy, a small tree, wood used for posts.

LAURUS CAMPHORA, *Linn.*

Camphora officinarum, *Nees.*

Kaya Kapur. JAP.

A native of Japan, Formosa, and of China, principally near Chin-Chew in the province of Fo-kien. It yields one of the camphors of commerce, to obtain which, the wood, split into billets, is boiled in water in an iron pot, covered with earthenware heads filled with straw, on which the camphor concretes. The wood of this tree is made into boxes, which are valuable as a preservative against insects.—*Royle, Eng. Cyc., Fortune's Residence, Riddell.*

LAURUS GLANDULIFERA, ? ? *Wall.*

Martaban Camphor wood. | Burmese Sassafras wood.
Tree galanga.

This is a very large tree, according to Dr. Wallich very like *Laurus glandulifera*, which furnishes the Sassafras, and Camphor wood of Nepaul. It grows scattered sparsely throughout the provinces in Amherst, Tavoy and Mergui. Its maximum girth 3 cubits, rarely 4, and maximum length 20 to 30 feet. It is not very abundant but procurable, from Amherst to Mergui, all along the sea-coast at Yea, Henzay and other places. When seasoned, it floats in water. It has the odour of Sassafras, is often used in house carpentry, also for interior of junks, for inside works of drawers, boxes, &c., as its odour repels insects. It is a durable wood, when seasoned and worked up, remarkably tough and strong, excellent for planes, helves, and handles of tools generally, and would be valuable for almirahs in which to keep serge, hospital clothing, &c.—*Captain Dance, Dr. Mason.*

LEGUMINOSÆ. In this family, in Burmah, Captain Benson mentions the following, as valuable timber trees: Acacia stipulata; two species of Acacia not named, used by the Burmese for naves and spokes of wheels. Acacia stipulata is a valuable wood for general purposes, its middling girth and scarcity would, however, render it useless except in small quantities and scantling. Dalbergia, species, resembling Bombay blackwood; Cassia fistula, Inga xylocarpa and Pterocarpus Indica are of this order. Cassia fistula a beautiful ornamental tree, wood useful for furniture, naves and spokes of wheels and tool handles; Inga xylocarpa is a dense wood, resembling Cassia fistula, used for windlasses, block sheaves and for parts of gun carriages; was found too brittle to resist concussion—Pterocarpus Indica is therefore preferred and generally adopted. The family is rich in trees, but not much so in temperate climates.—*Major Benson.*

LEP-DWAT, Burm. In Amherst, a timber used for spear-handles and sword-sheaths: it is a fine grained, white wood, fit for turning purposes and picture-frames; it is probably the same kind of Nauclea which is used for similar purposes as in Bengal.—*Captain Dance.*

LIEUN, Burm. In Amherst, a timber used for house posts and rafters. It is a most valuable compact wood, homogeneous and very heavy, of deep-brown colour and fine grain, and exempt from attacks of insects.—*Captain Dance.*

LIEP-YO, Burm. In Amherst, a timber used for making carpenter's tools; it is a very compact and heavy but small sized, timber.—*Captain Dance.*

LIMBO, Uria. Melia azadirachta? Under these names, Captain Macdonald describes a tree of Ganjam and Gumsur, extreme height 70 feet, circumference 5 feet and height from ground to the intersection of the first branch, 22 feet, and he adds that it is the margosa tree. Idols are usually made of its wood because it is not liable to be attacked by insects. The bark is used medicinally for fever, small pox, and worms. An oil which is extracted from the seeds of this tree, is used for itch and other cutaneous diseases. The tree is tolerably common and is burnt for firewood.—(*Note*, is this the Azadirachta Indica?)

LIMONIA, a genus of plants belonging to the natural order *Aurantiaceæ*, so called from the original hindi names, of the lemon, neemoo and leemoo. Most of the family abound in essential oil, the leaves of some of the Limonias are fragrant, and the fruit, though small, of *L. acidissima* and *L. crenulata* is very acid. *L. laureola* is remarkable as the only plant of this family found on the tops of cold mountains. The people of the Himalayas, remarking its highly fragrant leaves, fancy that it is by feeding on them that the musk-deer acquires its strong and peculiar flavour. Wight gives Limonia missionis: L. caudata, *Wall.*, grows in the Khassia hills.—*Voigt, Eng. Cyc., W. Ic.*

LIMONIA ACIDISSIMA, *L. D.C.*

Limonia crenulata, *Roxb., Cor. Pl.*

Torelaga. Tel.

Grows at the falls of Gokak: common on sandstone hills at Padshapore, in the forests of the Godavery, at Hurdwar, Monghir and Assam. Wood very hard, and worthy of attention.

LIMONIA ALATA. *Wight, Ill.* 41.

Kat yelloo mitcha maram. Tam.

Tree small, but the wood is remarkably close grained, hard and heavy. It is pale yellow or straw coloured, and if procurable of adequate size would be very valuable. Is found in the southern ghat forests of the Bombay presidency, above and below, where the wood has all the qualities attributed to it by Dr. Wight; but it is not a common tree.—*Drs. Wight and Gibson.*

LIMONIA PENTAGYNA—?

Chitraka. Tel.

A large timber tree, a native of the Circars, Bengal, &c.—*Mr. Rohde, MSS.*

LINGOA or AMBOYNA WOOD. This wood is very durable, and takes a high polish. It was imported from the Moluccas in considerable quantities at the time when the latter were British possessions; it is very abundant, and may be had in any quantity. Very large circular slabs are obtained from the lower part of the tree by taking advantage of the spurs, or lateral growths; they are sometimes as large as nine feet in diameter. A circular disk of wood thus obtained, nearly seven feet in diameter, as well as some other specimens, were exhibited in 1851 by Messrs. Almeida of Singapore, and were deemed deserving of a Prize Medal by the Jury. It is from the Pterospermum Indicum. *See* Kayaboka wood, Java woods, Pterospermum Indicum.

LIQUIDAMBAR ALTINGIA, *Blume.*

Nan-tar-uk. Burm.	Rasamala. Jav.
Liquid amber tree. Eng.	Rasamala. Malay.
Liquid storax tree. "	

A native of the forests of Java, at elevations of 2,000 and 3,000 feet above the level of the sea, and indigenous on the Tenasserim coast. In some parts, it is quite abundant and a considerable stream in Mergui derives its name from this tree.—*Eng. Cyc., Dr. Mason.*

LIQUIDAMBAR CERASIFOLIA, *Wallich.*

Sedgwickia cerasifolia, *Griff.*

Grows in Assam, but it is not known if it yields any balsam.

LITSÆA FUSCATA, *Thw.*

A tree growing 20 feet in height in the Central province of Ceylon, at an elevation of 6,000 to 8,000 feet.—*Thw. En. Pl. Zeyl. p.* 258.

LODH, Hind. A tree of Chota Nagpore, with a soft, white wood.—*Cal. Cat. Ex.* 1862.

LOOKKEE. Tel. In the Nalla Mallai, a fine grained wood, of a greyish color; found in small quantity.—*Mr. Latham.*

LŒNDIA, Mahr.? A Nagpore wood, said very closely to resemble, "Thevus" another

Nagpore wood and to be equally good. It is probably, therefore, a valuable timber.—*Captain Sankey.*

LUMNITZERA LITTOREA.

Pyrrhanthus littoreus, *Jack.*

A tree of Pulo-Dinding and Penang.

LUMNITZERA RACEMOSA, *Willde.*

Petaloma alternifolium, *Roxb. Fl. Ind.*
Bruguiera Madagascariensis, *D. C.*

Kara kundal. MALEAL.

A tree of Madagascar, grows on the banks of salt water creeks in the Konkan, also in the Sunderbuns, and in several parts of the two peninsulas of India. Its wood is strong and durable, and used for posts and other purposes in house building, but, in Calcutta, chiefly for fuel.—*Voigt, Useful Plants.*

LUNU MIDELLE, *Singh.*

Common Bread tree. ENG.

A tree of the western parts of Ceylon. A cubic foot of its wood weighs 15 feet and it is said to last 8 to 20 years. The small sticks and branches are used in common buildings, and as out-riggers for dhonies and fishing boats; the timber for panels of carriages, buoys, targets, &c.—*Mr. Mendis.*

LUZAR, BURM. A log of a certain length.

M.

MABA BUXIFOLIA, *Pers.*

Ferreola buxifolia, *Roxb.; Cor. Pl.*

Irumbeli. TAM.
Pishanna. TEL.
Pisinika. „
Utti chettu. TEL.
Nalla muddee. „

A small tree of the Circar mountains and of the forests of the Godavery, furnishing a dark coloured wood, small but remarkably hard and durable.—*Voigt, Captain Beddome, Fl. Andh.*

MACARANGA INDICA, *R. W.*

Vutta thamare. TAM. | Putta thamara. MAL.

This tree grows on the Neilgherries and is common in Travancore. It produces a light crimson colored gum which is used in medicine, and for taking casts.—*Drury's Useful Plants.*

MACARANGA ROXBURGHII, *Wall.*

Osyris peltata, *Roxb.; W. Ic.*

Boddi chettu. TEL.

This is marked by Voigt as a shrub of the Circars. The Telugu name would indicate that it is a tree, and information on this point is required. All the young parts of this plant are covered more or less with soft resinous adhesive matter, smelling strongly of turpentine.—*Voigt.*

MACARANGA TOMENTOSA, *Wight's Ic.*

Kanda-gass. SINGH.

This tree is very abundant in Ceylon, up to an elevation of 3,000 feet. It grows, also, in Travancore and exudes a gum of character similar to that of M. Indica.—*Thw. En. Pl. Zeyl. p.* 274, *Drury's Useful Plants.*

MACREIGHTIA BUXIFOLIA, *Pers. A. D. C. Prod.; Wight Ic.*

Kaloo-habaraleya-gass. SINGH.

Of this there are four varieties *α*, *β*. microphylla; *δ*. angustifolia; var. *α*. and *β*. grow, in the hot drier parts of Ceylon, var. *δ*. in the Ambagamowa district, and near Ratnapoora. Var. *δ*. on the banks of rivers; woods not known. —*Thw. En. Pl. Zeyl. p.* 183.

MACREIGHTIA OBLONGIFOLIA, *Thw.*

A small tree of Ceylon, near Ratnapoora, and in the Singherajah and other forests between that place and Galle.—*Thw. En. Pl. Zeyl. p.* 183.

MADDANG KAMENHJIR. A Penang wood used by the Chinese for making boxes.

MADDANG TANDACK. A Penang wood, of a dark brown colour. Not used.

MADETIYE, SINGH. Adenanthera pavonina? Under these names, Mr. Mendis describes a tree of the western side of Ceylon, a cubic foot of which weighs lbs. 56, and is said to last 30 years. It is used in common house buildings. The tree produces a red seed which is roasted and eaten.—*Mr. Mendis.*

MADRAS PRESIDENCY, ITS TIMBER TREES AND FANCY WOODS. Amongst the earliest contributors to this department of the economic resources of the country, was Dr. Roxburgh, whose invaluable Coromandel plants were published, in 1795, in three folio volumes, by the East India Company, and nearly 20 years after his death, Dr. Wallich, in 1832, edited his Flora Indica, in three volumes 8vo. In 1813, appeared Dr., afterwards Sir Whitelaw, Ainslie's Materia Medica of Hindostan and Artlsan's and Agriculturist's Nomenclature in which are many useful notices of the timbers and fancy woods of South-Eastern Asia, and which reappeared in 1826, in his Materia Indica. Early in the beginning of this century, Mr. Edye, of the Survey department of the Navy, reported on the timber trees of Canara, Cochin and Travancore, on the Malabar Coast, and on those of the Island of Ceylon. His notice appeared in the Royal Asiatic Society's Journal in 1835. About that year, Lieut. Colonel Frith of the Madras Artillery made an extensive tour through the timber provinces of this presidency, during which he collected 187 of the woods of the country,—from Penang 45; from Palghat, 20; Tinnevelly 41, and Travancore 81,—one set of which were retained in the Grand Arsenal at Madras, and another forwarded to the India House. Each of his woods was accompanied by a note as to its quality and its specific gravity, and for conciseness and usefulness, these notes remain unrivalled. Subsequently, in 1850, when the Madras Central Committee were gathering together samples of the raw products of the country for the coming Exhibition of 1851, Dr. Wight, the author of the Icones and of the Illustrations of Indian Botany, furnished, from Coimbatore, extensive notes on 133 woods which he had identified in the Coimbatore and Palghat forests. He named these botanically, and added the vernacular synonyms that Ainslie and Edye had given. That list was sent to Mr. Rohde of the Madras Civil Service, who added valuable practical remarks, on 35 of the 133 woods that Dr. Wight had described. Mr. J. E. Chapman exhibited, in 1851, 20 of the timbers of Malabar, which he considered applicable for railway purposes and which had been collected by Dr. Gibson. Since then, our knowledge of the timbers and fancy woods of peninsular India, has been much extended. Dr. Cleghorn as Reporter to the Jury on woods, in the Madras Exhibition of 1855, reported on the 146 woods, whose names are given below. At the same time, Captain (now Major) Macdonald sent a list of 150 woods from the forests of Ganjam and Gumsur, and Captain Beddome, enumerated 108 of the trees of the Circars and of the forests of the Godavery. Dr. Gibson, the Conservator of the Bombay forests, gave continuous lists of 64 of the timber trees of Canara and Sunda, and, subsequently, of 157 of all the Bombay forests. Captain Sankey has added to our knowledge of the woods in the northern part of the peninsula, by furnishing notices of 22 of the woods of Nagpore. While this has been done for the peninsula of India, Captain (now Colonel) Simpson, and Captain Dance of the Madras Artillery, Major Benson of the Madras Infantry, in reports to the Ordnance and Commissariat Departments, on the timber trees of Burmah, Moulmein, Amherst, Tavoy and Mergui, and Dr. Mason's exhaustive works on the Natural products of Tenasserim and Burmah, have appeared, as also Drs. Wallich, Falconer, McClelland and Brandis' descriptions of the forests and timber trees of Pegu, and have done much to make known the many useful timbers of the Burmese provinces and of the Malay peninsula, where the Madras Troops serve. Captain Dance's notes embraced 114 woods; Dr. Mason's, 63; Dr. McClelland's 76; Major Benson's 31, and Dr. Brandis' 116; and there were, likewise, exhibited at the Exhibition of 1851, 90 woods from Amherst: 49 from Labuan; 32 from Singapore; 19 from Penang, along with 86 woods collected by Dr. Wallich, viz. 17 in Martaban and 69 from Tavoy; as, also, 10 from Moulmein by Mr. J. E. Colvin, and the 187 woods that Colonel Frith had collected in his tours. In forming the Government Central Museum Madras, I gave special attention to the timbers of the country and collected together specimens of every procurable wood. The collection in the Madras Museum is perhaps unrivalled. While forming it, Sir George Anderson, then Governor of Ceylon, sent a beautiful series of 96 of the woods of that island, collected by Mr. Adrian Mendis, Master Carpenter of the Royal Engineers Department there. But, as all Mr. Edye's list of Ceylon woods were in the vernacular, so, of Mr. Mendis' names several are in the Singhalese language, and the acceptance of some of his botanical terms requires much caution. When Mr. Thwaites completes his enumeration of the plants of Ceylon, it will be possible to identify botanically many of Messrs. Edye's and Mendis' woods, the importance of whose notes, however, even as they now are, cannot be over-rated—from the practical knowledge which these two writers possessed, and notices of many valuable timber trees are given in Major Drury's "Useful Plants" published in 1858. In the first edition of this work, published in the beginning of 1858, was gathered together the results of the labours during the previous 70 years, of the several contributors to this branch of economic knowledge. Mr. Latham of the Madras Railway, has recently noticed 87 woods in the Nalla Mallai mountains which border the eastern sides of the Cuddapah and Kurnool districts. Dr. Cleghorn's Forests and Gardens of South India has appeared, gathering together all his reports on the forests and their useful products. Dr. Bidie has, in 1862, given a list of 111 woods, and the Catalogues of the Calcutta and Madras Committees for the Exhibition of 1862, have given to the public the first list that has appeared of the woods of Mysore, contributed by Captain Puckle, accompanied by smaller Madras lists from Drs. Hunter and Shortt and from Mr. Pedro Coelho of South Canara, Dr. Brandis and the Moulmein Committee's lists of the woods of Pegu and Moulmein appeared in the Calcutta Catalogue, though Dr. Brandis' enumeration of, and invaluable practical remarks on, the woods of British Burmah, have been printed separately. The following is the list of the woods which Dr. Cleghorn reported on, at the Madras Exhibition of 1855:

1 Acacia Arabica.
Acacia catechu.
Acacia leucophlœa.
Acacia odoratissima.
Acacia speciosa.
Acacia sundra.
Adenanthera pavonina.
Ægle marmelos.
Ailanthus excelsa.
10 Alangium decapetalum.
Aquilaria agallocha.
Areca catechu.
Artocarpus hirsuta.
Artocarpus incisa.
Artocarpus integrifolia.
Atalantia monophylla.
Azadirachta Indica.
Bassia longifolia.
Bauhinia Richardiana.
20 Bauhinia tomentosa.
Bauhinia variegata.
Berrya ammonilla.
Bignonia suberosa.
Borassus flabelliformis

Briedelia spinosa.
Butea frondosa.
Cæsalpinia coriaria.
Cæsalpinia sappan.
Calophyllum inophyllum.
30 Careya arborea.
Careya sphœrica.
Caryota urens.
Casuarina equisitifolia.
Cathartocarpus fistula.
Cathartocarpus Roxburghii.
Cedrela toona.
Chickrassa tabularis.
Chloroxylon Swietenia.
Cicca disticha.
40 Citrus aurantium.
Cluytia collina.
Cocos nucifera.
Cordia latifolia.
Cyathea arborea.
Dalbergia latifolia.
Dalbergia sissoides.
Dalbergia sissoo.
Dillenia pentagyna.
Diospyros cordifolia.
50 Diospyros ebenaster.
Diospyros mabola.
Diospyros melanoxylon.
Ehretia lævis.
Elate sylvestris.
Emblica officinalis.
Embryopteris glutinifera.
Eriodendron anfractuosum.
Erythrina Indica.
Euphorbia tirucalli.
60 Euphoria litchi.
Eurya longifolia.
Feronia elephantum.
Ficus glomerata.
Ficus Indica.
Ficus infectoria.
Ficus nitida.
Ficus racemosa.
Ficus religiosa.
Ficus virens.
70 Gmelina aborea.
Gossypium acuminatum.
Grewia tiliæfolia.
Grewia Sp.
Guaiacum officinale.
Guatteria longifolia.
Guazuma tomentosa.
Hibiscus lampas.
Hæmatoxylon campechianum.
Hura crepitans.
80 Hydnocarpus inebrians
Inga dulcis.
Inga xylocarpa.
Jatropha multifida.
Jonesia asoca.
Kleinhovia hospita.
Kydia calycina.
Lagerstræmia microcarpa.
Lawsonia inermis.
Malphigia punicifolia.
90 Mangifera Indica.
Melia azadirach.
Mimusops elengi.
Mimusops hexandra.
Michelia Rheedii.
Morinda citrifolia.
Nauclea cadamba.
Nauclea cordifolia.
Parkia biglobosa.
Odina wodier.
100 Pavetta indica.
Pimenta vulgaris.
Poinciana regia.
Pongamia glabra.
Premna tomentosa.
Prosopis spicigera.
Psidium pyriferum.
Pterocarpus Indicus.
Pterocarpus marsupium.
Pterocarpus santalinus.
110 Pterospermum Indicum
Rottlera tinctoria.
Salmalia Malabarica.
Santalum album.
Sapindus emarginatus.
Schmidelia serrata.
Semicarpus anacardium.
Sethia Indica.
Soymida febrifuga.
Spathodea adenophylla.
120 Spathodea Sp.
Sterculia fœtida.
Sterculia guttata.
Stereospermum suaveolens.
Strychnos nux vomica.
Strychnos potatorum.
Syzygium jambolanum.
Tamarindus Indica.
Tecoma stans.
Tectona grandis.
130 Terminalia alata.
Terminalia belerica.
Terminalia Berryi.
Terminalia catappa.
Terminalia chebula.
Terminalia glabra.
Thespesia populnea.
Thevetia neriifolia.
Vachellia Farnesiana.
Vatica robusta.
140 Visenia umbellata.
Vitex alata.
Vitex altissima.
Wrightia antidysenterica.
Wrightia mollissima.
Wrightia tinctoria.
146 Zizyphus jujuba.

See Amherst, Burmah, Canara, Circars, Cuddapah, Ganjam, Moulmein, Mysore, Pegu, Penang.

MADU-KAH, the Tamil name of a Malabar and Canara tree, the wood of which is yellow and very small; its grain is close and heavy: it is not of much use or value.—*Edye, Forests of Malabar and Canara.*

MADURA. A district in the south of the Peninsula of India. The slopes of the Pulni hills and Cumbum valley are reported to contain valuable timber.

MAGADAMBOOM, Tam. A Travancore wood, of a white colour, specific gravity 0·462, used for light work generally.—*Col. Frith.*

MAH YUH GAH, Burm. A tree of Amherst, Tavoy and Mergui, maximum girth 2⅓ cubits, and maximum length 18 feet. Abundant all over the Tenasserim and Martaban provinces. When seasoned it floats in water. It is used for elephant bells; but is not a durable wood.—*Captain Dance.*

MAI KIN, Burm. A tree of Moulmein. Wood used as an ordinary building material. Fruit used in medicine.—*Cal. Cat. Ex.* 1862.

MAIKAY, Burm. MURRAYA, *Species?*

A timber of Amherst, Tavoy and Mergui, maximum girth 1 cubit and maximum length 15 feet. Abundant inland in Tavoy, but scarce near Moulmein. When seasoned it floats in water. It is too scarce for helves, but recommended for handles of planes, chisels, hammers, &c. It is used by Burmese for handles of knives and other weapons, and is a strong, tough wood, in grain like Box wood—(Vide Major Simpson's Report). It is recommended by the Ordnance carpenters as the very best wood, in the collection, for planes or for any purpose in lieu of box.—*Captain Dance.*

MAINABAN, Burm. A Tavoy wood, used for bows, lances, beams, rafters &c.

MAILAH, the Tamil name of a tree which grows to about twelve feet high, and twelve inches in diameter. It is generally curved, and is used in boat work. It produces a fruit which the wild pea fowl feed on; and is to be found in the forests of Malabar, and also in Ceylon.—*Edye, Forests of Malabar and Canara.*

MAI TAI YO. Burm. A tree of Amherst, Tavoy and Mergui, of maximum girth 2½ cubits and maximum length 22 feet. Found abundant all over the province. When seasoned it floats in water. Its wood is used for posts and many other purposes by the Burmese, and it is a particularly good wood for helves, being durable, light, and tough.—*Captain Dance.*

MALABAR, CANARA, COCHIN, TRAVANCORE and CEYLON TIMBERS. In the early part of this centnry, John Edye, Esq., of the Survey Department Royal Navy, described the forests of the Malabar coast and of Ceylon, and his essay descriptive of them and of their timber trees and fancy woods was read on the 16th May 1835 before the Royal Asiatic Society of Great Britain and printed at pages 324 to 377 of the second volume of their Journal. The 174 timbers and woods which he described were obtainable in the forests, above noted, which extend from Cape Comorin to Onnor (Honore), in the north part of Canara, being an extent of about 500 miles. The forests of Travancore and Cochin were and are still the property of native princes, but the northern parts and those of Ceylon belong to the British. Mr. Edye's descriptions were very complete in all relating to the qualities of the various woods, but the names he gave, were unfortunately in Tamil, Maleala, Canataka, Singhalese, Portuguese and Dutch, and the botanical names of only a few can be identified and a few more surmised. In the plan of this work, therefore, viz. describing each timber tree by its scientific name and subjoining the vernacular synonyms, there is much still to do, with Mr. Edye's list, if it is to be reduced to the botanical names. His list is as follows, and the few botanical names of recognisable trees are given.

Ahvi maram, MAL. Steam wood.
Ambalam, MAL. Wild mango.
Angely or Angilica, MAL. & TAM.
Anakuru, TAM.
Aralie, Porrel, Attu, Itti, MAL.
Ardda, MAL.
Atti, MAL.
Beati-maram, TAM. Bombay Black wood. ENG.
Bellerom, TAM. Kyndle, MAL. & CAN.
Bembur, TAM.
Boa or Boe, TAM. Poam, MAL.
Brallah, MAL.
Canjara, TAM. & MAL.
Cajom Mone, MAL. Cashew nut, ENG.
Chambogum, TAM.
Chari-maram, TAM. Acha maram, TAM. of Ceylon. Nuga-gaha, TAM. of Ceylon. Ebony. ENG.
Charu, MAL.
Chauna, MAL.
Cheru-puna, TAM. & MAL. or Real Mast Poon.

Of Peon, Poon or Puna, there are other four sorts:

Karapa puna, TAM. dark poon.
Malai puna, ,, hill ,,
Vellai ,, ,, white,,
Merchie ,, ,, which is very like American birch.

Chini, TAM., and Kasawha, MAL.
Choutal. MAL.
Curmbole, MAL.
Devedah, PORT., TAM. & MAL. Cedar of Libanus, ENG. Spanish cedar, ENG. Chittagong wood, ENG.
Dup-maram, MAL. & TAM. Nadenara, MAL.

Other two sorts of Dup-maram are

Macdenar, MAL.?
Paini Dup-maram, TAM.? Vatica Indica.

Edanah, TAM.
Eddellah, MAL.
Elavum, TAM.
Ellande, MAL.
Elupe-Maram, MAL.
Erupuna, TAM., and Erembui rapan, MAL.
Headie, MAL.
Horingi Tanga maram, TAM.
Horingi maram, TAM. Sapindus emarginatus. Soap nut. Soap apple.
Jambau, CAN.
Kadda Pilow, TAM. River side Jack wood.
Kahlaru, MAL.
Kajaw, MAL.
Kalayum, TAM., and Condle, MAL.
Kallow Mow, MAL.
Kaludumum, TAM.
Kalu vitte marda, TAM.?
Kamalah, TAM. Halmilile, SINGH. Somendille, SINGH.
Kangu Vittu, MAL.
Kara-Kundle, MAL.
Karangely, TAM., and Karakili, MAL.
Kareovam, MAL.
Karincolu, TAM., and Karinjurah, MAL.
Karindagarah, TAM.
Karingatta, MAL.
Karnara Vette.
Karuatagarah, TAM. & MAL.
Kathukevi, TAM.
Khounay, TAM., Kakay, MAL. & CAN.
Koir-pah, MAL.
Kulbagi, CAN.
Kurotu-palah, MAL.
Kurvah Tanga maram, TAM. Cinnamomum iners, Wild Cinnamon tree.
Madu-Kah, TAM.
Mailah, TAM.
Mangui or Mangoe, MAL. Mangifera Indica.
Marda, or Marthu, TAM. & MAL., and Martha, CAN.
Maruti, MAL.
Milulu, MAL.
Munchetty Maram, MAL.
Myhilenah, TAM., and Mylelu, MAL.
Myrole or Mirole, TAM. & MAL.
Nelu, TAM.
Nanah, TAM.
Narah, MAL.
Navellu maram, TAM. Tongue wood.
Nelle Pale, TAM. Emblica officinale.
Nidam Paini, MAL.
Nilam-pala, TAM.
Nila Pala, TAM.
Orupu-lingi-Maram, MAL.
Padri, TAM. & MAL.
Pallaga Payanye, MAL.
Pala Maram, MAL.
Paraty maram, TAM.
Patti Vayngu, MAL. Dogwood, ENG.
Penaru Palam Maram, MAL.
Perji, MAL.
Perra Maram, MAL., and Coia Maram, TAM.
Pong, TAM. & MAL.
Poreal Paini, TAM. & MAL.
Pulli Maram, TAM. Tamariud.
Punga Marum, TAM., MAL. and Puna Balle. Calophyllum *sp.*
Puoam, TAM.
Puoam Parasom, TAM.
Shini, TAM. & MAL. Buttress Tree, ENG.
Talle Tanga, MAL. & TAM.
Tambogum, TAM., and Vanponga, MAL.
Tani, TAM. & Jellam, MAL. Water wood, ENG.
Tanna, TAM.
Tawni, TAM., and Taniki Marum, MAL.
Tek or Teak, TAM. & MAL. Tectona grandis.
Telle or Payane, TAM. & MAL., also Dupi maram. TAM.
Tembow, MAL. Black Heart wood, ENG.
Tibelebu, CAN. and MAL. Nambogum, MAL.
Towtal, MAL.
Upputah, MAL.
Vardagour, MAL.
Vaw Karah, MAL.
Vayngie, TAM., and Mulu-Vengah, MAL. Pterocarpus marsupium.
Vellai Puna Pinu, TAM.
Vellai Venjah, TAM.
Velatti, TAM.
Velle-elow, MAL.
Velli-ellus. TAM.
Vellie Puna, MAL. Kat puna, MAL.
Vembah, TAM.
Venarah, MAL.
Vengendah, TAM. & MAL.
Veu-Teak, TAM., and Bellinger, MAL.
Vette Maram, MAL.
Villai Katti Marda, MAL.
Villai Marda, MAL.
Villa Vengah. TAM.?
Viram Pila or Jackwood, TAM. & MAL. Artocarpus integrifolia.

Timbers of Ceylon.

Attati, TAM.
Charlombi, TAM.
Chivendi, TAM.
Chomondri or Chalembry, TAM.
Ear gulie, TAM. or Iar gulie, TAM.
Hal, TAM.
Hatey or Arti, TAM.
Kandle, TAM.
Kanjurea, TAM.
Karangalle, TAM. Ebony. Charu maram, TAM. Acha maram, TAM. Nuga-gha. CAN.
Kartuma, TAM. Wild mango.
Kartu-Nedenari, TAM.
Kartu Tangie, TAM.
Kartu Toda, TAM.
Karucue-wach, TAM.
Karudu, TAM.
Katamanak, TAM., and Miniley, PORT.
Kauna, TAM.
Kayann, TAM.
Kuevea, TAM.
Kula, PORT.
Kuveama, TAM.
Maratina, TAM.
Mara-verie, TAM.
Marauda, TAM.
Margosa, PORT., and Vembu, TAM. & MAL.
Marvulinga or Marvilingum-Maram, TAM.
Mocheal, TAM.
Mulmuraca, TAM.
Mungevenah, TAM.
Mutherie, TAM. Buratu, PORT.
Nar-putte, TAM.
Naruvealy, TAM.
Narvell, Jambu, TAM. & PORT. Eugenia jambolana.
Odre, TAM.
Pali, TAM., Irambu, MAL., Palari, PORT. Iron wood, ENG.
Panichic, TAM.
Parcutille, TAM.
Pienche, TAM.
Piri, TAM.
Poverasie, TAM., and Santa Marie, PORT. Ceylon Tulip tree.

Puna, TAM.
Punde-cyann, TAM.
Pungul, TAM. Pongamia glabra.
Somendilla, TAM. & MAL. Halmile, DUT. PORT. Hameniel, „ „ Satin wood, ENG.
Tentukie, MAL.
Teru-Kundle, TAM.
Tiella, MAL. & TAM.
Vaghey, TAM.
Vanangu, TAM.
Vela Salu, TAM. White iron wood.
Velatte, TAM., and Ballanju, PORT.
Velcana, TAM.
Velle Aere, TAM. White Aere, ANGLO-TAM.
Velle Nealea, MAL.
Vell-viru, TAM.
Vengula-Cyam, TAM.
Veractal, TAM.
Veram Pelow, MAL. & TAM. Jack wood.
Verda-Canara, TAM.
Vernangu, TAM.
Vipenie, TAM.
Virey, TAM.
Vulocal or Vuloaylum Maram, TAM.
Yarvini, TAM. Crawn, PORT.

The descriptions given by Mr. Edye, of these woods, will be found under their respective Tamil, Canataka or Singhalese names, excepting the following woods, which have been accidentally omitted.

Akri Maram, in Malabar, is "steam wood," from its emitting steam when the root is cut. This tree grows to about ten inches in diameter, and fifteen feet long: it is a wood of little value. At times it is used for inferior purposes in the frames of native vessels, in repairs, &c. It is not very durable.—*Edye, Forests of Malabar and Canara.*

Ambalam, the Malayala name of a wood which produces a fruit considered by the natives to be the wild mangoe. The fruit is very acid, and, as well as the wood, is of no use.—*Edye, Forests of Malabar and Canara.*

Anakuru, the Tamil name of a tree which grows to about 30 feet long, and eighteen inches in diameter; at times the natives make small canoes of it, and use it in house building: it is not of much value.—*Edye, Forests of Malabar and Canara.*

Ardda, the Malayala name of a tree which grows to about ten inches in diameter, and twenty feet high: it is used in conjunction with the other woods, in country vessels, &c.—*Edye, Forests of Malabar and Canara.*

Atti, the Malayala name of a tree which grows to about twenty feet high, and from twelve to fifteen inches in diameter. It produces a sort of fig, which the natives use medicinally. The tree is rather scarce.—*Edye, Forests of Malabar and Canara.*

Beati-maram, or Bombay black-wood; a wood which grows in Malabar and Travancore to a large size; some trees five feet in diameter, and fifty feet long, have been brought from Travancore, but the wood is generally not more than twenty or twenty-five feet long, and from twenty inches to two feet in diameter. It might be procured in great quantities in Travancore and the Cochin forests. Much of this wood is used in England, and called rose-wood. Its general uses in India are for household furniture: great quantities are exported to Bombay, Madras, and Calcutta, for that purpose.—*Edye, Forests of Malabar and Canara.*

Bembur, the Tamil name of a tree which grows on the Coromandel coast: it is remarkably durable and strong. The few natives who build vessels on that coast prefer it to the other woods of the coast, which are not very abundant.—*Edye, Forests of Malabar and Canara.*

Brallah, the Malayala name of a tree that grows to about eight inches in diameter, and sixteen feet high. It is used by the natives on the coast for boats; and for timbers and knees in larger vessels: it is considered strong and durable.—*Edye, Forests of Malabar and Canara.*

Chambogum, the Tamil name of a tree, the most beautiful in appearance on the coast of Malabar; it is a very close-grained wood, and throws out rather a pleasant smell when cut. It is generally found in the forests of Travancore of about eighteen inches in diameter, and from twenty to twenty-five feet long, it produces a small round fruit which the natives use medicinally.—*Edye, Forests of Malabar and Canara.*

Chari-maram, the wood called ebony in England. (See Ceylon woods &c. named Achamaram, Nugagaha.)—*Edye, Forests of Malabar and Canara.*

Chauna, the name of a tree which grows in Malabar. It resembles the English beach, and is used by the natives for house work. It is not durable, nor is it remarkable for its growth, quality or uses.—*Edye, Forests of Malabar and Canara.*

Charu, the Malayala name of a jungle wood which grows to about forty feet high, and two feet in diameter. It is used in building native vessels, particularly for planks. It is not very durable, and is of little value except for those purposes. It is cheap and is easily procured from the banks of the rivers.—*Edye, Forests of Malabar and Canara.*

Chivendi, the Tamil name of a Ceylon tree which grows to about eighteen inches in diameter, and twenty feet in height. It is used in house work and for other purposes.—*Edye, on the Timber of Ceylon.*

Choutal, the Malayala name of a tree that grows to about forty feet in height, and eighteen inches in diameter. It is a wood which the coopers use in preference to the woods of the country for casks vats, tubs &c.—*Edye, Forests of Malabar and Canara.*

Devedah, is the Portuguese, Tamil, and Malayala name of a wood, known to Europeans by that of Cedar of Libanus, or Spanish cedar. This tree is to be found from Cape Comorin, south of Malabar, to the north part of Canara. It grows to a large size, from eighteen inches to two feet and a half in diameter, and from thirty to forty feet high. This may be considered a good wood, and might be found useful with the heavy woods in ship building. The texture of some trees is hard, and might be converted into good plank. It is much used by the natives for house work and furniture. It is imported into Ceylon, and to the coast of Coromandel, from Pegu and Rangoon and named Chittagong wood. I need not enter into any further detail of its qualities, as cedar is a common and well known wood to all Europeans.—*Edye, Forests of Malabar and Canara.*

There is also the "Vela-Devedah," or white cedar, which grows in the forests of Cochin and Travancore. It may be had in great quantities, and is said to be useful and durable. I know it to be a tough wood for boards and plank for boats and vessels, for which purpose it is generally used, as well as for house work. It grows to about two feet in diameter and from thirty to thirty five feet high: its grain resembles the red cedar, but it is closer grained and heavier.—*Edye, Forests of Malabar and Canara.*

The following 20 woods were collected, in 1846, by Dr. Gibson, Conservator of Forests in the Bombay Presidency, for Mr. Chapman, in connection with the projected "Great Indian Peninsular Railway."

Jamboo; a very heavy wood.	Seerass.
Kad kud.	Sood beebo.
Kelaho.	Sawree; a white, soft, close wood, very light.
Koompoly.	Teh pully.
Kendel; a heavy, strong, dark wood.	Jamboo or Jambu, Mimosa xylocarpa. This tree grows to a large size and is much valued in house building for its strength and toughness.
Kunganee.	Mairtee. Pentaptera coriacea. A very common tree both above and below the ghats, wood durable, and used in house, boat and ship building.
Kursing.	
Kumdee.	
Marlee; a very heavy, brown wood.	
Ombah.	
Pood goossa.	
Ruccuh korurah; a very straight-grained wood.	
Satannah; a light, soft, close wood.	
Sarrah.	

MALA-KA, BURM. A Tavoy wood, small sized, but strong; useful for handles.

MALA-KA BURM. In Amherst a timber used for gunstocks and carpenter's tools; it is a close, compact, but small sized wood, fit for hand-spikes, wheel-spokes, and the like.—*Captain Dance.*

MALAY PENINSULA. Notices of many of the timbers of this peninsula will be observed, under the heads of Amherst, Burmah, Moulmein, and Tavoy; and, doubtless, many of the woods used in Penang and Singapore, are brought from the mainland. The following is a list of 26 woods of the peninsula which were sent to the Exhibition of 1851, by the Singapore Committee.

Kledang.	Simpot ryah.
Beliong.	Merbow.
Changis.	Medangsi miniak.
Klat.	,, Buah yeah.
Timbusu.	,, konit.
Kaya brombong.	,, kitanahan.
Angsanah.	,, tandoh.
Tampinis.	Billion wangi.
Tanpang.	Jambu-ayer utan.
Kranji.	Peragah.
Slumar.	Kaya arang.
Simpoth bukit.	Leban.
Krantai.	Ranggas.
Kamuning.	

Singapore Catalogue of the Exhibition of 1862.

MALILER. In Penang, a small tree; wood white colour, used for boxes and ornamental work.

MALLY VELLY RAVAH. TAM. In Travancore, a wood of a light brown colour, specific gravity 0·664. Used for building houses only.—*Colonel Frith.*

MANDARA. A Penang wood, of a pale red colour, specific gravity 0·939. A small tree; used for ornamental furniture.—*Colonel Frith.*

MANEE AUKA, BURM. A tree of Moulmein. Wood used for ordinary house building purposes. The bark is used medicinally.—*Cal. Cat. Ex.* 1862.

MANEOGA, BURM. According to Major Benson, one of the Cinchonaceæ, its peculiarity of grain, which resembles oak, would make it useful for decorative purposes: very brittle.—*Major Benson.*

MANEEOGA, BURM. According to Captain Dance, stated by Burmese to be much used for rice pounders. Its maximum girth 4 cubits and maximum length 30 feet. Abundant all over the Tenasserim and Martaban provinces. When seasoned it floats in water. It is not a good wood, as, when stored, it soon dies and rots; the roots are used for medicine; the fruit is eaten by Burmese, and the wood is well spoken of, though favorable specimens had not been seen, by Captain Dance. *(Note*—Are the last three woods identical?)

MANGIFERA. A genus of plants belonging to the natural order *Anacardiaceæ.* Three or four species of this genus are enumerated—as *M. fœtida* of Loureiro, a native of Cochin-China and the Moluccas: *M. laxiflora,* indigenous in Mauritius; *M. Indica,* the mango tree of India, is cultivated everywhere, and *M. sylvatica* of Roxburgh, a native of the hilly districts bordering on Silhet, where it grows to a great size, and is called Lukshmee-Am. It bears a fruit which ripens in February and March, and is eaten by the natives, though not so palatable as even a bad mango. It is also dried and kept by them for medicinal purposes. *M. oppositifolia,* Roxburgh, a native of Rangoon, is proposed by Messrs. Wight and Arnott to be formed into a distinct genus. The following merit distinct notice as trees yielding timber.

MANGIFERA ATTENUATA.

Tawsa thayet. BURM.

Found in the Pegu and Tounghoo Forests, but scarce; wood dark brown.—*McClelland.*

MANGIFERA FŒTIDA, *Loureiro.* HORSE MANGO. This is a large mango cultivated at Mergui, and quite a favorite with the natives. It has an odour resembling the dorian, and like that has been introduced from the Straits. Wood not known.—*Dr. Mason.*

MANGIFERA INDICA, *Linn.; Roxb.; W. & A.*

Mangifera montana, *Heyne.*
,, domestica, *Gærtn., Rheede.*

Am. BENG.	Makandamu. SANS.
That-yat. BURM.	Ma maram. TAM.
Mavena. CAN.	Mamari. TEL.
Mango. ENG.	Mavi. ,,
Am. HIND.	Mamidi chettu. TEL.
Palam. JAV.	Ela (fragrant) mavi. ,,
Kapalam. LAMPUNG.	Gujju (dwarf) mamidi. ,,
Ampalam. MALAY.	Racha mamidi. ,,
Mampalam. ,,	Tiyya mamidi. ,,
Mava. MALEAL.	Ambo. URIA.

A tree generally diffused over all the warmer parts of Asia: but it extends as far north as 30° and has been successfully introduced into the West Indies. It grows to a great size, with an erect trunk, and dark coloured cracked bark. Its flowering time is January, February and March: the fruit ripens in May, June and July, and is one of the most grateful fruits of the tropical parts of Asia. The wood is of a dull grey colour, porous, yet pretty durable if kept dry, but soon decays if exposed to wet, of the effect of which it is very sensitive. In very large old trees it acquires a light chocolate color towards the centre of the trunk, and larger branches. This is hard, closer grained and much more durable. It is generally used for constructing massoolah boats and for packing cases, the cabinet makers at Madras prefer it to other wood for veneering on: it is also generally used by coach builders, cabinet makers and others, where common light wood is required, being the cheapest wood obtained. It is but little used in Coimbatore, as many much better woods are there procurable; but, in Southern India, is employed generally for packing cases, boarding and rough work. Mr. Rohde also mentions that the wood has the property of holding a nail faster than any other wood. In Madras, it is one of the most common woods used for backs and linings of furniture. Mr. Edye remarks that many trees are found three feet in diameter, and thirty feet high, that the wood is of a whitish colour, and is not durable or of much value, but that the natives make canoes of it. Dr. Gibson says it is a very serviceable wood for planks, when not exposed to wet, and is much used for house purposes, but much less for carts. It seems to bear the action of salt water better than that of fresh; is hence used for canoes. It could be readily creosoted. Captain Puckle mentions it is used in Mysore for the solid wheels of country carts, and rough furniture. The kernels are large and seem to contain some nourishment, they are however, made no use of excepting during times of scarcity and famine, they are then boiled in the steam of water and used as an article of diet. The engrafted fruit is much prized by Europeans. Propagating by layers, and grafting by approach, are the only modes of certainly continuing fine sorts, as well as of improving them. These have the advantage also of bearing when small in size, that is, only a few feet in height, and therefore well suited to culture in the hot-houses of Europe.—*Edye, Forests of Malabar and Canara, Captains Macdonald, Beddome and Puckle, Cal. Cat. Ex. of* 1862, *Elliot's Flora Andhrica, Mr. Rohde in Madras Cat. of* 1861, *also MSS., Eng. Cyc., Drs. Gibson, Wight and Cleghorn, Madras Ex. Jury Rep.* 1855, *Madras Cat. Ex.* 1862.

MANGIFERA OPPOSITIFOLIA.?

Mayan. Burm.

A tree of Moulmein. Wood used for building purposes. Fruit edible.—*Cal. Cat. Ex.* 1862.

MANJA CADAMBOO, Tam.? in Travancore, a wood of a light yellow colour: used for packing cases.—*Col. Frith.*

MANKADU. In Penang, a wood of a brown color. A kind of Dumarlout, much used for beams.

MANNY MAROOTHA, Tam. Wood of a flesh color, used for carts and in building houses. —*Col. Frith.*

MARATINA, the Tamil name of a Ceylon tree which grows to about twenty inches in diameter, and from fifteen to twenty feet in height. It is sometimes used by the natives for house and boat work. —*Edye, on the Timber of Ceylon.*

MARAUDA, the Tamil name of a Ceylon tree which is very heavy and close grained. It is one of the best sorts of Ceylon wood; of a dark brown colour, and grows to about twenty inches in diameter, and twenty feet in height.—*Edye, on the Timber of Ceylon.*

MARAVA, Can.? A wood of South Canara used for building purposes.—*Mad. Cat. Ex.* 1862.

MARA-VERIE, the Tamil name of a Ceylon tree which is much the same as the Vell verie in size and quality. It is used for natives' huts, &c., but is not of much value.—*Edye, on the Timber of Ceylon.*

MARDA or MARTHU, *Tamil, Malealo,* MARTHA *in Canarese.* This tree of Malabar and Canara is of large dimensions and perfectly straight, it is of a dark brown colour and very close grained; many trees are to be found on the banks of the Maletur river, of a hundred feet long, and about twenty-four inches in diameter. From the apparent qualities and native uses of this wood, there is no doubt that it might be converted with advantage into plank, thick-stuff, beams, &c. for ships, where strength is required, and where weight is of little consideration. It runs from sixty-two to seventy pounds the cubic foot, when green: the native carpenters use it with the teak for beams in the pagodas, &c.; it is considered durable; and contains a quantity of oil. The forests in Travancore abound with trees of this sort, which can be obtained on the rivers' banks, an important consideration in the expense of procuring such valuable wood. There is an inferior description which is named "Villai Marda," or White Marda; it much resembles the former tree, excepting in size and in leaf, both of which are considerably smaller, and it is said by the natives to be inferior in quality and durability; it is more like the English oak in grain than any wood Edye met with. These trees, and also the former sort, are found in patches of some hundred together, and generally on the banks of rivers. There is another sort named "Villai Katti Marda," which is the White Lump Marda. This tree grows to about twelve or fifteen inches in diameter, and twenty-five feet long. In Malabar there is another sort, which is well known to the natives by the name of "Kalu Vithe Marda," the Dark Stone Marda, and may be considered of the same quality as the last sort. It is used for the frames of vessels, and many other purposes, for which it answers well.—*Edye, Forests of Malabar and Canara.* (*Note*—These seem to be species of Terminalia, probably T. alata, T. Berryi, T. chebula and T. glabra.)

MARGOSA, the Portuguese name, and Vembu, the Tamil and Malayala names of a Ceylon tree, which grows from 18 inches to three and a half feet in diameter. In appearance it is much like mahogany, and is used by the natives for general purposes. It produces a fruit from which an oil is extracted which is used medicinally.—*Edye, on the Timber of Ceylon.* (*Note*—This seems to be the Azadirachta Indica.)

MARIBOT. A very large tree in Penang; wood of a purple colour; specific gravity 0·939. Difficult to work, but used for furniture.—*Col. Frith.*

MARUTI, the Malayala name of a Ceylon tree which grows to about fourteen inches in diameter, and from twenty to twenty-four feet high. It produces a fruit which the natives use as a medicine, and from which, also, they extract an oil which they use in lamps, and in anointing the body after bathing.—*Edye, Forests of Malabar and Canara.*

MARVULINGA, or MARVILINGUM MARAM, the Tamil name of a Ceylon tree which grows to about sixteen inches in diameter, and eight feet high. It is praised by the natives for sandals and toys &c. It produces a kind of pod, which, with the bark and leaves, is used with much success in cases of intermittent fevers.—*Edye, on the Timber of Ceylon.*

MARYA CADAMBA, TAM.? A Travancore wood, of a yellow colour; used for packing cases.—*Col. Frith.* (*Note*—Is this not a species of Nauclea?)

MAROOTHOO, TAM.? A Tinnevelly wood of a white brown colour, used in building in general.—*Col. Frith.*

MARTABAN TIMBER TREES. Dr. Wallich noticed the following timbers of this province.

Calophyllum, Thurappe. BURM., a large tree; used for masts and spars.

Careya, Zaza, used for posts, &c.

Cynometra, Maimegn, a small tree.

Diospyros? Ryamucha, used in house building.

Elæocarpus, very large timber: used for masts and house posts.

Fagræa fragans, Annah-beng, compact, hard, yellow, and very beautiful wood; little used.

Gordonia? Zaza, loose common timber.

Hopea odorata, Tengaun, an immense tree.

Meenabon, a durable pliant wood.

Pongamia atropurpurea, Legun, a noble tree used in boat and house building.

Quercus Amherstiana, Tirbbee, a large tree; used in boat building.

Tectona grandis, teak wood.

Terminalia bialata.

Xanthophyllum, Saphew, a very large tree; used for posts and rafters.

Pterospermum Indicum, Lingoa wood, or the Amboyna wood of commerce, is from Ceram in the Moluccas. It was imported in considerable quantities into Great Britain during the period in which the Moluccas were British possessions. This wood, which is very durable and capable of a high polish, is abundant at Ceram, New Guinea, and throughout the Molucca seas. It can be obtained in any quantity, if the precaution is taken of ordering it during the previous trading season. The Kaya Buka of commerce is the gnarled excrescence of this tree.

Large circular slabs of the Lingoa wood, from Ceram, 6 feet to 9 feet in diameter are obtained by taking advantage of the spurs which project from the base of the trunk, as the tree itself has not sufficient diameter to furnish such wide slabs. They are occasionally met with as large as 9 feet, but the usual size is from 4 to 6 feet.

Kaya Buka is obtained from the Moluccas, from the knotty excrescences which are found on the stems of the same tree. It is brought to Singapore by the Eastern traders from Ceram, Arru and New Guinea, and is sold by weight. It is much esteemed as a fancy wood.

MASKAW. A Penang wood of a light brown colour; specific gravity 1·016. Used for palankeens, carriages, furniture &c.—*Col. Frith.*

MASOODAH, TAM.? Qu. Maroodah? A Travancore wood of an ash colour, 2 to 3 feet in circumference; used for building.—*Col. Frith.*

MATHA, HIND.? A tree of Chota Nagpore, with a hard, white timber.—*Cal. Cat. Ex.* 1862.

MATHGIRIE VAMBOO, TAM. In Tinnevelly, a wood of a whitish brown colour when young, and is a strong light wood: used for general purposes. When old, it is of a red colour, but still is a strong light wood.—*Col. Frith.*

MA-THLOA, in Amherst, a timber used for house posts; probably Artocarpus integrifolius, or jack-wood.

MAWAN, HIND. A tree of Chota Nagpore, with a soft, grey wood.—*Cal. Cat. Ex.* 1862.

MAY-BYOUNG, BURM. A tree of Tenasserim, Amherst, Tavoy and Mergui, of maximum girth 3 cubits, and maximum length 18 feet. Not abundant, but found near the seaside, and near the mouths of rivers along the coast. When seasoned, it sinks in water. It is used for anchors of boats, and for the sticks of oil mills; it is an uncommonly heavy and a durable wood, but not tough enough for ordnance purposes generally, though from its hardness, it makes good planes and turns well. Dr. Mason says it is a hard, tough, knotty wood, which the Tavoyers select for anchors to their large boats, wooden anchors laden with stones constituting the greater part in use in 1832. He had never seen the tree.—*Captain Dance, Dr. Mason.*

MAY-KLIN, Burm. A Tavoy timber, used for rudders and anchors.—*Dr. Wallich.*

MAY-MAKA, Burm. A Tavoy timber, used in ship building.—*Dr. Wallich.*

MAY-RANG, Burm. A Tavoy timber, said to be very durable.—*Dr. Wallich.*

MAY-SHOUNG, Burm. A tree, of maximum girth 2½ cubits, and maximum length 18 feet. Scarce, but found on the sea coast from Amherst to Mergui. When seasoned, it floats in water. It is a short fibred, brittle, yet soft wood, called, but erroneously, a kind of Annan by the Burmese. It is not a durable wood, and, is, besides, too scarce for ordnance purposes.—*Captain Dance.*

MAY-TOBEK, Burm. In Tavoy, a wood used for the bottoms of ships; preferred to teak.—*Dr. Wallich,*

MAY-YAM, Burm.? A Tavoy timber, an indestructible, strong, heavy, dark red wood.—*Captain Dance.*

MAZA-NENG, Burm., or **MAGA-NENG**, Burm. In Amherst, a close grained wood, nearly allied to teak. It is used for house posts, carts, boats, paddles, oars, &c.

MEE-KYAUNG-KYAY, Burm. In Tavoy, a heavy wood, not attacked by insects.—*Dr. Wallich.*

MEENABAN, Burm. Tavoy Lance wood, Eng. Regarded by Dr. Mason to be one of the Apocynaceæ. A tree in Martaban, Tenasserim, Amherst, Tavoy and Mergui, of maximum girth 1½ cubits, even in Tavoy and Mergui where largest, and maximum length 12 feet. Found in moderate quantities in Tavoy, Mergui and the adjacent islands; also in smaller scanting and scarcer in Amherst province. When seasoned, it floats in water. It is used by Burmese for bows, spears, walking sticks, dhar and chisel handles, &c. and is an excellent tough, hard, elastic, pliant and durable wood, bears a beautiful polish, and makes excellent furniture, when wanted in but small size only. It is much recommended for handles of screw drivers, hammers, planes, and all kinds of tools; also for all purposes for which a close grained heavy wood is required, (*Vide* Major Simpson's Report.) Does not seem to stand exposure to the direct rays of the sun well, but under cover is found to be a thoroughly good wood for planes, for which this is especially recommended, also for screw drivers and all kind of turning. This is good for all those purposes for which box is now imported.—*Captain Dance, Dr. Wallich.*

MEEP-THUA-BAN, Burm. In Tavoy, a small sized, compact, grey wood: used for handles, &c.—*Dr. Wallich.*

MEET-GNYOO, Burm. or **NEET-GNYOO**, Burm. A fruit tree of Amherst, with a red coloured, useful, strong, heavy wood, probably a species of Acacia.

MEGEONE, Burm. In Tavoy a large tree used in building.—*Dr. Wallich.*

MEHRA FOREST, HAZARA. The following timbers were sent to the Exhibition of 1862:

Walnut. Juglans	Olive
Toon. Cedrela	Buroongi
Bear. Pinus longifolia	Umloke
Ash. Fraxinus	Mulberry
Reen. Quercus	Loon. Pyrus
Yew	Kungur or Kukker. Fraxinus
Kayan	Dear or Deodar. Cedrus deodara
Fir (Pinus longifolia)	
Kalanath. Cerasus	

Cal. Cat. Ex. 1862.

MELANORRHŒA USITATISSIMA, *Wall.*

Thit-si. Burm.	Lignum vitæ of Pegu.
Varnish tree. Eng.	Kheu of Munipur.
Burmese varnish tree. „	

This tree grows from Munipur southwards to Tavoy. It was first seen near Prome, but is found in different parts of Burmah and along the coast from Tenasserim to Tavoy, extending from the latter in 14° to 25° N. lat., and Dr. Wallich has identified it with the Kheu or Varnish-tree of Munipoor, bordering on the north-east frontier districts of Silhet and Tipperah. It grows, especially, at Kubbu, an extensive valley elevated about 500 feet above the plains of Bengal, and 200 miles from the nearest sea-shore and it attains its greatest size there, some of the trees having clear stems of 42 feet to the first branch, with a circumference near the ground of 13 feet. It forms extensive forests, and is associated with the two staple timber trees of continental India, teak and saul (*Tectona grandis* and *Shorea robusta*), especially the latter, and also with the gigantic Wood-oil tree, a species of *Dipterocarpus*. It is in full foliage during the rainy season, which lasts for five months, from the middle of May until the end of October. It is rare in the Irrawaddy valley, but common in the forests east of the Sitang river, particularly south-east of Sitang Town.* It is very common above the parallel of Tounghoo and grows there to a girth of six feet and it is plentiful in the Tounghoo and Prome Forests, especially in the former. It is found very abundant in Amherst province, and grows in Tavoy and Mergui. Captain Dance says that its maximum girth is certainly 3 and said to be 4 or 5 cubits and maximum length certainly 20 and said to be 30 feet; and Dr. Brandis tells us that, in a full grown tree on good soil, the average length of the trunk to the first branch is 30 feet and average girth measured at 6 feet from the ground is 9 feet. Its wood is the Lignum vitæ of Pegu, and is of a dark red color, or a dark brown, dense structure: and of particularly fine close grain. Of extreme closeness of grain and density of structure, it has a specific gravity so great, that it serves in place of iron as anchors for native boats. A cubic foot weighs lbs. 54, but it is not brought to Moulmein so heavy as Dr. McClelland describes it. When seasoned it floats in water. It is very strong, durable, hard and tough, it is found to answer well for cogs of machinery (Vide Artillery Records with report of woods by Captains Simpson and Babington, dated Moulmein 25th May 1842) and is used by the Burmese for tool helves and the stocks of their wooden anchors, &c. For, the anchors of Burmese boats are always of wood to which stones are lashed, the flakes being of Pyeng Khadoe and the stocks of Theetsee or of some other heavy wood. Its great hardness and weight prevent its being employed in house building; but, it would answer for sheaves or block-pulleys and other purposes connected with machinery, where great strength and density are required. It is therefore recommended for handles of tools, also of sheave blocks, for machinery generally, for railway sleepers, for gun stocks, for rammer heads, and for helves, *in short* for all purposes where a strong yet not very heavy wood is useful. It exudes a black gum which repels ants, and is used by the Burmese as a varnish. At Prome a considerable quantity of this varnish is extracted but very little at Martaban. It is collected by inserting a pointed joint of a bamboo, which is closed at the other end, into wounds made in the trunk and principal boughs, which are removed after 24 or 48 hours, and their contents, which rarely exceed a quarter of an ounce, emptied into a basket made of bamboo and rattan previously varnished over. The collecting season lasts from January to April. In its pure state it is sold at Prome at about 2*s*. 6*d*. for about 3½ lbs. avoirdupois. It is procurable in great quantities from Munipoor, where it is used for paying river-craft and for varnishing vessels designed to contain liquids. The drug, is conveyed to Silhet for sale by the merchants who come down annually with horses and other objects of trade. In Burmah, Dr. Wallich states that almost every article of household furniture intended to contain either solid or liquid food is lacquered by means of it. The process consists in first coating the article with a layer of pounded calcined bones, after which the varnish is laid on thinly, either in its pure state or variously coloured. The most difficult part consists in the drying. It is also much employed in the process of gilding; the surface, being first besmeared with this varnish, has then the gold leaf immediately applied to it. Finally, the beautiful Pali writing of the Burmese on ivory, palm-leaves, or metal, is entirely done with this varnish in its native and pure state.—*Voigt quoting Wallich, Drs. McClelland, Mason, and Brandis, Cal. Cat. Ex.* 1862, *Captain Dance.*

MELIA, *Species*.

Hulanhick. SINGH.

A tree of the central province of Ceylon, the wood of which is used in house building: a cubic foot weighs lbs. 39, and it is esteemed to last 50 years.—*Mr. Mendis.*

MELIA AZEDARACH, *Linn.; D C.; Roxb.; W. Ic.*

Bavena. CAN.
Bayvena. „
Lilac. ENG.
Bead tree. „
Persian lilac. „
Common bead tree. „
Pride of India. ENG.
Dek. HIND. ?
Nim. HIND. & MAHR.
Male vempu. TAM.
Vepa manu. TEL.
Turka vepa. „

Its flowers.

Nim ka phul. DUK.
Vaypum pu. TAM.
Vaypa puvvu. TEL.

This is one of the Meliaceæ, or Meliads, a natural order of 33 genera and 150 species of trees or shrubs, inhabiting all countries within the tropics, but very rare in colder climates: though this plant is now naturalised in the south of Europe. In general, the species are bitter and astringent, but they are sometimes dangerously poisonous, acting violently as emetics and purgatives. Notwithstanding this, the pulpy fruit of the *Lanseh* is esteemed in the Indian Archipelago; and that of *Milnea edulis* is eaten in Silhet where it seems to resemble the litchi and longan of China. This species grows in Syria, the north of India and in China, in gardens all over the south of India. When in flower it has some resemblance to the lilac, and its flowers are very fragrant. It flowers during the hot season; thrives luxuriantly, and becomes a large useful timber tree, of very great beauty. It has a soft reddish coloured, rather loose textured wood, which however takes a pretty good polish, and is much used in the peninsula for cabinet-making purposes, under the name of bastard cedar. The mature wood however is hard, durable and handsomely marked. It is used for common furniture, but it warps and splits.—*Voigt, Drs. O'Shaughnessy, Wight, Gibson and Cleghorn, Eng. Cyc.*

MELIA ROBUSTA, *Roxb.*

A large tree, native of the Konkan and Mysore and Malabar: in seven years the trunk of one raised in the Calcutta gardens attained a circumference of forty-four inches and a height of forty-six feet.—*Mr. Rohde, MSS.*

MELIA SEMPERVIRENS, *Roxb., Flor. Ind.*

Melia Bukayun, *Royle.*

Ban. AR.
Bam. ? „
Maha nimba. BENG.
Bukayun. ENG.
Ever green Bead tree. ENG.
Bukayun HIND.
Bukarjun. „
Daracht-i-azad. PERS.
Bukayun, Bukain. „

This is a smaller tree than the M. Azedarach—the flowers bluish. It is common at Ajmeer; as is also the large deciduous variety. This is the chief tree in Northern India compounds, being very ornamental when in blossom and odoriferous. It grows in Persia, Nepaul and Kumaon, and, so far as I have seen, is not known in Peninsular India. Nevertheless, Dr. Gibson thus notices the "Melia azadirachta," or "*Neem.*" The garden Neem; "our Melia sempervirens I take to be the one here meant. The wood is worthless, except for cabinet-work, for which it is fitted by its colour and grain," and at another place he says, that "Melia bukaen, "*Bukkun*" differs from Melia azadirachta in several respects. I have seen it only in the upper country. Though very similar to the last in leaf, and general appearance. The smoothness of the bark and smaller size of the fruit at once indicate a distinction. The tree is found only about cultivated holdings. The wood is very strong and valuable for beams, roof-dunnage for terraces, and many other purposes. It has also the useful property of shooting from the root when once cut down with as much vigour as teak does. It is a tree deserving of extensive increase." I am unable to reconcile these remarks.—*Voigt, Dr. O'Shaughnessy, pp.* 243, 244, *Genl. Med. Top. p.* 193, *Dr. Gibson.*

MELIA COMPOSITA, *Willde.*

Melia superba, *Roxb., Flor. Ind. p.* 396.

Neembara. MAHR.

A great tree, of Mysore, found near the Parr ghat and not uncommon in the Konkan jungles, and seen occasionally in Guzerat. Its wood is used in making frames for native drums. The wood is of good quality, but inferior in strength and durability to that of Azadirachta Indica, the common or mountain Neem.—*Dr. Gibson.*

MELICOCCA TRIJUGA.

Kobin. BURM.

A most valuable timber, employed by the natives of Burmah for cart wheels, oil-mills, and other purposes requiring great strength and solidity. It is found in greatest perfection on the banks of the Sitang in the Kareen forests above Tounghoo; but it is also found throughout the Pegu and Tounghoo forests in abundance, more particularly the latter. It is also found along with teak in Tharawaddy and Prome forests. It is a large tree, every where procurable, in the Southern forests of Pegu, affording a strong tough wood, of which the Burmese make their excellent solid cart wheels. Light brown wood.—*Dr. McClelland, No. IX. Govt. of India Report, p.* 2, *Cal. Cat. Ex.* 1862.

MELICOCCA TRIJUGA??

Gyoo Tha. BURM.

Under these names, there was sent to the London Exhibition of 1862, the timber of a tree of Moulmein. The wood of which is used for bows, being tough and elastic.—*Cal. Cat. Ex.* 1862. (*Note*—Is this Gyoo Tha, identical with Kobin?)

MELIUSA VELUTINA, *Hf. & Th.*

Tha-boot-kyee. BURM.

This tree grows all over the plains of British Burmah. Its wood is used for the poles of carts and harrows, yokes, spearshafts, oars, &c. &c. A cubic foot of it weighs lbs. 42. In a full grown tree on good soil the average length of the trunk to the first branch is 15 feet and average girth, measured at 6 feet from the ground is 5 feet.—*Dr. Brandis, Cal. Cat. Ex.* 1862.

MEMECYLON, a genus of plants of the East Indies, shrubs or small trees, M. cuneatum, is a small tree of the central province of Ceylon at an elevation of 3,000 feet. M. ellipticum, also a small tree between Galle and Ratnapoora. M. Gardneri and M. leucanthum, grow at a height of 2,000 to 5,000 feet in the central province. M. orbiculare and M. ovoideum, in Ambagamowa: M. orbiculare at Hinidoon Corle. M. parviflorum, in the central province at 7,000 feet, and M. rhinophyllum and M. rostratum at 3,000, and M. sylvaticum, is common in forests at an elevation of 4,000 feet.—*Thw. En. Pl. Zeyl.*

MEMECYLON TINCTORIUM, *Kön.; W. & A.; W. Ic.*

Memecylon ramiflorum, *Lam.*

Anjuna. MAHR. | Surpa? MAHR.
Kurpa. „

Voigt indicates this as a shrub of Sylhet, the western ghats, and Coromandel coast. But, Dr. Gibson gives two notices of woods under this botanical name. Writing from Canara and Sunda, he says, Memecylon tinctorium; Surpa, *Mahr.* Iron wood of two species. On the upper head of the ghats; wood very tough and strong for cart axles, &c. The beautiful flowers extensively used as a dye. Writing of the forests generally he says Memecylon tinctorium, "Kurpa," "Anjuna." A tree of rather a small size: common on the ghats above; not seen elsewhere. Wood is very strong and tough. Does not yield readily to wet. Is much employed, when procurable of sufficient size, for agricultural implements, cart-furnishing, &c.—*Gibson.*

MENG-BA, BURM., or MING-BA, BURM. In Amherst, a timber used for house posts and rafters. The wood looks like a kind of saul, and would answer all the purposes of that wood.

MERESINGHA, URIA. In Ganjam and Gumsur, a tree of extreme height 30 feet, circumference 2½ feet and height from the ground to the intersection of the first branch, 8 feet. It is tolerably common, and burnt for firewood. The leaves are used in curry stuff.—*Captain Macdonald.*

MESUA, *Species.* Pynaroo? *Tam.*, according to Dr. Gibson, is the Malabar name of a species of Mesua. The Pynaroo gives one of the finest woods he had seen.—*Dr. Gibson.*

MESUA, *Species.* Irool maram, *Tam.* Under these names, Mr. McIvor sent to the Madras

Exhibition of 1855, a wood from the Nelambore jungles : common, much used by the natives for building purposes : durable and not liable to be attacked by insects.—*Mr. McIvor in M. E. J. R.*

MESUA COROMANDELINA, *W. Ic.*

A tree of the forests between Galle and Ratnapoora, at no great elevation, wood not known.—*Thw. En. Pl. Zeyl.*

MESUA FERREA, *Linn ; D C.*

Mesua nagaha, *Gard.*	Nagassarium, *Rumph.*
Arbor naghas, *Burm.*	

Nag-keshur. BENG.	Kesaramu Naga sara. SANS.
Gungau. BURM.	Kinjalkamu. SANS.
Iron wood tree. ENG.	Irul Maram. ? ? ? TAM.
Nagkesar. HIND.	Chikati manu ? TEL.
Nag Champa. MAHR.	Naga kesara chettu. TEL.
Belietta-champagam. MALEAL	Suvarnam. „

This tree grows in Ceylon, in Peninsular and northern India, in Burmah, Tenasserim, and Java. It has several varieties, or it so varies in different localities, that botanists have given several names to it. Sir William Jones says that this tree is one of the most delightful on earth ; and that the delicious odour of its blossoms justly gives them a place in the quiver of Camadeva, the Hindoo god of love. It is found chiefly in gardens in Bengal, where it flowers in the beginning of the warm season. It is cultivated in gardens at Jaepoor, and is there very ornamental and the flowers fragrant. Dr. Gibson had not seen it in Bombay forests, but much about villages and Brahmins' gardens in the southern parts of the Bombay presidency. It is cultivated in Pegu on account of the beauty and fragrance of its flowers but is wild in Tenasserim. In the Bombay presidency the tree never reaches any great diameter, but the wood is very strong and tough. In Pegu, in a full grown tree on good soil, the average length of the trunk to the first branch is 20 feet, and average girth measured at 6 feet from the ground is 5 feet. A cubic foot weighs lbs. 69. The wood is said to be used for furniture. The dried anthers are fragrant ; the flowers and leaves are used in Bengal as antidotes to snake poison.—*Ains. Mat. Med.* 1813, *p.* 163, *Gen. Med. Top. p.* 199, *Dr. O'Shaughnessy, p.* 230, *Dr. Gibson, Dr. Brandis, Cal. Cat. Ex. of* 1862, *Dr. Mason, Thw. En. Pl. Zeyl.*

METROSIDEROS (from μήτρυ, the heart of a tree, and σίδηρος, iron), a genus of plants belonging to the natural order *Myrtaceæ* so named because of the hardness of their inner woods, *M. lucida,* a beautiful tree, occurs as far south as Lord Auckland's Islands, in lat. 50½ south. *M. polymorpha,* is a tree of the Sandwich Islands, and is said to be the plant from which are made the clubs and other weapons employed in warfare by the South Sea Islanders and M. verus, of China ? Java and Amboyna, is said to furnish the iron wood of China. It grows among rocks. The Chinese and Japanese value its wood for making rudders, anchors, &c., for their ships and boats. The bark is used in Japan as a remedy in mucous discharges, diarrhœa, and dysentery. It is usually mixed with some aromatic, as Penang cloves, or nutmeg.—*Eng. Cyc., Voigt.*

METROXYLON SAGO.

Sagus Konigii.

Rambaya. MALAY.

Is cultivated in the Eastern Archipelago, to obtain sago from its wood.—*Seeman.*

MEZZALE, BURM. A tree of Amherst, Tavoy and Mergui, of maximum girth 4 cubits and maximum length 30 feet. Found scattered, not very abundant, all over the provinces. When seasoned it floats in water. It is used by the Burmese for rulers, mallets and walking sticks ; is of very handsome streaked grain like palmyra wood, but not sufficiently durable to be recommended for ordnance purposes.—*Captain Dance.*

MIAUP-BOUT. Used for furniture, &c.

MICHELIA : a genus of plants of the order Magnoliaceæ, some of which furnish useful woods. Further information is required regarding M. aurantiaca, *Wall.*, a tree of Pegu : M. kisopa, *Buch.*, a tree of the forests of Nepaul, and M. oblonga, a tree of the Khassya hills.—*Voigt.*

MICHELIA CHAMPACA, *Linn.*

Champaka. BENG.	Sampenga chettu. TEL.
Champa. „	Champakamu, TEL.
Sumpaghy. CAN.	Champeyamu. „
Chumpa. DUK.	Gand'ha p'hali. „
Bongas jampacca, MALAY.	Hem an gamu. „
Champakam. MALEAL.	Heman push pakamu. TEL.
Schampakam. „	Kanchanamu. TEL.
Champaca. SANS.	Konchona ? URIA.
Sappoo. SINGH.	
Shembugha maram. TAM.	

A tree of the Moluccas, of Java, of most parts of India and Ceylon, which flowers and fruits mostly throughout the year. Captain Macdonald seems to describe this tree in Ganjam and Gumsur as "Konchona," *Uria.* Michelia champaca? Of extreme height 30 feet, circumference 2½ feet and height from the ground to the intersection of the first branch, 8 feet. Tolerably common. Ploughshares are occasionally made of the wood. The flowers are offered at the shrines of the hindoo divinities. There are two varieties of the tree called respectively the "Dhobo" and "Rongo." Its wood weighs lbs. 40 to the cubic foot and it is said to last 20 to 30 years :—In Ceylon it is used for carriages, palanquins and in buildings. Captain Puckle says, it makes very handsome furniture ; and polishes well, grows to a very large size, and has a yellow sweet scented flower.—*Voigt, Mr. Mendis, Captain Macdonald, Captain Puckle.*

MICHELIA DOLTSOPA, *Buch.*

A tree of the forests of Nepaul, wood fragrant, excellent, used in Nepaul for house building.—*Voigt.*

MICHELIA NILAGIRICA, *W. Ic. Zenk.*

Pila Champa. HIND.	Walsa-pu. SINGH.
Pila Champa. MAHR.	Shembugha maram. TAM.

This tree grows in the Central province of Ceylon up to elevations of 3,000 to 8,000 feet. It is rare in the Walliar forests, being alpine in its tendencies, and is common on the Neilgherries, but Dr. Gibson had not seen it wild in the Bombay forests, though, in gardens and about dwellings, it is common. Dr. Wight tells us, its wood is said to be good as regards strength, but too highly hygrometrical to be useful in other form than rafters or beams, though close and fine grained; and Dr. Gibson mentions that the wood is straight, and moderately close in grain, that it could be turned to account in house-building, and might with advantage be creosoted, but it is not sufficiently common to be extensively used.—*Thw., Drs. Wight and Gibson.*

MICHELIA RHEEDII, *Wight.*

Sumpaghy. CAN.	Sampanghy maram. TAM.
Siapangam. MALEAL.	Sempangam. TAM.

A large tree of Mysore, the wood is close grained and very handsomely marked in a mottled manner. At the Madras Exhibition of 1855 a remarkably large specimen was exhibited by Captain Cunningham, its dimensions were 11½ feet in length, 4½ feet in breadth and 3 inches in thickness, and was apparently derived from a tree of very great age.—*Dr. Cleghorn in Jur. Rep., Mad. Cat. Ex. of* 1862, *Capt. Puckle.*

MILLELE. A wood of Ceylon probably specifically identical with Sapoomilile, with which it coincides in very respect.—*Edye, Timbers of Ceylon.*

MILLINGTONIA, *Species.*

Ramenei delle. SINGH.

A tree of the western province of Ceylon, the wood of which weighs lbs. 48 to the cubic foot, and is esteemed to last 20 years. It is used in common house buildings. The sticks make excellent fences.—*Mr. Mendis.*

MILLINGTONIA SIMPLICIFOLIA, *Roxb.* This tree belongs to the order Millingtoniæ of Lindley, and grows in Madura, Nepaul, the Khassya hills, and is found in the forests of the Pegu valley, but scarce. Its properties as a timber are valuable from its weight and strength. Wood white colour and adapted for every purpose of house building.—*Voigt, Dr. McClelland.*

MILLINGTONIA HORTENSIS, *Linn. fil.*

Bignonia suberosa, *Roxb.*

One of the Bignoniaceæ. This grows in Ceylon, but is supposed to be cultivated there. Dr. Riddell says it is an elegant tree growing to the height of fifty feet, is in blossom towards the close of the rains, and the seeds ripen in March. The bark is of a soft spongy nature, the wood is white, firm, and close grained.—*Thw., Dr. Riddell.* *See* BIGNONIA SUBEROSA.

MILULU, the Malayala name of a Malabar and Canara tree that grows to about sixteen feet high, and ten inches in diameter. It is known as one of the jungle woods and is used by the native carpenters for boats, knees and timbers, on account of its strength.—*Edye, Forests, of Malabar and Canara.*

MIMUSOPS, *Species.*

Thubbæ. BURM.

A Tavoy wood used in ship building.

MIMUSOPS ELENGI, *Linn.; Roxb.; Cor.*

Bakula. BENG.	Bakula. HIND.
Kya-ya. BURM.	Mulsari ka jhar. ,,
Mugali mara. CAN.	Bakul. MAHR.
Minjulu ? ,,	Elengi. MALEAL.
Taindu. DUK.	Bakula. SANS.
Bacul. ,,	Moone Mulgass. SINGH.
Mulsari. ,,	Magiludam maram. TAM.
Bholsari. ,,	Mayugadi maram. ,,
Ape faced flower. ENG.	Pogada manu. TEL.
Bakula Tree. ,,	

This tree grows in Ceylon, throughout the peninsula and the north of India, in Burmah, Pegu, Tenasserim and the Moluccas. Dr. Gibson says that, in the Bombay forests, it is mostly found as a cultivated tree, more rarely wild, and then only below the ghats. It is an ornamental tree with dark green oblong alternate leaves, and white fragrant flowers; of moderate size, and often cultivated for the oil obtained from its fragrant flowers. This tree is very ornamental in compounds. Its small white sweet smelling flowers are celebrated in the Puranas and even placed amongst the flowers of the hindoo paradise. In Canara and Sunda, in the high jungles close above the ghats, it reaches a great size. It thrives well at Ajmeer, growing to a large size, the fresh flowers are delightfully fragrant, the wood is very hard and durable, and the foliage is beautiful and evergreen. The berries are eaten sometimes by the poor. In Burmah it is a rare ornamental tree, much valued by Burmese ladies, for its small delicate sweet-scented blossoms, which they string in chaplets for the head. It yields, in Canara, wood serviceable for houses, but not used in ships or boats. At Moulmein, it is a strong wood for any ordinary purpose. Dr. Gibson had used the wood for cart shafts, and found it strong, and rather durable. In Ceylon, it is used for house building and furniture. A cubic foot weighs lbs. 61 and it is esteemed to last 50 years.—*Drs. Wight, Gibson, Mason, Voigt, Cal. Cat. Ex.* 1862, *Madras Ex. Jur. Reports, Mr. R. Brown, Ains. Mat. Med. p.* 158, *Gen. Med. Top. p.* 190, *Mr. Mendis.*

MIMUSOPS HEXANDRA, *Roxb.; W. Ic.*

Kirni. DUK.	Pala maram. TAM.
Rajun. HIND.	Pattai. ,,
Kirni. MAHR.	Pala chettu, TEL.
Chiri. SANS.	Pala. ,,
Paloo. SINGH.	Pedda pala. ,,
Pallé. TAM.	

The Fruit.

Keerni ka phall. DUK.	Palay pallam. TAM.
Cheerie. SANS.	Pala pundoo. TEL.

This tree grows in the eastern province of Ceylon? it is common in the Deccan, where it is generally planted by mahomedans; it grows near the Godavery. It is common in Guzerat, where it reaches a great size, but is seldom found in other of the Bombay forests. The wood is rather strong, and much used for sugar mill beams and well-frames in Guzerat, but Dr. Gibson had not seen it used elsewhere. Captain Beddome tells us that the wood is much used where strength and toughness are required. It is hard, a cubic foot weighs lbs. 60 and it is said to last 10 to 70 years. It is used for rulers, knobs, handles of tools, such as chisels, &c., and other articles of turnery; and, in Ceylon, for oil presses, bridges and buildings. The berries are eaten when ripe, are nutritious and palatable.—*Ainslie, p.* 229, *Drs. Riddell and Gibson, M. E. J. R., Mr. Mendis, Captain Beddome, Voigt.*

MIMUSOPS INDICA, *A. DC.; W. Ic.*

Paloo-gass. SINGH. | Palava maram. TAM.

This valuable tree grows very abundantly in the hot, drier parts of the island of Ceylon. The timber is extremely hard, and strong, and very durable. Dr. Cleghorn informs us that it grows in Tinnevelly, but its felling is restricted as it is in large demand by the Madras Ordnance Department for gun stocks. Until recently it was not included among the reserved woods, and the tree accordingly was extensively cut for private purposes. Steps, however, have now been taken to prevent this wood being removed, and, in Tinnevelly, where the tree chiefly grows, the Collector has been requested to inform the subordinate revenue officers in his district, that all private cuttings of *Palava* is restricted.—*Thw. En. Pl. Zeyl. III. p.* 175, *Report Conservator of Forests,* 1859—60.

MIMUSOPS KAUKI, *Linn.*

Mimusops dissectus, *Spreng.*
,, hexandra, *Roxb.*
Achras dissecta, *Forst.*
,, baluta, *Aubl., Rheede, Rumph.*

Kirni. HIND. | Manil kara. MALEAL.

This middle sized tree grows in Malabar, in Northern India, the Malay islands, the Moluccas and New Holland. It is cultivated at Ajmeer and Kotah, where the tree becomes very large and is very handsome. In the Dekhan, this tree grows to a large size, and is generally planted in groves. The wood is fine grained and hard. The fruit, which is about the size of a small olive, is of a yellow color when ripe, after the rains, and contains a sweet clammy juice, eaten chiefly by the natives. In Burmah this dried fruit is occasionally seen among the Chinese, brought from Singapore.—*Voigt, Dr. Irvine's Med. Top. of Ajmur, p.* 190, *Drs. Riddell & Mason.*

MINJHAREE OR PALOODHONA, URIA. A tree abundant in Ganjam and Gumsur, extreme height 45 feet, circumference 5 feet and height from ground to the intersection of the first branch, 6 feet. Used on account of its lightness for rafts also for pacottah poles. The fruit and flower are both eaten. The bark and leaves are used medicinally for worms.—*Captain Macdonald.*

MIRABAN. A Penang wood of a light red colour. Much used for ship building, furniture &c.

MITREPHORA HEYNEANA, *Blume.*

Orophea Heyneana, *H. f. et T.*

A middle sized tree, growing at Haragam and other places on the lower Badulla road from Kandy, up to an elevation of 1,500 feet.—*Thw. En. Pl. Zeyl. p.* 8.

MOCHEAL, the Tamil name of a Ceylon tree which is about twenty inches in diameter, and eight or ten feet high. It is used in native boats, &c. It produces a fruit from which oil is extracted.—*Edye, on the Timber of Ceylon.*

MODDORO GOODEE, URIA. A tree of Ganjam and Gumsur, of extreme height 40 feet, circumference 2½ feet, and height from the ground to the intersection of the first branch, 8 feet. It is used for plough shares and rafters and burnt for firewood, is not very common.—*Captain Macdonald.*

MOEE, URIA. Garuga pinnata. This tree of Ganjam and Gumsur, is of extreme height 30 feet, circumference 3 feet, and height from the ground to the intersection of the first branch, 13 feet. Stakes are cut from this tree and planted in hedges where they spring up again. The bark is used in tanning leather. The tree abounds.—*Captain Macdonald.*

MOHOOLO, URIA. Bassia latifolia? Under these names, Captain Macdonald describes a tree of Ganjam and Gumsur, of extreme height 50 feet, circumference 8 feet, and height from the ground to the intersection of the first branch, 36 feet. Used for boats and the flooring of cattle sheds is often made of this wood, this tree is highly prized by the hill tribes on account of the intoxicating liquor which they distil from its flower. The latter is made into a sort of sweetmeat by the Ooriyas, who mix sugar and rice with it. The fruit in its unripe state is boiled and eaten as a vegetable. The fruit yields an oil termed "Jolo Jelo," this is purchased by the bukals for the purpose of adulterating ghee, which it somewhat resembles in appearance. This tree and the solopo palm are never destroyed by the Koonds when they clear a patch of jungle for the purpose of bringing it under cultivation, and in the time of the Gumsur rajahs, the rebellion of any of the hill tribes was often punished by cutting down all their mohoolo and solopo trees.—*Captain Macdonald.*

MOKETAMMATHA, BURM. Meaning Martaban wood. A tree of maximum girth 1 cubit, and maximum length 8 feet, found very abundant in Martaban and its adjacent jungles, also all over the provinces especially on the banks of rivers. When seasoned, sinks in water: uncommonly heavy. Stated to be used for the same purposes as chisel handle tree, but still stronger. —*Captain Dance.*

MOMA-KHA,? BURM., or MORNA-KHA,? BURM. In Amherst, a timber employed for gun stocks; it is a reddish, softish wood, close and compact, fit for turning purposes, and exempt from attacks of insects.

MONG-DAYAT NEE, BURM., or RED MONG DAYAT. A tree of maximum girth 2 cubits, and maximum length 15 feet. Not abundant, but found on the sea shore from Amherst to Mergui and on the Callagouk islands. When seasoned, it floats in water. Used for crooks, and straight parts also of ships, and boats: is a light tough wood with a good grain, but too liable to rot to be recommended.—*Captain Dance.*

MONG-DAYAT PEW, BURM., or WHITE MONG-DAYAT. A tree of maximum girth 2½ cubits, and maximum length 22 feet. Scarce, but found all over the Tenasserim provinces near the sea and in the mouths of the rivers. When seasoned, it floats in water. It is not a good wood, being very perishable.—*Captain Dance.*

MONOPORANDRA CORDIFOLIA, *Thw.* A moderate sized tree of Ambagamowa and Saffragam districts in Ceylon, at an elevation of about 3,000 feet. Wood unknown.—*Thw. En. Pl. Zeyl. I. p.* 39.

MONOPORANDRA ELEGANS, *Thw.* A moderate sized tree of Saffragam district in Ceylon, at an elevation of about 2,000 feet. Wood unknown.—*Thw. En. Pl. Zeyl. I. p.* 39.

MONOPORANDRA LANCIFOLIA, *Thw.* A small tree growing in Ceylon at Hellessee, in the Pasdoon Corle, at no great elevation. Wood unknown.—*Thw. En. Pl. Zeyl. I. p.* 39.

MOOKERSEY? TAM. In Tinnevelly, a wood of a red color, used for building in general.—*Colonel Frith.*

MOOLU VENGA, TAM. In Travancore, a wood of a copper colour, specific gravity 0·831. Used for common buildings.—*Colonel Frith.*

MOON-DIEN, BURM. This wood is fine grained, light, and recommended for furniture. Its breaking weight is lbs. 121. A cubic foot weighs lbs. 33 to 38. In a full grown tree on good soil the average length of the trunk to the first branch is 50 feet and average girth measured at 6 feet from the ground is 10 feet. It sells at 4 annas per cubic foot.—*Dr. Brandis, Cal. Cat. Ex. of* 1862.

MOORGAH, HIND? Of a light brown color, close-grained and takes a good polish, but is not a strong or serviceable wood. Occurs in the Santhal jungles from Raneebahal to Hasdiha, but rather scarce. Native articles of furniture are principally made from this wood.—*Cal. Engineers' Journal, July* 1860.

MOORGUL MARA.

Garcinia purpurea, *Wild Mangosteen.*

Kokeem.? MAHR.	Kokum.? MAHR.

Under these names, Dr. Gibson describes a beautiful tree of Canara and Sunda, mostly below and near valleys. Valued for its fruit which is extensively exported as a native condiment. The concrete oil also is much used. Its wood is good.—*Dr. Gibson.*

MOOTSOMAH—? This is a very plentiful tree of Akyab. It furnishes a very small wood, used for firewood.—*Cal. Cat. Ex.* 1862.

MORELE, HIND. A tree of Chota Nagpore, furnishing a hard, white timber.—*Cal. Cat. Ex.* 1862.

MORINDA, a genus of trees, indigenous and largely cultivated in India, producing hard and very durable woods, and useful dyes. The bark and root of *M. tinctoria, M. citrifolia* in India, and *M. exserta,* in Burmah, are employed to form a very valuable red dye, which is fixed with alum; and Dr. Buchanan mentions that the root of M. ternifolia in Mysore, is used for similar purposes. Most of the red turbans of Madras are dyed with the root of the Noona. The Karens prepare their red dyes most usually from the roots of two or three species. The *M. citrifolia,* is cultivated by the Burmese for a dye, but the Karens more commonly use *Morinda exserta,* the indigenous species. These form a very valuable red dye which is fixed with alum: the colour, though not brilliant, is far more permanent than many other colours.

MORINDA BRACTEATA, *Roxb.*

Rouch. BENG.	Yaiyoe.? BURM.
Mhan bin.? BURM.	

A small tree, native of Ganjam, the Andamans, and of the Phillippines and Moluccas in the Archipelago,—with large shining leaves. The tree is common throughout the province of Pegu. It is also cultivated about Phoungyee houses. Its wood, of a bright yellow colour, is found in the Bengal bazars under the name of *Rouch,* and is valuable as affording a bright yellow dye. —*Dr. McClelland, Mr. Robert Brown, Voigt.*

MORINDA CITRIFOLIA, *Linn.; Roxb.; W. & A.; Rheede.*

Togaree wood. ANGLO-TEL.	Barra-al. HIND.
Indian Mulberry? ENG.	Al. MAHR.
Al. HIND.	Bartondie. MAHR.
Ach. „	Kada pilva. MALEAL.
Ak. „	Manja pavattay maram. TAM.

Nonna maram. TAM.	Toguru chettu. „
Nuna maram. „	Mulugha, „
Maddi chettu. TEL.	Mulugu chettu. „

This small tree is common in Kotah and Boondee. It grows in the Madras Presidency, is much cultivated in that of Bombay, and grows in Pegu, Cochin-China and the Moluccas. It is not a common tree in the Bombay forests; but is more common about villages. The wood is of a deep brownish yellow and the roots are said to be used in dyeing. The quality of the wood, judging simply from the appearance, is little, if at all inferior, to Nauclea cordifolia; but the tree is much smaller. The wood is easily worked and used for common purposes Mr. Rohde has seen trees of this wood nearly 2 feet in diameter. It makes tolerable planks, but appears never to be used on the Bombay side, except for door-shutters and such like. A scarlet colouring matter is procured from the roots and bark and used for dyeing handkerchiefs, turbans, &c. It is used, also, to assist more expensive dyes in giving a red colour to yarn and cloth—the red thread used in carpet making is entirely dyed with it. The process of dyeing red yarns in the Circars is well described by Heyne. The roots of the awal tree of Malabar and other parts of India, *Morinda citrifolia*, and of *M. tinctoria*, are found abundant in all the Asiatic islands, and are extensively used as a dye stuff for giving a red color. It is usually grown as a prop and shade for the pepper vine and coffee tree. The coloring matter resides principally in the bark of the roots, which are long and slender, and the small pieces are the best, fetching 8*s*. to 10*s*. a maund. It is exported in large quantities from Malabar to Guzerat, and the northern parts of Hindostan, but seldom finds its way to Europe. The flowers have a very sweet scent and the tree would thrive well and be ornamental in compounds. In Coimbatore, Nonna maram, Tam., is the proper Tamul name for the *Morinda citrifolia*, but *Morinda umbellata*, a climbing plant, and hence unfit for use as a timber, has the same Tamul name.—*Voigt, Mr. Robert Brown, Drs. Wight, Gibson & Cleghorn, Gen. Med. Top., Mr. Rohde, Simmonds.*

MORINDA EXSERTA, *Roxb.*

Bun uch. BENG.	Togari mogilli. TEL. of the Godavery.
Mhan-bin ? BURM.	
Nya ? „	Mogilli. TEL. of Circars.

A small tree of the Circars, of Bengal and Burmah. Wood yellow, hard and useful, is fit for fancy work, and does not warp. In Pegu, M. bracteata and this are both small trees, only found about Phoungyee houses, in a cultivated state.—*Voigt, Captain Beddome.*

MORINDA TINCTORIA, *Roxb.*

Al. BENG.	Maddi chettu. TEL.
Ach. „	Mulugu chettu. „
Al. HIND.	Luagru. „
Ach. „	Togaru. „
Uchyuta. SANS.	

A small tree, supposed to be the same as M. citrifolia in its wild state. Its green fruit is pickled or eaten in curries. It is pretty common in every part of India. It is in flower and fruit the greater part, if not the whole, of the year. It is largely cultivated at Boondee, Kotah and Mewar. The woods of all the species are beautiful, hard and durable; and excellent for gun stocks. That of this species, possesses all these qualities, is variegated red aud white, and is employed for gun stocks in preference to all other kinds. The bark of the roots is used to dye red, the colour is fixed with alum, but it is neither bright nor durable. In some parts of India, it is cultivated for the sake of the roots. In the Circars the dyers use the bark of the fresh roots bruised and gently boiled in water for a short time. The cloth or yarn is prepared in a cold infusion of the powdered gall of Terminalia chebula, in milk and water; it is then dried and moistened with alum water, and again dried, and receives from the above decoction, a pretty bright, but fugitive red. Dr. Irvine says the root is extensively exported from Ajmeer as a red dye. The plant is not allowed to shoot up into the bush, but is dug up the third year after planting. The flowers are very fragrant.—*Dr. Roxb. Med. Top. of Ajmere, p.* 182, *Voigt, Mr. Robert Brown.*

MORINDA TOMENTOSA. *Heyne.*

Morinda mudia *Ham.*

Manjinate. MALEAL.

This tree grows to 20 or 30 feet high in Travancore. It is very common there and is frequently found in gardens as well as in the forests. It yields a yellow timber which takes a polish equal to Jack wood, and the interior wood of old trees yields a dye.—*Drury's Useful Plants, p.* 308.

MORRE, SINGH.

Eye ball. ENG.

A tree of the central province of Ceylon. A cubic foot of its wood weighs 62 lbs. and it is said to last 25 years. It is used for common house building and, next to Galmorre, Nephelium, furnishes the best firewood for lime and brick kilns. Berries eaten when ripe.—*Mr. Mendis.*

MOULMEIN TIMBERS AND FANCY-WOODS. Of the following timbers, forwarded to the Exhibition of 1851, from Moulmein, by J. R. Colvin, Esquire, Commissioner of the Province in 1847, under their native names, several were afterwards identified by Dr. Falconer, during his visit to the Teak forest of the Tenasserim provinces in 1848-49:—

Careya sphœrica, Bamboose, BURM.

Cyrtophyllum fragrans, Anan, BURM., one of the Nux vomica tribe; one of the hardest, most compact, and heaviest woods known.

Hopea odorata, Thengan, BURM., of the Dipterocarpeæ or saul tribe; a very strong but coarse-grained timber.

Indike. BURM., Ebony.

Inga xylocarpa, Pyangadeau, BURM. The Iron wood of the Arracan provinces, very hard, dense and durable.

Lagerstrœmia macrocarpa, pyen-ma, BURM., commonly known under the name of jarrool.

Pterocarpus Indica, Padauck, BURM., one of the Leguminosæ, called Rosewood. It is a very beautiful and hard compact timber, closely resembling the Andaman wood.

Pyen-ma and Kazaret, BURM., undetermined.

The following 114 woods were sent from Moulmein to the London Exhibition of 1862 :

(1) **Acacia**, Konk Koe, this wood is made into boats, carts, and other ordinary house-building material.

Acacia sirissa, Tseek Tha, wood reddish colour, used for furniture.

Ahline Ngai, used for ordinary house-building purposes ; leaf is eaten boiled as greens.

Ah See Eha, wood hard, used for making musical instruments.

Arborea ?? Bun Boay, a strong durable wood ; used for house-posts.

Arbus ? Youg Tha Ngai, used in ordinary building materials.

Artocarpus echinatus, Toun Phain, used for making boats and carts

Artocarpus echinatus, Toung Pain Nai, fruit edible, used in house-building.

Artocarpus integrifolius, Pain Nai, BURM. "Jack tree," Fruit eaten, wood yellow, used to dye the yellow Pongyee, (Burmese Priest) cloths.

(10) Bamboo, species. Dedoap Tha, this wood is made use of for ordinary house-building purposes.

Bignonia, Thau Thet Ngai, used in common purposes of building.

Bignonia stipulata, Ma Shoay, a strong wood for any ordinary purpose. Fruit edible.

Bombæ ? That Pan ? a strong wood for any ordinary purpose.

Bon Sone, the fruit is edible. Used for house-building purposes.

Cassia, species. Ngoo Tha, made into house-posts. Fruit and bark used medicinally.

Cassia Sumatrana ? Kyee, this wood is used in ordinary house-building.

Cassia Sumatrana, Mazalee, this wood is used in ordinary house-building.

Castanea martabanica, Thit Nya, the fruit eaten exactly like chesnuts.

Cordia myxa, Koan Tha Nath, this wood is used in ordinary house-building. The leaf is made into cigar wrappers.

(20) Dalbergia, Species. Myouk Shaw, this wood is used in ordinary house-building.

Dalbergia, species. Water Dalbergia, Thapya, this wood is used in ordinary house-building.

Dalbergia species, Youdine, a hard heavy black wood, used for furniture.

Dalbergia alatus, Tsouk Yoa, used for tool handles.

Dalbergia oonta, Tsouk Yo, a tough wood, much used for tool handles.

Dillenia, species, Zin Pyun Ngan, a strong wood for any ordinary purpose. Fruit edible.

Dipterocarpus grandis, Tugtha, converted into planks for building.

Ein Gyin, one of the Dipterocarpeæ, a very strong durable wood, as strong as Pyengado ; when kept long in water it is said to become petrified.

Ein Win, used for all ordinary purposes of building.

Eugenia, species. Sha Bya Gyin, wood soft, used in ordinary purposes of building material.

(30) Eugenia, Species. Sha Bya, a strong wood for any ordinary purpose.

Fagræa fragrans, Ah Nan, a strong wood, good for building purposes.

Ficus cordifolia, Nga Thingyee, a strong wood for any ordinary purpose.

Galex, species. Mohmagah, used in common purposes of building.

Garana speciosa, Balawa; used in common purposes of house building.

Garcinia, species. Young Zalai, this wood is made use of for ordinary house-building purposes ; fruit edible.

Gardenia floribunda, Thet Ya, this wood is made use of for ordinary house-building purposes.

Gardenia coronaria, Yin-gat, used for building purposes. Fruit edible.

Gmelina arborea, Yamana, used as an ordinary building material.

Gosy-pin-gyee, used in common purposes of house building, and also its seed as weights, in weighing gold.

(40) Goay Tha, used in common purposes of house building.

Grewia, species ? Bha Woon, converted into planks for building.

Grewia, species, Tha-ran, a wood used to make dancing dolls.

Grewia floribunda, Mya-ya-gyee, made into any common house-building material.

Gordonia, Anan Pho, a strong wood, good for building purposes.

Homalium tomentosum, Mouk Kyan, a strong wood for any ordinary purpose.

Hopea odorota, Thin Gan, a very strong, durable wood ; used for making canoes.

Inga species, Bom Mai Za, wood hard, used for making musical instruments.

Inga xylocarpa, Pyen-ka-doe, wood extremely hard ; used for house posts.

Ka Nat Tha, this wood is made use of for ordinary house-building purposes.

(50) Kay Yoob, used in ordinary building materials.

Khan Tha, this wood is made into any house-building material.

Koun Soay-dan, this wood is used in ordinary house-building.

Kya Nan, red wood, used generally by carpenters.

Kyan-pho, a strong wood, good for building purposes.

Kya zo, used for building material.

Lagerstrœmia, Species. Jarool, Pyen-ma-zoat-Gyee, wood soft, used in ordinary purpose of building material.

Lagerstrœmia reginæ, Pyen Ma Nee, or Jarul of Chittagong, wood used for boats and carts, also for flooring houses.

Lagerstrœmia, Pyen Ma Phoo, used for making oars and for rough house-building.

Mai Kin, used in ordinary building materials. Fruit used as medicine.

(60) Manee Auka, used for ordinary house-building purposes. Bark is used medicinally.

Mangifera Indica, Tha Yat, That Yat, this wood is used in ordinary house-building. Fruit edible.

Mangifera oppositifolia, Mayan, used for building purposes.

Mellicocca trijuga, GyooTha, this wood is used for bows, being tough and elastic.

Mimusops elengi, Kya Ya, a strong wood for any ordinary purpose. The flower is used medicinally and prized for its fragrance.

Moringa pterygosperma, ? Dhane Tha ? used for building purposes.

Moringa pterygosperma, ? Dain Tha, flowers, bark, and root used medicinally. Wood made into dolls.

Mya Ya Ngai, this wood is used for ordinary house-building purposes.

Myouk Ngo, Moulmein Lance wood, this wood is made into any house-building material.

Nat Gyee, used for posts and knife handles.

(70) Nauclea cadamba, Ma-oo-tha, used for building purposes.

Nux vomica tree, Kha Gyee, used for all ordinary purposes of building. Fruit used medicinally.

Nux vomica tree, Kaboung, used in ordinary building materials. Fruit used as medicine.

Nyoay Sha, used for building material.

Nyoung Tha, a strong wood for any ordinary purpose.

Nyoung Lan, used for building material.

Oan Naih, the fruit is edible. Used for house-building purposes.

Oak An, this wood is made into canoes.

Odina wodier, Na Bai, a red wood. Bark used medicinally.

Ouk Kyine, this wood is used in ordinary house-building.

(80) Paran Tha, wood soft, used in ordinary purposes of building material.

Phat Than, used for chisel handles.

Phyllanthus emblica, Yee Pye, used in common purposes of house building.

Pierardia sapida, Ka Na Oo, a very hard wood: used for wheel axles.

Pollypod, Oak-leaved; Zangyecoat-doup, used for all ordinary purposes of building.

Pterocarpus dalbergiodes, Padouk, a very strong wood, admirable for furniture, used by the Burmese to make their musical instruments.

Pune Tha, wood soft, used in ordinary purposes of building material.

Red jambo, Tha Bya Nee, used for building material.

Setphau, used in common purposes of house building.

Sonneratia acida, La Moo, an inferior wood for boats, which lasts but two or three years. The fruit is an article of food.

(90) Sonneratia assetata ? qu. acida ? Kama-la, an inferior wood for boats, which lasts but two or three years.

Terminalia bellerica, Phangah, is very hard and heavy. Used to make rice pounders, furniture, &c.

Tha Khoot, this wood is used in ordinary house-building.

Tha-man-tha, used in ordinary building materials.

Than-that-gyee, used for building materials.

Thet Kon Nyen, this wood is used in ordinary house-building.

Thet Lendah, used for all ordinary purposes of building.

Thin-win, used for house-building purposes. The fruit is edible. The root used medicinally.

Thit Nee, converted into boxes, tables, &c., &c.

Tonng Ma Yoa, wood smooth; used generally for Burmese slate or writing boards.

(100) Tsan-saypen, used for ordinary house-building purposes. Leaf is eaten boiled as greens.

Tsat Tha, used for building purposes.

Vatica, Species. Koung Mhoo, used for making carts and boats.

Vitex arborea, Tonk-sha-gyee, fruit eaten, the wood is used for any common purpose.

Vitex arborea, Tonk Tsa, a strong wood for any ordinary purpose.

Wiha Oung, used for all ordinary purposes of building.

Woot Tha, a strong wood for any ordinary purpose.

Xylocarpus echinatus, Ah Nan, a very strong wood, used for making gun stocks and scabbards.

Ya Ka Ngine, this wood is used in ordinary house-building.

Yamanie, this wood is used in ordinary house-building.

(110) Ya Tha Nat, an inferior wood for boats, which lasts but two or three years. The fruit is an article of food.

Ya-tha-pya, the fruit is edible. Used for house-building purposes.

Yin Yo, a strong wood, good for building purposes.

Za Padrup, a strong wood, good for building purposes.

Zinpyun Gyee, this wood is used in ordinary house-building.

MOU-THA-MA. A tree in Amherst; with a fine-grained, compact, red wood, but liable to split; it would answer for hand-spikes. It resembles Myrtus pimenta. Bark used for blue dye.—*Captain Dance.*

MUDAMALLAI FORESTS. The Bangalore barracks, railway, Neilgherry barracks, jail, and other works were supplied with timber from these forests.—*Conservator's Report.*

MULMURACA, the Tamil name of a Ceylon tree which grows to about twenty-four inches in diameter, and twenty-five feet in height. It is used by the natives for canoes, catamarans, and many other purposes. It produces a fruit which, with the leaves of the tree, is used medicinally. —*Edye, on the Timber of Ceylon.*

MUNCHETTY MARAM, the Malayala name of a tree which grows in Malabar and Canara, to about twenty-five feet in height, and eighteen inches in diameter: it is used by the natives for coasting vessels and house building: it is of little value.—*Edye, Forests of Malabar and Canara.*

MUNGEVENAH, the Tamil name of a Ceylon tree which grows to thirty inches in diameter, and eight feet long. It is close in its grain and light. It is used for gun-stocks, poles of palanquins, sandals, &c. It produces a fruit which is of little use. It is on the fruit of this tree that the monkeys, pea-fowl, &c. feed.—*Edye, on the Timber of Ceylon.*

MUNJADDY, TAM. A Travancore wood of a purple colour, specific gravity 0·667. Used for building houses only.—*Colonel Frith.*

MUNJET KERDDUM, TAM. A Tinnevelly wood of a light straw colour. Used for building in general.—*Colonel Frith.*

MUNNY MARTHA, TAM. A Travancore wood of a brown colour, specific gravity 0·607. 1 to 6 feet in circumference; used for furniture. —*Colonel Frith.*

MUROODOO, TAM. A Palghat wood of a light colour. A small tree; used for buildings. —*Colonel Frith.*

MURRAYA, *Species.* Burman box wood. The Karens sometimes furnished Mr. Mason with specimens of wood scarcely to be distinguished from the box-wood of Europe. Dr. Wallich found *Nauclea cordifolia* on the banks of the Irrawaddy, which has "wood coloured like that of the box tree, but much lighter, and at the same time very close grained." It may possibly be the same tree, although the Tenasserim wood is not light; or it may be a Tavoy tree, which he says has "a strong tough wood, in grain like box."— *Dr. Mason's Tenasserim.*

MURRAYA, *Species.* Maikay, BURM. In Tavoy, a tough close grained wood, used for handles.—*Dr. Wallich.*

MURRAYA, Ash leaved.

Etteiriye. SINGH.

Under these names, Mr. Mendis notices a timber tree of the eastern province of Ceylon, a cubic foot of the wood weighs lbs. 60 and it is said to last from 10 to 70 years. It is used for handles of mamoties, hammers and bill-hooks; and rafters for cadjan roofs.—*Mr. Mendis.*

MURRH NEEN, BURM. A tree of maximum girth 2 cubits and maximum length 15 feet. Found abundant all over the Tenasserim provinces on low grounds. When seasoned it floats in water. It looks exactly like deal, but is stated to have no durability.—*Captain Dance.*

MUSSEE, CAN. One of the Lauraceæ, grows in Mysore, where it is in general demand.—*Captain Puckle in Mad. Cat. Ex. of* 1862.

MUTHERIE. In Ceylon, the Tamil name of the satin-wood: called Buratu by the Portuguese. It is a handsome and valuable wood, and may be considered the most durable of any in Ceylon for general uses, provided it is seasoned in the shade: it may be converted into handsome furniture, &c. In consequence of its weight all trees are cut in lengths of from ten to twelve feet for the purpose of getting it floated down the rivers from the forests, which is done in canoes. Mr. Edye was of opinion that it may be obtained from twenty-five to forty feet long, but the largest diameter is thirty-six to forty inches. That which is in general brought to the dock-yard is about fifteen feet long and from eighteen to twenty-four inches in diameter, being cut to that size for the ease of conveyance.—*Edye, on the Timber of Ceylon.*

MUTTALLA, TAM. A Travancore wood of a brown colour. Used for light work.—*Colonel Frith.*

MYA-KAMAUN, BURM.? A valuable strong, black, Tavoy wood; used for knife handles.—*Wallich.*

MYAUN-NGO, BURM.? In Amherst, white sissoo; used for rafters.—*Cat. Ex.* 1851.

MYAUP-LOAUT, BURM.? In Amherst, a timber tree, a kind of superior Toon wood, supposed of the genus Cedrela.—*Cat. Ex.* 1851.

MYA-YA-NGAI, BURM.? A tree of Moulmein, wood used for ordinary house building purposes.—*Cal. Cat. Ex.* 1862.

MYA-YA, BURM. In Amherst a hard and close-grained wood, used for rafters; it is strong and durable, and would answer for beams, &c., being exempt from the attacks of insects.—*Cal. Cat. Ex.* 1851.

MYENG-TA-BEP, BURM.? A strong, bluish-greyTavoy wood; adapted for handles.—*Dr. Wallich.*

MYHILENAH in Tamil, Mylelu in Malayala. This Malabar and Canara wood is of a greenish tinge, and very close grained; it grows to about twelve or fifteen feet long, and two and a half feet in diameter. It produces a fruit like green pepper; its leaves resemble the mango: the wood is generally considered strong and durable, and the native carpenters procure from its branches the small crooks and for the knees and timbers of boats, &c., and the large limbs for the frames of native vessels. The tree is scarce in the north part of Malabar and Canara, and not known in Ceylon.—*Edye, Forests of Malabar and Canara.* (*Note*—Is this Colonel Frith's myle ellah?)

MYLE ELLA, TAM. ? In Travancore, a wood of an ash colour, used for carts, buildings, &c.—*Col. Frith.*

MYLE ELLAH, TAM.? In Travancore, a wood of a light green colour, specific gravity 0·896. Used for building houses only.—*Col. Frith.* (*Note*—Is this Edye's Myhi-lenah?)

MYOUK-NGO, BURM. Lance wood of Moulmein. A tree of Moulmein, wood is made into any house building material.—*Cal. Cat. Ex.* 1862.

MYRISTICA, *Species.*

Thounsanga. BURM.

In Tavoy, a large tree, used in boat building.—*Dr. Wallich.*

MYRISTICA, *Species.*

Koathoe. BURM. | Kunneen. BURM.

In Tavoy, a large tree, used in flooring houses.—*Dr. Wallich.*

MYRISTICA AMYGDALINA? and M. SPHÆROCARPA? Wild nutmeg tree. There are one or two trees, in the southern provinces of Tenasserim, belonging to the genus which contains the nutmeg. The fruit has none of the aroma of the nutmeg, but the timber, which is large, is used by the natives in house carpentry. Griffith found only one species, "apparently," he says, "referable to Louriero's genus Knema." Wallich however, met with two and referred both to Myristica.—*Dr. Mason.*

MYRISTICA CINEREA.

Ran Jai phal. MAHR. | Sandikai maram. TAM.

A great and straight tree, found in the Bombay green-wood jungles or Raees, above and below the ghats. It is not sufficiently common, nor found generally in situations easy of access, so as to allow of its being used for household or agricultural purposes. The wood is white and compact. In Coimbatore, its wood is straight grained, close, even grained apparently and of fine quality.—*Drs. Wight & Gibson.*

MYRISTICA MOSCHATA, *Thunb.* Common nutmeg. This small tree has been introduced into various parts of India from the Moluccas. It is chiefly valued for its aromatic fruit. The wood is said to be hard and close grained.

MYROLE, or MIROLE, in Tamil and Malayala, is a Malabar and Canara wood of much value, but scarce; it is very heavy and strong, and grows to about twelve inches in diameter, and fifteen or twenty feet high. It is generally used where strength and durability are required. —*Edye, Forests of Malabar and Canara.*

MYSORE WOODS. The forests at Nuggur contain valuable timber, and the large and extending timber trade on the Tumbudra, is forming a new and interesting feature in this country.

Captain Puckle sent the following Mysore woods to the Exhibition of 1862.

Bobbalu, CAN., Babul, Acacia arabica.
Bamboo, Bambusa arundinacea.
Hippay, Bassia longifolia, wood often curiously grained.
Red custard apple, Anona reticulata.
Ructa chandana, Adenanthera pavonina.
Trincomallee. Berrya ammonilla.

Boghy, CAN., Acacia, for furniture, is strong and tough.

Choojelly, CAN., Acacia, has great resilience, useful for all purposes.

Baghy, CAN., Acacia speciosa, for carriages, and house building.

Hoonasay, CAN., Tamarindus Indica, for naves of wheels, oil mills, mallets, rice pounders, &c., excellent for brick and tile burning. Heart-wood very hard.

Biti, CAN., Dalbergia latifolia, for furniture of every description.

Honagal, CAN., Terminalia, for furniture and house building.

Wulla Hoonay, CAN., Pterocarpus, for furniture and house building.

Nellee, CAN., Emblica officinalis, for veneering, good for well-rings, does not decay under water, well adapted for turning.

Nundee, CAN., Lagerstrœmia microcarpa, useful for a variety of purposes, has great stiffness, wooden bridges have been built of this. An excellent wood.

Billawar, CAN., Acacia odoratissima, has great toughness or elasticity, makes handsome furniture resembling walnut, and much used in carriage building for the frame work, felloes and spokes.

Rugta Hanay, CAN., Pterocarpus marsupium, makes handsome furniture, and resembles fine mahogany, but must be well seasoned, or it stains yellow.

Nowladdi, CAN., polishes well, is used for house building, and furniture, &c.

Hindiga, CAN., furniture, polishes and turns well, useful for the cabinet maker, and would do for veneering.

Jalari, CAN., Vatica laccifera, strong useful wood for a variety of purposes.

Kurramutti, CAN., Terminalia tomentosa, House building, bears a good transverse strain, a wood much esteemed for all railway purposes.

Jambay, CAN., Inga xylocarpa, furniture, shafts, plough heads, knees and crooked timbers in ship building, and railway sleepers.

Sagwan, CAN., also Teyaga, CAN., Tectona grandis, ship building, house building, furniture, &c.

Dindaga, CAN., Conocarpus latifolia, house building, shafts and yokes, and general use for railway purposes, but makes very good cabinet furniture.

Kuddavailoo, CAN., Nauclea cadamba, for various kinds of furniture.

Sumpaghy, CAN., Michelia champaca, very handsome furniture, and polishes well, grows to a very large size, has a yellow sweet scented flower.

Mauvoo, CAN., Mangifera indica, for solid wheels of country carts, and rough furniture.

Godday, CAN., Cedrelaceæ, polishes well, and is good for turning.

Bevoo, CAN., Melia azedarach, common furniture, but it warps and splits.

Mussee, CAN., Lauraceæ, in general demand.

Halasoo, CAN., Jack. ENG., Artocarpus integrifolia, furniture, chairs, tables, &c., but must be well seasoned, or it will warp and crack.

Yettaga, CAN., Nauclea cordifolia, polishes well, resembles box wood, and is good for turning, cracks and warps, is light and durable if kept from wet.

Thenoon, CAN., Cocos nucifera, ridge poles for temporary roofs, aqueducts, &c.

Somy, CAN., furniture; a handsome wood.
Baulay, CAN., Diospyros melanoxylon.
Thadsal, ,, A good fine grained wood.
Joghy, ,,
Sime Thengady, Satin wood.
Danum, CAN.
Noname, ,,

Naralay, CAN., Eugenia jambolana, used in ordinary house building.

Hoongay, CAN., Pongamia glabra.
Punaralay, CAN.
Seebay, CAN.
Gundugguraghy, CAN., Cedar.
Doddu Godda, CAN., Toon?

Casuarina muricata, a hard tough wood; grows fast, and useful for scaffolding poles.

Hooaeasee, CAN., Thespesia populnea. Heart-wood, fine, close grained, gun stocks have been made of it.

Dalchini, CAN., Cinnamon.

Davadary, CAN., Sethia indica. Timber short but good: the wood fragrant.

Gundha, CAN., Sandal wood, Santalum album.
Honda Bevoo, CAN., scented margosa.
Pathunga, CAN., Cæsalpina sappan.

Karachi, ,, Bauhinia. A good strong wood somewhat like black-wood.

Padrio, CAN.
Nullacrua, CAN.
Seemy thengady, CAN.
Chillala, CAN.
Chittay, ,,
Kittalay, Orange, Citrus aurantium.

Dr. Cleghorn, Conservator's Report, Capt. Puckle in Mad. Cat. Ex. 1862.

N.

NAGAKUNNY, TAM.? A Tinnevelly wood of a whitish brown colour, used for building in general.—*Colonel Frith.*

NA GHEE, BURM. A timber of Tenasserim, of maximum girth 3 cubits, and maximum length 15 feet. Abundant all over the Tenasserim provinces. When seasoned it floats in water. It is a tolerably good wood, used for mallets, but not durable enough to be recommended.—*Captain Dance.*

NAGISHVORO, URIA. Of Ganjam and Gumsur, supposed to be Mesua ferrea? Its extreme height is 30 feet, circumference 3½ feet, and height from the ground to the intersection of the first branch, 9 feet. A medicine, used for diarrhœa, rheumatism &c. is extracted from the flower. The flowers are also worn by the Oriyas and the Rajahs stuff their pillows with them. The tree is tolerably common, but no use seems to be made of the wood.—*Captain Macdonald.*

NAGPORE WOODS. Captain Sankey, in a report from Kamptee to the Ordnance Department, dated 23d Septr. 1852, notices the forest trees and forests of this province as they then existed. The Pachmurra jungles, lying all about the base of the range bearing the same name, and very dense to the East and West of it, though having a great profusion of fine timber, do not apparently furnish beams of equal scantling with those situated on a lower level. The difficulties to be contended with in clearing a path for the transport of the timbers to the Kanhan are very great: and that stream, even in the monsoon, presents so many rocky barriers, as to render it doubtful whether the beams could even then be navigated in rafts to Kamptee; and, again, the expense of land carriage would put the obtaining of beams from this source out of the question. From the jungles lying about Deogur, Jobnee, Jam, and generally the base of, and on that line of ghats, hitherto, the supply of jungle woods has been drawn, they furnish very fine timbers, but the difficulties of cutting and transport yearly increase from the precipitous nature of the hills on which they grow. These hills are for the most part of trap, resting on granite. These jungles will continue to supply the department with Bejasar, Eyne, and Arjoon for many years. Hitherto, land carriage has been employed to Kamptee from the obstacles to floating which the Kanhan presents in two or three places, but a more extended communication hereafter, might warrant an expenditure sufficient to overcome these. At Koomerpani a little to the East of the above, great quantities of young teak trees (estimated at no less than 15,000) have been observed; these, if carefully preserved for the next 25 or 30 years, would, after the expiration of that period, furnish nearly a century's supply for the present Kamptee demand. The difficulties of transport are at present enormous, and not worth the expense of overcoming in the young state of the jungle. But, when the trees shall have arrived at their full growth the clearing of a track to the Pench or Kanhan nuddees, would involve an expense inconsiderable with the value of the store opened up. The price of teak thus obtained would not probably be more than 5 annas the cubic foot, which would at once raise it to the first class either as a tie beam or rafter timber. Doongerthal, more to the East and South, will yield a supply of rafter timber, and from its nearness to Kamptee at a very moderate rate. The supply is however trifling. Langee, though formerly thought so much of as a place likely to yield an excellent supply of timber, has been almost completely denuded. Mundilla, from which the Seonee and Jubbulpore supply of teak is drawn, though abounding in fine timber, and especially with Saul, presents, from all accounts, too great difficulties for a supply being at present drawn from it for the Kamptee market. The Panawarras jungles south-east of Kamptee from which teak is drawn, are gradually getting cleared, and timber suitable for the public service can only probably be obtained for another 6 years. From the nature of the country the cutting and transport of beams is comparatively easy. Till this season we have been in the habit of carting the beams all the way to Sillapore on the Baug Nuddee, there forming them into rafts and floating them with the stream to Ambora (more correctly Ghat Kooraddee), where the Kanhan discharges itself into the Wyne Gunga. The ramifications of the Koragurh Nuddee, extend to nearly all the places Where the timber has been cut. The beams after entering the Wyne Gunga, will require to be drawn up against the stream to Kamptee. The Jouk, Leo, and other Nuddees which flow into the Mahanuddee, may, at a future period, bring timber from the vast forest in rear to the neighbourhood of the Baugnuddee, and thence to Kamptee; but at present, it is useless to speculate on such a case presenting itself. Boojung Row's Zamindaree, from which the future supply of teak must be drawn, is capable of affording an unlimited supply, but accurate information is wanting. It will be seen, says Captain Sankey, from the remarks, that a gap in the supply of teak timber, at a low price, will probably occur between the years 1858 and 1862 (6 years being the supposed limit of the capabilities of the present source and 30 years being the time required for the Koomerponi jungle to attain its full and proper growth), and, that it will be for the interest of Government to employ in a great measure jungle wood (particularly Eyne, Arjoon, and Bejasar from the Deogur, and Jobnee jungles), during the interval. But, again, the supply of junglewood will probably prove insufficient in quantity, and he directs particular attention to the Chandah districts (that part on the left bank of the Wyne Gunga) which, in that case, must be looked to for a supply of teak. There, according to all accounts, almost boundless forests of the finest timber exist. The means of transport, offering itself in the broad stream of the Wyne Gunga, are at hand, and nothing but accurate information is required about localities. That no such information is at present to be had is clear, from the country being written "unknown" on the very best charts; all apparently known is that Boojung Row's zemindaree is inhabited by a wild race of men. Even the position of Panawarras, the place where his supply, then, came from, was only hit upon by chance after very great labor. The Chandah jungles are only open from all accounts, for two months in the year, and he gives descriptions of the following timbers; which will be found entered under their respective heads.

Tectona grandis. Teak. ENG., Sagwan. HIND., Theaka marum. TAM.
Pterocarpus marsupium. Bejasar or Bejasal. HIND., Bheulah. MAHR., Vengay marum. TAM.
Pentaptera tomentosa. Eyne. HIND., Ain or Eyne. MAHR., Marudam marum. TAM.
Diospyros ebenum. Tendoo. HIND., Taimurum or Tendoo. MAHR., Toombie marum. TAM.
Gmelina arborea. Seevum or Seeven. HIND., Seevun. MAHR., Coommy marum. TAM.
Bassia latifolla. Mowah. HIND., Moho. MAHR.
Terminalia chebula. Hurra or Hurda. HIND., Kaducai marum. TAM., Pilla murdah marum. TAM.
Acacia ordoratissima. Sirsa. HIND., Chechooah or sunkœur (?) GOND., Sirris. MAHR., Curry vaugay marum. TAM.
Erythrina Indica. Paunjerah. HIND., Moochoo marum. TAM.
Conocarpus latifolia. Thoura. HIND. MAHR., Vellay naga marum. TAM.
Swietenia febrifuga. Rohun. HIND., Rohuni. MAHR.
Dalbergia sissoo. Seesum. HIND., Yette marum. TAM.
Acacia arabica. Bhubool. HIND., Bhabool. MAHR., Curvalia marum. TAM.
Butea Gibsonii. (?) Dhamin. HIND., Dhamun. MAHR.
Cedrela toona. Thoon. HIND., Thoon. MAHR., Thoona marum. TAM.
Pentaptera arjooona. Arjoon or Unjen. HIND., Azun. MAHR.
Dalbergia—(?) Thevus. HIND., Thevis. MAHR.
Kyem. HIND., Kem. MAHR.
Derea or Dareah. HIND., Bhera. MAHR.
Nauclea—(?) Bahdah or Behra or Bhada. HIND., Hirida. MAHR.
Dhewus Dhaves. HIND., Dhivus. MAHR.
Vatica robusta. Saul.

NALLA MALLA. *See* CUDDAPAH.

NA-KYEEN, BURM. In Amherst a timber employed for house posts and rafters. This is the soondrie wood of Calcutta, Heritiera minor, where it is so common as to serve for fire-wood, although, from its superior qualities for buggy-shafts, hankery or cart axles and wheels and other purposes requiring great strength and toughness, it is highly prized.—*Cat. Ex.* 1862.

NANAH, TAM. A tree which grows in Travancore and Malabar to about 12 feet in height, and 10 inches in diameter. It is generally curved in its growth, and very soft and light. It resembles the American red birch as to its silvery grain. The native carpenters use it for the frames of small vessels. It is of a little value in consequence of its early decay.—*Edye, Forests of Malabar and Canara.*

NANAMBOO, TAM.? A wood of Travancore, of a brown colour. Used for common buildings.—*Col. Frith.*

NANGKA, MALAY. *Jack*, ENG. This and the Champadah, are varieties of Artocarpus integrifolia, and differ from each other in the smaller size, and hairy stems of the latter.—*Low's Sarawak. p.* 73.

NAOO, BURM. In Amherst, a timber used for house posts: the leaves, flowers, and roots are said to be used for medicine. It is a brown, substantial, solid wood, not liable to the attacks of insects.—*Cat. Ex.* 1851.

NA PEW GEE, BURM. OR LET THOUK GEE, BURM. In Amherst, Tavoy and Mergui, a wood of maximum girth 1½ cubits and maximum length 14 feet. Abundant all over the provinces. When seasoned, it floats in water. It is a wood, of inferior grain, and not durable. —*Captain Dance.*

NARAH, the Malayala name of a Malabar and Canara tree that grows to about twelve feet high, and ten inches in diameter. It is curved in growth, and is used for the frames of vessels. It is not very durable, and ranks as one of the inferior sorts of jungle wood.—*Edye, Forests of Malabar and Canara.*

NAR-PUTTE, the Tamil name of a Ceylon tree which is used for canoes, planks of vessels, &c. It grows to about thirty feet in height, and twenty inches in diameter. It is not durable, and is of little use.—*Edye, Ceylon.*

NARVELL, a Ceylon wood, sometimes called Jambu, in Tamil and Portuguese. It grows to about eighteen inches in diameter, and from ten to fourteen feet in height. It is used for the frames of native vessels and boats, but is not considered a very durable wood. After it has attained its full growth it produces a berry which the natives use as food.—*Edye, Ceylon.* (*Note*— Is this a species of Eugenia, or the Dillenia speciosa of Thunb.)

NAT-GYEE, BURM. A tree of Moulmein, wood used for posts and knife handles.—*Cal. Cat. Ex.* 1862.

NA-THAT, BURM. In Pegu, a forest term for trees that have died from natural causes. The term seems to be applied also to seasoned timber, or to trees that have been girdled.— *McClelland's Report, No. XXVIII. p.* 2.

NAT-TA-MIN, BURM. A reddish grey wood of British Burmah, loose grained, and recommended for cigar boxes. Breaking weight 129 lbs; a cubic foot weighs 33 lbs. In a full grown tree on good soil the average length of the trunk to the first branch is 60 feet and average girth measured at 6 feet from the ground is 6 feet. It sells at 4 annas per cubic foot.— *Dr. Brandis, Cal. Cat. Ex.* 1862.

NAUCLEA ? ? *Species.*

Babdat. HIND.	Behra. HIND.
Bhada. „	Hirida. MAHR.

Under these names, Captain Sankey notices a nice clean working Nagpore wood, of a yellow color and straight grain, which has apparently but little essential oil. It is very scarce, but, when obtainable, is used by the natives for all purposes; in strength it ranks next to "eyne," and, therefore, if procurable, in large quantities, and of a proper size, would be a most valuable wood. The timber procurable ranges from 15 to 17 feet in length and is about 3 feet in girth. —*Captain Sankey*.

NAUCLEA *Species*.

Hagin Kae. CAN. | Hagin Mara. CAN.

A tree of Canara and Sunda. Flower not seen. It is frequent in the upper third of the ghats to the south. Wood described as being strong and serviceable for houses and implements.—*Dr. Gibson*.

NAUCLEA, *Species*.

Hteingalah. BURM.

A wood of British Burmah of a light chesnut color, recommended for furniture. Breaking weight 208 lbs. A cubic foot weighs lbs. 43 to 56. In a full grown tree on good soil the average length of the trunk to the first branch is 40 feet and average girth, measured at 6 feet from the ground is 6 feet. It sells at 8 annas per cubic foot.—*Dr. Brandis, Cal. Cat. Ex.* 1862.

NAUCLEA, *Species*.

Hteinthay. BURM.

A wood of British Burmah not used. Breaking weight 170 lbs. A cubic foot weighs 35 lbs. In a full grown tree on good soil, the average length of the trunk to the first branch is 30 feet and average girth, measured at 6 feet from the ground is 6 feet. It sells at 8 annas per cubic foot.—*Dr. Brandis, Cal. Cat. Ex.* 1862.

NAUCLEA CADAMBA, *Wall.; Roxb.*

Maoo-ka-doon. BURM.
Kudda-vailoo. CAN.
Kaddon. HIND.
Halamba-gass. SINGH.
Vella cadamba. TAM.
Kodombo TEL.
Rudrakshamba. „

This is a noble ornamental tree of India and British Burmah, with orange coloured flowers. It is common in Ceylon, up to an elevation of 2,000 feet. It is found in Travancore and in the Dekhan, where it grows to a large size near villages, also in Ganjam and Gumsur, and is plentiful in Kotah and Bondee, though rare at Ajmir and is sometimes cultivated in the Tenasserim provinces and grows at Moulmein. It attains a height of 70 to 80 feet, with a girth of from 6 to 12 feet. In Ganjam and Gumsur, its extreme height is 80 feet with a stem of 32 feet to the nearest branch. It is there made into boats, and its flowers are offered to the hindu deities. In Mysore, it is used for various kinds of furniture. In British Burmah, the wood is of a deep yellow color but loose grained. A cubic foot weighs lbs. 37. In a full grown tree, there, on good soil the average length of the trunk to the first branch is 70 feet and average girth measured at 6 feet from the ground is 15 feet. It sells, in Burmah, at 8 annas per cubic foot, and is suitable for furniture.—*Thw. En. Pl. Zeyl., Captain Macdonald, Dr. Cleghorn, Cal. Cat. Ex. of* 1862, *Captain Puckle in Mad. Cat. Ex.* 1862, *Irvine's Med. Top.*

NAUCLEA COADUNATA, *Roxb.; D C. Prod.*

Bakmee-gass. SINGH.

Common in the warmer parts of Ceylon: wood not known.—*Thw. En. Pl. Zeyl. II. p.* 137.

NAUCLEA CORDIFOLIA, *Roxb.*

H'nau. BURM.
Yetlay-ga? CAN.
Hedde. „
Hurdoo? HIND?
Hedoo. MAHR.
Colong-gass. SINGH.
Manje Kadambe. TAM.
Manja Kadamba. „
Daduga. TEL.
Holondho, of Ganjam and Gumsur.
Paspoo Karami. TEL. of the Godavery.
Bundaroo. TEL. of the Godavery.

This large tree grows in the hot drier parts of Ceylon, and abundantly in the mountainous districts of the peninsula of India. It is a common tree in the coast forests of the Bombay Presidency, but never found inland,—it is getting scarce in Ganjam and Gumsur. It is said to be a tree of Jubbulpore, abundant, and its wood much in request, being light and easily worked. Its strength is not great, but it is lasting if not exposed to the weather. In British Burmah it appears as a large tree of regular growth, but not very common. In Ganjam and Gumsur it attains an extreme height of 75 feet with a circumference of 7 feet, the height from the ground to the first branch being 36 feet: but, in British Burmah, in a full grown tree, on good soil, the average length of the trunk to the first branch is 80 feet and average girth, measured at 6 feet from the ground is 10 feet, and, there, a cubic foot weighs 42 lbs. and sells at 12 annas. The wood is pretty, yellow, rather close grained, and is soft, and easily worked. In Coimbatore, it is much used for common purposes, and sustains a weight of 320 lbs. In the Bombay Presidency, it is most extensively used for all purposes of planking in in-door work. The timber deteriorates from steeping, and therefore should not be floated to its destination. In Gumsur and Ganjam, on account of its size and lightness, it is used for boats, which are made of a single log of it by simply scooping out the inside and afterwards shapening in a rough manner. It is also used for the masts of native dhoneys, and bazar measures, and is cut into planks and made into doors, boxes, &c. It is best suited for work which is sheltered, bedsteads, &c., being much affected by alternations of dry and wet weather. It seems best suited for house-carpentry and furniture. In Burmah it is used for combs. Dr. Gibson, writing from the Bombay side of India, remarks that the timber could probably be creosoted with advantage. It is said to be a good wood for model work, it polishes well, resembles box-wood, and is good for turning; but it cracks and warps. It is light and durable if kept from wet.—*Thw., Drs. Wight, Gibson, Brandis,*

Captain Macdonald, Cal. Cat. Ex. 1862, *Madras do. do.*

NAUCLEA DIVERSIFOLIA, *Wall.*

Ringah ? BURM.	Pungah ? BURM.
Bingah ? "	

Wood of British Burmah, of a light yellow color, not much used but may be recommended for furniture. A cubic foot weighs lbs. 45. In a full grown tree on good soil, the average length of the trunk to the first branch is 60 feet and average girth, measured at 6 feet from the ground is 7½ feet. It sells at 8 annas per cubic foot.—*Dr. Brandis, Cal. Cat. Ex.* 1862.

NAUCLEA ORIENTALIS.

Kuta mura. CAN.	Kudum. MAHR.

A timber tree of Canara and Sunda, rather rare and found chiefly below. Wood strong and serviceable, used for gun-stocks. Not quite common enough for house or ship purposes.—*Gibson.*

NAUCLEA PARVIFOLIA, *Roxb.*

N. parviflora, *Pers.*
N. orientalis, *Gœrtn.*
Cephalanthus pilulifer, *Lam.*

H'tein. BURM.	Helembé. SINGH.
Hedoo mara. CAN.	Nir kuddembay maram. TAM.
Yetega. "	Buta Karamee. TEL.
Yetegal. "	Moondo-monde. URIA.?
Kuddum. MAHR.	

This large tree is found in the western and northern provinces of Ceylon, in the hot, drier parts of the island, where its close grained hard timber is used for common house building purposes. It weighs lbs. 42 to the cubic foot and is calculated to last 40 years. Dr. Wight, writing in Coimbatore, says, this is a strong fine grained timber, sustaining a weight of 400 lbs. Beams of considerable size are procurable. The wood is dark colored but, according to Dr. Roxburgh, soon rots if exposed to wet. From the fineness of its grain it seems well fitted for cabinet purposes, and has the advantage of being easily worked. It is also frequent on the Western coast, and is, valued there, for yielding flooring planks, packing boxes, &c. It is mentioned by Captain Macdonald as a tree of Ganjam and Gumsur, of extreme height 60 feet, circumference 4½ feet and height from the ground to the intersection of the first branch, 22 feet. The wood is, used there, occasionally for beams, planks, &c., but is not in much request and the tree is not very plentiful. Dr. Gibson says that, in the Bombay Presidency, it is rather a common tree in the coast forests; less so inland. It is found, however, in quantities in the dells above the ghats. The wood is reddish coloured, close grained, and rather valuable for gun-stocks, in the making of which it is chiefly used. This wood could not be easily creosoted. That of the Sunda and Canara forests is valued as affording the best plank for flooring of houses and house beams. It is found in the Nalla mallai and is a hard, tough wood, light red in color and, used there, as yokes, posts and small beams. In British Burmah, a cubic foot weighs lbs. 43, and it is used for planking. In a full grown tree on good soil the average length of the trunk to the first branch is 30 feet and average girth, measured at 6 feet from the ground is 6 feet.—*Mr. Mendis, Drs. Wight and Gibson, Captain Macdonald, Dr. Brandis, Cal. Cat. Ex.* 1862, *Mr. Latham, Thw. p.* 137.

NAUCLEA UNDULATA, *Wall.*

Ma-oo lettan. BURM.

A soft useless wood in British Burmah, decays in less than a year. Breaking weight 80 to 120 lbs. A cubic foot weighs 22 to 34 lbs. In a full grown tree on good soil the average length of the trunk to the first branch is 100 feet and average girth, measured at 6 feet from the ground is 15 feet. It sells at 2 annas per cubic foot.—*Dr. Brandis, Cal. Cat. Ex. of* 1862.

NAUNGOO, TAM. A wood of Tinnevelly, of a red colour, specific gravity 1·009. Used for building, wheel wrights' work, handspikes.—*Col. Frith.*

NAURVEALY, the Tamil name of a Ceylon tree which grows to about twenty inches in diameter, and fifteen feet in height, not of much use. It produces a small red fruit which is of a very glutinous nature, and much esteemed by the natives of Malabar. From the bark of this tree a kind of cordage is made, which is used for the purposes required in the hills, and in the conveyance of timber, &c.—*Edye, Ceylon.* (*Note*—Is this the Narwali or Narvali tree, Cordia angustifolia, found common near Severndroog where ropes are made of the fibres.—*M. E.*)

NAVELLU MARAM. The Tamil name of a Malabar tree which signifies "tongue-wood." It grows to about fifteen inches in diameter, and twenty feet high: it is considered a strong and durable wood, and more particularly so under water. The native carpenters prefer it for the frames of small vessels in consequence of its strength and durability.—*Edye, Forests of Malabar and Canara.*

NA-YOO-GA, BURM. A Tenasserim wood, of maximum girth 3 cubits, and maximum length 22 feet. Scarce, but found all over the Tenasserim provinces. When seasoned it floats in water. It is a durable, tolerably good wood with a curled grain; used by Burmese for oars, much like English oak in appearance, but deficient in tenacity. It is scarce, and equally good woods are abundant.—*Captain Dance.*

NBUBAY, BURM. A Burmese wood, one of the Anacardiaceæ, has a dense wood, and brittle.—*Major Benson.*

NEBEDE, SINGH. A wood of Ceylon, used for common house building purposes. The tree grows in the southern and western parts of the island. A cubic foot weighs 51 lbs, and it is esteemed to last 20 years.—*Mr. Mendis.*

NEBONG. A Penang wood of a dark colour. It is from a tall and thin, but straight tree; used for railings. See NIBONG.

NEELAHAMPELLAH, TAM.? A Travancore wood of a light brown colour. Used for house building, ceilings, &c.—*Col. Frith.*

NEELUMPALLAH, TAM.? A Travancore wood of a light brown colour. Used for light work.—*Col. Frith.*

NEEN THA, BURM. Very abundant along the sea coast near Tavoy and Mergui. When seasoned it sinks in water. It is used for rafters of houses, is a very heavy wood, but liable to split, therefore not recommended for ordnance purposes.—*Captain Dance.*

NEILGHERRY SHOLAS. The revenue from these in the hill stations of Ootacamund, Wellington and Coonoor, is derived from sales of contract for firewood and contract for sale of charcoal. There is a thriving fringe of Pinus longifolia on the west side of the old plantations, and this tree should be more cultivated. From the commencement of planting, in 1856, about 106 acres have been planted with 2,40,000 young plants, chiefly Acacia stricta and molissima, but there are also a few Eucalyptus trees growing very well.—*Dr. Cleghorn's Reports, Rep. Con. For. p.* 33.

NELLY, TAM. A Travancore wood of a light brown colour. Used for building in general.—*Col. Frith.*

NELU. The Tamil name of a Malabar tree which is of a dark red colour, and is considered a good wood for boat work; it produces a small fruit which the natives eat in a raw state.—*Edye, Forests of Malabar and Canara.*

NELLA POLEEKI, TEL. In the Nalla Mallai a light wood, of coarse grain, unserviceable except for temporary purposes.—*Mr. Latham.*

NEPHELIUM, *Species.*

Gal morre. SINGH.

A tree of the central province of Ceylon; the wood weighs 65 lbs to a cubic foot, and is calculated to last 30 years. It is used in house building. Its berries are eaten when ripe by the natives. It supplies the best kind of firewood for brick and lime kilns.—*Mr. Mendis.* (*Note*—It is not known to what species Mr. Mendis here alludes. Mr. Thwaites notices three in Ceylon, viz. Nephelium bifoliatum, *Thw.*, a moderate sized tree on the lower Badulla road from Kandy, at no great elevation which flowers in April; Nephelium eximium, a large tree, of the central province, at an elevation of 1,000 to 2,000 feet, flowers in May and fruits in July, and Nephelium erectum, *Thw.*, also of the central province, up to an elevation of 3,000 feet. —*Thw. En. Pl. Zeyl. I. p.* 57.)

NEPHELIUM LONGAN, *Camb.*

Euphoria Longana, *Lam.*
Scytalia Longan, *Roxb.*
Dimocarpus Longan, *Lour.*

Poovutty maram. TAM.

A tree of the peninsula of India, the Khassia hills, the Malay peninsula, Cochin-China and China. A moderate sized tree having a straight trunk and fine globular head. It occurs in Coimbatore, but is rare in the Bombay presidency, being confined to their Races or green-wood jungles. The wood is white, hard, and close grained, but it is not used in carpentry by the natives who seem to be unacquainted with it.—*Drs. Wight and Gibson.*

NERA, TEL? Mr. Latham, describing the Nalla Mallai, says this name is probably incorrect and is used for Nerar the Syzigium jambolana. He adds Balfour calls a Neredu, నేరేడు, Eugenia (Syzigium) jambolana.—*Mr. Latham.*

NERASO, URIA. In Ganjam and Gumsur a tree with an extreme height of 25 feet, and a circumference of 2¼ feet. Height from the ground to the intersection of the first branch, 8 feet. It is tolerably common and burnt for firewood. Ploughshares are sometimes made of the wood. The bark is used medicinally for wounds.—*Captain Macdonald.*

NERIUM ANTIDYSENTERICUM, *Linn.*

Wrightia antidysenterica, *R. Br.*

Duola kooda. MAHR.
Veppalei maram? TAM.
Kooda pallie maram? TAM.

A very common shrub, in waste places, and on hills all over the south Konkan, less so in the north Konkan, and the interior, though still common even there. It is met with in Coimbatore and in the south of India, where the wood is said to be excellent for cabinet making purposes. It is hard and fit for the turner, but never reaches sufficient size to render it fit for the carpenter. Its bark is used medicinally.—*Drs. Wight and Gibson.*

NERIUM ODORATUM, *Lam.*

Nerium Indicum, *Mill.*
,, odorum, *Ait.*
,, oleander, *Lour.*

Goonaieho. TEL.

Under these names, Captain Macdonald notices a tree of Ganjam and Gumsur, extreme height 25 feet, circumference 2 feet, and height from the ground to the intersection of the first branch, 6 feet. He adds, this is the oleander tree and is tolerably common.—*Captain Macdonald.* (*Note*—As the oleander is usually a small shrub, it is desirable to identify this tree.)

NERRELOO, Singh. Under this Singhalese name, to which he attaches the botanical name, Illecebrun latrum, Mr. A. Mendis describes a tree of the central province of Ceylon, the wood of which weighs lbs. 56 to the cubic foot and is said to last 40 years. It is used in common house building.—*Mr. Mendis.*

NGA-SOAY, Burm. In Amherst, a solid, very heavy, reddish wood, and answers for house posts and rafters.—*Cat. Ex.* 1851.

NGOO-BENG. In Tavoy, a strong wood used for posts and planking.—*Dr. Wallich.*

NGY-SOUNG-THA, Burm. A Tenasserim wood of maximum girth 3½ cubits and maximum length 22 feet. Abundant all over the provinces. When seasoned it floats in water. It is a wood of no durability or strength; splits readily, with a short grain, and is only fit for firewood.—*Captain Dance.*

NIBONG. At the time of Pigafetta's visit, the town of Borneo was built of wood on strong and substantial posts; it is now constructed entirely of nibongs, which soon decay, and is thatched with the nipah-leaves, of which the sides also are composed.—*Low's Sarawak, p.* 150. *See* Neebong.

NIDAM PAINI, the Malayala name of a Malabar tree which means long Paini. It grows to about two feet in diameter, and seventy feet high, and produces a sort of varnish which is used with wood oil for painting wood. The natives use the spars for rafting timber down the rivers, and for the yards of small vessels. It is a wood of little value being neither strong nor durable.—*Edye, Forests of Malabar and Canara.*

NILAM PALA, the Tamil name of a Malabar tree that grows to about twelve or fifteen inches in diameter: it is not of much consideration; it produces a small fruit which is used by the natives medicinally.—*Edye, Forests of Malabar and Canara.*

NILA PALA, the Tamil name of a small tree of Malabar, the wood of which is very close grained; it is used in house work. The root of this tree is used as a medicine, and applied in cases of rheumatism (which are very prevalent after the monsoon sets in); this tree is only found in Travancore, and there it is sacred.—*Edye, Forests of Malabar and Canara.*

NIPAH FRUTICANS — ?

Cocos nypa, *Lour.*

A low palm of the Archipelago, chiefly valuable for its leaves, which are much used as thatch for the roofs of houses. The pulpy kernels of the fruit (called buah atop) are preserved as a sweetmeat, but are entirely without flavour. —*Marsden's Hist. of Sumatra.*

NOALEE-LYENG, Burm. In Tavoy, a close grained, strong, heavy wood; useful for handles. —*Dr. Wallich.*

NOONIAREE, LOONIAREE or NOONO-NONEA, Uria. Under these names, Captain Macdonald notices a tree of Ganjam and Gumsur, of extreme height 36 feet, circumference 4 feet, and height from the ground to the intersection of the first branch 7 feet. It is a common tree, chiefly used for firewood, though ploughshares are occasionally made from this wood. The bark is employed medicinally in fever.—*Captain Macdonald.*

NOTELÆA LONGIFOLIA, the "*Iron-wood*" of Norfolk Island, is used in all wheel-wright's work, and is very hard and durable. It is also used for cabinet work, and, when French-polished, it is not excelled by any of the fancy woods.—*Keppel's Ind. Arch. Vol. II. p.* 283.

NOVA, Tam. A Palghat wood of a white colour, used for shafts, cart-poles, &c.—*Colonel Frith.*

NOWLADDI, Can. of Mysore. This wood polishes well, is used for house building and furniture.—*Captain Puckle, Cat. Ex.* 1862.

NUFFELL, Tam. A Tinnevelly wood of a red colour; specific gravity 0·717. Used for building in general.—*Col. Frith.*

NULAMPALLAH. Tam. A Travancore wood of a dark brown colour, 2 to 4 feet in circumference, and 30 feet long; used for common houses and carts.—*Col. Frith. (Note*—This is perhaps the Nila-pala above described.)

NURMANJEE, Tam. A Travancore wood of a bamboo colour; used for light work.—*Col. Frith.*

NUR-MARITHY. A Travancore wood of a brown colour, specific gravity 0·615; used for building common houses.—*Col. Frith.*

NYCTANTHES ARBOR-TRISTIS.

Hursing. Can.	Paghala mallie. Tam.
Keysur. Duk.	Manja-pu-maram. "
Sorrowful nyctanthes. Eng.	Poghada mullai. Tel.
Hursinghar. Hind.	Karcheea, of the Godavery.
Sephalica. Sans.	

The tree of mourning or sorrowful Nyctanthes tree, is a great favorite in India, for its delicate orange and white blossoms, which pour their delicious fragrance on the evening air, and then fall in showers bestrewing the earth's cold bosom with sweetness. It is a hard useful wood, though it does not attain much size. It is very abundant, wild at the foot of the Vindhya range, where its green tough stalks are used to make large grain baskets.—*Drs. Ainslie, Mason and Irvine, Captains Beddome and Macdonald.*

NYOAY-SHA, Burm. A tree of Moulmein, wood used for building material.—*Cal. Cat. Ex.* 1862.

NYOUNG-LAN, Burm. A tree of Moulmein, wood used for building material.—*Cal. Cat. Ex.* 1862.

NYOUNG-THA, Burm. A tree of Moulmein. A strong wood for any ordinary purpose. —*Cal. Cat. Ex.* 1862.

OAK, Eng.

Baalut. Arab.	Dab. Pol.
Eeg. Dan.	Roble. Port.
Eik. Dut.	Carbalho. „
Chene. Fr.	Dub. Rus.
Eiche. Ger.	Roble. Sp.
Quercia. It.	Carbalho. „
Quercus. Lat.	Ek. Sw.

In the tract of country from Asia Minor, along the north of Persia to China and Japan, also in the Tenasserim provinces, several kinds of Oak occur, but, in the presence of other valuable timber trees, their woods do not attract the same attention as that of English oak. An oak is mentioned in the Holy Scriptures, but it is not identical with the British oak, being either the evergreen oak (*Quercus ilex*), or a species nearly resembling it. Near Shechem there stood also a tree of the same genus which probably was remarkable for its size, being called in Genesis xxxv. 4, "The Oak which was by Shechem." In the war of 1812-13 and 14, the natives of the peninsula and the French both frequently fed on the acorns in the woods of Portugal and Spain. In Morocco and Algiers, the acorns of *Quercus ballota* are sold in the public markets, and the acorns "balut" of some of the oaks are met with in all the Indian bazars.—*John's Forest trees of Britain, Vol. I. p.* 51, *McCulloch's Commercial Dictionary, p.* 854. *See Japan.*

OAK-AN, Burm. A tree of Moulmein. This wood is made into canoes.—*Cal. Cat. Ex.* 1862.

OAN-NAIH, Burm. A tree of Moulmein. Used for house building purposes.—*Cal. Cat. Ex.* 1862.

ODDA-MARAM, Tam? A tree of Travancore, wood of a dark colour, 3 feet in circumference, used for tent-pegs, mallets, &c.; very strong wood.—*Col. Frith.*

ODDY-SAGA, Tam? A wood of Travancore, of a dark brown colour. Used for common building purposes.—*Col. Frith.*

ODINA WODIER, *Roxb.*

Hnan bai. Burm.	Hik-gass. Singh.
Na-bhay. „	Anni carra. Tam.
Na bai. „	Ooday maram. „
Mageer. Mahr.	Goompana chettu. Tel.
Hig-gass. Singh.	„ karra. „

A large tree which grows in the warmer parts of the island of Ceylon, up to an elevation of 1,500 feet. It is also a native of mountainous districts in the peninsula of India. It grows in Coimbatore, and it is found in the coast jungles of the Bombay presidency, but it is not common. In the Madras Presidency, it is grown from cuttings and planted in avenues, but it yields no shade in the hot weather, being without leaves till June. The tree is rather common on the hills of British Burmah. The heart-wood is red and used for sheaths of swords, spear handles, oil presses and rice pounders. A cubic foot weighs 65 lbs. In a full grown tree on good soil the average length of the trunk to the first branch is 50 feet, and the average girth, measured at 6 feet from the ground, is 12 feet. It sells in Pegu at 12 annas per cubic foot. The wood is very difficult to season, requiring to be kept, even in planks, 2 or 3 years: but, once well seasoned, it is a close grained, beautiful wood, well adapted for cabinet making purposes, the central reddish portions in particular. In the Bombay presidency, Dr. Gibson says it is deemed of no value; but this seems some mistake. This, or another species, occurs quite common from Moulmein to Toungoo, where it yields a valuable timber. It is much used at Shawaygyen, in the manufacture of oil presses and rice pounders. The tree sometimes attains a girth of twelve feet. A considerable quantity of gum exudes from the trunk of this tree, which the natives use as a medicinal application.—*Thw. En. Pl. Zeyl. p.* 78, *Drs. Wight, Cleghorn, Gibson, Mason and Brandis, Cal. Cat. Ex.* 1862.

ODOORAH VENGA, Tam.? A wood of Travancore, of a dark brown colour, specific gravity 0·853. 4 feet in circumference, and 40 feet long; a strong good wood, used for wheels, gun carriages, &c.—*Col. Frith.*

ODRE. The Tamil name of a Ceylon tree which grows to fourteen inches in diameter, and ten feet in height. It is used by the native carpenters for palanquins and coach work.—*Edye, on the Timber of Ceylon.*

OLAX ZEYLANICA.

Melle. Singh.	Maella. Singh.

Under these names, Mr. Mendis describes a tree of the Eastern province of Ceylon, the wood of which is used for common purposes of house building. A cubic foot weighs lbs. 64, and it is said to last 40 years.—*Mr. Mendis.*

OLEA, the Olive tree, is a genus of plants of which 20 species have been discovered in India, but the value of the timbers of the arboreous species is not known. The olive tree of Europe grows easily in India. O. attenuata, *Wall.* is a small tree of Martaban; O. glandulifera, *Wall.* is a tree, native of the Central province of Ceylon, 2,000 to 4,000 feet high, and of the mountains near Dehra Dhoon and Kamaon: O. grandiflora, *Wall.* is a tree of Nepal; O. Gardneri, a small tree of Ceylon; O. clavata, *G. Don*, is a small tree of China, and O. Roxburghiana, *Rœm* and *Sch.*, of the Circar mountains, is a small tree. Olive-wood is imported from the Mediterranean countries into Britain. It is veined with dark grey, and resembles box-wood in texture, but is softer. The knotted and curled roots are made into embossed boxes. This is done by means of pressure in engraved moulds of metal.—*Eng. Cyc., Voigt, Thwaites.*

OLEA, *Species.* The Olive. A tree of Bukkote, on the Jhelum, Hazara.—*Cal. Cat. Ex.* 1862.

OLEA DIOICA, *Roxb.*

Burra nuge. CAN.	Par jamb. MAHR.
Indian olive. ENG.	Koli maram. TAM.
Karambu. MAHR.	

This tree grows in Chittagong and Silhet, in Coimbatore, and is common in the forests of Canara and Sunda, on the ghats, but seldom below or inland above. The wood is white, strong, compact and useful, and might be creosoted with effect.—*Wight, Gibson, Voigt.*

OODOOGOO, TAM. A large tree of Palghat, wood of a red colour; used for ploughs and building.—*Col. Frith.*

OOME TEAK, TAM. of Palghat, wood of a dark brown colour. Third-rate teak.—*Col. Frith.*

OONNAY, TAM. A wood of Tinnevelly, of a red colour; specific gravity 0·928. A strong wood used for wheelwright's work, handspikes. —*Col. Frith.*

OOSULAY, TAM? A wood of Tinnevelly, of a light brown colour; specific gravity 0·832; building in general.—*Col. Frith.*

ORGOON.? A light brown coloured wood close grained and strong, grows in the Santhal jungles plentiful near Sooree and scarce beyond Ranee-bahal up to Hasdiha. Used by the natives for building purposes and might be used in the construction of timber bridges.—*Cal. Engineers' Journal, July* 1860.

OROPHEA. A genus of middle sized trees of Ceylon, O. coriacea, grows at Dimboola and Raxawa, in the central province, at an elevation of about 3,000 feet; O. obliqua, *Hf. et. T.*, in the Galle and Ratnapoora districts, at no great elevation, and O. zeylanica, *Blume*, in the central province, at an elevation of 2,000 to 3,000 feet; woods unknown.—*Thw. En. Pl. Zeyl. p.* 8.

ORUPU-LINGI MARAM. The Malayala name of a Malabar tree that grows to about twelve feet high, and ten inches in diameter: it is very close grained and durable.—*Edye, Forests of Malabar and Canara.*

OSHOKO, URIA. A tree of Ganjam and Gumsur of extreme height 50 feet, circumference 3 feet, and height from the ground to the intersection of the first branch, 8 feet. Scarce in Gumsur, but abounds in Bodogoda, where it is burnt for firewood. The flowers are offered at the shrines of the Hindoo divinities. The bark is used medicinally, in diarrhœa.—*Captain Macdonald.*

OSYRIS PELTATA.

Pha-oun. BURM.

This is found in Tavoy.—*Wall.*

OUK-GUAY, BURM. This tree is found all over the Tenasserim provinces, but it is scarce, and yields a perishable short grained wood. It is not heavy and floats in water when seasoned. Its maximum length is 15 feet and maximum girth 1½ cubits.—*Captain Dance.*

OUK-KYINE, BURM. A tree of Moulmein, wood used in ordinary house building.—*Cal. Cat. Ex.* 1862.

OUN-THUAY, BURM.? This white, soft, wood is met with in Amherst, where it is employed for common carpentry purposes. It is not subject to injury from insects.—*Capt. Dance.*

P.

PAD-DAN. BURM. In Amherst, a timber used for making drums and musical instruments. It is a kind of red sanders wood.—*Cat. Ex.* 1851.

PADRI. The Tamil and Malayala name of a Malabar and Canara tree which is about twenty feet long and eight inches in diameter: it produces a small white flower, in shape like the fuchsia (?) or rather the snow drop, which has a most powerful fragrance; they are prescribed in infusion as a cooling drink in fevers. The leaves, if steeped in a portion of lime juice, make a most grateful and cooling drink. This is one of the sacred trees, and considered the property of the pagoda; and the flowers are held sacred for the purpose of decorating the dancing-girls' heads on days of ceremony.—*Edye, Forests of Malabar and Canara.*

PA-KA-THAN, BURM. A timber in Amherst, Tavoy and Mergui, of maximum girth 2 cubits and maximum length 12 feet. Abundant, but widely scattered all over these provinces inland. When seasoned it floats in water. It is used by Burmese to make paddles, oars, &c.; is a tough, durable, good wood, but too widely scattered to be easily obtained, unless such a large quantity be ordered as would repay a search in the forest.—*Captain Dance.*

PALA.—? In Penang, a tall thin tree; wood used for planks.—*Col. Frith.*

PALA MARAM. The Malayala name of one of the jungle fruit trees of Malabar and Canara. It produces a fruit which the natives use medicinally, but as a timber it is of no value. —*Edye, Forests of Malabar and Canara.*

PALA UTAN.—? In Penang, a wood of light brown colour, from a large tree; only used for planks.—*Col. Frith.*

PALAVARAYNEE, Tel. In the Nalla Mallai, a light, yellow, hard, wood, which Mr. Latham thinks is the *Peda kalmesura* of the Northern Circars.—*Mr. Latham.*

PALAWAH, Burm. A beautiful red but heavy wood of British Burmah. A cubic foot weighs lbs. 52. In a full grown tree on good soil the average length of the trunk to the first branch is 45 feet, and average girth measured at 6 feet from the ground is 6 feet. It sells at 12 annas per cubic foot.—*Dr. Brandis, Cal. Cat. Ex.* 1862.

PALENGA ZEYLANICA, *Thw.*

Palenga-gass. Singh.

A tree 40 to 50 feet high, of the Ambagamowa district in Ceylon, at an elevation of about 3,000 feet.—*Thw. En. Pl. Zeyl. p.* 287.

PALI. In Tamil, Irambu in Malabar, Palari in Portuguese; is the Ceylon wood known in England by the name of Iron-wood. It grows to about thirty feet in height, and twenty inches in diameter. It is very useful for stocks of anchors, piles for jetty-heads, beams in store houses and places where strength is required; for such purposes it will be found useful and durable: it may be obtained in great quantities at a very moderate rate.—*Edye, on the Timber of Ceylon.* (*Note*—Is this a species of Mesua?)

PALLAGA PAYANYE. The Malayala name of a Malabar and Canara tree, which means "plank wood." It grows to about twelve inches in diameter, and fourteen feet in height. It is soft and light, and is used by the natives for country vessels and catamarans. This wood, and all the light jungle woods, are of little value, in consequence of their early and rapid decay.—*Edye, Forests of Malabar and Canara.*

PALM TREE WOODS. Notices of the palm woods will be found under the names of their respective trees, the principal of which are the Areca catechu; Borassus flabelliformis; species of Calamus; Cocos nucifera; species of Corypha, many products of which—their woods, leaves and fruits—are largely used in India. The palm woods are, however, sparingly employed in England for cabinet and marquetry work and sometimes for billiard cues which are considered to stand remarkably well; they are also turned into snuff boxes, &c. The smaller kinds are imported under the names of Partridge canes (called, also Chinese or fishing canes), Penang canes from the island of that name, together with some other small palms which are used for walking sticks, the roots serving to form the knobs or handles. The knobs of these sticks exhibit irregular dots something like the scales of snakes, these arise from the small roots proceeding from the principal stem; which latter shows dotted fibres at each end of the stick, and streaks along the side of the same. The twisted palm sticks, are the central stems or midribs of the date palm; they are twisted when green, and stretched with heavy weights until they are thoroughly dry: they are imported from the Neapolitan coast but are considered to be produced in Egypt. The shells of the cocoa-nut and coquilla-nut, and the kernels of the areca or betle-nut, and those of the corosos or ivory-nut, have likewise their uses in English workshops. But, only two or three varieties of the several hundred species are imported into Great Britain from the East and West Indies. They are known in England by the names, palm, palmetto, palmyra, and nutmeg, leopard, and porcupine wood, &c. from their fancied resemblances; for, when they are cut horizontally, they exhibit dots like the spice, and when obliquely, the markings assimilate to the quills of the porcupine. The trunks of palms are not considered by physiological botanists to be true wood, they are all endogenes, and all grow from within, and are always soft and spongy in the centre, but are gradually harder towards the outside: they do not possess the medullary rays of the proper woods, but only the vertical fibres, which are held together by a much softer substance like pith or cement, so that the horizontal section is alway dotted, by which they may be readily distinguished from all true woods. The colours and hardness of the two parts differ very materially.—*Tredgold.*

PANDAN, Hind.? A tree of Chota Nagpore, furnishing a hard, red timber.—*Cal. Cat. Ex.* 1862.

PANDOR, Hind.? A tree of Chota Nagpore, with a soft, white wood.—*Cal. Cat. Ex.* 1862.

PANEEOLLO, Uria. A tree in Ganjam and Gumsur, of extreme height 40 feet, circumference 2 feet and height from the ground to the intersection of the first branch, 8 feet. Tolerably common and burnt for firewood. The bark is used medicinally.—*Captain Macdonald.*

PA-NGAN, Burm. A compact white wood of Amherst, used for boats and oars, and for making musical instruments. It seems to be Gmelina arborea.—*Captain Dance.*

PANICHIE. The Tamil and Portuguese name of a tree which grows in Ceylon and Travancore, from thirty to sixty feet high, and ten to twenty four inches in diameter. In Ceylon, it grows tall and straight; in Travancore it is not more than twenty feet high, and is curved. It produces a fruit which resembles externally the small russet apple: when pressed it yields a very glutinous juice, which is used as a substitute for glue; and may be considered in that country as very superior to glue for the use of joiners. In Ceylon, this tree is converted into masts, yards

&c. for country vessels; and the native carpenters consider it the best sort of all the jungle woods for that purpose.—*Edye, on the Timber of Ceylon.*

PAN-LOUN. In Tavoy a close grained red wood: used for building.—*Dr. Wallich.*

PANOON. A large tree of Lucknow, grows spontaneously in the Tarace: its large timber is used for beams, &c.—*Cal. Cat. Ex.* 1862.

PANTHEET-YA. In Tavoy, a good, white, rough wood; useful for boat building.—*Dr. Wallich.*

PAPISRANG. From Penang, are two notices of woods of this name, viz.:

Papisrang, purple colour. A strong wood; used for beams.

Papisrang, wood of a pale brown colour. Six to nine feet in circumference, forty feet long; not good for beams; chiefly used for furniture.—*Colonel Frith.*

PARAN-THA, Burm. A tree of Moulmein. Its wood is soft and used in ordinary purposes of building material.—*Cal. Cat. Ex.* 1862.

PARANYAN? Champac? A tree of Akyab, which grows to a moderate size, and is procurable in the Sandoway district. Wood used as planking.—*Cal. Cat. Ex.* 1862.

PARATY MARAM, the Tamil name of a Malabar and Canara tree. It grows to about twelve inches in diameter, and twelve feet long, and produces a nut which the natives eat, and on which wild animals feed. It is not of much value.—*Edye, Forests of Malabar and Canara.*

PA-RA-WA. In Amherst, a hard, red, compact wood, with large fibre, and fit for gun-carriages or other similar purposes. It is exempt from attacks of insects. It is used for spears and arrows. (*See* Parrawa: are they identical and a species of Garcinia?)

PARCUTILLE. The Tamil name of a Ceylon tree which grows to about twenty-four inches in diameter, and fifteen feet in height. It is used by the natives in boats, houses, and other works: it is not of great value.—*Edye, on the Timber of Ceylon.*

PARKIA BIGLANDULOSA, *W. & A.*

Mimosa pedunculata, *Roxb.*

Chendu phul. Hind.	Sambrani manu. Tel.

A very elegant tree of the Malay Archipelago: wood not known. The Malays are said to be fond of the mealy matter which surrounds the seeds, and of the seeds themselves which taste like garlic. The flower buds resemble balls of red velvet.—*Voigt, Dr. Riddell.*

PARKIA BIGLOBOSA. A very elegant tree of large size, introduced from Africa, the legumes are filled with a farinaceous pulp, the wood is hard and promising. Surrounded by an astringent bark. A watery extract has been prepared, the value of which for tanning purposes has yet to be tested. A supply of timber is not yet procurable.—*Dr. Cleghorn in M. E. J. R.*

PARKIA ROXBURGHII, *G. Don.*

Mimosa biglobosa, *Roxb.*

A tree of Assam and Sylhet, wood not known. —*Voigt.* (*Note*—Are the last two identical?)

PARKINSONIA ACULEATA, *Linn.; W. & A.*

Barbadoes flower fence. Eng.	Genet epineux. Fr.
Jerusalem thorn. „	Sima jiluga. Tel.

A small graceful tree, with large yellow flowers, of the West Indies and South America domesticated in India. It grows 12 or 15 feet high and is seen every where in hedges of the Peninsula, springing up with less care than any other tree, is valuable for hedges, and furnishing abundant cuttings for fuel. A useful fibre is obtained from its stem, valuable as a paper material.—*Voigt, Drs. Riddell, Royle, Eng. Cyc.*

PARRAWAH, Burm. A timber of Amherst, Tavoy and Mergui, of maximum girth 3 cubits and maximum length 22 feet. Abundant all over Tenasserim and Martaban provinces. When seasoned it sinks in water. It is a durable smooth-grained tough wood; used by Burmese for sticks, helves for pickaxes, and hoes, handles of chisels and other tools &c. Recommended for helves and handles of tools generally.—*Captain Dance.* (*Note*—See Pa-ra-wa. Is this a Garcinia?)

PARSI, Hind.? A tree of Chota Nagpore. Hard red timber.—*Cal. Cat. Ex.* 1862.

PASA LINIJA. A Penang wood of a light brown colour. A large tree; used only for planks: soon decays.—*Col. Frith.*

PASELAY, Tam. A Tinnevelly wood of a whitey brown colour. Used for furniture.—*Col. Frith.*

PATKEALE. A tree of the western parts of Ceylon, a cubic foot of its wood weighs 42 lbs. and it lasts 40 years. It is used for common house building.—*Mr. Mendis.*

PATONWA, Uria. Gardenia, *Species*?? A tree of Ganjam and Gumsur, extreme height 20 feet, circumference 1 foot and height from ground to the intersection of the first branch, 5 feet. Used chiefly for firewood being tolerably common. The fruit thrown into a pond of water kills all the fish in it and is used for that purpose by the keyouts or fishermen. This mode of catching fish is designated "Macho Mohneebaro." The fruit is said to be poisonous, but the seeds are used medicinally for fever.—*Capt. Macdonald.*

PATTI VAYNGU (which means dog-wood), the Malayala name, in Malabar and Canara, of one of the inferior sorts of jungle wood: it is considered of little use or value.—*Edye, Forests of Malabar and Canara.*

PATSENG-NGO, BURM.? In Tavoy, a superior high-coloured aromatic wood, like mahogany.—*Mr. Blundell.*

PAULAY, TAM. In Tinnevelly a wood of a deep straw colour. Fancy work.—*Col. Frith.*

PAULGHAT WOODS. Colonel Frith notices the following woods, in this district:

Ab Eney.	Eroopoottooirvolly.	Nova
Bumboo	Ittee veittee.	Oome teak.
Benteak.	Kullen teak.	Oodoogoo.
Cedar.	Kurroovalagom.	Portia.
Cedar-root.	Kurroomardoo.	Teak.
Cautovanga.	Kuroonganlee.	Vangay.
Chadachey.	Muroodoo.	

PAUL-TEAK, TAM. In Travancore, a wood of a brown colour, specific gravity 0·739. Used for furniture, gun-carriages, &c.—*Col. Frith.*

PAUSEE. In Kimedy, a tree 60 feet in height, 5 feet in circumference and 30 feet to the first branch: furnishing a light hard wood used to make presses, wheels, &c.—*Captain Philipps.*

PAVETTA INDICA, *Linn.*

Ixora paniculata, *Lam.* | Ixora pavetta, *Roxb.*

Kookoor choora. BENG. | Pavetti. TAM.
Pavetta. SINGH.

Abundant in Ceylon, up to an elevation of 3,000 feet, and all over India, timber very small. —*Thw., Voigt, M. E. J. R.*

PAVETTA TOMENTOSA, Papirree, also Papatta, TEL. Wood hard but very small. It grows in the Godavery forests and at Tavoy.—*Captain Beddome, Dr. Mason.*

PAVIA INDICA, *Royle.*

Indian Horse Chesnut. ENG. | Pangla. HIND.
Kanour. HIND.

This is a lofty tree and not less ornamental than the English horse chesnut. It grows on the mountains in Kamaon, Gurhwal, Sirmore and Kanawar, also near the sources of the Ganges. The seed contains a large proportion of fecula, and though combined with some bitter principle, is eaten in the Himalayas.—*Royle's Illustr. Him. Bot. p.* 135.

PEE-DAUP, BURM. Mimosa, *Species.* A wood of Tavoy.—*Dr. Wallich.*

PEEDOO MARAM, TAM. A small tree wood used for building in Wynaad where it grows plentifully.

PEE MA PEW, BURM. White Peema, ENG. A tree of maximum girth 6 cubits and maximum length 30 feet. Very abundant all over the Tenasserim and Martaban provinces near the red Peema. When seasoned it floats in water. It is a tough wood, lighter than, but does not last for so long a time as, Red Peema, and rots in any position when shut out, as in the hulls of ships, in store &c.—*Captain Dance.* (*Note*—Is this Lagerstrœmia reginæ?)

PEGU TIMBER TREES, TIMBER AND FANCY-WOODS. Dr. McClelland noticing 76 timbers, of these forests generally, says

White Woods.—Eighty-five species are soft and useless, being only fit for fuel. Many of them however are valuable, either for their fruit, gums, oil-seeds or spices; others, for their close and compact structure, are employed in the manufacture of small ware, as a species of *Nauclea* is used for making combs and two species of *Erythrina* yields the light charcoal employed in the manufacture of gunpowder.

These light woods, useless as timber, belong to the families of *Urticaceæ* (including more than twenty species of *Ficus*,) and *Sterculiaceæ, Laurineæ, Rubiaceæ, Myristicaceæ, Anonaceæ, Spondiaceæ* and *Bignoniaceæ*, with odd species from other families.

The remaining white woods, twenty-five in number, are valuable for their strength and closeness of grain. Seventeen of these are fit for house-building, viz.

(1) Hibiscus macrophylla.
Kydia calycina.
Eriolæna tilifolia.
Counarus speciosa.
Grewia floribunda.
Grewia spectabils and G. Hookerii.
Sapindus rubiginosa.
Millingtonia simplicifolia.
Sandoricum Indicum.
(10) Amoora (Aglaia) rohitoca.
Juglans tricocca.
Geloxium bifarium.
Excæcaria agallocha.
Walsura piscidia.
Canarium geniculatum.
Indigofera sp.
Terminalia belerica and T. violata.

And eight, from the hardness and fineness of their grain, render them valuable as fancy woods for cabinet making, viz.

(18) Semecarpus anacardium.
Sibia sp. (glomerata.)
Casuaria pentandra.
Chaulmoogra odorata.
Strychnos nux-vomica.
Conocarpus robustus.
Bauhinia parviflora also B. brachycarpa.
(25) Elæodendron integrifolia.

Red-colored Woods.—These are twenty-five in number, seven of which, from their strength and solidity, are adapted for the various purposes of house-building; viz.

(26) Heritiera minor and H. litoralis.
Eugenia pulchella.
E. myrtifolia.
E. vulgaris.
E. ternifolia and E. jambolana.
Sonneratia apetala.
Terminalia chebula.
Lagerstræmia pymmah.
Aglaia spectabilis.
(32) Ulmus alternifolius and U. integrifolius.

Seven, from the elegance of their grain and colour, are suited to the various purposes of which mahogany is used, viz.

(33) Cedrela toona.
Swietenia chikrassa.
Armosia dasycarpa.
Pterocarpus dalbergioides.
Careya arborea.
Barringtonia acutangula and B. speciosa.
Castanea Indica.

And eleven are suited to the finer purposes of fancy cabinet work, viz.

(40) Adenanthera pavonina.
Calophyllum longifolium.
Dolichampia pomifera.
Pygium acuminata.
Photinia serratifolia.
Acacia stipulata.
Acacia catechu.
Acacia serissa.
Acacia elata.
Ricinus dicocca.
Antidesma paniculata.

Yellow Woods.—These are four in number, hard and fine grained, and suited to fancy purposes.

(51) Gmelina arborea.
Morinda bracteata.
Morinda exserta.
Garcinia cowa.

Dark-brown Woods.—These are twelve in number and are all valuable. Eleven are adapted for house-building, and probably for ship-building and one for special purposes requiring great strength and hardness.

(54) Pterospermum aceroides, also P. subacerifolium and P. acerifolium.
Pentaptera arjuna and P. glabra.
Melanorrhœa usitata Theetsee or Lignum vitæ.
Dalichampia pomifera.
Butea frondosa.
Mangifera attenuata.
Anacardium occidentale.
Zizyphus jujuba.
Averrhoa carambola.
Picrardia sapota.
Ancestrolobus carnea and A. mollis.
Rondeletia tinctoria.

Black Woods.—These consist of four different kinds, all of which are valuable for their strength and hardness.

(66) Dalbergia, *Species.*
Cassia Sumatrana.
Inga xylocarpa, and I. bijemina.
Diospyros melanoxylon.

Light-brown Woods.—There are nine varieties of this colored wood, embracing all the timber of most value in the Province, exclusive of Teak.

(70) Dipterocarpus alatus.
Dipterocarpus turbinatus.
Shorea robusta.
Melicocca trijuga.
Dillenia augusta, also D. scabra and D. speciosa.
Hopea odorata.
Azadarchta Indica.

The above list embraces all the useful timber found in the forests of the Pegu province, except teak. Besides timber well adapted for house-building, the list contains several promising kinds that have never yet been fairly tried for ship-building, and which in point of strength are equal to teak or oak. The timbers referred to more especially are Nos. 73, 68, 54, 55, 30 and 37, Nos. 25, 23, 19, 14, and 4 are also deserving of trial for ship-building, and No. 56 for any special purposes, where great strength and density are required. Until these trials are decided, the timber employed for house-building purposes should be restricted to other kinds.

The forests of Pegu and their timbers have been described by Drs. Mason, Falconer, McClelland and Brandis, and Dr. McClelland says that timber for ordinary purposes is most plentiful throughout all parts of the southern forests of Pegu. The following are the trees which may be had of any size and to any extent.

Sapindus acuminata,
Odina woodier.
Dillenia augusta.
Dillenia scabra.
Blackwellia spirale.
Blackwellia perpinqua.
Cuytia amœna.
Bombax pentandra.
Connarus, species.
Nauclea parviflora.
Nauclea cordifolia.
Nauclea undulata.
Nauclea cadamba.
Uvaria ventricosa.
Bignonia spathodea.
Bignonia coronaria.
Bignonia adenophylla.
Sterculia alata.
Sterculia ornata.
Sterculia ramosa.
Sterculia fœtida.
Sterculia balangas.
Sterculia guttata.
Ricinus dicocca.
Artocarpus incisa.
Artocarpus liquosa?
Terminalia bellerica.
Terminalia scevola.
Hibiscus macrophylla.
Grewia floribunda.
Ficus macrophylla.
Ficus lanceolaria.
Ficus congesta.
Ficus glomerata.
Ficus cordifolia.
Ficus nitada.
Ficus usophylla?
Ficus pilifera.
Ficus bifasia.
Ficus mamilaria.
Ficus oppositifolia.
Kydia calycina.
Eliodendron, species.
Celtis tetranthera.
Grewia nudiflora.
Strychnos nux vomica.
Garcinia cowa.
Dipterocarpus turbinatus.
Dipterocarpus alatus.
Walsura piscidia.
Waltheria velutina.
Macroclena spectabilis.
Sandoricum indicum.
Pentaptera glabra.
Pentaptera arjuna.
Diospyros melanoxylon.
Dalbergia robusta.
Dalbergia frondosa.
Lagerstrœmia pymmah.

—*Dr. McClelland in India Selections No. IX.*

See AMHERST, BURMAH, MOULMEIN.

PENANG WOODS. The following 18 furniture woods, grown in Penang or Prince of Wales' Island, were sent to the Exhibition of 1851.

1. Angsena, or Senna Baymah.
2. Baloh Bungah.
3. Kulim.
4. Baloh Bungah.
5. Betel-nut tree root.
6. Clove tree.
7. Cocoa-nut tree root.
8. Durian (wild).
9. Eboch-tree root.
10. Ebony.
11. Guava wood.
12. Ibool wood.
13. Kamuning.
14. Baloh.
15. Mirlimoh.
16. Penang Wood.
17. Ranggas.
18. Siam Wood.
19. Timbusi.

42 woods of Penang by Colonel Frith.

Brantey.
Banho.
Bintagor.
Curupas.
Cooran.
Chinjeritt.
Cumpas.
Cawa-Arang.
Canis.
Chiuracy.
Cocoa-nut.
China red wood.
Ceylon ebony.
Damarlout.
Duuorhung.
Drum.
Hama Raja.
Maddang Kamenhir.
Miraban.
Maddang Tandack.
Maskaw.
Mankadu.
Maliler.
Maribot.
Mandara.
Nebong.
Pasa Linija.
Pala.
Pinang Bach.
Pala Utan.
Papisrang.
Penang Teak.
Penang Jack.
Rangha.
Rokam.
Red wood.
Sankuang.
Satin wood.
Siam ebony.
Teak.
Tampinnis.
Tija.

PENANG JACK. Wood of a yellow colour. Used only for ornamental furniture.—*Col. Frith.*

PENARU PALAM MARAM, the Malayala name of a tree. It is used at times by the natives, but is of little value.—*Edye, Forests of Malabar and Canara.*

PENEBARROO, SINGH. A wood of the eastern province of Ceylon. A cubic foot weighs lbs. 61 and it is said to last 50 to 90 years. It is used for rafters, &c. Fences made of the sticks of this tree are the most durable of all.—*Mr. Mendis.*

PENG-LAY-BYUN, BURM. A small sized tough wood of Tavoy.—*Mr. Blundell.*

PENG-LAY-KABOAY, BURM. In Tavoy a heavy small sized wood; suitable for handspikes, handles, &c.—*Mr. Blundell.*

PENG-LAY-OUN, BURM. In Amherst, a timber used for spear handles; it is a most valuable wood, compact, homogeneous, very heavy, of a deep brown colour and fine grain, having no tendency to split, and exempt from attacks of insects.—*Cat. Ex.* 1851.

PENG-LAY-OUN, Burm. In Tavoy, strong, rough, red wood, like Mimosa serissa.—*Mr. Blundell.*

PENLAY-PEEN, Burm. A Tavoy wood, used in building.—*Dr. Wallich.*

PERJI, the Malayala name of a tree which grows in the forests of Malabar and Canara to about twelve feet in height, and ten inches in diameter. It is very hard and strong, and is used by the natives for knees and boat timbers; and is ranked among the jungle-woods of the coast. —*Eyde, Forests of Malabar and Canara.*

PERRA MARAM in Malayala, Coia Maram in Tamil, are the names of a tree that produces the guava fruit. Its wood is very hard and close grained. This tree grows to about twelve or eighteen feet high, and eight inches in diameter; it is used, in conjunction with the jungle-woods, for inferior purposes, but is generally known as a garden fruit tree.—*Edye, Forests of Malabar and Canara.*

PET-THAN, Burm. A tree, abundant in Tavoy; not procurable in Moulmein, found in Tavoy and Mergui. When seasoned it sinks in water. Maximum girth and length not ascertained. A very hard and durable wood, used by Burmese for wedges.—*Captain Dance.*

PEW-BOCK, Burm. A tree of maximum girth 3 cubits, maximum length 25 feet. Very abundant along sea coast near Tavoy and Mergui. When seasoned it sinks in water. It is a strong, tough, durable wood; recommended for helves. —*Captain Dance.*

PHASEE, Uria. A tree of Ganjam and Gumsur, of extreme height 60 feet, circumference 6 feet, and height from the ground to the intersection of the first branch, 30 feet. A light hard wood, used for sugar presses, rice pounders, and bandy wheels, and occasionally for making boats of. It is tolerably plentiful.—*Captain Macdonald.*

PHATAL PIPAL, Hind.? A tree of Chota Nagpore, with a hard, white timber.—*Cal. Cat. Ex.* 1862.

PHAT THAN, Burm. A tree of Moulmein, wood used for chisel handles.—*Cal. Cat. Ex.* 1862.

PHOBEROS HOOKERIANUS, *Wright.* A great tree of the central province of Ceylon, at an elevation of 4,000 to 7,000 feet.—*Thw. p.* 17.

PHŒNIX. A genus of palms, the species of which are found in the south of Europe, in the north of Africa, and in the south of Asia, eastwards to the Archipelago. As they do not furnish much useful timber or fancy woods, a mere notice of them and their products must here suffice.

Phœnix dactylifera. Linn., the famed date tree of Arabia, grows there to a height of 50 to 80 feet. Baskets are made of the leaf stalks.

Phœnix farinifera, Roxb., grows along the Coromandel coast. It has an edible fruit, and its stem contains a fecula which is used as food by the natives in times of famine. The leaflets are wrought into sleeping mats, and the common petioles are split into three or four and are used to make baskets of various kinds.

Phœnix sylvestris, Roxb., common all over India, is generally supposed to be the Ph. dactylifera, in its uncultivated state. Its juice is of great value, as palm wine, which is largely used as a stimulant, and is extensively converted into sugar. On the Bombay side, the trunks freed from the inner pith, are chiefly used as convenient and economical water conduits, and extensively used for the formation of embankments, temporary bridges and piers.—*Dr. Gibson, Eng. Cyc., Voigt.*

PHOTINIA SERRATIFOLIA?

Doukyat. Burm.

Found in the neighbourhood of Rangoon and along the banks of the stream in the Rangoon district, in the direction of the teak forests. It is a red wood and adapted to cabinet making. Voigt mentions Photinia (Mespilus) Bengalensis, *Wallich,* a small tree of Nepaul, the Khassya hills, Assam and Chittagong: and Photinia eugenifolia, *Lindl.,* a tree of the Khassya mountains: their woods are not known.—*Dr. McClelland, Voigt.*

PHUTKAL, Hind.? A tree of Chota Nagpore, with a soft, white wood.—*Cal. Cat. Ex.* 1862.

PHYLLANTHUS, *Species, Brandis.*

Nasha. Burm.

A light coloured wood exhibiting a natural shine or polish when planed. A cubic foot weighs lbs. 35. In a full grown tree on good soil the average length of the trunk to the first branch is 30 feet and average girth measured at 6 feet from the ground is 6 feet.—*Dr. Brandis, Cal. Cat. Ex.* 1862.

PHYLLANTHUS EMBLICA, *Linn.*

Emblica officinalis, *Gært.*

Amluj. Arab.	Amla ka. Sans.
Aonla. Duk.	Nelli-gass. Singh.
Aonli "	Topa nelli. Tam.
Aonla. Hind.	Oosarika. Tel.
Aonli. Mahr.	

This tree grows in Ceylon, in peninsular India, and northwards to the Jumma, in Bengal and the Moluccas. It is common in Ceylon, on exposed grassy places, up to 4,000 feet. In the Bombay side, it is pretty common, both inland and on the coast. Wood is hard and rather durable, particularly under water, but seldom obtainable sufficiently straight, except in gardens, where it is often grown. The bark is very astringent and used in tanning. Fruit is pickled or preserved in sugar.—*Thwaites, Gibson, Voigt.*

PHYLLANTHUS RETICULATUS.— ? A shrub of the Coromandel side of India, the Konkans, and Bengal, with a wood white and durable and employed by the hill people for various economical purposes. It is frequently employed for ornamental hedges. Cattle eat the leaves.

PHYOO, BURM. A tree of maximum girth $1\frac{1}{2}$ cubits, and maximum length 17 feet. Abundant in Tavoy and Mergui, also in less abundance in Amherst province. When seasoned, it floats in water. It has a tolerably good strong wood, but not with much tenacity of fibre.—*Captain Dance.*

PICHHRA, HIND. ? A tree of Chota Nagpore, with a soft white wood.—*Cal. Cat. Ex.* 1862.

PIENCHE, TAM. A Ceylon tree which is of a dark colour and very heavy and close grained. It grows to about twelve inches in diameter, and fourteen feet in height. From this tree the native carpenters make the frames of vessels, it being considered durable; it produces a fruit which is of no use.—*Edye, on the Timber of Ceylon.*

PIENMAHNE, BURM. A Tavoy tree, yields very strong knee-timber.—*Dr. Wallich.*

PIENMAH PUE, BURM. A Tavoy wood. —*Dr. Wallich.* (*Note*—Are these two species of Lagerstrœmia ?)

PIERARDIA, *Species. ?*

Kanna. BURM. | Kuzzo. BURM.

A timber tree of Tavoy.—*Dr. Wallich.*

PIERARDIA SAPIDA, *Royle.*

Kanayoe. BURM. | Luteo ? HIND.

A small tree of Tipperah and Burmah. A cubic foot weighs lbs. 61, in a full grown tree on good soil, the average length of the trunk to the first branch is 15 feet and average girth measured at 6 feet from the ground is 4 feet. Dr. Brandis says that the wood is not used, but Dr. McClelland notices, Pierardia sapota, Kanayoe, BURM., as plentiful in the Pegu and Tounghoo forests, as well as about Rangoon and with a wood dark brown in colour, and the Moulmein Committee sent to the Exhibition of 1862, a specimen of the wood of Pierardia sapida, Ka-na-oo, BURM., as a tree of Moulmein with a very hard wood: used wheel axles.—*Dr. Brandis, Dr. McClelland, Cal. Cat. Ex.* 1862, *Royle's Ill.*

PINANG — ? Bach — ? A Penang wood of a brown colour. A large tree, wood used for beams.—*Col. Frith.*

PINLAY JALLAT, BURM. A tree of maximum girth $2\frac{1}{2}$ to 3 cubits and maximum length 15 feet. Tolerably plentiful by the sea side and very near to the water's edge, in the Tenasserim provinces. When seasoned, it floats in water. Its wood is strongly recommended for fuzes, it is free from oil, and acid, and light, yet strong; it is much used for rockets of enormous dimensions and for wooden guns, and is used for the burning of the dead Phoongyes and on other occasions. —*Captain Dance.*

PINNAI, BURM. ? In Amherst, said to be a fruit tree; the wood affords a yellow dye, and is a compact, handsome, yellow wood, suitable for common cabinet purposes. It is probably an Artocarpus. Indeed, under the same Burmese name, Mr. Blundell describes an Artocarpus of Tavoy with a strong, close grained yellow wood.—*Cat. Ex.* 1851, *Mr. Blundell.*

PINATHA, BURM. ? In Amherst, Tavoy and Mergui, a tree of maximum girth 5 cubits and maximum girth 25 feet. Very abundant all over the Tenasserim provinces particularly in the old deserted towns. When seasoned it floats in water. It is a light wood with a yellow hue which darkens on exposure. Useful from the yellow dye which boiling extracts from it and which is permanent in cloth, and not affected even by boiling water. It is used by Phoongees. This wood has a fine tone when struck, and is used for musical instruments by the Burmese, it is used by English brush makers for the backs of hair brushes, being a handsome wood which takes a good polish.—*Captain Dance.* (*Note.*—Is this a species of *Artocarpus.* Is it the same as Pinnai ?)

PINUS. The Pine tree genus consists, for the most part, of timber trees, many of which are of great beauty and of much value on account of their timber. Many of them are growing along with fir trees (Abies), yew trees, and the larch (Larix) in the northern Himalayas, in China and Japan, and one or two in Burmah, one ? in Cochin-China and one in Arabia. These have been noticed by Drs. Wallich, Royle, O'Shaughnessy, Hooker, Mason and Brandis and Thunberg described others in Japan. The following may be noticed.

PINUS BRUNONIANA, *Wall.*

Pinus dumosa, *Lamb.*
Abies Brunoniana — ?

Silver Fir. ENG. | Semadoong.

A tree of Nepaul, Bhootan and Gossain Than, growing occasionally in dense and gigantic forests, 70 to 80 feet high, with a clear trunk of from 15 to 20 feet, and a spreading branching head. Dr. Hooker measured one 28 feet in girth.—*Eng. Cyc., Hooker's Him. Journ.*

PINUS DAMMARA, BURM. *Wall.* According to Dr. Wallich, in Tavoy, a very large tree, used in building.—*Dr. Wallich.*

PINUS DEODARA, *Lambert.*

Cedrus deodara.
Abies deodara.

Sacred Indian Fir. ENG. | Kelon ? HIND.
Deva-dara. HIND.

A magnificent tree with a trunk of 12 to 30 feet in girth, growing on the mountains of Kedarkanth, Nepaul and Thibet, at a height of 7,000 and 12,000 feet, as also in the woods of Almorah. Its wood is highly resinous and is very durable, lasting from 200 to 400 years.—*Royle, Ill. p.* 350, *Eng. Cyc., Hooker's Him. Journal. See* CEDAR, CEDRUS, DEODAR.

PINUS EXCELSA, *Wall.*

Tong-schi. CHIN. | Kuel of Sirmoor & Garwhal.

Resembles the Weymouth pine, and is remarkable for its drooping branches. It grows in West Nepal, not in East Nepal and Sikkim, but is common in Bhootan. It is found with the deodar, at Narainhutty, Theog. The wood is durable and close grained, and so resinous as to be used for flambeaux.—*Dr. O'Shaughnessy, p.* 612, *Dr. Hooker's Him. Jour. Vol. II. p.* 45, *Royle's Illustr. p.* 349.

PINUS GERARDIANA.

Neoza chilghoza, *Elphin.*

Neoza. HIND. in Kumaon. | Julgozeh. PUSHT.
Chilgozeh. PUSHT.

A tree with a lofty trunk, a native of the coldest forests of the Himalayas, confined to the northern and drier face. Its seeds form an article of food in Kunawar.—*Eng. Cyc., Dr. O'Shaughnessy, p.* 613, *Royle's Illust. p.* 350.

PINUS KÆMPFERI, *Lambert.*

Abies Kæmpferi.

A native of Japan, found wild on the mountains of Fako.

PINUS KHASYANA.

Tin-yoo-ben. BURM.

Found on the hills in British Burmah, between the Sitang and the Salween rivers at an elevation exceeding 3,000 feet. It is a stately tree, sometimes as high as 200 feet to the top but owing to the difficulties of transport from these hills no timber of this species has as yet been brought to Moulmein. The wood of both kinds is very rich in resin. In a full grown tree on good soil the average length of the trunk to the first branch is 80 feet and average girth measured at 6 feet from the ground is 9 feet.—*Dr. Brandis, Cal. Cat. Ex.* 1862.

PINUS LATTERI, *Mason.*

A tree of Amherst province, on the banks of the Thoungyeen river, 50 to 60 feet high, or more, and 4½ to 8 feet in girth. It is not found west of the Donaw mountains. The Karens make tar of its wood, which is excessively resinous.—*Dr. Mason, As. Soc. Journ. Jan.* 1849.

PINUS LONGIFOLIA, *Lamb.*

Cheer. HIND. | Thansa. HIND.
Sullah. „ | Surrul. „

Grows in the Himalayas, in the entrance to Nepal, in the Cheree pass, along the Tonse and Jumna rivers, and at elevations of 5,000 and 6,000 feet within the Himalayas. Growing at the lowest of the pine tree elevations, it is the most readily obtainable from the plains, and, as the wood is light, it is often employed as a substitute for English deal. It is full of resinous matter like the wood of the deodar, and both these are frequently employed in the hills for making torches.—*Royle Ill. p.* 349, 351.

PINUS MASSONIANA, *Lamb., Abel ?*

Tinyooben. BURM.

Is a moderate sized tree found in the forest of Dipterocarpus grandiflora (Eng. forest), east of the Salween river. Spars of this species have occasionally been brought down to Moulmein. In a full grown tree on good soil the average length of the trunk to the first branch is 50 feet and average girth measured at 6 feet from the ground is 6 feet.—*Dr. Brandis, Cal. Cat. Ex.* 1862. (*Note*—Is this Dr. Mason's Pinus Latteri ?)

PINUS PINDROW, *Royle ?*

Abies Pindrow, *Royle.*

Pindrow. HIND. ? | Morinda. HIND.

A magnificent species, even to the limits of the forests, and growing in Kemaon along with the deodar. It comes near P. Webbiana.—*Royle's Illustr.*

PINUS SMITHIANA, *Wall.*

Abies Khutrow — ?
„ Smithiana.

Indian Silver Fir. ENG. | Seh. HIND.

A spruce fir tree of enormous size on the slopes of the Himalayas. It has a dark and sombre appearance, but is peculiarly graceful owing to its symmetrical form and somewhat pendulous habit. Its wood is white, but considered indifferent though readily split into planks, and is used for beams and posts.—*Hooker's Him. Journ., Royle's Illust. Him. Bot. p.* 350.

PINUS WEBBIANA, *Wall. & Lamb.*

Pinus spectabilis, *Lamb.*
Abies Webbiana.

Webb's Fir. ENG. | Gobrea. HIND.
Purple coned Fir. ENG. | Sallur. „
Chilrow of Northern Himalaya. | Oonum. „

Grows at great elevations of the Himalayas, where it is one of the principal ornaments of the forests. It attains a height of 30 to 90 feet with a girth near the ground of 9 to 35 feet, and is unbranched at Choongthan for 40 feet. Its wood is white, soft, splits well, and is highly prized for its durability.—*Hooker's Him. Journ., Royle's Illust. p.* 350.

PIRI. The Tamil name of a Ceylon tree which grows to about twenty feet in height, and two feet in diameter. It is very close in its grain, and is used by the natives for the frames of vessels and in house work. It produces a fruit which is of no use.—*Edye, on the Timber of Ceylon.*

PITHECOLOLIUM SUBCORIACEUM, *Thw.*

Meemini mara. SING.

A large tree, growing, not uncommon, at an elevation of 4,000 to 6,000 feet in the central province of Ceylon: wood unknown.—*Thw. En. Pl. Zeyl.*

PITOLO, URIA? A tree in Ganjam and Gumsur, extreme height 30 feet, circumference 2 feet, and height from the ground to the intersection of the first branch, 6 feet. Abounds, but is only burnt for firewood.—*Captain Macdonald.*

PITTA KALOOCHIA, URIA? A tree of Ganjam and Gumsur, extreme height 36 feet, circumference 3 feet, and height from the ground to the intersection of the first branch, 15 feet. Used for posts, ploughshares and firewood as the kaloochia, but is a larger tree and very plentiful. —*Captain Macdonald.*

PLATANUS ORIENTALIS.

Doolb. ARAB. | Chinar. PERS.
Oriental Plane. ENG.

The Oriental Plane is indigenous in most of the countries of the Levant; from whence it was transported in the first instance to Sicily. It is a native of Asia Minor, but extends into Cashmere. Some of the trees in the Turkish dominions, are of so gigantic a size, that the largest specimens in England, if placed near them, would appear like small shrubs. This Plane was a great favourite among the ancients; they prized it particularly for the close shadow which its spreading foliage afforded, and celebrated many of their festivities beneath its branches. The wood is much like that of the beech, but it is less hard, has a finer and closer grain, and is more capable of receiving a good polish; it is, however, very apt to warp and split, is not durable, and is frequently attacked by the worm. Sinking the wood in water for several years, is said to improve its quality. According to Belon, the Greeks of Mount Athos were in the habit of making boats of a single piece, out of the trunks of the largest trees.—*Book of Trees, p.* 152, *Royle's Ill. p.* 344.

PLYE, is collected in the forests of Borneo. It is the root of a large timber tree of the same name. It is very light, more so than cork, and might perhaps be used for the same purpose.—*Low's Sarawak.* (*Note*—Is it the root of Sonneratia acida: is it the Polai of Singapore?)

POAM. BOA, OR BOE, sometimes called Poam by the people of Malabar, is a Malabar and Canara wood much like the timber called in Ceylon Palari, or Pali, and Irambu, or, as known by the English name, iron-wood. It is a strong, heavy wood, and is considered durable. It grows from 20 to 30 feet high, and from twelve to thirty inches in diameter.—*Edye, Forests of Malabar and Canara.*

POCHOBORO, URIA? A tree of Ganjam and Gumsur. Extreme height 30 feet. Circumference $2\frac{1}{2}$ feet, and height from the ground to the intersection of the first branch, 6 feet. Tolerably common, only used for firewood and charcoal.—*Captain Macdonald.*

PODADENIA SAPIDA, *Thw.*

Rottlera stylanthus, *Thw.*

A large Ceylon tree, growing at Ambagamowa and at Marai Çalai near Ratna povince, at an elevation of 1,000 to 2,000 feet: wood not known. —*Thw. En. Pl. Zeyl. p.* 274.

PODOCARPUS NERIIFOLIA—?

Theetmin. BURM.

The meaning of this Burmese name is "the prince of trees." These are large trees with stems not very regularly shaped, and found on the higher hills between the Sitang and Salween rivers, and on the range which skirts the coast of the Tenasserim provinces in British Burmah. The wood is close grained and may prove a substitute for box-wood. A cubic foot weighs lbs. 50. In a full grown tree on good soil the average length of the trunk to the first branch is 20 feet and average girth measured at 6 feet from the ground is 6 feet.—*Dr. Brandis, Cal. Cat. Ex.* 1862. (*Note*—Podocarpus latifolia occurs in the mountains of Sylhet, and Podocarpus macrophyllus in Nepal, Penang, Amboyna and Japan.—*Royle's Ill. Him. Bot., p.* 349).

POINCIANA ELATA, *Linn.*

Neerangi. CAN. | Sooncaishla. TEL.
Pade Narrayan. TAM.

This willow has been extensively and successfully used by Major Lawford, Madras Engineers, as a protection for the footings of rivers and channel banks, where it is not wanted to spread laterally and to cause obstructions. It should be planted in cuttings in December; it grows quickly; its wood might be used for basket boats. The tree affords a grateful shade, and though continually stripped of its leaves, which, in Cuddapah, are extensively used for manuring indigo fields, it quickly replaces them and that abundantly.—*Dr. Cleghorn.*

POJO HIND.? A tree of Chota Nagpore, with a soft, white wood.—*Cal. Cat. Ex.* 1862.

POLAI. A tree of Singapore. The wood is used to make floats for fishing-nets. It is a very remarkably light, white wood, and might probably be imported and used with advantage as a substitute for cork, and some similar substances. (*Note*—Is this the Plye of Borneo?)

POLAVA, TAM.? A Tinnevelly wood of a light brown colour. Used for musket stocks, and building purposes.—*Colonel Frith.* (Qu.—Is this the Careya arborea?)

PONASO, URIA ? A tree of Ganjam and Gumsur. It is the common jack tree, Artocarpus integrifolia. It is not very plentiful.—*Captain Macdonald.*

PONG. The Tamil and Malayala name of a Malabar and Canara tree which has a very heavy and remarkably strong wood. It grows to about eighteen inches in diameter, and twenty feet in height, and spreads its branches to a great extent. The native carpenters prefer this wood for the knees of vessels, and also for general uses where strength is required. The trunk of the tree is applied to the uses of the blockmaker, for shivers, blocks, &c.—*Edye, Forests of Malabar and Canara.*

PONGAH, TAM. ? A Travancore wood of a brown colour, specific gravity 0·988. Used for building houses.—*Colonel Frith.* (*Note*—Is this identical with Edye's Pong ?)

PONGAMIA, *Species, Brandis.*

Thinwin. BURM.

Not uncommon in the dry forests, in the plains, and on the hills of British Burmah. The heart wood, which is black and tough but rather small, is used for the cross pieces of Burmese harrows, the teeth being made of Sha (Acacia catechu), Myoukkhyau, (Blackwellia tomentosa), and Gyo (Schleichera trijuga). A cubic foot weighs 60 lbs. In a full grown tree on good soil the average length of the trunk to the first branch is 20 feet and average girth measured at 6 feet from the ground is 6 feet. It sells at 12 annas per cubic foot.—*Dr. Brandis, Cal. Cat. Ex.* 1862.

PONGAMIA, *Species, Brandis.*

Thitpagan. BURM.

A soft wood of British Burmah, said to be useless. In a full grown tree on good soil the average length of the trunk to the first branch is 40 feet and average girth measured at 6 feet from the ground is 9 feet. It sells at 4 annas per cubic foot.—*Dr. Brandis, Cal. Cat. Ex.* 1862.

PONGAMIA ARTOPURPUREA, *Wall.* DARK, PURPLE PONGAMIA. This tree is very common about Moulmein, and is a noble tree used in boat and house building.—*Drs. Wallich and Mason.*

PONGAMIA GLABRA, *Vent.*

Galedupa Indica, *Lam.*
Robinia mitis, *Linn.*
Dalbergia arborea, *Willde.*

Kurunja. BENG.
Karung. BURM.
Hoongay. CAN.
Kurunj. MAHR.
Poonga maram. TAM.
Kanuga chettu. TEL.
Korunjo. URIA.

This graceful tree grows all over India and in the two peninsulas, attaining a height of 40 to 50 feet. It is excellent for avenues; in good soil it attains a large size, and has beautifully varnished green leaves all the year round. It is very common in Southern India, flourishing equally well in the arid plains of the Carnatic and on the sub-alpine tracts of Mysore. It is common on the Bombay side, in forests chiefly, near and under the ghats, and will generally be found skirting streams. On the Godavery, its wood is said to be strong, but it does not appear to be used there. In Ganjam and Gumsur, its extreme height is 36 feet, circumference $4\frac{1}{2}$ feet, and height from the ground to the intersection of the first branch 22 feet. The tree is very common there, but seems to be used only for firewood; the oil extracted from the fruit is used medicinally for itch and other cutaneous diseases and is also employed as lamp oil. In Coimbatore, the wood is said to be only fit for fuel, though Dr. Roxburgh states that it is light and white and serves for a variety of purposes. Dr. Gibson thinks it may be of some use for household purposes. The boughs and leaves are extensively used as a strong manure, for sugar-cane especially. The bitter oil is much used on the Bombay side in the manufacture of native felt, and has great curative powers in itch and mange.—*Drs. Wight, Gibson and Cleghorn, Simmonds' Com. Prod.; Voigt, Captain Macdonald, Mr. Latham, Captain Beddome, M. E. J. R.*

PONGHU, TAM. ? ? In Travancore, a wood of a brown colour; specific gravity 0·960, 3 feet in circumference, used for building.—*Col. Frith.*

PONPATHERA, TAM. In Tinnevelly, wood of a whitey brown colour; specific gravity 0·683. Used for building purposes.—*Col. Frith.*

PONPOSO KOMAREE, URIA ? A tree in Ganjam and Gumsur, extreme height 30 feet, circumference 2 feet, and height from the ground to the intersection of the first branch, 8 feet.—*Captain Macdonald.*

PONNAM, in Malabar. *See* KUMARI.

POODY VAGA, TAM. ? A Travancore wood of a brown colour, specific gravity 0·400, 4 to 10 feet in circumference, 40 feet long; strong, never splits; used by wheelwrights.—*Colonel Frith.*

POOLYETTY, TAM. ? A Travancore wood of a black colour, specific gravity 0·858, 2 to 8 feet in circumference; a strong wood used for furniture.—*Colonel Frith.*

POON OR PEON. A commercial term, derived from some vernacular word, and seemingly applied to the timber of several distinct trees, used for masts and spars. The Calysaccion angustifolia, which grows in Canara and Sunda, in ravines of the ghats and below in sheltered valleys—is used there for "Poon" spars, and ought to be conserved every where and largely increased. Another of the supposed Poon spar trees, is the Calophyllum inophyllum, *Linn., Roxb.*; a beautiful tree, which grows in the western part of Ceylon where it is employed for the masts and cross sticks of Yettra dhonies and fishing boats and poles of bullock carts. A cubic foot of it, there, weighs 40 lbs. Dr. Wight says, that this tree is rare in Coimbatore, and that the wood is coarse grained, but very strong and durable, and on the coast is used in ship building. In the alpine forests, it attains a great size and furnishes the poon spars so valuable for shipping; but, so far as he could learn, there are two or three species of Calophyllum used for the same purpose under the general name of poon. It grows well in sandy tracts close to the sea, where few others thrive. Drs. Gibson and Cleghorn are of opinion that the Poon spars of commerce, are obtained from the Calophyllum angustifolium, and their decision is of the greatest weight. Dr. Gibson's words are, that to the best of his knowledge, Poon spars are furnished by Calophyllum angustifolium, which is a magnificent tree in the ravines of the southern ghats. Major Drury has long resided in Travancore. In his "Useful Plants," he does not name the Calophyllum inophyllum (Ponna, *Maleal.* and *Tel.*: Pinnay, *Tam.*,) as furnishing any of the Poon spars of commerce, but he adds that one kind of East Indian Tacamahaca is produced by Calophyllum inophyllum, though C. calaba and C. tacamahaca also furnish other kinds of Tacamahaca wood. Also, in 1850, in the proceedings of the Madras Central Committee, for the Exhibition of 1851, the Poon of commerce was supposed by Dr. Wight to be from the Dillenia pentagyna, "Rowadan" TEL., a large timber tree, a native of the Northern Circars; which flowers in March and April. The similarity of native names between this and Calophyllum inophyllum led Dr. Wight to suspect that some mistake had arisen. He observes that the wood of Dillenia pentagyna is said to be exceedingly strong and very durable, even when buried under ground, and, it is a stately forest tree, common on the face of the W. Ghats. Dr. Wight was, at that time, satisfied that D. pentagyna is the tree which furnishes the Poon spars, being a tall, and Calophyllum inophyllum a short stunted, tree. At the Madras Exhibition of 1855, Dr. Cleghorn in the Jury reports, noticing Sterculia fœtida, *Pinari maram*, Tam., *Guruppu badam chettu*, Tel., as a large tree in Mysore and on the western coast of the peninsula, adds that it is one of the trees believed to furnish the smaller Poon spars, and Major Drury, in Useful Plants, repeats that it furnished some of the masts known as Poon spars. Until botanical inquirers who visit the forests finally determine the trees which furnish all the Poon woods of commerce, it would be useless to pursue the subject further, here. The tendency of the evidence, therefore, is to establish Calophyllum angustifolia, C. inophyllum, Calysaccion angustifolia, Dillenia pentagyna and Sterculia fœtida, as trees which produce the Poon woods of commerce. The Bintangor wood of Penang, Malacca and Singapore, seems, also, to be the Calophyllum angustifolia, and, Dr. Cleghorn, in his forest reports seems to have no doubt that C. angustifolia, produces the Poon of Coorg, Mysore and Canara, where, he says, the trees are becoming very scarce, and the timber is consequently more valuable than teak. He enjoins their strictest conservation. In a special report on Poon spars, Dr. Cleghorn mentions that these are supplied entirely from Canara and Coorg. He tells us that in the ghats of Coorg and Malabar, the best timber has been cut away and the wood contractor is felling in more remote localities. Teak, black wood and Poon spars are every year becoming more scarce in accessible localities. There may, however, have arisen some of all this doubt, from several trees having similar Tamil and Malealum names. Thus, Poongum maram, TAM. Poongana, MALEAL., is the Pongamia glabra. Ponna, is the MALEAL, Pinnay maram, TAM.? Poonnay maram, TAM., of Calophyllum inophyllum. Pinnari, TAM., Sterculia fœtida, and Pinnay maram, TAM., Dillenia pentagyna.

This wood, as imported from the East Indies, into Britain, very nearly resembles a dull coloured and greyish specimen of mahogany, and would be useful for any purpose to which such kind of mahogany is applicable; besides having a greater degree of strength and stiffness compared with its weight. The Poon-wood, or Peon-wood of Singapore is of a light porous texture, and light greyish cedar colour; it is there used in ship building for planks, and makes excellent spars. Calophyllum angustifolium, Dr. Roxburgh says, is a native of Penang and of countries eastward of the Bay of Bengal, and yields the straight spars commonly called Poon, which in those countries are used for the masts of ships. Tredgold says its texture is porous, but uniform; and the mean weight of a cubic foot in the dry state is 405 lbs. The cohesive force of Poon is from 10,000 to 14,700 lbs. per square inch, the mean weight of the modulus of elasticity for bars of an inch square is 1,689,800 lbs. The specific gravity, and the relative strength, stiffness, and resilient power compared with Riga fir, as 1,000, from Mr. Fincham's experiments are, as under: –

Specific gravity.	Strength.	Stiffness.	Resilience.	
579	1380	1270	1400	Barlow.
647	1226	1230	1146	Fincham.
.613	1303	1250	1273	Mean of both.

From whence it appears that it is superior to Riga fir in the properties required for mast wood. Colonel Frith noticing a Poon in Travancore, says it is of a brown colour, specific gravity 0·623, 2 to 4 feet in circumference and 80 feet long and there used for masts. Poon is used for the decks, masts, and yards of ships, and it appears to be well adapted for these purposes, both by its strength and lightness.

Mr. Edye, writing on the Poon spars generally, says that the light-red peon from the forests of Coromandel and Mysore, which can be procured at the port of Mangalore, on the Malabar coast, is considered the best of the growth of India, for the general purposes of lower masts, top-masts, and yards. The peon masts, as to strength, compared with Riga &c. spars for masts, are superior to any; the weight of those of the proper sort is about the same as Riga fir, and their durability is very great; a set of lower masts would probably last for fifteen or twenty years. Mr. Edye, while in Canara, Malabar and Ceylon, thus described the following kinds of Poon, viz.:—

Cheru-Puna in Tamil and Malayala, which is the small-leaf peon. This wood is the real mast peon, which is preferred for the masts of ships or vessels. Peon, or Puna, consists of five sorts, all of which are similar in shape and growth; (*a*) the largest sort is of a light bright colour, and may be had at Mangalore, from the forests of Corumcul, in Canara, where it grows to a length of one hundred and fifty feet. At Mangalore, he procured a tree of this sort that would have made a foremast for the Leander, sixty-gun ship, in one piece, for the sum of 1,300 rupees, or 149£ sterling. Peon grows in the forests of Cochin and Travancore, but it is of a very inferior quality to that before stated; (*b*) one sort is named the *Karapa Puna*, which is dark peon; (*c*) another, *Malai Puna*, meaning the hill peon; and another sort, (*d*) the *Vallai Puna*, or the white peon, this sort is small, not more than twelve or eighteen inches in diameter, and eighteen or twenty feet long. In Canara, another sort, (*e*) named *Merchie Puna*, grows to twenty-eight inches, or three feet in diameter, and from thirty to fifty feet long; and is much like the American birch. It is generally defective and not durable, consequently it is never brought from the hills, for, when felled, it opens and splits at the top and butt for many feet in length. The weight of the peon may be said to be from forty to forty-eight pounds the cubic foot; but the lightest I had met with was thirty-four and three-quarters, and the heaviest fifty pounds, the cubic foot, when dry. The leaf of this tree is small and oval, about two by one and a half inches broad, and the fruit grows in bunches, it is about the size of coffee-berries; from this the natives extract oil, which is used for various native purposes.—*Edye, Forests of Malabar and Canara.* (*Note*—Cheru means bastard.)

Puna, in Ceylon, is the wood commonly called Peon in England. It is used for masts, yards, &c. This is the wood so much spoken of by persons from Ceylon, and it certainly is of a good quality, and superior to that of Malabar: but, from its small dimensions, its scarcity, and the trouble in obtaining it, is of little consideration. The largest said to have been found was eighteen inches in diameter, and sixty feet in height; but the largest Edye could discover was not more than nine inches in diameter, and thirty-five feet high. In quality it is much the same as the first sort in Malabar, which may be obtained at Mangalore from the native merchants at all times when the coast is open (viz. from November to April), of three feet in diameter, and one hundred and ten feet long, for the sum of 150£ sterling.—*Edye, on the Timber of Ceylon.*

Vellie Pura, a Malabar and Canara tree, known in Malabar as the white or *Cat Puna*. It grows to about eighteen inches in diameter and eighteen feet high; and is used by the native carpenters for the frames of vessels. It grows curved, and is not durable. It is not found in any quantity in the forests.—*Edye, Forests of Malabar and Canara.*

Vellai Puna Pinn, the Tamil name of a Malabar and Canara tree, which is the white peon pinu: it can be procured on all parts of the coast of Malabar. It grows to seventy and eighty feet long, and two to three feet in diameter; the natives use it for the masts and yards of dowes and country vessels. It is more like the American white pine, and the upright yellow wood at the Cape of Good Hope, (Antinaquatis), than any wood he had seen.—*Edye, Forests of Malabar and Canara.*

Puna Balle in Tamil, and Punga Marum in Malayala ("Calophyllum" species ?). This is a beautiful tree and of much value; it grows to about two and a half feet in diameter, and from ten to fifteen feet long, spreading its branches to a great extent, and into curves of various dimensions, which are valuable for native uses, particularly in building country vessels. It produces a fruit from which oil is extracted, and is used for lamps, &c. The Arabs prefer this oil to any other to mix with chunam, for the purpose of covering the bottoms of their vessels to preserve them from worms; it is also used for the purpose of curing rheumatic pains, by being applied warm with friction.—*Edye, Forests of Malabar and Canara, and Timbers of Ceylon, Major Drury's Useful Plants, Edye, Roxburgh, Mr. Mendis, Voigt, Drs. Wight, Gibson and Cleghorn, Tredgold, Colonel Frith.* See POREAL PAINI.

POONKEE, TEL., Gyrocarpus Jacquini. In the Godavery forests, a wood soft and light, much used for making cowrie boxes and toys, takes paint and varnish well. Tella poonkee "Givotea Rottleriformis" is used also for the same purposes.—*Captain Beddome.*

POONNAY, TAM. In Tinnevelly, a wood of a deep straw colour, used for building purposes.—*Colonel Frith.*

POOVERSOO, TAM. In Tinnevelly, wood of a red colour; specific gravity 0·860. Used for making bandies.—*Colonel Frith.* (*Qu.*—Thespesia populnea ?)

POPULUS, THE POPLAR.

Popelier. DUT.	Pappelbaum. GER.
Poplar. ENG.	Pioppa. IT.
Peuplier. FR.	Populus. LAT.
Pappel. GER.	Alamo. SP.

Plants belonging to the natural order *Salicaceæ*. The wood of the English species is soft and light, and not very durable, unless kept dry. In the Himalaya, the poplars flourish only at considerable elevations. P. ciliata, found at Kemaon, is common on the northern face of the Choor, at Muttiana, and at Seran in Lower Kunawar; P. pyriformis, Royle, occurs at Deobun; P. alba, Linn., common in Europe and the north of Asia, extends into the Himalayas; P. dilatata, the Lombardy poplar, grows in the Punjaub. It is the Arabic Ghurb: the Persian Wussuk and Sapedan; and Hindi Safeda. The character of their woods is not known.—*Eng. Cyc., Mr. Faulkner, Royle's Illust.*

POREAL PAINI. The Tamil and Malayala name of a Malabar and Canara wood which may be ranked among the best sort of the Dupi marams, or Painis, and next to the peons on the coast of Malabar. It might be used for small yards of vessels. At times this wood is called Puni Paini by some of the northern natives: it is of a light red colour, and grows to about eighteen inches in diameter, and sixty feet long.—*Edye, Forests of Malabar and Canara.* *See* POON.

PORTIA, TAM.? A small Palghat tree; wood of a brown colour, used for musket-stocks. *Col. Frith.* (*Note.*—Is this the Thespesia populnea?)

PORTO KOORWAN, URIA? A tree of Ganjam and Gumsur, of extreme height 20 feet, circumference 1 foot, and height from ground to the intersection of the first branch 5 feet. Chiefly remarkable on account of its seeds, called here Indrajebho, which are used medicinally and held in great estimation. The juice of the leaves is given to young cattle to destroy worms. The bark is also used medicinally. The tree abounds.—*Captain Macdonald.*

POTOOBAOLO, URIA? In Ganjam and Gumsur, a tree of extreme height 45 feet, circumference 4 feet, and height from the ground to the intersection of the first branch 12 feet. Occasionally used for bandy wheels and ploughshares. The leaves are eaten as a sort of vegetable by the hill people. Tolerably common.—*Captain Macdonald.*

POUK-THA OR THAN-YEN, BURM. Dr. McClelland reports probably Inga bijemina. Its maximum girth is 3 to 4 cubits, and maximum length 22 feet. Widely scattered, but abundant, all over the Tenasserim Provinces inland. When seasoned, floats in water. It is an excellent and durable wood, would do well for handles of tools. This wood is of the same nature as Pyeng Khadoe (Inga xylocarpa), of which it is said to be a variety.—*Captain Dance.*

POUK THEN-MAYEK KYOUK, BURM. A light coloured close grained wood of British Burmah, much prized by Burmans. A cubic foot weighs 58 lbs. In a full grown tree on good soil the average length of the trunk to the first branch is 15 feet, and average girth measured at 6 feet from the ground is 5 feet.—*Dr. Brandis, Cal. Cat. Ex. of* 1862.

POVERASIE, in Tamil, Santa Marie in Portuguese, and called by Europeans Ceylon Tulip tree. Is a Ceylon tree, used at times by the coach makers for wheels, &c. It is a tree generally planted to ornament walks in gardens, and is very common: it produces a yellow flower.—*Edye, on the Timber of Ceylon.* (*Qu.*—Thespesia populnea? *See* PORTIA. POOVERSOO.

PREMNA INTEGRIFOLIA, *Roxb.*

Premna hircina, *Buch.*

Chamaree. MAHR.	Ghebu nelli. TEL.
Appel. MALEAL.	Pinna nelli. „
Munnay maram. TAM.	

The greens.

Ugnie munda. SANS.	Passu-munna-kiray. TAM.
Munni kiray. TAM.	Ghebbu nelli kura. TEL.

The root.

Munni ver. TAM.	Ghebbu nelli veru. TEL.

A small tree, common in India, the timber is only fit for the most common purposes.—*Voigt, O'Shaughnessy, Ainslie.*

PREMNA LATIFOLIA, *Roxb.*

Nelli chettu. TEL.

A small tree of the Coromandel coast, wood white, firm, and used for various economical purposes.—*Mr. Rohde's MSS., Voigt.*

PREMNA PYRAMIDATA, *Wall.*

Kyoon-na-lin. BURM.

A small tree of British Burmah; wood strong, used for weavers' shuttles. A cubic foot weighs lbs. 52. In a full grown tree on good soil, the average length of the trunk to the first branch is 30 feet, and average girth measured at 6 feet from the ground is 5 feet.—*Dr. Brandis, Cal. Cat. Ex.* 1862.

PREMNA TOMENTOSA, *Willde; Roxb.*

Chambara. MAHR.	Navuru. TEL.
Kolcuttay teak maram. TAM.	Naooru. „
Nagara chettu. TEL.	Nagool. „

A small tree of Coimbatore, the Bombay ghats, and the Northern Circars. It has a pretty looking wood, hard and close grained, of a brownish yellow colour and well fitted for ornamental purposes.—*Drs. Wight & Gibson.*

PROME. The various kinds of trees associated with teak in the Prome forests are 22 in number, and are thus enumerated by Dr. McClelland, in the order of their numerical proportion:—

1 Acacia catechu.	13 Conocarpus robusta.
2 Odina wodier.	14 Hymenodictyon parviflora.
3 Pentaptera.	15 Bursera serrata.
4 Spondias acuminata.	16 Kydia.
5 Nauclea.	17 Dipterocarpus alatus.
6 Inga.	18 Blackwellia.
7 Tectona grandis.	19 Hopea odorata.
8 Careya arborea.	20 Pterocarpus dalbergioides.
9 Terminalia.	21 Pterospermum ? Heynianum.
10 Shorea robusta.	22 Melicocca trijuga.
11 Walsura piscidium.	
12 Strychnos.	

Thus, teak holds the seventh place. In other words, there are six other kinds of trees more numerous within the limits of the Prome teak forests than teak itself. *Acacia catechu* probably forms 40 per cent. of the whole trees in the forests; *Odina wodier* 10 per cent.; *Pentaptera* and *Spondias acuminata* 5 per cent. each; *Nauclea* and *Inga* about 4 per cent. each; *Tectona, Careya arborea*, and *Terminalia* 2 per cent. each; the remaining thirteen may be put down as bearing the proportion of 1 per cent. each, leaving 13 per cent. to be made up of other species, such as *Barringtonia acutangula, Acacia serissa, Galedupa arborea, Mimosa octandra, Erythrina, Dalbergia, Bombax,* and *Xanthoxylon alatum,* which are found in low grounds only.—*Dr. McClelland in Selec. Records Govt. of India, Foreign Dept. No. IX. p.* 103.

PROONBAJAH —? A tree of Akyab, and plentiful in Arrakan. Used for making wooden bells, &c.—*Cal. Cat. Ex.* 1862.

PROSOPIS SPICIGERA, *Roxb.*

Shami. BENG.	Parumbay maram. TAM.
Sounder. MAHR.	Janum Chettu. TEL.
Kunda. SINDI.	Chami. TEL.
Vunni maram? TAM.?	

A thorny tree of Coimbatore, in the black cotton soils of Mysore, common in the waste places and forests of Bombay, and common in Sind. It attains a considerable, even a large, size, in Coimbatore and Mysore, and the timber is straight grained, strong and hard, easily worked and used for bandy wheels and other common purposes. It never reaches such a large size on the Bombay side, as would afford a square log of more than 9 inches. In Sind, however, where it is common, it attains a large size, and its heart wood is strong, tough and dark coloured, and is commonly used for weavers' shuttles Dr. Wight found it sustain a weight of 592 lbs. Its pod is about an inch in circumference, and from 6 to 12 inches long, and when ripe it contains a quantity of a mealy substance which has a sweetish taste and is eaten by the natives. It is reverenced in the Dassera rites.—*Drs. Ainslie, Wight and Gibson.*

PRUNUS. A genus of plants, which produces the Apricot, *Prunus armeniaca ;* the cherry, *Prunus cerasus,* also *Prunus Bokhariensis,* Royle, *Prunus triflora,* Roxb. These grow abundantly in the North West parts of India —*Royle's Ill. p.* 205.

PSIDIUM. THE GUAVA TREES grow in the south east of Asia, but succeed also in the gardens of northern India. The Chinese or purple guava, Psidium Cattleyanum, *Sabine,* grows in China. The common red and white, round and pear shaped, guavas, are found everywhere in gardens of Southern Asia, and were probably brought to India from S. America through the Portuguese; the white is most cultivated and is planted in Tenasserim, perhaps, more extensively than any other fruit tree. It grows in all parts of the Deccan, is esteemed as a dessert fruit, but the scent when too ripe is unpleasantly powerful; it makes an excellent jelly, and is also prepared like damson cheese. The fruits have been brought to great perfection in some Indian gardens, and one variety almost divested of seed—perhaps by repeatedly propagating from layers. The fruit is generally preferred fresh from the tree in the early morning; as the heat of the day is supposed to injure its flavor.—*Drs. Ainslie, p.* 223, *Mason, Royle's Illustr., Cleghorn, M. E. J. R., Riddell, Mr. Rohde, MSS.*

PSIDIUM POMIFERUM, *Linn.*

Lal paira. BENG.	Lal Saffri-am. HIND.
Lal paira. ,,	Malaka pela. MALEAL.
Red guava. ENG.	Segapu varnam ? TAM.
Apple shaped guava. ENG.	

Grows in Peninsular India. Wood resembles that of the P. pyriferum.

PSIDIUM PYRIFERUM, *Linn. ; Roxb.*

Guava pyriformis, *Gærtn.*

Paira. BENG.	Supari-am. HIND.
Peyara. ,,	Supi-am. ,,
Sebe mara. CAN.	Pela. MALEAL.
Jam. DUK.	Manjal varnam. TAM.
White guava. ENG.	Coaya maram. TAM.
Pear shaped guava tree. ENG.	Jama chettu. TEL.

The fruit.

Jam. DUK.	Utchola. SANS.
Guava. ENG.	Coia pallum. TAM.
Pera kai. MALEAL.	Goia pandu. TEL.

Besides yielding fruit, the wood is useful for many purposes; as handles of tools, mallets, pegs, &c., it is very hard, but small, and has been used for wood engraving. Good gun stocks are made from the old wood.—*Dr. Riddell, Mr. Rohde, M. E. J. R., Dr. Cleghorn.*

PTERIDOPHYLLUM DECIPIENS, *Thw.,*

Rhus decipiens, *W. & A., Illust.*

Pehimbia-gass. SINGH.

Grows in the central province of Ceylon up to an elevation of 3,000 feet. It flowers in January and fruits in March. It is a very ornamental tree and, in Ceylon, the wood is used for building purposes.—*Thw. En. Pl. Zeyl. p.* 59.

PTEROCARPUS, *Species.*

Wulla Honnay. CAN.

Grows in the Mysore forests, and is used for furniture and house building.—*Captain Puckle.* (*Note*—Is this the species alluded to by Dr. Gibson, where he remarks that the Honei or Pterocarpus, garden, farmed some years ago near Tawunkutha, in the Bedee Talooka of Belgaum, is said to be making fair progress.—*Gibson's Bombay Forest Report of* 1857-58-59-60, *p.* 127.)

PTEROCARPUS *Species, Wall.*

Puddow. BURM.

In Tavoy, a large tree, used for furniture, &c. —*Dr. Wallich.*

PTEROCARPUS, *Species ?*

Jumbagum maram. TAM.	Chempaka manu. TEL.

A large tree, common about Nelambore and the Wynaad. Wood said to be durable and used for building and garden fences.—*Mr. McIvor in M. E. J. R.*

PTEROCARPUS, *Species ?*

Karu vagu. TAM.

A very common tree on the western ghats, wood strong, durable and much used for building. —*Mr. McIvor in M. E. J. R.*

PTEROCARPUS, *Species ?*

Nou maram. TAM. | Nagu maram. TAM.

A very strong and durable wood, common on the lower elevations of the Neilgherries; an ordinary sized tree.—*Mr. McIvor in M. E. J. R.*

PTEROCARPUS, *Species. ?*

Beejah. HIND. ?

A tree of Jubbulpore, grows to a large size, is found in all parts, but not very abundant, has an excellent wood, easily worked.—*Cal. Cat. Ex.* 1862.

PTEROCARPUS BILOBUS, *Banks.*

Vayngie wood. ANGLO-TAM. | Vayngie maram. TAM.

This is reckoned by the natives a very useful wood. It is of a reddish colour, and is employed in making doors and windows, and for other common purposes.—*Ains. Mat. Med. p.* 207. (*Note*—of what tree is this the synonym ?—Is it P. marsupium ?)

PTEROCARPUS DALBERGIOIDES, *Roxb.*

Padowk-wood. ANGLO-BURM | Red wood tree. ENG.
Padouk. BURM. | Andaman red wood tree. „
Hance ? mara ? CAN. | Tenasserim mahogany. „
Honce mara ? „ | Beebla. MAHR. ?

This large and handsome tree was introduced by Col. Kyd into the Calcutta botanic garden in 1791, whence it has been spread into the country. It is a native of the Andaman Islands, where it grows to an immense size, with a girth of 15 feet, and forms a valuable timber tree. Under the names Hance, *Can.*, Beebla, *Mahr.*, Dr. Gibson says it is common in large jungles; above and below in Canara and Sunda. It is found chiefly as a large tree about the neighbourhood of Prome and habited places to the north of that town, but rarely in the forests. Dr. Brandis and quoted in the Cal. Cat. Ex. of 1862 tell us that trees of the largest size of this strong and beautiful timber abound in the forests of British Burmah, east of the Sitang river, also in the valley of the Salween river and its tributaries, the Thoungyeen, Yoonzalen, Hlineboay, Houndraw and Attaran: but, is much less frequent in Pegu and entirely wanting in some districts. The wood is prized beyond all others for cart wheels. The trees are felled green, and are split up into short planks 3 feet 6 inches long, 2 feet wide and 9 inches thick. Three of these pieces make one wheel and a pair is sold on the spot in the forests of the Prome district at from 12 to 25 Rupees. Captain Dance mentions that, in the Tenasserim provinces, its maximum girth is 6 or perhaps 7 cubits, and maximum length 15 to 30 feet, that of great girth being always short. It is abundant but scattered all over the provinces. When seasoned, it sinks in water. It takes about two years to season; when cut it has a peculiar and fragrant smell, and he adds that another wood, called Peddowk, is procurable in abundance at Tavoy, which seems very strong but does not sink and is devoid of smell. The Padouk wood of the Pterocarpus dalbergioides of Roxburgh, is extensively used in the Gun Carriage Manufactories of India: in that of Madras, for light field beams, cheeks, axle cases, perches, poles, timber framing, waggon perches and framing, heavy field cheeks, transoms, axle cases, hand spikes, poles, braces, framing, &c., all parts of garrison carriages, garrison traversing platforms, as well as gun and mortar platforms, transport carriages and limbers, cart work of all sorts, and heavy and light field wheels. In Burmah, a cubic foot weighs 60 lbs. In a full grown tree on good soil the average length of the trunk to the first branch is 35 feet, and average girth measured at 6 feet from the ground is 9 feet. It sells at 12 annas per cubic foot. The wood is not unlike mahogany, but is more heavy, red and coarse grained, that of the root is beautifully variegated, closer grained and darker coloured. It is used for furniture, and, by the Burmese, to make their musical instruments.—*Voigt, Drs. Gibson and McClelland, Eng. Cyc., Mr. Robert Brown, Dr. Brandis, Cal. Cat. Ex.* 1862, *Mad. Cat.* 1862, *Royle Illust. p.* 195.

PTEROCARPUS DRACO, *Linn.*

Pterocarpus officinalis, *Jacq.*
„ hemiptera, *Gært.*
Dum-ul-uk-wain. AR.

Introduced into India, from the West Indies, in 1812. Produces the dragon's blood of the shops. Wood unknown.—*Voigt.*

PTEROCARPUS INDICUS, *Willde.*

Padouk. BURM. | Rosewood. ENG.

Grows in the Malay islands, in China and the Moluccas. It is a handsome tree with long waving branches and clusters of deep yellow flowers, which scent the air. It produces very fine timber, said to be white ? and not equal to the red padowk of the P. dalbergioides. This species also yields a gum kino. But, Dr. Wallich noticing it as a Moulmein tree says it is a very beautiful and hard compact timber, closely resembling the Andaman wood.—*Voigt, Dr. Cleghorn in M. E. J. R., Drs. Mason, Wallich.* (*Note* —Was the white wood, and red wood tree, the same, but of different ages ?)

PTEROCARPUS MARSUPIUM, *Roxb.*

Pterocarpus bilobus, *Don.; Mill.*

Yegy. BENG. | Ragta hanay ? CAN.
Vaygah. „ | Beula. DUK.
Pit sal. „ | Bia. „
Yegah ? „ | Bibla. „
Pedong ? BURM. | Vangay wood. ANGLO-TAM.
Whonay. CAN. | Yagesah wood. „ TEL.
Dhin daga ? „ | Bibla. HIND.

Pit shala. HIND.	Vengay maram. TAM.
Bejasar. HIND. of Nagpore.	Egisa. TEL.
Bejasal. " " "	Vegi. "
Bheulah. MAHR. of Nagpore.	Vegisa. "
Beeblah. " of Dekhan.	Yegassi karrah. TEL.
Karintha gara. MALEAL.	Pia salu. "
Vijaya. HIND. of Nepaul.	Yegis. "
Vangay maram. TAM.	Yegee TEL. of the Godavery.

This is a large and a very beautiful tree, especially when in flower in the beginning of the rains: for, its seed ripens about the close of the year. It is widely diffused, and yields one of the most abundant and useful timbers of S. India, also the valuable gum kino. It is one of the most lofty and striking trees in the Indian forests, with a very high trunk, which, however, is scarcely ever straight. It is met with from Cape Comorin to the Himalayas. Mr. McIvor says, it is common all round the foot of the Neilgherry ghats and two thousand trees were seen by Dr. Cleghorn along the roads through the Wynaad, notched in a V shaped form, for the extraction of kino which meets with a ready market on the coast and is exported in wooden boxes to Bombay. It grows luxuriantly on the eastern ghats, on the hills between Vellore and Salem, and on the Malabar and Canara ghats, where large quantities are collected of the resinous substance it yields, and sent to England under the name of "kino." The tree abounds near Tellicherry, and along the whole Malabar coast. Dr. Cleghorn has seen it both in the ascent of the eastern and western ghats. It is not generally common in the Bombay forests, but most so in the northern inland ones, and also in those of the extreme south, as in the Bedee talooka, but it everywhere reaches a great size. Dr. Wight sent to Dr. Cleghorn specimens of its gum from Coimbatore. Mr. Latham mentions it as occurring in the Nalla Mallai, and as furnishing there a darkish, coarse grained, serviceable timber. Dr. Roxburgh found it in the Northern Circars, and Captain Beddome in the forests of the Godavery; Captain Sankey mentions it in the Nagpore forests. It is noticed by Buchanan Hamilton under the name of *Vijaya* as occurring in Nepaul and Voigt mentions it in the Rajpeepla jungles and in Assam. In Nagpore, the average length of the logs is from 18 to 30 feet and from 4½ to 3½ feet in girth, it sells there at 5 annas a foot. Dr. Wight says the wood in Coimbatore, is dark coloured and strong, sustaining a weight of 370 to 400 lbs. but it is said to require being kept dry and Dr. Gibson adds that on the Bombay side of India, the wood is much used in house building, but does not stand exposure to wet. Mr. Rohde considers the timber useful for many purposes; it is very little inferior to teak, seems less liable to split after long exposure and is equally strong. He says that very great caution is, however, requisite in using this wood to obtain it sound, and adds that it is heavier than teak, more expensive than teak to work and, that, when sawn green, the outer planks bend considerably. When wet, or unseasoned it imparts a yellow stain and it gives out to wet lime (white wash for example), a dark rusty brown colour which depreciates it for house building. In Nagpore, Captain Sankey tell us, it is called Bejasar and has there a reddish coloured heart, surrounded by an outer ring of a white soft wood. This ring varies from ½ to 3 inches in thickness, so that it may be adzed off without very much diminishing the scantling of a full grown tree. It has a very close and frequently winding grain, but is subject to numerous faults of a coal black and charred appearance. Frequently a fault of 3 inches diameter and considerable length presents itself. On this account it might be a dangerous timber to use for joists. For all works, however, where such faults would not signify or would be exposed, as in rafters, bressumers, &c., &c., and, generally, pieces of small scantling, it would be found a most valuable timber. In strength it is much superior to teak, apparently always retains its essential oil, and, like it, door frames of 20 years standing are the only instances of white ants having attacked the red wood. From the large size which is procurable in Nagpore as well as the many excellent qualities of this timber, Captain Sankey classes it both as a tie beam and a rafter wood. Dr. Cleghorn tells us that this tree is greatly prized at Dharwar, not for its exudation, but for its timber, which was extensively used in the cotton gin factory. Mr. Rohde adds that vessels built in the Ganjam districts are planked with it and that the door panels and venetians of the neglected houses at Ganjam formed of this wood stood better than teak similarly situated. On the Godavery, the native dhol is often made of it. The timber has been fully tried as sleepers on the Madras railway, and found useful. It makes handsome furniture, and resembles fine mahogany, but must be well seasoned, to avoid its yellow stains. This tree yields from incisions the gum kino of commerce. It issues as a blood-red juice, which, on being simply exposed to the sun, hardens and then quickly cracks into little angular masses, and crumbling fragments which constitute, without further preparation, the kino of the shops. Specimens of the exudation sent by Dr. Cleghorn to Professor Christison in 1846 from Mysore, were considered by him "quite identical with the kino of commerce." The tree being thus widely diffused, and the exudation procurable in large quantity, it may possibly come into extensive use in dyeing and calico-printing. The product can be obtained with facility by simply incising the bark and requires no outlay save that of collecting.—*Dr. Roxburgh, Flora Indica, Vol. iii. p.* 234, *Coromandel Plants, ii. p.* 116, *Drs. Wight, Gibson, Royle, Cleghorn, Voigt, Eng. Cyc., Captain Sankey, Captain Puckle, Mr. Latham, Mr. McIvor, Captain Beddome, M. E. J. R., Madras Conservator's Report of* 1858.

PTEROCARPUS SANTALINUS, *Linn.; Roxb.; W. & A.*

Sundun? Ar.
Sundel-al-ahmar. Ar.
Rakto chandana. Beng.
Chendana. "
Na-sa-phiu. Burm.
Honnay. Can.
Whonnay. "
Saudel-hout. Dan.
Lal chandena. Duk.
Red sandal wood. Eng.
Sanders wood. "
Red sanders wood. "
Santale-rouge. Fr.
Sandal-holz. Ger.
Ruttunjee. Guz.?
Rakto chandana. Hind.
Chandana. Hind.
Sandolo-roso. It.
Rakt chandan. Mahr.
Uruttah chaudanam. Maleal.
Sandal surkh. Pers.
Bakam. Pers. ? ? ?
Racta chandana. Sans.
Ranjana. "
Ract-chundun. Singh.
Segapu chendanum. Tam.
Erra chandanam. Tel.
Ku chandanam. "
Rakta chandanam. "
" gandham. "

This tree grows abundantly in the Nagerry hills west of Madras. Its wood is sold by weight as a dye wood, and forms a regular article of export. In the Cuddapah forests, the red sanders may be had in any quantity, of a superior quality, both in logs, which are converted into posts for houses and which the natives prefer to any other timber, and in pieces and roots for export as a dye wood. A bandy will contain from 20 to 25 converted logs, which, at Madras, readily fetches from 2 to 2½ rupees the log. The value of a bandy load of red sanders at Madras is therefore from 40 to 50 Rupees. It grows also in Ceylon on the Paulghat hills, in Mysore, Malabar, on the Nalla mallai, and on the Pulicat? and Triputty? hills. It is not found on the Godavery forests, but grows in the island of Timor. It is brought to Coimbatore, in small quantities, from Mysore, and sells at an extravagant price, by weight, as a dye wood. It is a large tree; but, as brought into Madras since the past 12 years, its timber is in short billets, generally hollow, or in twisted or knarled masses, the billets 2 to 3 feet long and rarely 3 feet in girth, indicating that the forests are being exhausted. It is not, seemingly, used in Madras city, but is very largely exported to Calcutta. The billets are of a deep red colour, the concentric circles being divided by dark lines. With different mordants, it yields various shades of red, but these are said not to be permanent. The Madras exports for 1853-1854 amounted to 47,431 cwts., value 59,570 Rupees. In the 4 years 1852-53 to 1855-56, there was exported from Madras cwts. 1,79,815, value Rupees 2,20,983; the destination chiefly being the United Kingdom, Indian French Ports, Pegu, Bengal. Red sanders wood is principally shipped to England from Calcutta in logs from 2 to 10 inches diameter, generally without sap, and sometimes in roots and split pieces. This will explain much of the shipments from Madras to Calcutta, in which latter district the tree is not known to grow. The logs are often notched at both ends, or cut with a hole as for a rope, and are much worn externally from being dragged along the ground; other woods, as also indeed ivory tusks, are sometimes perforated for the like purpose. It is heavy, extremely hard, with a fine grain, and is very much used as a dye wood, and by colour manufacturers: also, often in turnery. It takes a beautiful polish. It is largely used in Bengal, for hindu images and in Ajmere for the suffumigations of hindu idols. It yields its coloring matter to alcohol and ether, but not to water.—*Tredgold, Mr. Rohde's MSS., Captain Beddome, Dr. Wight, Dr. Cleghorn in M. E. J. R. of* 1855, *Dr. Cleghorn in Conservator's Report, p.* 37-38, *Mr. Faulkner, Simmonds, M. E. J. R., Commercial Products of Madras Presidency, Useful Plants, Voigt.*

PTEROSPERMUM ACERIFOLIUM, *Willde*

Kanuk champa. Beng. | Nagee. Burm.

Pterospermum (from the Greek word πτερόν signifying a wing, and σπέρμα a seed), a small genus of plants found in the Indian Isles and the southern parts of India. All the species form handsome trees, and abound in mucilage. According to Voigt, this is a large tree, of the peninsula of India and Assam, but, it grows along with teak in the Pegu forests, though scarce. The timber is extremely valuable and is as strong as teak or oak, but its durability has never been fairly tested, as it has never been desiccated like teak. It attains a girth of 10 or 12 feet and rises to a lofty height. It has a dark brown wood.—*Dr. McClelland, Eng. Cyc., Voigt.*

PTEROSPERMUM ACEROIDES, *Wall.*

Tha-ma-jam-wai-zoke. Burm.

A timber tree of Martaban, and growing in the Pegu forests similarly to P. acerifolium, but plentifully: timber of the same qualities as P. acerifolium.—*Voigt, Wallich, McClelland.*

PTEROSPERMUM HEYNEANUM, *Wall.*

Pterospermum suberifolium, *Willde.*
Velago xylocarpa, *Gærtn.*

Nolika chettu. Tel.
Loluga kurra. "
Lolugu chettu. Tel.

A tree of Courtallum, of the Godavery forests, and the Ginji hills. Wood pinkish and hard, but is generally hollow in the centre.—*Voigt, Captain Beddome.*

PTEROSPERMUM INDICUM?

Kyaboka wood tree. Eng.
Kaiaboka wood tree. "
Amboyna wood tree. "
Lingoa wood tree. Eng.
Serioulout. Malay?

According to Holtzapfel, the botanical name of the Kyaboka wood tree has not yet been determined with certainty. But, it is generally believed to be the *Pterospermum indicum.* The Kyaboka is said by Prof. Reinwardt, of Leyden, to be the burr of the *Pterospermum indicum;* but, by others that of *Pterocarpus draco,* and to be brought from the Moluccas, the islands of Borneo, Amboyna, &c. The native name appears, from the specimen of Mr. Witson Saunders, to be "*Serioulout,*" the wood itself is of the same colour as the burr, or rather lighter, and in grain resembles plain mahogany. Col. Lloyd is quoted as saying that the root of the cocoanut tree is so similar, when dry and seasoned, to the bird's-eye part of the wood, termed kyaboca, that he could perceive no difference, the cocoa has a tortuous and silky fracture, almost like indurated asbestos. But, it is said, the comparison of the palm wood with the kyaboka, renders the question uncertain, as amongst the multitudes of ordinary curly woody fibres, that one cannot account for in a palm, there are a few places with soft friable matter much resembling it. The general belief is that P. Indicum throws out burrs or excrescences, and that which receives the name of

Amboyna wood or *Lingoa wood* seems to be the timber of the bole of the tree, sometimes along with that of the burr. The Lingoa wood, or Amboyna wood of commerce is abundant at Ceram, New Guinea, and throughout the Molucca seas, and can be obtained in any quantity, if the precaution be taken of ordering it during the previous trading season. It is very durable and takes a high polish. At the Exhibition of 1851, there was seen a circular slab of this wood, from Ceram, 6 feet 7 inches in diameter. But, such large circular slabs are only obtained by taking advantage of the spurs which project from the base of the trunk, as the tree itself has not sufficient diameter to furnish slabs of such widths. They are occasionally met with so large as 9 feet, but the usual size is from 4 to 6 feet. Amboyna or Lingoa wood was imported in considerable quantities into Great Britain during the period in which the Moluccas were British possessions; but Poole's Statistics of Commerce says it is now rarely seen in Britain.

The *Kyaboka wood* of commerce, on the other hand, is supposed to be from the knotty burrs or gnarled excrescences. It is brought from Ceram, New Guinea, the Arru and other islands of the Moluccas, to Singapore; and is much esteemed as a fancy or ornamental wood for cabinet-work; of late years, its estimation seems to have decreased in Europe, but it is still much valued by the Chinese, and is sold by weight. It is sawn off in slabs from 2 to 4 feet long and 2 to 8 inches thick. It resembles the burr of the yew, is very hard and full of curls—the colour being reddish brown, varying to orange. It is used for making small boxes, writing desks and other fancy ornamental work. It is tolerably hard, and full of small curls and knots, the colour is from orange to chesnut brown, and sometimes red brown. At the Madras Exhibition of 1855, a slab of Kyaboka wood, imported from Singapore, was exhibited by Dr. Sanderson. A small portion was polished, and in its marking showed well the highly ornamental appearance of the timber. The specimen exhibited the very knotty character and curly fibres of the wood, from which pieces of even a foot square, free from flaws, can rarely be obtained.—*Holtzapfel, J. R. M. E. of* 1855, *Cat. Ex.* 1851, *Sing. Cat. Ex.* 1861, *Poole's Statistics of Commerce.*

PTEROSPERMUM LANCÆFOLIA, *Roxb.*

A tree of Assam, with a dense strong wood.

PTEROSPERMUM SEMI-SAGITTATUM, *Buch.* A tree of Assam, which flowers in March, April and May, with large white fragrant flowers.—*Voigt.*

PTEROSPERMUM SUBACERIFOLIUM? Dr. McClelland, at p. 133 of No. IX. of the Records of the Government of India, thus remarks: *Pterospermum aceroides*, Tha-ma-jam-wai-zoke: also *P. subacerifolium*, and *P. acerifolium*, Najee, *Burm*, three species of large timber, found growing along with teak in all the forests of Pegu. The two first are plentiful but the third kind is scarce. This timber is extremely valuable and is as strong as either teak or oak. Its durability for purposes of ship-building has never been tested, because it has never been desiccated or killed like the teak. It attains a girth of ten or twelve feet and rises to a lofty height. Wood dark brown.—*Dr. McClelland.* (*Note*—Is this P. suberifolium?)

PTEROSPERMUM SUBERIFOLIUM, *Lam.*

Pterospermum canescens, *Roxb.*

Velenge. SINGH. | Taddi maram. TAM.

This is a native of the mountainous tracts all over India. In Ceylon, it is common up to an elevation of 2,000 feet, especially in the drier parts of the island. The wood is useful for many purposes where toughness is required, such as poles of bullock carts, betel trays, and gun stocks. A cubic foot weighs 36 lbs., but it is said to last only from 5 ? to 7 ? years. Flowering time the beginning of the hot season, March, April, and May. Trunk erect, growing to be a timber tree of middling size.—*Thw., Mr. Rohde, MSS., Mr. Mendis.*

PUL-I-SHINTA, TEL., Bauhinia, *species.* A wood of the Godavery forests. Said to be good and hard. Tree not apparently described. Legume filled with a scented pith.—*Captain Beddome.*

PULSUNDRA, TEL. This Nalla Mallai wood is of a reddish colour, strong and useful.—*Mr. Latham.*

PUNA KAD in Salem, *see* KUMARI.

PUNDE CYANN. The Tamil name of a Ceylon tree which grows to about twenty inches in diameter, and twelve feet in height. It is a close grained wood, and resembles the English pear tree. It is used by the natives for various purposes in making farming utensils.—*Edye, on the Timber of Ceylon.*

PUNE THA, BURM. ? A tree of Moulmein. Wood soft, used in ordinary purposes of building materials.—*Cal. Cat. Ex.* 1862.

PUNGUL. The Tamil name of a Ceylon tree which grows to about eighteen inches in diameter, and twelve feet in height. It is of little use. Its fruit, and also its juice, are used as applications to ulcers, &c. From the seed a fixed oil is prepared which is considered valuable in rheumatic pains, bruises, &c.—*Edye, on the Timber of Ceylon.*

PUOAM. The Tamil name of a Malabar and Canara tree, of a light red colour, much like the Spanish mahogany. It is generally curved in its growth, and is considered very durable. It grows to about twenty-four inches in diameter, and seldom more than twenty feet high. It produces a fruit which the natives pickle and from which also they extract an oil, which they use for rheumatic gout, bruises, and various complaints: it is considered by them to be valuable. The weight of this wood is about thirty-seven and a half pounds the cubic foot.—*Edye, Forests of Malabar and Canara.*

PUOAM PARASOM. The Tamil name of a Malabar and Canara tree with which the natives of Malabar are well acquainted, and which they use for the masts and yards of pattamahs. It grows to about sixty feet high, and fifteen inches in diameter: it may be considered inferior to the mast peon before described.—*Edye, Forests of Malabar and Canara.*

PUPRA, HIND.? A tree of Chota Nagpore. Hard, white timber.—*Cal. Cat. Ex.* 1862.

PURLA KIMEDY FORESTS. Capt. Philipps, writing in 1855, in describing the forests and woods of this district, says they now furnish sufficient timber for all local purposes and admit of large quantities being sent annually, principally by water, to Calingapatam, Chicacole, Poondy, &c. With proper management and control over the Sowrah population, the dread of violence from whom prevents the low country people very generally from entering the country, he believed that 4 or 5,000 logs of timber of all sizes, could be obtained between January and June ready on the banks of the two rivers, to be floated down in rafts to the coast at Calingapatam with the first floods. This number could be exceeded were a few elephants employed to drag the logs from the more distant hill sides, where the best timber trees now remain, to spots accessible to carts and oxen. The woods of Kemidy cover 400 square miles, the principal ones and those most accessible at present are found on both banks of the Vumshadura river above and below Buttely, Barsinghy, Jerangee, Giba, Cothoor, Jadoupully, and, indeed, the whole of the hilly tracts abound with fine trees, the only difficulty being their removal, when cut, through dense jungle and across ravines to the river bank. The zemindar of Kemidy owns these woods and forests, and no revenue is now derived from them. The teak tree was introduced some 25 years ago by the then Dewan; few of those planted have escaped the axe, but the remaining specimens thrive remarkably well and promise to become very fine trees in time. This may be attributable to the peculiar climate, which greatly resembles that of Burmah. The heat, rains, cold weather, mists and fogs are as intense and very similar to those experienced on the other coast. The indigenous trees are extremely numerous, the principal ones and those most in request are noticed in the annexed list. No regulation whatever exists as to the felling of timber in this zemindary, large trees and small alike are cut whenever a demand for such exists and latterly a very large quantity of both has been required for the public works, bridges &c. in course of construction at Chicacole and in the northern trunk road as well as in the Kemidy zemindary. The annual destruction of timber on the hill sides is very great as the "Sowrahs" seldom cultivate the same patch two seasons successively, being indebted for their scanty crop and for the quantity of charcoal deposited between the rocks and stones, by burning the timber and brushwood on the ground where it has been felled some three or four weeks before the commencement of the rains. This may be immaterial in remote hills, but he thinks that on the confines, especially near Sowacotta, the practice should, if possible, be put a stop to as the whole of the surrounding country is now destitute of timber. He found the average number of carts leaving Sowacotta with wood, during April 1855, to be 27 daily.

Achoo, URIA. Togaroo chettu, TEL., extreme height 36 feet, circumference of trunk 3 feet, height from ground to first branch 10 feet. A light wood, of which stocks of match-locks are made. Leather is dyed pink with the bark of the roots.

Ambeleetoba, URIA, extreme height 30 feet, circumference of trunk 1 foot, height from ground to first branch 6 feet. Made into charcoal and used as firewood.

Arjoono,* URIA, extreme height 90 feet, circumference of trunk 7 feet, height from ground to first branch 35 feet. When hollowed out with fire and axe, this tree makes a good ferry boat, being very buoyant—it is the best wood for catamarans. Its Telugu name is Vedda Sirissim chettu.

Baee Dimeree, URIA, extreme height 25 feet, circumference of trunk 2 feet, height from ground to first branch 9 feet, made into charcoal, and used as firewood.

Balliah, URIA, Ballidi chettu, TEL., extreme height 40 feet, circumference of trunk 4 feet, height from ground to first branch 15 feet. The nuts of this tree are eaten, and an oil is extracted from the seeds which is stated to have healing properties. It is also applied in rheumatism.

Barokolee, URIA, Regu chettu, TEL., extreme height 30 feet, circumference of trunk 3 feet, height from ground to the first branch 8 feet. Used for an infinity of purposes: the leaves pounded are considered a cure for rheumatism, and lac is obtained from it.

Baelo, URIA, extreme height 30 feet, circumference of trunk 3 feet, height from ground to first branch 10 feet. Made into charcoal and used as firewood.

Banjhonoo, URIA, extreme height 45 feet, circumference of trunk 5 feet, height from ground to first branch 22 feet. A very strong wood, of which bandy wheels, ploughshares, &c. are made.

Baygona, URIA, Navelli chettu, TEL., extreme height 18 feet, circumference of trunk 1 foot, height from ground to first branch 4 feet. Made into charcoal and used as firewoood.

Behenta, URIA, Tov Tolli yelga chettu, TEL., extreme height 28 feet, circumference of trunk 3 feet, height from ground to first branch 9 feet. A hard strong wood used for axle trees, oil presses, &c.

Bello, URIA, Maredu chettu, TEL., extreme height 30 feet, circumference of trunk $2\frac{1}{2}$ feet, height from ground to first branch 10 feet. The fruit of this tree is eaten, the leaves and a preparation of the wood itself is offered in the temples. (*Note*—Is this Ægle marmelos ?)

Bhayroo, URIA, Bhalloo chettu, TEL., extreme height 35 feet, circumference of trunk 3 feet, height from ground to first branch 18 feet. Used for axle trees, presses, rafters, &c., healing properties are said to exist in the leaves when applied to sores.

Bodaka, URIA. Teku chettu. TEL., extreme height 38 feet, circumference of trunk 3 feet, height from ground to first branch 14 feet. A somewhat similar wood to Goombaree. Palanquin poles, grain measures and boxes are made of it.

Bonokoniaree, URIA, extreme height 45 feet, circumference of trunk 3 feet, height from ground to first branch 9 feet. Used in the erection of village houses and as firewood.

Bouro, URIA, Bouroga chettu, TEL., from the roots of this, the silk cotton tree, a tonic is extracted, and the gum and bark is given as an astringent.

Charo, URIA, Chara-mamidi chettu, TEL., extreme height 36 feet, circumference of trunk 3 feet, height from ground to first branch 12 feet. A very common tree, used for many domestic purposes. (*Note*—Is this the Buchanania latifolia ?)

Dhamono or Tur curra, URIA. Tada Karra chettu, TEL., extreme height 39 feet, circumference of trunk $3\frac{1}{2}$ feet, height from ground to first branch 18 feet. A very long grained tough wood, pliant and light, used for doolies, cots, bandy wheels and poles, spear and axe handles, and for other purposes where strength and pliantness are desirable. Admirably adapted for fishing rods, lance handles. (*Note*—Is it the Grewia elastica.—*Royle*. It is very desirable that this wood be identified. Dr. Royle, *Ill.* Him. Bot. p. 103—4 says Grewia helicterifolia, tiliæfolia, and sapida—the last being the G. pumila, *Don.*, and G. nana, *Wall.*—Grow in Bengal and Assam in the forests at the foot of the mountains. That G. sclerophylla, didyma, oppositifolia and elastica, are found in the Kheree pass, in the Dhoon, as well as higher up in the Himalaya, particularly in the neighbourhood of villages. G. elastica, he adds, called "dhamnoo" by the natives, and common in the Himalayas and in northern latitudes at moderate elevations, affords timber which is highly valued for its strength and elasticity, and is therefore much used for bows, buggy shafts, bangy sticks, &c.)

Dhimeree, URIA, Bodda chettu, TEL., extreme height 40 feet, circumference of trunk 4 feet, height from ground to first branch 9 feet. Of little use, is considered sacred by the hill men, and the fruit is eaten by them.

Dhoon, URIA., extreme height 45 feet, circumference of trunk 5 feet, height from ground to first branch 20 feet. A common tree, of little value save as firewood.

Dolosinga, URIA, extreme height 22 feet, circumference of trunk $1\frac{1}{2}$ feet, height from ground to first branch 7 feet. Used in the erection of village houses and as firewood.

Gondopolaso, URIA, extreme height 40 feet, circumference of trunk $2\frac{1}{2}$ feet, height from ground to first branch 8 feet. Used in the erection of village houses and as firewood.

Goombaree, URIA. Gummudu chettu, TEL. extreme height 50 feet, circumference of trunk $4\frac{1}{2}$ feet, height from ground to first branch 20 feet. A wood in great request, used for every purpose. White in color and very light.

Gooroohado, URIA, extreme height 22 feet, circumference of trunk $2\frac{1}{2}$ feet, height from ground to first branch 10 feet. Used in the construction of houses generally.

Gouharea, URIA. Tuma chettu, TEL., extreme height 45 feet, circumference of trunk 5 feet, height from ground to first branch 13 feet. A very strong wood, from which plough-shares, rice pounders, sugar mills, oil presses, wheels, &c. are made. (*Note*—Is it the Acacia arabica.)

Haredha, URIA. Kara Kaia chettu. TEL., extreme height 42 feet, circumference of trunk 4 feet, height from ground to first branch 18 feet. Used for rafters and beams, and to burn into charcoal.

Hinjolo, URIA. Kanapa chettu, TEL., extreme height 30 feet, circumference of trunk $4\frac{1}{2}$ feet, height from ground to first branch 6 feet. A common wood of great use in bridge or anicut building, where wells have to be sunk into the soil: the frame work on which the masonry is built, is generally of this wood, and it is almost imperishable under water.

Holondho, URIA. Kumba chettu, TEL., extreme height 70 feet, circumference of trunk 7 feet, height from ground to first branch 32 feet. A light wood used for making boats and masts at Calingapatam, and for many other purposes.

Jamoo, URIA. Neradi chettu, TEL., Myrtus cyminum? Eugenia jambolana? extreme height 70 feet, circumference of trunk $6\frac{1}{2}$ feet, height from ground to first branch 30 feet. The ferry boats on the Kimedy river are made of large logs of this timber hollowed out; it is very light and is used for many other purposes. A decoction of the bark is a favorite remedy for bowel complaints.

Joontia, URIA., extreme height 40 feet, circumference of trunk 4 feet, height from ground to first branch 15 feet. A white wood, but very hard, and seldom used.

Joree, URIA. Buddi chettu. TEL., extreme height 50 feet, circumference of trunk 5 feet, height from ground to first branch 8 feet. The seeds of this tree are eaten by the Sourahs in times of scarcity, and the wood is made into bandies, &c.

Jundamaree, URIA, extreme height 60 feet, circumference of trunk 4 feet, height from ground to first branch 9 feet. Used in the erection of village houses, and as firewood.

Kaloochia, URIA., extreme height 25 feet, circumference of trunk $2\frac{2}{3}$ feet, height from ground to first branch 10 feet. Of little value.

Khoiro, URIA. Chandara chettu. TEL., *Acacia catechu,* extreme height 25 feet, circumference of trunk $2\frac{1}{4}$ feet, height from ground to first branch 6 feet. A hard wood used for ploughshares, rice pounders, sugar mills, oil presses, wheels, &c.

Kindhoo, URIA, Chinna Tumi chettu. TEL., extreme height 50 feet, circumference of trunk $4\frac{1}{2}$ feet, height from ground to first branch 25 feet. A hard black wood, writing desks or boxes are often made of it. (*Note*—Is this an ebony? or Acacia odoratissima?)

Kodoro, URIA, extreme height 30 feet, circumference of trunk 2 feet, height from ground to first branch 9 feet Used in the erection of village houses and as firewood.

Kokhoondia, URIA, extreme height 30 feet, circumference of trunk $1\frac{1}{2}$ feet, height from ground to first branch 8 feet. Used in the erection of village houses and as firewood.

Koombee, URIA, Aray chettu, TEL., extreme height 35 feet, circumference of trunk 3 feet, height from ground to first branch 6 feet. A light wood used in making bandies, the bark spun into twine, is used throughout the hill country as a slow match. (*Note*—Is this the Careya arborea?)

Konchona, URIA, Kanchanapu chettu, TEL., extreme height 30 feet, circumference of trunk $2\frac{1}{4}$ feet, height from ground to first branch 9 feet. Used in the erection of village houses and as firewood.

Kossaye, URIA, extreme height 23 feet, circumference of trunk 1 foot, height from ground to first branch 6 feet. Made into charcoal and used as firewood.

Koossoomoo, URIA., extreme height 45 feet, circumference of trunk 4 feet, height from ground to first branch 11 feet. A heavy hard wood used for oil and other presses, the seeds afford an oil, and they gather from the bark, a description of lac. (*Note*—Is this the Schleichera trijuga? Dr. Royle, *Ill. Him. Bot. p.* 138, says—this tree is called *Kusoombha* and *Guosum,* in distant parts of India, where it is indigenous, and where, as in the Doon, in April, it may readily be recognised at a distance, by the red colour of its young leaves. The wood is hard and used as timber and the pulpy sub-acid aril, forms a grateful fruit. (*See* KOOSOOM, KOOSUMBH, also MELICOCCA TRIJUGA, and SCHLEICHERA TRIJUGA.)

Korada, URIA, Vadisay chettu, TEL., extreme height 30 feet, circumference of trunk $3\frac{1}{3}$ feet, height from ground to first branch 7 feet. A light wood used in building huts and making toys. The leaf cures itch and ring worm, the bark of this tree is poisonous, and long thin stripes of it, well saturated in the juice or decoction of the bark, is neatly bound round the head of the Sourah's arrow, with which he destroys the largest animals.

Korra, URIA, Mushidi chettu, TEL., *Strychnos nux vomica,* extreme height 45 feet, circumference of trunk 4 feet, height from ground to first branch 18 feet. Wheels, ploughs and many other things are made out of this timber.

Korunjoo, URIA, Kagoo chettu, TEL., extreme height 36 feet, circumference of trunk 4 feet, height from ground to first branch 20 feet. Oil is extracted from the fruit of this tree, which is a remedy for itch: it is also burnt.

Kosee, URIA, extreme height 45 feet, circumference of trunk 4 feet, height from ground to first branch 20 feet. Used in the construction of houses generally.

Koeto, URIA, Vellaga chettu, TEL., extreme height 50 feet, circumference of trunk 5 feet, height from ground to first branch 9 feet. This wood is manufactured into bandy wheels, and its gum also is in request for many purposes.

Kotoko, URIA, Endupa chettu, TEL., extreme height 40 feet, circumference of trunk 4 feet, height from ground to first branch 10 feet. This wood is used to make ploughs and bandy wheels; the seeds are sold in the bazar and used to clear muddy water. (*Note*—Is it Strychnos patatorum?)

Kubate, URIA, Grouhonee TEL., extreme height 80 feet, circumference of trunk 6 feet, height from ground to first branch 12 feet. Affords good planks, but is little used, the bark is given in diseases of the stomach.

Mahalimboo, URIA, extreme height 70 feet, circumference of trunk 4 feet, height from ground to first branch 20 feet. Not much used, but the fruit and bark are considered remedies for fever.

Minjharee, URIA., extreme height 43 feet, circumference of trunk 4 feet, height from ground to first branch 6 feet. A very common tree, wood light and used in various ways, where strength is not required.

Mohooloo, URIA, Ippa, TEL., extreme height 70 feet, circumference of trunk 7 feet, height from ground to first branch 33 feet. This wood is made into boats or canoes and used by the fishermen. Collectors of the water lily leaves and flowers, on all the large tanks in the country, gather its flowers and leaves. The Kimedy people always eat off this leaf, and offer the blossom in their temples. A very intoxicating liquor is made from the Mohooloo blossom, which is also sold in the bazar as a sweatmeat when mixed with other ingredients. The unripe fruit is made into curry, and greatly esteemed. (*Note*—Is this the Bassia latifolia?)

Moondomonde, URIA., extreme height 50 feet, circumference of trunk 4 feet, height from ground to first branch 20 feet. This tree is scarce, and little used for any purpose.

Mooneearee, URIA, extreme height 30 feet, circumference of trunk $3\frac{1}{2}$ feet, height from ground to first branch 6 feet. Used to erect village houses and as firewood.

Nerusoo, URIA, Ali chettu, TEL., extreme height 25 feet, circumference of trunk 2 feet, height from ground to first branch 8 feet. Used to erect village houses and as firewood.

Oshoko, URIA, Asoka chettu, TEL., extreme height 45 feet, circumference of trunk 3 feet, height from ground to first branch 9 feet. Made into charcoal and used as firewood.

Patoowa, URIA, Karubalasu chettu, TEL., extreme height 15 feet, circumference of trunk 1 foot, height from ground to first branch 4 feet. Used to erect village houses and as firewood.

Patrokoorwan, URIA., extreme height 20 feet, circumference of trunk 1 foot, height from ground to first branch 5 feet. The seeds of this tree are collected with great care, as it forms one of the principal medicines of the country: the bark and leaves are also held in repute for some diseases.

Pausee, URIA, extreme height 60 feet, circumference of trunk 5 feet, height from ground to first branch 30 feet. A light hard wood used to make presses, wheels, &c.

Pia Saloo, URIA. Maddi or marri chettu. TEL., extreme height 80 feet, circumference of trunk 5½ feet, height from ground to first branch 20 feet. So great has been the demand for this timber for household building and other purposes, that but few trees are now found within an easy distance of the river banks. It is plentiful in remoter places.

Pitta Kaloochia, URIA, extreme height 33 feet, circumference of trunk 2½ feet, height from ground to first branch 12 feet. Made into charcoal ana used as firewood.

Potoobalo, URIA, Nakari chettu, TEL., extreme height 40 feet, circumference of trunk 3 feet, height from ground to first branch 10 feet. Used to erect village houses and as firewood.

Rayee, URIA, extreme height 30 feet, circumference of trunk 3 feet, height from ground to first branch 15 feet. Used in the erection of village houses and for firewood.

Sahada, URIA, Barinika chettu, TEL., extreme height 30 feet, circumference of trunk 2 feet, height from ground to first branch 7 feet. Used in the erection of village houses and as firewood.

Sahajoo, URIA., extreme height 60 feet, circumference of trunk 5 feet, height from ground to first branch 25 feet. A very useful wood and plentiful, it is used in house building, sawn into planks, and generally burnt into charcoal.

Salora, URIA, extreme height 20 feet, circumference of trunk 1 foot, height from ground to first branch 5 feet. Used in the erection of village houses and for firewood.

Salwa, URIA. Guggalapu chettu. TEL., extreme height 85 feet, circumference of trunk 6 feet, height from ground to first branch 33 feet. This is the dammar tree. Only a small quantity of its resin is brought in for sale by the hill men to Kimedy, and that is purchased by the hindoos to burn in their temples. The price of it is Rs. 3 per maund. The seeds are boiled and eaten by the Sourahs, when their crops fail, and they also consider them a remedy for bowel complaints.

Sidha, URIA, extreme height 45 feet, circumference of trunk 3½ feet, height from ground to first branch 20 feet. A common wood, of which rafters, &c. are made, the bark is used to tan leather and the natives ascribe strange medicinal qualities to it.

Sirisee, URIA, Sirissan chettu, TEL., extreme height 60 feet, circumfererence of trunk 4½ feet, height from ground to first branch 25 feet. A light hard wood used to make presses, wheels, &c.

Sisooca, URIA. Yeridi chettu. TEL., Dalbergia sisso, extreme height 40 feet, circumference of trunk 4½ feet, height from ground to first branch 16 feet. A most useful wood, being that used in the manufacture of every description of household furniture.

Sohn, URIA. Somide chettu. TEL., extreme height 50 feet, circumference of trunk 5 feet, height from ground to first branch 12 feet. A very heavy wood, and so hard that white ants make no impression on it. Little use is made of this valuable timber in consequence of the Ooriah superstition that bad luck attends its use in any but sacred buildings; its bark has astringent qualities, and is used for tanning and medicinally.

Soonaree, URIA, Nelli chettu, TEL., extreme height 25 feet, circumference of trunk 3 feet, height from ground to first branch 9 feet. Ploughshares are made of this wood: the fruit is given as an astringent in bowel complaints.

Soondoragoonde, URIA, Vassantagoonda chettu, TEL., extreme height 15 feet, circumference of trunk 2 feet, height from ground to first branch 5 feet. The fruit of this tree yields a dye which is sent for sale to Berhampore in small quantities. (*Qu.* Rottlera tinctoria?)

Tanghany, URIA. Tangadu chettu., extreme height 40 feet, circumference of trunk 3 feet, height from ground to first branch 15 feet. Used in building, for firewood and charcoal.

PUTRANJIVA ROXBURGHII, *Wall.*

Jewun-pootr. MAHR. | Kurroopallay maram. TAM.

This tree grows on the mountains of the Coromandel coast, in the ravines at Nagotnah and Khandallah: in the Kennery jungles, at Salsette, in the jungles to the north and east of Belgaum, in the Konkans, Sylhet, Assam and Oude, and is common along the foot of the Himalayas. Dr. Wight had not seen this tree in Coimbatore, but Roxburgh describes it as a large timber tree with an erect straight trunk, and with wood white, close grained and very hard. Dr. Gibson tells us it is not common as a forest tree on the Bombay side, and is found only in the coast jungles. He had never seen it of any size, but the wood appears hard, strong, and durable. It is good wood for turning. The nuts are threaded as necklaces and amulets.—*Voigt, Drs. Wight & Gibson.*

PYAUNG-PYION, BURM.? In Tavoy. a compact, heavy, yellow wood.—*Mr. Blundell.*

PYEEN-MA, BURM. In Amherst, a timber used for house posts, carts, boats, paddles, oars, &c. It is a capital wood, a kind of saul? and would answer for all the purposes of common saul; specific gravity 0·920.—*Cat. Ex.* 1851, (*Note*—Is this the Lagerstrœmia? the Peemah?)

PYENG-KHADO, BURM.? In Tavoy, a small sized, heavy, close grained, red wood.—*Mr. Blundell.* (*Note*—Is this the Inga xylocarpa?)

PYGIUM ACUMINATA. Scarce, but found on the banks of streams in the Tounghoo district attaining a girth of five or six feet. Wood red and adapted to cabinet making.—*Dr. McCelland.*

PYGIUM CEYLANICUM, *Gærtn.*

Kankoombala-katteya-gass. SINGH.

A moderate sized tree of the moister parts of Ceylon, at an elevation of 3,000 feet.—*Thw.*

PYGIUM WIGHTIANUM, *Blume.*

Oonoonoo-gass. SINGH.

A middle sized tree growing at an elevation of 4,000 to 8,000 feet in the central province of Ceylon.—*Thw.*

Q.

QUERCUS. THE OAK. Oaks are found in the Himalayas, Nepaul, Kumaon and Sylhet, and in many parts of the S. E. of Asia. All travellers in the Himalayas, testify to the abundance of their oaks. The people employed by Dr. Wallich gathered a considerable number of species, and Dr. Royle assures us that they are found from moderate elevations up to the limits of trees. He adds that they are found from the northern to the most southern parts, on the mountains of Sylhet, and in Chittagong, Penang and Taong Dong and from moderate elevations, as in the case of Q. incana—from 5,000 to 7,000 feet,—to the limits of the forest where Q. semecarpifolia disappears; but at 10,000 and 12,000 feet,on the southern face of the Himalayas, as at Choor, Kedarkanta, and Changshel, the Quercus semecarpifolia generally forms the forests at their highest limits, though other species of Quercus are found below, with Taxus, Betula, Deodara, Pinus excelsa, and morinda. Dr. Hooker tells us that oaks grow in the valleys of the eastern Himalaya, in eastern Bengal, and in the Malay peninsula. No oak nor chesnut, he says, ascends above 9000 feet in the interior of Sikkim, where they are replaced by a species of hazel (Corylus); in the north Himalaya, on the other hand, an oak (*Quercus semecarpifolia*) is amongst the most alpine trees, and the nut is a different species, more resembling the European. On the outer Sikkim ranges, oaks (Q. annulata ?) ascend to 10,000 feet, and there is no hazel. It is not generally known, he adds, that oaks are often very tropical plants; not only abounding at low elevations in the mountains, but descending in abundance to the level of the sea. Though almost unknown in Ceylon, the Peninsula of India, tropical Africa, or South America, they abound in the hot valleys of the Eastern Himalaya, East Bengal, Malay Peninsula, and India islands; where, perhaps, more species grow than in any other part of the world. Such facts as this, he remarks, disturb our preconceived notions of the geographical distribution of the most familiar tribes of plants, and throw great doubt on the conclusions which fossil plants are supposed to indicate. The evergreen oaks observed by Mr. Fortune in the Himalayas, were *Quercus dilatata* and *Q. semecarpifolia*: also, the *Quercus sclerophylla* and *Q. inversa*, the last two with large and glossy leaves, not unlike the Portugal laurel at a distance. Captain Gerard tells us of three species of oak in Kunawar the leaves of all being lance shaped, more or less serrated, and some exactly like holly. They are the Monroo and the Khursoo which grow at 12,800 feet, and the Ban (Q. incana), which disappears at 8,000 feet. Major Benson, writing in British Burmah, remarks that Quercus fenestrata, Quercus turbinata, and Quercus velutina, produce good, durable, timber, resembling that of the Dillenias in density and elasticity, though the trees do not grow of that size to make the timber of the same value as the Dillenias, "Zinbuin." And the Dillenias are not only valuable as timber trees, but for ornamental purposes. Dr. Mason tells us that Dr. Wallich found seven different species of oak growing in Burmah and on the Tenasserim Coast, all of them yielding useful timber, though inferior to the English oak, and 23 species are named in Japan, but many of the Javanese kinds, appear to be peculiar to the Indian Archipelago, or only occur near the south eastern angle of Asia, where they reach their most southern limits, being scarcely known in a wild state, in the southern hemisphere. Dr. Wight gives, in his Icones, Quercus acuminata; armata; castanicarpa: fenestrata: ferox; lanceæfolia, lappacea; semi-serrata, squamata; turbinata.—*Gerard's Account of Kunawar p.* 67. *Royle's Ill., Him. Bot. pp.* 17 *to* 345. *Dr. Mason's Tenasserim. Hookers Him. Jour. Vol.* 1, *p.* 87 *and* 11, *pp.* 114, 436. *Hodgson's Nagasaki p.* 342. *Dr. O'Shaughnessy, p.* 607 *and Ben. Phar. p.* 217. *Roxb. Fl. Ind. Vol. iii., p.* 633 *to* 641.

QUERCUS, *Species.*

Reen Wood. ANGLO-PUSHTOO ?

An ever-green oak, bearing acorns. A tree of the Mehra Forest, near Abbottabad, Hazara. It is a large spreading tree, and supposed to be the American Oak.—*Cal. Cat. Ex.* 1862.

QUERCUS AMHERSTIANA. A large tree of Martaban, used in boat-building. It grows also in Tenasserim and Burmah and affords useful timber though inferior to English oak.—*Dr. Mason.*

QUERCUS ANNULATA. The Ring Cupped Oak grows in the outer ranges of the Sikkim Himalayas, to the height of 10,000 feet.—*Eng. Cyc.*

QUERCUS CHINENSIS. Chinese Oak. This beautiful species is found in mountainous places in China, and is said to have exactly the habit and appearance of a Spanish chesnut.—*Eng. Cyc., Royle's Ill.*

QUERCUS DILATATA. A fine evergreen oak of the Himalayas.—*Fortune.*

QUERCUS FENESTRATA, *Roxb.* Grows in the Khassya hills, is a native of the mountains in the vicinity of Sylhet, and grows in Burmah and the Tenasserim provinces not fifty feet above the level of the sea. It affords useful timbers though inferior to English oak.—*Major Benson, Dr. Mason. Roxb. Fel. Ind. p.* 633.

QUERCUS INCANA.

Himalayan Ilex. Eng. | Ban of the Himalaya.
Munroo, in Kumaon.

Is found in Kumaon at moderate elevations. —*Royle's Ill., Gerard's Kunawar.*

QUERCUS INVERSA, an ever-green oak, of the Himalayas, with large glossy leaves, not unlike the Portugal laurel.—*Fortune.*

QUERCUS LANATA. The Woolly leaved Nepaul oak, is found wild in the Himalayas, and is one of the hardest oaks yet discovered.—*Fortune,*

QUERCUS LANCEÆFOLIA, *Roxb.* A tree of the Garrow hills and Assam. Wood light-coloured like the English oak but harder and reckoned, where it grows, one of the most durable timbers.—*Voigt. Roxb., Flor. Ind. p.* 634.

QUERCUS LAPPACEA, *Roxb.* A tree of the Khassya mountains. Wood strong, in colour like that of the common oak, but hard and more close grained.—*Voigt., Roxb. Fl. Ind.*

QUERCUS LUCIDA, *Roxb.*, and Q. muricata, *Roxb.* are Penang trees.

QUERCUS PRINODES, *Linn.*

Quercus serrata, *Roxb.* | Shingra, Hind.

A tree of the Garrow hills, yields a useful timber.—*Voigt, Roxb. Fel. Ind.*

QUERCUS SCLEROPHYLLA. An ever-green oak of the Himalayas, with large glossy leaves, not unlike the Portugal laurel at a distance.—*Fortune.*

QUERCUS SEMECARPIFOLIA. One of the most alpine trees of the north Himalaya. It is an ever-green species.—*Royle.*

QUERCUS SEMISERRATA, *Roxb.*

Thitkya. Burm.

Grows in the Garrow and Khassya hills and in British Burmah: wood used for plugs or pins to join together the three pieces which compose the body of a Burmese cart wheel. A cubic foot weighs lbs. 48. In a full grown tree on good soil, the average length of the trunk to the first branch is 20 feet and average girth measured at 6 feet from the ground is 4 feet.—*Roxb., Dr. Brandis, Voigt.* (*Note*—Is this Q. prinodes, above ?)

QUERCUS SPICATA, *Buch.* A tree of Nepal, of the Garrow hills, the Khassya mountains and Chittagong. Wood lighter colored than English oak, but equally close grained and apparently as strong.—*Voigt.*

QUERCUS TIRBBÆ ? ? Grows in Burmah and the Tenasserim provinces. It affords useful timber though inferior to English oak. (*Note*—Is Tirb-bæ not a Burmese term for one of the oaks ?)

QUERCUS TURBINATA. Grows in Chittagong : in Burmah, it affords useful timber though inferior to English oak. Roxburgh says it is only used for fuel.—*Roxb. p.* 636.

QUERCUS VELUTINA. Grows in Burmah and the Tenasserim provinces. It affords useful timber though inferior to English Oak.

R.

RACKA NASTA, Can.? Stunted teak : a forest term.

RAJAMUNDRY WOODS. The following woods were sent from this district, to the Exhibition of 1851. Karra, కఱ్ర in Telugu, meaning " wood."

Acacia cinerea, ఏలుతురి కఱ్ర Yeluturi karra.

Agisti karra అగిసి కఱ్ర.

Alangium hexapetalum, ఊడుగ కఱ్ర Uduga karra.

Auneng karra. ఆనెంగ్ కఱ్ర.

Artocarpus integrifolia, పనస కఱ్ర Panasa karra.

Azadirachta Indica, వేప కఱ్ర Vepa karra.

Bassia latifolia, యిప్ప కఱ్ర Ippa karra.

Bombax malabaricum or heptaphylla, బూరుగ కఱ్ర Booroogа karra.

Careya arborea, కంబ కఱ్ర Kamba karra.

Cassia auriculata, తంగేడు కఱ్ర Tangadu karra.

Chloroxylon Swietenia, బిల్ల కఱ్ర Billa karra.

Cordia myxa, నక్కేరు కఱ్ర Nakkeru karra.

Cratæva, ఉలిమిడితిగె Oolimiditige.

Cratæva Roxburghii or tapia, తెల్ల ఉలిమిరి కఱ్ర Tella oolimiri karra.

Diospyros chloroxylon, నల్ల ఉలిమిరి కఱ్ర Nalla Oolimiri karra.

Diospyros montana ? యిరుగుడు చావ కఱ్ర Irugoodu chava karra.

Diospyros melananoxylon, తుమ్మెద చావ కఱ్ర Tummeda chava karra.

Erythrina Indica, బాడిద కఱ్ర Badida karra.

Feronia elephantum, వెలగ కఱ్ర Velaga karra.

Ficus racemosa, బొడ్డ కఱ్ర Bodda karra.

Ganara karra, గనర కఱ్ర.

Gata karra, గాంత కఱ్ర.

Gmelina arborea, గుమ్ముడు కర్ర Gummudu karra.

Isakarasi karra. ఇసకరాసి కర్ర

Mangifera Indica, మామిడి కర్ర Mamidi karra.

Mimusops elengi, పగడుపు కర్ర Pagadupu.

Morinda citrifolia, తొగరు కర్ర Togaru karra.

Nauclea cordifolia, దాడుగ కర్ర Daduga karra.

Nauclea purpurea, బొగద కర్ర Bogada karra.

Odina wodier, గుంపెన కర్ర Goompena karra.

Penemu karra, పెనెము కర్ర.

Paya karra, పాయ కర్ర.

Pentapteratomentosa, నల్లమద్ది కర్ర Nallamaddi.

Pentaptera glabra, తెల్లమద్ది కర్ర Tella maddi.

Pongamia glabra, కానుగ కర్ర Kanuga karra.

Pterocarpus marsupium, యేగిశ కర్ర Yegisa

Pterospermum Heynii? లోలు కర్ర Lolu karra.

Rottlera tinctoria, పొన్న కర Ponna karra.

Sapindus emarginatus, కుంకుడు కర్ర Koonkudu karra.

Swietenia febrifuga, సోమిద కర్ర Somida karra.

Spondias mangifera, జాడుమామిడి కర్ర Jadu mamidi karra.

Strychnos potatorum, ఇందుగ కర్ర Indooga

Syzygium jambolana, నేరేడు కర్ర Neredu

Tada karra, తడ కర్ర.

Teli karra, తెలి కర్ర.

Thespesia populnea, గంగరావి కర్ర Gangaravi

Vatica tumbugaia? గుగ్గిలపు కర్ర Googgilapu karra.

Vandooroo karra. వండురు కర్ర

Wrightia antidysenterica, అంకుడు కర్ర Ankudu.

Zizyphus jujuba, రేగు కర్ర Regu karra.

RAJAW—? A plentiful tree of Akyab. It is a small wood, used in house building.—*Cal. Cat. Ex.* 1862.

RALL, or, ROSIN TREE. Sir Richard Jenkins states in his report on the Nagpore territory, that the Rall or rosin tree, as also other large wood, is obtained in the forests of Kakir (probably Conkair) and in the hills north of Ruttenpore. When Captain Sankey visited the Pachmurra range, Dr. Jerdon and he met with the "Vatica tumbugaia" which is probably Sir R. Jenkin's Rall tree, though it does not seem, in those jungles, to attain a large size.—*Captain Sankey.*

RAMBABHA — ? A very plentiful tree of Akyab which grows to a large size, and is sometimes used for planks.—*Cal. Cat. Ex.* 1862.

RANDIA, *Species.*

Nalla Manga, TEL. of Circars.

A good sized, armed, tree, of the Godavery forests: furnishing a very hard and close grained wood, good for turnery.—*Captain Beddome.*

RANDIA DUMETORUM, *Lam.*

Gardenia spinosa, *Linn.*
Pasoqueria dumetorium, *Roxb.*
Ceriscus malabaricus, *Gaertn.*
Randia longespina, *D. C.*
Canthium coronatum, *Lam.*
Gardenia dumetorium, *Retz.*

Jooz-ul-kueh. ARAB.
Bush-Randia. ENG.
Muen-phal ka-jhar. HIND.
Myn. HIND.
Gehela. MAHR.
Maru karang. TAM.
Madu karray maram. TAM.
Manda. TEL.
Mauga. TEL.

This is a shrub or small tree, thorny, and branching, met with in the hotter parts of Ceylon; in Coimbatore, where it seldom exceeds the size of a large shrub, and, it is one of the most common trees of the Bombay forests, but the wood never reaches any size. It is, however, strong, hard and close grained. It grows, also, in Guzerat and northwards in the Dehra Dhoon and the Kheree Pass. The fruit is used in Malabar to poison or intoxicate fish, which are still considered good for eating.—*Drs. Wight and Gibson, Voigt, Thwaites, O'Shaughnessy.*

RANDIA LONGIFLORA, *Lam.*

Posoqueria longiflora, *Roxb.*
Gardenia longiflora, *Willde.*

A tree of Chittagong and Penang with large flowers, white the first day, but, on the second, becoming yellow. Wood not known.—*Voigt.*

RAN-FANNAS, MAHR.

Artocarpus sylvestris.

A tree of the Bombay forests.—*Dr. Gibson.*

RANGHA-AS—? A Penang wood, of a light brown colour, used for furniture.—*Col. Frith.*

RATAN KHAUR HIND. ? A tree of Chota Nagpore, furnishing a hard, white timber.—*Cal. Cat. Ex.* 1862.

RAUNG-THMOO, BURM? This is a wood of Amherst, and it is said to be a kind of teak. It is used for house posts.—*Cat. Ex.* 1861.

RAY. HIND. ? A tree of Chota Nagpore, furnishing a hard timber.—*Cal. Cat. Ex.* 1862.

RAYEE, TEL? A tolerably plentiful tree of Ganjam and Goomsoor, which attains an extreme height of 30 feet and a circumference of 3 feet. The distance from the ground to the outer section of the first branch is 15 feet. It is only used for firewood.—*Captain Macdonald.*

RAILWAY SLEEPERS. Railway operations in India, are largely thinning the forests near which the lines run; and, as roads are projected over a large part of India, it may be of interest to mention the experience acquired from that at

Madras. At one time, it was thought that the forests of the south of India would furnish numerous timbers suitable for sleepers and the following, 22 in number, were the woods of highest promise, viz :—

Tectona grandis, Teak.	Soymida febrifuga, Som maram.
Shorea robusta, Saul.	Acacia odoratissima, Karroo vangay : also, Chella woongay maram.
Dalbergia sissoo, Sissoo.	
Pterocarpus Indicus, Pedowk.	
Zizyphus glabrata, Kurkuttah.	Prosopis spicegera, Perumbay maram.
Terminalia glabra, Karra marda.	Inga xylocarpa, Irool, Erool, or Eroovaloo maram.
Terminalia alata, Maruthi maram.	Acacia speciosa, Vel-vangay maram.
Hardwickia binata, Acha maram.	Artocarpus integrifolia, Pila maram.
Pterocarpus marsupium, Vengay maram.	Bassia longifolia, Dud eloopa maram.
Terminalia chebula, Kadukai-maram.	Acacia Arabica, Karu-velam maram.
Nicani maram.	Kombadri.
Myladi maram.	Katu-voye maram.

But these hopes have not, as yet, been fulfilled; no timber used, has been found capable of resisting the combined effects of the heat and moisture of thesouth of India, and only on the woods of three trees, the Erool, *Inga xylocarpa ;* Karra marda, *Terminalia glabra ;* and Vengay, *Pterocarpus marsupium,* is any great reliance now placed, and iron sleepers are very extensively in use on the Madras line. Hitherto, taking an average of the various woods in use on this road, the duration of its sleepers has been about 3½ years, and annually about 340 sleepers per mile have been required to be replaced. On these points, Mr. Pinson, acting chief engineer, in a letter to the agent and manager, dated 14th August 1862, furnishes the result of the experience upon the 1st or Madras division of the south west line, in the form of the following statement, which gives the average lives of sleepers of various woods, taken out of the line in a state of decay, and replaced by iron pot sleepers, up to the present date.

Distinguishing Mark.	Names of woods.	Average life.
A.	Aucha	4 years 7 months.
F.	Kurrah murdah	3 „ 10 „
C.	Combadrie	4 „ 2 „
K.	Cadookoy	4 „ 1 „
S.	Saul	4 „ 2 „
E.	Dud eloopay	3 „ 10 „
Y.	Eroovaloo	2 „ 8 „
V.	Vangay	4 „ 3 „
P.	Paulay	2 „ 10 „
R.	Auray	2 „ 6 „
M.	Myladee	1 „ 5 „
H.	Myroothy	4 „ 3 „
D.	Katvoy	4 „ 4 „
B.	Karavalum	4 „ 2 „

The general average, therefore, has been 3 years and 8 months. Mr. Pinson is awaiting returns from the engineers of the other divisions on the south-west line, to enable him to ascertain the durability of Erool, which was confidently expected to turn out to be the best description of wood for sleeper purposes. He adds that the creosoted sleepers of Baltic fir, which had been received from England from time to time, are, as a rule, exceedingly durable. Recently, there was occasion to take some decayed ones out of the line near Sholinghur, which were ascertained to have been in the road for a period of nearly 6½ years. But the cost of such sleepers, he remarks, interferes materially with their extensive use in this country. The prices paid for sleepers for the Madras railway have ranged, according to the various woods, from Rs. 1½ to Rs. 3, for the timbers of the south of India; but those of Burmese and Australian woods have cost Rs. 5: and, where timber sleepers are used, there must be added the cost of two chairs, say annas 14. But, a pair of iron sleepers, with fittings complete (answering to one timber sleeper), delivered in Madras, cost about Rs. 7-8; and, while the cost of labour in laying an iron road is much less than for a wooden one and the labour cost of its maintenance also much less, the duration of the iron road is greatly longer than that of a road of any of the woods, as hitherto tried. Several years ago, I expressed my conviction that if mining and smelting operations ever be carried on with activity the most extensive forests in India would diminish and disappear; and the experience just detailed shows that, as the operations have, hitherto, been conducted, the forests are not inexhaustible for railway purposes, and leaves the impression that there are no woods in India which can compete with a road on iron pot sleepers. From recent correspondence, on this subject, elicited in consequence of Major Morgan's remarks in his forest report for 1860-61, it would also appear that the success of the iron sleepers on the Enniskillen and Londonderry railway, has been most favourable; and, on the Egypt line, where they use Greaves' cast-iron, pot, bell, or cup sleepers, for it has all these appellations, the success of that kind of road, in an alluvial soil, has been unquestionable. In the report alluded to, Major Morgan added that one cause of wooden sleepers not lasting is that under the chair a hollow forms, in which water lodges and causes rapid decay, and he thinks that a small piece of galvanised sheet-iron fitted over the part, would prevent the formation of a hollow. But, Mr. Smart has replied that the wood sleepers give way not only under the chair, but everywhere else. From this remark, and from the longer lives of the Baltic fir sleepers, it would seem that in using the woods of this country, the defect, for the sleepers of the Madras line, has been insufficient seasoning. I have never heard that the timbers of the country have been stored for years, to allow their juices to escape: but, so far as is known, soon after the trees have been felled, they have been laid on the gronnd as sleepers, and no known timber could withstand so severe a trial. With the rapidity of the operations on this line, for the first turf was cut on the 9th June 1853 and there was no previous gigantic stacking of timber, to admit of the requisite seasoning—because, it requires 3 to 5 years seasoning to render green wood fit for use, and at least two years should have been allowed for seasoning, before any use, whatever, was made of the timbers of the countries—perhaps, the Baltic fir alone, of all the timbers that have been tried, was seasoned wood. With our present knowledge, it would be wrong to condemn the many valuable timber trees of this country, or to assert that Baltic fir can possibly, compete with them.—*Beresford Anderson, Esq., Engineer, Madras Railway, M.SS., John A. Pinson, Esq., in Records of Consulting Engineer, M. R., R. B. Elwin, Esq., Manager, in Records of Consulting Engineer, Madras Railway, favoured through Captain Prendergast, Royal Engineers, W. G. Smart, Esq., Chief Engr., Henry J. Rouse, Esq., in Proceedings of Madras Government, Dr. Cleghorn's Reports on the forests, Major Morgan, in Madras Conservator's Report, Balfour's Report on the Iron ores of the Madras Presidency, Madras*, 1855.

RED WOOD. This, like the ebonies, the iron woods and rose woods of commerce, is a term applied to the woods of different trees, and many nations have a wood to which this English term is applied. Amongst others may be mentioned, the

Red wood of Japan.

Fa-ang. JAP. | Tsiampan. JAP.

This wood is a product of Coy or Kiu, in Thunbergs' time, belonging to the king of Siam. It was also obtainable in Bambilisoo, on the coast of Cambodia, and from Bimen island, between Bali and Timor. It was imported into Japan, where, Thunberg remarks, "this wood rubbed with some lime and water, yields the finest violet colour we could wish to see." —*Thunb., Hist. of Japan, Vol. I. p.* 42-43. (*Note*—Is it the Pterocarpus santalinus or the Cæsalpinia sappan? "Useful Plants" gives *Tsjapangam* as Malealam of C. sappan.)

Red dye wood. A wood of this English name, occurs in the Vizianagrum zemindary. (*Note*—Is this the red sanders wood, the Pterocarpus santalinus ?)

Red wood. A wood of this English name occurs in Penang where it is in general use for furniture Its colour is red, and its specific gravity 1,000.—*Col. Frith.* (*Note*—Is it a Pterocarpus ? marsupium ? Wallichii ? or dalbergioides ?)

RENGA, TEL. Zizyphus jujuba.

REYGATTI, TEL. Capparis grandis.

RHIZOPHORA, *Species.*

Leafy mangrove. ENG. | Kadol. SINGH.

This mangrove is found in the western and northern provinces of Ceylon, chiefly near the mouths of the rivers. The wood weighs lbs. 65 to the cubic foot, and is used for common house building purposes. It is calculated to last 20 years. A dye is extracted from the bark, and used for colouring leather, nets, sails, &c.—*Mr. Adrian Mendis.*

RHIZOPHORA, *Species.*

Hiri-koddol. SINGH.

This mangrove grows in the western and northern provinces of Ceylon, and is used for common house building purposes. A cubic foot weighs lbs. 49, and it is estimated to last 35 years. A dye is extracted from the bark.—*Mr. Adrian Mendis.*

RHIZOPHORA CONJUGATA. *Linn.*

Rhizophora candelaria, *W. & A.; Blume.*

A small tree of Ceylon, Malabar, Tenasserim and Java.—*Thwaites, p.* 120, *Voigt, p.* 41.

RHIZOPHORA MUCRONATA, *Lam.; W. Ic.*

Rhizophora mangle, *Linn.; Roxb.?*
,, candelaria, *W. & A.*
,, macrorrhiza, *Griff,*

Bhora. BENG.
Oopuponna. ,, Qu: uppu-ponna?
Manggi-manggi? MALAY.
Kaya api api? ,,
Pukandel. TAM.
Adavi ponna. TEL.
Pukandel. ,,
Uppu ponna. ,,

Grows in Madagascar, Mauritius and Arabia, at Trincomalie, Calpentyn, Negumbo and other parts of the Ceylon coast, along with R. conjugata,—also in Malabar, the Sunderbuns and Java. The wood is dark reddish, hard and durable. The flowers are large, white and sweet scented. Bark used for tanning.—*Voigt, p.* 41, *Thw., p.* 120.

RHUS. This genus includes some true poisons, as R. venenata, perniciosa, radicans, and toxicodendron; and, though most are inodorous, others, R. suaveolens and aromatica, exhale a pleasant odour; while some of the species have acid berries as R. coriaria; bucki-amela, and Schinus molle. Thus Rhus cotinus or Red sumach, has wood, called young fustick, which, as well as the berries, is astringent, and R. coriaria, known in India as in Europe, by the name of Sumach, and as a powerful astringent, is chiefly employed in tanning leather, but also in Indian medicine. The seed of R. parviflora, tuntereek, is frequently substituted in India for that of the sumach. R. glabra is considered a febrifuge. Rhus vernix, a Japanese tree, exudes a whitish resinous juice, which soon becomes black in the air. R. succedania and vernicifera, both common to the Himalayas and Japan, are said, in the latter, to yield a similar product. Species of other genera as, of Schinus, contain a resinous matter. —*Royle's Ill. Him. Bot. p.* 179.

RHUS? *Species?* One of the Terebinthaceæ. Coongilliya maram, TAM. Dr. Wight remarks, regarding this Coimbatore wood, that it is the Chloroxylon dupada of Buchanan and Ainslie, an undescribed name and, judging from the leaves, one not required, which are clearly those of a Rhus very nearly allied to Roxburgh's R. Bucki-amela but distinct. The qualities of the timber are unknown. The outer sap-wood is white, fine grained and heavy, apparently very good.—*Dr. Wight.*

RHUS BUCKI-AMELA, *Roxb.*

Rhus amela, *G. Don.*
„ semialata, *β. Roxburghii.; D C.*

Grows in Kumaon and Shreenuggur and the peninsula of India; but, Dr. Gibson says, it is not found in the Bombay presidency.—*Voigt, Drs. Wight and Gibson.*

RHUS DECEPIENS, *Wight.*

Pehimbive. SINGH. | Kattu puvaras maram. TAM.

Grows in the central province of Ceylon and in the south of India. Dr. Wight says, it yields a very fine, close grained, light coloured wood, and, if procurable of good size, the wood must be of considerable value. In Ceylon, Mr. Mendis says a cubic foot of it weighs 68 lbs., and it is used there for buildings, lasting 50 years.—*Dr. Wight, Mr. Mendis.*

RHUS MYSORENSIS. The chief representative of this tribe in the barren hills of that territory, is Rhus Mysorensis, a scrubby shrub, fit only for firewood.—*Dr. Gibson.*

RICINUS DICOCCUS, *Roxb.*

Taw-the-din-bin. BURM.

This grows in Amboyna and in British Burmah, but it is scarce and found only on the banks of streams in the Pegu and Tonghoo districts. It yields a very tall large timber. The wood is red and adapted to cabinet making.—*Voigt, McClelland.*

RHUS VERNICIFERA, *DC.*

Rhus juglandifolia, *Wall.*

The varnish tree of Japan is common in the Himalaya, in Kumaon, Nepaul and Gurhwal.—*Royle, Ill. Him Bot.*

ROKAM—? A light red coloured wood of Penang, used for boxes and furniture.—*Cat. Ex.* 1851.

RONDELETIA TINCTORIA.

Tamayoke. BURM.

In Pegu, a small timber which, together with Mangifera attenuata, Anacardium occidentale, Zizyphus jujuba, Averrhoa carambola, Pierardia sapota, Ancestrolobus carnea, Ancestrolobus mollis, are adapted, from the fineness of their grain and elegance of colour, for common work. Its wood is a dark brown in colour.—*Dr. McClelland, p.* 134.

ROORADEA, URIA? A tree of Ganjam and Gumsur, extreme height 12 feet, circumference 1 foot, and height from the ground to the intersection of the first branch 3 feet. The fruit is eaten; but no use is made of the tree.—*Captain Macdonald.*

ROHANA, URIA.? TEL. A tree of Ganjam and Gumsur, of extreme height 30 feet; tolerably common and burnt for firewood; wooden pestles and ploughshares are sometimes made of this wood.—*Captain Macdonald.*

RORI, HIND. A tree of Chota Nagpore, with hard, white timber.—*Cal. Cat. Ex.* 1862.

ROSEWOOD.

Bois du rose. FR.	Leno de rosa. SP.
Rozen-holz. GER.	Yerra goodda-chava curra. TEL.
Legno rodie. IT.	
Pao de rosada. POR.	

Like to iron-wood, blackwood &c., this is a commercial term given to the timbers of several trees. That used in Britain, is produced in the Brazils, the Canary Isles, the East Indies, and Africa. It is imported in very large slabs, or the halves of trees which average 18 inches wide. The best is from Rio de Janeiro, the second quality from Bahia, and the commonest from the East Indies: the latter is called East India black-wood, although it happens to be the lightest and most red of the three; it is devoid of the powerful smell of the true rose-wood, which latter Dr. Lindley considers to be a species of mimosa. The pores of the East India Rosewood appear to contain less or none of the resinous matter, from which the odour, like that of the flower of Acacia armata, arises. Rose-wood contains so much gum and oil, that small splinters make excellent matches. The colours of Rose-wood are from light hazel to deep purple, or nearly black: the tints are sometimes abruptly contrasted, at other times striped or nearly uniform. The wood is very heavy; some specimens are close and fine in the grain, whereas others are as open as coarse mahogany, or rather are more abundant in veins. The black streaks are sometimes particularly hard, and very destructive to the tools employed on it. Next to mahogany, it is, in England, the most abundant of the furniture woods. A large quantity is cut into veneers for upholstery and cabinet work, and solid pieces are used for the same purposes and for a great variety of turned articles of ordinary consumption. Mr. Poole, in his recent Statistics of Commerce, describes it as a highly esteemed dark brown colored fancy wood, principally used in veneering and making costly furniture. That delivered in England, he says, is imported chiefly from Bahia and Rio de Janeiro, into London and Liverpool. It is in the form of the halves of trees averaging 18 inches wide, and in height 2½ cwt., called planks, of which the import in 1851 was 2,000 tons. Price, ordinarily, £9 to £19, but rising occasionally to £90 per ton. The Rosewood of the Tenasserim provinces, is a very beautiful, hard, compact timber, resembling "Andaman wood," and is occasionally seen in the bazar of Calcutta. From Siam, a rosewood is largely exported by the Chinese; and other places. These woods are generally esteemed according to the degree in which the darker parts are distinct from the purple red, which forms the ground.

A Rosewood, is the *Lignum Rhodium, Aspalathus.*

The *Chinese Rose-wood,* called by the natives Tze-tau, is odorous, of a reddish black colour, streaked, and full of fine veins, which appear as if painted. The manufactures of this wood are more valued in China than the varnished or japanned. There are baser kinds of Rose-wood of inferior value.

East Indian Blackwood or Rose wood, from a species of Dalbergia, is an excellent heavy wood, suited for the best furniture. It can be procured in large quantities, and of considerable size; the wood contains much oil, which was exhibited in 1855, by the Ganjam Local Committee. In large panels it is liable to split.—*Faulkner's Commercial Dictionary, The Hon'ble Mr. Morrison's Compendious Description, M. E. Jr. Rep., Dr. Mason's Tenasserim. Holtzapfell, Poole's Statistics of Commerce.*

ROTTLERA, a genus of plants named in honour of Dr. Rottler. It is found in the tropical parts of Asia and throughout India, and contains handsome moderate sized trees. *R. tetracocca* grows in Silhet, and yields a hard and valuable timber. Rottlera digyna, Thw. (*Chloroxylon digynum,* Wight, Ic. t. 1884—c. p. 2,190), is a small tree growing at Caltura in Ceylon. Rottlera eriocarpa, Thw., grows in Ceylon, in the hot, and drier parts of the island, but is not very common, and Rottlera fuscescens, Thw., another small Ceylon tree, is not uncommon up to an elevation of 2,000 feet. And, in Ceylon, also, is found R. muricata, *Thw.;* R. oppositifolia, *Blume,* and R. rhombifolia, *Thw.,* all small trees.—*Thw. En. Pl. Zeyl. p.* 272.

ROTTLERA, *Species.*

Ya-gine. BURM.

A moderate-sized tree of British Burmah, common on the low ground near streams. Breaking weight from 153 to 170 lbs. A cubic foot weighs lbs. 35. In a full grown tree on good soil the average length of the trunk to the first branch is 30 feet and average girth measured at 6 feet from the ground is 6 feet. It sells at 4 annas per cubic foot.—*Dr. Brandis, Cal. Cat. Ex.* 1862.

ROTTLERA, *Species.*

Otte. SINGH.

This wood, which is used for common house building purposes, is the product of a tree growing in the western province of Ceylon. It weighs 36 lbs. to the cubic foot, but is little durable, lasting only 10 years.—*Mr. Mendis.*

ROTTLERA, *Species.*

Mimasko. BURM. Qu: mimasho?

A Tavoy tree, represented as furnishing a timber.—*Dr. Wallich.*

ROTTLERA, *Species.*

Keoun lae. BURM.

In Tavoy a large tree, the timber of which is used for rudders.—*Dr. Wallich.*

ROTTLERA TETRACOCCA, *Roxb.; Fl. Ind. III. p.* 826, *c. p.* 2118.

Boo-kanda-gass. SINGH.

Grows in Silhet, and, in Ceylon, is common up to an elevation of 2,000 feet. It yields a hard and valuable timber.—*Voigt, Thw. En. Pl. Zeyl. p.* 272.

ROTTLERA TINCTORIA, *Roxb.; Cor. Pl Rheede.*

Croton coccineum, *Vahl.*
" punctatum, *Retz.*

Tung. BENG.
Corunga munje mara. CAN.
Sarnakassary mara. "
Shendri. DUK.
Tung. "
Toong. "
Monkey faced tree. ENG.
Kamal. HIND. Qu: kamala?
Cupala. "
Punag. "
Tukla. "
Kapila. "
Sendri. MAHR.
Poonagam. MALEAL.
Punnaga. SANS.
Hamparandella-gass. SINGH.
Kapilapodi. TAM.
Chéndúrapu chettu. TEL.
Sinduri chettu. "
Kunkumapuvvu. " "
Punnagamu. " "
Vasanta gundu. " "
Veligáram. " "
Soondoro-gundi. URIA.?
Koomala-gundi. "
Bosonto-gundi. "

A tree of moderate size, not uncommon in the hotter parts of Ceylon. Grows in the northern Circars, in the Dekhan, the inland and coast jungles of the Bombay Presidency, and extending to the forests of northern India, in the Kotah and Mewar jungles. Writing regarding this tree, in Ganjam and Goomsur, Captain Macdonald tells us that, the "Soondorogoondee, Koomalagoondee, or Bosontogoondee, is of extreme height 15 feet, circumference 2½ feet, and height from the ground to the intersection of the first branch, 5 feet. The fruit of this tree, he adds, yields a valuable dye which is extensively used for dyeing silk &c., and is exported in large quantities to Calcutta and other places. It is very expensive and is eagerly bought up by the mahajuns who send their gumashtahs to purchase it of the Khonds. The tree is very scarce in many parts of Goomsur but is tolerably common in any of the frontier mootahs such as Juggernathprasaud, Kurcholy and Coocooloobah. It is found in greater abundance in the Bodogodo jungles, and is said to be tolerably plentiful about Chotapaud, but is far more common on the Bengal side of the frontier and is said to abound in Boad and Duspullah." Dr. Cleghorn, in M. E. J. R., says the wood is soft and inferior. Dr. Gibson says it is of fair quality when not exposed to wet, and that it is not readily attacked by worms. Its capsules are covered with short stiff hairs, which when rubbed off have the appearance of a powder of a fine red colour, which is employed in India in dyeing silk of a scarlet colour, and therefore forms an article of commerce. Dr. Royle states that this strigose pubescence is also employed in India as an anthelmintic in the same way that cowhage is and like it probably acts mechanically in expelling the worms.—*Royle, Him. Bot., Thwaites, Voigt, Flor. Andhr., Captain Macdonald, Eng. Cyc., Dr. Gibson, Dr. Cleghorn.*

ROUMEA HEBECARPA, *Poit.*

Katambilla. SINGH.

A moderate sized Ceylon tree, at Condasalle, Maturatte, &c.—*Thw. p.* 18.

S.

SALIX, the Willow. There are 15 species of willows in India,—5 in the peninsula, 1 in Bengal, 2 from Oude, and the rest in the Himalayas. The earliest mention of the willow which occurs in any composition is to be found in the Pentateuch, where the Israelites were directed at the institution of the feast of tabernacles to "take the boughs of goodly trees, branches of palm trees, and the boughs of thick trees, and willows of the brook, and to rejoice before the Lord their God seven days." At a later period, the Psalmist describes the captives as thus lamenting—" By the rivers of Babylon, there we sat down, yea, we wept, when we remembered Zion. We hanged our harps upon the willows in the midst thereof. For there they that carried us away captive required of us a song; and they that wasted us required of us mirth." Dr. Hooker tells us that the willow is not commonly found below 8,000 feet elevation on the Sikkim mountains, where it grows on the inner Himmalaya only, and some kinds ascend to 16,000 feet: like the poplars, the willows are valuable for their timbers or economic purposes.—*John's Forest trees of Britain, Dr. Hooker, Himalayan Journal, Vol. II., p.* 240.

SALIX TRETRASPERMA, *Roxb.*

Panee-juma. BENG.	Momakha. BURM.

This peculiar species of willow is common at Rangamally in the Terai, in the Kheree pass, and along the foot of the mountains: it grows in Bengal and the peninsula of India, likewise in British Burmah. The wood is not used in Burmah. A cubic foot weighs lbs. 37. In a full grown tree on good soil the average length of the trunk to the first branch is 10 feet and average girth measured at 6 feet, from the ground is 3 feet.—*Drs. Brandis and Hooker, Him. Jour., Vol. I., p.* 400, *Dr. Royle's Ill., Bot. Him., p.* 343, *Voigt.*

SALIX BABYLONICA.

Weeping willow. ENG.	Khilaf-i-balkhi. HIND.
Bet-i-majnoon. HIND.	Seil-i-majnoon „

A small tree of Greece, Asia Minor and Nepaul. It is cultivated in gardens at Ajmir and Calcutta, and is common in gardens in northern India, as is S. Ægyptiaca, while the polyandrous S. tetrasperma, *Roxb.*, is found in the Kheree pass, along the foot of the mountains and in other parts of India as Bengal and the peninsula.—*Dr. Irvine's Medical Topography, p.* 210, *Royle's Ill., Him. Bot., p.* 343.

SALMALIA MALABARICA, *Sch. & End.*

Bombax malabarica, *D C.: W. & A.; W.*
„ heptaphyllum, *Roxb.; Cav. Rheede.*
„ ceiba, *Burm. ?*
Gossampinus rubra, *Ham. ?*

Rakto shimool. BENG.	Elavam maram. TAM.
Mullelavu. CAN.	Pula maram. „
Red cotton tree. ENG.	Konda búruga. TEL.
Mulelavu. MALEAL.	Pinna búruga. „
Katoo-imbool-gass. SINGH.	

This is a large tree with flowers of a beautiful red colour, common in the warmer parts of Ceylon and from one end of India to the other particularly along the foot of the Himalaya. It is one of the most abundant of the forest trees of Tenasserim. The wood is light and spongy and very inferior, but used by moochies in their work. In Tenasserim, the silky down that envelopes the seed, is used to stuff mattresses and pillows and has occasionally been made into cloth.—*Dr. Cleghorn and Mr. McIvor in M. E. J. R., Dr. Mason, Voigt, Thwaites.*

SALORA, URIA. A tree of Ganjam and Gumsur, extreme height 22 feet, circumference 1 foot, and height from the ground to the intersection of the first branch, 5 feet. A common tree, only used for firewood. The leaves are eaten.—*Captain Macdonald.*

SALVADORA INDICA, *Royle; Roxb. W. Ic.*

Salvadora Wightiana, *Herb.; Hook.*
„ Persica, *Roxb.; Fl. Ind. not Linn.*

Mahomedan tooth brush tree. ENG.	Irak. PERS.
	Miswak. „
Jal. HIND.	Peda vara goki. TEL.

Grows towards the sea coast in the north part of the island of Ceylon, and near the sea, in both the Concans. It is found in the Punjab and on the banks of the Jumna, and from Delhi to Saharunpore. The leaves "Rasuna," resemble the lanceolate senna, and are also purgative; the fruit called *Peel* and *Pinjood*, is said to be eatable. It is not known whether the root bark possesses acrid properties. The twigs of this tree are used as tooth-brushes. Character of the wood not known.—*O'Shaughnessy, p.* 527, *Thirty-five years in the East, by Dr. Honigberger, p.* 339, *Thwaites.*

SALVADORA PERSICA, *Linn.; W. Ic.*

Rivinia paniculata, *Forsk.*
Cissus arborea, „

Chardal. AR.	Kurjal. HIND.
Chardul. „	Peeloo. MAHR.
Khardal. „	Khardalo. SYRIAC.
Mustard tree of Scripture.	Ughai. TAM.
Chardul of the Talmud.	Pinna qu ? chinna ? vara gogu. TEL.
Sinapis. GR.	Ghunia. „
Kharjal. HIND.	
Pilu. „	

This tree grows in Arabia, the Persian gulf, and is very common in Ajmir and Marwar. It is not a tree common on the Bombay side of India, except at Mahomedan durgahs and places of worship; but it grows wild on the coast in the Hubshee's country of Janjirah, and in the southern Maratha country, but seldom reaches any size. In Sind it is more common, and grows considerably larger. It thrives well in every soil, and is in flower and fruit all the year round. Trunk generally crooked, from eight to ten feet high to the branches, and one foot in diameter. It is supposed to be the mustard tree of Scripture. Dr. Gibson is inclined to think that the wood of this tree is well worthy of an extended trial, as it seems rather strong and of compact grain. The bark of the root is very acrid, and if applied to the skin soon raises blisters; it promises to be a stimulant of very great power.—*Drs. Irvine, O'Shaughnessy, Roxb., Gibson, Royle.*

SALWA, URIA. Guggalapu chettu. TEL. A tree of Purlah Kimedy, extreme height 85 feet, circumference of trunk 6 feet, height from ground to first branch 33 feet. This is the dammar tree. Only a small quantity of its resin is brought in for sale by the hill men to Kimedy, and that is purchased by the hindoos to burn in their temples. The price of it is Rs. 3 per maund. The seeds are boiled and eaten by the Sourahs, when their crops fail, and they also consider them a remedy for bowel complaints.—*Capt. Philipps.*

SALWA, URIA. SORUNGHEE, URIA.

Sal. HIND.	Gúgulapu chettu. TEL.

A tree of Ganjam and Gumsur, extreme height 90 feet, circumference 6 feet and height from the ground to the intersection of the first branch, 33—38 feet. This is the well known sal or dammer tree, and is one of the commonest as well as one of the most useful trees in these jungles. It is used for beams, rafters, posts and for almost every description of wood work required in house building; it is made into masts for native dhonies, is used for bandy wheels and ploughshares and has recently been exported in large quantities to supply the demand for railway sleepers. The large logs are cut into planks for doors, windows and other purposes. The branches and less useful portions of the tree are burnt for firewood and for charcoal. The tree, before being used, is usually stripped of its bark; it is then designated Jhora or Jhangherree and is not liable to be attacked by white ants. A well known resin (bdellium) termed here Jhoona or Sodaloso exudes from the tree when it has attained a large size. This is burnt at the shrines of all the village goddesses, is used by native jewellers for filling up the hollow portions of ornaments, and is in great request among ship owners and boatmen for their vessels. The leaves of this tree are used for eating rice from. The seeds are used medicinally and are said to have an astringent property. They are also boiled, dried and pounded into a sort of rice, which is eaten by the Khonds and poorer classes of Oriyas in times of scarcity. This tree abounds everywhere, the largest specimens are to be found in the Gumsur forests, but the timber of Bodogoda appears to be more highly prized in the native market, not, it is said, on account of any intrinsic superiority in the wood, but because large quantities of a uniform size are more easily procurable in that zemindary. It forms an important article of traffic in Bodogoda, large quantities of it being annually floated during the rains down the Jhoroo and the Patna towards Sooroda, and thence, after the junction of these streams with the Kooshkoolliah, to Aska, Pitala and Ganjam, besides which a considerable quantity of timber is carried on bandies to Shergoda, Coorlah and Berhampore.—*Captain Macdonald.* (*Note*—This from Ganjam and Gumsur, seems identical with that of Captain Philipps from Purlah Kimedy, and both appear to be the Shorea robusta).

SAMADERA INDICA, GÆRTN.

Karin gota. MALEAL.	Samadara-gass. SINGH.

A large tree of Ceylon, and the south of India, and the Concans. Wood not known. Its fruit and root are used medicinally; its bark is the Niepa bark of commerce.—*Thw., Eng. Cyc., Useful Plants.*

SAM-MARM, TAM. A wood of Tinnevelly, of a red colour, used for furniture of any description.—*Colonel Frith.* (*Note*—Is this Soymeda febrifuga?)

SAMPAYA-PAULAY, TAM. A wood of Tinnevelly, of a light brown colour, specific gravity 0·792, used for building purposes.—*Colonel Frith.*

SANDORICUM, *Species.*

Thittoo. BURM.

A Tavoy wood, used for furniture.—*Dr. Wallich.* (*Note*—Is this S. Indicum?)

SANDORICUM INDICUM, *Cav.*

Trichilia nervosa, *Vahl.*

Theit-to. BURM.	False mangosteen. ENG.
Indian sandalwood. ENG.	

This elegant timber tree grows to a large size in the south of India. In British Burmah, it is scarce in the forests, but is large and plentiful near all villages both in the Rangoon and Toungboo districts, where it is cultivated by the Burmese for its fruit, which is of the size of an orange, and has a fleshy acid pulp. It grows also in Penang, the Moluccas and Philippines. The wood is white colored and adapted to every purpose of house building. The pulp of its fruit is eaten raw by the natives of Tenasserim who esteem it excellent. It makes a good jelly. Its root is bitter and used in medicine in bowel complaints.—*Eng. Cyc., Drs. Mason and McClelland, Voigt.*

SANKUANG, a Penang wood, of a pale brown colour, used only for ornamental work.—*Col. Frith.*

SANTALUM ALBUM, *Linn.; Roxb.*

Ayasru. AMBOIN.
Narti. ANNATOM ISLAND.
Niat. „
Sandal abiad. AR.
Chandana. BENG.
Sanda-ku. BURM.
Sri-ganda. CAN.
Gandaga mara. „
Tan-heong. CHIN.
Tan-muh. „
Kaya-yndhan. COCH.-CHIN.
Sandel. DUK.
Chunduna. „
Ghundasaru. „
Sandal wood. ENG.
White sandal wood. „
Yellow „ „ „
Sandale. FR.
Jarse. FIJI.
Sundul sukur. GUZ.
Sandal Sakar. „
Chandana. HIND.
Kat chandan. „
Sandal. „
Sakar? „
Sandalo. IT
Chandan. MAHR.
Jindana. MALAY.
Chandana. „
Chandana mara. MALEAL.
Bua-alu. MARQUESAS.
Nassau. NEW HEBRIDES.
Turi-turi. OPARO-ISLANDS.
Sandal safed. PERS.
Hia-hi. SANDWICH ISLANDS.
Chundana. SANS.
Mala-yaja. „
Sandan. SINGH.
Nebissi. TANNA ISLANDS.
Eimeo. TAHITI.
Ahi. „
Chandanam. TAM.
Shandanam. „
Chandanam. TEL.
Chandanapu chettu. „
Tella chandanam. „
Krishna. „ „
Rakta krishna. „ „
Aika menil. TIMOR.

There are three kinds of Sandal woods known in commerce, the white, the yellow, and the red. The latter is from the Pterocarpus santalinus, *Linn.*, also called saunders wood, or red sandars wood, but the white and the yellow are from the Santalum album, now under notice. It is a small or moderate sized tree which grows in both the Indian peninsulas, in Assam, Cochin-China, China and, as the various names will show, in many of the islands of the Eastern Archipelago. It is much sought after for its wood which in southern India, where it grows in a wavy tract from S. Canara southwards into Mysore and Coimbatore, is cut into billets of 50 to 70 lbs., and sold by weight in that state. It is burnt as a perfume, in houses and temples, both in India and China, and used in the funeral ceremonies of the hindus. The wood is chiefly remarkble for its agreeable fragrance and is employed for trunks, almirahs, &c., as a preservative against insects. It is much used in making work-boxes, walking sticks, pen-holders and other small articles of fine ornament. Ground into powder, it is a favourite cosmetic with hindus, and with Chinese and Burmese ladies, and hindus use it to form the sectarian marks on their foreheads. It is much used among the Chinese in cabinet work, and in the manufacture of fans, and other ornamental articles. A valuable oil, used as a perfume, is distilled from its wood. The Sandal wood trees in Mysore, Canara, Coimbatore, Salem, and some in North Arcot, received much attention from Dr. Cleghorn, who remarks that its spontaneous growth has increased to a considerable extent, and he thinks it certain that with the vigilant supervision of local officers and slight assistance to nature in clearing the heads of young plants, which are often matted down by strong creepers, an addition might accrue to the revenue of these provinces. From information received from the late Assistant Surgeon Drew, he was enabled to communicate to the Commissioner of Mysore the existence of a large band of smugglers in an unfrequented path near the Carcoor pass, who were captured by the Mysore horse to the number of 78, with the Sandal wood tied on their backs. This seizure effectually stopped a long continued system of robbery on the Malabar frontier. In Ossoor and Denkinakotta are Sandal wood jungles. In the system now adopted in Mysore for the preservation of young plants and the means of ensuring a regular revenue, Colkars are employed to destroy the strong creepers which tend to choke the young plants springing from seed dropped in hedge rows by birds. It is their duty also to cut, annually, all the ripe trees, 20 years old and no other, and to take care that the billets are properly prepared and sorted, and brought into the sandal godown. The Sandal tree grows to perfection in Mysore, Denkinacotta, Andyar, Collegal, and Suttimungalum and yields a large annual revenue to the State. It also thrives well in some parts of Salem, Coimbatore and North Canara. Dr. Gibson (Report p. 162) mentions that the Sandal wood appears to grow freely without any cultivation in all parts of the Bombay Deccan and may be seen in quantities in waste gardens, and even in some of their grass preserves, and trees may be seen in numbers of the hedges along the water-courses in western Khandesh. But, the northern Bombay Sandal wood has not the high qualities of that found in the more southern provinces. In the Dharwar collectorate there are about 153,000 trees, a number which much exceeds that found in the whole length and breadth of the more northern provinces. From the facility with which the tree is raised, and the great abundance of the seed which it furnishes, Dr. Gibson is of opinion that its extension should be kept in view. Sandal wood is very liable to the heart-shake which decreases its value twenty to thirty per cent. In North Canara, there are many stills for making Sandal wood oil. There is a current belief that the fragrance of the wood, depends on the local circumstances of its growth and that it is much modified by peculiarities of soil and elevation. A Chinese merchant mentioned that the Sandal wood growing on rocky mountains contains the greatest quantity of oil. That of North Canara is not of the first quality and Dr. Gibson, when at Hungul, tried the fresh Sandal wood by cutting into several of the ripe trees, and, he remarks, (Report p. 58), "I can safely say that I did find the wood very deficient in fragrance as compared to that of Mysore." Dr. Cleghorn tells us that there is a depôt for this wood in the forests near Denkinacotta, which the poojalies, for a few months of the year, work very laboriously and cheaply, felling, cleaning, shaving and cutting the trees into billets of 2½ to 3½ maunds of 25 lbs. each for one Rupee and bringing the same to the nearest store. Mr. Bennet mentions that the Sandal wood tree grows slowly and irregularly, in the Archipelago, where it generally attains a height of 8 feet without branches and 30 feet with branches and 2 feet in diameter. It is the heart of the tree, he adds, which yields the oil and one pound of the wood will yield about 2 drams. The wood increases in fragrance in age. The Sandal wood of the Sandwich group is from two other species of the same genus, S. freycinetianum and S. paniculatum. And, the name of Sandal wood is also given to the wood of the Exocarpos latifolia, which grows in the Percy Islands, Repulse Bay, Cape-Upstart, Palm Islands &c. &c., but it is useless as a substitute. In 1847 nearly 1,000 tons of the true Sandal wood, procured chiefly from New Caledonia, the New Hebrides, &c., were exported, from Sydney to China, where it is burnt with other incense in the temples. The Sandal wood trade in these islands gives employment to about six small vessels belonging to Sydney. In China, it realizes about £30 per ton.—*Dr. Gibson, Conservator's Reports* 1849 *to* 1856, *p.* 162, *and* 1857 *to* 1860, *p.* 58, *Dr. Cleghorn's Conservator's Reports, p.* 41, *McGillivray's Voyage, Vol. I. p.* 97-8, *Dr. Wight, Bennet's Wanderings in N. S. Wales.*

SANSIO, JAP., a middle sized tree of Japan, with prickles. They make use of its bark and husks instead of pepper or ginger, and they eat the pleasant tasting aromatic leaves. (v. Amœn. Ex. p. 892, where this tree is described and figured.)—*Thunberg's History of Japan, Vol. I., p.* 115.

SAPINDUS, a genus of plants of the natural order Sapindaceæ, names derived from Sapo Indicus or Indian soap, the berries of several of the species being employed as a substitute for soap. Several species furnish useful timbers, and edible fruits. Sapindus laurifolia, *Roxb.*, is a stout, very shady tree, of various parts of India: S squamosus, *R.* is a native of the Malay Archipelago and of the island of Nassau-laut. S. longifolia and S. fruticosus, *R.* and S. serratus, *R.* are trees of the Moluccas.—*Willde.*

SAPINDUS, *Species.*

Koote legree. CAN. | Khete. MAHR.

This is common, in Canara and Sunda, in the ravines below, but is not common on the high lands of Canara, wood is not used in the arts, but for building purposes, is of average quality. —*Dr. Gibson.*

SAPINDUS, *Species.*

Tsheik khyee. BURM.

This species is found on the hills, and in the forest skirting them in British Burmah where the wood is prized for house posts, ploughs, &c., Its color is grey, with a beautifully mottled grain. A cubic foot weighs 66 lbs. In a full grown tree on good soil the average length of the trunk to the first branch is 40 feet, and average girth measured at 6 feet, from the ground is 6 feet.—*Dr. Brandis, Cal. Cat. Ex.* 1862.

SAPINDUS DETERGENS, *Roxb.*

Ritha. BENG., DUK., HIND. | Urista. SANS.

This tree grows to a height of about 20 feet, in Bengal. The fruit is used for washing; character of its wood is not known.—*Voigt., p.* 94, *Roxb., Vol. II, p.* 280.

SAPINDUS EMARGINATUS, *Vahl; Roxb; W. & A.; Ill. Graham.*

The Tree.

Buro ritha. BENG. | Penela. SINGH.
Thaly marathu. CAN. | Puvandi. TAM.
Soap nut tree. ENG. | Pounanga. TAM.
Riti-ka-jhar. HIND. | Pucha cotta maram. TAM.
Arceta. MAHR. | Kunkudu. TEL.
Rarak. MALAY. | Kunkudu karra. TEL.

The Wood.

Soap nut wood. ENG. | Kankadu chettu. TEL.
Kunkudu wood. ANGLO-TEL. |

The Nut.

Ritah. DUK. | Rarak. MALAY.
Rishta. „ | Arishta. SANS.
Soap nut. ENG. | Phenila. „
Kithi-ki-binj. HIND. | Ponnang cottai. TAM.
Bindake. „ |

The Oil.

Soap nut oil. ENG. | Pungum yennai. TAM.
Rithay-ka-tel. HIND. | Kuncudu nuna. TEL.
Puvandie cottay yennai. TAM. |

This handsome tree grows in the peninsula of India, and in Bengal. In the Madras presidency, it is met with in the villages, and the fruit is sold in all bazars as a detergent, and in many cases yields a more profitable return than any other fruit tree. In the Bombay presidency, it is found planted near mahomedan buildings and is not known to occur in the forests. The wood is white, and Dr. Gibson had seen it used only for fuel, but information regarding it is wanted, for Captain Beddome describes it as a yellowish, prettily grained wood and adds that it is tolerably hard.—*Drs. Roxb. Wight, Gibson, Cleghorn, Captain Beddome.* (*Note*—It seems to be this tree which Mr. Edye notices under the name of Horingi maram, as the Tamil, "for a tree which produces the soap nut, or rather the soap apple, which the natives use as a substitute for soap." This tree is common on the Malabar coast, and grows to about eighteen inches in diameter, and twenty feet long. It is used by the carpenters for many purposes. There is another sort named Horingi tanga maram, which is the jungle or wild soap tree. The apple is very inferior in size and quality to the former, and the tree nothing more than a jungle or underwood. These soap apples are gathered and sold in the bazar at all seasons of the year, and answer the purposes of soap for washing.— *Edye, Forests of Malabar and Canara.*)

SAPINDUS RUBIGINOSUS, *Roxb. p.* 282, *W. & A., Willde.*

Sapindus fraxinifolia, *D C.*
Moulvisia rubiginosa, *G. Don.*

Hseik-kyi. Burm.
Rusty soap nut. Eng.
Rithi-ka-jhar. Hind.
Mani pungum. Tam.
Isakûrási manu. Tel.
Ishi-rashi. Tel.
Undurugu manu. Tel.

This tree grows in both the peninsulas of India, it is found, though not very plentiful, in the Pegu district, where it attains a girth of three or four feet, growing tall in proportion and straight. There, its wood is white coloured and adapted for every purpose of house building. Dr. Roxburgh says that the wood of this tree is large, straight, strong and durable, and useful for a great variety of purposes. When dry it has something the appearance of teak, but, he says, towards the centre it is chocolate coloured. Its Tamil name is derived from the quantities of silex or sand it contains, particularly near the bark, and which injures tools used in working it.—*Voigt, Hort. Cal. Cat. Mr. Rhode's MSS., Dr. McClelland, Flor. And., Roxb., Vol. II, p.* 283.

SAPINDUS UNIJUGUS, *Thw.* A large tree, in the Hewahette district of Ceylon, at an elevation of 3,000 to 4,000 feet. Wood not known.—*Thw. En. pl. Zeyl. p.* 56.

SAPINDUS ACUMINATUS, *Wallich, Royle.*

A tree of the valleys of the Himalaya, of Nepal and the Khassya mountains: wood not known.—*Voigt.*

SAPOTA, *Species.*

Lawoloo. Singh.

A tree of the western province of Ceylon, the berries of which are eaten by the natives. The wood is little durable, lasting only 10 years, but it is used in common house building purposes. A cubic foot weighs 39 lbs.—*Mr. Mendis.*

SAPOTA, *Species ?*

Palaepean. Burm.

In Tavoy, a very large tree, used in building.—*Dr. Wallich.*

SAPOTA ELENGOIDES, *A. D C. ; Prod.*

A tree of the hot, drier parts of the island of Ceylon.—*Thw. En. Pl. Zeyl. p.* 175.

SARAKONTAY, Tam. A wood of Tinnevelly, of a whitey brown colour, used in building in general.—*Col. Frith.*

SASSAFRAS WOOD.

Sassafras. Arab. Eng. Fr. Ger. Lat. Sp.
Cayavang-dec.? Coch.-Chin.
Sassafraso. It.

The true Sassafras wood is from the S. officinale, the Sassafras laurel of North America. But, at the Madras Exhibition of 1855, the Jury remarked two specimens of wood, like Sassafras, both from Mergui, very fragrant, and containing an essential oil of value in medicine. Dr. Mason, indeed, says that a species of Sassafras abounds in the Tenasserim jungles, which seems to possess all the properties of the Sassafras of America. But he had never met with the tree in fruit or flower, and the leaf, he adds, shows that it is not the *Sassafras officinarum ;* in another place, he mentions that a species of laurus with the odour of Sassafras, is, in Tenasserim, often used in house carpentry. It is probably the Camphora glandulifera, and Dr. O'Shaughnessy tells us that the Sassafras of Assam, is perhaps the bark of the Camphora glandulifera. *q. v.* It is fully equal to the American kind, and may be introduced accordingly, although its source is as yet not perfectly ascertained.—*Beng. Phar. p.* 279, *Dr. Mason Tenasserim, M. E. J. Rep.* 1855.

SASSAFRAS PARTHENOXYLON, is a lofty timber tree growing in the forests of Sumatra. The bark is rough and brown. The fruit has a strong balsamic smell, and yields an oil, considered useful in rheumatic affections. An infusion of the root is used in medicine.—*Eng. Cyc.*

SARRA or SARRAH, Tel. A wood of the Nalla mallai, of a dark grey colour and appears to be readily attacked by the worm.—*Mr. Latham.*

SATIN WOOD, has been sufficiently noticed under its botanical name, Chloroxylon Swietenia, and it will suffice here to mention that very fine Satin wood occurs at Kutapatti, in the Tengrikottah talook of Salem. It is used for the naves of gun carriage wheels and is the best suited of all the Indian woods for fuses. The price is nearly the same as that of teak and black wood. Colonel Frith mentions a Satin wood of Penang, of a straw colour and a beautiful wood for ornamental furniture, &c.: but, it is not known that the tree grows there.—*Dr. Cleghorn's Conservator's Report* 1859-60, *p.* 15, *Col. Frith.* See Chloroxylon Swietenia.

SAUVADY MARAM, TAM. A timber of Coimbatore.—*Dr. Wight.*

SCHLEICHERA TRIJUGA, *Willd.; Roxb. W. & A.; Gr.*

Melicocca trijuga, *Juss.; D C.*
Stadmannia „ *Spreng.*
Cussambium pubescens, *Buch.*
Schleichera „ *Roth.*
Melicocca? „ *D C.*

Koon. BENG.
Gyo. BURM.
Saguri mara. CAN.
Kusoomb. MAHR.
Koosoombh. „
Cong-gass. SINGH.
Puvu maram. TAM.
Pu maram. TAM.
Mayi. TEL.
Posuku. „
Rotangha. „
Kola-koosoomoo. URIA.
Ghuntiah „ „

This tree, noticed under Melicocca, grows in the warmer parts of Ceylon, up to an elevation of 2,000 feet. It grows in Coimbatore and is common in Canara and Sunda, though most so below the ghats where it reaches the size of a large tree. It is not uncommon in the Dundelee forest and in the forests of the South Konkun, and common in those of the North Konkun. It is said to be very abundant in the Godavery forests and to occur in Ganjam and Gumsoor, but, there are two Koosoomo trees in the last district, the Kola koosoomo and Ghuntiah koosoomo, the former of which abounds and is larger and more useful than the latter which is not so common, (also that either of these are the S. trijuga requires confirmation). It attains an extreme height of 50 feet with a circumference of 4½ feet. The height from the ground to the intersection of the first branch, is 9 feet. It produces a red, strong, hard and heavy wood, which, in Coimbatore, is generally rather small and used to make pestles, spokes for bandy wheels and other purposes where much strength in small space is required: but, in the Bombay forests it reaches a size so large that it is used for making screw rollers for sugar mills, cotton presses, &c. In Ganjam and Gumsur the wood thus named koosoomo is used for oil presses, sugar crushers and the axletrees of bandies and ploughs. It is always preferred for sugar and rice mills. The seeds yield an oil which is used for burning, and in Ceylon and Ganjam a considerable quantity of lac is obtained, gathered from the young branches and which in Ganjam, is in request among native jewellers. It is one of the heaviest woods known in Burmah, where it is common in the plains as well as on the hills, and is there used for cart wheels, the teeth of harrows, the pestles of oil mills, &c. &c. A cubic foot there weighs lbs. 70. The trunk of a full grown tree on good soil attains an average length to the first branch of 25 feet, and its average girth measured at 6 feet from the ground is 12 feet.—*Drs. Wight, Gibson and Brandis, Captain Macdonald, Voigt, Hort. Cal. Cat., Thwaites, p.* 58. *See* KOOSOOMB, KOOSOOMBHA, *also* Purlah Kimedy wood KUSSOOMB, MELICOCCA TRIJUGA.

SCLEROSTYLIS ATALANTIODES, *Blume.*

Limonia bilocularis, *Roxb.*
Arawi-nim. TEL.

This small tree or shrub is found in the Circars. Its wood is yellow, and is always very small, but is very hard and might be used as a substitute for box.—*Voigt, Captain Beddome.*

SCLEROSTYLIS CEYLANICA, *Wight, Ill.*

Sclerostylis Arnottiana, *Wight, Ic.*
Rissoa Ceylanica, *Arn. Pug. p.* 6, (324,) *c. p.* 1196.
Yucca-naara-gass. SINGH.

A tree of the warmer parts of Ceylon, not uncommon: wood not known.—*Thw. En. Pl. Zeyl. p.* 46.

SCLEROSTYLIS ROTUNDIFOLIA, *Thw.* A small and not common tree, growing in Ceylon, at an elevation of 4,000 feet and upwards.—*Thw. En. Pl. Zeyl. p.* 46.

SCHMIDELIA SERRATA, *DC.; W. & A.*

Ornitrophe serrata, *Roxb. Cor. Pl.*

Rakhal phul ka jhar. HIND.
Korra chettu. TEL.
Taulika. TEL.
Tantisa. TEL.
Tavatiké. „

Schmidelia is a genus of plants, one of the Sapindaceæ, which are shrubs or small trees; the only one requiring mention is the S. serrata. It is a straggling shrub, or small tree, with ternate leaves. It grows in the peninsula of India, and Bengal. Timber very small, its fruit is eaten by the natives. Its root is used in diarrhœa by the Teling physicians.—*Voigt, M. E. J.* R.

SCHREBERA SWIETENIODES, *Roxb.*

Weavers beam tree. ENG.
Mava-lingum maram. TAM.
Moga „ „
Mukodi. TEL.
Makadoo chettu. TEL.
Makkam. TEL. of the Nalla Mallai?

A large timber tree, a native of the valleys of the mountainous parts of the Rajahmundry circars, the Bala ghat mountains, the Thull ghat near Bhewndy, Jowar, and the Hala mountains west of the Indus. Its wood is of a grey colour, very close grain, heavy and durable. It is much employed by weavers for beams and for many other purposes of their looms. It is said not to be liable to warp or bend: and was recommended by Roxburgh as a substitute for box, in the scales of Mathematical Instruments.—*Roxb. Fl. Ind. Vol. I., p* 109, *Captain Beddome, Mr. Latham.*

SEAFORTHIA SAPIDA. The Norfolk Island cabbage tree is a handsome palm of Norfolk Island. The young unfolded leaves are used for making hats.—*Keppell, Vol. II., p.* 283.

SEET-SEEN, BURM. An Amherst wood, used for the construction of religious houses. It is a red, compact, very ponderous, and highly valuable wood.—*Cat. Ex.* 1851.

SEECURANEE, TEL. A Nalla mallai wood, white colored, light and straight grained, and would be useful for temporary purposes.—*Mr. Latham.* (*Note*—Is this the Is-akaras-i, *Tel.* the Sapindus rubiginosus ?)

SEGUR. This Neilgherry forest has been much exhausted and there is very little teak or black wood at present fit for felling. It should be allowed to recover, as it is the main source of supply to Ootacamund for house building purposes.—*Madras Conservator's Report, p.* 2.

SEMECARPUS. A genus of plants, of the south-east of Asia, of the sub-order Anacardieæ. They are moderate sized or large trees and many furnish woods and other useful products. Semecarpus acuminata, *Wall.; Thw.*, is a middle sized tree in the forests of the Ratnapoora, Galle and Ambagamowa districts of Ceylon at no great elevation and it grows also in Chittagong. S. cassuvium, *Roxb.*, the Cassuvium silvestre of Rumphius, is a tree of the Moluccas, where its tender leaves are eaten and the acrid juice of its stem is employed to varnish shields, canes, &c. Semecarpus coriacea, *Thw.*, is a moderate sized tree of the central province of Ceylon, at an elevation of 5,000 to 7,000 feet. Semecarpus Gardneri, *Thw.* Badoolla-gass, SINGH., is a moderate sized tree, very common in the central province of Ceylon, up to an elevation of 3,000 feet. S. humilis, *Wall.*, occurs at Prome, Semecarpus Moonii, *Thw.*, is a moderate sized tree of Ceylon, in the south of the island, at no great elevation. S. nigro-viridis, *Thw.*, is a moderate sized tree in the central province of Ceylon, at an elevation of 2,000 to 4,000 feet. S. odoratus, *Wall.*, in the Royal Garden, Ceylon. S. oblongifolia, *Thw.* Badoolla-gass, SINGH., is a moderate sized tree, common in the hot, drier parts of the island of Ceylon, up to an elevation of 3,000 feet. S. obovata, *Moon.* is a moderate sized tree of Ceylon, growing at Caltura, and near Ratnapoora. S. obscura, *Thw.*, a moderate sized tree growing at Deltotte, in the central province of Ceylon, at an elevation of 3,000 feet. S. parvifolia, *Thw.* Heen-badoolla-gass, SINGH., is a small sized tree of Ceylon, in the Hinidoon Corle, in the Galle district. S. pubescens, *Thw.*, is a small sized tree of the Ratnapoora district in Ceylon, at no great elevation. S. subpeltata, *Thw.* Maha-badoolla-gass, SINGH., is a large tree of Ceylon, 30 to 40 feet high, in the Singhe-rajah and other forests between Ratnapoora and Galle. As to the woods of most of these, information is required.—*Thw. En. Pl. Zeyl. p.* 75, *Voigt, Hort. Cal. p.* 271, *Roxb., Fl. Ind. Vol. II. p.* 85.

SEMECARPUS ANACARDIUM, *Linn.; Roxb.; W. & A.; W. Ic.*

Anacardium latifolium, *Lam.*
" officinarum, *Gært.*

Beladur. AR.	Gheru. CAN.
Bhela. BENG.	Kampira. MALEAL.
Bhela taki. "	Arushkara. SANS.
Bhola taki. "	Bhalataka. SANS.
Chai-bin. BURM.	Shayng cottay maram. TAM.
Ghera mara. CAN.	Shayrang cottay. TAM.
Bhalawan. DUK.	Bhallatiki. TEL.?
Bhela. DUK.	Bhallatamu. "
Marking nut tree. ENG.	Nalla jidi chettu. TEL.
Bellawa. GUZ.	Jidi chettu. "
Bhelawan. HIND.	Tummeda mamidi. "
Bhela. HIND.	Nellajidi. "
Beebwa. MAHR.	Jidighiuzalu. "
Biboo. MAHR.	Bhalleah. URIA.

This is a common tree in the Madras presidency, and on the skirts of the Bombay forests; but it also grows in Berar, Silhet, Assam, to Dera doon and Kyarda. It is common in the Pegu and Toungoo forests, where it grows to be a middle sized tree. The juice is, however, so acrid that wood cutters are unwilling to cut the tree until after it has been killed, by ringing the bark. Dr. McClelland says that the wood is adapted for fancy work and cabinet making, but to Dr. Wight it was reported to be of no value. The softness of the wood and its acrid juice, which renders it dangerous to work, detract from its value. The nuts are exported from the Dekhan and Mysore as a mordaunt.—*Drs. Wight, McClelland, Gibson, and Cleghorn, Voigt, Roxb., Vol. II. p.* 85.

SEMECARPUS CUNEIFOLIUS, *Roxb.*

Biboow-a. MAHR.	Bibwa. MAHR.

This tree grows in the Bombay ghats, Lanowlee Grove, Khandalla, and about Parr; also in Hindustan, Nepaul, and the Himalaya. Dr. Gibson says, the wood is not of any value, but might be turned to some account by being creosoted, of which the openness of its fibres would admit.—*Dr. Gibson, Voigt, Roxb., Vol. II. p.* 86.

SESBANIA ÆGYPTIACA, *Pers.*

Æschynomene sesban, *Linn.: Roxb.*
" Indica, *Burm.*
Coronilla sesban, *Willd.; Roxb. E. I. M.*
var. *a.* Sesbania bicolor. var. *β.* Sesbania concolor.

Jaianti. BENG.	Kedangu. MALEAL.
Buro-janti. "	Karun chembai. TAM.
Juyuntee. HIND.	Sominta. TEL.
Jet. "	

This is a small tree which grows in Ceylon, in both the Indian peninsulas, in Bengal, Assam, and Saharunpore. Voigt, quoting Dr. Gibson, says it is cultivated in the plains of the Dekhan, and extensively used as a substitute for bamboo. Its wood is said to make the best charcoal for gun-powder.—*Voigt, Roxb., Fl. Ind. Vol. III. p.* 332.

SESBANIA PALUDOSA.?

Æchynomene paludosa, *Roxb.*

Kath-sola. BENG.	Muntajiluga mokka. TEL.

An annual, but has the appearance of an elegant tree, it is a native of wet marshy places, in the south of India.—*Roxb.; Flor. Ind. Vol. III. p.* 333.

SETHIA ACUMINATA, *Arn.*

Batta-kerilla-gass. SINGH.

A Ceylon tree, in the Ambagamowa and

Saffragam districts, at an elevation of 1,000 to 2,000 feet, wood not known.—*Thw. En. Pl. Zeyl. p.* 53.

SETHIA INDICA, *D C.; W. & A.; W. Ill.*

Erythroxylon monogynum, *Roxb.*
" areolatum, *Ains. and Wight.*
" sideroxyloides, *Roxb.*

Deodaru. DUK.	Sima natti. TAM.
Sembu linja maram ? TAM.	Devadaram. "
Sembu-linga maram ? "	Adavi gerenta. TEL.

A small tree of the drier parts of Ceylon, with timber resembling sandal wood. Dr. Gibson had not seen it in the Bombay forests. Dr. Wight believes this is the *Erythroxylon areolatum* of Ainslie; when largest, it is still but a small tree, Ainslie states that the wood is so fragrant, it is used in Mysore as a substitute for sandal wood. Mr. Ondaatze informed Mr. Thwaites that an empyreumatic oil or wood-tar, used for preserving timber employed in the construction of native boats, is obtained from the wood of this tree.—*Thw. En. Pl. Zeyl. p.* 53, *Drs. Wight and Gibson, Voigt, Ains. p.* 213.

SHALIMBO-BANSO, TEL. Extreme height 40 feet, circumference $2\frac{1}{2}$ feet. Two species of bamboo which abound in the Ganjam and Gumsur forests.—*Captain Macdonald.*

SHIM, is the Tamil and Malayala name of a tree, commonly known as the Buttress tree. It grows to an enormous size. Edye saw one forty-five feet in circumference, and one hundred and ten feet long. It has a soft, spongy sort of wood of a white colour; not durable, nor of much use, unless it be oiled, when it may last for five or six years for canoes or catamarans, provided they are taken out of the water when not wanted. If it be kept in water, two years, it will render it water-logged and useless.—*Edye, Forests of Malabar and Canara.*

SHOREA, *Species.*

Nyaung-lan. BURM.

This grows in Amherst. It is of a peculiar kind, employed for beams, rafters, and boat building. The root is used as umbrella stocks.—*Cat. Ex.* 1851.

SHOREA ? *Species ?* a tree is noticed by Dr. Mason, as the largest in the Tenasserim provinces, but, he was doubtful as to its being a Shorea, and says it is principally used for making large boats. Its places of growth are usually of difficult access by water, and it is not in very general use. He quotes Mr. O'Riley as saying, " it is well adapted for spars for vessels."—*Dr. Mason.*

SHOREA, *Species.* Under the term lard or hogslard shorea, Dr. Mason describes a species as growing on the mountains in the interior of Tenasserim, which produces an oil of the consistence of lard. Wood not known, but being of the same genus as the Sal tree, he deemed it worth inquiring regarding.—*Dr. Mason.*

SHOREA CAMPHORIFERA, *Roxb.; Flor. Ind., Vol. II, p.* 616.

Dryobalanops camphora, *Royle.*

This remakable tree affords both the camphor and camphor-oil of Borneo and Sumatra. Mr. Prince, of Tappanooly, on the western coast of the latter island, writes that this tree grows spontaneously in the forests, and is to be found in abundance from the back of Ayers Bongry as far as north of Bacongan, a distance of twenty-five miles. It is one of the largest trees that grows on that coast, several being six or seven feet in diameter, though others are only two and a half.—*Roxb.; Flor. Ind. Vol. ii. p.* 616, *Royle Ill. Him. Bot. p.* 106.

SHOREA LACCIFERA, *Heyne.*

Vatica laccifera, *W. & A.*
Shorea robusta, *Roth. not Roxb.*
" talura, *Roxb.; Flor. Ind.*

Jalin ? CAN.	Talara. TAM.
Jalari ? "	

A large timber tree of Mysore and of the Bala ghat mountains, where it blossoms during the dry winds and ripens its seed in June. It yields a strong useful wood for a variety of purposes.—*Captain Puckle in Mad. Cat. Ex. of* 1862, *Useful Plants, Roxb., Flor. Ind., Vol. II, p.* 616.

SHOREA OBLONGIFOLIA, *Thw.* A large tree of Ceylon, growing at Saffragam and other districts in the south of the island, at no great elevation.—*Thw. En. Pl. Zeyl. p.* 36.

SHOREA OBTUSA, *Wall.*

Theya. BURM.

This wood grows in the Eng forest and on the brow of hills in Pegu, valued equally with Engyin or Sal. A cubic foot weighs lbs. 75. In a full grown tree on good soil the average length of the trunk to the first branch is 50 feet and average girth measured at 6 feet from the ground is 7 feet. It sells at 12 annas per cubic foot.—*Dr. Brandis, Cal. Cat. Ex.* 1862.

SHOREA ROBUSTA, *Roxb.*

Vatica robusta, *W. & A.*

Saj. AR.	Uswukunida. SANS.
Eing-gyin. BURM.	Sala. TEL.
Saul tree. ENG.	Gugalu. TEL.
Sal. HIND.	Guggalam chettu. TEL.
Sal. MAHR.	Salwa. URIA.
Sala. SANS.	Soringhi. URIA.

Its resin.

Ral. HIND.	Dhoona. HIND.
Rala. "	Guggala. TEL.

· This valuable timber tree is alluded to in ancient hindu writings. In the Hindoo Theatre (Vol. II., p. 100), Madhava speaking of the coming rainy season, says :—

" * * * * The days approach
" When the long line of clouds shall shed on earth
" Their amaranthine drops—trembling in the breeze
" That from the east comes powerful, and embued
" With the rich odours of the Sâl and Arjuna."

It grows, it is said, in the Palghat (qu.? Balaghat) mountains and to a limited extent on the west coast. In Gumsur, west of Burhampore and Russelcondah, the Sal forests are the most valuable tract of wood on the eastern coast of peninsular India. In the taluk of Gumsur and in the zemindari of Bodogoda, the Sal forests are important and accessible; for, these districts are traversed by rivers and during the short freshes timber can be rafted to the coast. But, the Sal forest of Gumsur, though valuable, is still scarcely equal in value to a second class forest of the western coast. In Gumsur, the tree grows remarkably straight and tall in the forests. In open places, however, it yields a thick trunk, throws out branches, and becomes umbrageous. Its seed has the utmost susceptibility of germination, with a vitality so limited in duration that it will not survive many days unplanted. It ripens at the commencement of the rains and after the first shower falls actually sprouting from the tree. In consequence, young plants come up in the utmost profusion forming patches of forest, which are literally impenetrable, till thinned by the woodsman. Captain Beddome found it abundant on the Indrawatti. In Nagpore, Sal is procurable from 25 to 60 feet in length, with a girth of 4½ to 3 feet. Captain Sankey says that the Sal of Nagpore, resembling Bejasar somewhat in colour, differs peculiarly from it in the construction of its grain, and in its freeness from the faults to which the other is so subject. In strength, size, and all the qualities of good timber, it appeared to him to stand first, of all those procurable in the Nagpore territories, as a tie beam or rafter wood; but, unfortunately, the price, a rupee the cubic foot, from the cost of transport, renders it little available. The Nagpore Sal, he adds, does not appear to lose its essential oil for a long time, and always exhibits small surface cracks, which widen or contract with the change of season. The increasing means of communication in Nagpore may, perhaps, diminish the cost of carriage. Further to the north, a thick forest of Sal grows or grew on Parasnath. The Sal forests of northern India, according to Dr. Falconer, extend in a nearly unbroken belt along the Terai from the Ganges at Hardwar to the Burhamputar: and it occurs, also, in the Morung hills, and in Assam; but, in many parts, at the foot of the Himalayas, the forests are said to have become much exhausted. When Dr. Royle wrote, about 26 years ago, Shorea robusta extended all along the foot of the Himalaya, to the neighbourhood of the Jumna, forming vast forests, frequently unmixed with any other tree, but generally confined in the most northern parts within the first range of the hills. The trees of this family of plants he adds, are conspicuous for their size, and beauty, and for the excellent timber which most of them afford: and, Shorea robusta furnishes the best and most extensively used timber in the north of India. In Pegu, the tree is found chiefly on the Shan side of the Tounghoo district, and in the forests north of Tounghoo, and it is abundant inland in the Amherst and Tavoy provinces. Sal timber suffers much from exposure,—splitting and warping greatly. The wood is hard, of a light brown colour and is in great repute: it is most valuable for house and ship building, as vats for liquids, door frames, and for the rails and battens of doors; it is not suited for planks, it twists, shrinks, and warps whenever the surface is removed, even after many years' seasoning. This wood is in general use for building purposes in the Ganjam and Vizagapatam districts. The Jury's Reports for the Exhibition of 1851, observed from Colonel Baker's excellent experiments, that it appears, compared with teak, its strength is about 1121 to 869. From Major H. Campbell's valuable experiments, unseasoned Sal broke with a weight of 1,308 lbs., seasoned Sal with 1,319 lbs., and teak wood with 1,091 lbs., and added that it is unquestionably the most useful known Indian timber for engineering purposes. It is useful for wedges, is possessed of considerable elasticity and resists the action of white ants. This wood should have a second seasoning after it is manufactured into half-wroughts, as there is a material shrinking immediately after the piece has been cut out of the wood and shaped. In the Madras gun carriage manufactory, it is used for beams of gun and howitzer carriages; light field axle cases of all kinds; all parts of carts; transport carriage cheeks; handspikes of all sorts; perches of waggons; poles short; perches; braces, framing and splinter bars of limbers, gun and waggon; and framing of all carts. The character of this wood, as it occurs in the Tenasserim provinces, is described by Captain Dance as thoroughly good and valuable and, as one of the most durable in those forests, tough, elastic, large, and extremely heavy. It is used for bows and for all kinds of purposes, by the Burmese, &c.; and, he recommends it for rammer heads; for handles of hammers, chisels, and other tools, also for sheave blocks, cogs, and machinery in which great strength is required. Also for government buildings, wharves, &c, especially for railway sleepers, from its abundance and large girth. He says it is too heavy for helves. It is said to harden by exposure to water and even to strike fire with steel, after having been kept in water for a length of time. The Tenasserim sal, he adds, appears a closer grained, better, and probably a heavier wood than the sal of India. He says its maximum girth, in Amherst, Tavoy and Mergui, is certainly 3 and said to be 5 cubits: maximum length, certainly 20, said to be 30 feet, and when seasoned it sinks in water. Major Benson writing of it, in Moulmein, says, it is a wood of dense structure, elastic and well adapted for the manufacture of gun carriages, being stronger and less brittle than padouk. Dr. Royle quotes Mr. Colebrooke's remarks, regarding Shorea robusta and S. tumbugaia, that they and perhaps other species of the genus, yield in great abundance the resin, called by the Hindoostanees dhoona, and by the English in India, dammer, which is very generally used as a substitute for pitch for marine purposes. The natives of India also employ it in their temples, as an incense.—*Roxb. Fl. Ind., Voigt, Dr. Mason's Tenasserim, Dr. Cleghorn's Conservators Reports, Ains. Mat. Med., p.* 210, *Dr. Hooker's Him. Jour., p.* 21, *Captain Beddome. Colonel Maitland in Mad. Cat. Ex.* 1862, *Dr. McClelland No. IX Indian Records, Royle Ill. Him. Bot., Major Benson, Captain Sankey, Captain Dance : Jur. Rep. Ex.* 1851, *Wilson's Hindoo Theatre.*

SHOREA STIPULARIS, *Thw.* A great tree of Ceylon, between Ratnapoora and Galle, at no great elevation, character of wood not known.—*Thw. Enum. Pl. Zeyl. I., p.* 36.

SHOREA TUMBUGAIA, *Roxb.*

Vatica tumbugaia, *W. & A.*

Thumbugum. Tam. | Tumbugai. Tam.

A large timber tree, a native of the Bala ghat? mountains, which blossoms in the beginning of the hot season and ripens its seed in June. In the Balpalli jungles, in the Cuddapah district, the tree abounds, particularly on the ridges of the hills from Balpalli to Yerra gunta Cottah, in short over all the ridges of the hills in the Cuddapah district, growing to a height from 30 to 35 feet, and from 6 to 7 feet in circumference. It is there chiefly used for house building purposes, being much prized by the natives of the district, on account of its durability. Its wood is used for fuses. It yields a large quantity of the resin called "dammar," which is employed in marine yards as a substitute for pitch, but used also as benzoin in temples for incense.—*Roxb. Fl. In., Voigt, Dr. Appavoo, Assistant Conservator of Forests, in charge,—in letter No.* 1236*A. of 6th Nov.* 1862.

SIBIA, *Species.* Thit-phew, Burm. This tree is very plentiful in Prome, Pegu, and Tounghoo, as well as about Donabew. It yields a compact and close-grained wood, seven or eight feet in girth, and is a timber that deserves to be attended to with a view of bringing it into use, being adapted for fancy work and cabinet making.—*Dr. McClelland.*

SIBIA GLOMERATA.

Thayat-pew tha or White Thayat. Burm.

A tree of Amherst, Tavoy and Mergui. This seems to be the same as the last, Captain Dance says its maximum girth is 5 cubits, and maximum length 30 feet, and that it is found abundant on the sea coast from Amherst to Tavoy, and Mergui. When seasoned, it floats in water. He remarks, the term, Thayat-pew, should bec ancelled as Thayat Pew, meaning white wood, is a name equally applicable to "Calophyllum longifolium," "Dillenia speciosa," to a species of Dalbergia and to other woods. The wood is called "Yemam-nee" is often styled by this name.—*Captain Dance.*

SIDDHA, Tel.? Uria. A tree of Ganjam and Gumsur of an extreme height 45 feet, and circumference of 4 feet, the height from ground to the intersection of the first branch, 22 feet. This wood is said to be not liable to be attacked by insects. It is used chiefly for making rafters of and being rather plentiful, is burnt for firewood. The bark and leaves are employed in tanning leather and are also used medicinally.—*Captain Macdonald.*

SIKHAMHAT, Hind.? A tree of Chota Nagpore, has a hard, yellow timber.—*Cal. Cat. Ex.* 1862.

SIMAN, Hind.? A tree of Chota Nagpore, with hard, grey timber.—*Cal. Cat. Ex.* 1862.

SIMJANG, Hind. A tree of Chota Nagpore. Soft, yellow wood.—*Cal. Cat. Ex.* 1862.

SIND. Of the forests scattered throughout Sind, particularly those in Lower Sind, the greater number are planted—not natural forest. In passing over the hills from Sonda en route to Jerruck, the noble river is seen at the distance winding its way through gigantic woods. The forests, under the rule of the Ameers, were mere hunting preserves, and were admirably adapted, from the thickness of their underwood, for the cover of wild animals of every sort. No attention whatever was paid to their timber. The forests in number amount to about 72, including the Sind forest jungles in Upper Sind (not walled in like those in Lower Sind) of bhan or poplar, which spring up spontaneously on the river bank when the inundation subsides. The forests cover an area of about 1,59,688 acres, under cultivation about 34,555, waste land 55,385, and wood area 69,753. The products of the forests are timber, firewood, charcoal, gum lac, bark, babul seeds, grass and reeds for mats. The common woods found are babul, bhan, kunda, tali (Sissoo of Upper India), tree tamarisk, jamul, sirme? sirree? and mountain or bitter neem. These have been turned to economic purposes since British occupation of the country. The grazing alone is much appreciated by the natives, and brings in a revenue of between eight to nine thousand rupees per annum. The supply of fuel to the Indus Flotilla was about 90,000 maunds per annum, and, with the other products, giving a gross revenue of not less than 1,20,000 rupees. It is said the forests are yearly diminishing in size from their being washed away by the encroachments of the river and from the canals, which run through them, not being cut, as they used to be during the time of the Ameers, to admit water for watering the trees. The Sirree is the Madras blackwood, and the Tale or blackwood of Upper India, and it and the guz or tree tamarisk, are found in many of the forests, but in small numbers. Dr. Gibson (Reports 1857—60 page 20) mentions the successful efforts made by Captain Hamilton to restore the much destroyed forests of Upper Sind, and that officer's opinion concurred in by the Commissioner, of the importance of appropriating for forest all the new land thrown up by the river. In the report for 1859-60, submitted to Government on the 23rd of April 1860, by Mr. Dalzell, Forest Ranger in Sind, it is shown that the revenue from the Sind forests in 1859-60 was Rs. 98,884-2-0, against Rs. 72,150-5-0 the previous year. The net surplus was Rs. 43,884-2-0 being nearly double that of 1858-59. The chief item in the receipts was that for firewood, which amounted to Rs. 44,000, the next was "grazing fees," which yielded Rs. 30,700. The price of firewood was raised, owing to the increased price of labour, by 20 per cent., except when intended for steam navigation. The price of rafters in the forests near a market was raised 25 per cent. Mr. Dalzell thinks that while the appropriation of forest land for purposes of cultivation would not benefit the revenue, as regards climate, the interests of agriculture, the progress of commerce, and the general prosperity of the province, doing so would gradually lead to the most serious consequences. And, in these views the Government concur, for Sind is a thinly inhabited country and no good plea for regarding the existence of forests as injurious can possibly exist. The indiscreet destruction of the forests of any country is apt to bring upon future generations three calamities, the want of fuel, the want of water and the want of timber—three things peculiarly necessary to Sind. Every steamer on the Indus, while under steam, consumes one ton of fuel per hour. It would be too hardy an assertion to say that the existence of forests in Sind causes any increase in the fall of rain, as they certainly do on the summits and slopes of mountains, yet in Sind not only is the rain that falls economised and prevented from rapid evaporation, but the water of inundation also, which sinks deep into the ground, is being continually pumped up from great depths by the roots of the trees, and exhaled by the leaves, thus actually moistening the neighbouring atmosphere in the driest weather, and benefiting the crops of the neighbouring fields, without the ignorant zemindar, who considers forests a nuisance being aware of the blessing. In passing through a tamarisk jungle early in the morning, even in the driest weather, the whole of the foliage is found dripping—not from dew, but from the water of exhalation brought up from great depths by the vital processes of vegetation; the whole of this passes into watery vapour in a few hours. If the forest were cleared away, the neighbouring fields would be exposed to the violence of parching winds, and liable to be covered with drifting sand, while the cattle of the cultivator would find no grazing and no shelter from the scorching heat. It has been found, that forests and plantations in England yield in the long run a much higher rental than if the ground on which they stand had been given up for cultivation. Land under wood in Great Britain will, at the end of sixty years, under good management, pay the proprietor nearly three times the sum that he would have received from any other crop upon the same land. Even in Sind those forests which are tolerably near to a market will bear comparison in point of profit with some of the most favoured Zillahs of the province. To take a fair example; a certain district in the valley of the Indus contains 2,24,586 beegas, of which 1,65,008 are culturable and 42,601 or one-fifth, actually cultivated in 1858-59. The revenue of this district was in that year Rs. 32,240, or deducting charges Rs. 29,000 which is equal to two annas per beega. The forest of Oomerpoor contains 18,000 beegas, yielding after deduction of all expences of establishment, &c., a nett profit of Rs. 4,500, or four annas per beega. The forest of Meeanee yields the same. In their resolution on the report, Government say that they fully recognise the importance and advantages arising from the conservation of the forests of this country.—*Scindian, July* 12, 1856, *Annual Indian Administration, March* 1861.

SINGAPORE WOODS. These from Singapore and the Malay peninsula, at the 1851 Exhibition, consisted of about one hundred specimens, many having no labels; those named were as follows :—

1 Angsanah.	Arangi Klat.	Medansi Konit.
Biliong.	Kayu Brombong.	Polai wood.
Biliong Wangi.	Kledang.	Peragah.
Bras Bras.	Lakah wood.	Ranggas.
Bitangor wood.	Leban.	Simpoh Ryah.
Changis.	Meosbon.	Simpoh brekit.
Glam.	Medansi Miniak.	Slumar.
Jambu-ayer-utan.	20 Medansi Buah yeah.	30 Tan Pang.
Kayau Arang.	Medansi Tandoh.	Tampenis.
10 Kamuning.	Medansi Kitanahan.	Timbusu.
Krautai.		
Arangi.		

SI-PAIT, MALAY. Meaning the "bitter wood," is the root of a tree of Sarawak. In substance, appearance and lightness, it precisely resembles the Plye; but, while Plye is tasteless, Si-pait is very bitter to the taste.—*Low's Sarawak.* (*Note*—Pait, in Malay, means bitter).

SIPHONANTHUS INDICA—?

Putri. HIND.?

A tree of Chota Nagpore, with a soft, white wood.—*Cal. Cat. Ex.* 1862.

SISAGI, HIND. A tree of Chota Nagpore, with hard, white timber.—*Cal. Cat. Ex.* 1862.

SITPHAN, BURM., ALSO SETPHAN, BURM. A tree of Moulmein. Its wood is used in common purposes of building.—*Cal Cat. Ex.* 1862.

SOHOJO MAREE, TEL? URIA? A tree of Ganjam and Gumsur of extreme height 25 feet, circumference 1½ feet, and height from the ground to the intersection of the first branch, 8 feet. Tolerably common in Bodogoda, where it is burnt for firewood but not in Gumsur. The bark is used medicinally.—*Captain Macdonald.*

SOMENDILLA, the Tamil and Malabar name of a tree yielding the best and most useful wood in Ceylon for naval purposes. It is commonly called Halmilile and Hameniel, by the Dutch and Portuguese. It grows straight, from twenty to forty feet high, and from twelve to thirty inches in diameter. This tree, with the satin wood is the most plentiful and valuable found in Ceylon; and can be obtained at a moderate rate to answer the demands of the navy in India: it may be considered superior to any wood for capstain bars, cross and trussel-trees, cask staves, battens for yards, fishes for masts, boat building, &c. At Madras, it is highly valued for coach work from the toughness and fineness of its grain.—*Edye, on the Timber of Ceylon.* (*Note*—Mr. Mendis says Hal-milile is the Berrya ammonilla, the Trincomallee wood of commerce).

SONNERATIA ACIDA, *Willde, Linn.*

Rhizophora caseolaris, *Linn.*
Mangium caseolare, *Rumph.*

Orchaka. BENG. | Blatti. MALEAL. of Rheede.
Sour sonneratia. ENG. | Gedde killala-gass. SINGH.

This tree yields a light soft wood. It grows in Ceylon, on the coast at Caltura and Negombo and, other places; grows also on the western and eastern coasts of peninsular India, at Salsette and, in the delta of the Indus, the supply is said to be inexhaustable. It grows in the northern Circars and, also, in the deltas of the Ganges and of the Irawady. Indeed, in British Burmah, it abounds in the mangrove swamps and on the banks of almost every stream on the coast as far as tide-waters reach, the natives use it for various economical purposes, and it is said to be "a better substitute for coal in steamers than any other kind of wood." It grows, in Malacca, Penang, and Singapore.—*Wight and Arn., Vol. I., p.* 327, *Roxb. Fl. Ind., Voigt, Dr. Mason, Mr. Thwaites.* (*Note*—Is it the Polai of Penang and Singapore, and the Plye of Borneo?)

SONNERATIA ACIDA.?

La moo. BURM.

A tree of Moulmein. An inferior wood for boats, which lasts but two or three years. The fruit is an article of food.—*Cal. Cat. Ex.* 1862. (*Note*—What is this tree?)

SONNERATIA APETALA, *Buch.*

Khoura. BENG. | Kumbala. BURM.
Keora. " |

A pretty large and elegant tree, which grows in the Bombay side of India, in the delta of the Ganges, and is found under the parallel of Rangoon. It flowers in the hot season. It yields a strong hard wood of coarse grain. It is the timber of which boxes for packing beer and wine are made in Calcutta, is of a red colour, strong and adapted for house building.—*Roxb., Voigt, Dr. McClelland, W. & A., Vol. I. p.* 327.

SONNERATIA? *Species?*

Thaumma. BURM.

A small tree of Tavoy, wood not known.—*Dr. Wallich.*

SOOGOONDHI, URIA? A tree of Ganjam and Gumsur; of extreme height 25 feet, circumference 2 feet, and height from the ground to the intersection of the first branch, 7 feet. This tree is tolerably common, but no use is made of the wood except for firewood, the leaves are used medicinally for rheumatism and wounds of long standing.—*Captain Macdonald.* (*Note*—This has been supposed to be a species of Calophyllum, and requires to be identified.)

SOORYA, SINGH. A timber tree of the central and western provinces of Ceylon, wood admirable for carriages, hackeries, and gun-stocks, also useful for blocks and buildings. A cubic foot weighs 49 lbs., and it is calculated to last 20 to 40 years.—*Mr. Mendis.*

SOORIYA MARA, SINGH. Under this name, Mr. Mendis describes, as a species of Mimosa, a plant of the central province of Ceylon, the wood of which is used for buildings and common furniture. A cubic foot of it weighs 42 lbs. and it is calculated to last 20 to 30 years.—*Mr. Mendis.*

SOROOPOTTREE MOEE, URIA,? TEL.? A tree of Ganjam and Gumsur, extreme height 40 feet, circumference 2½ feet, height from the ground to the intersection of the first branch, 18 feet. Used for planks, doors, boxes, posts, and ploughshares. It is tolerably common.—*Captain Macdonald.*

SOONDA. A district in the south of the Bombay presidency, bordering on north Canara. It contains large forests, which, up to 1855, were under the charge of the Bombay Conservator, but were then transferred to Madras. Dr. Gibson's Reports (1849 to 56, page 60, and 1857 to 1860, page 17) indicate that the timber has greatly decreased in amount. In the transfer of Canara to Bombay, this district has been retransferred along with it.

SOONDOROGOYAN BANSO, TEL.? URIA.? In Ganjam and Gumsur, circumference 3¼ feet, extreme height 30 feet, two species of bamboo which are not common.—*Captain Macdonald.*

SOWAY DO, BURM. A tree of maximum girth $1\frac{1}{2}$ cubits and maximum length 10 or 12 feet, very abundant on the sea coast and on the banks of rivers in the Tenasserim provinces. When seasoned it floats in water. The wood is much recommended for gun-stocks with but one fault; that it is crooked and therefore not more than ten or twelve feet can be procured between the bends. This wood is commonly sold to Burmese at half a rupee for a piece large enough to make one gun-stock.—*Captain Dance.*

SOW-YEW, BURM. The Egg tree of the KARENESE, and Chisel handle tree of the English in Burmah. This is stated by Dr. Mason to be of the genus Dalbergia, *species* unknown. Its maximum girth $2\frac{1}{4}$ cubits and maximum length 10 feet. Found scattered all over the Amherst, Tavoy and Mergui forests inland; always found in undulating ground only, not near water. When seasoned it floats in water. It is used by Burmese in preference to any other for handles of chisels and tools, also for helves of axes, and hatchets. It is a very hard, fine grained wood, which is strongly recommended for helves and handles of all kinds of tools, and is unequalled for those tools, such as chisels, which are struck with a hammer or mallet. This wood is of a yellowish white in colour with patches of black interspersed, looking as if iron had in some manner been drawn from the soil, and incorporated in the wood. Though widely scattered, it is in such demand as always to be procurable in the markets.—*Captain Dance.*

SOYMIDA FEBRIFUGA, *Ad. de, Juss.*

Swietenia febrifuga, *Roxb. Cor. Pl. W. & A.*
„ rubra, *Rottler.*

Rohuna. BENG.	Rohuni. MAHR.
Rohan. „	Wonga maram. TAM.
Red wood tree. ENG.	Shem maram. „
Bastard cedar. „	Choar Kullie maram. TAM.
Rohuna. HIND.	Wond maram. TAM.
Rohitaka. „	Sumi. TEL.
Rheya. MAHR.	Somida manu. TEL.

This large forest tree, is a native of several of the mountainous districts of India, in the Coimbatore and Cuddapah districts, of the Godavery forests and the Rajahmundry circars; also, in the northern Bombay forests, where it is more common in those inland, as on the Satpura range, than in the forests of the coast. It is in considerable abundance, however, in various parts of Guzerat, also at the Sindhwah ghat and in the Adjunta and Jowar jungles. It is very abundant in Nagpore, and grows in the Chunar hills and in the jungles south of Hazareebagh, indeed in all the central and southern parts of India. The wood is light and easily worked, and is reckoned durable and strong, and good for indoor or cabinet purposes, but not adapted to those requiring exposure to sun and weather. Captain Beddome, however, says it never rots under ground. In the Cuddapah district it is much used in buildings. Writing of it in Nagpore, Captain Sankey quotes a writer in the Bengal Gazette, as remarking that the Rohun is a mahogany furnishing a febrifugal bark, and believed to be one of the most durable and heavy woods known, and of a "blood-red colour." The specimens which Captain Sankey obtained, he says, might be called somewhat darker in colour than here described, and in Nagpore the logs are obtainable from 17 to 20 feet long and 4 to $3\frac{1}{2}$ feet in girth, at 5 annas the cubic foot. In weight, the wood is much greater than water, but by all native accounts it is, there far from a durable wood, on exposure splitting greatly, and when seasoned becoming extremely brittle. It nevertheless he adds, has a fine straight grain, and is not so difficult to work as its great weight and compactness would lead one to imagine. But, notwithstanding this and the fact that it rivals the finest English oak in strength, he hesitates to recommend it has a building material. The bark is a useful tonic in intermittent fevers. —*Drs. Wight, Gibson, O'Shaughnessy and Cleghorn, Voigt, Roxb. Fl. Ind., Vol. II., p.* 398, *W. & A., Vol. I., p.* 122, *Captain Sankey.*

SPATHODEA, *Species?*

Thit-linda. BURM.

A white wood of British Burmah, not much used. A cubic foot weighs lb. 63. In a full grown tree on good soil, the average length of the trunk to the first branch is 50 feet, and average girth, measured at 6 feet from the ground, is 6 feet. It sells at 8 annas per cubic foot.—*Dr. Brandis.* (*Note*—Is this any of the species now of the genus Bignonia? q. v.)

SPATHODEA ADENOPHYLLA. Palol, SINGH. A small tree, occasionally found in Ceylon gardens. It was introduced into the agri-horticultural gardens at Madras.—*Thwaites, Cat. Madras Gardens.*

SPATHODEA ARCUATA, *Wight, Icon.* 1340.

Mer-singi. MAHR.	Ran-palai maram. TAM.

A small or middle sized tree, common in the Walliar forests of Coimbatore and in the forests on the Bombay coast. It furnishes a strong wood, used by the turner.—*Drs. Wight and Gibson.*

SPATHODEA CHELONOIDES, *D C. Prod. W. Ic.*

Loonoo-madala-gass. SINGH.

This tree is very abundant in Ceylon, near the sea, but occurring up to an elevation of 2,000 feet.—*Thwaites.* (*Note*—This has been noticed under its synonym Bignonia chelonoides, which see.)

SPATHODEA LONGIFLORA.

Daanga. SINGH.

This arboreous plant has large yellow and very

fragrant flowers. According to Mr. Mendis, it grows in the northern and western divisions of Ceylon, where its wood is used for buoys for fishing nets, but this point seems to require confirmation. It is said, in the English Cyclopædia, to be plentiful on the hills of the Malabar and Coromandel coasts, and its wood is described as high coloured hard and durable, and of much use among the inhabitants of the hills.—*Mr. Mendis, Eng. Cyc.* (*Note*—What is this plant: it is not mentioned in Roxburgh's Fl. Ind., Wight and Arnott or Voigt?)

SPATHODEA RHEEDII, *Spreng.*

Spathodea longifolia, *Kent.*
Bignonia spathacea, *Roxb.; Fl. Ind.*
„ falcata, *Kœn's MSS.*

Tha-khoot-ma. BURM.	Vodi. TEL.
Nir pongilam. MALEAL.	Udi. „
Deya danga-gass. SINGH.	Wodi. „

This small thin tree, a native of the west of Ceylon, in the hotter parts of island and in the forests of the coast, is met with in the peninsula of India, in the forests of the Northern Circars and of the Godavery and in British Burmah. The trunk is very irregular. In a full grown tree on good soil, the average length of the trunk to the first branch is 30 feet, and, at 7 feet from the ground, the average girth is 7 feet. A cubic foot of the wood weighs lbs. 35. It is strong, of a whitish colour, and in Burmah, where it sells at 8 annas the cubic foot, it is used for yokes and cart poles. —*Thwaites, Roxb. Fl. Ind., Eng. Cyc., Dr. Brandis, Captain Beddome.*

SPATHODEA ROXBURGHII, *Spreng.*

Bignonia quadrilocularis, *Roxb.: Cor. Pl. II. & Fl. Ind.* 3 *p.* 107.

Baro kala goru. HIND.? TEL.?

A large tree, with a straight trunk and of considerable height. It is a native of the Northern Circars, flowers in the hot season with spreading branches and large rose coloured and delightfully fragrant flowers, and is remarkable for its leaves. Roxburgh says its wood is used for many purposes by the natives, but other accounts describe it as worthless. Buffaloes are very fond of the leaves.—*Roxb., Fl. Ind. iii. p.* 107, *Voigt, Captain Beddome, Eng. Cyc.* (*Note*—This has been noticed under its synonym, Bignonia quadrilocularis, which see).

SPATHODEA STIPULATA, *Wall.*

Bignonia stipulata, *Roxb.; Fl. Ind. iii. p.* 108.

Paet-than. BURM.

A large tree of British Burmah, wood used for bows and spear handles, also for paddles and oars. A cubic foot weighs lbs. 48. In a full grown tree on good soil the average length of the trunk to the first branch is 20 feet and average girth measured at 6 feet from the ground is 4 feet.—*Roxb., Fl. Ind. iii. p.* 108, *Dr. Brandis.* (*Note*—This has been noticed under its synonym, Bignonia stipulata, which see).

SPATHODEA SUAVEOLENS, *D C.* (*c. p.* 1960.) This has been noticed under its synonym, Bignonia suaveolens. In the south of Ceylon it is sometimes to be found in the neighbourhood of Buddhist temples, but Mr. Thwaites could not hear of its occurring truly wild. Its roots are much valued by the natives as a tonic medicine, and they attribute the same properties and give the same name ("Palol") to those of Spathodea adenophylla, which is occasionally found in gardens.—*Thwaites. See* BIGNONIA SUAVEOLENS.

SPONIA? *Species?*

Tella kaka mushtee. TEL. of Circars.

Captain Beddome says that this appears to be Celtis Wightii of Wight's Icones, and is one of the hardest woods he had ever met with—light colored and well worthy of attention.—*Captain Beddome.*

SPONIA ORIENTALIS, *Voigt.*

Papyrus sphærica, *Kœmpf.*
Celtis orientalis, *Roxb. Fl. Ind. Vol. II., p.* 65.

Chicon? BENG.	Morali chettu. TEL.
Jeebun. „	Budu muru. „

A small erect tree of Ceylon, the Coromandel coast, common along the foot of the ghats, and occurs in the Kennery forests, Salsette, in Nepal, Bengal, Sylhet, and Assam. Roxburgh says it is neither useful nor ornamental. Voigt mentions that the under bark consists of numerous reticulated fibres, and forms a natural cloth used by the Garrows, and that its leaves are used for polishing horn.—*Roxb. Fl. Ind. ii. p.* 65, *Voigt, p.* 294, *Flor. Andh.*

SPONDIAS ACUMINATA, *Roxb.*

Ambut. DUK.

A most elegant middle sized tree, with shining leaves. It grows on the western side of India, being sufficiently common in all the Bombay forests, both coast and inland. The wood, in its natural state, is not of any value, but could be creosoted with advantage.—*Roxb., Fl. Ind. ii. p.* 453, *Dr. Gibson.*

SPONDIAS MANGIFERA, *Pers.; Roxb.; W. & A. Vol. I. p.* 173.

Spondias amara, *Lam.*
„ amra, *Ham.*
„ paniculata, *Roxb. in E. I. C. M.*
Mangifera pinnata, *Kœn.*
Poupartia mangifera, *Blume.*
Condondong of *Rumph.*

Amra. BENG.	Kat maaam maram. TAM.
Ambalam „	Mirri-mangi maram. „
Jaugli am. DUK.	Kát mavu. TAM.
Wild mango tree. ENG.	Ambara. TEL.
Hog plum tree. „	Amra. „
Amra. HIND.	Ambála chettu. „
Ambalam. „	Jvuru mamidi. „
Amb. MAHR.	Pita vrikshamu. „
Ambalam. MALEAL. of Rheede	Amatum. „
Kat ambalam. MALEAL.	Adavi mamidi. „
Amrataca. SANS.	Ambud'ha? URIA.?
Canana amra. „	

This is a large tree in the Coromandel mountains, but as a cultivated plant, it is small. It flowers in the hot season. It grows in various parts of India in some, as in Ganjam and Gumsur, is sufficiently common. It there has a straight trunk and attains an extreme height of 30 feet, with a circumference of 2½ feet, and its height from the ground to the intersection of the first branch, is 7 feet. The wood is soft and of little or no use, except for firewood. From wounds made into the bark, in the beginning of the hot season, very large quantities of a transparent juice issue, which soon hardens into a mild insipid gum, like gum-arabic. Ainslie tells us that the fruit got its name from its resemblance to a mango, but it is harsh and little deserving of notice: and, that Rheede informs us, on the Malabar coast, the root is considered as emmenagogue; the bark is supposed to be of use in dysenteric affections and a decoction of the wood serviceable in gonorrhœa.—*Ainslie, p.* 222, *Roxb., Vol. ii. p.* 451, *Wight and Arnott, Vol. i. p.* 173, *Voigt, p.* 148, *Captain Macdonald.*

STEMONOPORUS, *Thwaites.* A genus of Ceylon plants, small or large trees, but the character of their woods is not known. The S. affinis, *Thw.*, is a large tree, growing in the Hunasgiria district, at an elevation of 4,000 feet. S. canaliculatus, *Thw.*, a moderate sized tree, of the Hinidoon and Reigam corles, at no great elevation. S. Gardneri, *Thw.*, a great tree, near Adam's peak, at an elevation of about 5,000 feet. S. lanceolatus, *Thw.*, is a small tree near Ratnapoora, at no great elevation. S. Moonii, *Thw.*, near Maturatte. S. nitidus, *Thw.*, at Pasdoon corle, a middle sized tree, at no great elevation. He also mentions, S. oblongifolius, S. petiolaris, S. reticulatus, S. rigidus, and S. Wightii, a great tree, the Vateria Ceylanica of Wight, and S. apicalis, a great tree of the damp forests, at an elevation of 1,000 to 2,000 feet, the "Ooroo-kannoo gass" of the Singhalese.—*Thw. p.* 43.

STERCULIA. A genus of plants, many of them large trees, of which several species are found in India. Sterculia urens, is a native of the mountains on the coast of Coromandel, as well as of Hindoostan, and yields a gum exceedingly like tragacanth, which has been imported as such into England. S. guttata yields a bark that the Malabars convert into a flaxy substance of which the natives of Wynaad make a sort of clothing. As the seeds of Sterculia chicka are eaten by the Brazilians, so, in India, are those of S. balanghas, S. urens and S. fœtida, after being roasted.—*Roxb. Fl. Ind.* 3, *p.* 149, *Royle, Ill. Him. Bot. p.* 102.

STERCULIA, *Species.*

Ku-nu-nu, BURM.

An enormous tree of Tavoy.—*Dr. Wallich.*

STERCULIA, *Species.*

Thi-ka-doo. BURM.

A Tavoy tree.—*Dr. Wallich.*

STERCULIA, *Species.*

Kodalo. TEL.

A tree of Ganjam and Gumsur, extreme height 39 feet, circumference 3 feet and height from ground to the intersection of the first branch, 8 feet. Gives a light wood, used for planks, doors, boxes and scabbards; it is also used for firewood, being tolerably plentiful.—*Dr. Cleghorn, Captain Macdonald.* (*Note*—It is not S. fœtida.)

STERCULIA, *Species.* A nar or bast from a species common on the higher elevations in Wynaad, is as durable as ordinary, but inferior to the best, Russian bast.—*Mr. McIvor, M. E. J. R.*

STERCULIA ALATA, *Roxb., Vol. III, p.* 152.

Buddhs cocoanut. English in Burmah. | Dodelee mara. CAN.

Grows to an immense height in Canara and Sunda, in deep ravines and sheltered places below the ghats but is used there only as a support for pepper vines. The wood is said to be too spongy for spars, for which its height and straightness otherwise well fit it. It is described, by Dr. Mason, as a handsome tree of the Tenasserim provinces, bearing a large fruit whose winged seeds are sometimes eaten by the natives.—*Drs. Gibson and Mason, Roxb., Vol. III, p.* 152.

STERCULIA AUGUSTIFOLIA, *Roxb.*

Southwellia angustifolia.

A middle sized tree, a native of Nepal.—*Roxb., Vol. III, p.* 168.

STERCULIA BALANGHAS, *Linn.*

A tall and straight tree, of the hotter parts of Ceylon: common in the forests of the Bombay coast, where it may readily be distinguished, at certain seasons, by its large pink fruit. The wood is of open grain, so that it probably could, by being creosoted, be made useful in various ways. The seeds are described by Rumphius, as being roasted and eaten by the natives of Amboyna and the capsules burned for the preparation of the colouring matter called by the natives kussumbha.—*Dr. Gibson, Thwaites, Eng. Cyc., W. & A., Vol. I, p.* 62.

STERCULIA COLORATA, *Roxb.*

Bhai. ? DUK. | Karaka. DUK ? TEL.

A large tree of the Dekhan and in the Godavery forests, which is deciduous in the cold season, and flowers in March and April. Grows at Courtallum, the wood is said to be useless.—*Dr. Riddell, Captain Macdonald, Captain Beddome, W. & A., Vol. I, p.* 63.

STERCULIA FŒTIDA, *Linn.; Roxb.; W. & A.; Ic.*

Jangli badam. BENG.	Telembhoo. SINGH.
Let khop. BURM.	Kudrapdukhu. TAM.
Fetid sterculia. ENG.	Pinnari maram. „
Horse almond tree. „	Pinata maram. „
Bastard poon. „	Pinary maram. „
Klompan boerong. MALAY.	Gurrapu badam chettu. TEL.
Karill. MALEAL.	

The oil.

Gudira pusjun yennai. TAM.

This large tree is very common in the central province of Ceylon, where a cubic foot weighs 26 lbs. and grows in the peninsula of India, generally, but chiefly on the western coast in Malabar and Mysore. On the Bombay side of India, it is not common in the forests, but more frequently found about cultivated holdings on the coast, where it grows up small and very straight. It is common on the hills and plains of British Burmah, where a cubic foot weighs lbs. 33. In a full grown tree, on good soil, the average length of the trunk to the first branch is 50 feet, and average girth, measured at 6 feet from the ground is 10 feet. Dr. Brandis tells us that the wood is not used there. But, in Ceylon, it is used for common house-building purposes, on the western coast and in Mysore, it is applied to a number of useful purposes, and is one of the trees believed to furnish the smaller poon spars of that coast: indeed, Dr. Gibson tells us that it is used as a substitute for the true poon spars in small country vessels. The seeds are eaten by the Singhalese.—*Ainslie, Mr. Mendis, Dr. Brandis, Dr. Gibson, M. E. J. R., Dr. Riddell, Wight and Arnott, Vol. I, p.* 63, *Thwaites, p.* 29.

STERCULIA FOLIIS DIGITATIS, *Ains.*

Hill cocoanut. ENG.	Conda than-kaia. TEL.
Malai taynga. TAM.	

The edible seeds of this tree are eaten by the poor. They are contained in follicles, each of which is nearly as large as two hands joined.—*Ainslie, p.* 227. *(Note*—Is this not S. fœtida ?)

STERCULIA GUTTATA, *Roxb.*

Goldar. DUK.	Ramena pu maram. TAM.
Pi maram. TAM.	

A large forest tree, of Ceylon, and Malabar, but occurring in the Dekhan. The character of its wood is not known. Its inner bark abounds with very strong, white, flaxen fibres, which are chopped up and converted into a flaxy substance, that the natives of the coast, below Wynaad, contrive to make into a sort of clothing.—*Dr. Riddell, Mr. Rohde, Dr. Wight, Roxb., Vol. III, p.* 149, *W. & A., Vol. I, p.* 62, *Useful Plants, p.* 399, *Royle, Fib. Pl.*

STERCULIA PARVIFLORA, *Roxb.*

Ram-julparee. HIND.

A middle sized tree, a native of the hills east of Tipperah: wood unknown.—*Roxb., Vol. III, p.* 147.

STERCULIA POPULARIFLÒRA *Roxb.*

This tree is a native of the Coromandel side of India. The bark is peculiarly smooth in young trees.—*Roxb., Vol. III, p.* 148.

STERCULIA RAMOSA. A tree of Pegu. The inner bark affords a strong and durable rope, in common use.—*Dr. McClelland.*

STERCULIA URENS, *Roxb.*

Buli. ? BENG.	Velle butallé maram. TAM.
Kateria kuli ? HIND.	Vellay putalli maram. TAM.
Kur kutila. „	Kavali. TAM. ?
Katira. „	Thabsi. TEL.
Kundol. MAHR.	Kavali. „ of the Godavery

The gum.

Tshaw. BURM.	Katila ka gond. HIND.

This large tree is a native of Ceylon and of most parts of India—occurring in the peninsula, on the western coast, common in the inland and coast forests of Bombay, growing in the Ajmer hills and Kotah, and in the mountainous countries of India generally. It may always be recognised by its peculiar bark, which looks as if painted of a light colour. Wood, according to Roxburgh, is soft, spongy, and loose grained, only fit for the most common purposes. According to Dr. Gibson, it is worthless. Seeds are roasted and eaten by the natives, and the leaves and tender branches are of great use in certain cattle diseases. The leaves when soaked in water, render it ropy and glutinous. The bark yields a gum resembling tragacanth.—*Drs. Wight, Gibson and Irvine, Thwaites, Roxb. Vol. III, p.* 145.

STERCULIA VILLOSA, *Roxb., Vol. III. p.* 153.

Oodal. ASSAM.

A large tree of the Dekhan and of the mountainous countries to the eastward of Bengal. It has a straight trunk with a smooth bark. The wood is not known. The bark is made into rope most readily; the bark, or rather all the layers, can be stripped off from the bottom to the top of the tree with the greatest facility, and fine pliable ropes may be made from the inner layers of bark, whilst the outer yield coarser ropes. The rope is very strong and very lasting—wet doing it little injury.—*Dr. Riddell, Dr. Royle, English Cyclopædia, Roxb., Vol. III, p.* 153.

STEREOSPERMUM CHELONOIDES, *W. Ic.*

Tha-koop-poo. BURM.	Vela-pathri maram. TAM.
Padri. HIND.	„ padri „ „
Padul. MAHR.	

This, though not a large, is a very handsome tree, with very fragrant beautiful pinkish flowers. It grows in Coimbatore, it is not common in the forests of the Bombay presidency, it is found, especially in those of the coast and ghats, but has not been observed in the inland jungles. Its wood is there used for interiors of buildings but is seldom procurable of a size fit for anything but posts. The wood in British Burmah is used in house building. In a full grown tree on good soil, there, the average length of the trunk to the first branch is 30 feet and average girth measured at 6 feet from the ground is 5 feet. It sells, in Burmah, at 8 annas per cubic foot.—*Drs. Wight, Gibson and Brandis, Cal. Cat. Ex.* 1862.

STEREOSPERMUM SUAVEOLENS.

Oolognanthri mara. Can.
Padeel ? Mahr.
Purrul. „
Padul ? Mahr.
Padri maram. Tam.

A middle sized tree, with pinnatic leaves, and panicled inflorescence, frequent in the Walliar jungles in southern India. It abounds in the Soonda forests; is very rare in other Bombay forests, but is occasionally found in the Konkun, near a temple, where it has evidently been planted for the sake of its beautiful flowers. The wood is dark coloured, strong and serviceable, is said by Dr. Wight to be elastic and fitted for making bows.—*Drs. Wight, Cleghorn and Gibson.*

STILLINGIA SEBIFERA, *Willde; Micheaux.*

Sapium sebiferum, *Roxb., Fl. Ind. Vol. III, p.* 693.
Croton sebiferum, *Linn.*

Chelat pipul. Beng.
Mom China. „
Tallow tree of China. Eng.

This tree, which Voigt says had been domesticated about Serampore, grows all over the eastern part of China and in Chusan, and when fully grown is a beautiful tree, resembling the aspen in shape and foliage, and with a straight trunk. It was introduced into India, and in Dr. Roxburgh's time was common near Calcutta. It grows to the height of a pear tree, with trunk and branches like the cherry and foliage like the poplar. Its kernels are coated with a pure white tallow, which is steamed off and collected. It is used for candles, as oil for lamps, but Dr. Roxburgh says it is not equal to cocoanut oil. Character of wood not known, but in Bengal it was only considered an ornamental tree.—*Voigt, Roxb., Fl. Ind. Vol. III, p.* 693, *Dr. Williams, Dr. Rawes.*

STRYCHNOS, a genus of plants, growing in Ceylon and India. Mr. Thwaites mentions, as Ceylon plants, S. cinnamomifolia, *Thw.*, of the Hantani district, S. colubrina, *Linn.*, in the hot, drier parts of Ceylon, S. laurina, *Wall.*, at Galle and Korne-galle. S. minor, *Blume*, at an elevation of 6,000 feet, and S. nux-vomica.

STRYCHNOS COLUBRINA, *Linn.*

Kuchila lata. Beng.
Snake poison nut tree. Eng.
Snake wood tree. „
Bois de couleuvre. Fr.
Lignum colubrinum. Lat.
Modira kaniram. Maleal ?
Pao-de-cobra. Port.
Naga musada. Tel.
Naga musadi. „
Modira canoram. Rheede.

A scandent plant with a stem of a great size, often 8 to 12 inches in diameter, growing in the hot, drier parts of Ceylon and in Malabar. The wood is of a light grey colour, hard, and intensely bitter. It forms one of the woods known in Britain as snake wood, along with those of the Ophioxylon serpentinum of Amboyna, Ophiorhiza mungos of Java. The Teling physicians regard the wood of the root as a remedy in snake bites.—*Dr. O'Shaughnessy, Eng. Cyc., Thwaites, Roxb., Fl. Ind. Vol. i. p.* 577, *and note,—ibid.*

STRYCHNOS NUX VOMICA, *Linn. Roxb. Fl. Ind. Vol. i. p.* 575.

Khanck ul kalb. Ar.
Falus mahi. „
Kuchila. Beng.
Kha bouug. Burm.
Kha gyee ? Burm. of Moulmein ?
Kuchila. Duk.
Snake wood tree. Eng.
Vomit nut „ „
Poison nut „ „
Nux-vomica tree. „
Kuchla. Hind.
Kuchila. „
Lignum colubrinum. Lat.
Jhar-katchura. Mahr.
Kariram ? Maleal.
Izaraki ? Pers.
Culaka ? Sans.
Cutapa. „
Vesha-mushti bijum. Sans.
Kudaka dornatta ? Singh.
Goda-kadaru. ? „
Gada-kadooroo-gass „
Yetti maram. Tam.
Mutti ? Qu ? Yetiimaram.
Yetti-cotay maram. Tam.
Musadi. Tel.
Mesidi. „
Mushti. „
Musada. „
Mushti ganga musidi. Tel.
Korra Tel. ? of Ganjam and Gumsur.
Kunjaram of Travancore.

A small or middling sized tree, with a short crooked trunk, which grows in the hotter parts of Ceylon, common in every part of the Madras presidency; common in the south Konkan, particularly in shady ravines, but, on the Bombay side, does not reappear either north of the Savitri or inland. It is a native of the southern parts of the Bengal Presidency and near Midnapore, is a very common tree throughout the forests of Pegu and extends into the Archipelago. In a full grown tree, the average length of the trunk to the first branch, is 15 feet or 20 feet, and average girth measured at 6 feet from the ground is 3 feet. Its timber is strong and close grained, but never of large size: wood hard and of a white or ash colour, specific gravity 0·706. A cubic foot weighs 52 lbs. It is used for ploughshares, cart wheels, in Travancore, for making cots, and is adapted for fancy work and cabinet making. It furnishes one of the snake woods of commerce. It produces the poison nut or nux vomica of commerce, the favourite food of the Buceros Malabaricus, or Malabar hornbill. Iron tools are sharpened on blocks of this wood. White ants will not touch it.—*Drs. Wight, Cleghorn, Gibson, Brandis and Mason, Colonel Frith, Captain Macdonald, Cal. Cat. Ex.* 1862, *Roxb., Fl. Ind. Vol. I, p.* 575, *Thw. En. Pl. Zeyl.* 201.

STRYCHNOS POTATORUM, *Willde.*

Nirmali. Beng.
Chilbinj-ka-har. Duk.
Clearing nut tree. Eng.
Nirmali. Hind.
Chil binj. „
Tettam parel maram. Maleal.
Katake. Sans.
Injini-gass. Singh.
Tettan cottay maram. Tam.
Chillaghinzalu chettu. Tel.
Chilla chettu. „
Indupu „ „
Katakamu. „

The wood.

Indaga wood ? ANGLO-TEL. | Indaga karra. TEL.
Chilbinj-ki lakri. HIND.

The tree.

Clearing nut tree. ENG. | Tatan maram. TAM.
Chillbinj. HIND. | Chilla ginja chettu. TEL.
Nirmul. " | Indapa chettu. "
Nirmuli. " | Kotoko of Ganjam and Gumsur.
Nir malli. MAHR.

This tree grows in the drier, and especially the northern, parts of Ceylon. It is found in various parts of India and grows to a moderate and even large size, larger than the S. nux vomica and scarcer. It is found in Coimbatore and other parts of the Madras Presidency, on mountains and in woods of great extent; on the hills of the Satpoora range, near Arrawad and in the jungles of Doordi, on the Gutpurba river. The wood is hard and durable, and though of small size, is used in several economic purposes. In Ganjam and Gumsur, its extreme height is 40 feet, circumference 4 feet, and height from the ground to the intersection of the first branch, 9 feet. In Ganjam and Gumsur, it is chiefly used for firewood, though bandy wheels and ploughshares are occasionally made of it. The seeds have the curious property of purifying muddy water, and are constantly used for that purpose by the natives who rub the inside of their lotas and brass pots with them. The fruit is used medicinally.—*Drs. Wight, Gibson and Cleghorn, Captain Macdonald, Thw. p.* 201, *Roxb. Fl. Ind. Vol. I., p.* 576

STRYCHNOS SANSCTI IGNATII.

Ignatia amara—?

St. Ignatius' bean tree. ENG. | Papita. HIND.

A branching tree, a native of the Philippine Islands, character of wood not known. Its seeds or beans are of the size of a large olive, and contain treble the quantity of strychnine of the nux-vomica nut.—*Dr. O'Shaughnessy.*

STYLOCORYNE WEBERA, *A. Rich.*

Webera corymbosa, *Willd. Roxb. Fl. Ind.* 2, *p.* 533.
Canthium corymbosum, *Pers. Rheede.*
Rondeletia asiatica, *Linn.*
Cupia corymbosa, *D C.*
Tarenna Zeylanica, *Gærtn.*

Kommi chettu. TEL. | Konda papata. TEL.
Bomma papata. "

The wood of this shrub or small tree is small, but hard: is prettily marked, and much esteemed by the natives. This tree is met with on the Godavery. Its leaves and fruit are used in medicine.—*Capt. Beddome, Roxb. Fl. Ind.* 2, *p.* 533, *Voigt, p.* 377.

STYRAX BENZOIN, *Dryander.*

Husse-ul-jawi. ARAB. | Gum benjamin. ENG.
Benjamin. ENG. | Luban. HIND.
Benzoin. " | Husse luban. PERS.

This tree is a native of Sumatra, Siam and Java, and yields the gum benjamin of commerce: character of wood not known.—*Voigt.*

SUVANDE, SINGH. A wood used in Ceylon, for common house building purposes. It grows in the western province of that island. A cubic foot weighs 56 lbs., and the wood is said to last 30 years.—*Mr. Mendis.*

SUMATRA. The Sumatra forests contain an inexhaustible store and endless variety of timber trees, many sorts of which are highly valuable and capable of being applied to ship-building and other important purposes. On the western coast, the general want of navigable rivers has materially hindered both the export and the employment of its timber; but, those on the eastern side, particularly Siak, are more favorably situated.

Red bintangur. For masts and yards the wood preferred is the *red bintangur,* a species of Uvaria, which in all the maritime ports of India, has obtained the name of poon or puhn, from the Malayan word signifying tree in general; as puhn upas, the poison tree, puhn kaya, a timber tree, &c. (*qu.?* a species of Calophyllum ? *See* BINTANGOR. *Note.*—*Puhn,* MALAY, a tree, seems to be the source of the commercial term for the Poon or Peon spars.

Camphor wood, useful for capenters' purposes.

Kayu pindis or *Kapini,* a species of Metrosideros, is named also *Kyau besi,* or iron-wood, on account of its extraordinary hardness, as it turns the edge of common tools.

Marbau, the Metrosideros Amboinesis, R. grows to a large size, and is used for beams both in ship and house building, as well as for other purposes to which oak is applied in Europe.

Pinaga is valuable as crooked timber, and is used for frames and knees of ships, being also very durable. It frequently grows in the wash of the sea.

Juar, Ebony, called in Batavia "kayu arang," or charcoal wood, is found here in great plenty.

Kayu gadis, a wood possessing the flavour and qualities of the sassafras, and used for the same purposes in medicine, but in the growth of the tree it resembles rather the British elm than the laurus, to which latter tribe the American sassafras belongs. It is very common in the plains near Bencoolen.

Kayu arau, the Casuarina littorea is often termed a bastard pine, and, as such, gave name to the Isle of Pines discovered by Captain Cook. By the Malays it is usually called kayu chamara, from the resemblance of its branches to the ornamental cow-tails of Upper India. It has been already remarked of this tree, the wood of which is not particularly useful, that it delights in a low sandy soil, and is ever the first that springs up from land relinquished by the sea.

Rangas or *Rangi,* commonly supposed to be the manchineel of the West Indies, but perhaps only from the noxious quality of its juices, is the Arbor vernicis of Rumphius, and is particularly described in the Batav. Trans. Vol. V., under the name of Manga deleteria sylvestris, fructu parvo cordiformi.—*Marsden's History of Sumatra, p.* 162.

SUMSIHAR, HIND., OR SAMSIHAR, HIND. A tree of Chota Nagpore. Hard timber.—*Cal. Cat. Ex.* 1862.

SUTSHER. A dark coloured wood, close grained, strong and heavy, grows from Sooree to Hasdiha in the Santhal jungles, but scarce. Furniture and posts are made from this wood.—*Cal. Engineers' Journal, July* 1860. (*Note.*—Is this name correct?)

SYMPLOCOS, *Species.*

Kam-tha-pho-gee. BURM.

A timber of Tavoy, used in boat building.

SYMPLOCOS RACEMOSA, *Roxb.; Fl. Ind. ii. p.* 539.

Lodh. BENG.	Savura lodhra. SANS.
Lodh. HIND.	Loddugu. TEL.
Hoora. MAHR.	Erra loddugu. „

This small tree, from ten to twelve feet high, and with a trunk about 20 inches in circumference, is a native of Nepal and Kemaon and of Burdwan and Midnapore in Bengal. It grows also in the Kotah jungles, but, in the Bombay Presidency, it is found only in the jungles of the highest ghats. Its wood is yellowish, but appears strong and compact, and might be used for cabinet as well as for other purposes. The bark of the root is sold at 4 seers the rupee, and is used in Rajputanah, for dyeing red. It is also used in medicine, being considered heating and promotive of the secretions. It is used also in the mesalihs for animals. The bark furnishes one of the red powders, known as "abir," scattered by hindus in the festival of the hoolee.—*Roxb. Fl. Ind. ii. p.* 239, *Irvine, Gibson, Voigt.*

SYZYGIUM, a large tropical genus of plants, some of which are now referred to other genera, particularly Eugenia, and notices of E. acris; E. alternifolia; E. amœna; E. bracteata; E. caryophyllifolia; E. caryophyllata; E. cerasoides; E. jambolana; E. jambos; E. laurina; E. Malaccensis and E. obtusifolia, will be found under these names, but, particular attention is directed to the remarks against Eugenia jambolana. And, as Dr. Wight, in Icones, gives Syzygium carophyllaceum; densiflorum; jambolanum; lanceolatum; nervosum; oblatum; rubicundum; rugosum; salicifolium and Zeylanicum, it will be understood how different botanists mix up the genera. Mr. Thwaites notices Zyzygium assimile, Z. Gardneri, Z. micranthum; Z. rotundifolia; Z. sclerophyllum; Z. spathulatum and S. umbrosum, all growing in the central province of Ceylon, at elevations of from 2,000 to 8,000 feet. S. oliganthum, *Thw.*, a small tree of the Ambagamowa district, at an elevation of 3,000 to 5,000 feet. Z. jambolanum, which will be found noticed under its synonym E. jambolana (and Mr. Thwaites gives as its synonyms, *Syzygium caryophyllifolium*, D C. E. (S.) caryophyllifolia, [E. (S.) jambolana? var. microcarpa], Wight, t. 553. E. caryophyllifolia, Lam. Roxb.; Fl. Ind., II. p. 486. Calyptranthes cumini, Moon's Cat. p. 39—c. p. 1584) It is the Madang-gass, SINGH., is common in Ceylon, up to an elevation of 3,000 feet. Mr. Thwaites gives, *Syzygium polyanthum*, ENG. (S. polyantha, Wight, Ill. ii. p. 17; Ic. t. 543.) And S. balsameum, Wall. Wight, III. ii. p. 16. Calypt. caryophyllifolia, Moon's Cat. p. 39—c. p. 2081, the Batta domba-gass of the Singhalese, as a large tree common in Ceylon up to an elevation of 3,000 feet. And, *Syzygium sylvestre*, ENG. (S.) sylvestris, W. Ic. t. 532. Calyptranthes jambolana, Moon's Cat. p. 39—c. p. 2862, the Aloobo-gass of the Singhalese, as a large tree, common in Ceylon, up to an elevation of 3,000 feet. The woods of several of these trees are employed for economic purposes.—*Wight Icon., Voigt, Thw. En. Pl. Zeyl. p.* 116.

SYNDESMIS TAVOYANA, *Wallich.*

Ka-tha. BURM.	Mergui red wood. ENG.
Tavoy red wood. ENG.	

A very large tree of British Burmah. The wood makes handsome furniture, and is used for building, boxes, &c., and, in Tavoy, for similar purposes to what the gum kino wood is applied at Moulmein. It is, occasionally, a beautifully variegated wood, well adapted for furniture and ornamental purposes. It contains a dye, and is in great abundance in the islands on the coast and near Moulmein. When the wood is steeped in ferruginous mud, it turns jet black and looks like ebony. The large cylindrical knobs, one or two inches in diameter, so often noticed in the ears of Karen women at Tavoy, are made of this wood after the color has been changed.—*Captain Dance, Drs. Mason and Wallich.*

T.

TABERNÆMONTANA CITRIFOLIA.

Nagin koora. CAN.

Common on the hills near and below the ghats of Canara and Sunda. Wood white, but tough and strong. Never large.—*Dr. Gibson.*

TA KEEP-NEE. In Tavoy, a very strong, close grained, heavy, light coloured, wood.—*Mr. Blundell.*

TA-KOUK THA, BURM. OR YAY MI-NE, BURM. A tree of Amherst, Tavoy and Mergui, of maximum girth ½ cubit and maximum length

7 feet. Abundant all over the provinces. When seasoned it floats in water. It is a durable wood, likely to make good helves or to be useful in turning. Too small in size however to be recommended. —*Captain Dance.*

TABOOT—? A tree of Akyab, wood used for making banghies and other fine work. It grows to a moderate size, but is not very plentiful.—*Cal. Cat. Ex.* 1862.

TAG-NYENG. In Tavoy, a useful furniture wood.—*Mr. Blundell.*

TAIA-BOUK-BHA—? A tree of Akyab. It is a small wood, is plentiful, and is used for firewood.—*Cal. Cat. Ex.* 1862.

TALAZ—? A tree of Akyab. It is plentiful and is used for oars and banghies, and in house building.—*Cal. Cat. Ex.* 1862.

TALLE TANGA, the Malayala and Tamil name of a Malabar and Canara tree, which grows to about two feet in diameter, and thirty feet high. It is the tree that produces the jungle-almonds, on which the monkeys and other animals of the forest feed. The natives cut this wood into boards for boats and house building, they also make it into canoes, which are said to be durable. The boats are sewed together by coir yarns.—*Edye Forests of Malabar and Canara.*

TAMARINDUS INDICA, *Linn.*; *Roxb.*; *W. & A.*

Tamarindus occidentalis, *Gærtn.*

Tamr-i-hindi. Ar ? ?	Cheetz. Mahr.
Tintori. Beng.	Asam. Malay.
Ma-gyi. Burm.	Kamal. „
Huli shena. Can.	Balam puli. Maleal.
Oonara mara. „	Darakht tamr-i-hindi. Pers.
Hoonsay ? „	Sigembela. Singh.
Tamarind-tree. Eng.	Pulia maram. Tam.
Amli ka jhar. Hind.	Chinta chettu. Tel.

The Fruit.

Amli. ? Ar.	Asam. Malay.
Imli. Cash.	Jawa. „
Umbuli. „	Kranji. „
Cay-me. Coch.-Chin.	Kamal. „
Imli. Duk.	Neghka. Maleal.
Tamarind. Eng.	Tamr-i-hindi. Pers.
Tamarins. Fr.	Amlika. Sans.
Tamarinden. Ger.	Tintili. „
Amli. Guz.	Maha-siambala. Singh.
Amli. Hind.	Tamarindo. Sp.
Tamarindo. It.	Puli pallam. Tam.
Kamal. Jav.	Chinta pandu. Tel.
Tamarindus. Lat.	Demer-hindi. Turk.

This is a very handsome tree of slow growth, but attains a great size. It is not a tree common in forests, but is met with in gardens, near old temples, where it has been planted. It is a graceful avenue tree and its fruit is in great request. The wood is hard, dark coloured, durable, and often finely veined, and the heart wood of old trees is dark coloured, resembling ebony. It is apt to be hollow in the centre, which prevents large slabs being obtained. It is used in the manufacture of oil mills, mallets, rice pounders, and for furniture and building purposes, but carpenters are very unwilling to work it up, on account of the great damage it causes to the best tempered tools. It is valuable for brick and tile burning. Mr. Edye says there are two sorts of the tamarind, the light and the dark. The trees grow to about seven or eight feet in diameter at the butt, while that of the body of the tree is about five feet. This part is seldom more than ten feet long when it branches out into curves of various dimensions. It is considered valuable from the quantity of fruit it produces, which is used medicinally. The acid is used in cookery. These trees are cultivated in gardens, and spread their branches to a great extent. The timber is remarkably heavy and hard, much like Lignum vitæ, and is used generally for shivers in blocks, and such purposes.—*Edye, Forests of Malabar and Canara, Drs. Wight, Mason, Cleghorn and Gibson, Mr. Mendis.* (*Note.* —Mr. Edye, in saying that there are two sorts of tamarind, the light and the dark,—must allude to the West Indian red and East Indian white varieties; several large trees of the former with red fruit, grow in the south of India, and I have largely distributed the seeds through the Madras Board of Revenue).

TAMARIX, the Tamarisk. Of this genus, the more common species are the T. gallica, *Linn.* the "*jhao*" of northern India, which grows on the Coromandel coast, on the banks of the Jumna and Ganges, the banks of the Indus, in Cutch and Sind, where it is commonly used for firewood:—also T. dioica, *Roxb.*, a shrub of the Sunderbuns and found in the beds of the Konkun and Dekhan rivers: it is the "Lal jhao of India. Dr. Royle remarks that bitterness and astringency are the properties ascribed to the Tamariscineæ and hence the occasional employment of the European species as a tonic, and as a substitute for hop in making beer in Denmark. In India, also, the twigs of T. Indica and dioica, are considered astringent, but the plants are more valued on account of the galls which are formed on these and on T. Furas, as on T. orientalis in Egypt, and which, being highly astringent, are now, as in former times, used in medicine and dyeing, those formed on T. Furas, are called "Sumrut-ool-aul" or "Chotee-muc"; and of the jhao, "Sumrut-ool-toorfa" or "buree-muc," they are chiefly imported from Mooltan, but he had found them on the Furas in Delhi. The ashes of T. gallica and Africana, when growing near the sea, contain a large proportion of sulphate of soda, so that they may be profitably burnt to obtain this salt, and its abundance explains the utility of some of these plants as diuretics. The T. Indica grows to the size of a middling sized tree, with a trunk the thickness of a man's body. A product very different from any of these products, is the manna produced on a species of tamarisk.

This has been ascertained by Ehrenberg to be produced by the puncture of Coccus maniparus, on a variety of T. gallica, growing on Mount Sinai. This manna has long been known by the name of Arabian, to distinguish it from Persian manna, the produce of Alhagi maurorum, the toorunjbeen (v. p. 194,) of Arabian authors. This is called Guzunjbeen, from Guz or Kuz, one of the names of T. gallica or a species of tamarisk.—*Royle, Ill. Him. Bot. p.* 214, *Roxb. Vol. ii p.* 101.

TAMBAGUM. TAM. A Travancore wood of a brown colour, specific gravity 0·910, 5 feet in circumference, a very strong wood, used for houses, blocks, &c.—*Col. Frith.*

TAMBOGUM in Tamil, and Vanponga in Malayala. This Malabar and Canara tree is remarkably heavy and close grained, and may be considered very similar to the timber now imported into the dock yards from Africa, named African teak, No. I. It grows from thirty to fifty feet long, and about thirty inches in diameter, and is used by the natives where strength and durability are required, and weight is of no consideration. It produces a fruit or berry, which the natives reduce to meal, with which they make cakes, curry, &c.: the berry is much like coffee in shape and size.—*Edye, Forests of Malabar and Canara.* (*Note.*—Are the Tambagum of Colonel Frith and the Tambogum of Mr. Edye identical. Is it Shorea tambugaia ?)

TAMPINNIS, A fruit tree of Penang, of a light red colour used for ornamental furniture, billiard cues, &c.—*Colonel Frith.*

TANGNET-NA, BURM. A Tavoy wood.

TANI in Tamil, Jellam in Malayala, which means water-wood. This tree grows to about two feet in diameter, and forty feet high. It is remarkably soft and porous, and contains a great quantity of water. When it is felled it is of little use; and is considered as one of the inferior kinds of jungle wood.—*Edye, Forests of Malabar and Canara.*

TAN-LABET—? In Amherst, a heavy white timber, employed for house posts and other common purposes. It is not liable to injury from insects.—*Cat. Ex.* 1851.

TANNA, the Tamil name of a Malabar and Canara tree, which is hard and heavy. It is used by the natives in house work, and for implements of agriculture when it can be procured, but, it is very scarce.—*Edye, Forests of Malabar and Canara.*

TANTHEYA, BURM. A Tavoy wood.

TAREE MARA, CAN. Yehela, MAHR. Terminalia bellerica. In Canara and Sunda, common both above and below, and is one of the greatest trees in the forest. Wood serviceable for houses but not first rate; used also for plank.—*Dr. Gibson.*

TAUP-SHA. An Amherst wood, employed for house posts, and would answer for common carpentry, but it is liable to split; the bark is supposed to be medicinal.—*Cat. Ex.* 1851.

TAVOY WOODS. Our knowledge of the woods of this province is derived from two lists of specimens, one by Dr. Wallich and one by Mr. Blundell, which were sent to the Exhibition of 1851; and, from the extended notices of the timbers of this province, which Captain Dance furnished. The names of Captain Dance's contributions, will be found under the head of Amherst, Tavoy and Mergui. And his detailed descriptions alphabetically. The names in the lists of Dr. Wallich and Mr. Blundell are as under: and notices will be found in the alphabetical arrangement.

The trees and woods of Tavoy by Dr. Wallich.

Acacia: Popeeah, *Burm.*
Acacia: Paingadoo. *Burm.*
Anacardium. Thubbamboo, *Burm.*
Artocarpus. Thouenben, *Burm.*
Artocarpus, *sp. Burm.*
Artocarpus: Pynyathe or tannabeng, *Burm.*
Bignonia, Thathee, *Burm.*
Bignonia: (?) Thuggainee, *Burm.*
Bignonia: lainbha, *Burm.*
Calophyllum: Turra-phee, *Burm.*
Carapa: Taila-oon, *Burm.*
Careya: Kaga, *Burm.*
CastaneaMartabanica, Norne or zitha, *Burm.*
Cerbera manghas, Kulloon, *Burm.*
Dillenia. Zimboon, *Burm.*
Dipterocarpus grandiflora, Ain or aintha, *Burm.*
Dipterocarpus grandiflora, ? Kunnean phin, ? *Burm.*
Euphorbiaceæ, Yamula, *Burm.*
Eurya, Thaun, *Burm.*
Excœcaria, ? Thurrotha, *Burm.*
Ficus, Thubboo, *Burm.*
Ficus, Thuppan, *Burm.*
Garcinia, Pulloua, *Burm.*
Grewia, Minya, *Burm.*
Heritiera fomes, Kunnazoo, *Burm.*
Hibiscus macrophyllus.
Hibiscus macrophyllus. (?)
Hopea floribunda, Thanthe-ya, *Burm.*
Lagerstrœmia, Kuenmounee or puma, *Burm.*
Laurus, Kullowa or kurrowa, *Burm.*
Laurus, Panatha, *Burm.*
Laurus, Maythen, *Burm.*
Laurus, Keemna, *Burm.*
Laurus, Thuggoo, *Burm.*
Laurus, Thitya, *Burm.*
Laurus, Kayzai, *Burm.*
Mimusops, Thubbae, *Burm.*
Mimusops, elengi.
Murraya, Maika, *Burm.*
Myristica, Thounsanga, *Burm.*
Myristica, Koathoe or Kuuneen, *Burm.*
Osyris peltata, Phaoun, *Burm.*
Pierardia, (?) Kunna or Kuzzo, *Burm.*
Pinus Dammara, *Burm.*
Pterocarpus, (?) Puddow, *Burm.*
Rottlera, Mimasko, *Burm.*
Rottlera, Keoun lae, *Burm.*
Sandoricum, Thittoo, *Burm*
Sapotea, (?) Palæpean, *Burm.*
Sonneratia, (?) Thaumma, *Burm.*
Sterculia, (?) Kununu, *Burm.*
Sterculia, Thikadoo, *Burm.*
Symplocos, (?) Kain-thaphogee, *Burm.*
Syndesmis, Tavoyana, Katha *Burm.*
Syndesmis, Kunnuu keunka; Kunnuu keunla, *Burm.*
Terminalia, Thuphanga, *Burm.*
Ternstrœmia, Puzzeen zwa, *Burm.*
Uvaria, Thubbor, *Burm.*
Wrightia antidysenterica Lathou, *Burm.*
Xylocarpus, Keanuan, *Burm.*
Zizyphus, Zeethee, *Burm.*

Vernacular names.

Ahnaun, *Burm.*
Bah-mah-thoa, *Burm.*
Con-moo *Burm.*
Kaantha, *Burm.*
Kaungo kurra.
Keahnaun, *Burm.*

Kuddoot alaim, *Burm.*
Kuddoot-nu, *Burm.*
Kummi, *Burm.*
Mainaban, *Burm.*
May-klin, *Burm.*
May-maka, *Burm.*
May rang, *Burm.*
May-tobek, *Burm.*
Megeone, *Burm.*
Peulay-peen, *Burm.*
Pieumahne, *Burm.*
Pienmah pue, *Burm.*
Tantheya, *Burm.*
Tangnet-na, *Burm.*
Teatha, *Burm.*
Thauga-et thittoo, *Burm.*
Thau-baunpo, *Burm.*.
Thau baun thau-lay, *Burm.*
Theyah, *Burm.*
Thounmynga, *Burm.*
Thymbro, *Burm.*
Town pine, *Burm.*
Mr. Blundell's list.
Annan.
Bep--than.
Bep-won.
Bhan-bhway.
Bha-ta-ka.
Daup-yan.
Eng-beng.
Cedrela? Kad-wot-nu, *Burm.*
Kanna-tso.
Ka-nyeng kyaung khyay.
Ka-nyeng-pyan.
Katso Like toon.
Kaung-thmoo ysepsay.
Kengthep-guyung-ywept.
Kengthep-pheoot-kyay.
Khamoung-nee.
Khamoung-pyion.
Kharaway-nu.
Kouk-ko.
Kyay-tsay-gyu-khy-ay.
Kyay-tsay-bayoun.
Kyep-yo.
Kywon-bo.
Kywon-ma.
Lienman.
Mala-ka.
Ma-yam.
Mee-kyaung-kyay.
Meep-thua-bau.
Miaup bout.
Mya-kamaun.
Myeng-ta-bep.
Ngoo-beng.
Noalee-lyeng.
Pan-loun.
Pantheet-ya.
Patseng-tsway.
Patseng-ngo.
Peng-lay-byun.
Peng-lay-oun.
Peng-lay-kaboay.
Mimosa, Pee-daup, *Burm.*
Artocarpus, Pinnay, *Burm.*
Pyaung-pyiou.
Pyeng-khado.
Tag-nyeng.
Ta keep-nee.
Tha-bhan.
Tha byny-nee.
Tha-byoo.
Theet-ta-gyee.
Theet-ya-han.
Theet-ya-nee.
Theet-ya-pyiou.
Thiem.
Thingan-kyaup.
Thmeng-ba.
Thmeny-tshout.
Toung-bhaut.
Toung-bhien.
Toung-byeng.
Toung-byion.
Toung-kha-ray.
Tseng byiou.
Tsoay-dan.
Wonthay-khyay.
Yow-ma-lay.
Zoo-lat.

Cat. Ex. 1851.

TAYET KHYEE. BURM. This timber tree, of maximum girth 2 cubits and maximum length 15 feet, is abundant all over the Tenasserim provinces. When seasoned it floats in water. It yields a pretty wood in grain, but one which rots when it dies readily. It is of no durability.—*Captain Dance.*

TAY-THA. BURM. A timber tree of Amherst, Tavoy and Mergui, maximum girth 3 cubits and maximum length 15 feet. Scarce in Amherst, but abundant towards Tavoy. Found inland also along the sea coast all over the provinces. When seasoned it floats in water. It is subject to the dry rot when seasoned, is a useless wood and not recommended.—*Captain Dance.*

TAY YO THA. ? A timber tree of Amherst, Tavoy and Mergui, of maximum girth 2 cubits and maximum length 18 feet. It is very abundant on the sea coast and adjacent islands of these provinces. When seasoned it floats in water. It is used for oars and masts of boats. When this wood is cut, a very acrid caustic juice or sap flies from it which will destroy sight, if it touch the eye; or, if it fall on the face, it raises blisters. A wood dangerous to work, and not durable.—*Captain Dance.*

TECTONA GRANDIS. The Teak tree.

Saygun. BENO.
Kuyon. BURM.
Shuldoona of Jubbulpore.??
Sagwan. HIND.
Saya. MAHR.
Jati. MALAY.
Tek maram. TAM.
Teku chettu. TEL.

Localities. For the purposes of the public service, this majestic forest tree is perhaps the most largely used of any of the woods of south-eastern Asia and merits, therefore, a notice of some length. It is found in Bundelcund, on the Aravalli and Satpoora and on the banks of the Taptee river. It grows as a majestic forest tree on the western side of India, from Nassik, N. W. of Bombay southwards to Severndroog: in the forest west of Vingorla, near Sawuntwarie: in the forest between Dharwar, Sunda and Sedashegur and in smaller patches above the ghats, in Canara, Malabar, Cochin, Travancore and Coimbatore, in the Anamallai. In Ceylon, the Dutch largely planted teak, which has attained considerable size: a small quantity occurs in the Nalla Malai mountains between Nellore and Cuddapah. North-east of this, it is known in the Nagpore and the Hyderabad territories, on the Godavery and its feeders, viz., east of Chanda, on the left bank of the Paen Gunga and north of the Indrawatti river in 20° N. L. also on the 18° N. L. close to the right bank of the Godavery, east of Warungul and, further east, on the right bank of the Sebbur river. In Burmah and the Tenasserim provinces, also, at the forks of the Salwen river, and west of Moulmein between the Martaban river and the Menam, nearly as far south as Tavoy, teak forests occur of great value. Further south and east it only reappears in Siam and in the mountainous parts of Sumatra, Celebes, Sumbawa and Java. Between Japara and Sourabaya, several extensive teak forests occur, which are of vast importance to the island: as the timber is well adapted to ship-building, being very durable and easily worked. Indeed, there is no other kind of wood in the Archipelago, which will endure so well, in the water. But, Java is the only island in the Archipelago possessing teak forests which are, at present; available to any extent for the purpose of ship-building; for, though teak is found in Sumatra, Celebes and Sumbawa, the forests in these islands, are so far distant from the sea, that the expense of land carriage prevents the natives deriving any great advantages from their export.—*Mr. Earl, p.* 44 *to* 45.

Bombay west coast, Dr. Gibson, Report 1845 to 1856, pages 5 and 6, tells us that in the Bombay Presidency, from many destructive processes, such as burning, hacking, &c., many provinces formerly abounding in Teak-wood trees are now bare. They are still, however, found at Gond, Barnunbulee, Mawlinga, Berchee, &c. above the ghats, and in other parts of Yellapore talook: a few trees in Honore, north of the foot of Hosul-Mukki ghat; and about 18,000 small, estimated in Ankolah and Honawur divisions. These teak forests continue to be worked for the naval department, and afford a few logs of upwards of eight khundies, and having a length of above forty feet. These are technically called superiors and are calculated for kelsons, &c., of ships of the line. In his Report, 1857 to 1860, p. 45, Dr. Gibson estimated the Teak trees fit to be cut, without reference to those below three candies each, and available, as under:

	Trees.	
I.—For Sedasheghur.		
A—From Tareemullapoor up to Shidungoor, about......	2,000	
B—Goond Teak, where there will be scarcely any rejected wood...................	40,000	42,000
II.—For Gungawullee.		
A—As far as Coddlooguddy.	1,000	
B—From Coddlooguddy till Mogore and Soondat......	1,000	2,000
III.—For Tuddry, about................		2,000
IV.—For Honore.......................		2,000
Total number of Teak trees......		48,000

And, taking the trees at the average of only three candies each, he estimated that there could be 1,44,000 candies cutting of these yearly, so that they could supply Bombay with 2,430 candies, and the supply would last for 55 years more. Dr. Gibson's Report, 1849 to 1856, p. 166, tells us that in Ankola talooka of the Bombay Presidency, teak extends over mountain lands in thirty-two villages, and in Kownaee over forty villages, including those of the mahal of Trimbuk.

Malabar coast. Dr. Cleghorn tells us (*Report* 1858, *p.* 3,) that along the whole length of the Malabar coast from Goa to Cochin, there is now very little teakwood in a ripe state on Government land below the ghats, and there are only three localities above the ghats, viz. the Anamallai forests in Coimbatore; Wynaad and Hegga-devin cottah; and the Gund plateau, North Canara, near Dandellie where he found Teak in abundance and of good size. The chief reserve remaining is a forest in the Gund plateau. Indeed, Teak scantling of large size is becoming more and more scarce all along the West coast, and in Malabar first class logs are not easily procurable. That of Canara is even of smaller size: and, it is every where found too expensive for ordinary railway purposes. But, it is not teak only that the Canara forests produces; for,

the following timbers were supplied from the Canara forests in the year 1859.

To what department supplied.	Teak.					Blackwood.					Junglewood.					Total.				
	Logs.	Candies.	Qrs.	G.	T.	Logs.	Candies.	Qrs.	G.	T.	Logs.	Candies.	Qrs.	G.	T.	Logs.	Candies.	Qrs.	G.	T.
Bombay Dockyard.	409	904	2	4	10	12	45	2	4	10	...	...	...	...	...	421	950	1	4	...
Hyderabad Sinde Engineer.	37	118	2	2	10	...	...	...	...	...	...	...	...	...	...	37	118	2	2	10
Darwar Engineer.	187	344	2	1	5	...	...	...	...	...	538	842	...	4	...	725	1,186	3	...	5
Belgam do.	88	146	1	1	0	...	...	...	...	...	375	160	...	3	17	463	306	1	4	17
Lingasur. do.	103	188	3	2	17	...	...	...	...	...	16	23	...	1	1	119	211	3	3	18
Darwar factory.	...	...	...	...	...	...	...	...	...	...	30	43	3	4	15	30	43	3	4	15
Belgam barrack.	215	417	1	2	6	7	6	3	1	3	531	907	3	3	11	753	1,332	...	2	...
Tuddy workshop.	100	38	2	3	13	...	...	...	...	...	...	...	...	...	...	100	38	2		
Edulgee Government Contractor	9	38	1	4	19	...	...	...	...	...	25	21	2	...	...	34	40	...	...	...
Total......	1,148	2,177	2	3	0	19	52	2	...	13	1,515	1,998	3	...	11	2'682	4,229	...	...	3

Teak plantations have been formed in several places, but the most important are those on the Nelambur river in the Ernaad taluq of Malabar. Dr. Gibson tells us (*Report* 1848—56, *p.* 4) that the number of trees planted there by Mr. Conolly, is said to have been about four hundred thousand, and they were then of ages varying from sixteen to four years. Advantage had been taken of the proximity of the Nelumbur river with a view to future operations. The locality is about forty-eight miles inland from Calicut, near to the short or bridle-road to the Neilgherry hills. The success which had attended the measure appeared to Dr. Gibson to be complete. The trees had run up with a straight and clear stem, and some had reached the height of thirty-five feet, with a circumference of from eighteen to twenty-four inches below. They were at that time thickly planted, in order to secure a straight stem and for mutual protection from the winds. When Major Morgan visited the Nellumbur Teak plantations in December 1861, more than 50,000 saplings were marked and cut, to relieve the plantations, many of which were suffering severely from overcrowding, as detailed in his report in May 1861.

The ***Wynaad and Heggadevincottah forests***, on the borders of Mysore and Malabar, Dr. Cleghorn says (*Report* 1858, *p.* 4) are of great value. They are about 40 miles long by 30 broad, and were estimated by him as able to supply 2,000 bandy loads annually (or say 40,000 cubic feet of Teak) without apparently injuring the resources of the forest. There being no cultivation and a very scanty population, and the timber consequently not being required for local purposes, he urged that this forest should be reserved. From the situation and natural slope of the country, the timber must be carried eastward and will be extremely valuable for military purposes in Bangalore: the new barracks of which were then being built of this Teak. And, he thought it probable that this forest timber would come into use also to meet the increasing demand at Ootacamund: but, no means of transport exists by which the crooks and other naval timber found in the forest can be conveyed to the coast, where they would be extremely valuable. The expense of carriage by the usual route to Mysore and Manantoddy and down the Perriah Ghat to Tellicherry is altogether prohibitory. The average price of teak at the quarterly auctions held at Mysore had been almost exactly the same as at Anamallai, viz.,—about one rupee per cubic foot.

Mysore. The Teak forests in Wynaad, says Major Morgan, lie along the Mysore frontier, from Mudumallai in the south to the confines of Coorg in the north, a distance of about forty miles. The belt of Teak, on an average, is about six miles in breadth. But, this belt also contains an abundance of very fine blackwood, honah and muttee. The central portion is the broadest and richest in Teak. There, it grows straight and to a good height, and contains fully fifty good Teak trees to the acre. The northern part of the belt from Bowally to Coorg is narrow, but is also very rich in fine Teak. In the days of Hyder and Tippoo, these forests were worked to a great extent: there are good track roads and outlets to the eastward, and timber is easily floated down the Cubbany river. The Wynaad Teak forests are now the first in importance, as Wynaad will soon have outlets towards the west to the sea coast. In 1855, the price of Teak at Mysore was from 6 to 8 annas a cubic foot, which gave the wood merchants, who worked the forests (as they chose), not less than 25 per cent. profit, and, if taken to Bangalore, fifty per cent. more. The Mysore Government, some years ago, stopped the system of "Gootty Kanum," or stump fee, and worked their forests by their own servants, and now obtain at least one rupee per cubic foot profit. (Rep. Con. For. 1861-62, p. 21.) The price of Teak at Mysore, in consequence of that Government taking the working of the forests into its own hands, had considerably increased at the time Major Morgan wrote. During the last three quarterly sales at Mysore, Teak, 20 feet long 12 × 2; 10 feet long 21 × 21, and 15 feet long 18 × 10, cut in the forests which adjoin those of Wynaad, the receipts per foot of first, second, third, and fourth class, by auction quarterly, had been on an average as follows:— × × ×

August 1861	at Rupees	1	9	3½	per cubic foot.
Dec. 1861	at do.	1	12	7	do.
March 1862	at do.	1	6	4	do.

The Teak forests of Mysore are contained in the eastern Umshoms or parishes of Moonenaad, Ganapatty vattam, Elloornaad, Poolputty dasum of Koopatode. The following is a list of the Teak forests in the belt from Mooroogal or Moogoodoo in the north, on the confines of Coorg, to Tippoo Caudoo in the south, on the high road to the Neilgherry hills.

Iyapenpara Kukary, possessing teak in abundance, claimed by the Tiruelly temple.

Kooteray Cotta, possessing teak in abundance: Government property.

Masaul, possessing teak, but young. This forest having been exhausted of prime teak: Government property.

Susyvile, Hoolhully, Pambray, Kaper and Poolpully, commonly called the Veddykynaad, possessing teak in abundance, claimed by Poolpully temple.

Koorcheadoo, Kallymallay, Mungigal, Toromungal, Hurrygoonge and Echecoon, commonly called the Veddykynaad escheat, possessing teak in abundance, Government property escheat.

Edditoracottah, Kalamungul and Bene, possessing teak in abundance, but not easily to be got at, Government property escheat.

Nardimallay, Tippoocaudoo and Caroor, possessing teak in abundance, easily worked, Government property escheat.

Moodoomallai, possessing teak in abundance, teak nearly worked out by Government who obtained it on lease, claimed by the Nellumbore Rajah, but the Umshom is an escheat.—*Major Morgan's Report*, 1861-62, *p.* 23.

Cuddapah, little is known of the small quantity available, in the *Nalla mallai*, on the north-east border of the Cuddapah district.

On the *Godavery*, Captain Beddome's opinion was unfavourable to the existence of a large quantity of Teak within the limits of British territories: but, Dr. Cleghorn thought that the officials in the Nizam's country and those engaged in the timber trade had been unwilling to lead Captain Beddome into the deeper recesses of the forest where alone ripe timber now remains.—(*Report* 1858, *p.* 13.)

In *Nagpore*, says Captain Sankey, there are

two varieties of teak procurable one of a light, the other of a dark colour. The former seasons quickly, apparently does not lose its essential oil, and, by all accounts, is a better and stronger wood than the darker variety, which, drawn from the Langee jungles, was that formerly employed in the Government departments. Door frames of 20 years standing had on removal, been found ant-eaten, but these were the only instances of such having taken place. The natives of Nagpore use it particularly for the construction of bowries (by placing rough mortised frames one over the other as in the shaft of a mine) and they say that when immersed continually in water, it lasts in an extraordinary manner. (*Note*—This is the case with most woods E. B.) They moreover construct all terrace roofs, ferry boats, solid wheels of bandies, &c., from it, as well as use it extensively for furniture. Of the teak procurable, the average length was 30 feet, with a girth of 5 feet, and the maximum 64 feet with a girth of 4½ feet, and it was then selling at from annas 7½ to annas 12 per cubic foot.

In the *Jubbulpore* province, according to the Calcutta catalogue for the exhibition of 1862, one kind of this timber is there called, by the natives "Oil Teak" or "Seba Sagoon," and is found, it is believed, almost exclusively on the Vindyas, north of the Nerbudda, and is the best in the Jubbulpore provinces. Another kind, called by the natives "Patthareea Sagoon" or "Stoney Teak," is found in the more hilly tracts, and is shorter and more knotty than the first. A third kind, called by the natives "Doodheea Sagoon" or "Milky Teak," is found chiefly south of the Nerbudda, on the Satpoora, and is the softest timber. The differences in the above three woods are said to arise from the soils in which they grow.

The *Pegu province*, on the 20th December 1852, was proclaimed annexed to the British territories. It has ever been a principal mart for teak, indeed, this wood constituted the most important article of trade ever since the foundation of Rangoon by Alompra in the year 1775, and Teak is, still, the staple timber of the Tenasserim provinces, and from its abundance and its valuable property of being impervious to the white ant, Dr. Mason tells us, it is used in Moulmein almost exclusively, both for building purposes, and for furniture. In 1848, eighteen thousand tons of this timber were exported, and Mr. E. Riley estimated that more than three thousand tons were used for home consumption ; the total value of the whole falling little short of a million of rupees. A public journal recently commented on the Pegu Teak forest Report, for 1860-61, as an item of Revenue as follows :—"The Commissioner says that the total number of first class teak trees is estimated at a million and a half in the whole of the Pegu forests, and proceeds to say that of these Dr. Brandis considers that 30,000 may be girdled annually. We conclude that there is some error here—this increase in the number of first class trees could scarcely be as much as a million in four years. And again the Conservator, by his scheme shows that only 25,000 would be obtainable even in 1869-70. These discrepancies may be perhaps susceptible of explanation :—it is difficult to comprehend the figures as now presented. The number of logs sold during the year 1860-61, appears to have been 8,834, and in the previous year 15,416; and the sums realized approximately were Rupees 2,20,850 and Rs. 2,31,240, the logs of 1860-61 having been of larger size. The total revenues from the forests, however, from all sources, amount to Rs. 2,49,752, and the total expenditure to Rs. 2,76,753. The excess of expenditure is in part accounted for by the purchase of 40 elephants, forest improvements, &c., —but the deduction nevertheless is inevitable, that the forests do not yet yield a revenue to Government. When discussing this subject, now some months back, we pointed out that the footing on which these forest matters were established and conducted was not financially satisfactory, and we then showed that Government was paying more for the timber it required, through one agency or other, than it could have obtained it through private contractors and permit holders. The present report from the Commissioner does not satisfy us that matters have been altered to any manifest advantage. It is time, we conceive, that some indication of remunerative working should at the present day be exhibited, after such large disbursements annually, and so many years of unprofitable outlay. It is true that the Commissioner has an assumed set off in the shape of stock on hand, amounting to, he calculates to 1,08,000 Rupees—but by the period this stock is disposed off, and money recovered, another annual expenditure on account of the Conservancy Department will have been incurred. This item may be constantly recurring, and we do not see our way well out of this dilemma. There is no reason to expect that the disbursements will be less in 1861-62, than set down for 1860-61." Dr. Brandis, tells us, in the Calcutta Catalogue for the Exhibition of 1862 and his separate re-print, that the best Teak forests in British Burmah are on the hills between the Sitang and Irrawaddy rivers and in the Thoungyen valley ; but, even these forests are poor compared with extensive tracts, covered with Teak producing forests, to the north of the British boundary, especially on the feeders of the Sitang and Salween rivers and on some of the tributaries of the Meenam or Bankok river. The trees also are, as a rule, much larger and the shape of the stem more regular, in the forests of the Burmese empire, the Siamese kingdom and the Karenny country. The tallest Teak tree measured in Pegu was 106 feet high to the first branch.

—*Selections from the Records of Government of India, Foreign Department, No.* XXVIII, *p.* 11.

Even in the Teak forests of Burmah, however, Teak forms only a very small proportion of the forests; the greater part of which consists of various trees, mostly growing much faster than Teak and much more able to propagate themselves by natural means, but almost all of which are, in comparison with Teak, at present of very little or no value. It is, however, says Dr. McClelland in the hill forests of Pegu alone, that teak appears in perfection. It is only found on the southern and western declivities where it is exposed to a strong sun. On the open and exposed ridges, it becomes scarce, and it disappears altogether on the northern sides of hills. It is this peculiar partiality it exhibits for the southern and western slopes that renders the distribution of Teak so partial and limited. Its immediate associates in the forests are Spondia acuminata, Swietenia chaplas, Inga xylocarpa; Dalbergia robusta, and D. emarginata, Blackwellia propinqua and B. spirale, Pentaptera arjuna, and P. glabra, Sterculia alata, Careya arborea, Terminalia seevola, T. bellerica, Phyllanthus, Cluytia spinosa and Conocarpus acuminata, all large timber rivalling the Teak itself in magnitude and far out-numbering it in quantity. The soil of the Teak forests presents the same uniformity as to geological structure. In the forests where the best Teak is found, the soil is a grey stiff sandy clay, derived from the dark slaty sand-stone and slate clay, the particles passing downwards into comminuted slaty rhomboidal fragments. In the lower forests, where the soil is composed of laterite, Teak is not found in the same perfection; but, whether the difference be owing to the soil, or to the want of shelter and radiated heat from the immediate vicinity of hills, Dr. McClelland was not able to say, but nearly all the other varieties of timber associated with Teak partake of the same peculiarity and attain a much larger size in the hills than they do in the lower forests. Teak is diffused throughout the general forest in the proportion of about one to five hundred of other trees. In what are called the teak forests, strictly speaking, it is found in the proportion of about one to three hundred, not equally diffused, but confined to certain localities of small extent where it constitutes the prevailing tree for a few hundred yards, seldom for a mile continuously. These localities are the warm southern or western slopes; sometimes it ascends to ridges, and when these are sheltered to the north and east by higher hills presenting a free south-western aspect, the teak assumes its largest and most lofty size. It must be quite obvious, therefore, that a tree depending on so many local peculiarities for its full development, cannot occur continuously to any great or general extent, yet the quantity of teak in these forests has been, and, when Dr. McClelland wrote, still was very great, although the lower forests have been heavily worked and the best teak is now only to be had high up in the forests from whence its removal will every year be attended with increased difficulty. This observation applies more particularly to the Thounzai and Oakkan, although it is more or less applicable to all the other forests. Still from the canal-like character of the Choungs, and the absence of any very formidable rocky impediments, the facilities they afford for floating timber in the rainy season is very great, even from their extreme sources. But even in these remote places the sources of the forest in full grown timber are limited, and in the Phoungyee forest almost quite exhausted. There are few inhabitants in these teak forests, certainly not above two or three to twenty square miles. Dr. McClelland also tells us that teak occurs in the outer forest on the Hlaine valley growing on laterite soil along with other trees, but whether from the facilities afforded for its removal or other causes, it is of small size compared with the dimensions it attains in the hills. In some places it assumes, from the number collected together, the character of teak forests, but every tree, on attaining a marketable size, had been removed. Steps were taken to prevent this as far as possible, and he hoped that in the course of a few years, when the instructions given are attended to, it will be seen whether these lower forests are really capable of yielding large teak or not.—*Selection Records of Government of India, Foreign Department, No. IX, from p.* 12 *to* 13.

Dr. Brandis informs us that Teak trees, though scattered and of inferior growth, are not uncommon in the lower parts of the Tharawadie district. The forest Tahpoon, the teak near Minhla-yoah and that below Seppadan on the Beeling are the nearest to the upper Hlaine or Konktlean river that had been observed. In Dr. Brandis' survey of the Pegu teak forests, he classified the trees in the following manner:—

a. of 6 feet or 4 cubits in girth and above.

b. of 4 feet 6 inches or 3 cubits in girth and above.

c. of 3 feet or 2 cubits in girth and above.

d. of a girth under 3 feet, and seedlings,

and, he adds, that the Burmese are accustomed to classify trees according to the number of cubits which the girth of a tree measures.

We are told that a forest patch of teak, when in full bloom, has much the appearance of a field of ripe corn, with a few spots of green interspersed. By this appearance, persons who work the forests are enabled to distinguish, at a distance, the teak patches from other trees. The leaf of the teak tree is large and round, in shape resembling a cabbage leaf, about ten inches in diameter, but very thin, although its fibres are strong. The blossoms and berries are produced in large bunches: when in bloom, they may be compared to hops; when in seed, as to size, to a bunch of grapes. The nut is of a dark russet brown, and very hard; when ripe, it falls to the ground, and plants itself. It is of rapid growth, and the trunk grows erect, to a vast height, with copious spreading branches. In 20 or 25 years, the teak attains the size of two feet diameter, and is considered serviceable timber, but it requires 60 to 100 years to arrive at maturity: after 20 years, however, a teak plantation would probably yield a valuable return in thinning. On the Coromandel coast, it flowers in June and July, and the seeds ripen in September and October. It grows straight and lofty with cross armed panicles of showy white flowers.

On this point, *the growth of Teak*, Dr. Brandis, who has watched the trees from year to year, observes that the rate of growth of teak, like that of all other trees, is exceedingly variable, according to the locality and soil where it occurs. The tree grows fastest in forests of deep alluvial soil. Here the roots can spread far, and the leaves remain green during a considerable part of the dry season. Thus, some of the largest seedlings on the Thingan-nee-noung plantation had within 2 years attained a girth of from 10 to 13 inches near the root or of 8 inches at 6 feet from the ground, which in other localities would correspond to an age of from 4 to 5 years. And, in a similar locality on the banks of the Zimmay river (near Punko village) 9 trees were measured stated to be 7 years old with an average girth of 1½ feet, usually the size of trees 10 years old. Also, the growth of the sprouts from stumps in the Kjoonchoung forests was an instance of unusually fast growth. Nine sprouts, estimated to be 25 years old, had an average girth of 4 feet 5 inches which girth teak trees generally attain with 35 years only. Further, six teak trees of different sizes in girth between 3 feet and 15 feet were measured in the Thoukya-ghat forests in 1856. The same trees were measured again in 1859, and showed an average annual increase of 1 foot 6 inches, which rate usually is observed only in trees below 3 feet in girth. But, on the other hand, teak has a very slow growth on arid hills, with poor soil or with rocks near the surface. Here, often not a single tree is to be found, exceeding 4 feet in girth, although the forest has never been interfered with either by cultivators or timber cutters. The large number of Nathat trees, (trees that have died) shows that the tree remains stunted and dies off before reaching a good size. Teak of this description is found on the hills between the Pahchoung and the Karenee country and on the dry hills of the Prome district near the frontier on both sides of the Irrawaddee. In the Bombay forests, he adds, teak 14 years old is said to attain a girth of 8 inches in the hills and of 14 inches in the plains. Both are remarkable instances of slow growth.—(*Selections from the Records of the Government of India, p.* 145.) Still more recently, Dr. Brandis remarks that teak when young grows rapidly, and he mentions that two stems dug out in July 1858, at the Thenganenoung nursery, in the Attaran forests, had been sown in March and April 1856. The plants therefore were two years and three months old. The largest seedlings had a girth of 13 inches, measured at 1 foot from the ground, and of 8 inches at 6 feet from the ground. They were 32 feet high, but this was an instance of commonly rapid growth. Trees ten years old, have usually a girth of 18 inches measured at 6 feet from the ground, with 22 years a girth of 3 feet is attained; but full grown trees of 9 feet in girth cannot be supposed to be less than 160 years old. In a full grown tree on good soil the average length of the trunk, to the first branch is 90 feet and average girth measured at 6 feet from the ground is 18 feet.—*Dr. Brandis, and Cal. Cat. Ex.* 1862.

Dr. McClelland, also (*Selections from the Records of the Government of India, Foreign Department, No. IX, p.* 107), tells us that teak is a tree of rapid growth when placed in a favourable soil. The first year the seedling attains the height of twelve inches, throwing out two large leaves; the second year it springs up to the height of three or four feet, after which it goes on increasing rapidly and bears seed in the eighth year of its growth, when it has attained the height of twenty-five feet and upwards. It is for the first four or five years, while the young plants are liable to suffocation from long grass and bamboos, that cultivation would be most requisite until the young trees secured possession of the ground. After that, all that would be necessary would be to protect the forests from fire and the unlicensed use of the axe. He adds that the lengthened period ascribed to the growth of teak, by writers on the Moulmein forests, was owing to their having been guided in their calculation by the number of what are called annual rings, exhibited by a section of the trunk. But Mr. Griffith, who is the best authority on questions of this nature, states that in tropical climates, where the alternations of seasons is less marked than in Europe, no dependence is to be placed in this test of the age of trees. Where no accidents of this nature occur, he considers fifty years to be about the period required for teak to attain its full size. In the Malabar forests, he adds, sixty years has been found by experience to be the time required for teak to acquire its full size. But, there can be no doubt that the period will be found to vary much in different forests, and to depend greatly on the early treatment that the young tree meets with, either in the shape of cultivation or accident.

Dr. Brandis mentions (*Selection from the Re-*

cords of Government of India, Foreign Department, No. XXVIII. p. 56,) that teak belongs to that class of tropical trees, the wood of which is not uniform, but distinctly divided into concentric rings. It is evident that the growth of teak is not uniform, the yearly increase for the first six years being: $10\frac{3}{11}$ lines in diameter, that for the next sixteen years $5\frac{8}{11}$ lines in diameter. By interpolation and diminishing proportionately the yearly increase in the years after the age of 70, a more complete scale of the growth of teak had been obtained, the rate of growth, as calculated from his observations, in Calcutta and Moulmein, is slower than that given for the Tenasserim provinces in the plains, but more rapid than the growth of trees 1,100 feet above the sea.

TABLE. 2.

Statements of the measurement of a number of Teak trees of different ages.

Localities of the trees measured.	Number of trees measured.	Aggregate sum of these girths at 3 feet from the ground.	Average girth of one tree.	Average diameter of one tree.	Age of the tree.	Increase in one year. From the age of	To the age of.	In girth in inches.	In diameter in lines.
		ft. in.	Inches.	Inches.				..	..
H. C. Gardens, Calcutta,	19	25 4	16	5 1-11th	6	0	6	2¾	10 2-11ths
Private Garden, Moulmein,	15	48 94	40	12 8-11ths	22	6	22	1¼	8 8-11ths
H. C. Gardens, Calcutta,	8	52 8	79	25 3-22nds	70	22	70	1 3-16ths	3

Estimated average rate of growth of Teak in the forests of the Pegu, Tenasserim and Martaban Provinces.

Age of Trees. As assumed in report for 1856.	As at present assumed.	Girth of Tree at 6' from ground.	Diameter of Tree at 6' from ground.	Cubic contents of a pole 30' long calculated on the round log in cubic feet.	Annual increase of girth.	Average annual increase of timber in a pole 30 ft. long in cubic feet.	Corresponding age of other trees grown in Europe on good soil. Oak.	Beach.	Larch.	Age of Teak trees actually measured. Age.	Girth.	No.	Where measured.
Yrs.	Yrs.												
...	...	...	...	...	1·8	0·534	...	...	...	... 2	... 8	... 17	Thinganneennoung Teak Plantation, measured in 1858.
										6	1·4	9	Calcutta Botanic Gardens, measured in 1856.
										7	1·6	9	Near Punko Village Attaran, measured in 1856.
7	10	1·6	$5\frac{8}{11}$	5·34	1·5	1·35	23	17	17	14	1·2	...	Bombay Forest plains (communicated by Dr. Gibson.
										14	8	...	Do. Hills do.
18	2	3	$11\frac{5}{11}$	21·5	1·2	1·78	34	32	27	22	3·4	15	Maulmain Private Garden, measured in 1858.
										25	4·5	9	Sprouts from Stumps Kyoon Choung Forests, Attaran do.
										25	3.2	...	Java taken from Tunghuhu's work on Java, Vol I, p. 253.
40	37	4·6	$17\frac{2}{11}$	48·25	0·72	1·51	43	41	36	...	...	...	
62	62	6	$22\frac{10}{11}$	86·	0·45	1·20	56	56	43	70	6·7	8	Calcutta Botanic Gardens, measured in 1856.
										82	7·10½	4	Hundrow Forests in the plains, age calculated from No. of annual rings taken from summary of papers on Tenasserim Forests, page 106.
										93	6·9	6	Hundrow Forests in the Hills, do.
										100	12·6	...	Java, see above.
93	102	7·6	$28\frac{7}{11}$	134·25	0·30	0·98	68	76	70	216	10·7½	5	Hundrow Forests on the Hills (from summary of papers p. 106.
128	162	9	$34\frac{4}{11}$	193.25			115	89	110	246	12·8⅛	3	Do. do. do.

According to Dr. Brandis, the following is the rate of teak growth.

10 years growth,		18 inches at 6 feet from the ground.					
22	,,	,,	36	,,			
37	,,	,,	46	,,	,,	,,	,,
62	,,	,,					
93	,,	,,	76	,,	,,	,,	,,

Characters of Teak wood. Teak wood is of a brown colour and when fresh sawn has the fragrance of rosewood. It is very hard, yet light, is easily worked and though porous, is strong and durable. It is soon seasoned, it shrinks little and being of an oily nature, it does not injure iron. It is probably the most durable timber known and is therefore of great value to ship-builders. It is the best wood in south-eastern Asia for ship-timber, house carpentry, or other work where strong and durable wood is required. It is rarely attacked by white ants, and, from long experience, it is esteemed the most useful tree in South-eastern Asia,—superior to every other wood, whether in or out of water. And this durability as Mr. O'Riley observes renders it valuable in a climate like that of India, where the elements causing decay are so numerous and powerful, where dampness brings on rapid decomposition and the white ant devours without scruple. In general qualities, remarks Dr. Gibson, especially in endurance under exposure, it seems superior to all other Indian woods. Differences in quality, according to latitude, soil, or situation, are however very observable. It is commonly said that teak of the northern parts of the Bombay presidency is superior to that of Canara; that this again is of greater strength and endurance than the Malabar wood; and that the teak of Pegu is the worst of all. For these distinctions, he thinks, there is some foundation, but by no means to the extent alleged. He has seen some teak grown in the richer valleys of the northern Dang, inferior in strength and compactness of grain to that imported from the inland hilly parts of the southern peninsula, as, from the Annamallai forest, situated between Coimbatore and Malabar. There is, however, he adds, no doubt but that the eastern teak, from the Salem (?) and other rivers, is considerably inferior in strength and durability strength &c. to that of Malabar.

The *cohesive force* of teak wood varies from 13,000 to 15,000 pounds per square inch; the weight of its modulus of elasticity is 21,67,000 pounds per square inch, according to Mr. Barlow's experiments; and the weight of a cubic foot of seasoned wood, varies from 41 to 53 pounds. Representing the strength of oak by 100, that of teak will be,

the strength of oak by 100, that of teak will be,		109
Stiffness of oak by 100,	,,	126
Toughness of oak by 100,	,,	94

From which it appears that, except in toughness, it is much superior to oak in these properties, but these proportions are drawn from two or three experiments on teak, and probably were tried on very select specimens; whereas those for oak, were on a mean specimen, selected from pieces of oak of various qualities.

Dr. Brandis, moreover, tells us that the strength and density of the teak timber of British Burmah vary exceedingly, according to the locality where the trees grow. The extremes observed in preliminary experiments were 40 and 50 lbs. per cubic foot and 190 lbs. to 289 lbs. breaking weight. Mr. Rohde, who has paid much attention to these points, had frequently been struck with the want of strength in logs apparently sound, but had generally found the darkest veined wood the strongest. He says teaks will be found to differ in weight from thirty-nine pounds six ounces to fifty-two pounds fifteen ounces the cubic foot, when seasoned; and the heaviest, when green, were only fifty-seven pounds nine ounces the cubic foot. He had been told that some of the teaks from the Cochin forest weigh as much as sixty pounds the foot, when green. He adds, Major Campbell's experiments show that the weight of a cubic foot varies in the several specimens from 52 to 37 lbs., practical value of S. 92 to 51. In Dr. Wight's experiments, with Coimbatore teak, it was proved as regards the strength, as shown by the weight it was found capable of sustaining, that it is inferior to several other woods tried there. The average of 6 specimens was about, but under, 400 lbs. and Dr. Gibson remarks that, in strength, it is, as Dr. Wight observes, inferior to some other trees, of which Dalbergia Oojenenis or Tunnach may be mentioned as one. Mr. Edye remarked that the Malabar teak is considered the best, and is always most valued in the British Government dock yards, and it is now admitted that the teak in Malabar differs from that of the Annamallai.

Indeed, the varying qualities of the different teaks, have long been well known to practical men. The Malabar teak which grows on the western side of the ghat mountains has been generally esteemed the best and always preferred at the Government dock-yards. The second rate teak of Palghat was found by Colonel Frith of a light colour with a specific gravity of 0·852. The Ceylon teak, "Taikke Ceylemey" of Mr. Mendis, which grows in the western province of Ceylon, and is used there for bridges and buildings, weighs 44 lbs. per cubic foot, and was esteemed to last from 15 to 60 years. That kind is described as a rather hard, fine, close grained and somewhat heavy wood. He says of the Cochin teak "Taikke Cochini," which is used in Ceylon for carts and waggons, bridges, in building, and for arrack casks (and the wood of these casks imparts a fine colour and flavour to the arrack,) that it weighs lbs. 44 to the cubic foot and lasts from 15 to 90 years. Cochin teak is elsewhere described as a rather hard, though somewhat coarse and open grained, moderately heavy wood, of a lighter hue, rather coarser texture, and considerably more ponderous than the Moulmein teak. The hill teak of Tinnevelly, (qu ? kul teak ?) is described by Colonel Frith as of a light brown colour, and used for general purposes. The kullen teak of Travancore, is described as of a brown colour, and specific gravity 0·749, and as used for buildings, wheelwright's work, &c., and the kullen teak of Palghat, as of dark colour, as the best teak, and very strong and large. This kullen teak is perhaps identical with what Mr. McIvor describes as "kulteak," a variety of Tectona grandis, of the Wynaad about Sultan's Battery, as scarce, but considered superior to the common teak, and under the Tamil name oomy takoo maram, at Coimbatore, Dr. Wight felt, yet uncertain whether to view this as variety or a distinct species of teak. Specimens tested there proved very inferior in strength to the true teak, breaking with a weight of only 300 lbs., while the other sustained above 400.

Mr. Rohde tells us that the Godavery teak varies much in density : much of it is finely veined ; generally it is heavier than the Rangoon teak, but not equal to some from the Malabar coast. The dark or heavy teak of the mountains bordering on the Godavery is very little, if at all, inferior to that of Malabar, but a good deal of the Godavery teak is very open grained. The logs brought to market are always irregular in shape. Where strength, without any regard to size and shape, is required, the small heavy logs brought down by return bullock carts to Masulipatam may be used. There is a variety, says Dr. Roxburgh, which grows on the banks of the Godavery in the Deccan, of which the wood is beautifully veined, streaked and mottled, closer grained and heavier than the common teak tree, and which is well adapted for furniture. Some of the old trees have beautiful burrs, resembling the Amboyna wood, which are much esteemed. He had obtained an excellent specimen of the burr of the teakwood tree through the kindness of Dr. Horsfield, of the East India House.

Its value, says Mr. Edye, for the purposes of ship building, does not consist merely in its durability. A still greater advantage is that the ship is at all times ready for service, while ships of European wood, constructed with oak and fir, are constantly warping and crazy, and in forty-eight hours after the caulking of the top sides, are frequently as leaky as before. In such ships the health of the crew suffers, in consequence, at the change of the monsoon, from exposure to the damp of a tropical climate ; and, also, from this cause, the carpenters' crew are kept fully employed. But the teak ship, when well caulked, is always efficient for service, and dry and comfortable for the crew. Mr. Edye says that teak had been brought into use in the British Navy, at Bombay, Calcutta, and Cochin, and he gave the following list of ships of war, till that time, built of this timber : a list which could doubtless be now extended.

Ships of the Line.—Minden, Cornwallis, Melville, Malabar, Wellesley, Ganges, Asia, Bombay, Calcutta, Hastings.

Frigates.—Salsette, Amphitrite, Trincomallee, Seringapatam, Madagascar, Andromeda, Alligator, Samarang, Herald.

Sloops.—Victor, Cameleon, Sphynx, Cochin. It has been considered by many, that a ship built of this sort of wood would last good from thirty to fifty years, for which time, report says, many ships have been known to run in India. The old Milford, Bombay ship, in the country trade of India, was the oldest and best conditioned ship that ever came under Mr. Edye's notice. She had been, he says, built of teak timber about thirty-five years before he saw her ; she had been constantly at sea, and only had a small repair during that period. She was built of the Malabar teak.

This timber has been found ill adapted for gun carriages. Indeed, when it is observed how readily it splits, it is surprising that it has been for so many years applied to this purpose, especially for the felloes of the wheels. For ship building purposes, teak is superior to every other sort of wood, being light, strong and durable, whether in or out of water. (Note.—Lagerstrœmia microcarpa, or Benteak, is quite a different tree. Its wood is of light colour, specific gravity 0·591, inferior, and used for building and common carts. But, Dr. Gibson says Naneh or Benteak is brought to use in the Bombay dock-yard.—*Dr. Gibson*).

TABLE 3.

In one of Dr. Brandis' recent Reports he gives the following comparative Statement of the growth of Teak trees according to different observations.

Age of tree.	Yearly increase in girth.	Class.	1 Calcutta and Maulmein.		Under the supposition that one concentric ring corresponds to one year's increase. 2 The Attaran forests, in the plains.	3 The Houndrow forests 1,000 feet above the Sea.	Bombay forests. 4 In alluvial soil.	5 In the hills.	6 Java.
Diameter in inches.			Girth in	inches.	Girth in inches.	Girth in inches.	Gth. ins.	Gth. ins.	Gth. ins.
	"		"	"	"	"		"	"
0	2¾	I. Class. (0' 3' in girth.)	0	0	0	0	0	0	0
6			5 1-11th	16					
14	1¼		9 6-11ths	30	...	...	14	8	0
18		III. Class. (3' 4' 6' in girth.)	11 5-11ths	36	...	...	...	...	...
22			12 8-11ths	40	...	...	...	...	...
38	13/16		16 19-22ds	53	...	...	...	...	...
39		II. Class. (3' 4'6" to in girth.)	17	53 13-16hts					
40			17 7-22ds	54 10-16ths	...	...	...	...	...
61			22 15-22ds	71 5-16ths	...	...	...	...	...
62		I. Class. (above 6" in girth.)	2221-22ds	72 2-16ths	...	...	...	...	...
70			25 3-22ds	79	...	...	...	...	...
82			27 1 22d	85	94½	...	...	...	...
93			28 9-11ths	90½	...	2)81			
100			29 10-11ths	94	...	...	...	...	144
216			48 4-11ths	152	...	3)127¼	...	...	...
249			51 19-22ds	163	...	4)152¼	...	...	...

(1.) This number is obtained by taking the average of the data given in Nos. 1, 2, 4 and 5 of the table, page 106 of the "Report on the Teak forests of the Tenasserim provinces," viz., the average of the age and of the circumference of four trees respectively 82, 88, 86 and 80 years of age.

(2.) Obtained in similar manner from Nos. 6 to 12 of the same table.

(3.) Ditto ditto ditto Nos. 6, 8, 9, 10 and 13 of ditto.

(4.) Ditto ditto ditto Nos. 7, 11 and 12 of ditto.

In Mr. Edye's time, it was generally considered that there were three sorts of teak in use. And, first, that sort which grows to a very large size, is of an open, porous grain and very much resembles Dantzic oak : it is found in the forests at the foot of the ghats ; in valleys where the soil is deep and rich ; and on the banks of great rivers. On the bank of the Iruari river, near the ghats, about eighty miles from Cochin, he caused such a tree of teak to be felled. It was seven feet in diameter, and at seventy feet from the butt it was twenty-six inches in diameter. It was not deemed durable as timber; but, for planks and boards, such as the native carpenters use, it is preferred to any other of the small knotty woods.

It is a fact, he adds, which his experience in the country had taught him,* that all teak-timber, above twenty inches in diameter at the butt, has the heart shake from end to end, and consequently, requires much care to convert it to use; which

I

should be done by a saw-cut in the heart of the wood and then either of the two parts might be used as timber (A) or plank (B.)

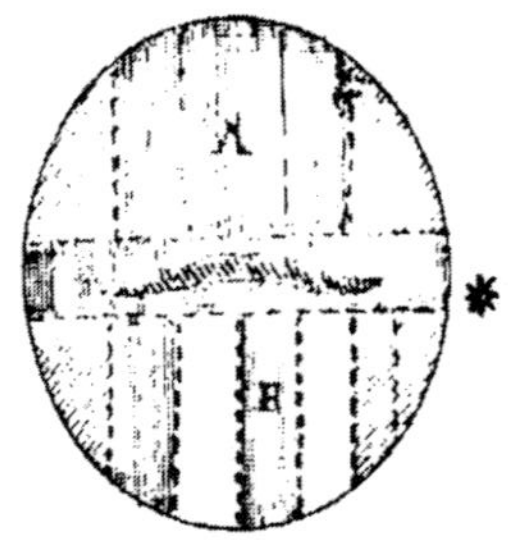

* Section of the tree 2½ feet diameter, with the heart shake shown. The dotted lines mark the best method for conversion by sawing it.

But teak generally grows straight, and, consequently, for the timber of a large ship its curve crosses the grain of the wood: the shake runs through the timber on the outside at the head and heel, and, in this inside, it follows the curve in the middle, nearly breaking through to the surface. This shake, if four or five inches broad and an inch or an inch and a half open in the heart of the timber, must be totally destructive to it; as must have been the case in the Minden seventy-four gun ship.

The next sort of teak on the coast, he says, is that which grows in the forests of the ghats. It is curved, hard and knotty, as the soil is not deep, its bed being rocky. This timber resembles in growth

2

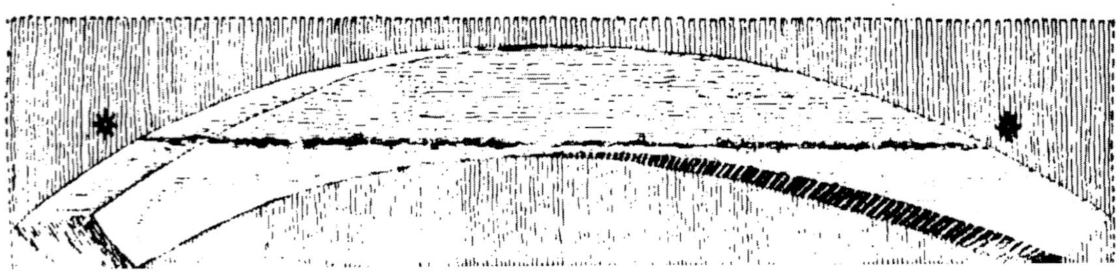

* Heart shake of a curved timber cut across the grain of the wood.

and appearance the English oak; its weight is very considerably more than that which grows to the large size; and the texture and durability of this timber is well known to those who are acquainted with the grain of woods.

The third sort of teak he continues, is procured from Pegu, Rangoon, Ava, and the Burmese territories. For ship building it is very inferior to that of Malabar. It is generally considered, by persons unacquainted with the nature of timber, that "the teak from that country is superior to any other in India," this is acknowledged by competent persons so far only as regards the size of the tree, and the free and clear grain of the wood. There can be no doubt that it is better for purposes of house building, and the general uses of the native carpenter, from the ease he finds in working

3

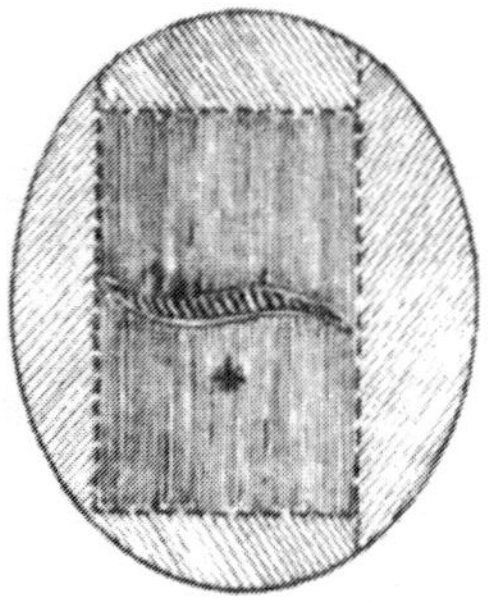

* The heart shake shown by the log being sided and converted from its full size.

J. [illegible] Rojoo. Del.

Lith.[d] by J. Dumphy, Govt. Lith. Press, Sept. 1862.

it. This timber, as well as that before described, grows in a rich deep soil, and, consequently, its maturity is rapid and its dimensions large; but the texture of the wood is as different from that of the forests of the ghats, as the American and Dantzic are from the English oak. At Rangoon and Pegu this timber is split in the heart shake into two parts, which the natives call shimbins, and this, Mr. Edye considers, shows the freeness of the grain of the wood. These pieces are priced according to their size; and this sort of teak is better known to the merchants and captains of the country trade than any other, on account of its use for the repairs of vessels, or as sea-shore timber."

Mr. Edye says the teak may be said to be the most valuable tree in India. It produces, he says, a good oil, which is used with paint as a substitute for linseed-oil; and which also makes a good varnish for paint or wood, and is known generally by the name of wood oil. The leaf of this tree is large and round, in shape resembling a cabbage-leaf, about ten inches in diameter, but very thin, although its fibres are strong. The blossoms and berries are produced in large bunches when in bloom, they may be compared to hops; when in seed, as to size, to a bunch of grapes. The nut is of a dark russet brown, and very hard; when ripe, it falls to the ground and plants itself. A forest patch of teak, when in full bloom, has much the appearance of a field of ripe corn when viewed from a distance, with a few spots of green interspersed; by this appearance the native hill people discover the trees of teak at this season, and cut around their roots to prevent the sap from ascending the next year. The persons who work the forests of teak on the side of the hills of western India, are thus able to distinguish at a distance those trees from the others, and cut them down for floating to the depôt there, which can only be done at the setting in of the monsoon, when the rapids fill the nallas; and then the tremendous torrents dash whatever may be thrown into them from one fall to another, from heights of fifty feet at a fall, until at last it reaches the depôt, having been brought down by a circuitous route of one hundred miles, from a height of from 1,000 to 2,000 feet above the level of the sea.

"Much, says Edye, might be said on the uses and durability of teak and foreign timber; but he adds it will be desirable to postpone that until its practical uses have been mentioned. Experience, he adds, proves that teak ships, if kept in India, or within the tropics, in actual service, would, at the end of seven or fourteen years, be in a better state than if kept in ordinary, subject to the changes of the climate of England. There cannot be a doubt that the climate and temperature of its native atmosphere is the most favourable to its durability. Its value, for the purposes of ship building does not, he says, consist merely in its durability; a still greater advantage is, that the ship is at all times ready for service, while ships of European wood, constructed with oak and fir, are constantly warping and crazy, and in forty-eight hours after the caulking of the top sides are frequently as leaky as before; the health of the crew-suffers, in consequence, at the change of the monsoon, from exposure to the damps of a tropical climate; and also, from this cause, the carpenters' crew are kept fully employed. But the teak ship, when well caulked, remains dry and comfortable to the crew and is always an efficient ship for service. The many contradictory reports of sailors on the state of ships of war on foreign stations, is to be placed to the want of knowledge of the true state of facts. It is well known in the dockyards that, by a continual caulking of the sides or decks of a ship, the wood is so completely compressed on the seams and edges of the plank by the caulking iron, that the oakum is forced through the seam into the ship, and that that seam can never be again caulked tight. From this cause, the oakum in the seam becomes wet and rotten; and the ship's crew are exposed to the injurious effects of inhaling the putrid air through the openings of the ship's timbers. The confined state of a ship under hatches in a tropical climate, is well known to all who have been on board one in the heavy tropical rains and gales of wind, when the monsoon sets in, and which lasts for days and weeks together."

Upon the whole, the Malabar teak seems the best. But that of Rangoon is lighter and more open and straight in the grain, and is preferred for masts and spars. It is also said that teak from Pegu, is of a lighter colour than that of the Peninsula of India But, in all these varying, and sometimes conflicting accounts, as to the strengths and weights of the teak woods grown in the several provinces of India, until we learn that the processes adopted, in killing, felling and seasoning, are similar, we shall not be in a position to judge as to the now reported differences. Major Morgan (Report 1861–2, para. 100) tells us that Malabar teakwood had been discontinued in Madras for the use of gun carriage wheels, by the superintendent, as it was found quite brittle. But he had explained to Colonel Maitland, and shown him that the manufactory must have been supplied with girdled teak. Good cross-grained Malabar teak, Major Morgan adds, is superior to any wood for wheels and the girdling of Teak, he says, has long ago been given up, as it makes the wood brittle and deprives it of its oil. Neverthless, writing in 1854, Dr. McClelland mentioned, as his opinion, that full grown timber requires to be killed at least two years before it is cut down, and in carrying this system out, he took the precaution, as early as November 1853, to have 800 full-sized trees killed in Thounzai forests, and 600 in the Oakkan forests; and, he adds, it will be necessary, without loss of time, to extend these provisions as far as the resources of the forests will safely allow, (*Selec. Records of Govt. of India, Foreign Department, No. IX. p.* 24.) Still more recently, (in para. 32 and 41, pages 11 and 13, *Selec. Govt. of India, No. XXVIII,*) we find the following course of operations laid down :—

1. "*Marking.*—All trees measuring 6 feet in girth and above in the first division, will be marked in 1857 in such a manner that the marks shall remain visible for 24 years.

2. "*Girdling.*—One fourth of the trees thus marked, will be girdled immediately by a circular cut through the bark, about one inch into the wood.

"The trees will always be allowed to stand three years before felling, which is one year longer than what is generally considered to be sufficient for seasoning in this climate.

"We must, for the present, therefore, limit our improvements to the rule which already forms an artilce of every forest contract concluded for this and the next year ; viz., that no tree, the lower part of which is not hollow, is to be felled higher than one cubit from the ground. And first, we must mention a few circumstances, that will tend to increase the number of trees to be girdled and felled. All trees of whatever size they may be, that show evident signs of decline and decay must be girdled at once. For trees that are beginning to be Nathat, this measure is desirable, because the timber of a Nathat tree is always inferior in appearance, and often in quality, to that of a sound tree. For those trees that show signs of decline from having been attacked by a parasitic ficus, which is particularly destructive to teak trees in this country, (Pegu) this measure necessary, if we wish to save their timber from destruction, as the timber therefore of a tree killed by a parasitic ficus is of little or no value.

Also, all isolated trees must be spared, in order to obviate a want of seedlings in places to which the seeds of other trees could not be carried by natural causes." Thus in the Pegu Province the girdling of teak seems to be in full operation.—*Dr. Brandis, Selec. from the Records of Govt. of India, No. XXVIII, p.* 10 *and* 13.

Uses.—Teak is used in house building, for beams, for furniture of every description, and largely in ship-building. In the Madras gun carriage manufactory, it is used for all parts of light field carriages (except the beams) ; waggons and their limbers (except poles and splinter bars) ; also for heavy field and garrison carriages ; garrison traversing platforms ; for gun and mortar platforms ; and for all parts of heavy and light mortar carts ; store carts (with the exception of poles and splinter bars) : platform, line, and water carts ; gins, and wheel work ; heavy and light field ammunition boxes : transport carriages and limbers and furniture work.—*Drs. Roxburgh, Wight, Falconar, Mason, McClelland, Gibson, Cleghorn and Brandis ; Mr. Edye, Mr. Rohde, Mr. Earl, Mr. E. O'Riley ; Cal. and Mad. Cat. Ex.* 1862, *Madras Proc. Ex.* 1851, *Major Morgan, Captain Sankey.*

TECTONA TERNIFOLIA, Buch.

Tectona Hamiltonia, *Wall.*

This species of teak grows on the banks of the Irrawaddy, at Segaen, Prome, Ava, and at the foot of Taong-Dong, and, from native descriptions, Dr. Mason imagines it is found in the province of Yay. It flowers in March, its wood is inferior to that of T. grandis.—*Dr. Mason, Voigt.*

TEE KA LOUNG or THA-KA-DAT-GHEE, Burm. A timber tree of maximum girth 3 cubits, maximum length 22½ feet. Abundant at Mergui and Tavoy. When seasoned it floats in water. It is used for bedsteads, and for house building. Recommended as a durable, tough wood for helves or for hammer handles.—*Captain Dance.*

TEKKEER ATTOVYE ANJELLY, Tam. A wood of Travancore, of a brown colour, specific gravity 0·528, 4 to 6 feet in circumference, used for house and ship building.—*Colonel Frith.*

TELEGA, Tel. A wood of the Godavery forests and Dekhan. (Gardenia, *species* ?) Wood very hard, would be very good for turning.—*Captain Beddome.*

TELEYA, Hind.? A tree of Chota Nagpore with a soft, red wood.—*Cal. Cat. Ex.* 1862.

TELLE or PAYANE, the Tamil and Malayala names of a tree on the Malabar coast and Travancore, about sixty feet in height, and two feet and half in diameter. It is an inferior sort of "*pine,*" and is named by natives Dupi maram. It produces an inferior sort of damah, or resin, which is boiled down with cocoanut oil. When thus prepared, it is a substitute for pitch or resin, but very inferior. The wood is used for the masts of pattamahs, catamarans, canoes, &c., but it is not durable.—*Edye, Forests of Malabar and Canara.* (*Qu. ?* Is this a Shorea or a Vateria ?)

TENBOW or Black Heart Wood. Grows in the Malabar forests to about eighteen inches in diameter, and from twenty-five to thirty-five feet in height. It is considered by carpenters a useful wood for general purposes, in house building, and for native vessels and implements of agriculture —*Edye, Forests of Malabar and Canara.*

TENASSERIM. The name of this province of the Empire has now merged into the more comprehensive term of British Burmah. But, the first edition of the Reverend Dr. Mason's invaluable work, was styled Tenasserim, and it seems suitable to give, here, the names of the timber trees which he noticed. They are as under :—

Tectona grandis.	Lagerstrœmia Reginæ.
Tectona Hamiltonia.	Grewia.
Bassia longifolia.	Calophyllum.
Inga xylocarpa.	Garcinia.
Fagrœa fragrans.	Gordonia floribunda.
Diospyros, *sp.*	,, integrifolia.
Diospyros, *sp.*	Bruguiera Rheedii.
Bauhinia, *sp.*	Rhizophora gymnorrhiza.
Swietenia mahogani.	Careya arborea.
Pterocarpus Wallichii.	Artocarpus echinatus.
,, dalbergioides.	Myristica amygdalina.
Syndesmis Tavoyana.	,, sphærocarpa.
Vatica robusta.	Bignonia.
Vatica, *sp.*	Sonneratia acida.
,, ,,	Laurus.
Hopea odorata.	Kyanan.
Vateria lanceolata.	Maybgoung.
Dipterocarpus lævis.	Casuarina muricata.
Dipterocarpus grandiflora.	Heritiera minor.
Dipterocarpus, *sp.*	Berrya ammonilla.
Terminalia.	Laurus (Sassafras.)
Vitex arborea.	Odina wodier.
Gmelina arborea.	Erythrina indica.
Cedrela toona.	Erythrina, *sp.*
Acacia sirissa.	Laurus.
,, stipulata.	Yamanee.
Acacia odoratissima.	Elœocarpus.
Dalbergia.	Dalbergia latifolia.
Quercus fenestrata.	Apocynaceæ.
,, turbinata.	Murraya.
,, velutina.	Zalacca edulis.
,, Amherstiana.	Agathis loranthifolia.
,, Tirbbæ. ? ? ?	Pinus Latteri.

These, adds Dr. Mason, are among more than a hundred trees in the Tenasserim provinces that furnish valuable woods, of which the selection of fifty or sixty would embrace the most useful.—*Dr. Mason.*

Mr. E. O'Riley remarks that the useful kinds of timber which abound in the forests, in addition to teak, are very numerous; many of these possess qualities superior to that timber in regard to durability under exposure to alternations of heat and moisture: and, unlike teak, when used as posts for houses, several are impervious to the attack of the white ant; their specific gravity, exceeding, for the greater part, that of water and their excessive hardness, forming the principle obstacles to their being more generally known. The principle trees are the following: some of them classed by Dr. Wallich, in his notice of the forests of these provinces.

1 Anan.	7 Padouk. Pterocarpus.
2 Thengan Hopea odorata.	8 Theet, kha.
3 Peengado Acacia.	9 Toung baing.
4 Bambwai.	10 Yin-dic or Bastard ebony.
5 Peemah: Lagerstrœmia.	11 Kuzee-tha, similar to Boxwood in grain.
6 Kouk H'moo.	

Several others of small dimensions are in general use with the natives for household and other useful purposes requiring a hard and close grained material.

Of the foregoing, he adds, the "Anan" stands pre-eminent in its characteristics as a forest tree of the largest dimensions, its straightness and freedom from internal decay, and more especially in its indestructibility under all circumstances of useful appliance. A specimen of this wood had been brought to Mr. O'Riley's notice which, for 60 years had formed the supports of a native bridge over a creek in his vicinity; embedded in mud and exposed to the alternations of wet and dry during each tide, it had undergone no change beyond the decay of the sap parts immediately below the bark, the posts of the bridge consisting of young trees cut on the spot and so applied at once. This unexampled durability renders the Anan of these provinces a valuable article for railway purposes; and, should the attention of parties be directed to it, the supplies to be obtained from these forests alone for railway sleepers are unlimited; it would also be found to answer admirably for such ship building purposes as to require extra strength and durability, and would afford the finest keel-pieces in the world.

Bambwai and Peengado possess the same property as Anan in resisting decay, but are less abundant, denser in grain, abound in knots and are smaller in size than that timber: they are, however, prized by the natives for their useful properties, and are with Thengan generally used in the whole tree as posts for monasteries, houses, &c.

The wood in most general use for almost all purposes, but principally for large canoes, which form the bottoms of the native trading crafts, is Thengan, this is owing to its being more plentiful than most of the others, easily worked; and, by killing the tree before felling as with teak, is rendered capable of floating; this process however is rarely observed, the tree selected for working is felled and hollowed on the spot, and the canoe removed to the neighbourhood of the water to undergo the process of widening by fire, some trees producing by this rude process canoes of 60 to 70 feet long by 6 to 8 feet breadth across the centre.

"Kouk h'moo," "Toung being" and "Theet kha" are also much sought after by the natives for boats, the former is also well adapted for spars for vessels, being straight, light, of large dimensions, and of long fibre.

"Toung being" is equally lasting with Thengan, but scarcer than the latter and of sizes to afford a large canoe.

"Theet kha" is a light timber, easily worked and, from its possessing the valuable property of being exempt from the attack of the "teredo," is in great request for small canoes: it is a scarce tree however. In common with "Theet kha," both "Anan" and "Peengado" are impervious to the destructive attack of the "teredo," the two latter may possess such property as the consequence of their closeness of fibre and extreme hardness, but the same reason cannot be applied to "Theet kha" from its opposite characteristics. In the latter case it is owing, in all probability, to the existence of some acrid principle in the wood (implied by its name " bitter wood") which, similar to oxide of iron, has the effect of repelling the insect.

" In the construction of wharfs and embankments on the river face, both " Anan" and " Peengado" would be found valuable for posts, and if proper care be observed in the selection of the timber and in freeing it from all the sap portions of the tree it would doubtless prove as lasting as brickworks.

" Padouk" affords a fine timber for many purposes, and from its large size and even texture has been brought into general notice. Several experiments have been made in the ordnance department of Madras to ascertain its fitness for gun carriages, but with what result, Mr. O'Riley was unable to state. As a substitute for teak, should it be found to answer for the above stated and other purposes, it is valuable, and from its large size, its even grain, rendering it susceptible of a high polish, and beauty of colour and pattern, it appears to be well suited to the manufacture of articles of furniture.

" The foregoing are the most generally known woods of the forests in common use with the natives, but to them might be added a list of forty to fifty others more or less useful. Of the remaining forest trees and shrubs the following possess valuable properties, adapted to a demand for Europe consumption.

Sapan wood, Caesalpinia, Teni-yeit, BURM.
Jack, Artocarpus, Teingnay, BURM.
Red-dye, Morinda citrifolia, Neepatsay.

" For many years past, a trade in Sapan wood from Mergui to Dacca has been prosecuted by the native boats, the article being obtained from the Sapan wood forests lying near the frontier hills, from the Eastern side of which large supplies are annually imported through Bangkok into Singapore. It is also found throughout the valley of the Great Tenasserim river and is said by the Karens to be plentiful in the vicinity of the head waters of the ' Hoin bwai,' and ' Dagyne.' In isolated patches it is found generally distributed throughout the whole provinces.

" The dye obtained from the wood of the ' Jack,' as prepared by the natives, is a brilliant orange yellow, which is obtained by the addition of an infusion made from the leaves of the ' Don-yat' producing a brilliancy of color not excelled by the best English dyers. The new sacerdotal dress of the Poongyees evince the effect of this process ; and were a specimen of the dyed article sent home it would be found to surpass most of the British range of dyes of its class, and as a process not requiring the application of any of the metallic bases as a mordant, would doubtless become an article of enquiry and consequent standard value.

" The red dye obtained from the roots of the Mordina citrifolia is equal in every respect to that of the Sapan wood ; it is in fact in general use with the natives for dyeing the yarn of the native cloths, both silk and cotton ; and with the exception of some specimens of Java dyes obtained from the same tree, I have rarely seen better single colors of the kind ; it must be borne in mind in relation to such a comparison, that the use of mineral mordant in the native process is unknown, and with the exception of weak leg made from the ashes of some of the animals of the jungles no other application is made beyond the simple solution of the extract from the wood itself."—*Dr. Mason's Tenasserim, Mr. E. O'Riley in Journ. Ind. Arch.*

TENG-KHAT, BURM. ? This is a heavy wood of Amherst, solid and fit for turning purposes ; used for rice-pounders, &c.—*Cat. Ex.* 1851.

TENTUKIE, the Malayala name of a Ceylon tree which grows to about twelve or eighteen inches in diameter, and twelve feet high : it cannot be considered valuable. It is sometimes used by the natives for inferior and common purposes.—*Edye, on the Timber of Ceylon.*

TENTOOLLEE OR KOYAN, URIA ? In Ganjam, the common tamarind tree ?—*Captain Macdonald.*

TETRANTHERA. A genus of plants, belonging to the Lauraceæ.

T. apetala, Roxb., Kookoor chita, Beng., is a tree of peninsular India, Bengal and Assam, and in the northern part of New Holland.

T. Gardneri, Thw. A tree 40 to 50 feet high of the central province of Ceylon, at an elevation of 4,000 to 6,000 feet.

T. glaberrima, Thw., a small Ceylon tree, at 4,000 feet elevation.

Also, may be mentioned, T. longifolia, T. ligustrina, T. iteodaphne, small or moderate sized trees of Ceylon. T. monopetala of peninsular India, and Oude, the *Buro-kukur chettu* of the Bengalese, the Nara chettu of Telingana and *Jungli Rai Am* of Hindustan, also T. nemoralis, and T. ovalifolia of Ceylon, the last a tree 30 to 40 feet high, with T. Roxburghii of India and Ceylon, the Bo-mee gass of the Singhalese.—*Voigt, Thwaites.*

TETRANTHERA NITIDA, *Roxb.*

A useful timber tree which grows in Assam, in the Garrow hills, from which canoes full fifty feet long are made.—*Voigt.*

TERMINALIA. This genus of plants is found in the tropical parts of Asia and America, and many of them furnish valuable timber and other useful products. The bark of Terminalia arjuna is used in India, in medicine, for its astringency, and in dyeing as that of Bucida buceros in Jamaica, and that of Terminalia benzoin in the Isle of France. The galls found on the leaves of T. chebula, are powerfully astringent, and used in dyeing yellow and black, the ripe fruit of T. bellerica is reckoned astringent, and that of T. Moluccana is like it. That of T. chebula, in an unripe state, and of different ages (v. Fleming, As. Res. XI, p. 182, 8vo.), has long been known under the names of black, yellow, and chebulic (Kaboolee from Cabool) myrobolans, and considered generally laxative. The fruit of T. citrina, as well as of T. angustifolia and T. Gangetica is like that of T. chebula, and employed for the same purposes. The kernels of T. catappa have the same hindi-persian name, "badam" applied to them, as to those of the common almond, they are eaten as such, and are very palatable; Dr. Royle had seen the tree as far north as Allahabad, in gardens. The kernels of T. Moluccana, and those of T. bellerica are also eaten. From the latter a gum exudes, as from Combretum alternifolium in south America: a milky juice is described as flowing from T. benzoin, *Linn. f.*, which, being fragant on drying, and resembling benzoin, is used in churches in the Mauritius as a kind of incense.—*Royle, Ill. Him. Bot., p.* 209.

TERMINALIA, *Species*. Thuphanga, BURM. A Tavoy timber tree.—*Wall.*

TERMINALIA, *Species*. Dr. Mason says, that the Tenasserim province yields the T. chebula, and two other species. One of these he describes as "the bitter wood of Tenasserim," (is it the Theet kha?) a small tree, used for boats in the neighbourhood of Amherst, and exempt from the attack of the teredo. Mr. Mason had never seen the tree, but its leaves and fruit were furnished to him by Mr. O'Riley, and they indicate it to be a species of terminalia, and of the section pentaptera. The good timber, and bitter bark assimilate it to Roxburgh's *P. Arjuna*, but the foliation is different.

The other species, a large timber tree, is common in the interior, and its winged fruit indicates its connection with Dr. Roxburgh's genus pentaptera.—*Dr. Mason's Tenasserim.*

TERMINALIA, *Species*. Hanagal, CAN. A Mysore wood, used for furniture and house building.—*Captain Puckle in Mad. Cat. Ex.* 1862.

TERMINALIA, *Species*. Kosee, TEL. A tree of Ganjam and Gumsur, extreme height 50 feet, circumference 4 feet, and height from ground to the intersection of the first branch, 22 feet. Used for posts, door frames and rafters, and burnt for firewood, being tolerably plentiful. —*Captain Macdonald.*

TERMINALIA, *Species*. Orjoono, TEL. Terminalia alata? T. glabra? A tree of Ganjam, extreme height 100 feet, circumference 8 feet and height from ground to the intersection of the first branch, 36 feet. This is used for making boats in the same way as the Holondho and Jamo. The tree is not very common in Gumsur, but abounds in the forests of Bodogoda.—*Captain Macdonald.*

TERMINALIA ALATA, *Ainslie, W. Ic.* 195.

Terminalia tomentosa, *Roxb.*

Kura-marthi mara. CAN.	Keenjul? MAHR.
Jungli karinj. DUK.	Kunjul? „
Maroodum tree. ANGLO-TAM.	Arjuna?? SANS.
Asan? HIND.	Kumbuk? SINGH.
Jungly karinj. „	Marudum maram. TAM.
Urjun??? „	Muddi chettu. TEL.

The bark.

Marudum bark. ENG.	Marudum pattai. TAM.
Arjuna. SANS.	Muddie patta. TEL.

A very large tree of the peninsula of India from Coimbatore north to Chota Nagpore? furnishing a useful timber which is employed, on the western coast, for house building and making canoes. Dr. Wight had not seen it in use in the Coimbatore district. He says that the tree only differs externally, from the Curri-murdah (Terminalia glabra?) by being hairy. Dr. Gibson seems to have been doubtful as to the identity of the tree, indicated by Dr. Wight, for, he thus remarks:—"Terminalia alata(?) Pentaptera paniculata, Keenjul (?) I believe that our Keenjul is here meant. It is common to the south, but not known to the northward. Wood is equal to the common Aeen. The Aurora cruiser was built of this wood." The wood of which a specimen was sent from Chota Nagpore to the Exhibition of 1862, as that of the Terminalia alata? T. tomentosa or Asan, HIND.? was described as a hard, brown timber.—*Drs. Wight and Gibson, Cal. Cat. Ex.* 1862.

TERMINALIA ANGUSTIFOLIA, *Jacq.*

Terminalia benzoin, *Linn.*
Catappa „ *Gærtn.*

Narrow leaved Terminalia. ENG.

The dried milky juice of this small tree is fragrant and resembles benzoin, for which it is used as a substitute in the Mauritius churches. Its fruit is used similarly to those of Terminalia chebula.—*Voigt.*

TERMINALIA ARJUNA, *W. & A.*

Pentaptera arjuna, *Roxb.*

Arjun. BENG.	Urjen. HIND.
Touk-kyan. BURM.	Kahua. „
Belee waulkee. CAN.	Kowah. „ of Jubbulpore.
Urjuna. DUK.	Arjoon. MAHR.
Urjun-sadra? DUK.	Sadura. „
White aeen. ANGLO-HIND.	Azun. „
Arjun. HIND.	

This tree grows in Bengal and in the Erra-waddi jungles S. E. of Surat. It grows in Canara and Sunda, but only by rivers and streams mostly below the ghats, and reaches, there, an immense size. As a forest tree, Dr. Gibson tells us, it is rare in the northern parts of the Bombay side, but very common in the south Konkan, from Ramghur southward and there, too, always found in the vicinity of streams and rivers. It reaches, everywhere, a very large size, and is esteemed equal to the Black Aeen, though the rapidity of its growth would hardly countenance this opinion. In the Nagpore territories, according to Captain Sankey, it grows, almost exclusively, on the banks of rivers, and to an enormous size; but, being in that province frequently rotten at the heart, it does not always reward the labour of cutting. In Pegu, Dr. McClelland mentions that next to teak, the most valuable kinds of timber found in abundance, in the southern forests of Pegu, are *Pentaptera glabra*, and *P. arjuna*, which present clean trunks of six to eight feet in diameter, and fifty to eighty feet high, without a branch; they would afford excellent mast-pieces and spars for naval purposes, and might be tried for gun carriages. Dr. Mason says, this valuable timber is found growing in all the teak forests of Pegu, and consists of two kinds, both of equal value. He adds, that its wood is dark brown, and the timber is as strong as teak and usually attains a girth of from seven to nine feet, with height in still more lofty proportion. This timber had never, he believes, been fairly tried for ship-building. In Nagpore, the timber of Arjoon is of a deeper red than Bejasar, more of a brown red. It is heavy, but splits freely when exposed to the sun's rays, white ants attack it seeming to prefer moist situations. Its strength is undoubted, and carefully selected specimens would, Captain Sankey thinks, be valuable. He classes it as a tie beam and rafter wood. In Nagpore, the length of the timber is from 18 to 30 feet, and girth from 4½ to 4 feet, and it sells there at 5½ annas the cubic foot. The bark is justly celebrated as an application to wounds.—*Voigt, Drs. Gibson, McClelland and Mason, Captain Sankey.*

(*Note*—Pentaptera arjuna ? Two specimens of woods of somewhat different character, were sent from Jubbulpore to the Exhibition of 1862, labelled as from this tree: thus

Saj, HIND. ? *Terminalia arjuna ?* A tree of Jubbulpore, timber very useful for beams and rafters, grows abundantly in all the districts to a great size, 40 to 50 feet long, and 2 to 3 feet broad, will not last if exposed to the weather.—*Cal. Cat. Ex.* 1862.

Kowah. HIND. ? *Terminalia arjuna ?* A tree of Jubbulpore, grows to a large size along the banks of rivers, all over the district; is an excellent lasting timber, somewhat similar in quality to ash.—*Cal. Cat. Ex.* 1862. (*Note.*—What are these two trees ?)

TERMINALIA BELERICA, *Roxb.; Cor. Pl; Rheede.*

Terminalia punctata, *Roth.* ?
Myrobalanus bellerica. ?

Beleyluj. AR.	Booloo-gass. SINGH.
Buhura. BENG.	Tandi maram. TAM.
Tit-seim. ? BURM.	Tani kaia maram. TAM.
Bulla. DUK.	Tonda maram. „
Bellerie myrobalan. ENG.	Cattu elupa. „
Beheyra ? HIND.	Tondi chettu. TEL.
Berda. MAHR.	Tadi chettu. „
Yehela. „	Katthu elupæ. „
Tani. MALEAL.	Bahadha. „
Beleyleh. PERS.	Bahadrha. „
Bahira. SANS.	

This very large forest tree has a straight trunk and a spreading head: the flowers have an offensive smell. It grows in Ceylon, up to an elevation of 2,000 feet, on the open grassy plains, and it is found in the peninsula of India and in Pegu. In Coimbatore, the tree is not uncommon in the Walliar jungles, but is considered of no value there. The wood is white and soft and though said by Dr. Roxburgh to be durable, it is not much used in that district. (It is conjectured by Dr. Wight that a large tree, of the same vernacular name in Malabar, which is hollowed out for canoes, which however are said not to be lasting and is perhaps the T. Berryi, which also attains a large size and is more nearly allied to the Karri murdah (Terminalia glabra ?) as belonging to the same section of the genus.) In the Bombay Presidency, this is one of the largest and finest looking trees in the forest and is found abundantly both in all the inland and the coast jungles but, although straight, and of great scantling, it is quite useless as a building timber, being immediately attacked by worms. In Ganjam and Gumsoor it is said by Captain Macdonald to be a tolerably common tree; it attains an extreme height of 50 feet, and from the ground to the intersection of the first branch, is 10 feet. The wood is said to be of no use there, but its fruit is used medicinally. It is common, Dr. Brandis tells us, throughout British Burmah, but the wood is not used. A cubic foot weighs lbs. 40, in a full grown tree on good soil, there, the average length of the trunk to the first branch is 80 feet and average girth measured at 6 feet from the ground is 12 feet.—*Drs. Wight, Gibson, Brandis, McClelland and Cleghorn, Captain Macdonald. Voigt.* (*Note.*—From these remarks, there seems some confusion as to this tree and its timber or its timber varies according to the place of growth. Dr. McClelland says that in the Pegu, Tounghoo, and Tharawaddy forests, it is a large timber tree with a white coloured wood, and would answer for all purposes of house building. Particular attention seems desirable, to ascertain the character of this wood.)

TERMINALIA BERRYI, *W. & A.*

Pentaptera angustifolia, *Roxb.*

Vellay murdah wood. ANGLO-TAM.	Vellai marudu. TAM.
	Vallay murdah maram. TAM.

This is a tree of the peninsula of India, which attains a very large size, especially at the foot of the western ghats, where it is used for canoes. It is not indigenous in the Bombay forests, and has been introduced into Coimbatore. The bark is quite smooth and nearly as green as the leaves. The wood is white, described as of ordinary quality, but used on the Malabar coast for canoes and for making the broad wooden platters in use among fishermen and ship lascars.—*Drs. Wight, Gibson, Voigt.*

TERMINALIA BIALATA, *Wall.*

Pentaptera bialata, *Roxb.*

Lein. BURM.

A tree of the mountainous parts of India, common in British Burmah and growing in Martaban, but the wood is not used. A cubic foot weighs lbs. 39. In a full grown tree on good soil the average length of the trunk to the first branch is 80 feet, and average girth measured at 6 feet from the ground is 12 feet.—*Voigt, Dr. Brandis, Cal. Cat. Ex.* 1862.

TERMINALIA CATAPPA, *Linn.; Roxb.; W. & A.; Rheede.*

Terminalia Moluccana, *Lam.*	Terminalia intermedia, *Spr.*
Terminalia myrobalana, *Roth.*	Juglans catappa, *Lour.*
Terminalia subcordata, *Willd.*	

Badam. BENG.	Catappa. MALAY.
Badam. DUK.	Ada maram. MALEAL.
Indian almond tree. ENG.	Ingudi SANS.
Country almond tree. „	Nattu vadom maram. TAM.
Bengal almond tree. „	Vadom. TEL.
Badami. HIND.	Badam chettu. „
Bengali badam. MAHR.	Badama „ „

The fruit.

Badam-i-hindi. DUK.	Natta vadom cottay. TAM.
Hinghudie. SANS.	Badome vittulu. TEL.

A beautiful tree common in the gardens of Europeans and Natives, of the Madras and Bombay presidencies. It attains a large size in Malabar, where the wood is much esteemed, and in the forests of the Godavery, it is said to be very strong. Dr. Gibson, however, says that the wood does not appear to him to be of average quality or fit either for public or domestic purposes, except as firewood. The English in India call it the Indian almond tree with reference to the oval and flattened shape of its fruit. The kernel, however, is cylindrical, it is eaten and palatable. Mr. Latham says, in Nalla mallai, it is a serviceable wood chiefly used as posts. Its colour is yellowish brown and it has a close grain. Captain Beddome says that as it occurs in the forests of the Godavery, the wood is very strong, and Voigt says the wood is good.—*Useful Plants, Voigt, Drs. Gibson, Wight and Cleghorn, Captain Beddome.*

TERMINALIA CHEBULA, *Retz.; W. & A.; Roxb.*

Terminalia reticulata, *Roth. in Useful Plants.*
Terminalia myrobalanus citrina, *Kœn, in do.*

Heliji Kabule. AR.	Hara. HIND.
Hari tuki BENG.	Umbed her. ? „
Kya zu ? BURM.	Heerda. MAHR.
Kayubin ? „	Heari. „
Pang ah. ? „	Kodorka maram. MALEAL.
Pilla-marrada. CAN.	Helileh-i-kalan. PERS.
Alali mara. „	Haritaka. SANS.
Alli mara. „	Aralu-gssa. SINGH.
Allibi kai mara. „	Pilla murda. TAM.
Hirda. DUK.	Kadukai maram. „
Huldah. „	Karaka chettu. TAM.
Pilla murda wood. ANGLO-CAN.	Karakaia chettu. „
Hordah. GOND.	Karkata sringi. „
Har. HIND.	Koreda. „

This tree grows in Ceylon, in both the peninsulas of India and northwards to Nepaul, and every where is a large tree; in Coimbatore, it is of gigantic size, furnishing planks three feet broad. There, its wood is of a dark colour, heavy and hard, sustaining a weight of about lbs. 400, but is very cross grained, and difficult to work. In Canara and Sunda, it abounds above the ghats, and the wood it yields is of average quality for houses. In the Bombay jungles it is more rare than on high table land on and near the ghauts. The wood there, also, is strong, and rather hard, but on that side of India it does not reach any great size, and is generally gnarled, owing to the exposed situations in which it grows. Also, Dr. Gibson is of opinion that in describing it as a most gigantic tree, Dr. Wight must have confounded the wood of Terminalia bellerica with that of this tree. Captain Beddome says its timber from the Godavery is very hard. In Ganjam and Gumsur, where it is tolerably plentiful, its extreme height is 45 feet, circumference 4½ feet, and its height from the ground to the insersection of the first branch is 20 feet, and it is employed for the beams and rafters of houses, but chiefly for firewood, on account of its abundance. On the Godavery it is said to yield a very hard valuable timber. In Nagpore, according to Captain Sankey, the average size of its timber is 16 feet with a girth of 4½ feet, and it sells there at 5¼ annas per cubic foot. There, the Hurda has a yellowish colored wood which becomes very dark on the outside in the process of seasoning, it is attacked by white ants, and is inferior in strength to teak, appears to have but little essential oil, and is said to be very subject to dry rot. Its value is principally from the ease with with which it works. According to Dr. McClelland, in Pegu, it is a large timber tree, plentiful throughout the teak forests, and yielding wood of a red colour strong, adapted for house building. Dr Brandis adds that it is common on the hills of British Burmah, and gives a valuable wood used for yokes and canoes, the heartwood being yellowish brown. A cubic foot weighs lbs. 53. In Pegu, in a full grown tree on good soil the average length of the trunk to the first branch is 80 feet and the average girth measured at 6 feet from the ground is 12 feet. It sells there at 12 annas per cubic foot. Dr. Cleghorn says that when used as sleepers for railways, in Southern India, it appears to be liable both to the attacks of fungi and of the carpenter bee. Its fruit is used by tanners. The leaves are punctured by an insect, and hollow galls are developed, which are powerfully astringent, and answer well for tanning and making ink. They also yield, for chintz painters and carpet weavers, their best and most durable yellow. (Roxb.) The fruit which is largely exported is well known for its dyeing properties, yielding also a black dye, and is substituted for gall nuts. It is also used medicinally. The astringent bark is also said to be employed in tanning. The fruit and galls are used by dyers and harness makers: with alum they give a durable yellow, with ferruginous mud, an excellent black, and they make useful ink. The unripe fruit are known as black, yellow and chebulic (*Kabuli*) myrobalans from their colours, which vary so, according to age.—*Drs. Gibson, Wight, McClelland and Brandis, Captain Macdonald, Voigt, Thwaites, Captain Beddome, Mr. Latham and Captain Sankey.*

TERMINALIA CITRINA, *Roxb.* ?

Myrobalanus citrina, *Gærtn.*

Huri tuki. BENG.

A very large and tall timber tree of Assam and the Khassya hills. The wood is very hard and shunned by insects. The fruit is used as that of T. chebula.—*Voigt, Roxb., Fl. Ind. Vol. II, p.* 436.

TERMINALIA CORIACEA, *W. & A.*

Pentaptera coriacea, *Roxb.*

Mairthee. CAN.	Aeen. MAHR.
Muddi. ,,	Arremuti maram. TAM.
Muttee. ,,	Karra maradu. TAM.
Ayni. ,, of N. Can.	

A large tree of peninsular India, and very common in Malabar, both above and below the ghauts. The wood, there, is very durable, and is used in house, ship, and boat building. In Canara and Sunda, it is the most common tree in the large jungles both above and below the ghats, and is there used for beams and pillars for houses: also for ships and boats. The heart wood is one of the most durable known. It seems to be regarding this tree that Dr. Gibson speaks when he mentions that several of the forest revenue officers have expressed their opinion that the exporting of Aeen for "keeta" or firewood, should be prohibited. It is employed by the Telegraph department for posts, along with sal and teak. It is a valuable, well known timber tree of the Godavery forests. It seems to be this wood to which Dr. Gibson alludes when he remarks that it has small dull yellow flowers, and its wood is strong, hard and heavy, and made into solid wheels for buffaloe carts.—*Drs. Gibson and Cleghorn, Forests and Gardens, p.* 267, *Voigt, p.* 38, *Captain Beddome.* (*Note*—The Aeen or Ayni of Malabar, is the Artocarpus hirsata.)

TERMINALIA GANGETICA, *Roxb.*

A tree of the banks of the Ganges.—*Roxb., Vol. II, p.* 437.

TERMINALIA GLABRA, *W. & A.*

Terminalia crenulata, *D. C.?*
Pentaptera glabra, *Roxb.*
,, obovata, *D. C.*

Took kyan. BURM.	Vel maroodum maram. TAM.
Curry murdah wood. ANGLO-TAM.	Karai marudu maram. ,,
Aeen?? MAHR.	Tella maddi chettu. TEL.
Mairthee?? MAHR.	Maddi chuttu. ,,
Koombook-gass. SINGH.	Sahajo. URIA.

A valuable timber tree with a large and lofty trunk, a native of Sylhet, Monghyr, and it grows throughout the peninsula of India, south to Ceylon, where it is very abundant up to an elevation of 2,000 feet. It is a large tree, procurable in Coimbatore, and found most abundantly in all the coast jungles of the Bombay Presidency, as also in those above the ghauts. The wood is dark coloured, very hard, heavy and strong, inch bars bearing from 430 to 450lbs., and large beams of it were, in 1850, readily procurable for house building, for which and many other purposes it is valuable. It is a good wood for trenails, but they should have a second seasoning after they are manufactured, as there is a material shrinking immediately after the piece has been cut out of the log and shaped and their ends should be dipped in tar to preserve them. According to Captain Macdonald, in Ganjam and Gumsur, its extreme height is 60 feet, circumference 4½ feet and height from the ground to the intersection of the first branch, 30 feet: is one of the commonest trees in those jungles, cattle sheds are sometimes floored with it, and rice pounders are also said to be occasionally made of it; it is extensively used for firewood and in making potash. The bark is used for tanning.—*Drs. Wight, Cleghorn and Gibson, Voigt, Thwaites, Captains Beddome and Macdonald, Mr. Latham.*

TERMINALIA MACROCARPA, *Brandis.*

Htoukgyau. BURM.

One of the largest trees in Pegu, and very common; the stems are of very regular shape, heartwood dark brown, and used for house posts and planking. A cubic foot weighs lbs. 58 in a full grown tree on good soil the average length of the trunk to the first branch is 80 feet, and average girth measured at 6 feet from the ground is 12 feet.—*Dr. Brandis, Cal. Cat. Ex.* 1862.

TERMINALIA MOLUCCANA, *Willde.*

Kala drooma. SANS.

A native of the mountainous countries of the N. E. of Bengal.—*Roxb. Fl. Ind. Vol. II, p.* 433

TERMINALIA PANICULATA, *W. & A.*

Pentaptera paniculata, *Roxb.; Fl. Ind.* 2, *p.* 462.

A tree of Malabar, of the valleys of the Concan rivers near their sources, at Courtallum and abundant in the jungles south east of Surat. Its timber is good —*Voigt, Roxb.*

TERMINALIA PARVIFLORA, *Thw.*

Hampalanda-gass. SINGH.

In Ceylon, this tree is found on the margins of woods in the central province, up to an elevation of 4,000 feet, and abundant in the Ambagamowa district.—*Thw. En. Pl. Zeyl., p.* 103.

TERMINALIA PROCERA, *Roxb.*

A tree of the first magnitude, of the Andaman islands, a charming species.—*Roxb. Fl. Ind. Vol. II, p.* 429.

TERMINALIA RUBRICA ?

Beleyleh. AR.	Taudra maram. TAM.
Buhira. BENG.	Tandi. TEL.
Vibbituka. SANS.	Tani. BHEED.

TERMINALIA TOMENTOSA, *W. & A.*

Pentaptera tomentosa, *Roxb. Fl. Ind.*

Ashan. BENG.	Asan. HIND.
Aans. ? ? „	Eyne. „ of Nagpore.
Piya-shal. BENG.	Eyn. MAHR.
Madi. CAN.	Eyne. „ of Nagpore.
Karrai mutti. CAN.	Maradu maram. TAM.
Piasal. DUK.	Carru maradu. „
Asan. „	Nalla maddi. TEL.

Common in the ghauts of the Malabar coast, grows in the Concans, and at Monghir, Rajmahal and Oude, grows in abundance in the Nalla mallai and is a well known valuable timber in the forests of the Godavery. In the Madras presidency, it is used for house building, it bears a good transverse strain and is a wood much esteemed for all railway purposes. The Asan tree of Lucknow grows spontaneously in the Taraee jungles, and its wood is considered durable and elastic and, for many purposes, preferable to sal. Writing of it as it occurs in Nagpore, Captain Sankey says, that like Bejasar this timber has white wood surrounding the body and heart, which is of a blackish colour; the ring however in this case does not exceed 1½ inch in breadth. The dark wood is exceedingly heavy, being exactly of the same weight as water, and has a much more winding grain than Bejasar. In strength it is far superior to all its forest congeners, and from the strength given by Barlow for American teak, it even appears to excel that celebrated timber. Unfortunately, he adds, its length, in Nagpore is limited, seldom furnishing more than a 20 feet tie beam, from the crooked manner in which the tree grows. It is a difficult timber to work up, splits freely when in exposed situations, and by all accounts is very subject to dry rot. Were the latter defect overcome by the steeping process, and the former guarded against, he knows of no timber which can bear a comparison with it; for the joists of a terraced roof it would be invaluable. White ants will not attack it. He ranks it both as a tie beam and rafter wood. He says that, in Nagpore, its average length is 18 feet, and average girth 4½ feet, and the maxima 28 to 24 feet, and its selling price 5 annas the cubic foot.—*Captain Sankey, Voigt, Captain Beddome, Cal. Cat. Ex.* 1862.

TERMINALIA VIOLATA, *McClelland.*

Laib-wai. BURM.

A large timber tree, plentiful throughout the Pegu, Tonghoo, and Tharawaddy forests. Wood of a white colour and well suited for all purposes of house-building.—*Dr. McClelland.*

TERNSTRŒMIA, *Species.*

Puzzeen zwa. BURM.

A large tree of Tavoy, used in building.—*Dr. Wallich.*

TERRUWALI. CAN.? A wood of S. Canara, used for building purposes.—*Madras Cat. Ex.* 1852.

THAB BAN. BURM. This Amherst timber is used for boat-building and making carts; timber sometimes 70 feet long: it is a teak, but rather heavier than the usual kind. Specific gravity 0·814.—*Cat. Ex.* 1851.

THA BHAN. A timber of Tavoy used for canoes.—*Mr. Blundell.*

THABIA KING ? A tree of Akyab, but not plentiful. It is a large wood, but not much in use.—*Cal. Cat. Ex.* 1862.

THA BONG PEW. BURM. A timber tree, of maximum girth 2 cubits and maximum length 15 feet, abundant on the sea coast from Amherst to Mergui. When seasoned it floats in water. It is liable to attacks from worm, rots readily, and is a brittle inferior wood.—*Captain Dance.*

THA-BOTE-KEE. BURM. A Tenasserim timber tree, of maximum girth 3 cubits, and maximum length 18 feet. Scarce, but found all over the province near the sea and at the mouths of rivers. When seasoned it floats in water. It is a short fibred, brittle, yet soft wood, and not durable.—*Captain Dance.*

THA-BWOT-GYEE. BURM. In Amherst a good heavy valuable timber, somewhat like ironwood.—*Cat. Ex.* 1851.

THA-BYA—? A tree of Akyab, which grows to a large size, and is plentiful. It is sometimes used for planking.—*Cal. Cat. Ex.* 1862.

THA BYAY-NEE. BURM. In Tavoy, a strong, close grained, brownish grey wood; used for house posts.—*Mr. Blundell, in Cat. Ex.* 1851.

THA BYAY-NEE. BURM. In Amherst, Tavoy and Mergui, of maximum girth 3 cubits, maximum length 23 feet, found very abundant all over the Tenasserim and Martaban provinces, when seasoned it floats in water. It is an inferior brittle wood, used by Burmese in short pieces for the props of houses.—*Captain Dance*.

THA BYA NEE, Burm.

Red jambo. Eng.

A tree of Moulmein, used for building materials.—*Cal. Cat. Ex.* 1862. (*Note.*—Are the last three woods identical ?)

THA-BYION. In Amherst, a useful timber, probably a Eugenia.—*Dr. Wallich.*

THA-BYAY-YNET-GHEE, Burm., meaning with large leaves. A tree of maximum girth 3 cubits, maximum length 22 feet, widely scattered inland, all over the provinces of Amherst, Tavoy and Mergui. When seasoned it floats in water. It is a tolerably good and tough wood, and is spoken of by Dr. McClelland as a strong and close grained timber.—*Captain Dance.*

THA-BY-KE or THA-BAY-KYA, Burm. Described as a kind of oak growing in Amherst, Tavoy and Mergui, of maximum girth, 1½ cubits and maximum length 16 feet. Not abundant, but scattered in all forests inland, all over the provinces. When seasoned, it floats in water. It is a sufficiently light, yet durable, straight grained, tough wood; used by Burmese for posts, building purposes generally, and various other objects. This wood is recommended as likely to prove excellent for helves, and if it could be procured in sufficient quantities, would be unrivalled for shot boxes.—*Captain Dance.*

THADOOP—? A plentiful tree of Akyab, furnishing a small wood, but not much in use.—*Cal. Cat. Ex.* 1862.

THA-KHWOT. This Amherst wood is useful for sandals ; it is a kind of white teak.—*Cat. Ex.* 1851.

THAMMAI. A native of Amherst, a strong, handsome wood, like Ægiceras, or box-wood.—*Cat. Ex.* 1862.

THA-KHOOT, Burm. A tree of Moulmein, wood is used in ordinary house building.—*Cal. Cat. Ex.* 1862.

THA-MAN-THA, Burm. A tree of Moulmein, wood used as an ordinary building material.—*Cal. Cat. Ex.* 1862.

THANDRAIKYA, Tel. In the Nalla mallai, an ash coloured wood, resembles hickory in fibre, is close and tough, and would be a very useful wood.—*Mr. Latham.*

THA-NAT-KHEE, Burm. A timber tree of Amherst, Tavoy and Mergui, of maximum girth 3½ cubits, and maximum length 30 feet. Said to be abundant all over the provinces, but has not been easily obtained in Moulmein. When seasoned, it floats in water. It is a durable, yet light wood with a very straight grain ; used for every purpose by the Burmese, and much recommended for helves.—*Captain Dance.*

THA-NAT. In Amherst, is a kind of grey teak.

THA-NAT-THAYT-PEW-THA, Burm. A very abundant timber tree in Amherst, Tavoy and Mergui, of maximum girth 2 cubits, and maximum length 15 feet. -*Captain Dance.*

THAN-KYA, Burm. A native of Amherst, the fruit of this tree is employed for ring-worm. The wood is like that of the Saul, Shorea robusta.

THANNA-DAN, Burm. A native of Amherst, and said to be a fruit tree ; it has a reddish-brown, heavy wood, fit for machinery or other purposes requiring great strength ; it is totally exempt from attacks of insects, but somewhat liable to split.—*Cat. Ex.* 1851.

THAN-THAT, Burm. Very difficult to procure, but found inland up the Gyne and Attaran rivers, in the Tenasserim provinces. When seasoned it floats in water. It is a capital wood, very durable ; used by Karens for bows, for shoulder yokes, spear handles and many other purposes. Excellent for hammer handles from its tough fibre.—*Captain Dance.*

THAN-THAT. An Amherst wood, used for stocks of various instruments ; it is a capital wood, and seems to be a kind of Saul.—*Cat. Ex.* 1851.

THAN-THAT-GYEE, Burm. A tree of Moulmein ; used for building materials.—*Cal. Cat. Ex.* 1862.

THA-PYKE-THA, Burm. A tree of Amherst, Tavoy and Mergui, of maximum girth 5 cubits, and maximum length 30 feet. It is very abundant along the banks of rivers, all over the provinces. When seasoned, it floats in water. It is a wood of no durability.—*Captain Dance.*

THARANCHILLY, Tam. A Travancore wood of a bamboo colour, 5 to 8 feet in circumference ; used for canoes only.—*Colonel Frith.*

THARANJULLA, Tam. A Travancore wood of a bamboo colour, specific gravity 0·576 ; used for common building.—*Colonel Frith.*

THAU-BAUN-PO, Burm. A wood of Tavoy, an inferior wood, used for common canoes.—*Mr. Blundell.*

THAUGAET-THITTOO, Burm. An inferior wood of Tavoy.—*Mr. Blundell.*

THA-YAY BEW, Burm. Maximum girth 2 cubits, and maximum length 20 feet. Not very abundant, but found inland all over the provinces of Amherst, Tavoy and Mergui. When seasoned, it floats in water. It is not a durable wood.—*Captain Dance.*

THA-YIN-GEE, Burm. A small tree of Amherst, Tavoy and Mergui, of maximum girth ½ cubit, and maximum length 6 feet. Abundant all over the provinces. When seasoned it floats in water. It is utterly useless except for firewood. —*Captain Dance.*

THAY-KYA-BA, BURM. In Amherst, Tavoy and Mergui, of maximum girth 3 cubits, and maximum length 24 feet, very abundant, but straggling inland all over the provinces. When seasoned, it floats in water. It is used for house posts, but is not a durable wood.—*Capt. Dance.*

THAY-THA, BURM. In Amherst, Tavoy and Mergui, of maximum girth 3 cubits, and maximum length 22 feet, widely scattered inland all over the provinces. When seasoned, it floats in water. It is a tolerably good and tough wood, liable to rot in store, and therefore not recommended.—*Captain Dance.*

THAY-YO-THA, BURM. In Amherst, Tavoy and Mergui, of maximum girth 5 cubits, and maximum length 25 feet. Very abundant all over the Tenasserim and Martaban provinces. When seasoned, it floats in water. It is a useless wood; rots very quickly, and is only used for temporary buildings.—*Captain Dance.*

THAYET KYA, BURM. A Tenasserim wood, of maximum girth 2 cubits, and maximum length 20 feet. Not very abundant, but occasionally procurable inland near the back of hills near Moulmein and here and there all over the provinces. When seasoned, it floats in water. It is durable and light, and a good wood for helves. —*Captain Dance.*

THEE KHYA THA. A timber of maximum girth 1 cubit, and maximum length 12 feet. Very abundant all over the Tenasserim and Martaban provinces, in Amherst, Tavoy and Mergui: when seasoned, it floats in water. It is a very crooked grained perishable wood; and not recommended.—*Captain Dance.*

THE-LA-BAY, BURM. A timber tree of Amherst, Tavoy and Mergui, of maximum girth 3 cubits, and maximum length 20 feet. Not very abundant, but obtained from Tavoy, Mergui and Yea. When seasoned it floats in water. It is a brittle, useless wood for ordnance purposes, though employed by Burmese for house posts and to support the shafts of wells.—*Capt. Dance.*

THEET-PHYIOU. This is a native of Amherst, is used for fan handles; it is a useful white wood, and would answer for common carpentry; it resembles Acacia serissa.—*Cat. Ex.* 1851.

THEET-TA-GYEE. A Tavoy wood, suitable for common carpentry.—*Mr. Blundell.*

THEET-TO. This is a native of Amherst, is said to be a fruit tree; it is a dark-brownish grey, hard, heavy wood, and employed in boat building, making carts, &c.—*Cat. Ex.* 1851.

THEET-YA-HAN. In Tavoy, a close grained teak, used for posts.—*Mr. Blundell.*

THEET-YA-NEE. In Tavoy, a close grained brown wood; rather shaky.—*Mr. Blundell.*

THEET-YA. In Amherst, employed for rice grinders or pounders. It is a superior, compact, close, tough, brown wood, fit for any thing requiring great strength and durability.—*Cat. Ex.* 1851.

THEET-YA-PYIOU. A heavy strong wood of Tavoy.—*Mr. Blundell.*

THEIM, BURM.? A timber of Amherst, used as house posts, rafters and general purposes of carpentry.—*Cat. Ex.* 1851.

THEM-MAI-THA, BURM. A very abundant wood, found all over the provinces of Amherst, Tavoy and Mergui, on both sides of the Moulmein river and on the sea coast. Its maximum length is 12 feet and maximum girth 2½ cubits; and, when seasoned, it floats in water. It burns with an intense heat, and is therefore used in preparing salt, and is recommended as an excellent wood for fuel for steamers, and probably would be a good charcoal wood.—*Capt. Dance.*

THENG-GAN, BURM. This wood, a native of Amherst, is employed for house posts, carts, boat building, paddles and oars. It is an excellent compact wood, fit for gun carriages.—*Cat. Ex.* 1851.

THEWGANET, (Tilsa?) A tree of Akyab. A very good wood, used for work of all kinds. Grows to a large size, and is very plentiful in the Akyab and Ramree districts.—*Cal. Cat. Ex.* 1862.

THEP-YENG, BURM. This, a native of Amherst, is said to be a fruit tree: the trunk affords a compact, fine grained wood.—*Cat. Ex.* 1851.

THET LENDAH, BURM. A tree of Moulmein, used for all ordinary building purposes.—*Cal. Cat. Ex.* 1862.

THEVAHDARUM, TAM. Or cedar wood. a timber of Travancore. Wood of a flesh colour, specific gravity 0·457, 2 to 8 feet in circumference, and used for palanquins, cabin fittings, furniture, &c.—*Colonel Frith.*

THEVETIA NERIIFOLIA, *Juss.*

Cerbera thevetii, *Linn.*
„ thevetis, *Don. Mill.*

Exile tree. ENG.

A garden shrub of Madras, called the "Exile." The wood said to be worthless.—*Cat. Madras Gardens.*

THEYAH, BURM. An inferior wood of Tavoy.—*Mr. Blundell.*

THESPESIA POPULNEA, *Lam.; W. Ic.; W. & A.*

Hibiscus populneus, *Roxb.*
Malaviscus populneus, *Gærtn.*

Poresh. BEN.
Poo-arasoo. CAN.
Paras pipal. DUK.
Tulip tree. ENG.
Portia tree. „
Bendi. MAHR.
Surya-gass. SINGH.
Pursa muram. TAM.
Pursung kai maram. TAM.
Puvarasa maram. „
Gangaravi. TEL.
Muni gangaravi. „
Gangaravi wood tree. ANGLO-TEL.

This tree is generally met with in Ceylon and in Southern India, in avenues or lining roads, but is in most abundance near the sea. It is of quick growth and yields a good shade, but is inconvenient on road sides and in gardens, from the quantities of leaves it sheds, and the numerous large flowers which fall. It is commonly planted from cuttings, from which cause, perhaps, it is often hollow in the centre. It yields, when ripe, a very strong, hard and durable timber, with a colour like mahogany; but, its use is limited from the difficulty of getting it of large size. It is used for chairs in Madras. On the Bombay side, where it is found only near the coasts, it is much used in the construction of cart wheel spokes, and for the timbers of native boats. The shoots are also in extensive use there, as rafters for houses, and at all times fetch a good price when sold for this purpose. The Bombay Government formed two plantations of this tree at Sakuria in Alibagh, at Sat Tar, and in Colaba. Those at Sat Tar not favorable, but the trees growing in the alluvial soil of Sakuria, were said to be in a good state. Dr. Gibson tells us, that the increasing scarcity of this tree is such, that wheel-spokes were, sometime ago, being paid for by the gun-carriage department at 12 annas each. There are a pretty large number of Bendy trees within the village precincts of many of the cultivators in the Concan, but these are mostly reserved for the supply of choice rafters, afforded by the straight shoots of the tree, while the stem is most frequently hollow; and therefore the ripe-wood, or such of it as remains, is worthless for ordnance purposes. Dr. Gibson imported some years ago, a number of Bendy trees which were rejected by the arsenal by reason of this hollowness. Nevertheless, he cut up a few by way of experiment, and found that many available spokes of wheels might have been turned out from them. As it is, they were sold as rejected materials, and the price realised just sufficed to cover charges. Dr. Gibson has noticed the value of his tree, for years, but though of rapid growth its wood is not in much use.—*Voigt, Drs. Wight, Gibson and Cleghorn, Captain Beddome, Thwaites.*

THIEM, Burm. A serviceable wood of Tavoy.

THIET-NEE, Burm. A tree of Moulmein; wood converted into boxes, tables, &c. &c.—*Cal. Cat. Ex.* 1862.

THING—? A tree of Akyab, which grows to a large size, and is very plentiful. Its wood is used in house building.—*Cal. Cat. Ex.* 1862.

THINGAN-KYAUP, Burm. A Tavoy wood, a close grained, heavy, strong wood, used in ship and house building, for carts, &c.—*Mr. Blundell.*

THIN-WIN, Burm. A tree of Moulmein. The root is used medicinally.—*Cal. Cat. Ex.* 1862.

THIT-NEE, Burm. A beautiful red, but heavy wood, of British Burmah. A cubic foot weighs lbs. 80. In a full grown tree on good soil, the average length of the trunk to the first branch is 50 feet, and average girth measured at 6 feet from the ground is 8 feet. It sells at 12 annas per cubic foot.—*Dr. Brandis, Cal. Cat. Ex.* 1862.

THIT-POUK, Burm. One of the Leguminosæ, a light wood of British Burmah, not much used. A cubic foot weighs lbs. 35: in a full grown tree on good soil, the average length of the trunk to the first branch is 20 feet, and average girth measured at 6 feet from the ground is 4 feet. It sells at 8 annas per cubic foot.—*Dr. Brandis, Cal. Cat. Ex.* 1862.

THMENG-BA, Burm. A timber of Tavoy, like red Jarool; used for posts and cotton rollers.—*Mr. Blundell.*

THMENY-TSHOUT, Burm. *Qu.?* Thmeng-tshout. A small heavy coarse, brown wood of Tavoy, used for door frames and boat beams.—*Mr. Blundell.*

THOKAY. Tam. A wood of Tinnevelly, of a red colour, specific gravity 0·950; used for building purposes.—*Colonel Frith.*

THOONGUN. A tree of Akyab. It is plentiful but is a small wood, used for oars and baughies.—*Cal. Cat. Ex.* 1862.

THOTHA-KUTTY. Tam. A wood of Tinnevelly, of a red colour, used for furniture of every description.—*Colonel Frith. (Note.*—Is this not an illustration of the errors arising from using vernacular names. Does it mean garden knife ?)

THOUNMYNGA. Burm. A wood of Tavoy, used in building.—*Mr. Blundell.*

THOUNG-THA-LAZ? A tree of Akyab which grows to a large size, but is not by any means plentiful. Its wood is used for oars and sometimes in house-building.—*Cal. Cat. Ex.* 1862.

THUN-NA-KA. Tam. A wood of Tinnevelly of a whitey brown colour, used for making trunks.—*Colonel Frith.*

THY—? A tree of Akyab, which grows to a large size, and is plentiful in the Ramree and Sandoway districts. Its wood is used for posts and firewood.—*Cal. Cat. Ex.* 1862.

THYKADO—? A tree of Akyab, which grows to a large size, but is not very plentiful. It is used for furniture.—*Cal. Cat. Ex.* 1862.

THYMBRO. Burm. A good strong durable wood of Tavoy, used in boat building.—*Wall.*

THYNAN—? A tree of Akyab, a small wood used in house-building. It is not very plentiful. —*Cal. Cat. Ex.* 1862.

THYZAUHOONG—? A tree of Akyab. It is small and plentiful, and its wood is used for colouring thread.—*Cal. Cat. Ex.* 1862.

TIBELEBU, the name of a tree in Canara and Malabar, also named Nambogum. The wood is close grained, and very durable for general house building purposes: the carpenters use it generally as a strong durable wood. It may be procured in Malabar and Canara, in quantities from eight to thirty-six inches in diameter, and from twenty to thirty-five feet long.—*Edye, Forests of Malabar and Canara.*

TIELLA in Malayala and Tamil, a Ceylon tree not much known. It grows from eight to twelve inches in diameter. It is used by the natives in the frames of country boats and, from its strength and durability, is found to answer the purpose well.—*Edye on the Timber of Ceylon.*

TIJA. A Penang wood of a light brown colour, used for furniture, boxes, &c.—*Col. Frith.*

TIMBER, from Saxon, Timbrian, to build.

Aruuyavu. CAN.	Chob. PERS.
Lakaru. GUZ.	Arunuyum. SANS.
Nath'h. DUK.	Davou. „
Lakra. HIND.	Kadu kambu. TAM.
Arunuyum. MALEAL.	Mar'm. „
Lakara. MAHR.	Chettu. TEL.
Aruneya. „	Karra. „
Hez'm. PERS.	Koia. „

In contradistinction to dye-woods, woods for engraving, ornamental woods, &c., says Tredgold, wood felled and seasoned and fit for building purposes, is called timber. It is met with in commerce in various forms. Mr. Poole in his statistics of commerce, mentions that the trunk of a tree, with or without boughs or branches undressed, is termed round timber; when hewn into logs square; when quartered, billets; when split, staves and lathwood; when sawn, deals, battens, planks, boards and scantling. The stems or trunks of several kinds of young trees are called spars, poles and rickers; also prop wood and postwood. In India, there are peculiar terms applied to timbers of different kinds. Reepers, in southern India, are the split stems of the palmyra tree. Timbers are also sometimes classed according to the purposes to which they are applied; oak, teak, green heart, black mara, are designated ship-building woods; teak, saul, padouk &c., are recognised ordnance woods; while, Trincomalee rosewoods, red-woods, satin wood, snake wood, mahogany, ebony, kyaboca, zebra, tulip and other furniture woods, are usually called fancy woods: Timbers, says Tredgold, are also spoken of as hard, soft and tough, but there are no established degrees of these qualities, and Tredgold in defining them merely says, that a hard wood yields less to a stroke or impression than a soft wood, and that wood is the toughest which combines the greatest degree of strength and flexibility. The timbers of commerce are, also, recognised as from the sap wood or heart wood. Sap wood is that part of the wood next the bark, and the Heart wood is near the centre of the bole or stem. Sap wood is softer and generally lighter coloured than heart wood, and is found to decay more rapidly and to be more subject to attacks of insects. The proportion of sap wood varies much in different trees. In many trees, such as those that produce the ebonies of commerce, the line of demarcation between the heart and sap wood is so strongly defined as to arrest attention and permit the application of those two parts of the timber to different economic purposes, and the sap woods and heart woods in such cases, though the products of the same tree, receive in commerce distinct names. In other trees, the change from the sap wood to the heart wood is gradual; but, in all cases, the sap wood preponderates in young trees and the heart wood in the old. Also, he says, according to Buffon and Duhamel, in trees that have not arrived at maturity, the hardness and solidity of the wood are greatest at the heart and decrease towards the sap wood. But, in the mature or perfect tree, the heart wood is nearly uniform while that of a tree on the decline is softer at the centre than it is next the sap wood; Tredgold quotes the opinion of Sir Humphry Davy (Agricultural Chemistry, p. 220, 4th Ed.) that the decline of trees is caused by the decay of the heart wood. And, in India, where vegetable life abounds, the correctness of that opinion can be testified to by every observer. As with the animal world, so with the vegetable creation, trees have the three stages of infancy, maturity and old age, and Tredgold (p. 196) tells us, that the oak and chesnut trees, under favourable circumstances, sometimes attain an age of about 1000 years, beech, ash and sycamore to half that age. The plain tree, the Chinar of north-western Asia, is said to live to a great age. In forestry, therefore, the rule deducible from our knowledge of these principles and facts, as indicated in Tredgold (p. 197), is to fell timber trees when in their maturity. For, if felled too young, there is much sap wood and even the heart wood has not acquired proper degree of hardness: and such timber cannot be durable. On the other hand, if the tree be not felled, till on the decline, the wood is brittle and devoid of elasticity: is tainted and discoloured and soon decays. The rule therefore is to fell the mature tree, when the quantity of sap wood is small, and the heart wood nearly uniform, hard, compact and durable, but too early is worse than too late. Therefore, for south-eastern Asia, a tabular statement, showing the ages at which its various timber trees reach maturity, is very necessary, though still a desideratum. Dr.

Brandis tells us that, in British Burmah, a full grown teak tree of 9 feet in girth, cannot be supposed to be less than 160 years old, and I think, have seen it some where mentioned that it is not to be cut for timber under 80 years of age. In England, as Tredgold tells us (p. 198) oak is never cut for timber under 50, nor above 200 years of age. Dr. Brandis tells us that the strength and density of teak timber vary exceedingly, according to the locality where the tree is grown. The extremes observed in preliminary experiments were, as to weight, lbs. 40 to 50 per cubic foot, and 190 lbs. to 289 lbs., breaking weight. It is well known that the timber of those trees which grow in moist and shady places, is not so good as that which comes from a more exposed situation, nor is it so close, substantial or durable. The preservation of timber naturally arranges itself into the preservation of growing timber, and that of timber when felled. Since the close of the last century, it has been a growing belief that the climate of a country is greatly modified by the scarcity or abundance of its trees and forests. Some years ago, in 1845, I furnished to the Madras Government, a memorandum of all existing information on this subject, and it was a matter of enquiry at one of the meetings of the British Association. Other writers, since then, have written on the connection between the amount of rain fall and the number of trees in a country, and it is now generally recognised that they do exercise a powerful influence on the climate of the region or district in which they grow. In a tropical country like India, therefore, the preservation of existing trees, and their extension, in arid districts is a matter of much climatic importance. Dr. Cleghorn, in his Report for 18 , gives on this point, the following extract of a letter. "The higher sholas clothing the ghauts on both sides are of the utmost importance, and the climate is believed to suffer the greatest detriment from their removal. I would therefore suggest that the high wooded mountain tops overhanging the low country (such as Hoolicul) should be preserved with rigid care, the forest there should not be given over to the axe, lest the supplies of water may be injured. It is the opinion of many persons, in which I concur, that the vast clearings which have taken place have had a share in producing the irregularity of the monsoon which has of late years been so much complained of in Coimbatore. In order that the course of the rivulets should be overshadowed with trees, I conceive that the hills should be left clothed to the extent of about half of their height from the top, leaving half of the slope and all the valley below for cultivation; this available portion would far exceed in extent the higher ridges which should be considered." It is not, however, merely from legitimate use, that the forests are decreasing :—all the Conservators notice the conflagrations which arise naturally, and are caused by the wild races who, alike in India and in Burmah, effect a clearance by fire, in order to obtain a fresh soil for a temporary cultivation. Dr. Cleghorn, in one of his reports says, that "the forest conflagrations in the Madras Presidency, are of frequent occurrence; the unextinguished fire of a camp of Binjaris, the sparks from the torches or cheroots of travellers, the spontaneous ignition from friction of bamboos, but much more frequently, the wilful burning of grass by the hill tribes, as heather is burnt in Scotland, in order that the ashes of the herbage may nourish the roots of young grass, and thus improve the forage of their cattle are, he says, among the causes of this devastation which extends annually over large tracts. The largest trees skirting the forest suffer more or less from these fires, the saplings are scorched and mutilated and the smaller seedlings perish. If the same spot is again visited by conflagration in the following year, the largest trees which escaped the first time are often consumed."—*Madras Conservator's Report, p.* 8, *Tredgold on Carpentry, Balfour on the effect of Trees on the Climate of a Country.*—*See* TABLES APPENDED.

TOBICA WOOD. Tobica kurra, TEL. A wood of north Canara.??

TO-DOORYAN, BURM. FOREST DOORYAN, ANGLO BURM. In Amherst, Tavoy and Mergui, a soft, light, useless timber, liable to rot readily. Its maximum girth 3 cubits, and maximum length 18 feet: scarce, but found on the sea coast of those provinces and adjacent islands: when seasoned it floats in water.—*Captain Dance.*

TO-NUGGAGAW—? A tree of Akyab, grows to a large size, and is not very plentiful. Its wood is sometimes used for planks.—*Cal. Cat. Ex.* 1862.

TOON. The timber of the Cedrela toona: this extends over every part of India, and may be seen all along the foot of the Himalaya. The specimens from Nepaul having frequently a sixth part added, Dr. Wallich was induced to call that variety Cedrela hexandra. There is, however, a distinct species, Cedrela serrata, which may be readily recognized by the great length of its racemes of flowers, and may frequently be seen with Sapindus acuminatus growing in the close valleys within the Himalaya.—*Royle's Ill. Him. Bot., p.* 142.—*See* CEDRELA TOONA.

TOPA, HIND? A tree of Chota Nagpore, with hard grey timber.—*Cal. Cat. Ex.* 1862.

TOUNKATSEET. BURM. One of the Leguminosæ. A tree not uncommon on the hills of British Burmah; wood used for canoes. A cubic foot weighs lbs. 45, in a full grown tree on good soil the average length of the trunk to the first branch is 50 feet, and the average girth, measured at 6 feet from the ground is 10 feet.—*Dr. Brandis, Cal. Cat. Ex.* 1862.

TOUNG-MA-YOA. BURM. A tree of Moulmein, wood smooth, and used by the Burmese as a slate or writing board.—*Cal. Cat. Ex.* 1862. (*Note.*—Is it Alston iascholars?)

TOUNG-BHAUT. BURM. In Tavoy, a rough, knotty wood; used for knife and spear-handles. —*Mr. Blundell.*

TOUNG-BHIEN. BURM. A light, porous wood of Tavoy, used for common carpentry.—*Mr. Blundell.*

TOUNG-BIEN. BURM. In Amherst, a wood used in boat-buliding and for making carts. It is a strong, heavy wood, well adapted for handles of tools, &c; it is probably a kind of teak.—*Cat. Ex.* 1851.

TOUNG-BYENG. BURM. In Tavoy a kind of red saul.—*Mr. Blundell.* (Are these three the same?)

TOUNG-BYE-NAY. In Tenasserim, a brittle short-grained wood. Not the mountain jack though similar to it in name, maximum girth 5 cubits. Maximum length, 30 feet. Scarce but found along the banks of rivers all over the provinces. When seasoned it floats in water.—*Captain Dance.*

TOUNG-BYIOU. ? A close grained, brown shaky wood of Tavoy.

TOUNG-THA-BYIOU. ? BURM. In Amherst, used for house posts; it is a strong, red, heavy wood, a kind of Acacia.—*Cat. Ex.* 1851.

TOUNG-THAU-GYEE. BURM. In Amherst, a hard compact wood of a dark brown colour.—*Cat. Ex.* 1851.

TOUNG-THA-KHWA. BURM. In Amherst, this is a capital wood for any purpose; used for gun-carriages or gun-stocks.—*Cat. Ex.* 1851.

TOUNG-KHA-RAY. BURM. A wood of Tavoy where it is called Red Jarool; used in boat-building.—*Mr. Blundell.*

TOWNI in Tamil, Taniki mara in Malayala. This Malabar and Canara tree grows to about three and a half feet in diameter, and from thirty to forty-five feet long; it is of a whitish colour, and is used by the natives for catamarans, canoes, &c. It produces a fruit which the native doctors use as a purgative in cases of fever, &c., the timber is not durable or of much use.—*Edye, Forests of Malabar and Canara.*

TOWN-PI-NE, BURM., in Tavoy, a good wood, used in boat building.—*Dr Wallich.*

TOWTAL, the Malayala name of a Malabar and Canara tree, which grows to about two feet in diameter, and thirty feet high. It is remarkably light, but not very durable, and is used by the natives for catamarans, &c.—*Edye, Forests of Malabar and Canara.*

TREE, ENG.

Pohun. ADANG (Murut) of Borneo.	Pokoh. MALAY of Borneo.
Shajr. AR.	Mara. MALEAL.
Nakl. BENG.	Akak kaya. MALU of Borneo.
Puhn. BISAYA, LANUN, MALAY.	Basoh. MILANAU "
Ghidayau ? CAN.	Karing. PAKATAN "
Mara ? "	Darakht. PERS.
J'har. DUK. HIND. MAHR.	Vrukchum. SANS.
J'hara. GUZ.	Pohn. SEA-DYAK of Borneo.
J'hada. "	Gass. SINGH.
Guas. IDAAN of Borneo.	Maram. TAM.
Keioh. KAYAN "	Cherri. "
	Chettu. TEL.
	Manu. "

—*St. John's Forests, &c.*

TRENAILS. See TERMINALIA GLABRA.

TROPHIS ASPERA, *Retz.*

Achymus asper, Soland., *MS.S.*
Epicarpurus orientalis, *W. Ic.*
Streblus asper *Lour.*

Sheora. BENG.	Barinika. TEL.
Shasa-gach'h BENG.	Barranki. "
Kurrera. MAHR.	Bari venka. "
Sahadra. URIA. ? TEL. ?	

This tree is so very plentiful in Ganjam and Gumsur, that it is chiefly used as firewood. It there attains an extreme height of 30 feet, and a circumference of 2 feet. The height from the ground to the nearest branch is 6 feet. It is more common in Guzerat, than in the other parts of the Bombay country. It is rare in the forests there. The wood is there reckoned of good quality, for small purposes, for it will seldom square above 4 inches. It is said to be used in Ganjam for bandy wheels. Its leaves are said by Dr. Royle, to be used to polish horns, and ivory &c. The bark is used medicinally, the leaves and sap are used for wounds and for a disease of the eye termed Jokia in Oriya, said to be peculiar to children.—*Dr. Gibson, Captain Macdonald, Royle, Ill. Him. Bot., Voigt, Eli. Fl. Andh.*

TROSUM, HIND. A tree of Jubbulpore with good timber, but the tree does not occur in any quantity.—*Cal. Cat. Ex.* 1862.

TSAN-SAY-PEU ? BURM. ? A tree of Moulmein, the wood is used for ordinary house building purposes. Leaf is eaten boiled as greens.—*Cal. Cat. Ex.* 1862.

TSAT-THA, BURM. A tree of Moulmein, the wood is used for building purposes.—*Cal. Cat. Ex.* 1862.

TSEET. A timber of Amherst employed as house posts and in boat building. It is said to be sal of small calibre.—*Cat. Ex.* 1851.

TSEKKA-DOUN. A timber of Amherst, said to be of a fruit tree, the wood is used for house posts, rafters and boat-building, it is like teak, but much disposed to split.—*Cat. Ex.* 1851.

TSENG BYIOU. In Tavoy a compact greyish-brown wood, suitable for common carpentry. —*Mr. Blundell.*

TSHAN-TSHAY. In Amherst, a useful wood, but liable to attacks of insects and to split.—*Cat. Ex.* 1851.

TSHAUP-YO. A timber of Amherst, used for house posts and musket stocks. It is a heavy white wood exceedingly strong, but liable to attacks of insects.—*Cat. Ex.* 1851.

TSHIET-KHYEEN. A timber of Amherst, used for house posts. A superior kind of crooked grained Sal.—*Cat. Ex.* 1851.

TSHWAI-LWAI. A timber of Amherst used for musket stocks and sword sheaths, it is a hard, red, crooked grained wood, fit for cabinet work. —*Cat. Ex.* 1851.

TSOAY-DAN. A wood of Tavoy, used for gun-stocks.—*Mr. Blundell.*

TSOAY-DAN. In Amherst a heavy, hard, tough wood, not subject to insects, and, being tough and short, it is suited for wheels, musket-stocks, &c.—*Cat. Ex.* 1851.

TSWOT-BA-LWOT, A timber of Amherst, this is said to be from a fruit tree, the wood resembles Jarool or Lagerstrœmia.—*Cat. Ex.* 1851.

TUKKUL, a system of temporary clearing.—*See* KUMARI.

TUNYEEN OR TUNYEEN DHA, BURM. Scarce near the Moulmein and Sittang rivers, more abundant near Tavoy and Mergui, of maximum girth 5 cubits, and maximum length 30 or 40 feet. When seasoned it floats in water. It is used for the construction of the very large boats which go from Moulmein to Tounghoo; hence in much demand at Moulmein, but not so much so on the sea coast. The wood when cut, has a peculiar and fragrant smell, is tough and oily, and likely to make excellent planes, handles, &c., &c.—*Captain Dance.*

TYE YOO THA OR LAN THAH, BURM. This timber is of maximum girth 2 cubits, and maximum length 22 feet. Found scarce in Tavoy and Mergui, also in less abundance in Amherst province. When seasoned it floats in water. It is a bad brittle wood, and readily splits and warps.—*Captain Dance.*

U.

ULLOOMBUL MARAM. TAM. A wood of Coimbatore. *See* VADEN COORNIE.

ULMUS, the Elm. A genus of plants, the type of the natural order Ulmaceæ. The various species of elm are wild in Europe, North America, India and China, and nearly 20 species have been enumerated, five of which occur in India, but it is now generally recognised that the seeds of the elm do not produce plants precisely like their parents, and on this account there are many recorded varieties of the species which are cultivated for ornament or timber.—*Eng. Cyc.*

ULMUS ALTERNIFOLIA, *McClelland.*

Thalai. BURM.

One of the largest trees in the Pegu province; found about towns and villages in the Prome district, but not below that latitude. The elms, to which family the tree in question belongs, afford valuable timber. The wood of this tree is red-colored, strong and adapted for house-building.—*Dr. McClelland, Voigt.*

ULMUS INTEGRIFOLIA, *Roxb.; Cor.; Pl.*

Holoptelœa integrifolia, *Planch.; Ann. Des. Sci. Nat.; W. Ic.*

Thalai. BURM.	Navili. TEL. of Nalla mallai.
Indian elm. ENG.	Namille. „ „ „ „
Wowlee. MAHR.	Navara. „
Aya maram. TAM.	Nowlee. „
Tambachi „ „	Nullee TEL.
Nali. TEL. of Nalla mallai.	Nalli. „

The class to which family this tree belongs, affords valuable timber. This, wherever growing, in Ceylon, and India, is a large timber tree. In the Circar mountains, where it is a native, it flowers in the cold season, leaves deciduous about the end of the year at the close of the wet season, and come out again in March. It occurs in the drier parts of Ceylon and grows in Coimbatore. It is rather common in the Konkan, but less so in the jungles than near to villages and towns, and it grows near Bombay, at Hurdwar, and at the foot of the Himalaya. In Pegu, it is one of the largest of the trees, and is found about towns and villages in the Prome district, but not below that latitude. The wood of this tree is reckoned of a good quality by natives of the Circars, and is employed for a variety of uses for carts, door frames, &c. It is of a red colour, strong, and adapted for general purposes but does not bear exposure well though it could probably be creosoted. Mr Latham says it is a light colored wood and said to yield a peculiar odour to boiling water which when mixed with common arrack gives it the flavour of the more expensive palmirah arrack and enables the vendors to obtain better prices for their adulterated article. The forks of the branches are used by the natives to protect their straw from cattle.—*Drs. Wight, Gibson and McClelland, Mr. Rohde, Thwaites, En. Pl. Zeyl., p.* 268, *Voigt, Mr. Latham.*

ULMUS VIRGATA, *Roxb.* A small tree of

China, Nepal, Kamaon, Mussooree, wood not known. But, the elms, to which family the trees in question belong, afford valuable timber. —*Voigt.*

UNCARIA GAMBIER, *Hunt.*; *Roxb.*

Gambier. MALAY. | Unkoodoo karra. TEL.

Grows in Ceylon near Colombo, and at an elevation of 3,000 feet; but it is a native of Malacca, Penang, Sumatra, &c. The substance called in commerce, gambier terra japonica, and catechu is prepared from it. The Malays chew it with the betel-leaf, as the Indians do the areca-nut. It is prepared from the leaves of the shrub and somewhat resembles true catechu. Its taste is exceedingly astringent. The water extract forms a good leather of a red or orange colour.—*Thw. En. Pl. Zeyl. p.* 133.—*Ainslie's Mat. Medl p.* 264.

UNDI MARA, CAN. Goolumb, MAHR. Samus of 2 species, abundant in the southern ghat jungles above the Canara and Sunda forests large and straight. Wood good as it abounds in an aromatic oil, which preserves it from insects. It is mostly in situations too remote from water for the wood merchant.—*Dr. Gibson.* (*Note*—What trees are these to which Dr. Gibson alludes ?)

UNONA. A genus of plants of south eastern Asia. U. longiflora is an elegant tree with smooth, pointed, and undulate leaves which is much cultivated in some parts of India to form avenues and to afford shade. It is sometimes called 'Deodara' which is properly the name of the celebrated Himalayan pine, Cedrus deodara. U. tripetala, U. unicinata, U. odirata, are natives of the Indian islands, and U. esculenta a native of the Indian peninsula, has fruit which is edible, but of their timber nothing is known, U. sylvatica is said to be valuable for its timber, U. longiflora, Roxb., is a small tree of Sylhet.—*Voigt, Eng. Cyc.*

UNONA DISCOLOR, *Vahl.*

Uvaria monolifera, *Gærtn.*

A tree of the Circars, Chittagong, Tavoy and Penang. Wood used for rafters.—*Roxb., Voigt.*

UPAS ANTIAR. The Upas tree.

Antiaris toxicaria, *Lesch.*
Ipo „ *Persoon.*

Upas tree. ENG. | An char. MALAY.

A native of Java, where it grows in the forests often over 100 feet in height. It yields the Upas poison. The character of its wood is not known.—*Voigt, Dr. O'Shaughnessy, Crawfurd.*

UPPUTAH, the Malayala name of a Malabar wood, which is hard, strong, and heavy. It grows to about twelve feet high, ten inches in diameter. It is used by the native carpenters for the frames of boats, of coasting-vessels, and similar purposes, where strength is required.—*Edye, Forests of Malabar and Canara.*

UVARIA. Of this genus of moderate sized or small trees little is known as to the value of their timbers. Marsden says that a Uvaria, in Sumatra, furnishes the Poon spars of commerce. But, it may be that he misapplied the Malay wood "Puhn" which signifies any tree.

UVARIA, *Species.*

Karee. HIND ?

A tree of Jubbulpore, wood used by natives for making toys.—*Cal. Cat. Ex.* 1862.

UVARIA, *Species.*

Beta goonda. CAN.

Grows in the Canara and Sunda forests, and on the jungles inland of Nilcoond. Wood of rather superior quality, being straight and tough. —*Dr. Gibson.*

UVARIA, *Species.*

Thub-bor. BURM.

A large tree of Tavoy, its wood is used for boat-building.—*Mr. Blundell.*

UVARIA, *Species.*

Hoom. MAHR.

Occurs on the Canara and Sunda forests, in jungles east of Kursulee on Black river; runs tall and straight. Wood strong and useful, it is not much known.—*Dr. Gibson.*

UVARIA MACROPHYLLA, *Roxb.* A small tree of Sylhet and Chittagong.—*Voigt.*

UVARIA ODORATA, *Lam.*

Unona odorata, *Dun.*

A small tree of the Tenasserim provinces, Sunda, the Moluccas and China.—*Voigt, Dr. Mason.*

UVARIA TOMENTOSA.

Pedda chilka dudugu. TEL.

A very strong yellow wood, much similar, but superior, to "Nauclea cordifolia." Cowars are made from it—also used in house building—it does not warp.—*Captain Beddome.*

UVARIA TRIPETALA, *Roxb.*

Unona tripetala, *D C.*

A tree of the Moluccas.—*Voigt.*

UVARIA VENTRICOSA, *Roxb.* A tree of Tippera.—*Voigt.*

UKBEIRIVE. SINGH. A tree of the southern provinces of Ceylon, its wood weighs 51 lbs. to the cubic foot, and it is said to last 80 years. It is in common use for house-buildings.—*Mr. Mendis.*

VACHELLIA FARNESIANA, *W. & A.; W. Ic.*

Mimosa farnesiana, *Roxb. Fl. Ind.*
,, Indica, *Poir.*
Acacia farnesiana, *Willd.*
,, Indica, *Desv. D C.*

Gooya babula. Beng.	Vaday valli maram. Tam.
Jali mara. Can.	Peetumma. Tel.
Guya-babula. Hind.	Kampu tumma. Tel.
Iri babool. Mahr.	Kasturi ,, ,,
Urimeda. Sans.	Arimedamu. ,,
Veda vully maram. Tam.	Naga tumma. ,,

This has already been noticed under its synonym Acacia farnesiana, and is again noticed to give further synonyms. It grows throughout south eastern Asia, from Sind and the Himalayas to Malacca. It is an armed shrub, very common in the Dekhan, Mysore and Coimbatore It furnishes a good, hard, tough, wood, greatly resembling that of the babool " Acacia arabica," but the size is very small. It makes excellent ship knees and tent pegs, and it exudes much gum.—*Drs. Wight and Cleghorn, in M. C. C. and M. E. J. R., Voigt.*

VAGHEY, the Tamil name of a Ceylon tree which grows to about twelve inches in diameter: it yields a strong wood, and is used by the natives for wheels of carts, &c.—*Edye, on the Timber of Ceylon.*

VAIMBOO, Tam. A Travancore wood of a flesh colour, specific gravity 0·483, 2 to 4 feet in circumference, and used for tables, &c.—*Colonel Frith.*

VAKANATTY, Tam. A Tinnevelly wood of a whitey brown colour, used for building in general.—*Colonel Frith.*

VALLY CANJARM, Tam.? A Travancore wood of a brown colour; specific gravity 0·703, used for building common houses.—*Colonel Frith.*

VAMBOO, Tam. A Tinnevelly wood of a light straw colour, specific gravity 0·795, used for building in general.—*Colonel Frith.*

VANANGU, the Tamil name of a Ceylon tree which grows to about eighteen inches in diameter and twelve feet in height. Its wood is used by the native carpenters in house work &c., and produces a fruit which the natives eat.—*Edye, on the Timber of Ceylon*

VANGAY, a Palghat wood of a light brown colour, specific gravity 0·788. A small tree, used for beams and carts.—*Colonel Frith.*

VANKAY, Tam. A Tinnevelly wood of a light brown colour, specific gravity 0·888, used for building in general.—*Colonel Frith.*

VANPUGGALAH. A Travancore wood of a light yellow colour, specific gravity 0·604, used for light work.—*Colonel Frith.*

VARDAGOUR, the Malabar name of a small Malabar tree which is remarkably hard and strong. It is used by the natives for spears, weapons of defence, and such purposes as require the hardest kinds of woods. This tree is known as junglewood only.—*Edye, Forests of Malabar and Canara.*

VAROODAH. A Travancore wood of a yellow colour, specific gravity 0·855, used for building houses.—*Colonel Frith.*

VATALOO. A Travancore wood of a purple colour, used only for firewood.—*Colonel Frith.*

VATANBOO. A Travancore wood of a light brown colour, 2 feet in circumference, used for railings, fences, &c.—*Colonel Frith.*

VATERIA, *Species.*

Le-toak. Burm.

A handsome wood plentiful in the Tenasserim provinces suited for cabinet work, the purposes of the turner and other purposes requiring a wood of dense structure.—*Major Benson.*

VATERIA CEYLANICA, *Wight, Illust.*, p. 88, p. 3415.

Stemonoporus Wightii, *Thw.*

A great tree in the forests between Galle and Ratnapoora, and at Palmadolla, near the latter place: wood not known.—*Thw. En. Pl. Zeyl.*, p. 37.

VATERIA INDICA, *Linn.*

Elæocarpus copalliferus, *Retz.*
Chloroxylon dupada, *Ains. Buch.*

Dupa maram. Can.	Hal. Singh.
Piney varnish tree. Eng.	Hal-gass. Singh.
Indian copal tree. Eng.	Piney maram. Tam.
White dammar tree. Eng.	Kondricam. ,,
Peini mara. Maleal.	Vela kondrikam. Tam.
Vella kondrikam. Maleal.	Chadacula. Tel.
Payani. ,,	Dupada chettu. Tel.

The oil.

Piney tallow. Eng.	Piney yennai. Tam.
Dupada oil. ,,	

A large and stately tree, which grows to the height of about 60 feet, with entire, smooth, coriaceous leaves, and terminable panicles of white flowers. It is common in the hotter parts of Ceylon, up to an elevation of 2,000 feet, it grows in Canara and all along the Malabar coast: it is found also in Mysore, and in the western provinces of Ceylon, its wood weighs lbs. 26 to the cubic foot, and its timber is said to last 10 years. In Ceylon, its timber is used for packing cases, ceilings, coffins, &c, but, on the western coast of India, it is said to be an excellent and valuable building timber, as not liable to be attacked by the teredo and much employed in ship building. Mr. Edye says, that the Paini dupmaram (which seems the Vateria indica, for he says it produces a sort of resinous gum), is found in the Cochin and Travancore forests, but is rarely cut down, as the damah taken from it is valuable, and when mixed with the wood oil makes the Paini varnish. This tree produces the resin in India called Copal, in England known by the name of gum anime, as very nearly approaching the true resin of that name. The best specimens are employed as ornaments, under the denomination of amber (kahroba), to which it bears external resemblance, in its recent and fluid state it is used as a varnish called Piney varnish, in the south of India (Buchanan's Mysore, ii, p. 476), and, dissolved by heat in closed vessels, is employed for the same purpose in other parts of India. Another plant of the same genus, V. lanceæfolia, affords a resin from which hindus prepare one of the materials of their religious oblations (As. Res. xii, p. 539). This is an article of export to China from Sumatra, where this tree also grows to a height of thirty to fifty feet and from two to four feet in diameter, and in greater abundance than on the coast of Malabar. When the bark is wounded, a pellucid, fragrant, acrid, bitter resinous fluid, called piney varnish, "pundun" or liquid copal exudes, which, in the rays of the sun, becomes yellow and fragile like glass. It is in this state that it is well known in commerce, and in England receives the name of gum anime, as above noticed. In India it is usually called copal, also East Indian copal. It occurs of all shades of colour, between pale green and deep yellow, and in India the finest pieces are sold as amber (kah rubah Arab. Pers.) The resin is used in Ceylon as incense. A solid oil is prepared from the seeds and is called Piney tallow or dupada oil, Piney yennai, Tam., which is used for lamps, but is very suitable for soaps and candle making.—*Eng. Cyc., Captain Hawkes in M. E. J. R., Mr. Adrian Mendis, Thwaites, En. Pl. Zeyl. p.* 37, *Royle, Ill. Him. Bot. p.* 106, *Voigt.*

VATERIA LANCEÆFOLIA, *Roxb.*

Moal of Sylhet.

A large tree, common in Sylhet, and growing in Assam and the Khassya mountains. It has entire, smooth, coriaceous leaves, and terminal panicles of white flowers. It flowers in April and May and fruits in July and August. It is valuable as a timber tree. It exudes a clear liquid from wounds &c. in the bark, which soon hardens into an amber coloured resin. From this the natives distil a dark coloured and strong smelling resin called Choa, also Chova, and gond ? or gum, in Hindi. The brahmins use it as an incense.—*Voigt, Royle's Him. Bot., Eng. Cyc. Dr. Mason.*

VATERIA LANCEOLATA ? ?

Pan-they-ya. BURM. | Pan-thit-ya. BURM.

This tree is noticed by Captain Dance, but it may be the same as V. lanceæfolia. He says it is found along the coast near Amherst : and is abundant in Tavoy and Mergui but scarcely procurable in Moulmein. Its maximum length is 60 feet and maximum girth 6 cubits, and, when seasoned, it floats in water. It is often called white thengan, but it is closer and heavier than the thengan. It is, he says, an excellent wood for tool handles and planes, but has not sufficient spring for helves. The Burmese use it for all purposes to which thengan is applied, especially in junks, but the Burmese of Amherst say it is not quite so good or durable as thengan.—*Captain Dance.* (*Note*—Dr. Mason in his Tenasserim speaks of a species of Vateria as a common timber tree in the Provinces of Tavoy and Mergui. The timber, he says, is whiter than hopea, and equally good. Indeed it is often, he says, called white thengan, or white hopea, the woods being only distinguished in commerce by their colour. Wallich in his list of Indian woods mentions *Hopea floribunda* as known at Tavoy by the Burmese name of *tantheya.* This tree is called at Tavoy *pantheya,* but pantheya is said to be not a species of hopea. Its flowers, in white fragrant panicles, are often seen in the Tavoy bazar, and are very unlike the yellow secund flowers of the hopea.—*Dr. Mason.*)

VATICA, *Species.*

Koung mhoo. BURM.

A tree of Moulmein : wood used for making carts and boats.—*Cal. Cat. Ex.* 1862.—(*See* SHOREA.)

VATICA TAMBUGAIA.

Congo wood. TAM. | Thambagum. TAM.

This has been briefly noticed under Shorea tambugaia, it may be added, here, that it has a strong heavy wood, close grained, but splintery, superior in strength and finer in grain than Sal, too heavy for gun carriages, but would answer for all purposes where great strength is necessary.

VAW-KARAH, the Malayala name of a Malabar and Canara tree which produces the country olives, to which the natives are very partial. This fruit is also eaten by the wild beasts and birds of the forest, the tree grows to about eighteen feet high, and twelve inches in diameter.—*Edye, Forests of Malabar and Canara.*

VAYNGIE, in Tamil and Mulu Vengah in Malayala. This Malabar and Canara tree is of a dark olive and light brown colour, it is very strong and tough, it sometimes grows crooked, and to about two feet in diameter, and from thirty to thirty-five feet long, it is used by the natives both for houses and vessels. This sort has a single leaf in the shape of a pear, but the Vella-Vengah, which is the white or light coloured, has a long leaf, and grows to about eighteen inches in diameter, and twenty feet long. The natives prefer this wood for boat-crooks, and the curved parts of the frames of pattamahs and native vessels.—*Edye, Forests of Malabar and Canara.*

(*Note.*—This seems to be the Pterocarpus marsupium.)

VEKKALI TREE WOOD.

Vekkali maram. TAM.

A variegated hard close grained serviceable wood employed by the natives in house building and also for making doors, windows, handles of instruments, &c. &c.—*Ains. Mat. Med.*

VELASALU. The Tamil name of the Ceylon white iron-wood, which grows to about fourteen inches in diameter, and ten feet high. It is used by the natives for huts, poles, &c., and where strength and durability are required.—*Edye, Ceylon.*

VELATTI, the Tamil name of a wood of Malabar and Canara, which resembles the English pear tree. It grows to about twelve inches in diameter, and fifteen feet high, it would answer well for carved-work, from the fineness of its grain.—*Edye, Forests of Malabar and Canara.*

VELATTE, the Tamil name, Ballanju, in Portuguese, of a Ceylon tree, which grows to about fourteen inches in diameter, and eight or ten feet in height. It is remarkably strong, and is used by native carpenters in vessels. It produces a fruit which is eaten by the natives.—*Edye, Ceylon.*

VELCANA, the Tamil name of a Ceylon tree which grows to about twelve inches in diameter, and eighteen feet in height. In appearance it resembles English oak. The native carpenters use it in boats and vessels' frames, knees, &c.—*Edye, Ceylon.*

VELLAH AHGUILL. A Travancore wood of white colour, specific gravity 0·602, 2 feet in circumference, 50 feet long, used for furniture.—*Col. Frith.*

VELHA AHGUILL, TAM. A wood of Travancore, of a light brown colour, 2 to 4 feet in circumference, used for furniture—*Col. Frith.* (*Note.*—Are these two identical ?)

VELLA CARDUNTHA, TAM. A Travancore wood, of a brown colour, 3 to 6 feet in circumference, 40 feet long, a strong wood, used for furniture.—*Col. Frith.*

VELLAI VENGAH, the Tamil name of a Malabar and Canara tree, the wood of which is of a light colour, and very tough and strong. It is used by the natives for the frames of vessels, or where strength is required; it grows to about eighteen inches in diameter, and twenty feet long, and the small branches make good boat crooks.—*Edye, Forests of Malabar and Canara.*

VELLA-LAVA, TAM. A wood of Travancore of a brown colour, used for light work.—*Colonel Frith.*

VELLA-NEER-MARADOO, TAM. A wood of Travancore of a light yellow colour ; specific gravity 0·573, used for furniture.—*Colonel Frith.*

VELLE AERE, the Tamil name of a Ceylon tree which is white Aere. It grows to about twelve or eighteen inches in diameter, and twenty feet in height. It is a light wood, and is generally converted into catamarans, being considered useful for that purpose only.—*Edye, Ceylon.*

VELLE-ELOW, the Malayala name of a Malabar and Canara tree that grows to about sixteen feet high and eight inches in diameter, it is used by carpenters for the frames and knees of country vessels, it produces a white seed which the natives use medicinally.—*Edye, Forests of Malabar and Canara.*

VELLE NEALEA, the Malayala name of a Ceylon tree which grows to about ten inches in diameter, and ten feet in height. The branches of this tree are very strong, and are used for the frames of native vessels.—*Edye, Ceylon.*

VELLIELLUS, a Malabar and Canara tree, little used except by the natives for house work, its growth is small, and it is rather scarce. —*Edye, Forests of Malabar and Canara.*

VELL VIRU, the Tamil name of a Ceylon tree which is about fourteen inches in diameter, and eight feet in height. Its strength and durability induce the natives to prefer it to other wood for the purpose of supporters to their huts. —*Edye, Ceylon.*

VELTY MARAM, TAM. A Travancore wood of a purple colour, specific gravity 0·623, used only for firewood.—*Colonel Frith.*

VELTY TADDY, TAM. A Travancore wood of a brown colour, specific gravity 0·635, used only for firewood.—*Colonel Frith.*

VEMBAH, the Tamil name of a tree which grows in Travancore ; it is close grained and of a yellow tinge, and grows to about twenty feet long, and fifteen inches in diameter ; it is used for native purposes. The bark of this tree is steeped, and used by the natives in cases of eruptions in the skin ; and also to purify the blood after fevers, for which it is considered most valuable.—*Edye, Forests of Malabar and Canara.*

VEM-MARAM, TAM. A Tinnevelly wood of a brown colour ; specific gravity 0·786, used for building in general.—*Colonel Frith.*

VENERAH, the Malayala name of a jungle tree of Malabar which grows to about twenty-four feet in height, and eighteen inches in diameter. It is used in building native vessels and for other native purposes.—*Edye, Forests of Malabar and Canara.*

VENGA MARAM, TAM.

Yepi ? vriksha. CAN. | Yapa chettoo. TEL. ?

This is reckoned by the natives of the Circars a very useful wood, it is of a reddish colour and is employed in making doors and windows and other common purposes. It is in common use both for building and for furniture in the Masulipatam district, it is a very heavy wood, but not strong, when used for rafters, it should be cut very broad in comparison to its thickness.—*Mr. Rohde*. (*Note*.—Is it Pterocarpus marsupium?)

VENGENDAH, the Tamil and Malayala name of a Malabar tree which the natives use for catamarans and in rafts for heavy timber, it is remarkably soft and spongy, and not of much use or durability.—*Edye, Forests of Malabar and Canara.*

VENGULA CYAM, the Tamil name of a Ceylon tree of little value. It grows to about twelve inches in diameter, and six feet high, and produces a fruit which is not made use of.—*Edye, Ceylon.*

VEN-PALLA, TAM. A Travancore wood of an ash colour. Only used for carved figures, sandals, &c.—*Col. Frith.*

VEN-TEAK, in Tamil and Bellinger in Malayala. This Malabar tree is much used by the native carpenters for house building and masts for dowes, pattamahs, and other country vessels. It grows to ninety and one hundred feet long, and from twelve inches to three feet in diameter, it is perfectly straight and without branches, excepting at its top; the leaves are small and very thick. This wood is not so durable as the poon, but it may be considered of the same texture, although it is very much lighter in colour, and in this respect much resembles the American red oak.—*Edye, Forests of Malabar and Canara.* (*Note.*—This seems the Lagerstrœmia microcarpa.)

VERAETAL, the Tamil name of a Ceylon tree which grows to about fourteen inches in diameter, and eight feet high. It resembles mahogany, but is capable of a more brilliant polish, the natives use it for superior purposes. It produces a kind of fruit which is of little use. —*Edye, Ceylon.*

VERAM PELOW, the Malayala and Tamil name of a Ceylon tree known by the name of Jackwood. It is common throughout India, and of great value to the natives, its fruit and nuts forming a part of their food. The wood when cut is yellow, but, when exposed to the air, turns as dark as mahogany, to which it is superior in brilliancy. It is generally used in articles of furniture for the Europeans, and for house work, and is considered handsome, the largest tree of this kind which Mr. Edye had seen was about three feet in diameter, and from thirty to thirty-five feet high, in Canara, this was the wood which Tipu Sultan used for his vessels at Honore, where his naval depot was formed.—*Edye, Ceylon.* (*Note.*—This seems the Artocarpus integrifolia.)

VERDA CANARA, the Tamil name of a Ceylon tree which grows to about twenty inches in diameter, and from thirty to sixty feet high. At times, some of the country vessels get their masts from this tree, it is not durable or strong. —*Edye, Ceylon.*

VERNANGU, the Tamil name of a Ceylon tree which is also named mast-wood. It is light and is used by the natives for the masts and yards of small vessels. It grows to about twenty inches in diameter and from twenty to forty feet in height. It produces a fruit or seed similar to that of the Poon.—*Edye, Ceylon.*

VETTI MARAM, the Malayala name of a Malabar tree, that grows to about twelve feet high, and eight inches in diameter. Its wood is much admired on account of its handsome dark streaks of black and brown, with white and yellow ground. It is very much like ebony in grain, and also in leaf. It produces a flower which is considered sacred; and is used for decorating the women on days of ceremony at the pagodas.—*Edye, Forests of Malabar and Canara.*

VEROOSOO, TAM. A Tinnevelly wood, of a whitey brown colour; used in building in general. —*Col. Frith.*

VEYTTY, a Travancore wood, of a light brown colour. Used for making carts, ceilings, &c.—*Col. Frith.*

VIPENIE, the Tamil name of a Ceylon tree, which grows to fourteen inches in diameter, and from twelve to fifteen feet high. It is used for boat work and house furniture.—*Edye, on the Timber of Ceylon.*

VIREY, the Tamil name of a Ceylon tree which grows to about twenty inches in diameter, and twelve feet high. This is a very handsome hard wood. It produces a kind of seed which is very mealy and which the poorer class of the natives eat as a substitute for rice.—*Edye, on the Timber of Ceylon.*

VISENIA VELUTINA, *W. Ic.*

Riedelia velutina, *D C.*
Glossospermum velutinum, *Wall.*
Visenia umballata, *Blain.*

A considerable tree of Java and Mauritius, of great beauty, with rose coloured flowers and velvety leaves; introduced from Sumatra into the Society's Garden, by Dr. Wallich.—*Voigt, Dr. Cleghorn in M. E. J. R.*

VITEX *Species*. A tree of considerable size, a native of the forests in the interior of Coromandel.—*Mr. Rohde's MS.S.*

VITEX, *Species*.

Kjeyoh. BURM.

This wood of British Burmah is used for tool handles, and is much prized, but rather scarce; a cubic feet weighs lbs. 45. In a full grown tree on good soil, the average length of the trunk to the first branch is 15 feet; and average girth measured at 6 feet from the ground is 3 feet.—*Dr. Brandis, Cal. Cat. Ex.* 1862.

VITEX ALATA, *Roxb.*

Mel-ilow. MALEAL.

A small tree found in the Naggery hills, leaves ternate, petioles winged. It occurs in the Bombay presidency, but is rare. Both it and V. leucoxylon have a white compact wood, apparently good for turning, as well as for cabinet work.—*Drs. Cleghorn and Gibson.* (*Note.*—It would be desirable to learn more of this tree.)

VITEX ALTISSIMA, *Linn.; Roxb.; W. Ic.*

Katu mellau mara. MALEAL.	Mililla-gass. SINGH.
Meeyan mililla-gass. SINGH.	Kat miella maram. TAM.

In Ceylon, it is common in forests, up to an elevation of 3,000 feet, In Coimbatore, it is a large tree, of great beauty when in flower, and frequent on the slopes of the western ghats. But Dr. Wight was not acquainted with the timber, except in so far as could be learned from a small outside specimen which seemed close grained. It was reported to him as fit for cabinet purposes. Under this name, Dr. Gibson says, he is not sure as to the species which Dr. Wight had in his eye, when he remarked on this. There are in the Bombay presidency two species of the genus, V. alata and V. leucoxylon. In Ceylon, this tree produces one of the most valuable timbers in the island for building and other purposes. The Ceylon Meean millile is very hard, fine close-grained and heavy.—*Thw. En. Pl. Zeyl., p.* 144, *Drs. Wight, Cleghorn and Gibson.*

VITEX ARBOREA, *Roxb.; Rheede.*

H'tonk Sha. BURM.	Nevali adugu. TEL.
Tonk-t'sa, „	Nawel busi, eragu „
Chaste tree, ENG.	Neval adugu manu, „
Katta mellalu, MALEAL.	Nowlee eragu, „

A native of the mountainous parts of the circars, of the forests of the Godavery, growing in Silhet, Chittagong; very common at Moulmein and found at Tavoy, Penang and Singapore, its flowering time is the hot season, and the seed ripens during the rains. In the Circars and Chittagong it grows to be a very large tree, and at Moulmein it furnishes a valuable small timber. Its wood is hard, of a yellowish brown colour, and when old is chocolate coloured, very hard and durable, which renders it useful for various ordinary purposes.—*Voigt, Roxb., Captain Beddome, Dr. Mason, Cal Cat. Ex.* 1862.

VITEX LEUCOXYLON, *Roxb.*

Karril. MALEAL.	Karril, CAN. of RHEEDE.
Neva-ledi. TEL.	

A native of the hotter parts of Ceylon, both peninsulas, Coromandel, Assam, the mountains of Chittagong; flowering time April. According to Dr. Gibson, Vitex leucoxylon is not uncommon by the edges of streams in the south Konkun, and the ghaut jungles of the Bombay presidency. According to Dr. Brandis, it is a large tree, very common in the plains of British Burmah, wood grey, deserves attention for furniture, used for cart wheels, breaking weight 142 lbs. A cubic foot weighs lbs. 42. In a full grown tree on good soil, the average length of the trunk to the first branch is 30 feet, and average girth measured at 6 feet from the ground is 12 feet. It sells at 8 annas per cubic foot.—*Thwaites, Voigt, Drs. Gibson and Brandis, Cal. Cat. Ex. of* 1862.

VITEX NEGUNDO, *Linn.; Roxb.; W.; Ic.;*

Vitex paniculata, *Lam.*

Fenjengisht. AR.	Sindhuka. SANS.
Nishinda. BENG.	Soodoo Nikka gass. SINGH.
Nergundi. „	Vella nuchi. TAM.
Shumbali. DUK.	Veyala chettu. TEL.
5 leaved chaste tree. ENG.	Waynlaku. „
Nisinda. HIND.	Wyala. „
Ban nuchi. MALEAL.	Nalla vavali. „
Sinduya. SANS.	

A small tree common in Ceylon on the banks of rivers, up to 3,000 feet in the peninsula of India, Bengal, the Dehra Dhoon and the Moluccas—*Thw. p.* 244, *Voigt. p.* 469.

VITEX PUBESCENS, *Vahl; Wight Ic.*

A Ceylon tree.—*Thw. En. Pl. Zeyl. p.* 244.

VITEX TRIFOLIA, *Linn.*

Ussel ke abi ? ? AR.	Jala nergundi. SANS.
Kara nuchi. CAN.	Sinduvara. „
Nirgunda. DUK.	Sappos milile ? SIND.
Pani ke shumbali. „	Meean „ ? „
3 leaved chaste tree. ENG.	Caba „ ? „
Indian prenet. „	Nir nochi. TAM.
Nisinda. HIND.	Vavili chettu. TEL.
Seduari. „	Tella vavili. „
Nishinda. „	Caranosi. RHEEDE.
Kara nuchi. MALEAL.	

This botanical and vernacular name is given by Mr. Mendis to a tree which grows in the western provinces of Ceylon, its wood weighing lbs. 56 to the cubic foot and lasting 20 to 90 years. Edye describes the Mean milille, as a very hard, fine, close grained, heavy, Ceylon wood and Mr. Mendis says, it is used for bridges, water-casks, paddle boats, carts, waggon-wheels, bullock carts, water tubs and house buildings. Under the name of Caha milile he describes the V. trifolia as occurring in the southern and western districts of Ceylon and as Sappoo milile in the western and southern districts, but weighing 49 feet to the square foot and lasting 10 to 40 years. There seems some confusion in the Singhalese synonyms, which perhaps are not applied to the correct plant; for Mr. Thwaites merely says, the V. trifolia is not uncommon near the sea, in Ceylon. It is a small tree, found in south-eastern Asia.—*Mr. Edye, Mr. Mendis, Thw. En. Pl. Zeyl. p.* 244. *See* V. ALTISSIMA.

VITMANNIA TRIFOLIA.

Samadera. SINGH.

Under these names, Mr. Mendis notices a tree of the western province of Ceylon, the wood of which weighs 26 lbs. to the cubic foot and which is used for buoys, &c., it is said to last 60 years.—*Mr. Mendis.*

VIZAGAPATAM. Large supplies of Sal

(Shorea) and Yegis (Pterocarpus marsupium) timber find their way to the coast in the north part of the Vizagapatam district, and in the whole of Ganjam. It is desirable to ascertain the sources of this supply, the method of transport and the rules under which the timber is cut. —*Conservator's Report, p.* 12.

VOODAGA WOOD. A wood of the northern circars.

VUTTY MARITHY, TAM. A Travancore wood of a brown colour, specific gravity 0·595, used in building common houses.—*Colonel Frith.*

VUDDAMBA. A Travancore wood of a brown colour, specific gravity 0·750, used in building common houses.—*Colonel Frith.*

VULOEAL, OR VULOAYLUM MARAM. In Ceylon, the Tamil name of a strong wood which is used by the natives in making farming utensils. It grows to twenty inches in diameter, and twelve feet in height. The bark of this tree, with the maradum bark and ginger, is used by the natives for cleaning and preserving the teeth.—*Edye, on the Timber of Ceylon.*

W.

WALSURA PISCIDIA, *Roxb.; W. & A.; W. Ill.*

Joe-boe. BURM. | Válarasi. TEL.
Walsura. TAM. | Wallurasi. TEL.

This tree grows in the Circars. It is very plentiful in the Pegu and Tounghoo forests, as well as in the Tharawaddy forests. The timber is large, heavy and strong. Wood, white colour and adapted for every purpose of house building. In India, the bark is thrown into ponds to kill fish, which, coming to the surface, are easily taken, and not considered injurious to be eaten. —*Royle, Ill. Him. Bot., p.* 143, *Voigt, Dr. McClelland.*

WALUKENE, SINGH. A tree growing in the western and southern districts of Ceylon, it weighs 39 lbs. per cubic foot, and lasts about 10 years. It is used for masts of dhonies.—*Mr. Mendis.*

WARDAH RIVER. Timber rafts can be floated down this river.—*Madras Conservator's Reports, p.* 4.

WEDGES. *See* SHOREA (VATICA) ROBUSTA.

WEBERA CERIFERA.

Tarrene. SINGH.

Under these names Mr. Mendis mentions a tree which grows in the northern provinces of Ceylon, it weighs 57 lbs. to the square foot, and is said to last 30 years. It is used for roofings and in the construction of fishing boats and dhonies.—*Mr. Mendis.*

WIHA OUNG, BURM. A tree of Moulmein, used for all ordinary purposes of building.—*Cal. Cat. Ex.* 1862.

WON-THAY-KHYAY. In Tavoy, a small, strong, compact, yellowish white wood.

WOOD ENGRAVING. The following Madras woods have been found suitable, viz:—

Guava, Psidium pyriferum; the best.

Palay, *Tam.* Mimusops hexandra. A good wood, but liable to be attacked by insects.

Vepalley, *Tam.* Wrightia antidysenterica. A fine close-grained wood, not quite so hard as the guava, but improving with age.

Jujube or Ber fruit tree, Zizyphus jujuba; rather soft.

Wood apple tree, Feronia elephantum, too coarse in the grain.

Satin wood, Swietenia chloroxylon. A close grained wood, but apt to split.—*Dr. Hunter.*

WOOT-THA, BURM. A tree of Moulmein. A strong wood for any ordinary purposes.—*Cal. Cat. Ex.* 1862.

WOON, URIA. A tree of Ganjam and Gumsur, extreme height 60 feet, circumference 5 feet, and height from the ground to the intersection of the first branch, 5 feet. No use is made of the wood, the tree is prized on account of its fruit which is pickled and eaten in other forms, the leaves are used for eating from; the flowers are eaten. The tree is scarce.—*Captain Macdonald.*

WORMIA TRIQUETRA, *Rottl., (H. f. et. T., I. c. p. 67)—c. p.* 1013.

Deeyapara. SINGH.

A moderate sized tree, common in Ceylon in the moist warmer parts of the island, up to an elevation of 2,000 feet.—*Thw. En. Pl. Zeyl. p.* 4.

WRIGHTIA, *Species.*

Beejee kooroowan. URIA.

A tree of Ganjam and Gumsur, extreme height 25 feet, circumference 2 feet and height from the ground to the intersection of the first branch, 8 feet. Tolerably common, and burnt for fire-wood. The milky juice is used for wounds.—*Captain Macdonald.*

WRIGHTIA, *Species.*

Toungzalat. BURM.

A beautiful wood of British Burmah. A cubic foot weighs lbs. 55. In a full grown tree on good soil the average length of the trunk to the first branch is 40 feet and average girth measured at 6 feet from the ground is 5 feet.—*Dr. Brandis and Cal. Cat. Ex.* 1862.

WRIGHTIA ANTIDYSENTERICA. *R. Br.*

Nerium antidysentericum, *Linn.; Ains.; Roxb.*

La-thou. BURM.	Kalingamu. TEL.
Conessi bark tree. ENG.	Kodisa pala chettu. „
Inderjau. HIND.	Kodisa chettu. „
Vepali. TAM.	Kodisa pala. „
Veppaula. TAM.	Kola mukki chakka. „
Kodaga pala. TEL.	Kutajamu. „
Pala chettu. „	Manu pala. „
Girimallika. „	Pedda ankudu chettu. „

The wood.

Palavarani. ENG.	Veppallay. TAM.
Palay wood. „	Palava renu. TEL.
Dudhii-ke-lakri. HIND.	

The bark.

Conessie. FR.	Corte-de-pala. PORT.
Curayia. GUZ.	Chiri. SANS.
Curuja. „	Kutaja. „
Curayia. HIND.	Veppalei. TAM.
Curaija. „	Pala codija. TAL.
Codaga pala. MALEAL.	Manupala. „
Palapatta. „	

The seed.

Lisan-ul-assafir. AR.	Indrayava. SANS.
Indrajow. GUZ.	Veppalei arisi. TAM.
Ahir. PERS.	

A small tree of common occurrence in Mysore and the hilly parts of southern India, and occurs also in Tavoy: the wood is of little value but its medicinal virtues are worthy of attention, the bark was formerly in request under the name of *Conessi* and is still esteemed a valuable drug by the natives in dysentery and bowel complaints. It appears to have lost its value in commerce, by not being distinguished from the bark of Wrightia tinctoria which grows in the same places.—*Voigt, Fl. Andh. Faulkner.*

WRIGHTIA MOLLISSIMA. Grows in Kemaon and on the Naggery hills; the yellow juice might be turned to account, but the timber is of no value.—*Dr. Cleghorn.*

WRIGHTIA TINCTORIA, *R. Brown; W. Ic.*

Nerium tinctorium, *Roxb.*

Kala koodoo. HIND.	Chitti ankudu. TEL.
Kala koodoo. MAHR.	Amkadu. „
Pallay maram. TAM.	Tedla pala. „

A small tree, found in the Coimbatore, Godavery and other forests of the Madras Presidency, and very common in all the forests of Bombay. It affords a very beautiful wood, white, hard and close grained; in the words of Dr. Roxburgh "coming nearer to ivory than any I know." In the Coimbatore jungles, where it is common, it attains a considerable size, but is not much in use there, but that of the Godavery is described as most valuable for turning. The leaves are said to afford an inferior kind of Indigo, hence the Mahratta name. It is extracted by scalding.—*Drs. Wight, Gibson and Cleghorn, Captain Beddome.* (*See* NILAM PALA.)

WRIGHTIA TOMENTOSA, *R. A. D C. Prod.; W. Ic.*

Nerium tomentosum, *Roxb.*

Koila mookree. TEL.

A small tree not very uncommon in the central province of Ceylon. Grows in the Circars and lower Godavery jungles. Wood not used—it appears close grained. The juice is a permanent yellow dye. Bark given internally for scorpion bites.—*Thw. En. Pl. Zeyl. p.* 193, *Captain Beddome, Voigt.*

WYNAAD FOREST LANDS. The Madras Conservator of forests mentions that these lands are principally contained in the four Umshoms adjoining the teak forests, viz., Moonanad, Ganaputhy vuttum, Ellornad, Poolpully dasum of Koopatode. They contain blackwood, &c., and much bamboo land, in many places, the land is well fitted for coffee. He says the destruction of these forests not containing teak for the bonâ fide cultivation of coffee may be considered legitimate, but not so for raggee, which spoils the land for ever from being cultivated for coffee. At least, if raggee is cultivated on lands unsuited for coffee, it should be done on a pattah, with permission of the deputy collector and taxed at a low rate. This system is carried to a great extent in the Umshoms of Ganaputhy vuttum and Moonanad in bamboo and tree jungles. The extent of Government lands in Wynaad is not known, but Government also possess some forest lands towards Periah and Teriate, and in fact in several spots over Wynaad. In the teak belt are several bands of Coorumburs some of the Jani and others of Moolly caste they amount to about,

Coorumburs..........	200	Panniars and Pooliar.	100
Gurcheas............	50	Chettys and Squatters.	50

The former live entirely in the forest. They are the only axemen, nd without them it would be difficult to work a forest. The Coorumburs, through their headmen, are held responsible, and the Chettys are also responsible for their Panniars or farm slaves. He recommends that the Assistant Conservator be armed with powers to fine for wilful waste and destruction of Government forest, and which no amount of planting will counteract. The Coorumbur has no lack of labor. His services are constantly called for by the wood contractor and the planter. They will not leave their haunts in the forests for any time. From Korchat in the east to Kooderykote in the west, a distance of some forty miles, past clearings for raggi have from time to time taken place, and there is hardly a square mile where traces of the Tukkul, temporary clearing system may not be seen, but owing to the richness of the soil, and moisture of the climate, the teak tree has, in most places, defied all efforts at extirpation. In some parts suckers from the old stoles, shooting up some fifty feet, straight as a fir, may be counted by thousands. In other parts it is lamentable to see the destruction caused by Coorumburs; acres and acres of girdled Teak trees of every size, from the sapling six inches in diameter, to the noble tree upwards of three feet.

It is the sale of these girdled trees, from which at present, revenue is derived, and to clear out the forests thoroughly, it will take at least three years, so numerous are the girdled trees. Very high prices have been realized for this dry Teak, as it is called, eight annas a cubic foot, or on an average ten Rupees a tree, some of the trees being small, this rate may be considered as very remunerative.—*Rep. Con. For. p.* 26 *and* 1861-62, *p. I.*

X.

XANTHOCHYMUS OVALIFOLIUS, is found in Rangoon, Pegu and Tounghoo districts, but is rather scarce, it was at one time supposed to yield gamboge.

XANTHOCHYMUS PICTORIUS, *Roxb.*

Stalagmitis pictorius, *G. Don.*

Dampel. HIND.	Chitaka mraku. TEL.
Eeswara mamidi. SINGH.	Tamalamu. „
Iswara mamadi. TEL.	Rata. GHORKA.
Dampel ? „	

Is very plentiful in the Rangoon, Pegu and Tounghoo districts. It was formerly supposed to be one of the trees yielding gamboge, but the product is found not to possess the elements of gamboge.

XANTHOPHYLLUM, *Species.*

Sa-phew. BURM.

A very large tree, growing in Martaban, where it is used for posts and rafters. There are two other species of Xanthophyllum in Tenasserim.

XANTHOPHYLLUM FLAVESCENS, *Roxb.*

A large tree, a native of the hilly parts of the province of Chittagong.—*Roxb. ii. p.* 222.

XANTHOPHYLLUM VIRENS, *Roxb.*

Gundee. BENG.

A large timber tree of the forests of Sylhet, wood remarkably hard and useful.—*Roxb. ii. p.* 221.

XANTHOXYLUM. This now includes Fagara, extending northwards into the temperate zone, and species of the same genus occur in China and Japan, and extend in India to Simla in 31° N. latitude, where X. hostile, differing little from X. alatum, is found. Other species run southwards along the Himalayas to Nepal and Silhet, and then to the Malayan and Indian peninsulas, whence we may trace them to the African islands on the east of that continent. So in India X. Budrunga, Rhetsa, alatum, and hostile, are used, wherever they are indigenous, for the warm spicy pepper like pungency of their capsules, a property which is participated in by their bark, and other parts. The capsules and seeds of X. hostile, called tej-bul by the natives are employed in northern India for intoxicating fish, and chewed as a remedy for tooth-ache; they are also given as the Faghureh of Avicenna, as Z. piperitum and Avicennae, are in China and Japan, and are considered an antidote against all poisons. Dr. Royle has no doubt that in many cases they would be of considerable use as a stimulant remedy.—*Royle, Ill. Him. Bot. p.* 157.

XANTHOXYLON BUDRUNGA, *DC.*

Fagara budrunga, *Roxb.; Fl. Ind.*

Toung-than. BURM.	Young-tha-ji. BURM.

A tree of Assam, wood not known.—*Voigt.*

XANTHOXYLON RHETSA.—*DC.; W & A.; Rh.*

Fagara rhetsa, *Roxb.*

Mulila. MALEAL.	Rhetsa maram. TAM.
Kattoo-keena-gass. SINGH.	Rachcha manu. TEL.

Grows in the central province of Ceylon and near Colombo, also on the coast hills of peninsular India. This tree so precisely corresponds with Roxburgh's description that there can be no doubt of its being the *Fagara rhetsa* of that author: wood not known.—*Thw En. Pl. Zeyl., I. p.* 69, *Voigt, p.* 185.

XANTHOXYLON TRIPHYLLUM, *Juss.; W. Ill. and Ic.*

Xanthoxylon zeylanicum, *DC. Prod.*
Evodia triphylla, *DC.*
Fagara „

Loonoo-ankenda-gass. SINGH.

Very abundant in Ceylon up to an elevation of 5,000 feet, var. β.—near Ratnapoora.—*Thw. En. Pl. Zeyl. I. p.* 69.

XYLOCARPUS, *Species.*

Ke-an-nan. BURM.

A tree of Tavoy, furnishing very durable timber. It seems to be the same as that described by Dr. Mason as growing on low lands near the sea coast, and producing a red wood which turns black on being anointed with petroleum. It is much used for sandals, and canoes are occasionally made of it. This tree grows in Tavoy, is found very abundant all along the sea shore from Amherst to Mergui, and in the Mergui Archipelago. It is very common in the mangrove swamps. Its maximum length is 20 feet, and maximum girth 4 cubits, and when seasoned it floats in water. It is a very good, fine and strong wood, splits with difficulty. It is used by Burmese for all parts of houses, posts, flooring, walls, &c., and is recommended by Captain Dance for hand-spikes, helves, spokes and handles of tools, also for shot boxes and packing cases. Its inedible fruit is not, says Dr. Mason, that of the Cocos de mer, but as the tree grows near the shore, the fruit falls into the sea, on which it floats.—*Dr. Mason, Captain Dance.*

XYLOCARPUS ECHINATUS ? ? ?

Ah Nan ? ? ?

A tree of Moulmein, a very strong wood, used for making gun stocks and sword scabbards.—*Cal. Cat. Ex.* 1862.

XYLOCARPUS GRANATUM, *Kœn.*

Carapa Moluccensis, *Lam.*

Puroos. BENG.	Penlay-oong. BURM.
Pen-lay-pyoun. BURM.	Sea cocoanut. ENG.
Pen-lai-ung. "	

Grows in the south of Ceylon and in the forests of the delta of British Burmah; wood used for house posts and musket stocks. A cubic foot weighs lbs. 47. In a full grown tree on good soil, the average length of trunk to the first branch is 20 feet and average girth measured at 6 feet from the ground is 12 feet. Captain Dance also says its maximum girth is 4 cubits and maximum length 20 feet. Very abundant all along the sea shore from Amherst to Mergui. When seasoned it floats in water. It is used by Burmese for all parts of houses, posts, flooring, walls &c., is a very good, fine, strong wood, and splits with difficulty. Recommended for hand-spikes, helves, spokes, and handles of tools, also for shot boxes and packing-cases—*Dr. Brandis, Cal. Cat. Ex.* 1862, *Thwaites, p.* 16, *Captain Dance.*

Y.

YA-KA-NGINE, BURM. A tree of Moulmein, wood used in ordinary house building.—*Cal. Cat. Ex.* 1862.

YAKAULEY, TAM.? A Tinnevelly timber, of a light brown colour, used for building purposes.—*Col. Frith.*

YAMANEE, BURM. A tree on the hills of Tenasserim, which furnishes a remarkably light, white timber, resembling mootchee wood, of which the natives often make canoes. The Karens say it bears a yellow flower, and a small plum, which is a favorite food with the barking deer.—*Dr. Mason. See* YEMMANEE.

YAMANI, BURM. A tree of Moulmein, wood used in ordinary house building.—*Cal. Cat. Ex.* 1862.

YAMMANDY, BURM. In Amherst, a useful and valuable wood, used for carving images and making drums.—*Cat. Ex.* 1851.

YANGY, TAM. A Tinnevelly timber of a light brown colour, used in wheel-wrights' work.—*Colonel Frith.*

YARVINEY, TAM. Crawn in Portuguese and Dutch of Ceylon. This Ceylon tree grows tall and straight, from twenty to forty five feet high, and from twelve to thirty inches in diameter. It may be obtained in great quantities, and answers many purposes in ship and house work.—*Edye, on the Timber of Ceylon.*

YA-THA-NAT, BURM. A tree of Moulmein. An inferior wood for boats, which lasts but two or three years. The fruit is an article of food.—*Cal. Cat. Ex.* 1862.

YA-THA-PYA, BURM. A tree of Moulmein. The fruit is edible. Used for house building purposes.—*Cal. Cat. Ex.* 1862.

YA-THITS. In Pegu, Dr. McClelland says, the cutting of Yathits should be, as far as practicable, prohibited. He adds that however desirable it may be to forbid or enforce such a rule, he is at a loss to know how much impediment can be attempted or laid without stopping the trade of yard-pieces, which are just as much in demand as mast-pieces. He is of opinion that a large consignment of timber might be realized, and duty received on them, and it will facilitate the growth of the under sized trees.—*Selection Records of Government of India, Foreign Department, No.* IX, *p.* 47.

YEENGA, BURM. A very abundant but small timber tree found at Moulmein and scattered over the Tenasserim provinces. Its maximum girth is 2 cubits and maximum length 15 feet, and it sinks in water when seasoned. It is a very pretty white wood for furniture, and is used by the Burmese for helves and for mamoties, and though not so strong as Chisel-handle-tree, it possesses similar properties, though in an inferior degree. It sells at Rs. 45 per 50 feet by 1 foot square.—*Captain Dance.*

YELLAREE, TEL. This wood of the Nalla Mallai is used in small quantities, but it appears a useful wood: it is of a light brown colour with a good grain.—*Mr. Latham.*

YERRA POLEEKI, TEL. A hardish wood of the Nalla Mallai of a red colour and very useful.—*Mr. Latham.*

YELLOW-WOOD. In England, there is a fine East India wood thus called, it appears to be larger and straighter than box wood, but not so close grained. Holtzapfel thinks it would be found to be a valuable wood for the arts.—*Holtzapfel.*

YEMMANEE, BURM. This tree is very abundant. The Karens say, it bears a yellow flower and a small plum which is a favourite food with the barking deer. It is found on the hills of Tenasserim, inland near the banks of the Gyne and Attaran rivers, and at the back of the mountains near Moulmein. Its maximum girth is 4 cubits and maximum length 20 to 30 feet. It furnishes a remarkably light white timber resembling mootchee wood, which, when seasoned, it floats in water. It is a slightly scented wood, free from cracks and the lightest of Captain Dance's collection, who mentions that it is quite free from acid or from a tendency to rot. It is very durable: the Burmese often make canoes of it and use it for boats, and it is employed by the king of Ava for his carved furniture. Captain Dance says it is excellent for fuzes.—*Dr. Mason's Tenasserim, Captain Dance.*

YENG-BYWOM, BURM. Employed in Amherst for house posts. It is a useful wood, equal to Jarool.—*Cat. Ex.* 1861.

YENG-TAIP, BURM. In Amherst, it is a strong useful wood for posts and common carpentry.—*Cat. Ex.* 1861.

YETHA-BYAY. This Amherst wood is used for house posts and boat building; it is a strong wood, suited for door-frames and common carpentry.

YEW-WOOD. A tree of Mehra forest, near Abbottabad, Hazara. Natural order, *Taxinidæ.* —*Cal. Cat. Ex.* 1862.

YIN-YO. A tree of Moulmein. A strong wood, good for building purposes.—*Cal. Cat. Ex.* 1862.

YOGA-THEET, BURM. A timber tree of Amherst. This wood is used for carved images, and the bark used as soap.—*Cat. Ex.* 1861.

YOMAH MOUNTAINS. Dr. McClelland mentions that these, the central chain of Burmah proper, are extended into Pegu and form the spine, as it were, of the province with the valley of the Irrawaddy on the west, and that of the Sitang on the east; and the several minor valleys lying between the off-shoots by which the chain is terminated on the south, as the valley of the Zamayee or Pegu river, the valley of Hlaine or Line river, together with the intermediate valley of the Phoungee river or Paizoondown creek, lying between the Hlaine and Pegu rivers. One of the most southern points of the Yomah lies between the Hlaine and Paizoondown, of which the Pagoda hill at Rangoon may be considered the last elevation, marking the direction of the chain or line of local disturbance. The most elevated portion of the Yomah chain appears to be that from whence these southern branches radiate, where the Oakkan and Thounzai Choungs derive their source, falling into the Hlaine rivers on the west, and the Zamayee and Phoungyee rivers, on the east and south. This part of the chain, Dr. McClelland estimates at about 2,000 feet above the sea, presenting steep and inaccessible declivities.—*Dr. McClelland, Selections Records of Government of India, Foreign Department, No.* IX, *p.* 6 *and* 7.

YOUNG-THA, BURM. This tree is found in moderate quantities along the sea coast near Tavoy and Mergui. Its maximum girth is 3 cubits and maximum length 30 feet. The seasoned timber sinks in water. It is a heavy durable wood, used for posts and planks of houses, and not bad for planes or handles, though surpassed for these by other woods of Amherst, Tavoy and Mergui.—*Captain Dance.*

YOW-MA-LAY, BURM. In Tavoy, a strong, heavy, rough, white wood; used for house-posts. —*Mr. Blundell.*

Z.

ZALACCA EDULIS. The light Selung boat in which the Selungs of the Mergui Archipelago shoot over their waters, owe their buoyancy to the stems of the edible zalacca, which form their sides. These stems are as light as, and of the consistency of cork, for which they are often substituted; and the Selungs are skilful in uniting them together to serve instead of planks, so as to make an unequalled sea boat, that floats on the waves like a swan.—*Dr. Mason's Tenasserim.*

ZANGYEEOAT-DOUP, BURM. Oak-leaved Pollypod.(?) A tree of Moulmein, used for all ordinary purposes of building. Fruit used medicinally.—*Cal. Cat. Ex.* 1862.

ZA PADRUP, BURM. A tree of Moulmein, a strong wood, good for building purposes.—*Cal. Cat. Ex.* 1862.

ZEE-BYION. This is a compact, close grained Amherst wood, like Lagerstrœmia, or white Jarool. It is used for house posts, and is liable to split, but is free from the destructive influence of insects.—*Cal. Cat. Ex.* 1862.

ZINPYUN GYEE, BURM. A tree of Moulmein; wood used in ordinary house building.—*Cal. Cat. Ex.* 1862.

ZIZYPHUS, *Species.*

Zi-thi, BURM.

Grows in Tavoy, and yields a hard and durable wood.—*Dr. Wallich.*

ZIZYPHUS, *Species.*

Contaya-kulli. TEL.

This large creeper common in Ganjam and Gumsur, has a circumference of 1½ feet. The charcoal used in making country gun powder, is made by burning this tree. The chatty used in pacottahs is placed in a frame work made of this. —*Captain Macdonald.*

ZIZYPHUS GLABRATA, *Heyne.*

Zizyphus trinervia, *Roxb.; Fl. Ind.*

Kurkutta wood ENG. | Kurkutta maram TAM.
Ran-bor. MAHR. | Karukuva. TAM.
Kurkatta maram. TAM. | Kakupala. TEL.

This tree grows in the peninsula of India. In the Bombay presidency, it is most common in cultivated lands and in alluvial soil on the banks of rivers. It is less common on the Bombay sea coast, than inland. Dr. Wight had seen trees, in Coimbatore, that would yield 12 inch planks, but it is commonly a moderate sized tree, though its timber, of a light brownish colour, is excellent, hard and close grained and takes an excellent polish. The bark affords a quantity of kino like gum, both by exudation and by decoction.—*Drs. Wight and Gibson, Voigt.*

ZIZYPHUS JUJUBA, *Lam.; Roxb.; W and A.; W. Ic.*

Zizyphus sororia, *Schult.*
Rhamnus jujuba, *Linn, Rheede.; Rumph.*

Ziruf. AR.	Bor. MAHR.
Usslie suddir. AR.	Elentha. MALEAL.
Koolgach BENG.	Perin todali. "
Bher. "	Yellandy maram TAM.
Kul. "	Ellendi "
Hyi-bin. BURM.	Regu manu. TEL.
Elanji mara. CAN.	Ganga regu. "
Guly mara. "	Regu chetta. "
Bher. DUK.	Karkandhava. "
Jujube tree. ENG.	Renga. "
Bher. HIND. MAHR.	

The fruit.

Unab. AR.	Elandei pallum. TAM.
Ber ka phal. DUK.	Regu pandu. TEL.
Budderie. SANS.	

This tree is found in Ceylon, throughout British India and in the Archipelago in Sunda and the Moluccas, but growing to various dimensions. Mr. Masson found the Ber tree generally throughout the tract between Saiyad Wala and Lahore, a distance of 40 miles, not confined to the vicinity of villages, and attaining a much larger size than he had elsewhere seen, as also does its fruit, which is there sweet and palatable. In the Bombay presidency, Dr. Gibson failed to find any specific difference between the wild and cultivated species. It grows there to a large size, fit for planks or sleepers, for which latter it might answer well in the dry climate of Sind, where the tree is common. In Coimbatore, it is usually of small size, but the dark brown wood is fine grained, strong and hard, and fitted for cabinet making purposes, for saddletrees, and implements of husbandry and sandals. In Burmah, it is scarce only found near large towns, rarely in the Pegu and Tounghoo forests.—*Drs. Gibson, Wight, Cleghorn and McClelland, Mason, Vol. I, p.* 403, *Voigt, p.* 145, *Thw., Mr. Latham, Captain Beddome.*

ZIZYPHUS LUCIDA, *Moon.* In the Matele and Kornegalle districts, of Ceylon, very abundant.—*Thw. En. Pl. Zeyl.*, I, *p.* 74.

ZIZYPHUS XYLOPYRUS OR GLABRA.? Ghattoo, HIND.? Under these names, as a fine large tree of Jubbulpore, there was sent to the Exhibition of 1862, a scarce wood, but close grained and excellent.—*Cal. Cat. Ex.* 1862.

ZIZYPHUS XYLOPYRUS, *Willd; Roxb.; W. & A.*

Zizyphus elliptica, *Roxb.*
" caracutta, *Roxb.*
" orbicularis, *Schult.*

Gumun mara. CAN.	Gatte chettu. TEL.
Guti. MAHR.	Gotte chettu. "

This tree grows in Ceylon and throughout the south of India, and can always be recognized by the pale colour and softness of the under surface of its leaves. It is most common below the ghauts in Canara and Sunda, but it never grows to a very large size. Its wood is used for implements and its fruit is employed in the arts, being much used by shoe-makers to blacken leather and to make blacking.—*Dr. Gibson, Voigt, Thw. p.* 74.

I have been favoured with the following Tabular Statements from Beresford Anderson, Esq., of the Madras Railway, Major Benson, Major Macdonald, Captain Philipps, Captain Puckle, of the Madras Army. Tables will also be seen collected from Dr. Wight's Report, Colonel Frith's list, from the Reports of Captain Dance and Colonel Simpson of the Royal Artillery, from experiments by Captain Best of the Madras Engineers, and by Messrs. Goldingham and Rohde of the Madras Civil Service. The results of their experiments are each recorded.

TIMBER AND FANCY-WOODS OF EASTERN AND SOUTHERN ASIA.

Dr. Wallich is the only author we shall quote on the subject of the woods of Asia generally, and we give his Catalogue here, as furnishing places of growth, the weight per cubic foot and specific gravity of the principal of the woods of which we have already given the list.

No.	NAME.	Place of growth.	Weight per cubic foot. lbs.	oz.	Specific gravity.
1	Acacia—? (Popceah,) ...	Tavoy, ...	23	3	.371
2	do do ...	do. ...	23	3	.371
3	Ægle marmelos (Bellee), ...	Ceylon, India.	49	1	.784
4	Anacardium latifolium Bhela	Gualpara, ...	37	0	.592
5	Andrachne apetala, ...	India, ...	33	14	.542
6	Artocarpus chaplasha, ...	do ...	34	12	.556
7	Artocarpus hirsuta (Anjelly-wood), ...	Cochin, ...	36	14	.590
8	Artocarpus integrifolia (Jack wood), ...	Travancore, ..	35	10	.570
9	Artocarpus—? (Pynyathe Tanabeng), ...	Tavoy, ...	...		...
10	Aultoovanchee, ...	Travancore, ...	31	6	.502
11	Auyanny, ...	do ...	32	11	.523
12	Averrhoa carambola, ...	India, ...	39	11	.635
13	Bah-nah-thoa, ...	Tavoy, ...	...		...
14	Betula Bhojpattra, ...	Nepal, ...	35	5	.565
15	Bignonia chelonoides, ...	do ...	42	8	.680
16	Bignonia—? (Thathee), ...	Tavoy, ...	49	8	.792
17	Bignonia (Thuggainee), ...	do ...	40	4	.644
18	Cadooca Marum, ...	Travancore, ...	38	3	.611
19	Calophyllum—? (Thurappe; chopee), ...	Martaban, ...	43	0	.688
20	Cambagum, ...	Travancore, ...	28	11	.459
21	Canoo, ...	... ...	36	0	.576
22	Cannal, ...	Travancore, ...	47	6	.758
23	Cannao, ...	do	58	7	.935
24	Caragagaloo,... ...	do	33	0	.528
25	Carapa—? (Tai-la-oon), ...	Tavoy, ...	36	0	.576
26	Careya—? (Kaza), ...	Martaban, ..	46	0	.736
27	Careya (Kombo), ...	Gualpara, ...	42	12	.684
28	Caringosha, ...	Travancore, ...	45	5	.725
29	Carivagah, ...	do	33	10	.538
30	Caroogha, ...	do	44	10	.7 4
31	Caroo Marum, ...	do	47	11	.763
32	Carintha, ...	do	34	4	.548
33	Cassia, ...	India, ...	41	9	.661
34	Castanea indica, ...	do ...	39	0	.624
35	Castanea tribuloides (Cotoor; chisee, Makoo; shingali).	Nepal, ...	62	0	.992
36	Catunguin, ...	Manilla, ...	42	11	.683
37	Caultoo mooroonga, ...	Travancore, ...	45	14	.734
38	Ceder, ...	India, ...	25	2	.402
39	Cedrela Toona (Toon, Tunga, Poma Jeea), ...	Gaulpara, ...	36	0	.576
40	Cedrela Toona (Toon, Tunga, Poma Jeea), ...	India, ...	32	9	.521
41	Chambagum,... ...	Travancore, ...	37	11	.603
42	Chana, ...	do.	20	7	.327
43	Chinchona gratissima (Tungnusi), ...	Nepal, ...	23	0	.368
44	Chorangaree,... ...	Travancore, ...	29	11	.475
45	Cæsalpinea sappan (Sappan)	do	60	14	.974
46	Coombool, ...	do	31	14	.510
47	Coturnba, ...	Ceylon, ...	23	5	.373
48	Cou-moo, ...	Tavoy, ...	...		...
49	Cynometra polyandra, ...	India, ...	52	10	.842
50	Cynometra—? (Maingya)...	Martaban, ...	48	7	.775
51	Dalbergia lanceolaria (Neddoon, Nedum, Nander-wood)	Ceylon, ...	45	7	.727
52	Dalbergia latifolia (East India ebony),... ...	India, ...	66	8	1.064
53	Debool, ...	Ceylon, ...	38	3	.615
54	Diospyros melanoxylon (Black ebony), ...	... ...	61	2	.978
55	Diospyros racemosa, ...	India, ...	34	11	.555
56	Diospyros—? (Ryamucha choomullo),... ...	Martaban, ...	50	8	.803
57	Dipterocarpus—? (Kunneanphew), ...	Tavoy, ...	25	3	.403
48	Domba, ...	Ceylon, ...	33	3	.531
59	Dombeya melanoxylon (St. Helena-ebony), ...	St. Helena, ...	71	9	1.145
60	East India Ebony. See Dalbergia.				
61	East India Rosewood, ...	India, ...			
62	Ehretia lævis, ...	Botanic Garden, Calcutta.			
63	Ekebergia—? (Jiyakohi),...	Gualpara, ...	39	1	.625
64	Eleocarpus serratus (Weraloo), ...	Ceylon, ...	33	8	.536
65	Eribotrya japonica (Loquat).	India, ...	46	11	.747
66	Eugenia malaccensis (Jamboo), ...	Ceylon, ...	30	4	.484
67	Eugenia malaccensis (Jamboo), ...	do ...	30	14	.494
68	Excœcaria, ...	Tavoy, ...			
69	Fagræa fragrans (Annahbeng, Burm),... ...	Martaban, ...	52	8	.840
70	Ficus—? (Thubboo), ...	Tavoy, ...	21	0	.336
71	Gadehoo, ...	Ceylon, ...	21	3	.339
72	Galloopah, ...	Travancore, ...	53	0	.848
73	Garcinia—? (Tullowa), ...	Tavoy, ...	45	8	.728
74	Garcinia—? (Purrah wah).	do ...	45	8	.726
75	Gmelina arborea, ...	India, ...	32	3	.515
76	do do ...	do ...	32	6	.516
77	Go-na, ...	Ceylon, ...	24	8	.392
78	Gordonia—? (kaza), ...	Martaban ...	37	10	.603
79	Guacua, ...	India, ...	41	14	.670
80	... ...				
81	Gundrucy, ...	India, ...	34	15	.559
82	Heritiera—? (Soondree),...	do ...	57	15	.927
	do do ...	do ...	49	15	.799
83	Hibiscus macrophyllus, ...	Tavoy, ...	27	13	.445
84	Hibiscus macrophyllus, ...	do ...	28	0	.448
85	Hibiscus, ...	do ...			
86	Hopea floribunda (Tantheya)	do ...	27	11	.443
87	Hopea odorata (Tengaun, Thaeu gong), ...	Martaban, ...	38	0	.608
88	do do do	Tenasserim Coast, ...	40	12	.652
89	Hune, ...	Burmah, ...			
90	Indian Wood,... ...	do. ...	45	6	.726
91	Jerah, ...	India, ...	36	11	.587
92	Juglans pterococca, ...	do. ...	39	14	.638
93	Juniperus excelsa (cedar of Himalaya), ...	... ...	34	7	.551
94	Kaantha, ...	Tavoy, ...			
95	Kain-tha-pogee. See Symplocos.				
96	Kaunzo-kurro, ...	do ...	43	0	.688
97	Kaza. See Careya, also Gordonia,				
98	Keahnaun, ...	do ...			
99	Keaza Perroun, ...	do ...			
100	Kuddoot-alain, ...	do ...	53	3	.851
101	Kuddoot-nee,... ...	do ...	34	0	.554
	do do ...	do ...	34	3	.547
102	Kunneen-keunkee. See Bignonia, ...	do ...			
103	Kunneen-keunla. See Symplocos, ...	do ...			
104	Lagerstrœmia reginæ, ...	India, ...	46	8	.744
105	Lagerstrœmia—? (kuenmounee; Peema), ...	Tavoy, ...	37	9	.601
106	Laurus camphora ? Camphor wood), ...	China, ...	35	14	.574
107	... ...				
108	Laurus—? (Kayzai),... ...	Tavoy, ...	43	3	.691
109	Laurus—? (Kullowa, also kurrowa), ...	... ...	30	0	.480
110	do do ...	Tavoy, ...	30	0	.480
111	Laurus—? (Lumpatch, Chasepoo), ...	Nepal, ...	34	0	.544
112	Laurus—? (Panatha), ...	Tavoy, ...	43	0	.688
113	Laurus—? (Sassafras), ...	India, ...	33	12	.536

No.	NAME.	Place of growth.	Weight per cubic foot.		Specific gravity.
114	Laurus—? (Thuggoo),	Tavoy,			
115	Manga chapui,	Manilla,	41	15	.671
116	Maroothee,	Travancore,	37	7	.599
117	Maunthaen or Sassafras,	Tavoy,	36	10	.586
118	Maymaka,	India,	51	12	.828
119	May rang,	Tavoy,	48	9	.777
120	Megeongee,	do	38	16	.617
121	Melia Azadirachta,	India,	46	1	.739
122	Metrosideros vera (iron wood),	China,	53	0	.848
123	Mimosa odoratissima,	India,	45	6	.726
124	Mimosa polystachya,	Botanic Garden, Calcutta.	32	0	.512
125	Mimusops Elengi,	Tavoy,	46	0	.736
126	Moluvo or Moloba,	Manilla,	51	3	.819
127	Moonga Vallah,...	Travancore,	38	5	.613
128	Mootoocorandy,...	do.	38	13	.621
129	Morinda citrifolia,	Botanic Garden, Calcutta	28	10	.458
130	Morung saul. See Shorea,				
131	Munha cadamboo,	Travancore,	38	15	.623
132	Murraya—? (Maikay),	India,	60	13	.973
133	Myrsine capitellata,	Nepal,	21	11	.349
134	Nar, or sacred wood,	Ceylon,	55	0	.880
135	Neerovallum,	Travancore,	24	5	.389
136	Nelle,...	Ceylon,	34	8	.552
137	Netty, or Nelley...	Travancore,	42	5	.677
138	Nerium tinctorium,	India,	39	14	.638
139	Nun Poungoo,	Travancore,	56	15	.611
140	Odina Wodier,	India,	41	0	.656
141	Osyris peltata (Phaoun),	Tavoy,	29	10	.474
142	do do	India,	30	8	.488
143	Pah-doubh,...	...	60	0	.960
144	Palah,...	Travancore,	14	9	.230
145	Palai,...	Borneo,	23	13	.381
146	Palm,...	India,	57	9	.921
147	Palmist,	do.	62	7	.929
148	Panacha,	Travancore,	44	14	.718
149	Pen lay oun,	...	32	0	.512
150	Penlaly peen,	Tavoy,			
151	Peroomarum,	Travancore,	27	14	.446
152	Pienmahne,	Tavoy,			
153	Pienmah-pue,	do			
154	Pierardia ? (kunna, also kuzzo),	do	37	12	.604
155	Pinus dammara,...	do	39	0	.627
156	Pinus longifolia,...	Nepal,	...		...
157	Pinus Webbiana,...	...	21	0	.336
158	Poomaram....	Travancore,	29	8	.472
159	Poomdroo,...	do	40	13	.653
160	Poonah,	do.	50	15	.815
161	Pothiree,	Travancore,	35	4	.564
162	Premna hircina (chikagambhari),	Gaulpara,	43	0	.691
163	Psidium pomiferum (Guava).	Travancore,	44	3	.704
164	Pterocarpus santalinus (Red Sanders),...	India,	46	14	.750
165	Pterocarpus ? (Thounkheea).	Martaban,	51	9	.826
166	Pterospermum indicum (Amboyna),	East India Islands.	39	10	.634
167	Quercus Amherstiana, Tirbbae, Ryakle,...	Martaban,	57	10	.922
168	Quercus fenestrata,	India,	47	0	.752
169	Quercus lanceaefolia,	do.	41	10	.666
170	Quercus lappacea,	do.	51	4	.820
171	Quercus semecarpifolia (Ghese cusroo)	Nepal,	22	0	.352
172	Regal wood,	Thibet,	54	6	.870
173	Rhizophora decandra,	India,	46	6	.736
174	Rottlera ? (keounlae,)	Tavoy,	37	9	.601
175	Sandoricum—? (Thittoo,)...	do.	28	6	.454
176	Santalum album...	India,	47	13	.765
177	Sapotea ? (Palaepean),	Tavoy,	41	0	.656
178	Shytalia longa...	India,	44	8	.712
179	Scytalia trijuga,...	do	60	0	.960
180	Scytalia—? ,...	do	39	6	.630
181	Shorea robusta (Indian saul)	do	52	10	.842
182	(Morung saul)...	Nepal,	43	14	.702
183	...	do.	45	14	.734
184	Sonneratia ? (Thaumma),...	Tavoy,	42	0	.672
185	Sophora robusta,	India,	42	4	.676
186	Sterculia ? (Kuneenee),	Tavoy,			
187	Swietenia chloroxylon (satin wood Booroota),...	Ceylon,	51	0	.816
188	Swietenia febrifuga,	India,	54	14	.378
189	Symplocos floribunda,	Nepal,			
190	Symplocos ? (kaintha phogee),	Tavoy,	34	7	.551
191	Symplocos ? (kunneen keunkee, kunneen keunla),	do	34	4	.548
192	Syndesmis tavoyana (keetha)	do			
193	Tantheya,	do	44	0	.704
194	Taxus virgata, (Dheyn also Lolsi),	Nepal,			
195	Tectona grandis (Teak, Taaka, Tekka),...	Ceylon,	47	3	.755
196	do. do. do.	Travancore,	42	8	.680
197	Tectona grandis (East Indian teak),	Malabar Coast	37	14	.606
198	do. do.	Moulmein,	31	9	.505
199	do. do.	do.	32	1	.513
200	Terminalia catappa,	Botanic Garden Calcutta.	32	0	.480
201	Terminalia chebula,	India,	42	10	.682
202	Terminalia citrina,	do.	60	2	.962
203	Terminalia—? (Thaphaugo)	Tavoy,	50	5	.805
204	Ternstromia—? Puzzeinzwa.	do.	36	7	.783
205	Tetranthera nitida,	India,	34	4	.548
206	Teutha,	Tavoy,	54	0	.864
207	Thallarwoo,	Travancore,	44	0	.704
208	Thambuvoo,	do.	55	6	.886
209	Thaun-bau-po...	Tavoy,			
210	Thau-baunthawlay,	do.			
211	Toun-mynga,...	do.	48	0	.768
212	Thymboo,	do.	17	7	.279
213	Thymboo, Thau-baunpo,	do.	17	3	.275
214	Town-pine,	do.	28	13	.461
215	Town-suggah,...	do.			
216	Une,...	do.			
217	Vallathorashel,...	Travancore,	22	1	.353
218	Vanava,	Manilla,	42	11	.683
219	Vanneemooringa,	Travancore,	40	10	.650
220	Vateria lanceæfolia,	India,	53	15	.863
221	Vavoolagoo,	Travancore,	29	4	.468
222	Vellilagoo,	do.	28	8	.456
223	Velty, or Vetty,...	do.	40	11	.657
224	Venga,...	do.	47	1	.753
225	Vinnee,	do.	15	18	.248
226	Vinny marum,...	do.	11	3	.179
227	Vyashanthak,...	do.	41	0	.656
228	White dammar lout,	India,			
229	Xanthophyllum—? (Sapheu, Choomuna),...	Martaban,	33	10	.538
230	Xylocarpus—? (Keannan).	Tavoy,	46	9	.745
231	Zizyphus—? (zeethee),	India,	35	11	.571

CEYLON WOODS.

The late SIR GEORGE ANDERSON sent us the following list of 96 *Timber Trees* in *Ceylon*, drawn up by Mr. ADRIAN MENDIS, Mohandiram of Moorrotto, and Master Carpenter, Royal Engineer's Department.

NAMES. Cynghalese. Botanical.	Locality. Provinces.	Weight per cubic foot.	Durability.
		lbs.	years.
A			
1 Andere. Acacia Vera.	Eastern.	71	15
2 Madetiye. Adenanthera pavonina.	Western.	56	30
3 Kebelle. Oblique Euginea.	Northern.	40	20
4 Cottamba. Almond.	W. & Southern.	38	30
5 Welipiyanna. Anissaphyllum zeylanicum.	Western and Northern.	35	40
6 Cocatiye. Aponogeton crispum.	Western.	56	30
7 Puwak. Areca nut.	Western, Eastern and Southern.	57	60
8 Patta Del. Artocarpus sps.	Southern.	34	30
9 Cos. Jack. Artocarpus integrifolia.	South Eastern and Western.	42	25—80
10 Del. Artocarpus pubescens.	E. S. & Western	40	25—50
11 Aludel. Artocarpus pubescens.	Western.	51	35—70
B			
12 Bairiye.	Northern and Western.	57	10—30
13 Mee, Bassia longifolia.	Northern.	61	25—80
14 Petan. Bauhinia tomentosa.	Eastern.	57	
15 Lunu Midelle. Common Bead tree.	Western.	15	8—20
16 Hal Milile. Berrya ammonilla.	Northern and Eastern.	48	10—80
17 Tal. Palmira. Borassus flabelliformis.	Northern and Eastern.	65	80
18 Calukeale. Butea frondosa.	Central.	38	30
C			
19 Calu Mediriye. Calamander. Diospyros hirsuta.	Southern and Western.	57	80
20 Waldombe. Calophyllum acuminatum.	Western.	89	20
21 Gorrukeence. Calophyllum calaba.	Western.	44	25
22 Dombe. Sweet scented Calophyllum.	Western.	40	5—10
23 Mahadan. Calyptranthes cumini.	Northern and Western.	36	20
24 Battedombe, Clove tree leaved Calyptranthes.	Western.	45	20
25 Alubo. Jambolana Calyptranthes.	Central.	49	20
26 Kahatte. Careya arborea.	W. & Southern.	88	10—20
27 Davette. Carallia zeylanica.	Western.	42	25
28 Kittool. Nepara. Caryota urens.	W. & Southern.	71	30—90
29 Dawol kuroendo. Cassia cinnamomum.	Central.	39	20
30 Arremene. Sumatra Cassia.	Central.	57	50
31 Hedde woke. (Choecarpus pungens ?)	Western.	58	50
32 Burute. Satin. Chloroxylon Swietenia.	Southern and Eastern.	55	10—80
33 Mal burute. Flowered Satin. Chloroxylon Swietenia.	Northern and Eastern.	57	80
34 Nelly. Cicca disticha.	Central.	49	30
35 Cocoanut. Cocos nucifera.	Sea coast generally.	70	20—50
36 Wea warene. Cratæva religiosa.	Central.	62	60
37 Hal Mendora. Branch flowered Cynometra.	Western.	56	8—20
38 Gal mendora. Branch flowered Cynometra.	W. & Southern.	57	15—60
D			
39 Nendoon. Dalbergia lanceolaria.	W. & Southern.	56	60—80
40 Daminne.	Eastern.	44	40
41 Gode parre. Toothed Dillenia.	Western.	51	60
42 Horre. Turbaned Dipterocarpus.	Western.	45	15
43 Doon. Dipterocarpus sp.	Central.	29	50
44 Dive parre.	Western.	44	20
E			
45 Caluvere. Ebony.	N. and Eastern.	71	80
46 Kadoembeiriye. Bastard Ebony.	Western.	45	40
47 Kiri walla. Lance leaved Echites.	Northern.	35	30
48 Book attene. Echites scholaris.	Western.	26	
49 Timbery. Embryopteris glutinifera.	Northern.	45	20
50 Walboamboo. Eugenia laurina.	Central.	36	15
51 Naw, Iron wood. Mesua ferrea.	Western.	72	10—60
52 Kiripelle. Indian fig tree. Ficus indica.	Southern.	30	20—30
53 Hunukirille, Grewia paniculata.	Southern.	44	25
54 Belygobel. Telia leaved hibiscus.	Western.	38	20
55 Nerreloo. Illicebrum latrum.	Central.	56	40
56 Dive ratembela. Jonesia asoca.	Northern.	58	25
57 Katie kale.	Eastern.	42	25—50
58 Murute. Lagerstrœmia reginæ.	W. and Southern.	42	30—40
M			
59 Hulanhick, Melia sp.	Central.	39	50
60 Rameneidelle, Millingtonia, sp.	Western.	48	20
61 Sappoo. Michelia champaca.	Central.	42	20—50
62 Sooriva Mara. Mimosa.	Central.	42	20—30
63 Moone Mal. Mimusops elengi.	Southern.	61	50
64 Paloo. Mimusops hexandra.	Eastern.	68	10—70
65 Morre. Eye ball.	Central.	62	25
66 Etteiriye. Ash leaved Murraya.	Eastern.	61	10—70

EXPERIMENTS ON TIMBER AT ERODE, CONDUCTED BY T. B. FRENCH, ESQ.

Names. Cynghalese. Botanical.	Locality. Provinces.	Weight per cubic foot.	Durability.
N		lbs.	years.
67 Helembe, Nauclea parviflora.	W. & Northern.	42	40
68 Nebede.	Sou. & Western.	51	20
69 Gal morre. Nephelium, sp.	Central.	65	30
O			
70 Koang. Ceylon Oak.	Southern.	42	5—10
71 Melle. Olax Zeylanica.	Eastern.	64	40
P			
72 Patkeale.	Western.	42	40
73 Penebarroo.	Eastern.	61	50—90
74 Sooriya. Persian.	Central and Western.	49	20—40
75 Velenge. Pterospermum ruberifolium.	Central.	36	5—70
R			
76 Hirikoddol. Rhizophora. Sp.	W. and Northern.	49	35
77 Cadol. Leafy mangrove, Rhizophora.	Northern and Western.	65	40
78 Pehimbive. Rhus disipium.	Central.	68	50
79 Otte. Rottlera, sp.	Western.	36	10
S			
80 Lawoloo. Sapota, sp.	Western.	39	10
81 Pamburoo. Limonia citrifolia.	Southern.	48	40
82 Daanga. Long flowered Spathodea.	N. and Western.	23	
83 Telemboo, Sterculia fœtida.	Central.	26	30
84 Suvande.	Western.	56	30
85 Siyembela. Tamarindus Indica.	North Eastern and Western.	80	80
86 Teak, Ceylon. Taikke Ceylemey. Tectona grandis.	Western.	55	15—60
87 Teak, Cochin. Taikke Cotchive.	Cochin.	44	15—90
88 Teak, Maulmein. Taikke Molmine.	Maulmein.	42	15—90
89 Ukbeirriye.	Southern.	51	80
90 Hal. Vateria indica.	Western.	26	10
91 Caha Milile. Vitex trifoliata.	Southern and Western.	56	15—80
92 Meean Milile. Vitex trifoliata.	Western.	56	20—90
93 Sappoo Milile. Vitex trifoliata.	Western and Southern.	49	10—40
94 Samedera. Vitmannia trifoliata.	Western.	26	60
95 Walukeene.	W. & Southern.	39	10
96 Tarrene. Webera cerifera.	Northern.	57	30

EXPERIMENTS on Timber at Erode Workshop, Madras Railway, September 1861, Conducted by T. B. FRENCH, Esquire.

The timber upon which the experiments were tried, were Teak, Vangay, Vellanagay, and Karoomarodoo. Each piece was one inch square and fifteen inches long, and supported at each end, having a bearing of 1½ inch on the supports, so that the length unsupported was one foot.

Two pieces were placed on the supports at the same time at about three feet apart, and a bar of iron 2 inches square was laid over them, bearing exactly in the centre of each on this bar, other bars were placed transversely, so that the entire weight was on the centre two inches of the beam.

Result of Experiments.

Timber.	No. of experiments.	No. of lbs. which broke two pieces.	Breaking weight of one piece.	Remarks.
Teak....	No. 1	1,146	573	
	2	833	416	
	3	827	413	
Average......	...	...	467	Broke short.
Vangay....	1	876	438	The Vangay was rather green.
	2	999	499½	
	3	1,196	598	
Average......	...	...	511	
Vellanagay....	1	1,350	675	Well seasoned, very tough.
	2	1,352	676	Do.
	3	1,811	905	Do. white wood.
Average......	...	...	752	
Karoomaroodoo....	1	1,942	971	
	2	1,692	846	
	3	1,658	829	
Average......	...	...	881	

EXPERIMENTS on the strength of the undermentioned various specimens of Teak and other Timber produced in the Tenasserim provinces, the weights being applied by half hundred weights.

Date.	Number marked on Specimen.	Number tested.	NATURE OF WOOD.	Length. Feet.	Dimensions square.	Specimens. Weight of lbs.	ozs.	drs.	Deflection. 5 Minutes with 224 lbs.	5 Minutes with 448 lbs.	5 Minutes with 606 lbs.	5 Minutes with 830 lbs.	Broke with lbs., including weights of scales and Esses. Last weight. lbs.	Last curve of deflection.	After Minutes.	Specific Gravity Temperature of the water in which immersed 79.	REMARKS.
			TEAK TIMBER.		Ins.				224 Ins.	448 Ins.	672 Ins.	868 Ins.					
13th Sept	1	1	Young Thounggeen killed	3	1 1/2	2	0	12	1/4	1/2	13/16	1 1/8	884	1 1/8	1/2	·721	Long firm good fibre, well interlaced, but rather coarse.
,, ,,	2	2	Zemi, very large	3	1 1/2	1	9	8	1/2	1 1/8	532-1 3/4	0	543	1 3/8	2	·776	Bad fibre, short and carotty.
,, ,,	3	3	Zemi large, burnt tree	3	1 1/2	1	10	8	5/16	3/4	642-1 5/8	0	665 1/3	1 5/8	3 1/2	·600	Firm fibre, not long, but sound.
,, ,,	4	4	Thounggeen, young tree.........	3	1 1/2	1	15	12	3/8	5/8	1 3/16	714-1 3/8	736 2/3	1 3/8	2	·727	Long, very good fibre.
,, ,,	8	...	"*Padouk*" killed, seasoned ...	3	1 1/2	2	14	8	1/4	1/2	1 1/16	1 1/4	930 1/4	1 5/8	3 1/2	1·018	Excellent fibre, but specimen knotty.
15th Sept.	5	5	Thounggeen, dead tree, large...	3	1 1/2	1	10	8	1/2	1 1/8	0	0	543 3/4	1 1/2	2 1/2	·581	Fibre long, but coarse, and exhibiting a fine almost impalpable powder along the fibre.
,, ,,	6	6	Thounggeen, dead tree	3	1 1/2	1	10	8	7/16	7/8	0	0	594 1/4	1 1/4	2	·592	Long fibre, but not very strong.
,, ,,	7	7	Thounggeen, very large tree killed	3	1 1/2	1	14	0	5/16	5/8	7/8	1 7/8	868 1/4	1 7/8	1 1/4	·696	Very good fibre, broke with long splinters.
,, ,,	8	8	Thounggeen, large tree killed.	3	1 1/2	1	8	0	5/8	1 1/16	0	0	459 3/4	1 1/16	1/2	·569	Short fibre, no splinters.
,, ,,	9	9	Thounggeen, young tree killed.	3	1 1/2	1	12	0	1/2	1 1/16	0	0	597 3/4	2	1	·641	Very good fibre, promised a better result.
,, ,,	10	10	Thounggeen, dead tree	3	1 1/2	1	12	8	5/16	11/16	0	0	602 3/4	1 1/2	1/2	·590	Good fibre, specimen imperfect.
,, ,,	11	11	Thounggeen, large tree killed...	3	1 1/2	2	0	0	3/8	5/8	1	1 1/4	984 1/5	1 7/8	4	·724	Particularly long, tenacious fibre, broke gradually.
,, ,,	12	12	Thounggeen, large tree killed...	3	1 1/2	1	14	8	3/8	5/8	7/8	1 1/8	912 1/4	1 3/4	1 3/4	·693	Very good strong fibre.
,, ,,	13	13	Thounggeen, dead tree	3	1 1/2	1	13	12	1/2	7/8	1 5/16	0	721 1/2	1 7/8	1 3/4	·635	Very fine fibre, and had it been a killed tree, would have given good result.
,, ,,	14	14	Zemi-large, killed by fire	3	1 1/2	1	12	4	3/4	0	0	0	280 1/4	7/8	1/2	·659	Short, dry fibre, broke short.
7th Oct.	22	15	Best specimen of Zemi Timbers.	3	1 1/2	2	1	0	7/16	1 1/16	0	0	573 1/3	1	1	·688	Coarse fibre, killed when full of sap.
,, ,,	23	16	Best specimen of Zemi	3	1 1/2	1	14	8	3/8	1	0	0	461 1/3	1	1 1/2	·640	Do. do. do. do. do.
,, ,,	16	17	Thounggeen, dead tree	3	1 1/2	2	0	8	3/8	4/8	5/8	1	925 1/5	1 3/8	1/2	·706	Very long fibre, long splintering fracture.
,, ,,	19	18	Thounggeen, very large tree ...	3	1 1/2	1	15	8	3/8	4/8	5/8	15/16	913 1/8	1	1	·706	Very good fibre, long fracture.
,, ,,	15	19	Thounggeen, young killed tree, best specimen.........	3	1 1/2	2	1	0	5/16	4/8	11/16	1 1/16	929	1 1/8	1/4	·687	Excellent fibre, long and tenacious, killed when full of sap.
,, ,,	17	20	Thounggeen, killed tree	3	1 1/2	1	12	8	7/16	5/8	1 1/8	0	743 1/4	1 1/8	1/4	·692	Very good fibre, tree killed when full of sap.
,, ,,	18	21	Thounggeen, killed	3	1 1/2	1	14	8	5/16	4/8	1 1/8	15/16	857 1/4	1 3/16	1 1/2	·695	Good fibre, long and tenacious.
,, ,,	21	22	Best specimen of Zemi	3	1 1/2	1	15	8	4/8	7/8	0	0	517 1/3	7/8	2 1/4	·686	Long fibre, but very coarse.

Date.	Number marked on specimen.	Number tested.	NATURE OF WOOD.	Length. Feet.	Dimensions square.	Specimens. Weight of lbs.	ozs.	drs.	Deflection. 5 Minutes with 224 lbs.	5 Minutes with 448 lbs.	5 Minutes with 606 lbs.	5 Minutes with 830 lbs.	Broke with lbs., including weights of Scales and Eases. Last weight. lbs.	Last curve of deflection.	After minutes.	Specific gravity, temperature of the water in which immersed 79.	REMARKS.
7th Oct.	20	23	Thounggeen, very large dead tree	3	$1\frac{1}{2}$	1	15	4	$\frac{5}{16}$	$\frac{4}{8}$	$\frac{6}{8}$	$\frac{7}{8}$	$915\frac{1}{4}$	$2\frac{3}{8}$	$\frac{3}{4}$	·696	Excellent, long and tenacious, broke very gradually.
" "	24	24	Zemi Timber, best specimen.	3	$1\frac{1}{2}$	1	14	8	$\frac{11}{16}$	0	0	0	$348\frac{1}{2}$	$\frac{11}{16}$	$\frac{1}{4}$	·680	Short, carotty fibre.
Commissariat Specimens																	
These specimens are of Timber furnished for Arsenal purposes by the Commissariat Department.	1	25	Thounggeen Timber.	3	$1\frac{1}{2}$	2	1	0	$\frac{3}{8}$	$\frac{5}{8}$	0	0	630	$\frac{7}{8}$	0	0	Short bad fibre, broke across.
	2	26	Zemi Timber	3	$1\frac{1}{2}$	2	3	8	$\frac{6}{8}$	0	0	0	404	$1\frac{1}{8}$	1		Short bad fibre, broke across.
	3	27	Zemi Timber	3	$1\frac{1}{2}$	2	3	8	$\frac{11}{16}$	$1\frac{1}{8}$	0	0	460	$1\frac{1}{8}$	$\frac{1}{4}$		Coarse, rather long fibre, do. do.
	4	28	Zemi Timber	3	$1\frac{1}{2}$	2	2	12	$\frac{4}{8}$	$\frac{13}{16}$	0	0	550	$1\frac{1}{4}$	$\frac{1}{10}$		Short fibre, broke across.
	5	29	Thounggeen Timber	3	$1\frac{1}{2}$	2	1	0	$\frac{3}{8}$	$\frac{5}{8}$	0	0	570	$\frac{5}{8}$	$\frac{1}{10}$		Coarse fibre, full of sap.
	6	30	Zemi Timber	3	$1\frac{1}{2}$	2	1	0	$\frac{7}{16}$	$\frac{6}{8}$	0	0	575	$\frac{5}{8}$	$\frac{1}{10}$		Firm fibre, but rather short.
	7	31	Thounggeen......................	3	$1\frac{1}{2}$	2	3	0	$\frac{3}{16}$	$\frac{3}{8}$	$\frac{5}{8}$	$\frac{13}{16}$	$745\frac{1}{2}$	0	3		Long fibre, broke very gradually.
	8	32	Padowk, seasoned	3	$1\frac{1}{4}$	2	10	0	$\frac{3}{8}$	$\frac{4}{8}$	$\frac{6}{8}$	$\frac{7}{8}$	$1085\frac{3}{4}$	$1\frac{7}{8}$	$\frac{1}{2}$	1·008	Firm hard fibre, great tenacity.
	9	33	Anan Timber	3	$1\frac{1}{2}$	2	11	0	$\frac{3}{8}$	0	0	0	$460\frac{1}{2}$	0	1	·932	Fibre good and firm, specimen, imperfect.

(Signed) G. W. Y. SIMPSON, Captain,

Commanding Artillery, Tenasserim Provinces.

MEMORANDUM of various specimens of the Forest Timbers of the Tenasserim Provinces, tested at Moulmein by the Commissariat Department.

Numbers.	NAMES. Burman.	Talien.	Karen.	Botanical.	Specific gravity in lbs.	Breaking weight lbs.	Deflection in inches.	Girth of tree in feet.	DESCRIPTION.
1	Seet............			Acacia stipulata....	$48\frac{13}{16}$	997	$2\frac{1}{8}$ In.	5 to 6 ft.	These three specimens are nearly identical, corresponding with Nos. 45, 47, 48, page 132 of Dr. McClelland's report, useful for ornamental purposes. Nos. 11 and 23, subject to the attacks of insects; not very abundant.
11	Koko............	Sycthan.	Poomah.	Acacia. *sp*..........	38	758	$1\frac{2}{10}$,,		
23	Seet, No. 2...			do.	56	600	$1\frac{1}{4}$,,		
2	Yendaik........			Dalbergia, *sp*......	83	1000	$1\frac{7}{10}$,,	$2\frac{1}{2}$ to $3\frac{1}{2}$,,	Strong, dense, variegated grained wood, useful for naves of wheels, block sheaves, tool handles, and also for turning.
$2\frac{1}{2}$	Kyœ..........			Syndesmis Tavoyana...	..	646	1 ,,	$2\frac{1}{2}$ to $3\frac{1}{2}$,,	Pretty coloured red wood, useful for furniture, a brittle wood.
$3\frac{1}{2}$	Theetsie........	Soothan.	Kiahong.	Melanorrhea usitatissima.	$61\frac{1}{2}$	509	$1\frac{1}{8}$,,	6 to 8 ,,	Handsome wood, particularly adapted for furniture, too brittle for most other purposes requiring strength.
10	Thabotghee .			N. O. Leguminosœ.	60	807	$1\frac{3}{4}$,,	5 to 6 ,,	A tough wood, useful for tool handles, furniture and other purposes where larger scantling and great strength are not required.
15	Eing or Aeng.	Sooahn.		Dipterocarpus lœvis	46	758	$1\frac{1}{2}$,,	6 to 9 ,,	Three species of the wood oil tree, all of which are abundant, of great size and length, low specific gravity, does not stand exposure to wet and breaking weight equal to Teak, a valuable wood for house building purposes when not exposed to wet and damp, in the latter case perishable.
24	Eingdah.... ...		Talahung.	,, turbinatus.	52	747	$1\frac{1}{2}$,,		
46	Kanyeennee...			,, elatus......	46	702	$1\frac{1}{2}$,,		
17	Thubbu yen...	Sookreoung	Mee.	Dillenia ornata....	$44\frac{1}{2}$	808	$1\frac{3}{4}$,,	6 to 8 ,,	A wood most plentiful, well adapted for all purposes of carpentry, house and ship building; strongly recommended for trial.
56	Kyet Zinbain.	Kaloonoot.	Koung.	,, scabrella...	$44\frac{1}{2}$	691	$1\frac{1}{2}$,,		
58	Zinbain.........	Carllow.		,, speciosa....	55	930	$1\frac{1}{2}$,,		
20	Meenaban......			Pavetta Indica....	66	980	1 ,,	2 to $2\frac{1}{2}$,,	A strong wood, useful for ornamental or cabinet work, and handles of tools, spokes of wheels, and splinter bars.
25	Mancoga......			Cirae honucea, *sp*:	$44\frac{1}{2}$	772	1 ,,	2 to $2\frac{1}{2}$,,	A wood too brittle for any purposes otherwise than cabinet and ornamental work, resembles oak.
27	Bambooay....	Kabooay.	Tagooyee.	Careya arborea......	50	950	2 ,,	3 to 5 ,,	A tough wood, good for furniture and most purposes of carpentry.
33	Nubbay......			N. O. Leguminosœ.	60	795	$1\frac{1}{2}$,,	5 ,,	A handsome wood for furniture and general purposes of carpentry, also tool handles naves of wheels, it requires a long time to season.
35	Pethan.........			Bignonia stipulata.	$73\frac{1}{2}$	1678	$2\frac{1}{3}$,,	3 to 4 ,,	The strongest wood of all the specimens, well adapted for carriage poles, splinter bars, naves of wheels, blocks and all purposes where size and great strength is required, strongly recommended.
40	Letoak........			Vateria, *sp*..........	60	906	$1\frac{3}{4}$,,	3 to 6 ,,	A handsome wood, plentiful; suited for cabinet work, turning and other purposes requiring a wood of dense structure.
53	Pangah.........	Kuchaa.	Mourdah.	Terminalia, *sp*......	58	1000	$1\frac{3}{4}$,,	3 to $6\frac{1}{2}$,,	A strong elastic wood, strongly recommended for all purposes where strength and dense structure is required.
60	Toakiah.........	Chouchong.		do.	$71\frac{1}{2}$	969	$1\frac{1}{2}$,,	3 to $6\frac{1}{2}$,,	A dense structured wood; useful as the above.
100	Therapee			Calophyllum Burmanni	45	590	$1\frac{3}{4}$,,	5 to $7\frac{1}{2}$,,	A useful wood for general purposes, very plentiful.
101	Paranah.......			Garcinia speciosa.	71	927	$1\frac{3}{4}$,,	3 to 4 ,,	A handsome grained wood of too small scantling, to be of general use, also too valuable, being an edible fruit tree.
102	Pedowk........			Pterocarpus indicus	71	1000	$2\frac{1}{4}$,,	5 to 9 ,,	Too well known to require comment.
103	Pyenkadoo. .			Inga xylocarpa.....	83	1153	2 ,,	5 to 8 ,,	Do. do. do.
104	Pawoon.........	Socksone.	Kathong.	Byttneria, *sp*.	72	1351	$3\frac{1}{2}$,,	5 to 8 ,,	The strongest and most elastic wood of the collection, plentiful; most strongly recommended for gun carriage purposes, being superior, either to the Pedouk or Saul—the specific gravity given here is of a green specimen and therefore too high—if seasoned would be less than Pedouk which is another advantage.
105	Peemah.......			Lagerstrœmia......	38	822	$1\frac{1}{2}$,,	6 to 10 ,,	Too well known to require comment.
106	Engyeen.			Shorea robusta......	72	1043	$2\frac{1}{4}$,,	6 to 10 ,,	Do. do do.
8	Tayet khya. ..			Castanea, *sp*........	37	392	$1\frac{3}{8}$,,	3 to 5 ,,	A soft wood resembling deal; useful for packing cases and similar purposes.
39	Fentha......			do.	42	738	$1\frac{3}{8}$,,	3 to 6 ,,	Similar to the above but stronger; might perhaps be suited for fuzes.

A LIST of the most useful of these Woods selected and placed consecutively according to their relative breaking weight.

No. in List.		Names.	Breaking weight, lbs.	Remarks.
35	1	Pethan................	1,678	
104	2	Pawoon...............	1,351	Strongly recommended as an unexceptionable timber.
103	3	Pyenkadoo.	1,153	
106	4	Engyeen..............	1,043	
102	5	Pedowk..............	1,000	
53	6	Pangah..............	1,000	
2	7	Yendaik..............	1,000	
20	8	Meenaban...........	980	
1	9	Seet..................	997	
60	10	Toukiah..............	969	
27	11	Bamboay............	950	
58	12	Zinbain..............	930	Good wood for general purposes.
40	13	Letoak...............	906	
105	14	Peemah..............	822	
17	15	Thubbu..............	808	
15	16	Eing..................	758	
38	17	Eentha..............	738	
2½	18	Kyœ..................	646	
100	19	Theerapee..........	590	
3½	20	Theetsie	509	

Captain Macdonald's List of Ganjam and Gumsur Woods.

Names.	Extreme height. Ft.	Circumference of trunk. F.	Height from the ground to the intersection of the first branch. Feet
Salwa or Sorunghee.	90	6	38
Piasalo.......	90	6	22
Sisoowa... ...	45	4½	15
Kendhoo	60	4½	30
Gombharce...	50	4½	18
Holondho.....	75	7	36
Jamo...... ...	75	7	36
Sohn..........	50	6	12
Bodoka.......	35	3	15
Ponoso...	0	0	0
Jhoontiah. ...	45	4½	15
Koossoomo..	50	4½	9
Moondomondee.......	60	4½	22
Orjoono......	100	8	36
Mohoollo.....	75	8	36
Achoo.........	36	2½	10
Ambo.........	0	0	0
Kodalo........	39	3	8
Mahalimbo...	70	5	22
Limbo...... ...	70	5	22
Soroopottree Moee... ...	40	2½	18
Siddha.......	45	4	22
Sahajo	60	4½	30

Names.	Extreme height. Ft.	Circumference of trunk. F.	Height from the ground to the intersection of the first branch. Feet
Kaloochia....	25	2½	12
Banjhono. ...	45	5	22
Dhamono. .	35	3	20
Kosee.........	50	4	22
Tanghany....	40	3	18
Gouharea. ...	45	4½	15
Pitta Kaloochia..... ...	36	3	15
Khoiro........	25	2	6
Dhobo Khoiro	25	2	6
Minjbarec or Paloodhana..	45	5	6
Tentoollee or Koyan.....	0	0	0
Sirisee........	30	4½	22
Boro	0	0	0
Phasee......	60	6	30
Oshrosto... ..	0	0	0
Dhoou...	45	4½	22
Koombee.....	36	3	6
Bouro.........	0	0	0
Baelo	30	3	15

Names.	Extreme height. Ft.	Circumference of trunk. F.	Height from the ground to the intersection of the first branch. Feet
Soondorogoondee Komalogoondee or Bosontogoondee...	15	2½	5
Korunjo.....	36	4½	22
Soogondhee..	25	2	7
Bhayroo......	40	3	20
Bello...	30	3	10
Borokolee ...	30	3	8
Ollakolee.....	40	4	15
Moee.........	30	3	13
Behenta.......	30	3	10
Korada... ...	30	3	8
Dhobee.......	36	3	15
Charo.	36	3	15
Poeechandea	48	5	9
Grouhonee Kubatee...	80	6	12
Horedha......	45	4½	20
Bahadha......	50	4	10
Soonaree.....	36	3	10
Bhalleah......	40	4	20
Dhimeree. ...	40	4½	8
Boincho.. ..	15	1	5

Names.	Extreme height. Ft.	Circumference of trunk. F.	Height from the ground to the intersection of the first branch. Feet
Choonokolee	10	1	5
Brahmonea. .	15	1½	7
Sahadha... ...	30	2	6
Gotho..... ...	20	2½	7
Gondhona....	25	7½	6
Rayee........	30	3	15
Ankoolo......	30	2½	12
Patonwa......	20	1	5
Ambaleta.....	12	1½	3
Kotoko... ...	40	4	9
Potro Koorwan....	20	1	5
Patolee.......	20	1½	12
Pamphoonea	20	1	8
Nooniaree Looniaree or Noonononea......	36	4	7
Gooroohado.	22	2	10
Hinjolo... ...	30	4½	6
Lodhoka Sijhoo....... ...	20	2	6
Salora.........	22	1	5
Khakodha....	30	2	9
Khookoondea.........	30	2	9

TABLE OF EXPERIMENTS, BY MR. BENJAMIN COUCH.

Names.	Extreme height.	Circumference of trunk.	Height from the ground to the intersection of the first branch.
	Ft.	F.	Feet
Killakooro o-wan...... ...	20	1	6
Koeto..... ...	50	5	10
Mosanea.....	15	2½	4
Gongosheo-lee or Don-deepoholo.	25	3	7
Pendoora.....	20	2	1
Ambhota.....	20	2	7
Kopassea.....	20	2	7
Potoobaolo...	45	4	12
Joree	60	5	8
Chochena. ...	60	5	9
Bokmo..... ..	36	2	8
Ghunteoh Patoolee...	22	1⅓	10
Choraycgo-dee.........	22	1½	6
Ambodha. ...	30	2½	7
Kontabaolo..	30	2	7
Borodha... ..	30	2	8
Ghoralanjea or Tentara?	30	3	10

Names.	Extreme height.	Circumference of trunk.	Height from the ground to the intersection of the first branch.
	Ft.	F.	Feet
Kodumbo....	80	6	32
Rooradea.....	12	1	3
Hadokonka-lee..........	12	2	4
Goonaieho.. .	25	2	6
Biahmonea..	15	1½	7
Gooroobolee.	18	2	4
Kodoro... ..	30	2½	12
Gondopolaso	45	2½	8
Sohojo Ma-ree....... ..	25	1½	8
Mohanea.....	25	1½	8
Kolce Kou-radea... ...	25	1½	8
Dalosingha or Taloo-singhee...	25	1½	6
Meresinha...	30	2½	8
Konchona....	30	2½	8
Boroona......	40	5½	9
Neraso.... ..	25	2½	8
Nagishvoro..	30	3½	9
Rahana... ...	30	1½	1

Names.	Extreme height.	Circumference of trunk.	Height from the ground to the intersection of the first branch.
	Ft.	F.	Feet
Pochoboro....	30	2½	6
Ponposo Ko-maree... ...	30	2	8
Kolasahajo...	50	4	18
Pitolo.	30	2	6
Choureeona..	30	3	8
Chalodhona..	30	2	6
Pancollo.	40	2	8
Dharonjo....	60	4	8
Beejee Koo-roowan...	25	2	8
Oshoko... ...	50	3	8
Korra.....	50	5	20
Baygoona. ...	21	1	5
Solopo..	40	3	28
Shyalee......	0	1⅓	0
Polaso	0	1½	0
Contayecool-lee..........	0	1½	0
Pichoolee....	0	1¼	0
Shalimbo-banso.	40	2⅓	0
Conta banso.	80	1½	0

Names.	Extreme height.	Circumference of trunk.	Height from the ground to the intersection of the first branch.
	Ft.	F.	Feet
Bolungee banso......	25	⅙	0
Soondorogo-yan banso.	30	¾	0
Bono Konia-ree.........	50	3	10
Baee Dhime-ree.........	30	2½	8
Moddoro goodee.....	40	2½	8
Babolo........	25	2	8
Jundamaree.	30	2½	6
Woon.........	60	5	5
Koromonga..	36	3½	9
Dhosora Khendhoo.	60	5	18
Ambeleetoba	30	1	6
Modoroo to-ba......... ...	30	1	9
Kheero Ko-lee........ ...	30	3	6
Naringhee....	30	3	7
Kossaye......	22	1	7

TABLE OF EXPERIMENTS

Instituted in order to ascertain the weight of a cubic foot of different kinds of Wood; the foreign when first imported, those of the growth of England when felled: also, the weight of each when fully seasoned; showing, at the same time, the loss sustained in dimensions during the process of seasoning.

By Mr. Benjamin Couch of His Majesty's Dock-yard, Plymouth.

Species (in the language of commerce.)	Country where produced.	What part of the tree the pieces experimented on were cut from.	Dimensions. When first planed for experiment. Length.		Dimensions. When first planed for experiment. Breadth and thickness, or diameter.	Dimensions. When seasoned. Length.		Dimensions. When seasoned. Breadth and thickness, or diameter.	Weight in air, of a cubic foot avoirdupois. When first planed for experiment.	Weight in air, of a cubic foot avoirdupois. When seasoned.
			Ft.	In.	Inches.	Ft.	In.	Inches.	Ounces.	Ounces.
Poon	East Indies.	Butt. ...	4	0	17 diameter.	4	0	16¾ diameter	651	576
		Top... ...	6	0	9 by 9	6	0	9 by 8⅞	771	695
Teak		Butt......	4	0	12 diameter	4	0	12 diameter	662	657
		Top... ...	4	6	6½ by 6½	4	6	6½ by 6½	688	675

Barlow's Essay, p. 9 *to* 11.

Experiments on the transverse strength of Seasoned Woods from the Forests of Western Mysore; the weight was suspended from the centre of each specimen, which was 24 inches long and one inch square, and supported at both ends for one inch—so that the bearing was just 22 inches.

N.B.—THE EXPERIMENTS WERE PERHAPS CARRIED ON TOO QUICKLY TO GIVE THE BEST RESULTS.

No. in list.	No. of specimens.	NAMES OF WOOD.	Deflection in Inches and Tenths. 1. lbs. 126.	2. lbs. 238.	3. lbs. 350.	4. lbs. 462.	Breaking weight in lbs.	Ultimate deflection.	Specific gravity.	Description.	Uses to which applied, &c. &c.	Whether likely to be attacked by insects or not.	Kind of fracture.	Average size of rough squared log procurable, and if abundant, or not.	Remarks.
I	1	*Can.* Boghy...	0·10	0·20	0·40	0·80	462	0·90	915	Dull brown, close grain.	For furniture, is strong, and tough.	No.	Short fibrous.	12×1×¾. Yes.	No. 2 Cracked at 330 lbs.
		Tam.													
		Lat. Acacia (probably.)	0·10	0·20	0·30	0·60	686	0·90							
	2	*Tel.*													
II	1	*Can.* Soojhel... ...	0·17	0·37	0·58	.....	...	...	973	Bright brown, long grain, rather open.	Has great resilience—useful for all purposes.	No.	Long fibrous.	8×⅓×¾. Yes.	No. 1 Deflected 0·68 with lbs. 380—0·72 with lbs. 400—0·98 with lbs. 446—1·02 with lbs. 456—It was then unloaded, and recovered its shape all but 0·100 of an inch.
	2	*Tam.*	0·10	0·25	0·40	0·60	658	1·70							
	3	*Lat.* Acacia (probably.)	0·25	0·40	0·60	1·00	574	1·60							
	4	*Tel.*	0·20	0·40	0·60	0·80	462	0·90							
	5	... ...	0·2	0·4	0·63	......	400	0·75							
III	1	*Can.* Boghy...	0·05	0·25	0·40	0·55	630	1·55	904	Light reddish brown, and with minute cavities, filled with secretion.	For carriages, and house building.	No.	Long fibrous.	12×1×¾. Yes.	Cracked at 460 lbs.
	2	*Tam.* Vaghay..... ...	0·10	0·30	0·50	1·00	480	1·40							
	3	*Lat.* Acacia speciosa...	0·20	0·30	0·50	0·60	582	1·10							
	4	*Tel.*	0·1	0·2	0·4	0·6	639	1·2							
IV	1	*Can.* Hoonsay	0·12	0·38	.....	......	294	0·60	1323	Heartwood is red, and black, streaked; close-grained, knotty.	For naves of wheels, oil mills, mallets, rice pounders, &c., excellent for brick and tile burning.	No.	Short fibrous.	10×1¼×1. Yes.	No. 4 Did not break quite through. No. 1 Broke in two after ¾ minute's suspension, specimen bad. No. 2 Was not a fair specimen, it had a longitudinal crack; but it sustained the weight, 40 seconds. Yields the best Charcoal for Gunpowder, the stones pounded, and boiled with thin glue, make best wood cement.
	2	*Tam.* Poolia Marum...	0·10	0·20	0·45	0·75	602	0·95							
	3	*Lat.* Tamarindus Indica.	0·20	0·30	0·50	0·70	486	0·80							
	4	*Tel.* Chinta Chettoo...	0·[illegible]	0·22	0·3	......	345	0·45							
V	1	*Can.* Biti, ...	0·10	0·20	0·40	0·60	574	0·70	818	Black, and streaked red, like rosewood, rather open grain.	Furniture of every description.	No.	Short fibrous.	18×1½×1¼. Yes very.	No. 1 Broke after sustaining weight, 20 seconds. No. 2 Cracked at lbs. 518, but sustained the last weight for one minute. Much larger timber is procurable in the Forests of Malabar, where it grows to a stately and handsome Tree, but in the largest specimens, earth is often found embedded. A fixed oil is procured from the seeds, and the root is medicinal.
	2	*Tam.* Yeti Marum ...	0·07	0·15	0·30	0·50	602	0·95							
	3	*Lat.* Dalbergia latifolia.	0·15	0·30	0·45	0·60	522	0·80							
	4	*Tel.* Eroopootoo. ...	0·1	0·2	0·4	0·6	597	1·1							
VI	1	*Can.* Honagul.	0·10	0·37	0·70	......	450	1·20	913	Dark straw color, compact.	Furniture & house building.	No.	Long fibrous.	17×¼ 1. Yes.	Did not break quite through. No. 1 Cracked after sustaining lbs. 448 for one minute, but broke through with an additional 2 lbs. No. 2 Cracked and broke through, to neutral axis only. No. 3 Broke straight through. This is perhaps the most abundant tree in the Forests.
	2	*Tam.*	0·10	0·25	0·40	0·70	480	0·85							
	3	*Lat.* Terminalia	0·19	0·20	0·35	0·55	576	0·60							
	4	*Tel.*	0·15	0·25	0·35	0·6	569	1·00							
VII	1	*Can.* Wulla Honay. ...	0·25	0·45	0·80	......	385	1·25	1020	Light colored, open grain, an excellent timber.	Furniture & house building.	No.	Rather long, and fibrous.	17×1¼×1. Yes.	A variety of the *Pterocarpus Marsupium*; this wood is lighter, but apparently as good, and does not stain yellow, as the Rugta Honay does. No. 1 Cracked in the centre, and broke (but not quite through) after sustaining the weight for a few seconds.
	2	*Tam.*	0·10	0·30	0·60	1·10	546	1·10							
	3	*Lat.* Pterocarpus... ...	0·15	0·33	0·65	1·30	574	1·30							
	4	*Tel.*	0·25	0·50	0·80	......	406	0·90							
	5	... ...	0·2	0·4	0·7	......	429	..							
VIII	1	*Can.* Nellee	0·20	0·30	0·48	1·00	490	1·20	1080	Dark flesh color, smooth, very close grain, compact and tough.	For veneering: good for well-rings, does not decay under water, well adapted for turning.	Yes.	8 inches long & fibrous.	8×1×¾. Yes.	No. 1 Broke in 2 pieces, after sustaining the weight ½ a minute. No. 2 Scarcely broke beyond neutral axis. The fruit (Country gooseberry) is pickled and preserved: the Bark is astringent and used in tanning—the young branches are often put in wells to purify the water.
		Tam. Nellee													
		Lat. Emblica officinalis.	0·10	0·25	0·40	0·80	574	1·30							
	2	*Tel.* Aseerki..													
IX	1	*Can.* Nundee	0·15	0·30	0·60	1·10	467	1·20	660	Light brown, rather open grain.	Useful for a variety of purposes, has great "stiffness"—wooden bridges have been built of this.	Yes.	Long fibrous.	18×1¼×1. Yes.	The fracture of No. 1 was a 6" long. This wood is much used in the Dockyard, but does *not* answer for sleepers, rotting quickly under ground.
	2	*Tam.* Benteak	0·10	0·20	0·40	0·50	574	0·70							
	3	*Lat.* Lagerstroemia microcarpa	0·20	0·25	0·50	1·20	462	1·20							
	4	*Tel.*	0·15	0·30	0·40	0·60	518	0·90							
	5	... ...	0·2	0·4	0·57	0·7	541	1·0							
X	1	*Can.* Billawar	0·10	0·30	0·45	0·65	546	1·30	730	Handsome grain, red & brown, streaked, rather open.	Has great toughness or elasticity, makes handsome furniture, resembling walnut, is much used in carriage building for the frame work, fellies and spokes.	No.	Short fibrous.	12×1¼×1. Yes.	No. 1 Cracked at lbs. 196 but sustained 546 lbs. for a second; at the moment of fracture, it deflected 2 inches; it broke very slowly, and not quite through. No. 2 Cracked after sustaining 475 lbs., broke through at lbs. 504.
	2	*Tam.*	0·10	0·30	0·40	0·65	504	2·20							
	3	*Lat.* Acacia	0·15	0·25	0·45	0·55	518	0·80							
	4	*Tel.*	0·10	0·25	0·40	0·60	578	0·80							
	5		0·1	0·2	0·3	0·5	711	1·2							
XI	1	*Can.* Rugta Honay ...	0·12	0·30	0·50	1·20	...	...	820	Do. do., but closer grain, and a little darker.	Makes handsome furniture, & resembles fine mahogany, but must be well seasoned, or it stains yellow.	No.	Short and rather splintery.	17×1×1. Yes.	No. 1 Cracked after bearing [illegible] few seconds: the weights were then taken off and the specimen remained whole. The tree, which grows to a large size, yields the Gum "Kino"—and is abundant in all the Forests of Southern India.
		Tam. Vengay..	0·20	0·40	0·60	0·70	518	0·70							
	2	*Lat.* Pterocarpus Marsupium	0·15	0·30	0·50	......	378	0·70							
	3	*Tel.* Yegass													
XII	1	*Can.* Nowladdi... ...	0·05	0·20	0·40	0·60	518	0·70	907	Greenish brown, dull, close grain.	Polishes well, is used for house building and furniture, &c.	No.	Long and rather splintery.	11×1×¾. Yes.	This is one of the woods used as sleepers in the S. W. Railway.
		Tam.													
		Lat.													
	2	*Tel.*													
XIII	1	*Can.* Handiga... ...	0·20	0·40	0·70	......	364	1·00	657	Light, mottled brown, long regular grain.	Furniture, polishes and turns well, useful for the cabinet maker, and would do for veneering.	No.	Splintery.	9×¾×¾. Not very.	No. 1 Bad specimen. No. 2 Cracked at lbs. 462 and broke after sustaining the weight one minute.
		Tam.													
	2	*Lat.*	0·15	0·30	0·50	1·10	462	1·20							
	3	*Tel.*													

Experiments on the transverse strength of Seasoned Woods from the Forests of Western Mysore, &c.

No. in list.	No. of specimens.	NAMES OF WOOD.	Deflection in Inches and Tenths. 1. lbs. 126.	2. lbs. 238.	3. lbs. 350.	4. lbs. 462.	Breaking weight in lbs.	Ultimate deflection.	Specific gravity.	Description.	Uses to which applied, &c. &c.	Whether likely to be attacked by insects or not.	Kind of fracture.	Average size of rough squared log procurable, and if abundant or not.	Remarks.
XIV	1 2	*Can.* Jalari ... ... *Tam.* Talura. ... ... *Lat.* Vatica laccifera ... *Tel.*	0·20 0·20	0·40 0·35	0·60 0·55	0·80 ...	40 43	1·00 0·70	689	Light yellow; long fibrous grain.	Strong useful wood for a variety of purposes.	No.	Short.	10×1×1. Yes.	A large tree, which the Lac insect attacks, the shell lac of commerce is procured from it.
XV	1 2 3 4	*Can.* Kurraymutti. ... *Tam.* Kurray maradah. *Lat.* Terminalia tomentosa ... ... *Tel.* Muddie	0·05 0·10 0·20 0· 1	0·20 0·30 0·30 0· 2	0·40 0·50 0·45 0· 4	1·00 1·00 0·60 0· 5	46 46 60 58	... ... 1·10 0· 1	892	Dark brown; open grain.	House building; bears a good transverse strain; a wood much esteemed for all Railway purposes.	No.	Rather splintery.	18×1¼×1. Yes very.	No. 1 Cracked at 406 lbs., very abundant everywhere.
XVI	1 2	*Can.* Jambay. ... ... *Tam.* Erool. ... ... *Lat.* Inga Xylocarpa .. *Tel.* Ezoovaloo... ...	0·15 0·10	0·35 0·25	0·60 0·65	... ...	35 40	0·70 0·70	934	Dull dark chocolate brown, with orange tint, close grain.	Furniture, shafts, plough heads and knees, and crooked timbers in ship building, and Railway sleepers.	No.	Long.	14×1×34. Yes.	No 1 Cracked at 550 lbs., and snapped with that weight after ½ minute. A large tree, the timber is hard, durable and in great demand. The bark is astringent, and used for dyeing black.
XVII	1 2 3 4 5	*Can.* Sagwan.. ... ... *Tam.* Theke Marum .. *Lat.* Tectona Grandis... *Tel.* Teka...	0·20 0·20 0·20 0·25 0· 2	0·40 0·48 0·40 0·55 0· 4	0·70 0·80 0·60	... ...	40 35 40 32 38	... ... 0·80 0·70 0· 5	684	Light brown, open grain.	Ship building, house do furniture, &c. &c.	No.	Splintery.	30×1¼×1¼. Yes. very.	No. 1 Broke in two, suddenly. No. 2 Snapped short in two, after sustaining weight for a few seconds. No. 3 do. do. N. B.—The Nuggur Teak appears not to be so good as that of the Mysore and Malabar Forests: sometimes timber of much larger scantling is procurable, but seldom longer.
XVIII	1 2 3 4	*Can.* Dinduga. ... ... *Tam.* Vella Nága ... *Lat.* Conocarpus latifolia. *Tel.* Siri Maun... ...	0·15 0·15 0·25 0· 1	0·35 0·30 0·40 0· 3	0·70 0·50 0·65 0· 5	... ... 0·90 0· 7	40 40 51 51	0·80 0·80 1·25 0· 8	1037	Close compact grain, yellowish, striped, and something like satin wood, very handsome.	House building, shafts and yokes, and general use for Railway purposes but makes very good Cabinet furniture.	No.	Splintery.	12×¾×¾. Yes. very.	Snapped like the preceding, but is much used in Bangalore.
XIX	1 2 3	*Can.* Kuddavailoo.. ... *Tam.* Vella Cadambay. *Lat.* Nauclea Cadamba. *Tel.* Rudrakshakamba...	0·10 0·15	0·35 0·60	0·80 ...	... ...	37 29	0·90 0·60	681	Brownish yellow, close compact grain, tough.	For various kinds of furniture.	Yes.	Splintery.	12×1½×¾. Yes.	Snapped like the preceding. A large and ornamental tree which yields extensive shade.
XX	2 1	*Can.* Soompaghy... ... *Tam.* Chumpaca. ... ... *Lat.* Michelia Champaca. *Tel.*	0·20 0·15	0·50 0·40	0·90 0·90	... ...	35 35	0·90 0·90	671	Rich brown, rather close grain.	Very handsome furniture; and polishes well, grows to a very large size, has a yellow sweet scented flower.	Yes.	Splintery.	15×3½×2½. Very.	No. 1 Snapped at 330 lbs., but there being a knot in the middle, it was not a fair specimen. This tree is highly venerated by the Hindoos, &c., dedicated to Vishnu, the bark is bitter and very acid.
XXI	1 2 3 4	*Can.* Mauvena ... ... *Tam.* Maah Marum... *Lat.* Mangifera Indica... *Tel.* Mamada Chettoo	0·10 0· 2 0·10 0·27	0·30 0· 3 0·30 0·50	... ... 0·70 0·60	... ...	29 31 35 85	1·00 0·45 0·70 0·60	597	Light greyish straw, open grain, and rather soft.	For solid wheels of the country carts, and rough furniture.	Yes.	11 inches long.	9×½×1½. Very.	Snapped suddenly. The wood is sacred, and used by the Hindoos for burning corpses, a reddish brown gum resin, hardening by age, and resembling Bdellium, is procured from this tree.
XXII	1 2	*Can.* Godda. ... ... *Tam.* ... ... *Lat.* Cedrelaceæ ... *Tel.*	0·40 0·20	... 0·40	... 0·30	... ...	18 35	... 0·85	639	Light flesh; close, even grain.	Polishes well, and is good for turning.	Yes.	Splintery, brittle.	9×¾×¾. Very.	No. 1 Deflected much, and broke in two, almost immediately at 182 lbs. No. 2 Snapped in 3 pieces, very suddenly.
XXIII	1 2	*Can.* Bayvena.... ... *Tam.* Vepa Marum. ... *Lat.* Melia Azadirach.. *Tel.* Taraka vepa. ...	0·30 0·20	0·70 0·60	1·00 ...	... ...	29 29	1·00 1·70	783	Light flesh, open grain, sweet scented.	Common furniture, but it warps and splits.	No.	Long splintery.	15×1½×1¼. Very.	No. 1 Cracked at 224 lbs., and broke after sustaining the last weight for one minute. No. 2 Broke near one end suddenly. The heart wood is good, but the branches are very apt to break, and snap off in high wind; Margosa oil is extracted from the yellowish green seeds, which are about the size of small gooseberries.
XXIV	1 2 3 4	*Can.* Mussee. ... ... *Tam.* ... ... *Lat.* Lauraceæ ... ... *Tel.*	0·30 0· 2 0·20 0·40	0·65 0· 5 0·50 0·57	... ...	... ...	29 [illegible] 22 11	0· 6 0·50 0·60 0·30	839	Very light brown, open grain.	In general demand.	No.	Shortish and rather splintery.	10×¾×¾. Yes.	Broke near one end suddenly—near a knot.
XXV	1 2 3 4	*Can.* [illegible] *Tam.* [illegible] *Lat.* Arto[illegible] integrifolia. ... ... *Tel.* Panasa...	... 0· 2 0·15 0·30	... 0·54 0·30 0·60	... 0· 8 ... 1·00	... ...	[illegible] [illegible] 2[illegible] 3[illegible]	0· 9 0·70 0·20	676	Yellow at first, but on exposure, it assumes a darker tint, approaching to dull mahogany.	Furniture, chairs, tables, &c., picture frames, &c., but must be well seasoned, or it will warp and crack.	Yes.	Splintery.	12×1×1½. Yes.	No. 1 Bad specimen, broke suddenly without sustaining the weights a single moment. Broke suddenly. Produces the large "Jack" fruit. Birdlime is manufactured from the juice of the Bark—and the leaves are greedily eaten by cattle, the roasted seeds are much used by the poorer people.
XXVI	1 2 3 4	*Can.* Vellayga. ... ... *Tam.* Manja Cadumbay. *Lat.* Nauclea Cordifolia *Tel.* Dudugu	0·45 0·40 0·40 0·45	0·90 0·90 0·75 0·70	... ...	... ...	[illegible] [illegible] [illegible] [illegible]	0·90 1·00 0·75 0·95	581	Dull yellow, close, short grain.	Polishes well, resembles Box wood, and is good for turning; cracks & warps, is light & durable if kept from wet.	Yes.	Very splintery and brittle.	14×1¼×1¼. Very.	No. 2 Snapped in two like a Carrot. No. 3 Do. after one minute's suspension. This is also used, but the Carpenter attaches it very much. No. 4 The last 8 lbs. caused it to snap like the others.
XXVII	1 2 3 4	*Can.* Thengana ... ... *Tam.* Thenga Marum. *Lat.* Cocos Nucifera ... *Tel.* Tenkaia...	0·20 0· 2 0·10 0·15	0·50 0· 3 0·30 0·40	.. 0·47	... ...	[illegible] [illegible] 2[illegible] 2[illegible]	0·50 0· 5 0·55 0·60	747	Light speckled, something like a nutmeg in the section; pithy.	Ridge poles for temporary roofs, aqueducts, &c. &c.	Yes.	Very fibrous.	25×¾×¾. Yes.	With 182 lbs. No. 1, deflected much, but it broke nearly through, after sustaining the weight (238 lbs.), and remained so, kept together by its stringy fibres, with a deflection of 3 inches. this tree produces the Cocoanut oil and fibre of commerce, the leaves are used for thatching houses, Toddy is also extracted.

Experiments on the transverse strength of Seasoned Woods from the Forests of Western Mysore, &c.

No. in list.	No. of specimens.	NAMES OF WOOD.	Deflection in Inches and tenths. 1. lbs. 126.	2. lbs. 238.	3. lbs. 350.	4. lbs. 462.	Breaking weight in lbs.	Ultimate deflection.	Specific gravity.	Description.	Uses to which applied, &c., &c.	Whether likely to be attacked by insects or not.	Kind of fracture.	Average size of rough squared log procurable, and if abundant or not.	Remarks.
XXVIII	1	*Can.* Somy ... ... *Tam.*	0·20	0·30	...	...	...	...	......	Handsome red, rather open grain, but it warps and cracks.	Furniture.	No.	Splintery.	Yes.	Neither specimen good.
	2	*Lat.* ... ... *Tel.*	0·30	0·60	...	...	294	0·80							
XXIX	1	*Can.* Baulay... ... ... *Tam.* Toombra... ... *Lat.* Diospyros Melanoxylon *Tel.* Toomica..	...	...	...	...	...	...	1200	....	....	No.		Yes.	
XXX	1	*Can.* Thadsal	0·10	0·20	0·30	0·60	558	0·90	......	Light close even grain.		Yes.	Straight, short fibrous.	16×1¼×1. Yes.	Apparently a very excellent wood.
	2	*Tam.*	0·12	0·3	0·4	0·7	533	0·8							
	3	*Lat.* ... ... *Tel.*													

Experiments on the transverse strength of Seasoned Woods from the Forests of Western Mysore; the weight was suspended from the centre of each specimen, which was 24 inches long and one inch square, and supported at both ends for one inch—so that the bearing was just 22 inches.

No. in list.	No. of specimens.	Names of wood.	Deflection in inches and tenths. 1. lbs. 126.	2. lbs. 238.	3. lbs. 350.	4. lbs. 462.	Breaking weight in lbs.	Ultimate deflection.	Specific gravity.	Description.	Uses to which applied, &c. &c.	Whether likely to be attacked by insects or not.	Kind of fracture.	Average size of rough squared Log procurable, and if abundant or not.	Remarks.
	1	Eng. Satin wood.	0·25	0·43	0·62	...	510	...	...	Light yellow long fibrous grain.	Makes handsome furniture.	No.	Long and rather splintery.	9×10×9. Yes.	
	2		0·3	0·43	0·62	100	489	...	...						
	3		0·37	0·62	...	...	329	1·12	...						
	1	Trincomallee ...	0·18	0·31	0·56	0·81	550	1·06	...	Light flesh colour smooth, Fibrous, close grain.	Furnitures and Coach building.	No.	Short and splintery.	21×1×1. Yes.	
	2	....	0·18	0·37	0·50	0·81	510	1·12	...						

N. B.—The size of the Logs is under, rather than over stated.

Extra experiments with woods of large scantling.

	Scantling.	Weights suspended in lbs.	Deflection in inches.	Remarks.
Hoonagul.	15′ × 3″ × 5.	1058 1658 1858 2258 2558 2782 3006 3230	2 3 3¼ 4 4½ 5 5½ 7½	On previous occasion, this piece of wood was suffered to remain 5 weeks with a weight of 1,600 lbs. suspended from the centre and exposed to alternate rain and sun. The deflection was three inches, but when the weight was removed, the wood regained its original position. Commenced to crack and broke after six minutes suspension, at a small knot a foot from the centre.
Kurramuttee.	15′ × 3″ × 5.	1058 2258	1½ 3	Commenced to crack and broke 1½ feet from the centre after two minutes suspension, not a good specimen.

J. PUCKLE, Captain,

Assistant to Chief Engineer in Mysore.

Experiments to test Comparative strength of Timber procurable on the Malabar Coast.

Beam supported at both ends and loaded in the middle and deflection taken there.

Price from Rs. 8 to 25 per Candy, 1st quality Teak.

Weights.

No. of experiments.	Size of Beam.	Weight.	Distance between bearing.	60	116	172	228	284	340	396	452	508	564	676	732	788	844	900	956	984	Remarks.
1	7' 0" × 2" × 2"	10" 00	6·0 def.	0·20	0·37	0·55	0·70	0·90	1·10	1·27	1·45	1·65	1·83	2·25	2·45						
2	Do.	11" 00	do. def.	0·18	0·32	0·48	0·62	0·77	0·90	1·10	1·25	1·40	1·55	1·95	2·17	2·45	2·86	3·35	3·60	4·30	
3	Do.	10" 00	do. def.	0·18	0·33	0·48	0·62	0·77	0·90	1·08	1·23	1·39	1·53	1·88	2·10	2·40	2·70	3·18	3·78	4·18	

Round Timber price per Candy 4-8-0.

I find this Timber will not stand hard driving, it is very liable to fly; have to use a rope wad between *Ram* and pile head, it is well adapted for large bearing Beams, Timber Bridges and excellent for Sleepers; it has but little or no sap, would make good Keys and Tree-nails.

ERROOL.

Weights.

No. of experiments.	Size of Beam.	Weight.	Distance between bearing.	60	116	172	228	284	340	396	452	508	564	620	648	676	704	732	760	788	816	844	872	900	928	956	984	1012	1040	Remarks.
1	7' 0" × 2" × 2"	13" 00	6' 0" def.	0·3[illegible]	0·47	0·70	0·85	1·15	1·40	1·60	1·80	2·05	2·30	2·55	2·75	2·90	3·05	3·30	3·55											
2	Do.	13" 20	do. def.	0·2[illegible]	0·35	0·51	0·67	0·82	0·95	1·17	1·34	1·49	1·66	1·80	1·89	1·98	2·08	2·15	2·28	2·38	2·48	2·59	2·84	2·99	3·16	3·32	3·57	3·82		Appearance compact, 956 lbs.
3	Do.	12" 50	do. def.	0·2[illegible]	0·12	0·47	0·62	0·77	0·95	1·10	1·25	1·40	1·56	1·70	1·80	1·88	1·95	2·0[illegible]	2·15	2·22	2·30	2·40	2·50	2·60	2·74	2·87	3·05	3·20	3·60	do. 1012.

Round Timber price per Candy 4-8-0.

This is equal to Errool when carefully selected; some of the trees have a large portion of sap, and this goes rapidly on exposure to sun and damp, but the sound heart of the wood is almost everlasting.

KURRAH MURDAH.

Weights.

No. of experiments.	Size of Beam.	Weight.	Distance between bearing.	66	116	172	228	284	340	396	452	508	564	620	676	732	788	816	844	872	900	928	956	984	998	1012	Remarks.
1	7' 0" × 2" × 2"	12" 25	6' 0" def.	0·2[illegible]	0·33	0·55	0·70	0·95	1·10	1·30	1·45	1·65	1·85	2·20	2·52	2·82	3·30										Signs of compression with 732 lbs.
2	Do.	13" 50	do. def.	0·13	0·30	0·45	0·57	0·72	1·85	1·00	1·15	1·30	1·45	1·60	1·75	1·95	2·25	2·3[illegible]	2·50	2·65	2·95	3·15	3·65	4·65	5·00	6·00	do. 900
3	Do.	13" 25	do. def.	0·1[illegible]	0·30	0·45	0·57	0·72	1·86	1·05	1·20	1·35	1·50	1·70	1·90	2·15	2·47	2·73	2·90	3·15	5·90						do. 900

Round Timber price per Candy [illegible] to 6 Rs.

Well adapted for house fitting, door windows in waggon building, find it warps and flies when exposed to the sun, the "white Ants" destroy this wood.

WHITE CEDAR.

Weights.

No. of experiments.	Size of Beam.	Weight.	Distance between bearing.	66	116	172	228	284	340	396	452	508	564	620	676	704	732	760	788	816	844	872	900	914	928	942	Remarks.
1	7' 0" × 2" × 2"	8· 00	6· 0" def.	0·18	0·32	0·50	0·65	0·70	0·95	1·15	1·30	1·45	1·60	1·82	2·22	2·32	2·47	2·7[illegible]	2·95	3·40	3·75	4·20	5·15	5·35	5·75	6·20	
2	Do.	9· 25	do. def.	0·13	0·30	0·42	0·57	0·71	0·82	0·99	1·12	1·30	1·40	1·57	1·75	1·92	2·00	2·2[illegible]	2·30	2·42	2·60	2·82	3·21	3·35	3·50		Signs of compression with 816 lbs.
3	Do.	8· 25	do. def.	0·28	0·48	0·68	0·87	1·13	1·33	1·38	1·75	2·10	2·48	2·78													do. 844

Round Timber price per Candy [illegible]-0 to 10 Rs.

A very useful Timber adapted for roofing stations, doors, windows and work generally.

BENTEAK.

Weights.

No. of experiments.	Size of Beam.	Weight.	Distance between bearing.	66	116	172	228	284	340	396	452	508	564	592	620	648	676	704	732	760	788	816	844	Remarks.
1	7' 0" × 2" × 2"	8· 25	6' 0" def.	0·[illegible]0	0·39	0·58	0·78	0·98	1·18	1·48	1·08	2·03	2·33	2·63										
2	Do.	9· 25	do. def.	0·25	0·43	0·61	0·80	1·01	1·21	1·62	1·81	1·90	2·20	2·35	2·68	2·90	3·10	3·3[illegible]	3·60	4·75	4·78	5·05	5·23	Signs of compression with 816 lbs.
3	Do.	10· 25	do. def.	0·1[illegible]	0·45	0·67	0·90	1·15	1·35	1·55	1·77	2·10	2·45	2·72	3·10	3·30	3·90	4·4[illegible]	5·55					do. [illegible]

MEMO.—Each piece on the average took 35 minutes in testing. They were cut from Timber which had been 5 months in stock, and were left 10 days after being sawn to scantling of 7' 0 × 2 × 2 before testing.

INDEX.

B.

C.

D.

E.

F.

G.

H.

I.

J.

K.

L.

M.

Murraya, Ash leaved Eteiriye, see Ceylon woods.
Murraya konigii, *Spreng.*, see Bergera konigii.
Muroodoo, **Tam.**, see p. 172.
Murrh neen, **Burm.**, see Amherst province, also p. 173.
Murukkai maram, **Tam.**, முருக்கை மரம், see Erythrina Indica.
Muruta, **Singh.**, see Lagerstrœmia reginæ.
Muruta-gass, **Singh.**, see Lagerstrœmia reginæ.

N.

O.

P.

Q.

R.

S.

T.

U.

V.

W.

X.

Y.

Z.

An index of such extent, with words almost wholly of foreign origin, could not, any where, be printed wholly free from typographical errors: and they would perhaps have been fewer, had I been able to revise the proof sheets as they were passing through the press, but this, I have not been able to do, as I have been serving in British Burmah, since the end of 1862, and, from page 280 to the end, could not be sent to me for revision.

EDWARD BALFOUR.

RANGOON, 12*th* *May* 1863.

DESIDERATA.

The following are subjects regarding which further information is desirable and the names of woods and timbers of which specimens should be obtained, and their botanical names duly determined.

Specimens of the woods of all unnamed trees yielding timber, with their several local names, are very necessary with a view of determining them botanically. For this purpose each specimen should be accompanied with a small shoot, bearing flower, fruit and full grown leaves, either together or separately, pressed and dried between folds of blotting paper.

A memorandum shewing the various uses to which each timber is used by the natives of the district will enhance the economical value of the specimens. The native names written in their own character and also in the roman character should be carefully attached to the specimens, the name of the locality in which the specimen is collected should also be given.

A tabulated statement showing the qualities, such as the specific gravity, strength of wood, power of supporting weight, deflection, &c. of the several timber trees is much required to serve as standard for future inquiries, arrived at from experiments with the woods from several logs. The specimens experimented on should be carefully labelled and deposited in a public place for reference.

In labelling a uniform system should be employed, viz. by recording.

Leguminosæ.
Tamarindus Indica *(Linn.) W. & A. Prod.* 884.
T. Occidentalis, *Gærtn.*
Nat. Name Pulia maram, *Tam.*
Chinta chettu, *Tel.*
Amli, *Hind.*
Quality. Wood strong and hard, used for oil mill.
Locality. All over India.
Contr. Dr. ———,

1st. The natural order to which the timber tree belongs.
2nd. Its botanical name referring to the best botanical description.
3rd. The scientific synonyms.
4th. Native name, which should be spelt in one uniform system.
5th. The quality of the wood.
6th. The localities in which the wood abounds.
7th. The name of the contributor.

Drawings of all timber trees (in one book in a portable form) is very desirable. The botanical books already published are either scarce or incomplete.

A map on a fixed scale showing the geographical distribution of the timber trees is much required.

ADENANTHERA ACULEATA, *Roxb.* a tree of the Coromandel Coast, *Vol. II. p.* 371.
AMYRIS SIMPLICIFOLIA, *Roxb.*, a small tree of Penang, *Vol. II, p.* 244.
,, ACUMINATA, *Roxb.*, a tree of Moluccas, *Vol. II, p* 246.
,, SUMATRANA, *Roxb.*, a tree of Sumatra, *Vol. II, p.* 250.
,, PUNCTATA, *Roxb.*, a tree of Chittagong, *Vol. II, p.* 251.
ANACARDIUM DUBIUM, *Roxb.*, a native of Sumatra, a large and beautiful tree, *Vol. II, p.* 313.
ANDERSONIA CUCULLATA, *Roxb.*, a considerable sized tree of the Delta of the Ganges, *Vol. II. p.* 212.
,, ROHITUKA, *Roxb.*, a small tree of Bengal, *Vol. II, p.* 213.
ARTOCARPUS LANCEÆFOLIA, *Roxb.*, a native of Penang, *Vol. III, p.* 527.
BAUHINIA PARVIFLORA, *Roxb*, a small tree of Coromandel, *Vol. II, p.* 323.
BERGERA INTEGERRIMA, *Buch.* a tree of the eastern parts of the mouth of the Megna, *Vol. II, p.* 376.
BHAN-BHWAY, Burm. Is this the Bhai-Bya?
BIGNONIA COMOSA, a native of the Moluccas, *Vol. III, p.* 103.
,, CRISPA, *Buch.* a native of Mysore, *Vol. III, p.* 103.
BINGTANGOR, is it a Calophyllum or Uvaria?
BOTANY BAY HE OAK, Is this a Casuarina?
BUCHANANIA LANCIFOLIA, *Roxb.*, a large and tall tree of Chittagong, *Vol. II, p.* 386.
CÆSALPINIA CORIARIA, wood of (not known) deserves attention.
,, RESUPINATA, *Roxb.*, a tree of the Moluccas, with a straight trunk, *Vol. II, p.* 362.
CALLICARPA ARBOREA, *Roxb.*, a stout tall tree, a native of Chittagong, *Vol. I, p.* 390.
,, LANATA, *Linn*, a pretty large tree, a native of the Circar mountains, and their valleys; trunk very straight, *Vol. I, p.* 391.
CALOPHYLLUM, *Species* one Thurappe, Burm. The other Turra-phee, Burm. } Are these identical?
,, BINTAGOR, *Roxb.*, the Bintagor maritima of *Rumph*, beautiful tree of the Mauritius, Amboyna and the Archipelago, *Vol. II, p.* 607.
,, SUIGA, *Buch*, a tree of the Circar mountains, *Vol. II, p.* 608.
CANARIUM SYLVESTRE, *Willde, Vol. III, p.* 137. A large handsome tree of the Moluccas, *Vol. III, p.* 138.
CAPPARIS BISPERMA, *Roxb.*, Goolee, Tel. A timber tree of the mountains, forest of the Circars, wood heavy, hard and durable, and employed for various purposes, *Vol. II, p.* 568.
CAREEMARADOO. Is this Terminalia glabra (karamarda)? or a species of Pterocarpus?
CARRIMARRIDDI. Is this identical with the above?

CASEARIA GLABRA, *Roxb.*, a small tree of the Molucca Islands, *Vol. II, p.* 421.
,, TOMENTOSA, *Roxb.*, a small handsome tree of the Circars not abundant, *Vol. II, p.* 421.
,, OVATA, *Willde*, a pretty large tree of the banks of the Hoogly, *Vol. II, p.* 420.
CASSIA RHOMBIFOLIA, *Roxb.*, a straight trunked tree of Ceylon, *Vol. II, p.* 334.
,, MARGINATA, *Roxb.*, a native of Ceylon, with a tolerably straight trunk, *Vol. II, p.* 338.
CELASTRUS VERTICILLATA, *Roxb.*, a tree of Nepal with a straight trunk, *Vol. II, p.* 624.
,, OBTUSIFOLIA, a tree of the Mauritius, *Vol. I, p.* 625.
CELTIS TRINERVIA, *Roxb.*, a middling sized tree of Chittagong, *Vol. II, p.* 65.
CERBERA ODOLLAM, *Gærtn.*, a pretty large tree of the salt swamps of India, *Vol. I, p.* 693.
CHAHOONG.? Is this Chakoong, or the Cordia myxa?
CHIONANTHUS RAMIFLORA, *Roxb.*, arboreous native of the Moluccas, *Vol. I, p.* 107.
CHOMONDRI or CHALEMBRY. Is this the Calamander wood, the Singhalese Kalu Medirye?
CINCHONA THYRSIFLORA, *Roxb.*, a tree of the interior of Bengal, flowers in June and seeds ripen in January, trunk straight, *Vol. I, p.* 130.
CORDIA GRANDIS, *Roxb.*, a native of Chittagong, a large quick growing tree, *Vol. I, p.* 593.
CONGO, a wood used in Madras for fuzes, what is the botanical name of this?
CORONILLA SESBAN? Coronilla picta? *Sohn*, URIA. The botanical names given are those of the Sesbania Ægyptica, *Pers.*, but according to the description it must be some other tree. Is it Soymida febrifuga?
CYNOMETRA POLYANDRA, *Roxb.*, Peng of Silhet, where it is a very large and useful timber tree, *Vol. II, p.* 372.
DALBERGIA, *Species*. Thevus, HIND. Thevis, MAHR. Is this D. Oojeinensis, *Roxb., Fl. Ind. Vol. III, p.* 220?
DALBERGIA EMARGINATA, *Roxb.*, a native of the Andaman Islands, *Vol. III, p.* 224.
,, ZEYLANICA, *Roxb.*, a large elegant timber tree of Ceylon, *Vol. III, p.* 228.
,, KROWEE, *Roxb.*, a large sized crooked tree of Silhet, *Vol. III, p.* 229.
,, OOJEINENSIS, *Roxb.* Is this the "Thevus" of Nagpore?
DHAMNA, URIA and HIND? these seem identical as to quality of timber, are they the *Grewia tiliæfolia?*
DILLENIA REPANDA, *Roxb.*, a native of Hindustan, *Vol. II, p.* 652.
DIOSPYROS EBENASTER, *Willde*, a Ceylon tree of considerable magnitude, *Vol. II, p.* 529. Is it D. ebenum?
,, GLUTINOSA, *Konig*, a middle sized tree of the moist valleys of the Circars, *Vol. II, p.* 533.
,, RAMIFLORA, *Roxb.*, the Origaub of Bengal, a Tippera tree with a straight trunk, *Vol. II, p.* 535.
,, RACEMOSA, *Roxb.*, "Goolal" of Silhet, where it is a middling sized tree, *Vol. II, p.* 536.
,, LANCEOFOLIA, *Roxb.*, "Goolal" of Silhet, a middling sized tree, *Vol. II, p.* 537.
,, SYLVATICA, *Willde*, tella godda, TEL., a native of the Circars, *Vol. II, p.* 538.
DIPTEROCARPUS INCANUS, *Roxb.*, the Gurjun of Chittagong, where it grows to a great size and furnishes abundance of wood oil, *Vol. II, p.* 614.
,, PILOSUS, a large tree of Mascal Island, *Vol. II, p.* 615.
ELÆODENDRUM INDICUM, *Gærtn*, a middle sized tree of the Mauritius, *Vol. I, p.* 640.
ELÆAGNUS ARBOREA, *Roxb.*, a large tree of the Garrow Hills called Sheu Shongow, *Vol. I, p.* 441.
ELÆOCARPUS ARISTATUS, *Roxb.*, the Randulia of Silhet, where it is indigenous and grows to be a tree of very considerable magnitude, *Vol. II, p.* 599.
,, RUGOSUS, *Roxb.*, the Bun julpai of Chittagong, where it is indigenous and grows to a great size with a scanty crown, *Vol. II, p.* 597.
,, RUBUSTUS, *Roxb.*, the Dulpai of Silhet, where it is indigenous and grows to be a very large tree, *Vol. II, p.* 598.
ERYTHROXYLON LAURIFOLIUM, *Willde*, a tree of the Mauritius, *Vol. II, p.* 449.
,, SIDEROXYLOIDES, *Lam.*, a native of Ceylon and Coromandel Coast, *Vol. II, p.* 449.
EUCALYPTUS MOLUCCANA, *Roxb.*, a tree of the Molucca Islands, *Vol. II, p.* 498.
EUGENIA LANCEÆFOLIA, *Roxb.*, "Poora jam" indigenous of Silhet, where it is one of the largest trees in the forests, and one of the most elegant and most useful of the genus, *Vol. II, p.* 494.
,, RUBENS, *Roxb.*, a large timber tree of the forests of Chittagong, "called the Kure jamb," *Vol. II, p.* 496.
,, MACROCARPA, *Roxb.*, the Chulta jamb of Chittagong, where it is indigenous in the forests among the timber trees, *Vol. II, p.* 497.
,, ZEYLANICA, *Willde*, a middling sized tree of Ceylon, Malabar and Silhet, where it is called Nagasun jam, *Vol. II, p.* 490. Is it E. bracteata, *Roxb.*?
,, VENUSTA, *Roxb.*, an elegant tree of Tippera, *Vol. II, p.* 491.
,, ACUMINATA, *Roxb.*, a small, but tall handsome tree in the Calcutta gardens, *Vol. II, p.* 492.
,, CYMOSA, *Roxb.*, a tree, the Buttee jam of Silhet, *Vol. II, p.* 692.
,, AQUEA, *Roxb.*, a tree with a short trunk native of the Moluccas, *Vol. II, p.* 492.
ALBA, *Roxb.*, a rather low sized tree, of the Malay Islands, *Vol. II, p.* 493.

EUGENIA CERASOIDES, Bottee jam of Chittagong, where it is indigenous, with a trunk so large as to furnish planks for various purposes, *Vol. II, p.* 488.
„ PRÆCOX, *Roxb.*, a stout tree of Chittagong, *Vol. II, p.* 489.
„ PANIALA, *Roxb.*, the Paniala jam of Bengal, a native of the forests of Chittagong, and one of the largest and most robust trees of the genus, *Vol. II, p.* 489.
„ LAURIFOLIA, *Roxb.*, a beautiful densely ramous small tree, *Vol. II, p.* 489.
„ TERNIFOLIA, *Roxb.*, a large tree native of Chittagong, *Vol. II, p.* 489.
„ ANGUSTIFOLIA, *Roxb.*, a small tree of Chittagong, *Vol. II, p.* 490.
„ PURPUREA, *Roxb.*, of the Malay Islands, with a straight trunk, *Vol. II, p.* 483.
„ AMPLEXICAULIS, *Roxb.*, a stately tree of Chittagong, *Vol. II, p.* 483.
„ OPERCULATA, *Roxb.*, a tree of Amboyna, *Vol. II, p.* 486.
„ BRACHIATA, *Roxb.*, is it the E. bractiata of authors, a native of Amboyna, *Vol. II, p.* 488.
„ CLAVIFLORA, *Roxb.*, a stout useful timber tree of Chittagong, *Vol. II, p.* 488.
EUNONYMUS GLABRA, a small tree of Chittagong, flowers in May, *Vol. I, p.* 628.
EUPHORBIA LIGULARIA, the mausa sij of Bengal, when 20 years old, trunk often a foot in diameter, *Vol. II, p.* 466. (Note.—Is it of any use?)
FAGARA BUDRUNGA, *Roxb.*, a large tree of Silhet, *Vol. I, p.* 417.
„ RHETSA, a very large tree of the mountainous parts of the coast, rhetsa manu, Tel., *Vol. I, p.* 417.
FRAXINUS CHINENSIS, *Roxb.*, arboreous, a native of China, *Vol. I, p.* 148.
GALEDUPA PISCIDIA, *Roxb.*, a small tree of Silhet, *Vol. III, p.* 240.
„ ARBOREA, } Are these identical?
——— INDICA, }
GARCINIA MANGOSTANA, *Willde*, a tree of the Malay Peninsula and of the Islands to the eastwards of the Bay of Bengal, *Vol. II, pp.* 618 and 619.
„ ZEYLANICA, *Roxb.*, a native of Ceylon, *Vol. II, p.* 621.
„ COWA, a middle sized tree of Chittagong, *Vol. II, p.* 622.
„ LANCEÆFOLIA, *Roxb.*, a small tree of Silhet, *Vol. III, p.* 623.
„ KYDIA, *Roxb.*, a tree of the Andamans, *Ib.*
„ PURPUREA, *Roxb.*, of the Archipelago, *Vol. II, p.* 624.
„ PEDUNCULATA, *Roxb.*, of Rungpoor, *Vol. II, p.* 625.
„ PANICULATA, *Roxb.*, of Silhet and G. pictoria of Wynaad, *Vol. II, pp.* 626 and 627.
GARDENIA ARBOREA, *Roxb.*, a native of the Circar mountains, *Vol I, p.* 708.
„ MONTANA, *Roxb.*, a small ramous tree of the Circars, *Vol. I, p.* 709.
„ CALYCULATA, *Roxb.*, a tree of Hyderabad in the Dekhan, *Vol. I, p.* 704.
GMELINA OBLONGIFOLIA, *Roxb.*, a tree native of the eastern parts of Bengal, *Vol. III, p.* 83.
„ VILLOSA, *Roxb.*, a tree of Penang, *Vol. III, p.* 86.
GREWIA ELASTICA. Is this the Dhamnoo of Kimedy, Ganjam and Goomsoor?
„ OPPOSITIFOLIA, *Roxb.*, a tree of Nepal, *Vol. II, p.* 583.
„ ASPERA, *Roxb.*, a tree of the Circar mountains, *Vol. II, p.* 591.
GUAREA BINERTIFERA, *Roxb.*, a tree with a straight trunk in the east of Bengal, *Vol. II, p.* 210.
GUETTARDA SPECIOSA, *Willde*, ravapu, *Rheede*, a tree on the coast of Coromandel, with an erect trunk, *Vol. I, p.* 686.
HARDWICKIA PINNATA, *Roxb.*, a tree of Travancore, *Vol. II, p.* 425.
HEYNEA TRIJUGA, *Roxb.*, a tree of Nepal, *Vol. II, p.* 390.
„ QUINQUIJUGA, *Roxb.*, a tree of the Moluccas, *Vol. II, p.* 391.
HONGE, Can. Is this a Bassia?
HOLIGARNA RACEMOSA, *Roxb.*, Am-jour of Silhet, a large tree on the Silhet, *Vol. II, p.* 82.
HOPEA EGLANDULOSA, *Roxb*, a very beautiful large tree, native of the Tipperah Hills, *Vol. II, p.* 611.
„ SCAPHULA, *Roxb.*, indigenous in Mascal Island, where its trunk is so immensely large, as to be made with canoes by the Mug inhabitants, *Vol. II, p.* 611.
HUMEA ELATA, *Roxb.*, The "Mas jot" of Chittagong, a truly majistic tree, with a straight trunk and of great size, being 15 feet in circumference 4 feet from the ground, *Vol. II, p.* 640.
HUNTERIA CORYMBOSA, *Roxb.*, a tree of Prince of Wales' Island, *Vol. I, p.* 695.
INOCARPUS EDULIS, *Linn*, a very beautiful ever-green tree of the Moluccas, timber unknown, *Vol. II, p.* 416.
JATI, Malay. Is it teak (Tectona grandis)?
JUGLANS PLEROCOCCA, *Roxb.*, a tree of Silhet of considerable magnitude, *Vol. III, p.* 631.
KA-THEE-THA, Burm. } Are these identical?
KA-THEET-THA, Burm. }
KAY-A BINTANGUR. Is this a Calophyllum?
KHUUR, Hind. Is this the *Kheir* (Acacia catechu)?
KLEINHOVIA HOSPITA, *Willde*, a tree of the Moluccas, with a straight trunk, *Vol. III, p.* 141.
KOANG, Singh. Is this identical with Koan?
KOES? or JACK? Artocarpus integrifolia?
KOOSSOOM, Uria, } Are these identical?
KOOSUMBH, Hind. }
KUMPADRI MARUM, used for sleepers on the Madras Railway, a specimen forwarded by *Mr. Robinson* from Kirkumbady, without flowers and fruit, appears to belong to Bignoniaceæ.

KYANAN, Burm. }
KYA-NAN, Burm. } Are these identical?
KYA NAN, Burm. }
KYDIA FRATERNA, *Roxb.*, a native of the Circars, *Vol. III, p.* 189.
KYEE, Burm. Is it Cassia Sumatrana?
LAGERSTRŒMIA GRANDIFLORA, *Roxb.*, a large tree of Chittagong, trunk erect and straight to the top of the tree, *Vol. II, p.* 503.
LIMBO, Uria. Is it Azadirachta Indica?
LIMONIA ARBOREA, *Roxb.*, *Cor.*, *Pl.*, a native of the Circar mountains, *Vol. II, p.* 381.
,, CRENULATA, *Roxb.*, *Cor.*, *Pl.*, a small elegant tree of the Coromandel and Malabar Coast, *Vol. II, p.* 381.
LIRIODENDRON GRANDIFLORA, *Roxb.*, a middle sized branching tree of Silhet, *Vol. II, p.* 653.
,, LILIFERA, *Willde*, The anoa champa of Silhet, a pretty large tree, *Vol. II, p.* 654.
LAURUS NITIDA, *Roxb.*, a native of Sumatra, with a straight trunk, *Vol. II, p.* 301.
,, OBTUSIFOLIA? a large tree of the mountains east of Bengal, *Vol. II, p.* 302.
,, DULCIS, *Roxb.*, an elegant tall slender tree, with a straight trunk, *Vol. II, p.* 303.
,, CAMPHORIFERA, *Willde*, a tree of Sumatra, like a fine old oak, *Vol. II, p.* 304.
,, CAMPHORIFERA, *Kæmpf*, a handsome tree of the Malay Islands, with a straight trunk, *Vol. II, p.* 306.
,, GLAUCESCENS, *Roxb.*, Syn. Sylvestris, *Buch.*, *Ham.*, a tree of the Circar mountains, *Vol. II, p.* 307.
,, VILLOSA, *Roxb.*, of Chittagong, *Vol. II, p.* 310.
,, BILOCULARIS, a tree of Tippera, with a straight trunk, *Vol. II, p.* 311.
,, LANCEOLARIA, *Roxb.*, a middling sized tree of Silhet, its wood is converted to various useful purposes, *Vol. II, p.* 309.
LUDIA SPINOSA, *Roxb.*, a native of Java, Sumatra and the neighbouring Islands, *Vol. II, p.* 507.
,, FŒTIDA, *Roxb.*, a tree of Amboyna, where it is called "somer-mera," it is about 30 feet high, with a straight trunk, *Vol. II, p.* 508.
MANGIFERA SYLVATICA, *Roxb.*, laxshmi am, a tall tree of great size of the mountains of Silhet, *Vol. I, p.* 644.
MANEE AUKA, Burm. }
MANEEOGA, Burm. } Are these identical?
MANEOGA, Burm. }
MARYA CADAMBA. Is it a Nauclea?
MARLEA BIGONIFOLIA, *Roxb.*, a small tree of Silhet, timber employed in native house building, *Vol II, p.* 261.
MELIA AZADIRACTA, *Willde.*
,, TOMENTOSA, *Roxb.*
,, SEMPERVIRENS, *Willde.*
,, AZEDARAK, *Willde.*
,, SUPERBA, *Roxb.*, a native of Somda.
,, ROBUSTA, *Roxb.*, a large tree of Malabar, *Vol. II, p.* 394 to 398.
MELICOPE TETRANDRA, *Roxb.*, a tree of Penang, *Vol. II, p.* 257.
METROSIDEROS VERA, *Roxb.*, a tree of great size in the forests of Amboyna and the other Molucca Islands, *Vol. II, p.* 477.
MILNEA EDULIS, *Roxb.*, a tree of middling size, a native of the Garrow Hills and Silhet, *Vol. I, p.* 637.
MIMOSA KŒRINGA, *Roxb.*, a large tree of Molucca, *Vol. II, p.* 543.
,, LUCIDA, *Roxb.*, a large beautiful tree, a native of the mountains N. E. of Bengal, *Vol. II, p.* 544.
,, HETEROPHYLLA, *Roxb.*, the Kawahurunee of Silhet, a large and useful timber tree, *Vol. II, p.* 545.
,, ELATA, *Roxb.*, a large, tall, most stately and excellent timber tree of the interior of Bengal, *Vol. II, p.* 546.
KALKORA, *Roxb.*, a large timber tree of Gwapara, *p.* 548.
PROCERA, *Roxb.*, the Pedda Patseroo of Tel., one of the largest timber trees of Coromandel, *Vol. II, p.* 548.
,, PULCHELLA, *Roxb.*, a most beautiful tree of Malabar, *Vol. II, p* 548.
,, STIPULACEA, *Roxb.*, the Amlooki of the mountains N. of Bengal and Roxburgh had seen a tree which at 5 feet above ground measured 13 feet in circumference.
,, SMITHIANA, *Roxb.*, the Suris the vernacular name of a very large tree of Silhet, *Vol. II, p.* 550.
,, PEDUNCULATA, *Roxb.*, an elegant tall large tree, a native of the Islands to the East of Bay of Bengal, *Vol. II, p.* 551.
,, BIGLOBOSA, *Jacq.*, a large tree native of the forests of Silhet, *Vol. II, p.* 551.
MOLINÆA CANESCENS, *Willde*, Sapindus tetraphyllus, *Vahl.*, Korivi, Tel., a tree of the Circar mountains with a straight but not thick trunk, wood white and not so useful as that of Sapindus rubiginosus, *Vol. II, p.* 244.
,, LÆVIS, *Willde.*, a handsome slender tree of the Mauritius, *Vol. II, p.* 244.
MURRAYA EXOTICA, *Mant.*, a small tree of China and the Northern Circars, *Vol. II, p.* 374.

MYHILENAH. Is this Myle Ellah of *Col. Frith?*
MYLE ELLAH. Is this Myhi-lenah of Edye?
NARVELL. Is this a Eugenia or Dillenia speciosa, *Thunb?*
NAUCLEA CORDATA, *Roxb.*, a tree, a native of Ceylon with straight trunk, *Vol. I, p.* 510.
,, MACROPHYLLA, *Roxb.*, a magnificent tree of Amboyna, trunk straight like the Pines, *Vol. I, p.* 511.
,, GLABRA, *Roxb.*, a native of the Moluccas, *Vol. I, p.* 512.
,, PURPUREA, *Willde.*, Bagada, TEL., a small tree of the Circars, *Vol. I, p.* 515.
,, SESSILIFOLIA, *Roxb.*, a large tree of Chittagong, *Vol. I, p.* 515.
,, ROTUNDIFOLIA, *Roxb.*, a tree of the forests of Silhet, *Vol I, p.* 516.
,, OVALIFOLIA, a tree of the Chittagong, *Ibid.*
,, TRETRANDRA, *Roxb.*, Shurut kudum, BENG., a small but elegant tree of Silhet, *Ibid.*
NERIUM TINCTORUM, *Roxb.*, a small sized tree, trunk of very irregular shape, wood remarkably white close grained very beautiful coming nearer to ivory in appearance than any other *Dr. Roxburgh* knew, *Vol. II, p.* 5.
,, TOMENTOSUM, *Roxb.*, a small tree of mountains of the Circar, *Vol. II, p.* 6.
OLEA PANICULATA, *Roxb.*, a small tree of the Circar mountains, flowers during the hot season, *Vol. I, p.* 405.
,, FRAGRANS, *Linn*, a native of China, blossoms during the cool season, *Ibid.*
,, DIOICA, *Roxb.*, Arboreous, Attajam in Silhet, also Chittagong, *Vol. I, p.* 106.
PALAVA, TAM. Is this Careya arborea or Mimusops Indica?
PARRAWAH, BURM. Is this a Garcinia?
PEE MA PEW, BURM. Is this Lagerstrœmia Reginæ?
PETALOMA ALTERNIFOLIA, *Roxb.*, kada kandel, *Rheede*, kripa, BENG., a pretty large tree of the Ganges Delta, the wood is remarkably strong and durable, used for posts and other parts of the houses of the natives, but in Calcutta for fuel, *Roxb., Vol. II, p.* 372, (is that the Acacia sundra???)
PIENMAHNE, BURM. } Are these identical?
PIENMAH PUE, BURM. }
PINATHA, BURM. Is this a species of Artocarpus?
PINUS MASSONIANA, *Lamb, Abel?* Is this *Dr. Mason's* Pinus Latteri?
POINCIANA ELATA, *Roxb.*, a tree of Coromandel with a straight trunk, *Vol. II, p.* 356.
PONGAH, TAM. Is this identical with Edye's Pong?
ROXBURGH'S FLORA INDICA, *Ed.* 1832, mentions the following trees some of them as Timber trees; but further information is desirable, viz.
PLYE. Is it the root of Sonneratia cicida? Is it the Polai of Singapore?
PREMNA SPINOSA, *Roxb.*, a tree of Calcutta, *Vol. III, p.* 77.
,, LONGIFOLIA, *Roxb.*, a tree of Bengal, *Vol. III, p.* 79.
,, MUCRONATA, *Roxb.*, a small tree of Silhet, *Vol. III, p.* 80.
PTEROSPERMUM SEMI-SAGITTATUM, *Buch.*, a large tree of Chittagong, *Vol. III, p.* 160.
,, CANESCENS, *Roxb.*, a tree of Ceylon, *Vol. III, p.* 162.
PYEEN-MA, BURM. Is this Lagerstrœmia Reginæ?
PYENG-KHADO, BURM.? Is this Inga Xylocarpa?
RHIZOPHORA MANGLE, *Willde, Roxburgh*, says wood of a dark reddish colour, hard and durable, *Vol. III, p.* 460, is it *Roxb.*, mucronata, *Sam.*
,, GYMNORHIZA, *Willde*, Kandel of *Rheede*, and kakra of the Ganges sunderbuns, a yellowish coloured wood hard and durable, used for post with which to construct native houses, *Vol. II, p.* 461.
RHUS PARVIFLORUM, *Roxb.*, a small bushy tree of Nepal, *Vol. II, p.* 100.
,, SUCCEDANEUM, *Willde*, a small tree of China, *Vol. II, p.* 98.
SAMARA PANICULATA, *Roxb.*, a tree, a native of the Circar mountains, *Vol. I, p.* 414.
SAPINDUS LAURIFOLIUS, *Willde.*, a stout very shady tree of various parts of India, *Vol. II, p.* 278.
SCYTALIA LONGAN, *Roxb.*, a Chinese tree, and on the mountains of the East of Bengal, *Vol. II, p.* 271.
,, RUBIA, *Roxb.*, a moderate sized tree of Silhet, *Vol. II, p.* 272.
,, TRIJUGA, *Willde*, a stout handsome middling sized tree of India, *Vol. II, p.* 272.
SEMICARPUS CASSUVIUM, *Roxb.*, *Cassuvium Silvestre, Rumph*, a tree of the Moluccas, *Vol. II, p.* 85.
SEM-MARAM, TAM. Is this Soymida febrifuga?
SEECURANEE, TEL. Is this the Is-akaras-i TEL. *(Sapindus rubiginosus)?*
SIDEROXYLON TOMENTOSUM, *Willde*, a small tree, flowers in the hot season, *Vol. I. p.* 602.
SONNERATIA ACIDA. Is this the Polai of Penang and Singapore and the Plye of Borneo?
Do. La-moo, BURM. What is this tree?
SHE OAK, is this Casuarina quadrivalvis.
SHOREA TALURA, *Roxb.*, a timber tree of the Balaghut mountains, *Vol. II. p.* 618.
,, LONGISPERMA, a native of Penang, *Vol. II, p.* 618.
SPONDIAS DULCIS, *Willde*, a large tree of the Society Islands, introduced into Calcutta, *Vol. I, p.* 452.
,, ACUMINATA, *Roxb.*, an elegant middling sized tree, native of Malabar, *Vol. II, p.* 453.
,, LONGIFOLIA, *Roxb.*, a Mauritius tree introduced, *Vol. II, p.* 453.
,, AXILLARIS, *Roxb.*, A native of Nepal, *Vol. II, p.* 453.

DESIDERATA.

STERCULIA LANCEÆFOLIA, *Roxb.*, a middle sized tree of Silhet, and S. Coccinea, a small tree Silhet, *Vol. III, p.* 150 & 151.
STYRAX SERRULATA, *Roxb.*, a small tree of Chittagong, *Vol. II, p.* 415.
,, BENJOIN, *Willde, Vol. II, p.* 416.
SUTSHER. Is this name correct?
SYMPLOCOS SPICATA, *Roxb.*, the Booree of Silhet, an indigenous tree of Sylhet of middle s *Vol. II, p.* 541.
TAMBAGUM of *Colonel Frith.*
TAMBOGUM of *Mr. Edye.* } Are these identical? *(Shorea Tumbugaia.)*
TERNSTRŒMIA SERRATA, *Roxb.*, Daloop of Silhet, where it is used for fuel, *Vol. II, p.* 521.
VELLAH AHGUILL,
VELAH AHGUIAL, } Are these identical?
VITEX ALATA, *Roxb.* It would be desirable to learn more of this tree.
VITEX HETEROPHYLLA, *Roxb.*, a tall slow growing timber tree, of the Tipperah forest, *Vol. III, p.* 7
,, SALIGNA, *Roxb.*, a tree of a considerable size of the forests of Coromandel, *Vol. III, p.* 75.
XANTHOCHYMUS DULCIS, *Roxb.*, a tree of the Moluccas, *Vol. II, p.* 631.
,, OVALIFOLIUS, *Roxb.*, a handsome branchy tree of Ceylon, *Vol. II, p.* 332.